EDITED BY
AHMET İÇDUYGU – KEMAL KİRİŞCİ

LAND OF DIVERSE MIGRATIONS
CHALLENGES OF EMIGRATION AND IMMIGRATION IN TURKEY

İSTANBUL BİLGİ UNIVERSITY PRESS

EDITED BY AHMET İÇDUYGU – KEMAL KİRİŞCİ
LAND OF DIVERSE MIGRATIONS
CHALLENGES OF EMIGRATION AND IMMIGRATION IN TURKEY

İSTANBUL BİLGİ UNIVERSITY PRESS 236
MIGRATION RESEARCH 10

ISBN 978-605-399-040-6

COVER PHOTO MERİH AKOĞUL

FIRST EDITION, İSTANBUL, FEBRUARY 2009

BİLGİ İLETİŞİM GRUBU YAYINCILIK MÜZİK YAPIM VE HABER AJANSI LTD. ŞTİ.
ADDRESS: İNÖNÜ CADDESİ, NO: 95 KUŞTEPE ŞİŞLİ 34387 İSTANBUL/TURKEY
PHONE: 0212 311 50 00 - 311 52 59 / FAX: 0212 297 63 14

www.bilgiyay.com
E-MAIL yayin@bilgiyay.com
DISTRIBUTION dagitim@bilgiyay.com

DESIGN MEHMET ULUSEL
INDEX BORA BOZATLI
ELECTRONIC PAGE MAKEUP MARATON DİZGİEVİ
PRINTER AND BINDER SENA OFSET AMBALAJ VE MATBAACILIK SAN. TİC. LTD. ŞTİ.
LİTROS YOLU 2. MATBAACILAR SİTESİ B BLOK KAT 6 NO: 4 NB 7-9-11 TOPKAPI İSTANBUL/TURKEY
PHONE: 0212 613 03 21 - 613 38 46 / FAX: 0212 613 38 46

İstanbul Bilgi University Library Cataloging-in-Publication Data
A catalog record for this book is available from the Istanbul Bilgi University Library

Land of diverse migrations: Challenges of emigration and immigration in Turkey /
edited by Ahmet İçduygu, Kemal Kirişci.
    p. cm.
    Includes bibliographical references and index.
ISBN 978-605-399-040-6 (pbk.)

1. Turkey—Emigration and immigration. I. İçduygu, Ahmet. II. Kirişçi, Kemal.
    JV8745 .L36   2009

LAND OF DIVERSE MIGRATIONS
CHALLENGES OF EMIGRATION AND IMMIGRATION IN TURKEY

EDITED BY
AHMET İÇDUYGU – KEMAL KİRİŞCİ

MIGRATION RESEARCH PROGRAM AT KOC UNIVERSITY

The Migration Research at Koc University (MiReKoc) was established in 2004 with the collaboration of the Foundation for Population, Migration and Environment (PME) of Switzerland. This program aims to encourage and support research on various cultural, economic, historical, social and political dimensions of emigration from and immigration into Turkey. So far MiReKoc has provided funding for more than thirty research projects. The findings of eight of these projects are covered by this volume, *Land of Diverse Migrations: Challenges of Emigration and Immigration in Turkey* edited by Ahmet İçduygu and Kemal Kirişci. The contributions to this volume address a range of historical as well as contemporary international migration issues involving Turkey.

MiReKoc
MIGRATION RESEARCH PROGRAM AT KOC UNIVERSITY

bmu
pme
stiftung für bevölkerung, migration und umwelt
foundation for migration, population and environment

ISTANBUL BİLGİ UNIVERSITY PRESS

Established in 2000, İstanbul Bilgi University Press publishes both original works in Turkish and translations from the major languages of the world in a wide range of areas such as political science, history, economics, sociology, psychology, philosophy, arts, and literature as well as textbooks. It also publishes scholarly works in the English language. It has published more than 240 titles since the time it was first established. The model of academic publishing that we seek to achieve rests on the principles developed by prominent and distinguished university presses, and we aim to combine these principles with the 150 years of experience of Turkish university presses.

İSTANBUL BİLGİ UNIVERSITY PRESS

Table of Contents

Tables

Figures

Charts

Maps

ŞEBNEM KÖŞER AKÇAPAR

Is a social and cultural anthropologist. Upon obtaining her PhD from the Catholic University of Leuven in Belgium, she started working as a visiting scholar at the Institute for the Study of International Migration (ISIM) at Georgetown University. Since 2007, she works as an assistant professor at the School of Foreign Service, Center for German and European Studies at Georgetown University, where she lectures graduate courses on Muslim communities in Europe and the USA. She also taught at the American University in Washington, DC at the School of International Service and KOGOD School of Business. Her research interests include the role of religion in international migration, skilled migration, immigrant organizations, feminization of migration, forced migrants, and transnationalism.

KELLY T. BREWER

Kelly T. Brewer is a doctoral candidate in Comparative Literature, and currently teaches in the Foundations Development Program at Sabancı University. His research interests include African migrants in Turkey, African diaspora studies, cultural studies and Hispanic literature.

YADİGAR COŞKUN

Is studying Demography as a research assistant since 1998 at Hacettepe University Institute of Population Studies. After graduation from Middle East Technical University Department of Sociology in 1998, he completed his master degree in Economic and Social Demography Program in 2002. He is interested in data quality in sample surveys and prepares his PHd thesis on the data quality of the Turkey Demographic and Health Surveys.

A. DİDEM DANIŞ

Is teaching sociology at Galatasaray University in Istanbul, since 2005. After receiving her BA degrees at political science and sociology departments of Boğaziçi University, she continued her studies at ODTÜ (Middle East Technical University) in Ankara, where she completed her master thesis on new suburbanization and urban fragmentation in Istanbul. From 1998 to 2002, she worked as a teaching assistant at Bilgi University. She is writing her PhD thesis on Iraqi transit migrants in Turkey where she studies the functioning of social networks, including transnational ones, in interaction with changing political reception mechanisms. She is also specialized on urban sociology and conducts researches on socio-spatial transformations in Istanbul.

AHMET İÇDUYGU

Has a Ph.D. in Demography from the Australian National University, Australia, 1991. Currently, he is Professor of International Relations in the College of Administrative Sciences and Economics and Director of Migration Research Program at Koc University. He was a faculty member and Associate Chairperson of the Department of Political Science and Public Administration of Bilkent University. He had been a Research Fellow at Stockholm University (1991-1992), Visiting Fellow at the University of Warwick (1998-2000), and Research Fellow and Visiting Professor at University of Manchester (1999-2000). Currently he serves as the national correspondent of Turkey to the SOPEMI-OECD, Paris, and as a member of the International Advisory Board of Mediterranean Migratory Observatory, Athens. He has conducted research for the international organizations such as OECD, IOM, UNHCR, and ILO. He teaches on the theories and practices of citizenship, international organizations, civil society, nationalism and ethnicity, migration, and research methods. In addition to his several articles in such journals such as *International Migration, International Social Science Journal, Global Governance, Middle Eastern Studies, Ethnic and Racial Studies, Population and Environment, Human Rights Quarterly, Citizenship Studies, Journal of Scientific Studies of Religion, Mediterranean Quarterly, Mediterranean Politics*, and *Journal of Southeast European and Black Sea Studies,* Prof. İçduygu has a book, *Citizenship in a Global World*, co-edited with Fuat Keyman (Routledge, 2005).

SELMİN KAŞKA

Received her Master's degree in Politics and Social Sciences from Marmara University and a second MA in Social Sciences from the University of Warwick, Comparative Labour Studies Programme. She obtained a PhD in Politics and Social Sciences in 2000 at Marmara University. Since then she has been working in the field of gender and migration. She is the co-author, with Prof. Dr Sema Erder, of an International Organization for Migration (IOM) research report, "Irregular Migration and Trafficking in Women: The Case of Turkey", published in 2003. She was a research fellow at Centre for Research in Ethnic Relations at the University of Warwick between April 2006 and October 2007 during which she conducted a research project on "Gender and Migration, Globalization of Domestic Work: the Moldovan Case in Turkey", supported by Marie Curie Intra-European Fellowships within the 6th European Community Framework Programme. She is currently working as an assistant professor in Department of Labour Economics and Industrial Relations at Marmara University.

KEMAL KİRİŞCİ

Is Jean Monnet Chair in European Integration, director of the European Studies Center, and a professor of international relations in the Department of Political Science and International Relations at Boğaziçi University in Istanbul. His areas of expertise include international relations theory, international politics, government, and society in the Middle East, Turkish foreign policy, international affairs since 1648, and refugee studies. From 1996 to 2000, he served as a member of the External Relations Advisory Committee of the United Nations High Commissioner for Refugees. Dr. Kirisci is a former Fulbright scholar and visiting associate professor in the Department of Political Science at the University of Minnesota, Minneapolis; a former visiting associate professor at the Center for Middle Eastern and North African Studies at the University of Michigan, Ann Arbor; and former faculty at the General Staff Armed Forces College, Istanbul. Dr. Kirisci received a B.A. in finance and management from Boğaziçi University; an M.A. in international relations from the University of Kent at Canterbury, England; and a Ph.D. in international relations from the Department of Systems Science at the City University, London.

RENK ÖZDEMİR

Is currently working towards a Dphil degree at the International Relations Department of the University of Sussex. Previously a Visiting Fellow at the Centre for Asia Minor Studies (Athens), she has conducted fieldworks on the late generation Grecophone Muslims and Turcophone Orthodox of the Greco-Turkish Population Exchange.

JEAN-FRANÇOIS PÉROUSE

After completing his studies in areas of social geography and Turcology, Associate Professor Jean-François Pérouse began to work at Toulouse University in France. He also taught at Marmara University and Galatasaray University in Turkey. Between the years of 2002-2006, Associate Professor Jean-François Pérouse worked as the director of "Istanbul Observation Center" of the French Institute for Anatolian Studies (Institut Français d'études Anatoliennes, IFEA) in Istanbul and conducted several research projects on urban studies with a specific focus on Istanbul.

LEVENT SOYSAL

Completed his Ph. D. at the Department of Anthropology, Harvard University. Before joining Department of Radio, Television, and Cinema at Kadir Has University as founding Chair, he held positions as Postdoctoral Research Fellow at the Berlin Program for Advanced German and European Studies, Free University-Berlin and as Assistant Professor of Anthropology at the John W. Draper Interdisciplinary Master's Program in Humanities and Social Thought, New York University, where he taught graduate courses in the area of *The City*, focusing on the contemporary urban spaces and cultures, and transnational movements of peoples, cultures, and goods. Soysal's topics of research and teaching interest include City; Globalization and the Metropolis; Transnationalism, Youth, and Migration; Spectacle and Performance; and Theories of Culture, Representation, and Media. His current research concerns the changing meaning and constitution of public events and the performance of identity. Soysal published articles in journals such as *New German Critique*, *Cultural Dynamics*, and *The South Atlantic Quarterly*, as well as in edited volumes. His recent publications include: "The migration story of Turks in Germany: From the beginning and to the end," in *Cambridge History of Turkey, volume IV: Turkey in the Modern World*, Reşat Kasaba, editor, 2008; and *Plausible Vielfalt. Wie der Karneval der Kulturen denkt, lernt und Kultur macht*, Co-editor (with Michi Knecht), Panama Verlag, Berlin, 2005.

CHERIE TARAGHI

After receiving her graduate degree from the department of Middle Eastern Studies at the School of Oriental and African Studies (SOAS) in London, Cherie Taraghi began to work at the International Catholic Migration Commission (ICMC) in Istanbul where she worked on issues of settlement, orientation, and integration of migrants from Middle East and North Africa. Ms. Taraghi currently works as a researcher at a private research organization in Istanbul where she also pursues her independent academic studies.

A. SİNAN TÜRKYILMAZ

Ahmet Sinan Türkyılmaz is an assistant professor at Hacettepe University, Institute of Population Studies, Ankara where he has received his master and Ph.D. Degrees on Technical Demography. He was graduated from Statistics department of Middle East Technical University, Ankara. He has worked as an associate researcher at University of Michigan, Institute for Social Research, Ann Arbor, USA and completed "Sampling Program for Survey Statisticians" as a fellow student. He is mainly specialized on survey and sampling methodology, and designed many nationwide sample surveys. He is also interested in mortality and migration.

BİLGE YAĞMURLU

Completed her Masters by Research at Middle East Technical University in 1998, with research focusing on adult and sibling influences on children's abilities to understand other people's minds. She received her Ph.D. in developmental psychology from the University of Melbourne, in 2003. Her studies investigate social and emotional development in children, and the role of within-child characteristics (e.g., temperament) and socialization (e.g., parenting, family context) in the development of socioemotional abilities. She also has a strong interest in acculturation and development of children in Turkish immigrant families.

DENİZ YÜKSEKER

Is assistant professor of sociology at Koc University. She has conducted research and published on the internal displacement of Kurds in Turkey, African migration to Turkey, and the informal trade between the former Soviet Union and Turkey.

INTRODUCTION

Turkey's International Migration in Transition

AHMET İÇDUYGU – KEMAL KİRİŞCİ

Traditionally, Turkey has been known as a country of emigration. Starting from the early 1960s and well into the 1970s, large numbers of Turkish nationals migrated to western European countries, particularly West Germany. This emigration continued until recent times through family reunification schemes and applying for asylum the asylum track. However, more recently, Turkey has also become a country of transit for irregular migrants from Asian countries such as Afghanistan, Bangladesh, Iraq, Iran, and Pakistan who are trying to reach the western world. Turkey is also becoming a destination country for EU professionals and retirees as well as regular and irregular migrants from former Soviet Bloc countries. Furthermore, a growing numbers of transit migrants are stranded in Turkey. Finally, Turkey is also a country of refuge for asylum seekers coming from neighbouring Middle East countries and beyond. The combination of Turkey's status as a 'transition country' as well as its efforts to become a member of the EU is creating pressures for an overhaul of Turkey's immigration policies.[1]

---

[1] For an earlier and detailed discussion over the term "migration transition", see, for instance, Castles (1998, 2007) and Castles and Miller (1997).

EMIGRATION IN TRANSITION

The first half of the twentieth century was very much marked by state and nation building, generating large waves of forced migrations and "un-mixing" of peoples of Europe as well as of beyond Europe (Marcus, 1985).[2] Turkey's case was not much different. In the final days of the Ottoman Empire and the first two decades of the Turkish Republic, the country's non-Muslim minority populations experienced mass emigration. Pull and push factors culminated in the majority of the members of non-Muslim communities to migrate to various countries around the globe (Akgündüz, 1998; Loizos, 1999; İçduygu et. al., 2008). In turn Turkey saw the arrival of large numbers of Muslims belonging to a range of ethnic groups from the Balkans. As a result of the "un-mixing" that took place, the demographic composition of the population of the Republic was substantially different from that of the empire it replaced. As Keyder (1987: 79) notes, '...before the war, one out of every five persons living in present-day Turkey was non-Muslim, after the war, only one out of forty persons was non-Muslim". While in the 1920s the population of non-Muslims in the country was close to three percent of the total, today it has dropped to less than two per 1,000 (İçduygu et al., 2008: 358) (see **Table 1**).

TABLE 1
Muslim and non-Muslim Population in Turkey, 1914-2005 (in thousands)

Year	1914	1927	1945	1965	1990	2005
Muslims	12,941	13,290	18,511	31,139	56,860	71,997
Greeks	1,549	110	104	76	8	3
Armenians	1,204	77	60	64	67	50
Jews	128	82	77	38	29	27
Others	176	71	38	74	50	45
Total	15,998	13,630	18,790	31,391	57,014	72,122
Percentage of non-Muslims	19,1	2,5	1,5	0,8	0,3	0,2

Sources: From 1914 to 1965, Ottoman and Turkish censuses and statistical abstracts; from 1990 to 2005, personal communication of the (opinion) leaders of non-Muslim communities to the authors.

---

2   For the notion of state formation provoking forced migrations, see Zolberg (1983).

Until the Second World War, emigration from Turkey by and large resulted from the out-mobility of its non-Muslim populations. They had a mostly urban as well as middle or upper class background. In the second half of the twentieth century, Turkey went through a massive economic and political transformation (Ahmad, 1993). This precipitated an ever growing proportion of Turkish rural population to move to urban centers beginning in the early 1950s.[3] This was, within a decade, accompanied by large-scale Turkish labor emigration to Europe that started as a result of an Agreement signed by the Turkish and West German governments in 1961.[4] The pact aimed to provide the booming German economy with temporary unskilled labor, while thinning the ranks of Turkey's unemployed. Turkey signed similar agreements with other European countries, including Austria, Belgium, Holland, France, and Sweden. It was expected that these 'guest workers' would return to Turkey with new skills and help reorient the Turkish economy from an economy based on rural agriculture to industry. However, many of them tended to settle down and bring their families to join them. Furthermore, it was often skilled laborers that ended up emigrating rather that the unskilled ones. The economic downturn in Western Europe in the 1970s ended the recruitment of labor from Turkey. However Turkish emigration to Europe continued through family reunification and family formation (see **Table 2**). Today, the number of Turkish nationals migrating to Europe is put at less than 50,000 (the net figure is even less when the number of migrants returning to Turkey is deducted) (İçduygu, 2006b).

In the late 1960s, the Turkish government, under pressure from growing unemployment, quickly began a search for new markets to sustain the labor exporting process. Indeed, Turkish emigration to Australia as well as to Arab countries started under these circumstances (İçduygu, 1991) (see **Table 2**). The timing of the bilateral labor recruitment agreement with Australia in 1967 reflected the efforts of

---

3   For a detailed elaboration of the rural-urban migration flows in Turkey, see Baydar (1998).
4   For an extensive coverage of labor emigration see Abadan-Unat (2002).

TABLE 2
Turkish Labor Migration by Destination, 1961-2005

Host Countries	1961-1974		1975-1980		1981-1990		1991-1995		1996-2000		2001-2005		Total	
	#	%	#	%	#	%	#	%	#	%	#	%	#	%
Europe	790,017	97,5	13,426	12,8	2,612	0,6	96,47	2,8	10,465	9,3	16,561	9,1	842,728	42,4
Arab Countries	2,441	0,3	74,181	70,6	423,208	97,7	208,274	60,4	32,195	28,5	57,974	31,9	798,273	40,2
Australia	5,806	0,7	2,647	2,5	2,478	0,6	1,324	0,4	515	0,5	176	0,1	12,946	0,7
CIS Countries		–		–		–	115	0,0	65,521	58,0	89,623	49,3	155,259	7,8
Others	12,235	1,5	14,792	14,1	4,875	1,1	125,238	36,3	4,256	3,8	17,533	9,6	178,929	9,0
Total	810,499	100	105,046	100	433,173	100	344,598	100	112,952	100	181,867	100	1,988,135	100

Source: Compiled by İçduygu (2006), based on various official sources in Turkey.

the Turkish emigration strategy of "falling back on another country if one showed signs of saturation and diminished absorption ability" in another (Bahadır, 1979). There was, of course, a significant contrast between the migration policies of Turkey and Australia at that time. While Australian immigration policy was based upon the expectation of permanent settlement of immigrants, Turkish emigration policy was guestworker-oriented. The signing of a migration agreement with Australia was a new step undertaken to maintain the continuity of emigration.

Europe's recession in the mid-1970s coincided with an economic boom in the Middle East. This allowed the Turkish government to channel labor emigration to countries such as Libya, Saudi Arabia, and Iraq as Turkish companies obtained major infrastructural construction projects (İçduygu and Sirkeci, 1998) (see **Table** 2). This emigration almost never involved family reunification. The Turkish presence in Iraq (and to a lesser extent, in other Arab countries) was reduced by the 1991 Gulf War. With the end of the Cold War and the dissolution of the Soviet Union an increasing number of Turkish companies won construction and industrial contracts in the Russian Federation and other parts of the Commonwealth of Independent States (CIS). This created employment opportunities for Turkish workers, engineers, and managers (see **Table** 2) and was accompanied by a growing number of small businesses, often in the form of bakeries and restaurants, set up by Turkish businessmen in these countries as well as Bulgaria and Romania.

Since the early 1980s, asylum seekers have been heading for Western Europe, fleeing from the consequences of the Turkish military intervention in civilian politics and the increase in the violence surrounding efforts to suppress the PKK[5], a separatist Kurdish movement in south eastern Turkey. According to the United Nations High Commission of Refugees' (UNHCR) statistics, between 1981 and 2005

---

5   The abbreviation of PKK refers to "Partiya Karkerên Kurdistan" (Kurdistan Workers' Party).

over 664,000 Turkish citizens applied for asylum, mostly in various European countries (see **Table 3**). The refugee recognition rates varied from country to country but have been very low as there were many who tried to make fraudulent use of the asylum channel to emigrate. Since the worst of the conflict between the armed forces and the PKK wound down in the second half of the 1990s, and following the gradual introduction of political reforms, asylum applications have fallen. However, an unidentified number of Turkish nationals, often of Kurdish origin, continued to attempt to enter EU countries illegally in search of jobs.

Today, it is estimated that there are approximately 3.3 million Turkish nationals living abroad, of whom about 2.7 million are in European countries. This is a substantial increase from 770,000 in the mid 1970s cited by Abadan-Unat (2002: 48). There are also some 100,000 Turkish workers in the Arab countries, some 60,000 immigrants in Australia, and over 75,000 workers in the CIS countries (see **Table 4**). In addition to these, there exists also more than a quarter million Turkish migrants in Canada and the United States. Thus, the equivalent of some six percent of today's Turkish population is residing abroad. There are also another almost 800,000 Turkish nationals that have taken up the citizenship of their host countries between 1991 and 2005 (see **Table 5**). This makes the Turks in Europe the largest immigrant community and a target for anti-immigrant feelings and xenophia. Against this background there are many in Europe who fear the arrival of further migration from Turkey if Turkey were to become a member of the EU. This fear is further aggravated by the social and cultural difficulties that Turkish immigrants encounter in integrating into the host societies. A significant proportion of second and third generation Turks abroad do poorly, especially in respect to education and employment. However there is a growing Turkish immigrant civil society in Europe which increasingly addresses the integration problems of the Turkish communities in major European countries.[6]

---

6   See for instance articles in the special issue of journal *Turkish Studies* by Erzan and Kirişci (2006); see also Kaya and Kentel (2005).

TABLE 3

Turkish Asylum-seekers by Destination, 1981-2005

Destination	1981-1985		1986-1990		1991-1995		1996-2000		2001-2005		1981-2005	
	#	%	#	%	#	%	#	%	#	%	#	%
Europe	45,620		185,797		175,557	98,6	141,226	97,9	107,534	97,2	655,734	98,7
Canada					755	0,4	1,919	1,3	2,451	2,2	5,125	0,8
Australia					780	0,4	928	0,6	332	0,3	2,040	0,3
USA					984	0,6	199	0,1	330	0,3	1,513	0,2
Total					178,076	100,0	144,272	100,0	110,647	100,0	664,412	100,0

Source: Figures are compiled by İçduygu (2006) from various sources of OECD and Eurostat.

TABLE 4
Turks Changing Citizenship in Europe by Country, 1991-2002

Country	1991-1993		1994-1996		1997-1999		2000-2002		1991-2002	
	# (x1000)	%	# (x1000)	%	# (x1000)	%	# (x1000)	%	# (x1000)	%
Germany	20,3	27,8	97,0	42,7	129,1	56,8	159,4	63,4	405,8	52,1
Austria	4,7	6,4	6,6	2,9	7,8	3,4	18,3	7,2	37,4	4,8
Belgium	7,2	9,9	13,0	5,7	17,5	7,7	31,7	12,6	69,4	8,9
Denmark	1,1	1,5	2,6	1,1	5,4	2,4	5,9	2,3	15,0	1,9
France	2,8	3,8	8,8	3,9	14,5	6,4	13,8	5,5	39,9	5,1
The Netherlands	29,5	40,4	87,6	38,5	39,9	17,6	10,2	4,1	167,2	21,5
The UK	0,2	0,3	0,5	0,2	2,0	0,9	2,5	1,0	5,2	0,7
Sweden	5,8	7,9	7,6	3,3	4,9	2,2	4,2	1,7	22,5	2,9
Switzerland	1,4	1,9	3,6	1,6	6,2	2,7	6,2	2,5	17,4	2,2
Total	73,0	100,0	227,3	100,0	227,3	100,0	252,5	100,0	779,8	100,0

Source: Figures are compiled by İçduygu (2006) from various sources of OECD and Eurostat.

TABLE 5
Turkish Migrant Stock Abroad in mid-1980s, mid-1990s and mid-2000s

	Mid-1980s		Mid-1990s		Mid-2000s	
	# (x1000)	%	# (x1000)	%	# (x1000)	%
Austria	75,0	3,1	147,0	4,4	127,0	3,8
Belgium	72,5	3,1	79,5	2,4	45,9	1,4
France	146,1	6,2	198,9	6,0	208,0	6,3
Germany	1400,1	59,3	2049,9	62,0	1912,0	57,9
Netherlands	156,4	6,6	127,0	3,8	160,3	4,9
Scandinavian Countries	41,2	1,7	73,0	2,2	51,6	1,6
Switzerland	51,0	2,2	79,0	2,4	79,5	2,4
Other European Countries	42,0	1,8	87,0	2,6	130,0	3,9
Total Europe	1984,6	84,0	2841,3	85,9	2714,3	82,1
Arab Countries	200,0	8,5	127,0	3,8	105,0	3,2
Australia	35,0	1,5	45,0	1,4	60,0	1,8
CIS Countries	0,0	0,0	50,0	1,4	75,0	2,3
Other Countries	140,0	5,9	245,0	7,4	350,0	10,6
Total	2359,6	100,0	3308,3	100,0	3304,3	100,0

Source: Figures are compiled by İçduygu (2006) from various sources of OECD and Eurostat.

Furthermore, there is also a growing recognition that host societies need to make an effort to encourage integration. There are also econometric studies suggesting that the number of Turkish nationals that might actually migrate to EU countries if membership with full freedom of movement were to occur is much less than what the general public fears (Erzan et. al., 2006). In addition, demographic studies show that by the year 2025, the economically active layer of the Turkish population (15-64 years of age) will start shrinking in proportion to the rest of the population (Behar, 2006). The mean age of this group will also be getting older. Hence, it is likely that in a growing Turkish economy it might become difficult to find large numbers of people prepared to migrate. Furthermore, those who will migrate will probably be the better educated. Finally, like in the case of Greece and Spain, it is possible that by then Turkey would have completed its 'migration transition' and become a net immigration country.

IMMIGRATION IN TRANSITION

The founding fathers of the Turkish Republic were very concerned about boosting the population of the country which in the 1920s stood at around 13 million, compared to 16 million in 1914 (Courbage and Fargues, 1998: 128). They were also concerned about creating a homogenous sense of national identity in an otherwise ethnically and culturally diverse country. This was very much driven by a deep-seated belief that the Ottoman Empire had collapsed because of its multi-ethnic and multi-cultural nature (Ahmad, 1993). Exclusive priority was therefore given to encouraging and accepting immigrants that were either Muslim Turkish speakers, or who were officially considered to belong to ethnic groups that would easily melt into a Turkish identity such as Bosnians, Circassians, Pomaks, and Tatars from the Balkans (Kirişci, 1996; 2000). From the establishment of Turkey in 1923 to 1997, more than 1.6 million immigrants came and settled in Turkey (see **Table 6**). These immigrants were successfully assimilated.

TABLE 6
Number of People Who Migrated to Turkey; by Region Between 1923-1997

Country	1923-1939	1940-1945	1946-1997	Total
Bulgaria	198,688	15,744	603,726	818,158
Greece	384	-	25,889	84,431
Romania	117,095	4,201	1,266	122,562
Yugoslavia	115,427	1,671	188,6	428,26
Turkistan	-	-	2,878	2,878
Others	7,998	1,005	8,631	17,634
Total	823,208	22,621	830,99	=1,676,819

Source: Complied from data obtained from the Foreigners Department of MOI.

After the 1970s, immigration began to be discouraged on the grounds that Turkey's population had grown enough and that land to distribute to immigrants had become scarce. Nevertheless, immigration did continue. In fact, the last major wave of immigration occurred when more than 300,000 Turks and Pomaks were expelled from Bulgaria in 1989. A third of these refugees returned soon after the regime change in Bulgaria in 1990 as the Cold War came to end, while the rest acquired Turkish citizenship. Since Bulgaria's recent accession to the EU, more and more of these immigrants as well as Turks of Bulgarian origin have been reclaiming Bulgarian citizenship in order to obtain the right to travel to Bulgaria and other EU countries without a visa.

Beginning in the early 1990s, Turkey has witnessed a new form of immigration involving nationals of neighboring countries, EU nationals, and transit illegal migrants (İçduygu, 2006b). Turkey allows nationals of Iran, the former Soviet Union as well as of Balkan countries to enter the country quite freely, either without visas or with visas that can easily be obtained at airports and other entry points (Kirişci, 2005). In 2007 there were almost 7.2 million people from the Balkans and the ex-Soviet world that entered Turkey, in 1980 the figure was under 100,000 (see **Tables** 7 and 8). Some of these people overstay their visa in Turkey and become involved in prostitution or work illegally on construction sites as well as in households looking after the children or elderly parents of professionals in large cities such as Istanbul, Ankara and Izmir. In 2002 the government introduced new legislation that has made it a little easier for foreign nationals to work as household help and in the tourism industry.

It is very difficult to estimate the number of irregular immigrants in Turkey. However, figures ranging from 150,000 to 1,000,000 are often cited (İçduygu, 2006b). To these groups must be added trafficked persons, particularly women. In August 2002, the government introduced new articles to the Penal Code criminalizing human smuggling and trafficking. It instituted stricter controls at borders and ports. In the meantime a project was put into action in cooperation with an NGO to bring social assistance for victims of trafficking. Currently there are two shelters for victims of trafficking, one in Istanbul and another one in Ankara. In May 2005, the police in cooperation with the International Organization for Migration (IOM)

TABLE 7

Entry of Persons From the Soviet Union and Former Soviet Republics Between 1964 and 2005

	1964	1970	1980	1990	1996	2000	2005
Soviet Union	414	4,824	40,015	222,537	—	—	—
Russia	—	—	—	—	1,235,290	677,152	1,855,900
Central Asian Turkie States							
Kazakhstan	—	—	—	—	31,373	38,939	106,167
Kyrgyzstan	—	—	—	—	8,052	8,789	31,017
Tajikistan	—	—	—	—	3,087	952	6,811
Turkmenistan	—	—	—	—	5,035	10,987	34,292
Subtotal	0	0	0	0	1,196,395	757,881	2,058,821
South Caucasus							
Armenia	—	—	—	—	5,345	17,549	36,633
Azerbaijan	—	—	—	—	100,249	179,878	411,111
Georgia	—	—	—	—	116,709	179,563	367,148
Subtotal	—	—	—	—	222,303	376,990	814,892
Western Newly Independent States (NIS)							
Belarus	—	—	—	—	474	9,622	77,029
Moldova	—	—	—	—	8,290	62,687	89,849
Ukraine	—	—	—	—	93,794	173,551	367,103
Subtotal	—	—	—	—	102,558	245,860	533,981
Total	414	4,824	40,015	222,537	1,621,256	1,380,731	3,407,694
General Total	229,347	724,754	1,057,364	2,301,250	8,538,864	10,428,153	20,275,213

Source: Complied from data obtained from the Foreigners Department of MOI and State Statistical Institute Annual Reports.

TABLE 8

Entry of Persons From the Neighbouring Balkan and Middle Eastern Neighbouring States, 1964-2007

Middle East	1964	1970	1980	1990	1996	2000	2003	2005	2007
Iran	12,796	14,247	42,082	219,958	379,003	380,819	484,269	957,244	1,057,987
Iraq	3,919	6,518	14,046	13,372	14,137	20,776	29,94	107,972	180,208
Syria	9,996	13,184	26,384	113,959	92,033	122,417	154,108	287,343	331,368
Gulf States	-	-	-	43,088	40,029	19,537	43,503	62,648	76,603
Pakistan	1,961	7,383	4,8	7,347	12,41	7,908	12,336	11,698	21,084
Subtotal	28,672	41,332	87,312	397,724	537,612	551,457	724,156	1,426,905	1,667,250
Balkans									
Albania	-	-	-	1,924	20,971	29,748	32,682	50,513	56,955
Bosnia	-	-	-		12,115	28,631	35,119	44,716	50,376
Bulgaria	693	18,214	26,523		139,648	381,545	1,007,535	1,620,939	1,238,280
Greece	3,042	11,313	19,477	203,72	147,553	218,092	368,425	548,268	404,847
Macedonia	-	-	-	-	41,269	108,928	117,819	119,157	93,672
Romania	-	-	-	352,034	191,203	265,128	184,182	201,807	388,132
Serbia-Montenegro	-	-	-	-	44,6	128,383	186,423	175,294	140,237
Yugoslavia	5,661	28,352	13,817	296,843	-	-	-	-	
Subtotal	9396	57,879	59,817	854,521	597,359	1,160,455	1,932,185	2,760,694	2,372,499
Total	38,068	99,211	147,129	1,252,245	1,134,971	1,711,912	2,656,341	4,187,599	4,039,749
General Total	229,347	724,754	1,057,364	2,301,250	8,538,864	10,428,153	13,461,420	20,275,213	22,249,775

Source: Complied from data obtained from the Foreigners Department of MOI and State Statistical Institute Annual Reports.

launched an awareness campaign and opened a telephone hotline for victims of trafficking.

Another problem that has confronted Turkey has been illegal transit migration. It is very difficult to estimate the actual number of illegal migrants that are transiting through Turkey. Between 1995 and 2007, the Turkish authorities apprehended more than 336,000 nationals of Afghanistan, Bangladesh, Pakistan, Iran, Iraq, and Syria (see **Table 9**). The Turkish government has been under massive pressure

TABLE 9

Breakdown by Nationality of Illegal Immigrants Arrested by
Turkish Security Forces, 1995-2007

Country of origin	Number of people
Afghanistan	44,525
Bangladesh	20,683
Palestine	13,064
Iran	26,327
Iraq	123,508
Pakistan	57,7
Somali	15,901
Syria	9,527
Unknown Origin	24,991
Sub-total	336,226
North Africa*	12,45
Former Soviet Republics**	133,607
Central Asian Countries***	12,901
Albania	4,496
Bulgaria	11,446
Romania	23,335
Turkey	33,322
EU	57,766
Others	105,644
Total	696,412

(*) Algeria, Egypt, Libya, Morrocco and Tunisia
(**) Russia, Ukraine, Moldova, Georgia, Azerbaijan, Armenia and Belarus
(***) Kyrgyzstan, Kazakhstan, Turkmenistan, Uzbekistan and Tajikistan
Source: Data obtained from the Foreigners Department of the Turkish Ministry of the Interior (MOI).

from a number of EU member countries to curb transit migration. Furthermore, the European Commission has been trying hard to get Turkey to negotiate and conclude a readmission treaty. Such a treaty would make it possible for EU member countries to send back illegal migrants that have transited Turkey. In turn, the Turkish government is trying to sign similar agreements with the governments of countries from where most illegal transit migrants come from (Kirişci, 2007).

Finally there is an increasing number of EU member-state nationals, professionals as well as retirees, who are settling in Turkey, particularly in Istanbul and some of the Mediterranean resorts.[7] They too constitute a relatively new phenomenon in terms of immigration into Turkey, and their numbers are estimated to be around 100,000 to 120,000. In 2006, according to figures provided by the Directorate of General Security, there were over 187,000 foreigners who resided in Turkey with residence permits. While 18 percent of them were people with work permits and 13 percent were students, the remaining portion of foreigners with residence permits were mostly people who are the dependants of working and studying foreigners (İçduygu, 2007).

ASYLUM IN TRANSITION

Turkey is also a country of asylum, and is among the original signatories of the 1951 Convention relating to the Status of Refugees. However, Turkey, together with Monaco, Congo and Madagascar, is among the only remaining countries that maintain a 'geographical limitation'. Accordingly, Turkey does not grant refugee status to asylum seekers coming from outside Europe and maintains a two-tiered asylum policy. The first tier of this policy is centered on Europe and is deeply rooted in Turkey's role as a western ally neighboring the Soviet Union during the Cold War. During that period, in close co-operation with the UNHCR, Turkey received refugees from the Communist Bloc countries in Europe, including the Soviet Union. Such refugees, during

---

7   For a detailed elaboration of the retirement migration to the the Mediterranean resorts in Turkey, see for instances, Unutulmaz (2007), Kaiser and İçduygu (2005).

their stay in Turkey, enjoyed all the rights provided for in the Convention. However, only a very small number were allowed to stay in Turkey, and many who stayed did so as a result of marriages that took place with Turkish nationals. The rest were mostly resettled to the United States and Canada. Although it is very difficult to obtain accurate statistics on their numbers, the Ministry of Interior (MOI) has indicated that some 13,500 asylum seekers benefited from the protection of the Convention between 1970 and the end of the Cold War. In addition, approximately 20,000 Bosnians were granted temporary asylum in Turkey during hostilities between 1992 and 1995 in the former Yugoslavia. Since the adoption of the Dayton Peace Plan, many of these refugees steadily returned to Bosnia. In 1998 and 1999, approximately 18,000 Kosovars fled to Turkey and enjoyed protection from the ethnic strife in their homeland. The majority have returned (Kirişci, 2001: 75-76).

The second tier of Turkey's asylum policy deals with people arriving from outside Europe. The new policy emerged after the Iranian Revolution in 1980 and subsequent to the growing instability in the Middle East, Africa, and south-east Asia in the late 1980s. This led to the composition of asylum seekers to change. For a long time, the government allowed the UNHCR considerable leeway to temporarily shelter these asylum seekers, with the tacit understanding that they would be resettled out of Turkey if the UNHCR recognized them as refugees. The understanding was also that those whose claims were rejected would be deported. However, the growth in the number of illegal entries into Turkey and in the number of rejected asylum seekers stranded in Turkey strained this practice. The situation was also aggravated by mass influxes of Kurdish refugees from northern Iraq, in 1988 and 1991, which amounted to almost half a million. It was against such a background that the government introduced a decree, the *Asylum Regulation,* in November 1994. The regulation aimed to bring status determination under the control of the Turkish government. It was primarily drafted out of national security concerns and hence introduced strict measures governing access to asylum procedures, with little regard for the rights of refugees.

However, the situation began to improve by the late 1990s, with the UNHCR and the Turkish government returning to the close cooperation that had characterized their relationship up until 1994. The government introduced amendments to the asylum regulation to prevent deportations in violation of the 1951 Convention. Most importantly, in 1997 the way to judicial appeal was opened against deportation orders. In addition, training programs were run for police officers and other officials dealing with asylum issues. Lastly, the officials increasingly began to work with NGOs.

Turkey has been under pressure to align its asylum system with that of the European Union. This would require Turkey to lift the geographical limitation and introduced a fully fledged national asylum system. At a time when Europe is tightening its own asylum system, Turkish authorities are concerned that Turkey could become a buffer zone. Accompanied with increasing refugee pressures from Iraq, Somalia and Sudan, Turkey too has been tightening its asylum policy.

According to Turkish government statistics, there were approximately 3,500 to 4,000 asylum applicants filed a year between 1995 and 2007. During this period a total of more than 50,000 asylum applications were received and about 25,000 of them were recognized as refugees (see **Table 10**). The overwhelming majority of the recognized refugees continue to be resettled out of Turkey. Those whose applications are rejected are supposed to be deported to their countries of origin, but many go underground and stay in Turkey or try to move on to European countries illegally.

THE VOLUME

This first book of MiReKoc Migration Research Series aims to address in greater detail some of the issues that arise as a result of Turkey becoming a "migration transition" country. It examines this develop-

TABLE 10

Applications Under the 1994 Asylum Regulation, 1995-2007

Country	Applications	Accepted cases	Rejected cases	Pending cases	Withdrawals and Secondary protection
Iraq	16,972	5,919	5,209	4,707	1,137
Iran	28,963	18,316	3,225	6,048	1,374
Afghanistan	1,48	312	280	860	28
Russia	80	15	43	15	7
Uzbekistan	231	70	76	73	12
Azerbaijan	36	3	24	1	8
Other Europe*	125	53	59	3	10
Other**	2,467	339	369	1,676	83
Total	50,364	25,027	9,285	13,393	2,659

(*) Includes Albania, Belgium, Bosnia, Bulgaria, Germany, Georgia, Greece, Italy, Macedonia, Romania, Switzerland, Ukraine and Yugoslavia

(**) Includes Algeria, Bangladesh, Birmania (Myanmar), Burma, Burundi, China, Congo, Egypt, Eritrea, Ethiopia, Ghana, Guinea, India, Israel, Ivory Coast, Jordan, Kazakhstan, Kenya, Kuwait, Kyrgyzstan, Lebanon, Liberia, Libya, Malaysia, Moritania, Morocco, Nigeria, Pakistan, Palestine, Philippines, Rwanda, Sierra Leone, Sri Lanka, Somalia, Sudan, Syria, Tunisia, Tajikistan, Turkmenistan, Uganda, United States of America, Yemen, Zaire

Source: Data obtained from the Foreigners Department of MOI.

ment and assesses some of its wider implications. These issues will be addressed by a new generation of promising Turkish researchers working on migration issues. The book is divided into two main parts, emigration from Turkey and immigration into Turkey.

Part I considers both historical and contemporary migratory flows from Turkey. It covers cases ranging from early twentieth century emigration of "Karamanlis" from Anatolia to Greece as well as the brain drain of Turkish professionals to the United States and the so-called guestworker experience of Turks in Germany. Renk Özdemir in **Chapter 1** draws attention to the continuous re-definition of identity borders involving the Karamanlis. The Karamanlis were members of the Greek Orthodox community in Anatolia who spoke Turkish and were included among the people that were exchanged with the

Muslims of Greece as a result of the mandatory population exchange stipulated in the 1923 Lausanne Convention. In an attempt to account for the continuous shift in the borders of belongingness to the Karmanli community identity before and after the Exchange, the study first takes an historical approach. It examines the dialectical relationship of this community to the ideological undercurrents taking place in the Ottoman Centre. This relationship is traced to the circumstances culminating in the final governmental 'decision' to include Karamanlis in the Exchange. Secondly, Özdemir in an effort to follow the spatial and socio-political rupture that the Karamanlis experienced, employs an anthropological approach and treats the information gathered from in-depth interviews with fifty Karamanlis to trace the complex re-identification processes. In so doing, Özdemir introduces the Mandatory Population Exchange to the literature as a metaphorical rite of passage. This enables her to account for the multiplicity of shifts in the borders of belongingness caused by a shift in one's socio-political setting and space.

In **Chapter 2**, Şebnem Köşer Akçapar, looks at the dynamics of 'brain drain' from Turkey to the United States. The US has traditionally been the key recipient of Turkish professionals, scientists, as well as graduate and post-graduate students, a significant number of which tend not to return to Turkey. Excessive 'brain drain' or emigration of highly skilled individuals is considered an important negative factor for the intellectual, academic, and labor productivity of any given country. This general observation is also pertinent in the case of Turkey, which is a net exporter of skilled migrants. This is a feature of Turkish emigration that is often overlooked. A particular strength of this chapter is that it relies on on-site observation and analysis in both the destination country and country of origin. The chapter focused on mainly three groups of highly skilled people from Turkey: the first are those who came in the 1950s-60s and who settled in the US; the second group are young professionals who come to the U.S. for further studies and decide to stay after finding work; and the third are Turkish doctoral students who have come in the last few years. The chapter questions the idea that all export of skilled individuals is inherently negative. Instead, it tries to show that migration of the highly skilled can produce balance between 'brain drain' and 'brain gain'.

Berlin can be considered the host city of the longest-standing Turkish emigrant community abroad. In **Chapter 3**, Levent Soysal focuses on the way in which the changing meaning and constitution of public events in Berlin interacts with the identity of migrants. He argues that the modes of immigrant participation in Berlin's public events reveal the elaborate connections between the social and cultural spaces of host and home countries. For the Turkish immigrants, these public spectacles occupy a significant place in ordering their everyday experiences in the social spaces of Berlin. This implicates them in a constant and often virtual movement between Turkey and Germany. At the heart of this study are the Carnival of Cultures, the May Day Parade, and the Turkish Day Parade, all of which attract significant participation of Turkish immigrants as audiences and performers. By subjecting public spectacles to anthropological analysis, Soysal aims to delineate the limits of identity as a concept and praxis, as well as tries to understand the changes in cultural production and civic participation in a world now imagined as increasingly "transnational and global."

A comparison of migrants and non-migrants often makes a powerful case for a better understanding of the impact that migratory context has over individuals. It is with this in mind that Bilge Yağmurlu in **Chapter 4** investigates the role of education in long-term socialization goals of Turkish mothers. Results indicate that all mothers endorse goals that enhance both autonomy and relatedness. However, as predicted, low-educated mothers emphasize the importance of relatedness and compliance more than high-educated mothers. High-educated mothers report that they value autonomy and self-enhancement, as well as emphasize these goals more highly than low-educated mothers. This chapter reveals similarities between socialization goals of the low-educated and high-educated Turkish mothers regardless of whether these mothers are migrants or non-migrants. Accordingly, both groups of mothers share similar concerns regarding love, decency and self-control related socialization goals. Overall, the comparative findings show the relative salience of constructs of autonomy and relatedness in the long-term socialization goals of low-educated and high-educated mothers both in the migratory and non-migratory context. This points to the fact that education is a potent source of within-culture variance in the attributes mothers want their children to attain. Results also provide support for Kağıtçıbaşı's Family Change Model that sheds light on the variations in family structure and familial relationship patterns in different socio-cultural-economic contexts.

Yadigar Coşkun, and A. Sinan Türkyılmaz try to demonstrate in **Chapter 5** that it is possible to make indirect estimations on the size of international migration into Turkey by using the 2000 Census data. Starting with the 1975 Census, the following question was asked to every household head: "how many members of this household who are not in the house now are (a) in the country, or (b) abroad?" The chapter with this question in mind, and assuming that the people who were abroad on the day of the 2000 Census and were reported as part of the households, attempts to estimate the number of emigrants. Coşkun, and Türkyılmaz recognize and discuss the difficulties associated with such an estimation but argue that this kind of an estimation can still be of use. This chapter also presents figures on the migratory flows considering the differentiations between the traditional five regions of Demographic and Health Surveys and for all three NUTS (The Nomenclature Units for Territorial Statistics) levels constructed by the State Planning Organization and State Institute of Statistics as part of the efforts of statistical adaptations to the European Union.

Part II covers a range of different categories and examples of recent immigration flows into Turkey and focuses thematically on their growing importance over the past two decades. Specifically, the case studies in this part also point to some specific features that help to explain the dynamics and mechanisms of immigration into Turkey. In **Chapter 6**, A. Didem Danış, Cherie Taraghi and Jean-François Pérouse refer to the period in which Turkey has acquired a central position in the international irregular migrations systems in the last decades and thus has become a crossing point on a regional and international scale. They elaborate the 'unofficial integration' models of four specific migrant groups in Istanbul, namely Iraqi, Afghan, Maghrebi and Iranian migrants. It is argued that given the weakness of state assistance and non-governmental organizations providing services for regular or irregular migrants, social networks have primary importance for migrants' survival and socio-economic incorporation in Turkey. The authors show how the migrants as soon as they arrive in Turkey become involved with informal reception mechanisms. The segmented incorporation of migrants via social networks is very precarious and contingent on policies as well as on the official treatment of foreigners in the country. Thus, such an incorporation, even though it is highly important for the survival of undocumented migrants, condemns the migrants to stay 'in limbo', unless a regularization in the migrants' status occurs. This chapter concludes that *de facto integration* of non-European migrants in Turkey may shed light on the mechanisms of socio-economic incorporation and thus contribute to the new policy making processes as well as the academic discussions.

In **Chapter 7**, Brewer and Yükseker present a survey of the African migrants and asylum seekers in Istanbul. They show their demographic characteristics, their reasons for migration, as well as their living conditions and problems. This chapter draws a number of conclusions. It observes that there is an increase in the numbers of Africans who arrive in Turkey as transit migrants and asylum seekers. These Africans in Istanbul should not be considered as a homogeneous group. There are instead migrants from all over the continent, and their motivations for migration are diverse, though often characterized by efforts to reach Western Europe. However, the difficulty of getting into Europe prolongs their stay in Turkey, leading them to engage in a variety of survival strategies. These strategies range from trying the asylum track with the hope to resettling out of Turkey, to seeking employment illegally while looking for means and ways of getting into EU. Finally, the chapter highlights how all these strategies are developed against a background of poor living conditions and extremely limited social services.

In **Chapter 8**, Selmin Kaşka focuses on the gender dimension of migration. She explores the new trends in the globalisation of household work in the Turkish context by focusing on female Moldovan domestic workers. In the last decade, these women migrants have joined the migration movements to Turkey mainly due to Moldova's geographical proximity, Turkey's liberal visa regulations and an informal vibrant labor market. Ethnicity also plays its role in the choice of Turkey as a destination country as most of the Moldovan women migrants are *Gagauz Turks*. This chapter also makes a contribution to better understanding how, in an informal economy, supply and demand for domestic work operates.

Finally, the concluding chapter lays out the challenges that are awaiting Turkey as a migration transition country. It also introduces a series of questions that might help to guide future research agendas.

REFERENCES

Abadan-Unat, N., 2002, *Bitmeyen Göç: Konuk İşçilikten Ulus-Ötesi Yurttaşlığa*, Istanbul: Publications of Istanbul Bilgi University.

Ahmad, F., 1993, *The Making of Modern Turkey*, London and New York: Routledge.

Akgündüz, A., 1998, "Migration to and from Turkey, 1783-1960: Types, Numbers and Ethno-religious Dimensions", *Jounal of Ethnic and Migration Studies*, 24(1): 97-121.

Bahadır, S. A., 1979, "Turkey and the Turks in Germany", *Aussenpolitic*, 1st quarter: 104-115.

Baydar, O., 1989, *75 Yılda Köylerden Şehirlere*, Istanbul: Tarih Vakfı Yurt Yayınları.

Behar, C., 2006, "Demographic Developments and 'Complementarities': Ageing, Labor and Migration", *Turkish Studies*, 7(1): 17-31.

Castles, S., 1998, "New Migrations, Ethnicity and Nationalism in Southeast and East Asia", paper presented at the School of Geography, Oxford University, June 12th, Oxford.

—, 2007, "Migration and Social Transformation", paper presented at the inaugural lecture for the Migration Studies Unit (MSU), November 15th, Clement.

Castles, S. and M. J. Miller, 1997, *The Age of Migration: International Population Movements in the Modern World*, 2nd ed., New York: The Guilford Press.

Courbage, Y. and Fargues, P. 1997 *Christians and Jews Under Islam*, London I.B. Tauris.

Erzan, R. and K. Kirişci, 2006, "Introduction", *Turkish Studies*, 7(1): 1-11.

Erzan, R., U. Kuzubaş and N. Yıldız, 2006, "Immigration Scenarios: Turkey-EU", *Turkish Studies*, 7(1): 33-44.

İçduygu, A., 1991, "Migrant as a Transitional Category: Turkish Migrants in Melbourne, Australia", unpublished Ph.D. thesis, Demography Department, Australian National University, Canberra.

—, 2006a, "Gaining from Migration: Case Study on Turkey", Paper prepared for the OECD Development Center, Koc University, Istanbul.

—, 2006b, "Turkey and International Migration", OECD Sopemi report for Turkey 2005-06, Koc University, Istanbul.

—, 2007, "Turkey and International Migration", OECD Sopemi report for Turkey 2006-07, Koc University, Istanbul.

İçduygu, A. and İ. Sirkeci, 1998, *"Changing Dynamics of the Migratory Regimes between Turkey and the Arab Countries"*, Turkish Journal of Population Studies, *20: 3-16.*

İçduygu, A., Ş. Toktaş and B. A. Soner, 2008, "The Politics of Population in a Nation Building Process: Emigration of Non-Muslims from Turkey", *Ethnic and Racial Studies*, 31(2): 358-389.

Kaiser, B. and A. İçduygu, 2005, "Türkiye'de Yaşayan Yabancı Uyruklular" (Foreign Residents Living in Turkey), A. Kaya ve T. Tarhanlı (der.), *AB Üyesi Ülkelerde ve Türkiye Gerçekliğinde Anayasal Vatandaşlık ve Azınlıklar (Constitutional Citizenship and Minorities in the Member Countries of the EU and Turkey)*, Istanbul: TESEV, ss. 171-184.

Kaya, A. and F. Kentel, 2005, "Euro-Turks: A Bridge or a Breach between Turkey and the European Union?", Istanbul: Center for European Studies.

Keyder, Ç., 1987, *State and Class in Turkey: A Study in Capitalist Development*, London: Verso.

Kirisci, K., 1996, "Refugees of Turkish Origin: Coerced Immigrants to Turkey since 1945", *International Migration*, 34(3): 385-412.

—, 2000, "Disaggregating Turkish Citizenship and Immigration Practices", *Middle Eastern Studies*, 36(3): 1-22.

Kirişci, K., 2001, "UNHCR and Turkey: Cooperating towards an Improved Implementation of the 1951 Convention on the Status of Refugees", *International Journal of Refugee Law*, 13(1/2).

—, 2005, "A Friendlier Schengen Visa System as a Tool of 'Soft Power': The Experience of Turkey", *European Journal of Migration and Law*, 7(4): 343-367.

—, 2007, "Border Management and EU-Turkish Relations: Convergence or Deadlock", CARIM-RR, European University Institute, Florence.

Loizos, P., 1999, "Ottoman Half-lives: Long-term Perspectives on Particular Forced Migrations", *Journal of Refugee Studies*, 12(3): 237-263.

Marcus, M. R., 1985, *The unwanted: European refugees in the twentieth century*, Oxford: Oxford University Press.

Unutulmaz, K. O., 2007, "International Retirement Migration in Turkey: Dynamics, Processes and Implications", MA Dissertation submitted to the Department of International Relations, Koc University, Istanbul.

Zolberg, A., 1983, "The formation of new states as a refugee-generating process", *ANNALS, AAPSS*, 467: 24-38.

PART ONE

Emigration From Turkey

1

Borders of Belonging in the 'Exchanged' Generations of Karamanlis

RENK ÖZDEMİR

INTRODUCTION

The mandatory transfer of whole populations between Greece and Turkey that took place at the beginning of the twentieth century was extraordinary, not only because of the immense size of the population subjected to the mandatory 'exchange' and its socio-political impact upon the receiving societies in its aftermath, but also because of the criterion upon which this 'exchangeability' was based in the Lausanne Convention. Foreseeing the mandatory transfer of whole populations on the basis of being Orthodox or Muslim, the Convention left the *"rationae personae* application of the Lausanne Convention ... unclear in that it possibly allowed for all co-religionists to be transferred (i.e. Albanians in Greece)" (Barutciski, 2004: 30, Ladas, 1932: 380, 381). While some groups, such as the Muslim Albanians in Greece, were kept exempt from the scheme (Ladas, 1932: 380), it was decided that a group from the Asia Minor interior who spoke Turkish and wrote it in Greek script, called the Karamanlis,[1]

---

1 *Karamanlı* in Turkish. Some of the informants also referred to the group as *Karamanlu*. The suffix *–lu* however is no longer used in modern Turkish. Also note that the suffix *–lar* indicates

would be included in the exchange scheme. This paper examines the processes that led to the realignment of the 'borders of belonging' in this particular group, whose 'key signifiers of belonging' have been the basis of their differentiation in relation to the changing micro contexts shared with their 'immediate others'[2] both before and after the Exchange. Accordingly in the first part, the study historically reflects on the societal context and the nationalization of belongings in the Imperial realm prior to the Exchange and, in the second part, it attempts to provide an examination of the processes involved in the gradual transformation of the 'borders of belonging'. In so doing, accompanying spatial and socio-political changes are treated within the framework of a metaphorical *rite of passage* in an effort to put two parallel processes into perspective, namely, the re-alignment of the geographical *and* mental borders of belonging.

Informed by a qualitative approach and through the use of ethnographic data collection, the study focuses on the process that has seen the reshaping of the borders of belonging in the late first and early second-generation Karamanlis and attempts to provide an outlook on their self/group perceptions, the Exchange and the changing image of 'the other'. Findings of the research are mainly based on the empirical data gathered through in-depth interviews with 38 second

---

plurality in Turkish. For this reason, one can also note the Turcophone group members referring to themselves as *Karamanlılar*. On the other hand, due to a specific grammar rule, the name *Karamanlı* (or *Karamanlu*) accommodates both the singular and the plural forms. The Turcophone informants preferred to refer to the community as *Karamanlı* or *Karamanlu*. On the other hand, Greek speakers refer to the group as *Karamanlides*, since the suffix *–des* denotes plurality in Greek. Within the framework of this study, the name is interchangeably used as *the Karamanli* (singular) or *the Karamanlis* (plural) in accordance with the English orthography. However, it would also be apt to refer to the group as the last Turcophone generations still refer to themselves, namely, as *Karamanlı*.

2 Term used to denote a category that the community has had *one to one contact* with. In this sense, the term differs from the general category of 'the other'. It is important to draw a distinction between the all-encompassing term 'the other' often conceptualized as the binary opposition of an extended collectivity with extended or imagined ties, as introduced by Benedict Anderson and the term 'the immediate other'. The term immediate other offers a tool to translate the subject positionings of 'us' versus 'the other' in micro contexts, underlining the one-to-one interaction processes.

and 12 first-generation Karamanli exchangees living in Nea Karvali (Kavala) and research conducted during the Visiting Fellowship period spent at the Centre for Asia Minor Studies (Athens).

LITERATURE REVIEW

> Written from the vantage point of nationalistic ideological concerns...the official histories in both countries appropriated the historical setting of this event from the very beginning and molded along the way the local ramifications of the Lausanne Treaty as a whole into the master narratives of their respective nations. Whereas Greek official historiography looked upon the events which led to and were associated with Lausanne as a collective tragedy and sanctioned them under the rubric of the Asia Minor Catastrophe, Turkish scholarship viewed these events as a triumphant recreation ...These two attitudes engendered, in turn, two discernible and diametrically opposed patterns in the representation of the Exchange, pointing at best to the use of history as an instrument of manipulating collective memory (Yıldırım 2002: 20).

Without doubt, this approach also applied to the treatment of the Karamanlis, in that various authors have taken "a conception inherent in the practice of nationalism" and "in the workings of the modern state system"[3] (Brubaker, 1996: 15, 16) and applied it retrospectively to communal identities presupposed to date back more than ten centuries. Whilst some of these accounts seem to be specifically formulated to build on the respective nationalisms' claims to a *continuum* in time and ethnic roots, other accounts belong to historians who simply make use of the categories of 'ethnic group' or 'nation' with the above-mentioned understanding.

It is no coincidence that the Karamanlis increasingly became an 'object of rivalry' between the Greek and Turkish nationalisms towards the conclusion of the 19th century. The historical develop-

---

3 Brubacker is referring to the 'realist cast of mind' dominating the studies of nationalism.

ment of these two rival nationalisms would soon culminate in a series of wars, reaching a climax with the Greco-Turkish wars of 1921 and 1922. Greek nationalism's interest in the ethnic origins of the peoples of Asia Minor dated back to the second half of the 19th century. The Karamanlis have been depicted as the 'unredeemed Greeks of Asia Minor' to be emancipated from Ottoman rule. They were depicted as ethnic Greeks who had lost their language but resisted the loss of 'the Greek religion' and preserved Orthodoxy (Benlisoy, 2002: 927, 930).[4] Greek nationalisms' ethno-linguistic line of explanation in relation to nationhood has made particular reference to the usage of Greek characters in the writing of Turkish, and extended this to the early presence and loss of Hellenism in the region basing its explanation on the continuum of an ethno-religious line of belonging.

Turkish nationalisms' views on the community on the other hand, would come to be expressed much later. From 1899 to 1923, successive articles on Turkish speaking communities were published in İkdam, Hakimiyet-i Milliye and Söz. Names like Şemseddin Sami and Cami Baykurt wrote extensively on the Turkishness of the Karamanlis, making reference to the linguistic basis of nationhood (Benlisoy 2002). References were made to the linguistic and cultural uniqueness of this group, tracing their ethnic roots to the Turkic tribes who had settled in greater Cappadocia before the war of Malazgirt in 1071 (Baykurt, 1932). This ethno-linguistic line of explanation set forth language as the primary key signifier of belonging to the 'corpus of the nation' and incorporated culture into its discourse just as the former did.

Arguably, the late 19th early 20th century debates repeated themselves in the 1960s and lately in the 2000s and writers from both strands continue to hold the floor with these broad arguments in addressing 'their' readership curious about the 'roots' of Karamanlis.

---

4 Benlisoy makes reference to Ilias Anagnostakis and Evangelia Balta, *La Découverte de la Cappadoce au Dix-Neuviéme Siécle*, Istanbul: Eren (1994). See also Alexis Alexandris "Η απόπειρα δημιουργίας Τουρκορθόδοξης Εκκλησίας (The Attempt of Establishing A Turco-Orthodox Chruch)", Δελτίο: Κέντρου Μικρασιατικών Σπουδών 4 (1983): 159-210.

Contemporary authors in search of 'proofs' vis-à-vis the 'ethnic roots' of the Karamanlis[5] refer exhaustingly but selectively to prominent historians whose work pertains to the early eras of Asia Minor/Anatolia.[6]

Among other reference points are the church records and kadi codices and the way the community members were referred to in these records. Then there are the travellers' notes. While there is no comprehensive study of the travellers' notes to date, it would be interesting to inquire whether earlier accounts were as hasty to endow this group with national categories – if at all – as the 19th and 20th century authors did. One of the earlier historical accounts is that of Dernschwam's travel notes, speaking of the Karamanlis as 'the Caramanos'. Having traveled through Istanbul and Asia Minor extensively in the mid-sixteenth century, Dernschwam provides that these people originated from Karaman, knew no Greek and spoke Turkish. Some were resettled by Sultan Selim I in Istanbul, (Dernschwam 1992: 78) mostly in the region between Yedikule and Samatya neighborhoods. Then, a century later, Evliya Çelebi refers to the Karamanlis of Antalya. De Planhol transfers knowledge from Çelebi. Accordingly, Çelebi in his 17th century writings mentions the *Rums*[7] in Antalya speaking only Turkish (De Planhol 1958: 111 cited in Faroqhi 2005: 92).

Among the contemporary contributions to the literature are the accounts provided by Richard Clogg, Janos Eckmann, Robert

---

5   This is not to suggest of course that the evaluation of the very reference points (at times archival data) provided by historians have been immune from the categorical lenses that Brubacker refers to.

6   Even the terminology used is highly politicized. Put crudely, while employment of the term Asia Minor refers to support of the Greek nationalist theses, usage of the term Anatolia denotes an alignment with the Turkish nationalist theses. Such is the case when referring to a place name with its Greek or Turkish equivalent (i.e. Constantinople in place of Istanbul and vice versa). Needless to say, such in-text implications are not the grounds for employment of vocabulary (i.e. place names) within the framework of this study.

7   In relation to the population sample at stake, the late first and early second now-bilingual generations referred to themselves as 'urum', with the addition of 'u' at the beginning (Fieldwork Notes, December 2005). 'Urum' is an older form of the term 'Rum' in Turkish. For the changing conceptualizations of the term Rum see Salih Özbaran, *Bir Osmanlı Kimliği: 14.-17. Yüzyıllarda Rum/Rumi Aidiyet ve İmgeleri*, Istanbul: Kitap Yayınevi (1994).

Anhegger, Gotthard Jaschke, Ioanna Petropoulu, Ilias Anagnostakis, Evangelia Balta, Alexis Alexandris, Semavi Eyice, Teoman Ergene, Turgut Kut, İsmet Hüsrev Tökin and Foti Benlisoy (Alexandris 1983; Anagnostakis 1994; Anhegger 1979-1980, 1983; Anhegger 1986; Balta 1990, 2000, 2003; Benlisoy 2002; Clogg 1999; Eckmann 1964; Ergene 1951; Eyice 1962; Jascke 1964; Kut 1987; Petropoulu 1993; Tökin 1984). Most of their articles can be found in journals like *Tarih ve Toplum*, *Belleten*, *Mnemon* and *Deltio*, namely the Bulletin of the Centre for Asia Minor Studies (Δελτίο Κέντρου Μικρασιατικών Σπουδών).

Without a doubt, this is an incomplete list and does not include all authors writing on the issue. However, as already mentioned, the aim of this study is to provide an overview of the processes involved in the reshaping of the 'borders of belonging' for this particular community rather than to contribute principally to the above mentioned literature.

On the other hand, it may still be possible to speak about the prevalent perceptions of the self and 'the other' and/or the ways in which the contending purveyors of the meta-narratives approached the issue and took their part in the eventual drawing of the borders of belonging for the Karamanlis. Oral history studies to be conducted with the last Turcophone generations may be of use in providing trans-ferred knowledge. Moreover, it is still possible to discover some of the Karamanli printed material produced for the consumption of the late Karamanli communities. Some of these are being sold in book-auc-tions or have taken their place in individual collections. This is because many of the Karamanlis sold their books and other heavy material in the provinces close by (i.e. in Aksaray) prior to their final departure from Anatolia, in order to make room in their oxcarts (Fieldwork Notes, December, 2005). This scatteredness is unfortunate for researchers, especially with regard to the materials that have not yet been recorded in the below-mentioned editions. This is in addition to the fact that most individual collections are not open for research and there is no system established for the willing individual collectionists to have their materials recorded.

Sévérien Salaville, Eugène Dalleggio, and Evangelia Balta have compiled and listed materials in Karamanli script that are *known* to the researchers to date. Needless to say, this is an ongoing effort. The first three of these editions were compiled by Salaville and Dalleggio and includes 333 printed materials in Karamanli script, printed between the years 1584 to 1900 (Salaville 1958, 1966, 1974). Balta made additions to this material with a similar effort and published them in 1987 (Balta 1987b). The same year, Balta published another compilation, this time composed of material published in the 20th century, the latest with a print-date of 1935 (Balta 1987a). In her compilations, Balta also included brief descriptions of each printed text, such as the printing date – where available, other editions, where it was printed, and the name of the printing house. Balta also added brief synopses of the content of the material.[8] Balta made the final compilation in 1997 (Balta 1997). This volume was the result of an ongoing project, the initial results of which she had published in 1991 (Balta 1991).

Most of the texts cited in these volumes were produced *for* the cultural, religious, and/or political consumption of the Karamanlis and only some were produced *by* the Karamanli *literati*. In other words, most of the material cited in these editions are translations (e.g. from Greek) into Karamanli script rather than being the production of the Karamanli literati themselves. In this regard, only some can be viewed as primary sources that reflect the views of individual members of the Karamanli literati.

---

8   Among other Karamanli material at the Centre for Asia Minor Studies (Athens) are Karamanli books, religious and literary brochures, community registers, church records, codices, and other related material, such as baptism documents in Karamanli script. There are also photographs dating back to the late 19th century, pictures of traditional wear, landscapes, and newly built state institutions (including the girl's school in Gelveri) and voice recordings (Karamanli songs) kept in the Musical Archives Section of the Asia Minor Folklore Archives. Lastly, there is an oral history archive under the heading 'Oral Tradition Archives', where oral testimonies of informants from Asia Minor are kept, taken under record from the mid-1930s onwards (Cited in the C.A.M.S. Brochure 2006).

For instance, 30 % of the Karamanli input was made by a single Karamanli literatus, Evangelinos Misailidis (Balta, 1993: 39). An important contribution to the literature would be to investigate the gradual changes in the views of this Karamanli intellectual through his articles in Anatoli, where he discussed various fashionable political ideals of the time and the possible ways in which the Karamanlis could fit into the picture. Other Karamanli intellectuals could also be included in this prospective study. However, the extent to which their views reflected the views of the consumers of their texts (i.e. the periphery Karamanlis, living – if not completely, then relatively – aloof from the socio-political milieu which had seen the production of these texts and the ideological undercurrents taking place at the Ottoman Centre and Athens) would be a matter of debate.[9]

Translations into Karamanli script are to a large extent of religious concern, but there is also material translated for cultural consumption (i.e. literary, educational) of a non-religious kind. Two authors, Robert Anhegger and Evangelia Balta, follow two different criteria of categorisation for the periodisation of these productions. While Anhegger opts to classify them as religious material, practical books of daily concern, and literary materials, studying them as productions of a) the period between 1718 and 1818, and b) the era between 1819 and 1900, Balta classifies them mainly as religious and

---

9   To review the material produced at the time and to examine the phases these authors went through would be an interesting exercise, taking into consideration the author and the publisher of the text, the contemporary ideological currents and the Centre/periphery relations. Evangelia Balta conducted a preliminary study on the prefaces of the Karamanlı books, in search of a national consciousness among the Turcophone Orthodox prior to the Exchange [Μπαλτα Ευαγγελία (Balta Evangelia), Οι πρόλογοι των καραμανλίδικων βιβλίων για τη μελέτη της "εθνικής συνείδησης" των τουρκόφωνων ορθόδοξων πληθυσμών της Μικρας Ασίας (Introductions of Karamanlidika Books for Studying the 'National Identity' of the Turcophon Orthodox Population in Asia Minor), σελ. 225-233]. A shortened version of this article was translated by Herculles Millas in 1990 into Turkish. See Evangelia Balta "Karamanlıca Kitapların Önsözleri." *Tarih ve Toplum* 13 (1990): 18-21. Note however, that Balta does not refer to a Centre and periphery *dichotomy* and does not draw a thick line between the eventual conceptualizations of belonging among the Karmanli literati of the Centre and the masses of the periphery.

'profane' books, studying them within the periods between 1751-1830 and 1831-1935 (Balta 1998). In this current study, we opt for the second classification, especially in relation to the re-constitution of the borders of belonging among the Karamanlis. Arguably, the changing percentages in the kind of printed material can be considered to reflect the increased outreach of the main producers of these translations (i.e. the Patriarchate, the private printing houses owned by the rising bourgeoisie in and abroad) to the grassroots, if not the changing trends in demand. The changing percentages in the kind of printed work may arguably be taken as mirroring the ideological undercurrents taking effect over these institutions' increasing quests of intervention in the socio-political sphere or the gradual withdrawal thereof. The gradual decrease in the production of religious books translated into Karamanli script by the Patriarchate for instance, may provide a partial perspective of this institution's universalist doctrinal influence (i.e. through the Ecclesiastical realm) gradually giving way or merging with the newly born nationalisms' quests of influence over these borderline communities. This process will be further discussed in the Analytical Part.

All in all, the above-mentioned six volumes leave us with 757 books, brochures, and other material in *Karamanli* script (Balta, 1991). However, to regard all these as *Karamanli* material or not depends on the criteria set for the definition of the term 'Karamanli'.

It is possible to take the region and/or the cultural characteristics (religion, speaking in Turkish but writing in Greek letters, the production of cultural artifacts such as songs, tales, monuments and so on) to define the Karamanlis. In this study, religion and language have been introduced as two key signifiers of belonging to account for the nationalization of belongings through these realms. In the literature however, more than often, one of these signifiers is brought to the fore as evidence of an essentially fixed form of belonging. In other words, the very selection/implication of the *core* criterion to define the Karamanlis (language, religion) -upon which all the rest gains meaning-, differs from author to author.

Moreover, the criteria themselves (or what they – i.e. religion and language – signify emically and ethically in terms of 'belonging' to a political or cultural entity) seem not to be fixed through time and space. Even the most solid departure point, i.e. the geographical categorization, seems far from being fixed. According to the geographical categorization, the Karamanlis have been accounted for as the:

> ...inhabitants of... a region with unstable [political] borders that differed from period to period. Its boundaries in relation to the subject in hand are: to the North as far as Ankara, Yozgat and Hüdavendigar, and to the South as far as Antalya and Adana, to the East as far as Kayseri and Sivas, and to the West as far as the borders of Aydın Province (Balta, 2003: 26).

This approximately provides for the outer borders of the cities, today named as Denizli, Burdur, Isparta, Konya, Karaman; with the eastern borders of Karaman, Niğde, Kayseri; the northern borders of Kayseri, Nevşehir, Aksaray –enlargening towards Yozgat and Kırşehir-Konya, Afyon, and lastly, the western borders of the neighbouring Denizli province. Vryonis points to approximately the same milieu (Vryonis, 1971: 452). Anhegger (1988) and Eckmann (1964), on the other hand, make additions to the Karamanli confines and include Roumeli, Macedonia, Syria, the Balkans, and the like remote regions (Anhegger 1988; Eckmann 1964).

Since the borders of these regions have changed over centuries, together with the names of the settlements, according to the dominant polity, it has been difficult to draw an historical topography of Anatolia. Place names changed along with the official languages of the subsequent polities that gained dominance. This process is further complicated by 'the use of different names referring to the same place, by authors writing in different languages' (Cahen 1994: 78).

Compounding the definitional problem is the difficulty of finding accurate information regarding the exact number of the Karamanlis. Both the overall numbers in the Exchange literature and the numbers provided for the Karamanlis in particular should be subject to vigilant reading. Although secondary sources generally refrain from providing numbers there are some reference points such as the Lausanne Conference proceedings and official reports. Among the secondary sources, Melpo Merlier cites the number of the exchanged-*Cappadocians* as 44.432 (Merlier 1963:xix). Then another account written by Triantaphyllides (1938) takes 'the 1928 census returns' as a basis and provides the number of the 'Turkish speaking Greeks of Anatolian origin settled in Greece in the 1930s' as 103,642 (Triantaphyllides 1928 cited in Clogg 1999: 133). Alternatively Richard Clogg provides the numbers of Karamanlis as ranging between 'perhaps as many as 300,000' (1999: 115) to 400,000 (Kontoglu in Clogg 1997: 74). The issue gets more complicated when one considers the primary sources. In a report dated May 10, 1922 (FO/371/7923/E2002)?[10] the numbers of the Turcophone Orthodox are provided as 500,000. Then, one comes across Lord Curzon's remarks at the Lausanne proceedings, when he mentions that '50,000 Anatolian Rums are expected to remain in Turkey anyway' (Session starting at 16.00, 12th December 1922, Lausanne Proceedings).

As for the earlier years, church records and *kadi* codices and similar credible sources may reveal numbers, but finding records under a centralized body remains problematic. For the period concerned, this was also the case elsewhere in the world. According to Drake (2003: 5), it wasn't until the 19th century that the European states started to "converge this sort of information at their disposal" and develop uniform practices "in the collection, analysis and presentation of demographic data" (Drake 2003: 5). In the case of the Ottoman Empire, it wasn't until the end of the 19th century that the state concentrated on recording 'those with tax liability; head of the

---

10 See also in A. Alexandris (1983). I would like to thank James Cronan from the Remote Enquiries Department of the British National Archives for his assistance in helping me to locate the report. The report was prepared by Arnold Toynbee, Arthur Boutwood and H. Pirie Gordon.

household; and those able to serve in the army' (Quataert 2002: 172). More importantly, tax liabilities differed from *millet* to *millet*, and the main basis for the collection of demographic data was religion, *not* language. This is the main reason behind the lack of preciseness as to the number of Karamanlis. All one is left with is the secondary sources that *claim* to give close estimates.

RESEARCH DESIGN

Hypothesis and Research Question

To date, the question for some still remains whether there is an 'essence' that is passed on through generations and that separates today's political categories or whether these identities are constructed upon cultural signifiers that in time become nationalized; signifiers that modernity's forces at work have seen become singularized in meaning and appropriated by respective national narratives. This study not only makes the latter statement but also claims to provide empirical evidence for this process. While the appropriation of cultural signifiers and attribution of additional/different meanings to existing ones by the contending meta narratives is explained by a Weberian (1968: 215) hypothesis that "rule is justified with reference to broader structures of meaning", testimonies and transferred knowledge from earlier generations reveal that the fixation of multiple forms of belonging to a national one owes to a plurality of processes created in the interplay of agency and structure. Thus, rather than searching for closed-events and essentially fixed identities, the study prioritizes the *continuous* transformation of the micro contexts that give way to the subject-positions of 'us' versus 'them', 'self' versus 'the other'.

Forced migration phenomena are usually dealt with as constituents of a 'rupture' from the communal identity and culture of the group left behind. The Exchange in this regard represents a unique example by being a forced displacement phenomenon followed by the granting of immediate citizenship to the group members who were expected to view this process as a repatriation process. Group members were immediately defined as parts of a new 'whole,' followed by the introduction of a new form of socio-political belonging through state institutions. Yet they experienced a series of disparities both in relation to their changing subject-positions and new otherization grounds as posed by their new 'immediate others' in particular and society at large. This applied especially to the Karamanlis.

This study examines the processes involved in the realignment of the borders of belonging in this particular group, whose key signifiers of belonging (religion and language) had been the basis of their differentiation in relation to the micro contexts shared with their 'immediate others' formerly in an Imperial realm and later in a national context. While the former (religion) had been the basis of their formal categorization during the time of the Ottoman Empire, language has since been the basis of their otherization within the borders of the subsequent nation-state.

Accordingly, in the first section of the Analytical Part, the study reflects on the societal context and the nationalization of belongings in the Imperial realm prior to the Exchange, while, in the second section of the Analytical Part, it attempts to provide an outlook to the gradual transformation of the borders of belonging after the Exchange. We therefore introduce the Exchange as a *metaphorical* 'rite of passage', and attempt to put two parallel processes into perspective: the re-alignment of the geographical *and* mental borders of belonging. As such, the Exchange represents not only a transition from one legal status to another and from one political sphere to another, but also a transition from one cultural realm to another, necessitating the re-alignment of the key signifiers of belonging in the dialectical relations of the Centre and the periphery, of the self and the 'new other'; attributing to the first and second- generation 'exchangees'[11] a

---

11 Throughout the study, the term 'exchangee' is used to underline the state-imposed and internationally supervised character of a regulatory mechanism that has come to drastically affect human lives.

borderline or *liminal* characteristic in the midst of socio-political and economic turbulences that paralleled their individual experiences.

Based on transferred knowledge and secondary readings, it is suggested that cultural domains were not always as bitterly contested or charged in terms of the key signifiers of communities being appropriated by state x's 'national' 'culture' and not by state y's. It is suggested that this was a belated process for the 'Near East'. The periods following the establishment of new regimes (i.e. the 1924 and 1923 Republican regimes in Greece and Turkey) have seen the continuation of efforts vis-à-vis the re-appropriation of the cultural signifiers of the pre-national eras, namely the nationalization of cultural realms and borders of belonging, via meta-narratives introduced through a downwards re-interpretation of culture. Oral history accounts reveal that this has not been a smooth process, especially if there has been a traumatic group dislocation and resettlement to a linguistically, socio-politically, and geographically segregated sphere.

The first generations having been through the most traumatic rupture in relation to the Exchange preserved their key signifiers of belonging and continued using Turkish, a practice that at times served to extend their social spheres of interaction in the presence of 'others'. Gradually, as of the second-generations, communities started to take an active role in the *selective* preservation of their key signifiers of belonging. In the case of the Karamanlis for instance, who spoke the language of 'the other', the bi-lingual late second-generations gradually started to opt for speaking in Greek, not only in social but also in private spheres of interaction in order to facilitate a less problematic process of assimilation for their children. Whilst publicly spoken, Turkish, as a societally contested key signifier of belonging, was gradually left to one side, societally accepted elements of the Karamanli culture were hyphenated. In that, religion has not simply been a plane of societal acceptance, making reference to an ethno-religiously shared belonging to the society at large, but it also served as a plane for the *translation* of the meanings attributed to their otherwise contested signifiers, such as language.

Methodology

The difficulty of dealing with identity-based questions in the Social Sciences owes to the insurpassibility of the agency/structure dichotomy. For instance, most studies in Migration that make use of the research methods and main paradigms of mainstream International Relations, Political Science, or Economics remain relatively limited in explaining identity-related phenomena by entering the same dead-ends, or by simply avoiding the issue of agency. Then there is the reverse inhibition posed by the employment of other disciplines' agency-based lines of inquiry. Strands of Sociology and Anthropology have interesting insights to bring to identity formation but may remain weak in bringing explanations to state level or systemic determinants and their transformative roles.

Efforts to untangle the complex processes of identity formation are ongoing. Take Anthony Giddens' problematization of the agency/structure dichotomy[12] and his endeavor to theorize their co-workings around the concept of 'structuration' for instance. Giddens' theory of structuration problematized the gaps in social theory and pointed to the complex processes involved in identity formation. However this time, 'the notion of structure had become rather diffused and even dissipated through the actions of the agency' (Singlewood 1991: 365).While culturalist approaches remained weak in bringing system level explanations, structuralists–apart from Goldmann and Bahtin –had trouble accounting for 'the complexity of the social structure and its transformations through collisions and collective actions' (Singlewood 1991: 363).

Because this project's purview cannot avoid the tensions of these ongoing methodological debates, it is limited to the same effects. Indeed, it is possible to depict the difficulties posed by the agency/structure dichotomy in the very organization of the study. Therefore, the project is divided into two main parts based on two different levels of explanation, interwoven around two metaphors. In the first part, a cen-

---

12   See Anthony Giddens, *Studies in Social and Political Theory*, London: Hutchinson (1985).

tre and periphery metaphor is used with a deviation from its neo-Durkheimian origins in Edward Shils and Serif Mardin.[13] In the second part, ethnographic data is processed around van Gennep's conceptualization of *rite de passage*. Still, theoretical explorations are kept to a minimum due to the ethnographic nature of the project.

This project constitutes part of a larger study that explores the various process*es* involved in modernization and the differentiated reflections of these processes onto the conceptualizations of belonging among the masses of the periphery. In this wider framework, ethnographic data is processed without divorcing the context from the infrastructural changes on the domestic *and* global planes. Accordingly, the notion of structure does not become dissipated through/in the actions of the agency. Moreover, neither the concepts of 'culture' nor 'agency' are read as autonomous in the roles they play in transforming the realms and contexts in which the borders of belonging undergo a *continuous* change. This leads to a specific understanding of the concepts of the Centre and the periphery.

While both Edward Shils who first introduced the dichotomy,[14] and Serif Mardin – who developed the metaphor to account for the social reflections of the modernization process in the Ottoman Empire – write about the overriding dynamics of how modernization affects the complex processes of identity formation, they each take a different approach. In their readings, the transformative role of structure is not taken into consideration in depth, if at all. Accordingly, the very notions of the Centre and the periphery are read as institutionally determined and somewhat domestically limited. In other words, contrary to the underlying premises of the study at hand, the dichotomy of the Centre and periphery is read as being aloof[15] from the global relations of production, domestically limited and fixed.

---

13 See Edward Shils. Center and Periphery: Essays in Macrosociology. The University of Chicago Press: Chicago (1975) and Şerif Mardin. "Türk Siyasasını Açıklayabilecek Bir Anahtar: Merkez-Çevre İlişkileri." *Türkiye'de Toplum ve Siyaset*, Makaleler-1, Istanbul: İletişim (1991).

14 -moving away from the Parsonian theory in the 1950s-

15 confined to the borders of one state.

While spatial limits and the subject matter of the project dictate that theoretical discussion be kept to a minimum, the overall reading is based on an understanding that emphasizes the role of structure in determining the realms and context(s) through which institutionalization takes place and wherein the agency can function.[16]

To recap, in the first and second sections of the Analytical Part a modernist line is followed to account for the nationalization of the micro contexts within the Imperial realm. Secondary sources are employed for this introductory part. The fourth section of the Analytical Party on the other hand, builds on the information collected through ethnographic methods of data collection, these being mainly group-observation and in-depth interviews.

Information was collected in both Turkey and Greece. First and second sections of the Analytical Part mainly comprise a review of secondary material gathered throughout the Visiting Fellowship period spent at the Centre for Asia Minor Studies, while the fourth section of the Analytical Part is extensively based on the findings of the fieldwork conducted in Nea Karvali in December 2005. For this latter part, data collection involved on-site observation and in-depth interviews with 38 early second and 12 late first-generation Karamanli exchangees.[17]

---

16 Once the overall understanding stresses the role of the infrastructure, then modernity for any given state is no longer an isolated process. This study also discusses a multiplicity of centres for the members of the Orthodox millet. In parallel to the inevitable structural transformations, the Ottoman Empire is continuously fragmented, giving way to a multiplicity of centres, if not in official, then in socio-political terms. The literati that had fallen within the borders of the new Greek monarchy did not stop to be effective vis-à-vis the shaping of a national consciousness among the masses in the periphery of the Ottoman Empire overnight. They were not the mere extensions of the Rum elite in the Ottoman Centre either. In this regard, modernization in the Ottoman Empire is neither an isolated nor a uniform process for the communities involved.

17 The researcher would like to thank the Director of the Centre for Asia Minor Studies (Athens), Dr. Stavros Anestidis, for his hospitality during the Visiting Fellowship period spent at the Centre throughout the first and third quarters of the academic year 2005/2006. The researcher would also like to acknowledge Mr. Geogrios Karageorigou's assistance throughout the fieldwork carried out in Northern Greece, Kavala and Ms. Evridiki Nasena's translations in Greek and German throughout the literature review process carried out in Athens.

Secondary sources have been used for triangulation purposes in relation to the information gathered through oral history accounts and on-site observation. Assistance was provided in the form of written and oral translation. Reaching secondary information proved problematic, especially in terms of numerical data. Records that Karamanli communities brought with themselves at the time of the Exchange, such as the community registers, codices and other documents of educational and religious concern are well kept but scattered. While some community registers, codices and educational and religious material are kept in the treasury of the archives of the Centre for Asia Minor Studies and a few similar initiatives, others are kept in various community centers like the one in Nea Karvali village (Stegi Politismou Neas Karvalis) and in the separate family archives of the village notables. This scatterdness is problematic for research. Moreover, the occupation of Northern Greece in the Second World War reportedly resulted in losing some numerical data, although numbers for the village of Gelveri remained intact. Information in relation to the village was provided by the Statistics Department of the Prefecture (Governorship) of Kavala.

This study will focus on the exchanged generations of Gelveri (Aksaray),[18] one of the mixed settlements of the Orthodox and Muslim populations of Asia Minor, reaching an estimate of 4000-4500 peoples before the Exchange. For the village of Gelveri, according to the cross-referenced oral testimonies, there were approximately 800 households. This amounts to an estimate of 4000 to 4500 people, out of which 400 were reported to be Muslims. As for the numbers of those who resettled in Nea Karvali, information gathered from the Statistics Department of the Prefecture (Governorship) of Kavala reveals that there were 1090 residents in the year 1928 and 1209 residents in the year 1951. This number held in relation to the numbers provided by E.S.Y.E – E.Σ.Y.E., namely, 600 families/2100 people for the year 1991,

---

18 Gelveri (Aksaray) is now referred to as Güzelyurt (Turkey). The Orthodox Karamanlis of Gelveri named their new village Nea Karvali, which is part of Kavala (Greece).

confirms the high degree of out migration and – in the early years of the post-Exchange era – high mortality rates in Nea Karvali.

Factors involved in this drastic fall are addressed under the fourth section of the Analytical Part. Yet, there are are no detailed studies accounting for the reasons for migration from Nea Karvali during the early years of settlement. Such is the case with both the emigration and immigration patterns in the latter 20th century, concerning which oral history accounts provide essential insights not only for the early years of settlement in Nea Karvali but also for the mobility in the following years (i.e. the massive emigration to Germany in the late 1950s and 1960s and the immigration wave from the ex-Soviet Republics to Nea Karvali from the 1990s onwards). Because oral history can only provide numbers approximate in value, triangulation was employed.

We gained entry to the field through contacts maintained with the gate-holders prior to the fieldwork, whose assistance greatly facilitated our research. Needless to say, due to ethical considerations regarding all compilation of data, we recorded, the informed oral consent of all interviewed individuals. Use of their names and/or pictures was subject to additional requests for permission.

The population sample was reached on the basis of snowball sampling in the Nea Karvali village. All individuals were either born in Gelveri or of (grand)parents born in Gelveri. This did not exclude, at times, one parent being from a neighboring village. Still, since the population sample interviewed had been resettled from one periphery settlement (Gelveri and/or the surrounding villages) to another (Nea Karvali), it constitutes a reliable representative sample for the experiences of the Karamanli populations living in the *periphery* settlements before and after the Exchange.

In-depth interviews were conducted with 12 late first-generation and 38 early second-generation exchangees with close representation of both genders. The grounds for receiving the 'late first-generation' title owes to their having experienced the Exchange in their *early childhood*. Attention has been paid to interview exchangees who have retained their mental faculties. Among the 12 first-generation members interviewed, we predominantly used the information gathered from Pantelis Akakiadis (1916) and Katina Hristoforidou (1919). The information from other first-generations, such as Makrina Hacıapostoulidou, Konstantinos Yousifidis, Elizabeth Sutluoglou (Demirci), Grigorios Hacatoglou, Orsiya Theofilaktou, Yorgos Hacıapostoulidis, Fotini Tomadiou, Minas Yousifidis, Anastasia Paytoncu, Grigorios Hacatoglou, and Arhelos Angelidis (Püsküloğlu) however, who were born in Gelveri between the years 1919-1922, has been treated as transferred knowledge rather than as first hand remembrance. Moreover, because the rest of the respondents identified one of them (who spoke a mixture of Bulgarian, Greek, and Turkish) as belonging to another group, calling him a *Tırhanlı*, – referred to as '*kuşdili* speaker' by the rest – his account has not been incorporated with the others.

Transferred knowledge gathered from the early second-generation exchangees born between 1924 and 1934 also proved to be valuable in relation to the experiences of the early first-generations. Information gathered from late second-generation[19] respondents, (born between the years 1934-1954), has been reserved for the separation phase only. Still, in the last section of the Analytical Part accounting for 1) the separation phase (separation from Gelveri, a three-day voyage by oxen, a train ride to Mersin, and a month long voyage by ship); 2) the transition phase (quarantine upon arrival in Greece, first contact with the Greek authorities, arrival at the first village where they would live two years, and resettlement to the second village) and 3) the reintegration phase into the new society, we have used the overall accounts of the first and second-generations.

In preparation for the semi-structured interviews, Kvale's

---

19 Disparities of age in this final population group owe to their (grand)parents' age disparities at the time of the exchange, owing predominantly to the tendency of young women marrying old men. This pattern is retained to a lesser degree.

(1996) design was taken as a loose reference point. Themes were depicted with a view to understand the changing conceptualizations of the 'self' and 'the other' and the processes involved in the reconceptualization of the borders of belonging. These processes were examined in relation to the subjects' resettlement to a new geographical and socio-political confine, religious re-institutionalization, the increasing centralization of the state, the teaching of a new language, and other socio-political variables involved at each phase.

Lastly, it should be noted that we were able to avoid lengthy discussions over the use of ethnographic methods of data collection and oral history as a credible source of information with the understanding that these are overridingly discussed by the contending approaches in the literature. Moreover, as repeatedly stated above, triangulation was maintained for all recorded material.

ANALYTICAL PART: RESULTS AND DISCUSSIONS[20]

'Borders of Belonging and Immediate Others' in the Last of the Imperial Realms

> The concept of 'the other' has taken different forms throughout history. For instance, the ancient Greeks envisioned 'the others' as the barbarians, in contrast to the civilized Greeks. Barbarians could have been valiant and brave but did not have the exact attributes of the Civilized. As for the Hebrew, they were the goy, those that fell outside of the chosen Hebrew community, those that were not Hebrew: 'the others'. As for the Ottoman Muslims, the concept of zimmi was another way of speaking about difference. They viewed the Christians and the Hebrew as ehl-i kitap (zimmi) or in other words those that have received the knowledge of the holy utterance, the word of God, prior to the arrival of the Prophet Muhammed and hence partially. In that, they regarded the zimmi as being in possession of religion, and thus civilization. But, the

---

20 Analyses and discussions in this Section will be interwoven owing to the overridingly qualitative nature of the project.

word of God was regarded as having been partially received and
hence non-Muslims were regarded as essentially different and infe-
rior in comparison (Quataert 2002: 253).

Similar generalizations are widely held in literature. However, the relational and contextual character of meaning maintains that the validity
of generalizing these views to essentially fixed totalities across centuries
is problematic. Is it then possible to know the extent to which/how
these views have been made inherent or were superseded by other 'otherizations' in different spatial and temporal settings, different cultural
milieus and socio-political contexts, with a view to understanding the
constructed nature of identities, contextual nature of meaning, and
thus the alternative readings of the self and 'the other'?

Clearly, perceptions of the self and 'the other' were not of a
national nature as conceptualized today, all throughout history. Oral
history accounts reveal that even at the end of the Ottoman era, which
had seen the rise of the essentialist understandings of the self and 'the
other' on the basis of ethnicity, individuals were capable of remaining
active in the interpretation process that saw the internalization of the
concept of 'the other'. Even when nationalisms took their effect in the
Near East, if conditions permitted, (for instance, for those who fell
outside the war zone of the Greco-Turkish armies), people were not
only able to exclude their co-villagers from externalizing narratives
vis-à-vis 'the other' but also kept seeing them as part of their immediate community (*köylüm/üz; co-villager*) a few generations later
(Fieldwork Notes, December 2005).

The Ottoman Empire dealt with its subjects as members of religiously defined communities called *millets*. Language or race did not
serve as signifiers of belonging to a millet. Ethnicity was not the basis
of the legal organization of millets and it did not become the basis of
societal otherization until later on.

Officially speaking, the Empire dealt with its subjects as members of these religiously defined communities. But in the Ottoman
Empire, the societal and legal organization of vocational segments

would cut through these religious amalgamations (Karpat, 1973: 113). Certain vocations were occupied by some millets and/or certain segments of one millet, but this developed rather conventionally among some of the major vocational categories such as the merchants and artisans who had an important numerical part in the vocational cake. For a majority of the population, vocations passed on from father to son (Karpat, 1973). This also applied to the Karamanli community in question.

While the borders of belonging for a Muslim were defined around religion, 'categories related to local belonging', as indicated by such terms as 'Konyevi' or 'Bursevi' [Konya dweller or Bursa dweller], and categories inseparable from 'the individual's occupation' (i.e. being 'a madrasah instructor, engraver, muralist, or farmhand') (Özbaran, 2004: 50), for an Orthodox these were, again, the religious criterion, namely the Orthodox faith, local belonging, and according to Augustinos (1997: 307) 'a third cultural confine mainly determined by language'.

But the linguistic picture, was more complex than asserted. The idea that language was a main signifier of a national form of belonging within the realms of the last monarchies of the Near East and the new Balkan states was problematic. This was not only the case for the tens of thousands of Karamanlis and "smaller numbers of Orthodox living in the eastern provinces of Asia Minor who spoke Armenian, Arabic, Kurdish and Syriac", but also for those in the Balkans and Macedonia. In these northern regions, there was a considerable number of "Albanian and Vlach speaking groups where Turkish, Albanian, Bulgarian and Ladino speaking Muslims and Jews lived" (Kitromilides, 1990: 43).

As a parallel process to the redefinition of the borders of belonging for the nationals of the Greek Kingdom, and the prioritization of the Greek language over the practice of Orthodoxy, the Greek speaking Orthodox groups that fell within the borders of the Ottoman Empire were now endowed with 'a separate linguistic group image'

(Jusdanis, 1998: 57). Hence it was, finally, religion, local belonging, and language that defined the borders of belonging for the periphery communities.[21]

However, until the rise of nationalisms, both Muslim and non-Muslim, Ottomans had intersecting definitions of 'belonging' within their shared micro-contexts which were not solely dependent on the linguistic variable (i.e. Ottoman being spoken as the lingua franca). Societal otherizations changed according to a myriad of variables, and the dialectical relation among them would change, if not the official other, the overtone. That is to say, the meaning attributed to the official other was not as fixed as it is depicted in the national meta-narratives today. The 'other' changed according to the context and changing levels of tension determined by such variables as: being of the centre or periphery, living in a mixed habitation or a segregated geographical confine, and/or speaking the language of 'the other' or not. To give an example, societally speaking, conceptualization of 'the other', even on the basis of the most clearly differentiated category, namely religion, had not been built around the official overtone only – and sometimes not at all. The 'other' changed according to the spatial, temporal, socio-political, and economic contexts, reflecting the changing levels of tension and relations of power among the members of certain sects within one religious community and their relation to that particular community's 'immediate other'. Take for instance, the relations between the late settlers of heterodox/orthodox Islamic belief (i.e. yörük[22]) and the settled Muslims/non-Muslims; the heterodox

---

21 Needless to say, for those who lived in the Centre, the linguistic variable and its role in the groups' self-identification was drastically different.

22 Nomadic tribes of orthodox or heterodox Islamic belief were referred as Yörük, their nomadic attribute being prioritized. It was interesting to come across the employment of the term '*yörük*' by some of the Karamanlis as an otherizing term, which did not indicate animosity but an in-between meaning. Some used the term when pointing to the late settlers of the village, their 'shared-others' with the settled Muslims. On another occasion, it was used by one informant to refer to her grandparents in a sarcastic tone as she told about the time they had burnt their clothes in resentment of their otherization ('Cepkenlerini çohalarını yaktı yörükler') smilingly indicating her feelings of loss, sadness, and anger (Athena Papadopoulou, 14th December 2005).

nomadic Muslims and the settled; the Orthodox and the Catholic; and the Gregorian etc.

In other words, neither the above-mentioned intersecting cultural milieus nor societal otherizations were shaped within the confines of the official *millet* categories only, which in the first place *did not have* solid borders in *cultural* terms. These people, living together in the upper or lower quarters of the same village and/or city, who entered into commercial transactions and spoke Ottoman as the *lingua franca*, shared not only the superordinate Ottoman Cultural milieu of the Centre and its otherizations, but also a multiplicity of intersecting subordinate micro cultural realms, sometimes shared more with the categorical-other than with those of the same millet. This was especially the case for small villages composed of mixed communities, such as the Gelveri village.

The very organization of society was complex. The societal structure was composed of "lateral and vertical associations, yet without full amalgamation; each segmentation being further divided into smaller units within itself and each unit being bound to another within a given hierarchical order while at the same time preserving its autonomy" (Karpat 2002: 34). It was this very structure that facilitated the existence of a multiplicity of belongings; shared borders of belonging and cultural milieus all feeding into one another, periodically intersecting or growing apart, according to such variables as the temporal and spatial characteristics or happenings in the overall Ottoman realm. As such the subordinate cultural realms continued to intersect with one another until a number of nationalisms started to come of age in dialectical relation with one another.

Officially speaking, the Empire foresaw a religious categorization of its subjects along communitarian forms of belonging. The state had 'enlivened the notion of the Caliphate', while the Sultan, among other titles and functions, bore the title of *gazi*, which came to mean 'warrior of Islam'. In this sense, individuals *were* 'deeply aware of the difference between Muslims and non-Muslims' (Quataert 2002: 253).

After all, the Muslims co-shared their main signifier of belonging, that is to say their religious belonging, with the Islamic attribute of the state apparatus.[23] But neither the state apparatus nor the religious institutions within its realms ascribed ethnicity, let alone race, to their religiously defined communities until nationalisms began to rise.

In order to ascertain how the Ottoman-representatives approached or stayed aloof from these cultural realms, one should have an in-depth understanding of both the official *and* societal organizations of the Empire.

Among others, the Sultan also took the title of '*Sultan-ı Rum*', the Islamic literati (*alimler*) were referred to as '*ulema-yi rum*', the raider soldiers (akıncılar) as '*gaziyan-ı rum*', the dervishes as '*abdalan-ı rum*', and poets as '*şuara-yı rum*' (Özbaran 2004: 47). In the macro context of the Ottoman Empire, connotations of the term *Rum* came to surpass the meaning it had carried when the territories of Eastern Rome had initially been taken over by the Ottomans, who referred to these territories as '*diyar-ı rum*'[the Roman states] and the residents as Rum, namely, 'the citizens of Rome' and/or those from the Roman states (Özbaran, 2004).

As for the micro contexts of interaction in small villages, the priest served as a mediator between the village community and the Ottoman authorities on the one hand, and between the former and the high clergy of the Ecclesiastical realm on the other (Karpat, 1983: 142). Moreover, due to the specific organization of the millet system and the autonomy of the Patriarchate in the regulation of educational and related matters, it was not the state that had the primary and only regulatory power over the cultural practices of these small communities (Jusdanis, 1998: 41).

This was the overall context in which one came to the understanding of the self, which was reflected in texts produced as late as

---

23 Quataert (2002: 253) makes reference to the sharing of the religious realm by the dynasty and a majority of the members of the Ottoman state apparatus. Quataert also makes reference to the fact that, until the mid 19th century, military service was mainly carried out by the Muslims.

the 19th century. Whilst a 'Turk could be anyone who belonged to the Muslim millet during the Ottoman period' (Karpat in Balta, 1990: 20), in 1891, I. Valavanis wrote about the Turcopone Orthodox masses in the interior of Asia Minor as follows:

> ...they wouldn't even know the name of their nation... if you asked a Christian, 'what are you?', s/he would say 'I am a Christian'. If you insisted and said 'but all the others, Armenians, Franks, Russians, too, are Christian'...s/he would say 'I wouldn't know... they too believe in Jesus Christ, but I am a Christian.'..If you insisted still and said 'Could you be Greek?', they would reply 'No, I am nothing as such, as I told you, I am a Christian' (Valavanis 1891 in Balta 1990: 20).

But this situation was to gradually change for all those who dwelt within the borders of the last monarchies of the Near East.

Nationalization of Belonging

One frequently cited determinant that played a role in the shifting of societal perceptions of the self and 'the other' is state-intervention in the socio-political sphere. While the Ottoman Empire was officially a theocracy, at the same time, there was a duality in the system of law . The *şer-i* (shar'i) law, or in other words the body of religious codes derived from the canonical law of Islam or the Shari'a, and the *örf-i* law, that is to say customary law, had set themselves forth almost as two separate systems in relation to the regulation of the political and societal realms (Ortaylı 2003, Quataert 2002).[24]

Gradually, not only religious affairs but also educational and administrative affairs were left to the *millets*[25] (Ortaylı, 2003: 175).

---

24 A group of authors headed by Ö.L. Barkan state that within the Ottoman state and society, customary law (established and applied by 'secular' authorities) overrode those of the Shari'a codes in practice. In that regard, they maintain that to entitle the Ottoman state as a Shari'a state is not that easy. In relation to this, Ortaylı (2003) maintains that, when state practice is observed, the situation does not nullify Barkan's views.

25 Needless to say, the Ottoman Empire dealt with its subjects as members of religiously defined communities called the millets. Race was not a basis for official categorization. Ortaylı (2003:

With the 1839 *Tanzimat* Edict (or the Noble Edict of the Rose Garden[26]) and later with the 1876 Constitution, the rights of non-Muslims would be institutionalized.[27] In due course, terms indicating *millet*, initially for the Christians and later for the Muslims, came to carry an in-between meaning as latent tensions led to definitions of 'the other' around increasingly ethnic lines. In due course, ethnic lines began to become synonymous with those of religion, which in turn was associated with language. In the end, as told in the grand-national narratives of the subsequent polities to the Ottoman Empire, the homogenization of nations was to be achieved over these two key signifiers of belonging. Yet this has been a gradual and differentiated process among members of different communities, with vast diversities, the least being their differentiation on the linguistic plane.

Moreover, transformations in the perception of the self and 'the other' did not take place through the one-way intervention of singled out state institutions.

Nationalization of Belonging in the Greek Kingdom
Going back to the period prior to the establishment of the Greek Kingdom, starting with the idealization of the Greek nation in Europe around the 18th century and in the Ottoman realm from the mid-18th century onwards, the whole struggle over education- which fell mainly under the responsibility of the Patriarchate of Constantinople but had also come to be an area in which Greek entrepreneurs[28] had invested considerable sums –was about getting hold of

---

177) maintains that 'in the millet organization, there was no differentiation on the basis of language or race... Turks, Albanians, Arabs were of Islam, Bulgarians and Rums were considered to be in the same millet, and the Armenians, even if they spoke the same language, were categorized on the basis of the Church they belonged to, namely as the Armenian, Armenian-Catholic, or, in the 19th century, as the Protestant millet'.

26 *'Tanzimat Fermanı'* or *'Gülhane Hatt-ı Hümayunu'*. Hereinafter referred to as the 1839 political reforms and/or as *Tanzimat*.

27 Literature on these two pivotal points (1839, 1876) abounds.

28 Diaspora Greeks, Greeks living in the newly established Kingdom and/or within the Ottoman realm.

the production of culture. At the end of this process, "by bringing together the nation and the Church as elements of the same symbolic universe, Greek nationalism caused a transformation in the whole Eastern Orthodox tradition" (Kitromilides 1990: 40) and alongside other factors, predestinated a redefinition of the territorial and mental borders of belonging not only for those who fell within the borders of the newly founded Kingdom but also for those who dwelt within the borders of the Ottoman Empire.[29] The Karamanlis would eventually become part of this new symbolic universe as well. But could this *process* possibly be presented as a closed event?

As a parallel process to the newly liberated Greek Kingdom's modernization programme, the identity of the new nationals has been redefined around the above-mentioned symbolic universe that brought together a national church and the nation. Nationalization, or a nationalist reading, of the cultural realms had already been under way with the combined efforts of the literati/intelligentsia of the Ottoman Centre, the prospering merchant class, and the strained situation of the agrarian Balkan communities.

Still, the most vivid examples of this modernization and nationalization programme happened between the period that saw the declaration of independence from the Ottoman state and the fifty years that followed. The Bavarokratia period was followed by the liberal Constitution of 1844, which forced modernization upon the King of Greece and prefigured 'the centralization of the state and a reshaping of the educational and legal systems around the French and German models' (Britannica 1995: 199). Prospective teachers and diplomats were trained at schools established in Athens, which was on the rise as a competing centre to Istanbul in the production of contending ide-

---

29   As a parallel process to the redefinition of the borders of belonging for the nationals of the new Kingdom, and the prioritization of spoken language over that of the practice of religion within the supra-national context of the Patriarchate -once comprising all Orthodox-, the Greek speaking Orthodox that fell within the borders of the Ottoman Empire were also endowed with a new linguistic group image (Jusdanis 1998).

ologies vis-à-vis the new forms of belonging (i.e. the national/citizen versus the subject).

In the new Greek Kingdom, 'rationalizing institutions' began to see a re-constitution and 'merging of the above-mentioned identity spheres around new formulae' (Augustinos, 1997: 307). However, this was not a flawless process. It was no easy feat to "thrust the institutions of a functionally differentiated societal structure into the existing stratified system" (Jusdanis, 1998: 59). This coupled with the fact that the regulation of these new institutions was now once again in the hands of rulers who were not Orthodox. Arguably, this created an antagonistic pattern, owing to which the masses responded to the state-induced, downwards rationalization process with a 'silent resistance' (Diamandouros in Jusdanis, 1998: 59). The state/nation tension would last until the ruler became Orthodox, or even later, due to regional loyalties and other similar obstacles that hindered the modernization process (Jusdanis, 1998), through which the conceptualization of the self, community, and the nation would transform.

While the Greek modernization project was to prove fruitful on the conceptual terrain, it followed nothing but a smooth line, undergoing a continuous tension between the traditionalist and modernist institutions/figureheads in the nexus of the newly established Kingdom, the Ottoman Empire, and Europe. Shifts in the approach towards the Turcophone Orthodox group lay bare a continuous tension among the institutions aiming to take control of the production of culture. Ethnographers of the newly founded Greek Kingdom would eventually refer to the Karamanlis as the 'non-Greek-speaking Greeks.'[30] However initially,

> Turcophone Christian Anatolia was not a subject of research for intellectual circles in Constantinople and Athens, since by defini-

---

30 For reference to non-Greek-speaking Greeks, see Haris Exertzoglu. 1999 "Shifting Boundaries: Language, Community and the 'non Greek speaking Greeks'", *Historein: A Review of the Past and Other Stories* 1. (1999: 75).

tion, it did not give arguments for Greekness; on the contrary, it undermined them (Balta, 2003: 33).

The extent to which the Karamanlis would be depicted as part of the corpus of the nation would depend upon the ultimate definition of nationhood. Nineteenth century intellectuals had long pondered the various formulae through which various identity spheres could be merged under one. Some of these ideologues championed the European ideals of the Enlightenment, in which language and culture were the primary signifiers of nationality,[31] while others continued to prioritize religion over the others. In part, this involved redefining the 'unredeemed Greeks' of the Balkans and Asia Minor.

Arguably, what caused a shift in state discourse vis-à-vis the issue of nationality in the 1870s was the European centre's performative discourse vis-à-vis nationalities in the Balkans (Kitroeff, 1989: 28). This would gradually transform the new Kingdom's definition of the non-Greek speaking Orthodox in its periphery. The newly crystallized attitude of the Great Powers depicting the region's Christian groups as *a number of* nationalities could undermine a legitimate enlargement of Greece in the region and "Greek ethnographers set about strengthening Greece's case" (Kitroeff, 1989: 28). While Orthodoxy could be the melting pot of a new and enlarged Greece, as the discussions surrounding the San Stefano Treaty of 1878 would show, the definition of national belonging would lay in the tensions posed by the prioritization of linguistic over religious criteria (Exertzoglou 1999).

In due time, this required ethnographers to quit 'insisting upon the older invocations of a fixed Greek racial and religious superiority'. According to this model, 'a multiplicity of races in the Balkans could readily be acknowledged' while 'their respective national claims were

---

31 One of the early intellectuals, Demetrios Katartzis was "probably the first among authors writing in modern Greek to use the Greek word for nation, ethnos, to describe a collectivity clearly delineated by its language and cultural heritage" (Kitromilides 1990: 27).

judged according to the stage they had reached on the conventional evolutionary *continuum*.' As such, the (re)emergence of 'ethnography represented a shift away from traditionalist views' and affirmed the shift in nationalist discourse (Kitroeff, 1999: 27, 28). During the 1870s, "reference to 'non-Greek-speaking Greeks' in Ottoman Macedonia and other Balkan provinces started to appear frequently" (Exertzoglou 1999: 75). The Greek state's new performative discourse vis-à-vis its Ottoman Christian subjects "depicted the Balkans as constituting nationalities with legitimate rights to nationhood and to statehood" on the basis of an 'evolutionary *continuum*' borrowed from the European ethnographic model of evolution (Kitroeff, 1989: 28). In a way, the shifts of emphasis over the religious and linguistic criteria were accommodated through the application of this evolutionary model.

Ethnographic, historical, linguistic, geographical and archeological studies of the Karamanlis (Balta, 2003) continued to stress the religious connotations of the Cappadocia region. In these studies, ethnographers depicted the Karamanlis as the heirs of Alexander the Great who had lost their language in a 'sea of Islam' but had resisted the loss of Orthodoxy (Benlisoy 2002). A number of schools were founded in the Cappadocia region where the Karamanlis were taught Hellenic culture as well as the Greek language (Kitromilides 1990).[32] However the field which saw the eventual transformation of the communal borders of belonging for those who lived within the borders of the Ottoman Empire (i.e. the periphery Karamanlis) remained in the nexus of tensions posed by the contending approaches, which emphasized a supra-national line of religious belonging on the one hand and the views of prosperous merchants and the new Kingdom's ideologues on the other.

---

[32] As will be further discussed in the fourth section of the Analytical Part, many of the informants transferred knowledge on how their schooled parents knew how to write Greek but how they were unable to speak fluently.

Nationalization of Belonging in the Ottoman Realm

As for the mission of Hellenization within the Ottoman realm, the tension between the Patriarchate of Constantinople (or to put it more correctly, its high ranking Orthodox clergy), and a considerable section of the *Rum* elite in the Phanar quarter of Istanbul[33] on the one hand and another section of the Greek elite in the Phanar – backed by the prospering merchants, now strong enough to take sides against the still powerful fragments in the Patriarchate–[34], proved resilient (see Runciman, 1968 in Jusdanis, 1998: 57). In the nineteenth century, however, these factions would converge around similar ideals, especially when the 1839 political reforms gave the merchants the upper hand in the gradual alteration of the composition of the Phanar elite[35] (Jusdanis, 1998) and when nationalisms made one another's rise inescapable rendering the converging of the formerly-contending fractions within the religiously defined communities ('*millet*s') a must. Still, in the second half of the 18th century, the fight over regulation of the cultural realm (e.g. through the school curricula) and the primacy of key signifiers that would draw the eventual borders of belonging for the masses continued.

The 'reformists' called for the recognition and dissemination of the ideals that shaped the new *Kingdom* (and its National Church). In

---

33 It was this faction that was in no rush to support the revolting *rayahs* in the Balkans. With the reforms made to the millet system (and the gradual change in the process that would see a shift in the individuals to occupy the positions of the high clergy) the views and ideals (i.e. nationalism) represented by the latter group have also come to be represented by the Phanar elites. At the beginning, the Phanar elites had predominantly taken their position on the traditionalist side (Runciman, 1968 in Jusdanis, 1998). However, when revolution became irreversible and the gradual change in the nomination system via the reforms of the mid 19th century took hold, their position was to change.

34 Note that with the reforms of the mid-19th century, the merchants and other factions in the society also started to play a role in their bringing into power. In a similar manner, note the downplaying of the Phanar elites after the Greek revolution. Still however, they were able to hold on to their traditional power positions in the regulation of the societal realm for another half a century.

35 A composition which had already been disturbed by the 1821 Revolution, rendering the Rum members of the Imperial Council, namely, the *Divan-ı Hümayun*, 'less trustable'.

other words, they advocated the preaching of a national form of belonging over that of a supra-national religious belonging – to the Patriarchate's flock through the Patriarchate's *own* schools. Nevertheless, the Patriarchate was careful to watch the line that would cause a shift in the flock's identification of itself due to these new factions' prioritization of the ethnic criteria over that of a once supra-nationally defined religious form of belonging. Although this approach showed shifts according to the voices that shaped its policies, including the Patriarchal Synod, the re-definition of its flock as an ethnically defined group was not reflected in the religious Karamanli texts using ethnic terms. In the Karamanli religious texts, "published between 1743-1918, the term 'Christians' increasingly gave way to the term, 'Orthodox Christians' (1718-1884) and/or to the 'Christians of the East' (1718-1883)" while ethnic vocabulary was *not* used to address the readership of these texts (Balta, 2003: 41, see also Clogg 1999: 127).

Moreover, agitated by the possibility of a prospective loss of the Patriarchate's regulatory power if it were to fall within the new Kindgom's sphere – with its own National Church established in 1833 – the ecclesiastics thought about ways to preserve the Patriarchate's authority in the Ottoman realm, if the supporters of the Ottomanism ideal were to stay in power, de-limiting the Sultan's power.

In the Ottoman Empire, modernization efforts had already given way to the adoptation of the 1839 Reforms, 'thereby initiating a process that saw a gradual abolition of the Ottoman state's compartmentalized administration of religiously defined groups, even though it is debatable that the reformists themselves had such an overarching abolition programme' (Ortaylı, 2003: 184).

Some state that Tanzimat is a belated nodal point to mention and that modernization – or its early signs – began with the state-induced modernization of the military, following the 1774 Treaty[36]

---

36   Toynbee takes the period between the 1774 Ottoman-Russia Peace Treaty and 1918 as the time when modernization/westernization began. Yet these early moves were more at the institutional

(Toynbee 1922: 52). But the initiative behind this nodal point can be seen more under a 'westernization of the military' rubric than as the conscious launching of a ceaseless process that would help redefine societal relations.

With the prevalent mode of societal and economic relations among these traditionally agrarian Muslim communities organized along "a symbolic representation of the world under the Caliphate" (Keyder, 2000: 16) and its political figureheads represented by the Palace and Ulema, early modernists were to face serious societal repercussions from the grassroots at large (Toynbee 1922: 52). Seen in this perspective, Istanbul, as the main hub of all these contending trends, 'became the clashing zone of all essentialist oppositions: East vs. West, Islam vs. Christianity, and local vs. global' (Keyder, 2000: 17). In that regard, the "figureheads of Turkish westernization" (initially the *Jeune Turcs*) had faced "a much stronger reaction from the obedient servants/satellites of the Sultan" (Toynbee, 1922: 53). The predecessors of these reformists (the Young Ottomans) would soon push the Sultan towards a Constitutional Monarchy. However the schism between the traditionalists (Islamic Monarchists/Islamists), and 'reformists' of the age (Constitutional Monarchists/the Young Ottomans) did not take on such clear-cut lines over-night and these contending visualizations of belonging came along gradually, in line with the changing micro and macro contexts.

Early reformists suffered from a semi-Islamist, semi-westernist dilemma (Ortaylı, 2003: 184). Towards the end of the 19th century, "the group named [the] Young Ottomans would be advocating Constitutionalism to result in the adoption of the 1876 Constitution, rendering the Ottoman Empire the first Islam state to have a written Constitution" (Kongar 1995: 55). Even though the Constitution would

---

level. It was the Tanzimat period that saw drastic political reforms with direct effects on new conceptualizations of belonging. Note also Toynbee's employment of the terms 'westernization' and 'modernization' in a synonymous manner. This approach is shared by the late authors (i.e. Niyazi Berkes) studying the modernization process in the late Ottoman, early Republican period.

be viewed by some as laying the groundwork for a laicist[37] state in a state of Islam, starting with the restructuring efforts through the 1839 Tanzimat, the dualism –not only in Law and the school system, but also in the 'mind-set of the 19th century thinkers and administrators caught up in a semi-Islamist semi-westernist dilemma' – would continue throughout the 19th century (Ortaylı 2003: 185).

In other words, this early faction gaining dominance in the Palace named the Young Ottomans did take a reformist turn and started advocating for the primacy of the civic notions of belonging. But for the Muslim masses, the Caliphateship continued to draw the symbolic borders of belonging and the extent of the community that they had become part of was still envisioned within this context.

Until the 1876 Constitution was suspended and an oppressive regime was established, the reformist ideal of Ottomanism found echoes among the figureheads of Muslim *and* non-Muslim communities living in the Centre. From the beginning of the 19th century onwards, especially with the new political reforms, the now-deemed-to-be-equal subjects of the Empire would be acquainted with new forms of belonging through the figureheads of their communities, the press, the new school curricula, and so on. Yet communitarian forms of belonging and the Centre/periphery dichotomy prevailed. Those living in the Centre would be introduced to these 'new' forms of belonging through their associations, the press, and a multitude of other channels while those living in the periphery, such as Gelveri, would be introduced to them through their family members living seasonally or permanently in the Centre, through the community notables, teachers appointed from the contending Centres of the era, and the school curricula shaped in the midst of the above-mentioned tensions.

Arguably, the resulting First Constitutional Monarchy estab-

---

37 İlber Ortaylı employs the term as the term had been understood at the specific socio-political setting of the time (Ortaylı, 2003: 184). These political reforms taking start with the Noble Edict of the Rose Garden in 1839 and resulting in a Constitutional Monarchy were crucial steps at the time.

lished through the promulgation of the 1876 Constitution during Sultan Abdulhamid II's reign, was noted as 'reformist' in the terminology of the supporters of the Ottomanist ideal[38] 'rather than being a consequence of nationalist ideals' (Güresin 1998: 7). In that regard, the traditionalist segments (represented by the Sultan and the Ulema as their political figureheads) would only 'bear with' the changes that the reformists imposed upon the Palace.

Among the newly prospering press some also discussed Ottomanism and the traditional order as an alternative. Still, the newly flourishing *Rum* press was to a great extent owned by the newly rising bourgeoisie advocating nationalist ideals. Starting with the second quarter of the 19th century, the traditionalists and ideologues of Hellenism took positions in the press only to converge near the close of the century.

The press was increasingly expressing nationalist ideals and when they faced enforced closure because of it, they would often establish a subsequent newspaper that continued in the same vein under a different title. Among the newspapers printed throughout the second quarter of the century was *Filos* ton *Neon*[39] was established in 1831 in Izmir and closed three months after its foundation. In a similar pattern, *Astir en ti Anatoli* (later *Filos ton Neon-Astir en ti Anatoli*), first published in 1832, was short-lived. Then *Mnimosini* which was first published in 1833 (Topuz 2003: 76, 77) published articles in favor of the reformist and nationalist ideals. Other newspapers, such as *Armonia* or *Anatolikos Astir* (published between 1862-1890) were closer to the traditionalist segments of the *Rum* community (the Patriarchate) and published articles discussing the possibilities of co-existence within the Ottoman realm and thus of

---

38 To later bear from among themselves the 1908 regime's dominant circles.

39 Regarded as the first Rum newspaper published in Greek. Some cite *Othomanikos Monitor* as the first newspaper in Greece, dating its first issue to 1832. But Topuz (2003: 77) dates its first print to 1835, stating that it was a translation of *Takvim-i Vakayi*, the Ottoman State's official gazette.

Ottomanism as a possible paradigm. Joining these discussions was a much-cited Karamanli author, publisher, and teacher, named Evangelinos Misailidis, whose newspaper, the *Anatolikos Monitor*, was first established in 1845 in Izmir and later moved to Istanbul in 1847 under the title, *Anatoli* (Topuz 2003).[40]

Soon, a contending nationalism was to rise among the Muslims, withdrawing all sides away from the consideration of Ottomanism as a possible alternative. In this era, the Karamanlis would increasingly become an "object of rivalry between the Greek and Turkish nationalisms" (Benlisoy, 2002: 927). Soon soldiers, bureaucrats, merchants of the Centre, and agrarians of the periphery, would have to take their conclusive positions regarding either one of the nationalist ideals of the age, as advocated by the 'reformist' segments of each group, and admit or be forced to admit new meanings or new lines of explanation vis-à-vis their key signifiers of belonging by one of the many contending factions fighting for ideological dominance in the region (among them the Patriarchate of Constantinople, the Turkish press, Catholic and Protestant missionaries, the Turco-Orthodox Church, and the new school curricula shaped around the Hellenic ideals of the Greek Kingdom, without any doubt, the former being the most dominant at all times). The Karamanlis, visualized within a single plane of attachment to either one of the national corpuses, found themselves increasingly subject to the propaganda of these factions, reaching them via printed or orally transmitted material.

Among the three ideologies of the era from Tanzimat onwards, Turkism rose among the Muslims. The Crimean War (1854-1855), the Ayastefanos Treaty, the Berlin Conference (1878), and the Balkan

---

40 It would be most interesting to note the different phases this individual went through from the early 1840s to 1900s. A thorough and separate study on Misailidis' complete works (articles in *Anatoli*, his books and pamphlets) should be conducted, as they reflect the changes that a Karamanli *literatus* of the Centre would have gone through during the second half of the 19th century. Such a study has not been undertaken to date. Only brief and selective references are made by the contending nationalist readings. Choosing Misailidis as the main figure of such a study would be important in terms of his popularity and the long period of time he wrote.

Wars all led to the rise of nationalism (Copeaux, 1998: 22). The fact that the Muslims were forced to flee to the remaining territories of the Empire added to the climax of Turkish nationalism. Among these fleeing Muslim masses were names that would later play important roles as the ideologues of Turkish nationalism. Ahmet Ağaoğlu and Yusuf Akçura, for instance, would be among the ideologues who emphasized language as the common denominator of nationhood. The Ottoman press at the turn of the century (*Sabah, Tercüman-ı Hakikat, İkdam*) became a plane of discussion for Turkism (Copeaux 1998: 23).

Names like Şemseddin Sami in İkdam and later, Cami Baykurt in *Hakimiyet-i Milliyet* or *Söz* wrote extensively on the Turkishness of the Karamanlis.[41] The first known article on the subject appeared on the 20th of March, 1899, under the title, "Turkishness (Turkishness) in İkdam". The article followed:

> it is to our knowledge that more than half a million of the Orthodox population that lives in Anatolia and speaks only Turkish originates from a mixture of the earliest settlers of Anatolia with the Turcomans, and has nothing to do with the Greeks. Since being a Muslim cannot be considered synonymous to being a Turk, being Orthodox cannot be considered synonymous

---

[41] The mainstream Turkish thesis about the Karamanlis followed these early authors in their approach to the *first* time that the Turkic origin peoples appeared in Asia Minor. The thesis was outlined by Cami Baykurt in *Osmanlı Ülkesinde Hristiyan Türkler ve Bizans İmparatorluğuna Dahil Olan Turanî Akvam [The Christian Turks Living in the Ottoman State and the Migrations of the Turkic Tribes to the Byzantium Empire]*. Accordingly, the Karamanlis were 'the descendants of the Turkic origin tribes that had migrated to Asia Minor in an irregular manner'. During the 9th and 10th centuries in particular, the migrating 'Turkic origin tribes were taken under arms by the Byzantium Empire, for the most part, as paid soldiers'. Consequently they were (re)settled by the Empire as semi-soldier, semi-agrarian communities in the buffer zones. They were Christianized in an irregular manner, either after they fell within the borders of the Byzantium Empire or before, through the Byzantium Empire's missionaries sent abroad. Arguably, it was during this time that much of the religious texts were made available to them in Turkish written in Greek letters. Baykurt referred to one mass conversion in particular, which was said to have taken place in the Caucasus during the time of Justinianos (i.e. in the 6th century) when Christian texts were translated into the languages of the Huns, Hazars and Kumans as it would later be done for the Kıptis, Syrians and Armenians in the seventh century (Baykurt 1932 [1922]).

to being a Greek. Religious dogma is based in belief and nationality is based in language (Kushner, 1977: 52-53).

This ethno-linguistic line of explanation had set forth language as the primary key signifier of belonging to a nation and incorporated culture into its discourse. On the other hand, as aforementioned, Greek nationalism's interest in the Karamanlis 'had been much earlier than that of its rival nationalism', dating back to the second half of the 19th century (Benlisoy, 2002: 927). Its ethno-linguistic line of explanation has not only made particular reference to the usage of Greek characters in the writing of Turkish, but extended this to the early presence and loss of Hellenism in the region and added to this explanation an ethno-religious line of belonging. The Karamanlis have been depicted as 'the unredeemed Greeks' of Asia Minor who had lost their language but resisted the loss of their religion and preserved Orthodoxy (Benlisoy, 2002: 927). According to this line of explanation, the preservation of Orthodoxy with an implied terrain of ethnicity, in addition to Alexander the Great's descendants' discourse, was especially important, since, on a societal level, the Karamanlis – like the rest of the masses – were to draw their new borders of belonging on a religious plane.[42]

---

[42] A. Aigidis' *The Greekness of Asia Minor and the Myth of the Turkish Orthodox* followed the same line of argument. It was published in the same year with the below-mentioned C. Baykurt's book titled *The Christian Turks Living in the Ottoman State and the Migrations of the Turkic Tribes to the Byzantium Empire*. In this respect, Aigidis' booklet was not only an outline of the Greek thesis but also a reply to the mainstream Turkish thesis outlined above. In explaining the way in which the communities in the interior of Asia Minor lost their *spoken* Greek skills, Aigidis followed that the Karamanli communities were 'isolated from the Aegean and the other Greek speaking regions'. This, 'coupled with other means of assimilation led to an inescapable fading away of the Karamanlis' spoken Greek skills'. The complete Hellenization of the interior of Asia Minor from the 4th century A.D onwards 'was attested by historical evidence'. Aigidis followed that 'even in face of the Turkish invasions, the Hellenic identity of the native communities (such as the Karamanlis) remained intact as clearly indicated by the community members' strong adherence to the Orthodox belief system, their ages-old customs, beliefs and rituals'. See Aigidis, A. 1922. Η Ελληνικοτης της Μικρας Ασιας και το Μυθευμα των Τουρκορθοδοξων *[The Greekness of Asia Minor and the Myth of the Turkish Orthodox]*. Athens: Τυπαις Δημητριαδου.

The dichotomy between the traditionalist and reformist segments within the Ottoman realm, in terms of their emphasis on an ethnic and (once supra-national) religious form of belonging converged in the late 19th century. This convergence ran parallel to the restructuring of the schooling system by the reformist/nationalist segments, whose ideas for the reshaping of the school curricula had gained more weight to follow the 1839 political reforms. Subventions were allocated from the Greek state, the municipality of Athens, banks in Greece as well as the prosperous Greek communities in Izmir, Istanbul and Egypt to fund schools (Clogg 1982: 197) where the new generations of the Turcophone Orthodox would be taught about the Hellenic culture, history and language (Kitromilides 1990: 48).[43]

On the other hand, the Turkish project to incorporate the Karamanlis into the national corpus had serious handicaps, such as the absence of an institutional network to reach the masses, the limited amount of time between the attempt to establish a Turco-Orthodox Church and the sending of its envisioned flock to Greece,[44] and most importantly, the earlier exclusion of Orthodoxy from the discourse of

---

43 Kitromilides notes that schools were founded as inland as Ankara. Within the realm of the Ottoman Empire the cultural societies (*syllogoi*) took active part in the teaching and spread of Greek much before 1894, when the Ottoman state required the minority schools to teach Turkish (Clogg 1999: 127, 128). "The Hellenic Literary Society of Constantinople alone, funded some two hundred schools". Upon graduation, Karamanli locals would be expected to return back to their communities (Clogg 1982: 197). Georges Perrot writing as early as 1864 noted that "the entire generation growing up now will talk Greek" Perrot, Georges. 1864. *Souvenirs d'un voyage en Asie Mineure*. Paris: Michel-Lévy frères. in Kitromilides (1990: 48-49). Indeed, some decades later, Stamatios Antonopoulos (the Consul General of Greece in Smyrna/Izmir) was reporting that the younger generations in Alasehir (Philadelphia) and Konya (Iconium) were starting to speak Greek despite the failed linguistic transitions in certain other settlements of the region. In his report, Antonopoulos complained about the fact that the authorities (the Church, the Greek state etc.) were not doing as much as they could in the teaching and spread of the Greek language and Greek patriotism (Antonopoulos 1907 in Kitromilides 1990).

44 Among the Turcophone Orthodox, apart from the ones that fell under the établi status (covered by Article 2 of the Exchange Convention), only Papa Eftim and his family were kept outside of the applicability of the Exchange Convention by a decree of the Turkish Grand National Assembly.

Turkish nationalism. The limited number of newspaper articles printed in Karamanli script or in Turkish and the political attempt to establish a Turco-Orthodox Church were the products of the last phase of
a now completely nationalized realm.

One after another, articles in support of the establishment of a
Turco-Orthodox Church[45] started to appear. However, even though the
Turkish press (such as *Ikdam, Hakimiyet-i Milliye* and *Anadoluda
Ortodoksluk Sedasi*[46]) started to publish articles on the subject, in practice there was no independent church until the end of 1921, owing to
the fact that the legal establishment of such a church could only come
about through the convening of high rank priests. The difficulty of finding clergy higher in rank than Papa Eftim, that is to say the leading figure in advocacy of a Turco-Orthodox Church in Kayseri,[47] was the main
reason behind this delay (Ergene, 1951). The efforts to convene the necessary number of priests of the required rank to establish a Turco-
Orthodox Church would be finalized on 28th May 1922, with the gathering of a Consultate, announcing the new rules of the 'Christian communities of Anatolia' (FO/_/35, sent to the Greek Representatives of
Lausanne, Athens, 10 January 1923, in Alexandris, 1983: 184). When
Papa Eftim eventually announced the independence of the Karamanlis
from the Patriarchate in Istanbul he did this in front of 50.000 supporters of the Kemalist revolution. In the meanwhile, there was the celebra-

---

45 The first document found regarding an independent Turco Orthodox Church appeared in
Hakimiyeti Milliye on the 1st May 1921. On the 3rd May 1921, Ikdam announced that 'the
Turkish Grand National Assembly passed a draft law upon the proposition of the establishment
of a Turco Orthodox Church and presented it to the Ministry of Interior' (Jaschke, 1969: 321
in Alexandris 1983: 177).

46 *Anadolu'da Ortodoksluk Sedası [Sound of Orthodoxy in Anatolia]* was published from July
1922 until April 1923.

47 It was also clear that 'the Kemalist factions had full confidence in control over Kayseri, designated as the centre of a Turco-Orthodox Church. Note for instance the time when the Greek
army was far inland in Anatolia in the summer of 1921. The Greek army had reached 125 miles
west of Ankara. Yet earlier in March 1921 Mustafa Kemal transferred the most important
archives of the revolutionary government from Ankara to Kayseri' (Thomas Milkoglu, KMΣ /
IB`, Archives of the Centre for Asia Minor Studies in Alexandris, 1983: 176).

tions of the war of Inonu (FO/371/7880/E3780, Rumbold to Foreign Office, Istanbul, 4 April 1922 in Alexandris, 1983: 182).

The British High Commissioner, Sir Horace Rumbold, writing to the Foreign Office on the 22nd November 1921, reported that the attempt to establish this Church was initiated by the Kemalist Government of Ankara (FO/371/6566/E8824, Rumbold to Foreign Office, Istanbul, 22 November 1921 in Alexandris, 1983: 177). What was peculiar was the simultaneous efforts of Papa Eftim to ban wearing of the clerical robe in public, outside duty, and declaring the requirements for the priests of the Turco-Orthodox Church, among them *not* to be involved in politics (FO/371/7880/E3780, Rumbold to the Office in Istanbul, 4 April 1922 in Alexandris, 1983: 182). These clearly fell parallel to the Turkish reformists' laicist ideals, foreseeing the eventual withdrawal of religious figures and codes from the regulation of the public sphere and politics.

When Ikdam started publishing articles on the issue of Karamanlis early in the beginning of the century, stating 'Orthodoxy cannot be considered synonymous to being Greek' (Ikdam, 20 March 1899), and that the Karamanlis were the descendants of the Turkic tribes, it had already been more than half a century since an increasing number of *syllogoi* and *literati* had advocated otherwise (See in Clogg 1982, Anagnostakis and Balta 1994).

These attempts on behalf of the Turkish ideologues were not only belated compared to the efforts of the contending nationalist ideology but also worked against the societal otherization grounds that had already been nationalized on the basis of religion. As such, the Papa Eftim incident became a case study employed in the deconstruction of the late Turkish nationalist thesis vis-à-vis the origins of the Karamanlis. On the other hand, the Turkish National Assembly's final decision to actually exchange the Karamanlis revealed the political considerations vis-à-vis the issue and put the last demarcation mark, if not to the ongoing public debates about their 'ethnic' roots, to the issue of the ultimate political body that they would make part of.

Crossing the Borders: The Decision to 'Exchange' The Karamanlis
Towards the end of the 19th century, historians began to categorize peoples' attributes based on new 'criteria of belonging' to the new and emergent polities of a now increasingly inter-*national* regime. Nationalist meta-narratives would soon marginalize people's previous key signifiers of belonging as the criteria of displacement while the ideologues of the prospective resettlement countries would search for rational explanations to account for peoples' categorical differences from the 'corpus of the nation'. Looking for answers as to why people carried the same attributes they had hitherto possessed, these ideologues had to decide which attribute (religion/language) was the 'natural' extension of their origins/bloodlines and which had been forced upon them, or lost in time –without, hopefully, having changed their 'common essence'. Authors of the prospective national histories would categorize peoples in one of the singular group belongings of the modern age, and write about their resettlement stories along the lines of their own political and analytical predispositions. In the case of the Exchange, the international community was involved in the final re-drawing of the political and geographical borders of belonging for many.

The League-supervised Exchange of Populations between Greece and Turkey was first brought to the table by Fridjof Nansen. On the 1st of December, 1922 during the First Commission's sessions of the Lausanne Conference, upon a call by Lord Curzon, Nansen took the floor.[48] Dr. Fridjof Nansen was appointed by the League of

---

[48] Fridjof Nansen was called into office by the League of Nations. He was held responsible for studying the population shifts and the related problems in the Near East (Fırat, 2001: 330). During the meetings that predated the Lausanne Convention, a sub-commission had been established to discuss the exchange of the civilian population and military personnel in Greece and Turkey. Accordingly, Nansen had prepared a draft-report following his visits to Turkey and Greece and presented the last version of this draft in the sub-committee on December 1st, 1922. Nansen stated that the economic situation in the Near East was devastating. Already more than one million people had left their cultivated lands. In this regard, Nansen claimed that an exchange of minorities could avoid the further worsening of the economic situation of both countries. In both Turkey and Greece, harvesting of agricultural products had to be completed

Nations to study the migration related 'problems' in the Near East (Fırat 2001: 330). The following sessions on this issue were framed within the larger issue of minorities and saw long debates in relation to the nature of the scheme; that is to say whether it would be a voluntary or mandatory exchange of populations. In the end, the Lausanne Convention and the Additional Protocol[49] regulating the population exchange was signed six months prior to the signing of the main body of the Lausanne Peace Treaty and the Karamanlis were not spared from its mandatory nature. All in all, the proposal of a prospective population exchange involved more than the two countries' leaders decisions. It was discussed on an international level and involved a set of variables, not the least of which were the economic balances in the Near East.

Following the implementation of the scheme, the Mixed Commission for the Exchange of the Greek and Turkish Populations (established by Article 11 of the Convention) maintained that a total of 354,647 Muslims were recorded to have left Greece and 189,916

---

by the end of the approaching summer. Accordingly, at least a part of the population exchange had to be realized before the end of February and within three months (Arı, 2000: 17).

49 In the original text of the League of Nations Treaty Series, the full name of the text serving as the legal grounding of the Mandatory Population Exchange between Greece and Turkey is, Number 807, Greece and Turkey, "*Convention* Concerning the Exchange of Greek and Turkish Populations and Protocol, signed at Lausanne, January 30, 1923." Later on, amendments were made during the preparation of the Lausanne Peace *Treaty*. The Lausanne Convention and the Additional Protocol regulating the population exchange had been signed on 30th January 1923, six months prior to the signing of the main body of the Lausanne Peace Treaty. Both the exchange of civilian populations and war prisoners had been settled by the same Convention and the Additional Protocol (Fırat, 2001: 33). Moreover, an International Commission for the Population Exchange had been established to regulate the population movements. Article 1 of the Convention and its Additional Protocol drew the main framework of the civilian population exchange. According to the Convention, "as from the 1st May 1923", "there was to take place a compulsory exchange of Turkish nationals of the Greek Orthodox religion established in Turkish Territory, and of Greek nationals of the Moslem religion established in Greek territory", excluding "the Greek inhabitants of Constantinople" and "the Moslem inhabitants of Western Thrace." For the full versions of Articles 1 and 2, see the original text of the Convention Concerning The Exchange of Greek and Turkish Populations, and Protocol, Signed at Lausanne, January 30, 1923.

Greeks were recorded to have left Turkey. But many had to flee before
the commencement date of the 'orderly exchange'. As regards the
Orthodox populations, who had left with the Greek army's withdrawal from Asia Minor, these numbers reached approximately
1,000,000, according to various sources. For instance, Pentzopoulos
states that approximately one million Greeks left Asia Minor *prior* to
the implementation of an orderly Exchange, mounting up to more
than 1,200,000 people in sum (Pentzopoulos 1962: 52-69). The numbers of the Muslims who had to leave Greece, mainly Macedonia, on
the other hand, are not known. Whilst these numbers increase up to a
total of 1,600,000 for the Orthodox and 800,000 for the Muslims
(Zolberg 1989 cited in Barutciski 2004: 28), the bottom lines in the
selective use of figures have more often than not been political. At
times, however, what appear to be overestimations of the numbers and
disparities in figures can be attributed to the changing criteria authors
employ in accounting for the numbers of the 'exchanged'. While some
take into consideration that the 1923 Convention foresaw that all displaced persons since the Balkan Wars would be considered to fall
within the status of 'exchangee' (Article III, Convention concerning
the Exchange of Greek and Turkish Populations and Protocol, Signed
at Lausanne, January 30, 1923) and calculate the overall numbers as
such, others take into account the numbers accounted for by the
Mixed Commission between the years 1923-1926. On the other hand,
foreseeing the problems associated with the mandatory transfer of
whole populations on the basis of being Orthodox or Muslim, the
Convention left the

> rationae personae application of the Lausanne Convention ...
> unclear in that it possibly allowed for all co-religionists to be trans-
> ferred. It was therefore necessary to establish that the signatory
> states intended it to apply only to co-religionists who were pre-
> sumed to share the national sentiments of the receiving country
> (see Eddy, 1931: 203; Ladas, 1932: 380). For example, Albanians
> in Greece who followed the Islamic faith were not to be included

in the exchange. However, the national sentiments of certain populations were not easily identifiable. Consequently, groups with questionable affiliations to the receiving country were included in the exchange. (Barutciski 2004: 30)

Seen in this context, the Karamanlis and similar communities were deemed to be subjected either to a *de facto* or *de jure* minority status. If they were to stay in Turkey, they would have been subjected to the minority regime established by the League of Nations, as stipulated by the Lausanne Peace Treaty signed six months after the Convention. If they were to be sent to Greece – which was ultimately the case – societal contestation of their identity due to their differentiated language use would – for a majority of them – entail a *de jure* minority status to last for the next two to three generations after the Exchange.

As already noted, many had already left by 1923. However, there were still Karamanli communities in inner Anatolia. The conclusive decision on whether or not the Karamanlis should be included in the Exchange scheme did not become clear until towards the end of the Lausanne negotiations.[50] When the financial (*rumi*) calendar showed the year 1339 (i.e., 1923), at a closed session of the Turkish Grand National Assembly, discussions would still continue. The Bolu deligate, Tunalı Hilmi Bey asked one of the representatives in Lausanne, Rıza Nur Bey, whether the Turkish Orthodox would be included into the Exchange or not. He underlined the fact that they (Papa Eftim) had founded a Turkish Orthodox Church and this made the issue even more complex. Rıza Nur Bey on the other hand replied, 'Sir, there is no clause (in Lausanne) indicating whether the Turkish Orthodox should be included or excluded from the Exchange. [We shall decide.]' (TGNA Closed Session, 2.3.1339, Second Session, Third Hearing).

---

50 For the Lausanne telegrams in relation to the establishment of a Turco-Orthodox Church, see the documents numbered 141, 150, 249, 259, 415 in Bilal N. Şimşir, *Lozan Telgrafları 1922-1923* (Lausanne Telegrams), Ankara: T.T.K. Basımevi (1990). From these telegrams, it is possible to depict that the Karamanlis' exchange was considered in relation to the Patriarchate.

In the end, the issue was considered in relation to the newly founded Turco-Orthodox Church in Istanbul, the possible abolition of the Patriarchate and the eventual definition of belonging to the corpus of the nation. The stipulations of the Convention were to be put into force as of 1st May. Hence, the Karamanlis found time to make order-ly preparations for the journey to take them to Greece. The Karamanlis were eventually transported to Greece from the ports of Izmir, Mersin and Istanbul (Arı 2000: 88).

The Resetting of the 'Borders of Belonging' Through a Metaphorical Rite of Passage

Within the framework of this study, the Mandatory Exchange of Populations is treated as a metaphorical *rite of passage*.[51] When van Gennep first introduced the concept, he designed it to explain how individual(s) deal with a major transformation in life such as "place, state, social position, age" (Van Gennep 1960 [1909]) through rites. In this current study, after examining the overall accounts provided by 38 second-generation and 12 first generation exchangees, we use van Gennep's conceptual terrain to frame the happenings, with particular reference to the separation, transition, and reintegration phases cov-ered by this concept. Below, following an introductory discussion on the partial incorporation[52] of van Gennep's concept into the overall framework, respondents' accounts will be set out in particular refer-ence to their conceptions of the 'self', the 'community' and 'the other' in relation to the changing contexts.

Here, the concept of 'rite' is used with a broad understanding, mainly to build on the conceptual framework provided by the overall

---

51 Original term introduced by van Gennep being *'rite de passage'* in French. Turner used *'rite(s) of passage'*.

52 Van Gennep's overall framework was developed within the disciplinary boundaries of early anthropology. But while both van Gennep and Turner –who later used van Gennep's concepts in his own work- refer to the possible applicability of the concept to modern conditions, this study takes the concept as an overall framework only and uses it as a metaphor, with the below-mentioned considerations.

understanding of the concept and its separation, transition, and reintegration phases. In that regard, the concept is used to stress *the continuous and cyclical transformation* of meaning and the process of
identity formation in relation to the Greco-Turkish mandatory population exchange.

According to van Gennep, the symbolic act of a rite involves a
public visualization of an individual(s)' transition, to be followed by a
different communal role (position/status/subjectivity) for the individ-
ual(s) in question. At the end of the rite, group members having witnessed the process (here, the Exchange and the simultaneous spatial
and contextual changes), internalize the transformation and their
prospective roles in relation to the new meaning(s) attributed to their
new 'place, state, and/or social position'.

The conceptual framework provided by the notion of *'rite de
passage'* builds on a dialectic that foresees cyclical change between
periods of order and disorder. The period envisioned to predate each
orderly period involves three phases, which see the 'release of the community members from structural rigidity in the shaping of their societal roles, statuses and the like' "only to return to structure" (Turner,
1969: 129). These phases are posed as the separation, margin (transition), and reaggregation phases.

In each of these phases, both the phase itself and the individuals experiencing them have a liminality attribute. Drawing from the
term 'limen', Turner elaborates on a 'liminality' attribute present in all
three phases, being most visible in the 'transition' phase (Turner 1969:
95). Hence, liminality appears as an attribute of these phases, *and* as
an attribute of the community members experiencing these phases.
The attributes of liminality or liminal personae ('threshold people') are
necessarily ambiguous, since this condition and these persons elude or
slip through the network of classifications that normally locate states
and positions in cultural space. Liminalentities are neither here nor
there; they are betwixt and between the positions assigned and arrayed
by law, custom, convention, and ceremony (Turner, 1969: 95).

Van Gennep suggests that the social classifications and cultural codes break down only to be re-classified and culturally re-coded, in this particular case, along national terms. In van Gennep, the breakdown of 'cultural codes' and 'social classifications' during periods of liminality and their re-arrangement during the reintegration phase is especially important. In this particular study, based on the accounts of exchangees, on-site observation, and secondary readings vis-à-vis institutional transformations, we suggest that a rearrangement of the symbolic borders of belonging involves either a re-arrangement of the *priority* given to certain key signifiers of a given communal identity or a re-definition of their constituents and/or meanings attributed to them.

The Exchange as a metaphorical rite of passage has also been accompanied by a parallel passage in space. This passage from one geographical threshold to another was paralleled not only by a transition from one legal status (subject) to another (citizen) but also by a transition from one cultural realm (of an Empire) to another (of a nation-state); from one socio-cultural context to another; from one political sphere to another; all rendering it necessary for the community members to redefine their symbolic borders of belonging (i.e. a selective preservation of some of the old signifiers of belonging) accompanied by a downwards introduction of new codes. Insofar as the transition and reintegration phases that followed the Exchange foresaw a re-arrangement of the prioritization of particular key signifiers of communal identity, a redefinition (singularization and rarely a multiplication) of certain meanings given to key signifiers – all taking place in the above-mentioned dialectical process – meant assigning first and second-generation Karamanlis a borderline/liminal characteristic.

It is suggested that the transition and reintegration phases necessitated a re-arrangement of the symbolic borders of belonging for the Karamanlis. The key signifiers[53] of belonging and the mean-

---

53 Language and the term Karamanlı as a key signifier of Karamanli identity are gradually left to one side as the new Grecophone generations opt to make reference to a 'Cappadocian' identi-

ings attributed to them have been reshaped through this metaphorical rite of passage. Or, simply, the very shift in the spatial, socio-political, and cultural context transformed the way in which a certain key signifier of belonging (i.e. religion) was perceived, both by the individual/community and the now different immediate others. To give an example, while it had been the Patriarchate's supra-national community that the 19th century Karamanlis visualized as the corpus that they had made part of in their pre-liminal status,[54] in their post-liminal status, it has gradually become the constituency of the National Church of Greece. Here the corpus has not only been de-limited but also nationalized.

All in all, in the case of the Exchange, it is possible to see a vivid reification of the rationale behind van Gennep's concept i.e., a group's transition from one status/state to another and the internalization of the new borders by the group members through a series of physical events and change of *locus*. Still, for evident reasons the *metaphorical* character of the concept is underlined.

Below, the separation, transition, and reaggregation (reintegration) phases are discussed in relation to the spatial and temporal changes and the overall contextual changes, i.e., the individuals' immediate others, socio-political changes, and happenings in Greece at large.

---

ty. Note that Cappadocia region has special connotations in Christianity. As such, employment of the term Cappadocian strengthens religion as a key signifier of belonging (above that of language). According to the testimonies, it was in the last two decades, that the term Cappadocian came to be in frequent use, thus replacing the term Karamanlı. Some of the now bi-lingual village notables also started to refer to their group as Cappadocians instead of Karamanlı and stressed the need to refer to the group as Cappadocian rather than Karamanlı during the interviews.

54 -which can be extended onto the era predating the rise of two contending Centres

Borders of Belonging and the Separation Phase[55]

'...You cannot go home again. Why? Because you already are.'

Marjorie Garber[56]

On the last day of departure, except for a few wealthy families who had left earlier, community members gathered at the churchyard and bid goodbye to their Muslim co-villagers. According to the testimonies, the churchyard was central to the village and was a traditional socializing space. Many of the Muslim co-villagers walked with them as far as the borders of the village whilst some rode with them a long way. In the interviews conducted with the late first and early second-generation Karamanlis from Gelveri, memories of separation were vivid, whether based on first-hand remembrance or on transferred accounts. A late first-generation woman, Katina Hristoforidou (1919) remembers the day:

> They walked with us, the remaining [Muslim co-villagers]. Women were crying. Some had prepared bundles of food for the road and baskets of grapes. It must have been the season. It was hot, very hot. Women were crying...'ne yer, ne icersiniz, ah nirelere gidersiniz' (indicating worry for the long journey and the uncertainty ahead). People bid goodbyes but everyone was at a loss, even though we had been preparing for the journey.

At the time, Hristoforidou was five years old. What was to follow was a three-day journey by oxcart, a train-ride to Mersin, and

---

55 Unless otherwise stated, all information in the following sections of the study is gathered from the on-site observations and in-depth interviews of a fieldwork conducted in December 2005 in Nea Karvali. Information on the separation phase is predominantly based on a group interview recorded at a sub-section of the Cultural Centre in Nea Karvali on the 13th December 2005 and on a separate interview conducted with Katina Hristoforidou. Specific interviews such as this one are cited with the informant's name. Cross-referenced information provided by a majority of the informants are interwoven in the discussion.

56 Marjorie Garber, *Shakespeare's Ghost Writers: Literature as Uncanny Casuality* London & New York: Methuen (1987): 159 cited in Iain Chambers, *Göç, Kültür, Kimlik* (Migrancy, Culture, Identity), Istanbul, Ayrıntı Yayınları, 2005 (1994).

then a month-long voyage to take the Orthodox members of the village to Greece in August 1924.

What the Turcophone Orthodox exchangees would leave behind was more than a geographical confine. They would leave behind the way in which they had conceptualized their borders of belonging in relation to their preliminal status. What they left behind were the intersecting micro-cultural contexts of an imperial realm, a different conceptualization of community in relation to the ecclesiastical realm that had related to the Orthodox community at large, and to them in particular. They left behind the peculiar way in which the periphery and the centre had been in relation with the intellectual currents that had reached them through printed material or in their spoken language. What was also left was a complex web of societal relations in a cultural realm shared with a unique combination of immediate others; shifting grounds in the way in which the Karamanlis had been otherized and/or accepted to a different societal whole; thus an entirely different mirror-image of themselves in relation to their use of language and religious belonging, indiscernible from Cappadocia.

According to the testimonies, the Gelveri village had approximately 800 households, of which 60 belonged to Muslims. The numbers indicated differed from 4,000 to 4,500 for the Orthodox, equivalent to approximately 800 households and 400 Muslims equivalent to 60 households. Many lived in stone-carved houses made by the muralists of the village.[57] Although Muslims lived in the upper quarters of the village, inter-communal interaction was vibrant. Villagers would get together at the Orthodox Easter festivities in the spring and it was not uncommon to see a Muslim woman light a candle for Saint Gregory the Theologian, the Patron Saint of Gelveri, for her child's illness or to be a nursing mother for an Orthodox family.[58]

---

57 The Karamanlis were renowned for their ability in construction. A traditional Karamanli house would often have a signature of the muralist/constructor inside the main room or on the door.

58 One informant indicated finding someone who was related to the nursing-mother to her family from before the Exchange on a visit paid to Turkey in the mid-1980s.

Still, the expressed differentiation line in terms of identity was religion. According to the testimonies, Muslim women would make use of the interior of the house more than their Christian fellow co-villagers and would not go out of the house without their head-scarves. Traditionally, Orthodox women, too, wore headscarves, but they were worn in a different style. Accordingly, the Orthodox would braid their hair and wear – in their own words – 'entari' (skirts) and 'üç etek' (traditional dresses made out of three separate pieces), and over these, 'yelek' (waistcoats). Second-generation women continue to do their own embroidery on their traditional dresses and wear them on special occasions.[59] Otherwise, during daytime, they wore traditional wear called 'çoha'. As for men, they would wear an 'uzun gömlek' (long shirt), 'cepken' (waistcoat), 'şalvar' (traditional baggy trousers worn in the Near and Middle East), and the 'kuşak' (thick traditional girdle worn over the baggy trousers) made out of thick cloth.[60]

Women would wear the 'üçetek' (traditional dress made out of three separate pieces) mostly during festivities such as the traditional fair, when everyone would get together. The 'üçetek' would also be

---

[59] Folkloric dance get-togethers are held once a week in the Cultural Centre (Stegi Politismou Neas Karvalis). But clothes are reserved for special events such as the Festival held for the Patron Saint of Gelveri on the 25th January every year.

[60] "Kadınlar çoha giyeridi...Türklerin pek çeşit değil idi. Bizler de, kücükler entari giyeridik. Yorgan gibi, 2 kol var. Urbamı giydim der, entarimi giydim. Yorgan gibiydi fistanımız. Yakası var biraz böyle. Burda yasak etti *daskala*lar" (Paisiyos Papadopoulos, 14th December 2005). Oral history accounts reveal that when the Karamanlis first came to Greece, the way they used to dress was also a basis of their 'otherization' by their new immediate others. What Papadopoulos refers to as 'daskalalar' is a half Greek half Turkish expression for 'teachers'. Note the period when the Karamanlis were first acquainted with teachers appointed from the Centre. Informants could not agree on what to call their sandals at the time. Some referred to them as 'çarık' but others were hesistant to use this term. They tried to clarify that theirs were different than what the Muslims wore. Men women alike, preferred to use the word 'urba' as a general term for 'dress'. Second-generation Atina Topsakal (Papadopoulu) –speaking of her grandparents- says 'cepkenlerini, çohalarını hep yaktılar yörükler' ('yoruks!! they burnt their clothes that they had brought from Anatolia') and quickly adds 'kızdığım için yörük dedim' ('I called them yoruks because I was mad at them'). From such remarks, we understand that the first generation have grown bitter for having been otherized on the basis of how they dressed when they first came from Anatolia.

worn in weddings. Accounts reflect vivid memories of Christians and Muslims joining in at the village centre for celebrations and, prior to that, cooking and preparing for the festivities.[61] Such festivities are remembered with nostalgia. Even though there are similar festivities still, older generations have revealed how they have been ripped out of the old contexts.

Other get-togethers would occur, for instance, during grape harvesting or similar activities in the fields or vineyards. Single Orthodox women whose husbands were away working seasonally in the Centre and Muslim women working on a paid or voluntary basis would get together.[62] Despite the uneasiness of the Muslim women's use of outside space downtown, they would take advantage of the gendered use of space. This was a rather informal but effective way of sharing the space. The traditional socialization places would be the fountain *('çeşme başı')* or the churchyard. But there were other places of interaction as well. Men would get together in the coffee-house close to the centre whilst women would mostly get together in the courtyards *('avlu')* of their homes, where they would make bread *('tandır ekmeği')* on a special hearth placed outside during summer

---

61 The 'nick names' that the villagers had called each person or family with are retained to date. A majority made use of these names when describing the village (i.e. the street of x or y person). Some of the villagers introduced themselves with the names that their Muslim co-villagers used to call them with. As a matter of fact, many of the informants introduced themselves with the names that they used before *and* after the Exchange. Some, like Pantelis Hristofouridis, also introduced themselves with their 'other' first names, namely, as they were called by their Muslim co-villagers. In this case as an equivalent to the Christian name Pantelis, the informant introduced himself as Bartın. His surname before the Exchange on the other hand was Hacıtotoroğlu. Needless to say, in most of the cases, second and third-generations were named after their (grand)parents. This is still a tradition both in Turkey and Greece. What is interesting is that they continued to be aware of and even make use of the Turkish equivalents made out of their Christian names as well as the nick names given after the Muslim and Orthodox families.

62 A few of the older generation women noted instances when Muslim and Christian women took snuff *('enfiye')* together in the field. It is not known whether these were singled out events or practiced regularly. Among the limited enjoyments of women were such singled out events, meeting in the Churchyard during Sundays or making bread together in the 'avlu' (courtyards) of their homes. Men on the other hand had spent their leisure time in the coffee house or in evening get-togethers when they would meet in one of the notables' homes from time to time.

and chat. These activities were not strictly confined to the members of one religion or another.

During winter, these get-togethers would take place in the interior where women would get together to exchange carpet or embroidery patterns or to simply chat. Some women still work[63] in their individual carpet looms in Nea Karvali whilst others have donated their looms and other devices to the Cultural Centre (*Stegi Politismou Neas Karvalis)*. The ones that continue making the carpets make use of the techniques learned from the elder women in the family. Most devices, including the looms, are brought from Gelveri. Probably the only difference between now and five or six generations ago is the use of synthetic dyes. Respondents told how carpet patterns and the embroidered dress patterns have been passed on from generation to generation. Women also worked in the fields to harvest the grapes for traditional wine making. Wine was kept in the storing unit dug out one floor below most of the stone-carved houses. They would also use the by-products of the production process and make other light liquors, still served in houses of the old.[64]

Until the Orthodox had left, wine making had been a major source of income for the village. Families had vineyards on both small and big plots of land. They also had cattle, sheep, and goats. While a minority had large plots of land, and were able to sell the excess product in Aksaray, others had just about enough to feed the household. Some Muslims worked, both on their own land and on that of others. In contrast to the case in the Balkan territories, in this part of Anatolia, Muslims worked for the Christians as farmhands. This was probably due to the Orthodox' practice in trade and their established networks with the Centre.

---

63 Patterns of lions and lionesses still predominate in these carpets, reminding one of the symbolic meaning attributed to lion by the heterodox belief systems in Cappadocia. Such cultural transitions/traits are readily observed.

64 Like many of the older generation Karamanlis, first generation Karamanli, Orsiya Theofilaktu, served home made liquor, welcoming the visitors to her house.

Some families also had horses. Horse raising was a beloved activity. After the Exchange, as soon as they could make a living, some bought horses.

> 'My grandfather raised them. As soon as I could, I bought horses too' (Paisiyos Papadopoulos, 1931).[65]

Women – and sometimes children – were responsible for herding the animals. There wasn't much wood to burn during winter so they would have to collect the excrement of the cattle and shovel it over the side of the walls so that it would dry in the sun. Then, they would use this to cultivate the land for heating and for cooking purposes, using a gadget they called a *'kürsü'* (lectern), which they placed in the middle of the house. Such devices were to become another aspect of 'otherization' or differentiation after their settlement in Greece, as 'these devices have also been used by the Turks'. To date, there are bitter remarks on how having the *'kürsü'* under the table would cause a smell, as they ate with their distinctive heavy clothing, all gathered around the table.[66]

Many in the village had double-occupations such as pottery making in the summer and tailoring during winter. These vocation-changes and migratory periods depended on the season, for the Karmanlis working seasonally in the central cities. Among some of the year round occupations were forging (blacksmithing), shoemaking, and other artisanships. For some, like construction, the Karamanlis have been renowned.[67] While there was no official differentiation for artisanship, it was traditionally the Orthodox who were occupied with

---

65 "Atları varmış dedemin. Ben de durumu düzeltir düzeltmez aldım." Paisiyos Papadopoulos, in an interview held on the 14th December 2005 in his house, expresses that as soon as he earned enough to make a living, he bought horses 'too', like his grandfather did in Anatolia.

66 A few similar remarks were made by the Pontiac 'brides', sharing the village with their families in law for over 40 years.

67 The person that would carve the rock house would write his name over the wall, either behind a brick on the wall or over the doorway. Such signatures remain to date in Gelveri.

commerce and artisanship. Most occupations were passed on from father to son. After the Exchange, for two to three generations to come, the Karamanlis of the periphery continued to preserve this father-to-son line in vocational training. Often, they took on their father's job, as most could not receive higher education, due to their Greek (especially *katharevousa* Greek) skills.

Most of the commercial activity was conducted by the Orthodox of the village, whether it be small-scale, such as buying and selling fabrics, clothes, or toys 'between the close by villages of Aksaray by three or four days donkey ride', or running small-scale businesses, such as *halvah* making, pickle selling, egg selling or charcoal selling in the city centres. Hence, the Orthodox had additional income sources via familial networks to the Centre. Most men worked either seasonally or permanently in Mersin or Istanbul. Nevertheless, despite disparities in income, differentiation on the basis of income was uncommon. This owed mainly to the organizational structure of communities in the Ottoman society. According to the testimonies, the most vivid visualization of the disparity between the wealthy and the poor was that the wealthy lived in the new brick-made rather than the traditional rock-carved Cappadocian houses, made by the Karamanli craftsman.

Almost all respondents had a relative working in Istanbul, either dealing with the above mentioned small scale businesses or with commercial transactions, goldsmiths and the like. The Karamanli of Gelveri had an association they named after their Patron Saint Gregory Naziansus. This association would help the newcomers to the centre as well as those back in Gelveri. For instance, 'if an orphan wished to continue into higher education, the association would help'.[68] Some others started to work in the newly flourishing factories of the modernizing Empire. There are accounts pertaining to relatives

---

68 When the Exchange took place, again, the Association and the Church helped the poor. Money was needed for hiring out horse-carriages and similar expenses and support was extended at this last phase as well.

working as foreman in these companies. One exchangee was still proud of having a relative work as a foreman in a notable company of the time.

> My father was a machinist in the Singer Company in Konya... He had craftsmanship, they made him a foreman (Minas Yousifidis, 1921)[69]

Nevertheless, perhaps owing to the short period between the time that modernization started to gradually take hold in the Ottoman centre and the Exchange, the mode of communal relations in this periphery community continued to display predominantly pre-modern characteristics. This remained so for two to three generations to follow the Exchange, despite the increasingly standardized education and the relatively slow industrialization wave taking effect in the Greek state's realm.[70]

While the Karamanlis had the chance to pack up as much as they could of their worldly belongings, their orchards (*'bağ-bahçe-miz'*), churches, homes and streets, in other words, all the *practiced places* of Cappadocia remained behind. Rupture from Cappadocia with its heavy religious and pre-modern connotations indiscernible from the conceptualization of the communal identity, was to prove traumatic. They would continue practicing these places via oral repetitions to one another, either in the secluded areas of their homes or via the plane provided by differentiated language use for decades to come.

---

69 "Babam Konya'da Singer Kumpanya'sında makinist... Zanaat sahibiymiş... ustabaşı" (Minas Yousifidis, 20th December, 2005).

70 Still, it should be noted that the parents/grandparents of most of the informants were recorded to have dealt with the above-mentioned small-scale businesses in the city centres and artisan-ships in the village. Those working on a waged basis in companies (like the person above, working in Singer) were small in number. Out of the 50 informants interviewed, only one (Minas Yousifidis' father) was recorded to work in such a company. Although this may be viewed to owe to snow-ball sampling at first, this observation falls in line with the views of other sources on the *relatively* slow wave of industrialization taking effect in the Ottoman realm at the time.

Borders of Belonging and the Margin/
Limen (Transition) Phase

> Everyone more or less is permanently in transit... Not so much
> 'where are you from?' but 'where are you between? (The intercul-
> tural identity question)
>
> (James Clifford 1992: 109)

Phases in a rite of passage vary (Turner 1982: 25). In the case
of the Exchange, the transition phase is observed to have been the
longest, diffusing effects of liminality over the reintegration phase as
well as the personae involved.

For the first-generations that experienced the Exchange and
even for the generation to follow them, this state of social limbo was
arguably ever-present. Throughout the Exchange and the happenings
that followed the Exchange, such as the great depression, the Metaxas
dictatorship, the Second World War, and the Bulgarian invasion of
Northern Greece, the collectivity experienced a 'breakdown of established social classifications and cultural codes' (Turner, 1982) followed
by their cyclical replacement with new ones. Language was but one of
these codes.

For the first ten years, the liminality phase was also paralleled
by a continuous transit from one 'non-place'[71] (Augé 1995) to another. Arguably, the first of these was the site of quarantine, where most
of them spent fifteen days to one month upon arrival in Greece.

For a majority of the Karamanlis, the journey started on August
15th 1924, by horse-carriage, taking them first to Aksaray then to
Ereğli. From Eregli onwards they took the train to Mersin, where they
met other Karamanlis from greater Cappadocia coming from the villages within the triangle between Aksaray/Nevşehir, Niğde and

---

[71] Augé (1995) defines a 'non-place' as in contradiction with the notion of place, in that a non-
place is "a space, which cannot be defined as relational or historical, or concerned with identity."

Kayseri[72] to wait for the ships that would take them to the ports in Greece, among them Piraeus and Salonika. Late first-generation exchangee, Pantelis Akakiadis (1916) remembers this journey as follows:

> We took off on the 15th of August. The grapes had barely ripened. With carriages we came... to Aksaray. We stayed on in Aksaray for one night. The following day we went on to Ereğli. I don't remember how many days we stayed on in Ereğli, maybe two maybe three days but not more than three days. There, at the centre...we waited at the station. The train came and we got on. (I remember) passing through [the] Bozantı Mountains... [which] the Germans had 'opened' during the war...we passed on from there, and came to Mersin. At the time, there was no port, no harbour in Mersin. The vessels had waited out in the deep sea. With little rowboats...they took us with little rowboats or with large barges. We had waited for fifteen days for the vessels to come.[73]

The ship voyage[74] would take them one month.

---

72 While the Karamanlis from Ankara were sent via trains to Istanbul and the ports of İzmir, those situated in Niğde, Kayseri, Nevşehir were transferred mainly to Mersin, which did not have a port at the time. The only way they could reach the ships waiting off shore was by getting into row boats.

73 "Ağustos'un 15'inde kalktık yola. Üzümler anca kararırdı yani... Ordan geldik, Aksaray'dan... Aksaray'da kaldık bir gece. Öbür gün Ereğli'ye gittik. Ereğli'de iki gün mü üç gün mü, bellemiyom, 3 günden fazla değil. Orda merkezde, istasyonda bekledik. Tren geldi, trene bindik. Trenlen Bozantı dağlarını filan... muharebede açmışlar Almanlar... büyük muharebede delmişler... ordan geçtik, Mersin'e geldik. Mersin'de o zaman liman yoğudu. Gemiler uzakta açıkta duruyordu. Ufak kayıklarınan, büyük mavnalarınan ehaliyi daşıyorlardı. Bir 15 gün bekledik orada" (Pantelis Akakiadis, 14th December 2005). Note the mixture of Istanbul Turkish and Aksaray dialect in his Turkish. Growing up, he had contact with relatives coming from Istanbul *and* Gelveri.

74 Some of the passengers described the voyage as having bad conditions including contagious diseases and a deadly flu. Of course, it is not possible to say whether it was a flu epidemic or not. A story about a girl 'probably having been kidnapped by the captains of the ship and taken back to Anatolia' repeated itself in three in-depth interviews and could well be about a dead body, being thrown out of the ship to avoid spreading of the virus. The fact here being unable to mourn and bury their dead via a religious ceremony and onto the soil of their village could have been the reason behind the transferal of bitter feelings of the journey and rupture to the immediate figures of authority, seen as part of the reason why they would soon be left to a land they

Vessels came. We set on to the sea with the ship...I don't know how many days...[75] We came to Pirea. (Pantelis Akakiadis, 1916).[76]

Following their one-month-long voyage, exchangees were taken to ports in Salonika and Athens and spent their first weeks in Greece in quarantine, followed by their resettlement to their prospective villages. Hence, the first non-place for a majority of them was the site of the quarantine. Pantelis Akakiadis (1916) remembers:

> What do they call it?...(speaking of the quarantine)..They cut all our hair and all. Our clothes..everything..they took hold of it all...They held the whole village one month in quarantine...But me and my family, we didn't stay that long...I had two older brothers in Istanbul...One of them had come to Pirea, the other had gone elsewhere. We stayed fifteen days..he came. We stayed a year and a half in Pirea...He took us to his hotel, fed us, changed our clothes..;We stayed on for a year and a half...and then came and found the whole village here (speaking of Kavala). They had come from before.[77]

Until the community's final resettlement in the government-built standard housing and even after their resettlement in this final village,

did not know and whose language they did not speak, away from their village. Still, borders of their local belonging to Gelveri would not fade, until the last Turcophone generation would pass away, eight to nine decades to follow the Exchange. Neither would their memory of a peaceful co-existance with their Muslim co-villagers and the experience of an extended community under the Patriarchate. Moreover, some of the second-generations still define themselves as Gelverili (from Gelveri). They kept on visualizing Nea (New) Karvali as an imitation and in due time, as an extention of their original village (Gelveri).

75 A majority of the informants provided that the voyage took one month.

76 Mr. Akakiadis and his family travelled with a different ship then the majority. Others noted landing in Salonika. Those 'with more money' were able to travel with a better ship. Those that did not have enough money were helped by their Association in Istanbul, named after the community's patron Saint, Gregory Naziansus.

77 "Ne diyorlar ona?.. Hepimizin saçlarımızı filan kestiler... Çamaşırlar filan... hepsi... tutuldu. Bir ay tuttular bütün köyü orada... Ama biz fazla durmadık... Benim 2 emmim vardı İstanbul'da. Emmimin biri Prea'daydı, öteki başka yerde. Biz 15 gün kaldık, geldi... Bizi aldı, yedirdi... oteline götürdü, çamaşırlarımızı filan değiştirdi... Biz Prea'da 1,5 sene kaldık... köyün geri kalanı gitmiş... sonra geldik bulduk buraları" (Pantelis Akakiadis, 14 December 2005).

the transitions imposed by the Exchange phenomenon not only entailed a change in space but was also accompanied by efforts on behalf of the community members to transform some of these non-places into practiced places; and, when possible via discursive practice, to relate the new to the old. Such would be the case when they named the new village after Gelveri, calling it Nea Karvali (New Gelveri). But until they resettled in their final village, many families changed more than one settlement. This applied to many exchangee communities. In the case of the Gelveri community at hand, testimonies reveal that families went to Salonika, Piraeus, Volos, and Neapolis. Once they reached their first destinations, the notables of the village took responsibility and searched for a suitable region until they found the right place. In the case of the Gelveri community, as in many others, this search would last a few years.

> Five to six of the elderly of the village took off (from the quarantine area) to look for a place... in Salonika... But they didn't like what the government showed them in Salonika... or in Athens... Then they heard that a farm-owner had donated land to the state... on the condition... that a village from Turkey would be resettled here (Paisiyos Papadopoulos, 1931).

Once the re-settlement to the first village was realized, it had become clear that resettlement to a new milieu was necessary, due to the dire conditions in the swamp[78] community, which experienced daily deaths, sometimes without even being able to conduct proper, separate funerals for their dead.[79] Some went a bit northwards, but conditions did not show any drastic difference.

---

78 Expressed as 'yabanın havasına suyuna alışamadı' ('could not get used to this foreign environment') in a number of interviews. The word 'yaban' was met with the word 'foreign'. However the word 'yaban' has other connotations in Turkish, including wilderness, strange deserted land, isolation and remoteness from homeland.

79 Informants stated that people from all ages would be buried on a daily basis owing to numerous reasons of death. Among these reasons, informants stressed 'gurbet acısı' (a term that could be translated as home-sickness yet with particular reference to the deep *agony* of those away from their motherland). Informants stressed that death of men was more common due to their inability to meet their roles as providers for their extended families and hurt feelings of pride.

> I don't know why it was called 'Çırpındı'... Perhaps because the
> environment 'beat' people like a rug...they didn't live here long you
> see... Maybe they named it 'Çırpındı' for that...[80] (Paisiyos
> Papadopoulos, 1931).[81]

Two years passed in this swamp before their prospective resettlement to their final village. With its predominantly modern government-built buildings, this place too would be in complete contrast to
remembrances of the homes left behind.

The Exchange of Populations itself was certainly, if not a direct
consequence, a part of the infrastructural changes that would soon
take effect through the modernization of the periphery. In its aftermath, modern housings built initially by the project managers assigned
by the Refugee Relief Fund[82] and later by the project managers of foreign companies started to transform the exchangees' new spaces
(Colonas, 2004: 168). The 'exchangees' on the other hand, made
every effort to turn these non-places into practiced spaces and form
relational contexts. This would sometimes take effect on the discursive
plane (such as naming the new village after Gelveri), while at other
times on the spatial and religious terrains. As soon as this final village
was established, villagers made themselves a church by placing rela-

---

80 "Çırpıyor muymuş, neymiş... yaşamıyormuş insanlar. Ondan mı dediler acaba adına çırpındı?"
(Paisiyos Papadopoulos, 14 December 2005). 'Çırpmak' in Turkish can be translated as 'to beat'
or 'to shake (off)'. But from the same root ('çırp') derives the verb 'çırpınmak' (to struggle) and
the adverb 'çırpıntılı' (slightly rough). Therefore the term 'çırpındı' makes reference not only to
the qualities of the land, the rough conditions of the environment and the dire living conditions,
but also to the people's struggle to survive.

81 On the other hand, oral testimonies are backed by the information in a brochure prepared by
a late establishment near Nea Karvali (the 'Akondisma'). The brochure provides that the name
Çırpındı (written in Greek as 'Tserpendi') came from a village present in this region from 1750
onwards. Accordingly, this was a mixed (Muslim-Orthodox) habitation. But the final owners
(Konstantinos and Athanasios Sismanoglu) of a large estate (çiftlik) left the estate -almost as big
as the village itself- to the Greek government, on the condition that the government would settle on this large plot of land, those coming from Anatolia.

82 The decision to set up the Refugee Relief Fund was taken by the Greek government on the 3rd
of November 1922. Its main mission, together with the Ministry of Health and Welfare, was to
set up housing for the incoming exchangees (Colonas, 2004: 168).

tional objects (the old church bell) and in so doing, held on to the religious plane. When a short lived foreign investment, a small carpet company, ceased to exist due to the economic depression in 1929, the villagers turned it into a Church and used it as such until material conditions allowed them to build a new one in 1950.[83]

Within less than a decade, space in Greece and Turkey would see a quick transformation as envisaged by the 'project' managers, from the reflections of which, the transformation and cyclical (re)production of the private/public and political sphere dichotomies would not be immune. It was as if the social engineering phase in both states ran in parallel to the architectural transformations. The results were spectacular. The immediate appearance of small settlements solidified in standardized housing in Northern Greece is still apparent.[84] Almost every settlement had the main transformative state or semi-state[85] institutions, such as the school, some type of a community or cultural centre, and a religious institution to serve as the main places of transformation (Fieldwork Notes, 2005). These were the main institutions that functioned through the transitory periods to establish the new codes. In the meantime, community members made every effort to turn these non-places into practiced spaces and worked in cooperation with the above-mentioned institutions in their struggle to relate to the new socio-political context.

The so-called[86] 'voluntary' acceptance of new meanings and

---

83 Paisiyos Papadopoulos (14 December 2005).

84 For plans of the standardized housing projects in Greece and Turkey and similar observations with regard to the parallelism between modernization and architectural transformation, see Vassilis Colonas "Housing and the Architectural Expression of Asia Minor Greeks Before and After 1923" in *Crossing the Aegean: An Appraisal Of The 1923 Compulsory Population Exchange Between Greece and Turkey*, ed. Renée Hirschon, Oxford: Berghahn Books (2004: 163-179) and Ali Cengizkan, *Mübadele Konut ve Yerleşimleri: Savaş Yıkımının, İç Göçün ve Mübadelenin Doğurduğu Konut Sorununun Çözümünde 'İktisadi Hane' Programı, 'Numune Köyler' ve 'Emval-i Metruke'nin Değerlendirilmesi İçin Adımlar*, Ankara: Arkadaş Yayıncılık (2004).

85 Taking their part in the reconstruction of the past and the selection of remembrances.

86 'So called' based upon the presupposition that the transformation was ultimately defined by the new context that the structural transformations had made inescapable.

codes took effect mainly on the religious plane, most vividly observed in the North. The Church served as the main plane of transformation, where communities would merge with the new extended society, the corpus of the nation. Nationalization of the religious realm worked in both ways. As such, it may be argued that transformation did not take place as a state-induced process *only*. Codes introduced from above with the help of the new state institutions were, in time, quasi 'voluntarily' internalized (e.g. the meanings attributed to the key signifiers of belonging among the *Karamanlı*).

Borders of Belonging and the Reaggregation (Reintegration) Phase

During the reaggregation or incorporation phase, the ambiguity associated with liminality throughout the transition phase had come to an end, in terms of the now re-established modes of societal relations, spaces, and other relational contexts, in this case the most important being language and religion.

Due to the hardships of daily life for the first six years of resettlement in Northern Greece (1924-1930), coupled with the global economic depression and the series of political crises that had to be endured, including the overthrow of Venizelos, the reign of King George, followed by the dictatorship of Metaxas, the invasion of Northern Greece by Bulgaria and the Civil War, the Karamanli of the late first-generation and early second-generation had to start over every four to ten years. Many from the first-generation did not endure these hardships and passed away. Pantelis Akakiadis (1916), who was eight years old when they arrived in Greece in 1924, experienced it all as a young man:

> I started to work for my household and myself since the 1950s. Before that...continuous losses...and trying to stand up... 1930s, 1940s... we were just about to get our business going. Then the war broke out. Whatever we ever had, cows, cattle, oxcarts, went to the military... Then, the military dispersed... half went away

with the government... the Germans... downward, it was the
Italians and the Germans and here... the Bulgarians came... Some
even stayed on in some of the houses in the village. You had to get
a paper to go to a village near by.

Due to these abrupt changes, the schooling of the first two generations was disrupted as well. Many of the respondents are recorded
as having had to stop school for reasons of civil unrest. Hence, until
the late second-generation started to come of age, the most important
criteria for social acceptance, namely language, remained a problem.
Later, when the late first and early second-generations learned demotic Greek (*dimotiki*), this time the difficulty of attaining fluency in
katharevousa Greek added hindrances for those who wanted to take
up official positions (Arhelos Angelidis (Püsküloğlu), 1921). This
added to the existing societal silences of the displaced Karamali.
Furthermore, the difficulties posed by a majority of the exchangees'
Venizelist position during the anti-Venizelist rule,[87] followed by the
Metaxas regime, increasingly drove the Turcophones to reserve spoken Turkish for the private confines of their homes.[88]

---

87 Except for the brief period of 1928-33

88 Until the village started to receive Greek speaking migrants and the schooled late-first and early
second-generations started to come of age -some among them marrying non-Turkish speakers
through inter-village marriages- Turkish has been the main spoken language in the village. To
date, early second-generations continue speaking Turkish or mix Turkish with Greek in their
daily encounters at the elderly people's gathering place 'Kapi', or at home. Informants provided that until the relative 'mixing of the village', Turkish had been the only spoken language. In
Katina Hristoforidou's (1916) words, the 'mixing' of the village took three different forms. First
the state joined the nearby villages, second, inter-community marriages occurred mostly with
the 'Pontiac', and lastly, after the dissolution of the Soviet Block, 'more Pontiacs came to the village'. Katina Hristoforidou's testimony is backed by the results of the 1996 census. Accordingly,
this year records the number of the 'Pontiac' people having arrived from the ex-Soviet Republics
as 150. The numbers in this census are cited in Stelaku (2004: 183). Moreover, in addition to
these in-flows, men started to go to work in the larger cities and later to West Germany. Late
third-generations do not speak much Turkish, even if they understand it. Some do not understand at all. Early third-generations born to Turcophone parents, on the other hand, speak
and/or understand Turkish depending on a set of variables (i.e. whether their parents' marriage
was an inter-community marriage or not, whether their parents made use of Turkish at home,
or whether they avoided it in general and used it only when they wanted to speak something in

As the Gelveri villagers came to resettle together, they enjoyed a rather large public and linguistic sphere wherein they could socialize among themselves. Yet this sphere grew narrower due to the new settlers that came to the village through mixed marriages,[89] the state's policy of joining the near-by villagers and with the 1990s in-flow of Greek- speaking Pontians from the ex-Soviet Republics. As for the bilingual second-generation Karamali, their increased presence in the Greek-speaking milieus (i.e. high-school, or the *'gymnasium'* in Kavala, serving in the military in another town, and in the 60s, going to work in Germany and being settled among the Greek-speaking communities there); and the coming of age of late third and early fourth-generation Grecophones, served as additional grounds for speaking Greek more often. A number of respondents recorded the gradual improvement in their spoken Greek skills as they went to 'gymnasium' (high school) in Kavala, despite the fact that they still felt insecure about making a mistake and being called names. A majority of the first and early second-generations remember being called the *'tourkosporoi'* (Turkish seeds) or *'giaourtovaftesmeni'* (the ones baptized in yoghurt).

Since community members grew close to one anotherwithin the secluded area in which they were placed and their nodal contact with

---

private etc.). Still, for the ones that do speak Turkish, it was noted that they had an accent and their pronunciation was not anywhere near to that of the native speakers, namely, their parents'. In due time, the schooled late-first generations and second-generations started to become bilingual, even if they had difficulties speaking Greek. As such, it would not be wrong to state that for the Gelveri village in particular Turkish as a native language was preserved by the first and second-generations *alone*. Since the time of the Exchange, most of them also changed their surnames from Turkish to Greek. Informants maintained that this transaction involved applying in person to the Prefacturate (Governorship) of Kavala. Among the expressed reasons were the informants' belief that having a Greek surname would facilitate their social mobility or would facilitate the new generations' societal acceptance and daily life (at school, in the army etc.). On the other hand, some others expressed that they did not opt to change their family names, underlining the fact that they were 'proud to be Karamanlis'.

89 This usually involved 'taking in' females from other communities (i.e. Pontiac). The first 'Pontiac brides' learned fluent Turkish instead of the other-way around (one 'bride' speaking of her mother in-law and many of her peers as "dying without having learned a word of Greek").

state institutions (school and police) was temporally and spatially limited and pre-determined, the initial generations after the Exchange continued to identify themselves along communal lines. It is interesting to note, however, the respective changes in the criteria of 'otherness' in the eyes of their immediate others before and after the Exchange. Whilst in the former period, the exchangees' otherness had without doubt been based upon the religion criterion, with their resettlement in the new nation state, linguistic unity was assigned increasing priority. A majority of the respondents had bitter remarks regarding the grounds for otherization (i.e. language) in the post-exchange era... According to the transferred accounts, their otherization stemmed not only from their speaking Turkish, which was not well received socially, but also from their poor skills in *katharevousa* and *dimotiki* (demotic) Greek. Some (like A. Angelidis) held that this decreased their chances of being employed in certain bureaucratic positions, while others shared information regarding the difficulties they have had with state figures like community school teachers appointed by the Greek Centre or their experiences during the mandatory military service.

Religion, on the other hand, came to be a prioritized key signifier of belonging, possibly even the main plane they shared with their new immediate others. As such, religious discourse provided not only a *continuum* in space but also served as the context in which they could take part in this new society, without much difficulty. The preserved and transferred body of Gelveri's Patron Saint, St. Gregory the Theologian, for instance, offered not only a temporal but also a spatial continuity, extending onto the corpus of the nation at large. Every 25th of January, people from all over Greece started to join in with their festivities.

All in all, it was the linguistic characteristics coupled with economic hardships,[90] that had become the main grounds for otherization

---

90 "The scarcity of arable land did not permit the allocation of viable plots to all...The issue of land distribution fuelled quarrels over disputed land throughout the inter-war period. In many mixed-villages serious clashes occurred" between the locals and the 'exchanged' (Kontogiorgi,

in the eyes of their new immediate others. As such, upon their coming into the Greek state's realm, the initial discourse of 'welcoming the parts of the nation', with connotations of the 'survivors of the Greek catastrophe', soon waned with the economic crises and the numerous dictatorships that followed the turbulent war years and, once again, the negative connotations associated with the term Karamanli[91] started to prevail. It was in this regard that the envisioned reaggregation phase, i.e. a full 'voluntary' assimilation of the Karamanli community into 'the whole,' would take more than one generation.

In that respect one needs to consider the larger transformations at work. Prior to the Exchange, a late wave of modernization taking effect in the Ottoman realm had gradually started to reflect upon the communities' conceptualizations of their immediate and extended communities, along with the newly introduced forms of subjectivity . This was especially the case for those living in the Centre. However, periphery populations also started to receive the new ideological undercurrents. For the periphery Karamanlis, familial networks with the Centre and their speaking of the *lingua franca* – as opposed to the case in post-exchange Greece – were but two of the previously mentioned elements that facilitated the gradual introduction of these new idealizations. In the Empire's realm, common language had opened the road for the Karamanli notables' prospective subjoining to the Centre, its cultural realm as well as a number of competing ideological undercurrents. In the last century of the Empire, the Karamanlis had long been prospering, due to the multiple incomes they had from agriculture and the capital inflow from their family members and other kin, living seasonally –or permanently- in the larger cities. The cultural *and* material capital of the Centre had started to reach them and the notables of the periphery settlements had gradually become the consumers of the ideological undercurrents of the modernization wave in Istanbul *and* abroad.

2004: 75). Here the term 'mixed-village' refers to the villages in which the government settled those coming from Asia Minor with the villagers already resident in Greece.

91 Met with adjectives such as the Tourkosporoi and the like.

With the Exchange, the Karamanlis had been uprooted from a context in which modernization and nationalization had been slowly under way, transforming the public sphere and conceptualizations of the immediate and extended totalities, such as the community and the nation. After the traumatic group dislocation of the Exchange, there followed a period during which all normal income differentiation and structured modes of social relations deteriorated. The gradual subjoining of the Centre and the Peripheral realms and the in-flow of intellectual currents was cut due to the Karamanlis' settlement in a segregated geographical[92] confine and a cultural milieu whose language they did not speak. To oversimplify, the gradual conceptual transformation from pre-modern forms of belonging into those of the modern was cut. Now the only way for these communities to come into contact with the outer currents was through a *downwards* introduction of culture and ideology. In that regard, while religion has served to facilitate the translation of old and the introduction of new codes through the transition and reintegration phases, language has remained an inhibitor to the introduction of newcultural codes from above.

For most of the periphery communities, the new modes of relations that have taken effect under a relatively recent wave of industrialization[93] have been reflected in the new conceptualizations of the self and the community. Arguably, this is not only the case for the periphery Karamanlis but for the communities resettled in Northern Greece, as well.[94] This pattern seems similar to the transformation experienced

---

92 Speaking in terms of the sample population and other communities in Northern Greece. The implementation scheme in Macedonia at the time was resettling whole villages together (Colonas, 1998).

93 For a brief account of the early economic development in the 19th and early 20th centuries' Balkans, see Michael Plairet, *The Balkan Economies 1800-1914: Evolution Without Development*, Cambridge: Cambridge University Press (1997).

94 Needless to say, most of the exchangees have been resettled to the Macedonia region (Colonas 2004: 170). It is equally important to note that the patterns of migration in the aftermath of the Exchange varied for the Karamanlis of the Centre (bilingual and coming from larger cities) and the Karamanlis of the periphery. Even if they were at times resettled together, the wealthy had the opportunity to migrate to larger cities near-by, to deal with commerce and the like activi-

two generations ago in the cities, in that, a 'late modernit*ies*' discussion is reified in the social, manifesting itself through the temporal and spatial variations of the Centre and periphery dichotomy. In other words, the infrastructural transformation is felt in the societal realm, seeing a gradual increase in individualistic conceptions of the self and the conceptualization of a singular attachment plane to the corpus of the nation, versus a communitarian view of the local.

DRAWING CONCLUSIONS AND POLICY IMPLICATIONS

> Political theory becomes rooted in political culture. It must recognize that there is no practical possibility of fully resolving disputed religious, philosophical and moral issues. Political theory should therefore not insist on providing substantive solutions; it should deal instead with issues of process and procedure (Bronner 1997: 20).

This approach is believed to apply to attempts at bringing fixed definitions to the fluid, ever-widening and changing notion of Culture, its deviations (i.e. 'national culture'), and its role in the fixing – if at all possible – of identity (i.e. 'cultural identity', 'national identity'), all subjected to a continuous reconstruction process within the dialectical relations as envisioned by the modernists *and* the micro-level analysts.

In its widest sense, culture is everything that cannot be transferred through the genes (Eagleton 2005: 46).[95] For some, simply the overarching act of entering on a quest to define cultural identity is based upon the belief that identity is what one is *taught* to be. The problem however, rests with the fact that this precognition is often contested by groups with essentialist claims to nationhood, appropriating cultural signifiers with claims to continuity in time and space.

As the modern/nation state played a part[96] in the ranks of social

---

ties. As such, these observations can relate with higher accuracy to the communities resettled in the periphery upon arrival from similar settlements.

95 For further discussion on the contemporary approaches to the idea of 'culture' see Eagleton, Terry, *Kültür Yorumları (The Idea of Culture)*, 2005, Translated by Ö. Çelik, Istanbul: Ayrıntı.

96 and mostly a superior place

and inter*national* organization, each state has bestowed upon its constituency not only a new form of subjectivity but also a singular form of belonging with the underlying premise that the assumed-collectivity has been 'preserved' in *essence* throughout time and space. Cyclical reference to a continuum in the constituent communities' common key signifiers of belonging such as language, religion and/or the practiced-space paralleled the societal and official exclusions of the 'unwanted' and/or the signifiers of the unwanted.

The modest attempt of this study has been to provide a brief account of an arguably ongoing process rather than a description of a closed event, from the perspective of those who were subjected to a mandatory population exchange. The period that followed the establishment of new regimes in the 'Near East' has seen a re-appropriation of the cultural signifiers of a pre-national era – nationalization of cultural realms and borders of belonging – via meta-narratives. This process involved a downwards re-interpretation of the meanings attributed to cultural signifiers and shifts in the prioritization of the key signifiers of belonging to the corpus of a new collectivity. Oral history accounts provided by community members 'otherized' on the basis of one of their key signifiers of belonging, both prior to and after the Exchange, reveal that this has not been a smooth process, especially if the traumatic group dislocation and resettlement was to a linguistically, socio-politically, and geographically segregated sphere.

The passage from one geographical threshold to another was paralleled by a transition from one legal status to another (subject to citizen); from one cultural realm to another; from one socio-cultural context to another; from one political sphere to another; all of which required a redefinition of the symbolic borders of belonging. It is in this regard that this paper has analyzed the 'Exchange' and introduced it to the literature as a *metaphorical rite of passage*, as a sequence of phases rather than a closed event. Overall, the Exchange itself can be seen as part of a process which saw the gradual fixing of the borders of belonging around new or re-translated codes. The spatial, temporal, and socio-political changes that the 'project' managers introduced continue to shape (divert and/or singularize) the meanings attributed to the key signifiers (i.e. religion, language, locality) of belonging. The process which saw the internalization of a new form of belonging was paralleled and fortified by subsequent periods of anti-structure, such as World War II, the Bulgarian occupation, and the meeting of new 'others' in national terms. The eventful transition and reintegration phases resulted in a re-arrangement of the symbolic borders of belonging for the Karamanlis, while assigning the first and second- generations a borderline characteristic in terms of identity.

It is concluded that the cultural domain was not always as nationally charged with certain signifiers appropriated by x state's national culture and not by y state's. We have introduced the Karamanlis in their immediate *pre-liminal* status as both the products and producers of a multitude of once-intersecting cultural realms. It was argued that much of the Karamanlis living in periphery settlements with mixed Orthodox and Muslim populations fell predominantly within the sphere of the Ecclesiastical realm[97] in their conceptualization of an extended community, while at the same time, sharing a variety of micro cultural realms with their co-habitants. The processes involved in the gradual transformation of the borders of belonging for the Karamanlis living in the Centre on the other hand, took place in the midst of a continuous tension created by the reformists and traditionalists of the age.[98]

Still, neither one of the rival interpretations (traditionalist/ reformist) of an extended community predominated in the masses' minds overnight. Moreover, this was a temporally differentiated process for those living in the Central and peripheral settlements.[99]

---

97 And its universalist doctrine, until the late transformations of the 19th century. Shifts of approach to the 'extended community' within the Ecclesiastical realm and the late nationalization of religious belongings have been discussed above.

98 As reflected in the Karamanli literatus Misailidis' writings

99 I.e. centralization of the state, state institutions' increased outreach to the periphery, print. An important note to make is that, although there were a few journals in Karamanli script pub-

According to the oral testimonies of the late first and early second-generation Karamanlis, religious, communal (Karamanlı) and local (Gelverili, Aksaraylı) identification among their (grand)parents continued to have priority over other forms of belonging and a divided sense of space continued to dominate their minds. This applied differentially to the late first and early second-generations as well, but the new generations have a more unified outlook at their borders of belonging as the late wave of modernization takes full effect in the North.

Today, in Turkey, it is still possible to come across books in Karamanli script being sold at book auctions, ending up in individual collections, and thereby closed to research. Nevertheless, this also comes to mean that it may still be possible to add new Karamanli material to the compilations made by S. Salaville, E. Dalleggio and Evangelia Balta with the combined efforts of institutionalized bodies and individual collectors. Existing collections of Karamanli books, religious and literary brochures, community registers, church codices, baptism documents in Karamanli script, photographs of traditional garments and the like can also be increased in number through the purchasing or donation of individual collections.[100] Institutionalized bodies of research should be increased in number, all manuscripts and printed material should be put on micro-film, existing voice recordings should be multiplied in copy and an inter-library loan system should be established between the institutions in Greece and Turkey.

The same holds true for the inspection and preservation of the artifacts and architectural products of the Karamanlis. Although the restoration of small chapels in the region have slowly begun to be undertaken in the last decade, extended projects focusing on the preservation of Karamanli cultural products (chapels, monuments,

---

lished in Greece after the Exchange, most periphery communities' relation with the Centre was *linguistically* cut as a majority of them could not speak Greek at all. Moreover, the post-Exchange decades of political turbulence added to the disturbance of schooling in the first and early second-generation Karamanlis.

100 C.A.M.S. Brochure 2006.

houses, and Karamanli script carvings on various artifacts) should also be conducted. They reflect more than the production and consumption of culture in a specific temporal, spatial, and socio-political setting at large. They stand as solid testimony to the possibility of co-exsitence between intersecting cultural universes and a multitude of belongings with openings to the possibility of heteroglossia in the interpretation of the world.

The question for some still remains whether there is an 'essence' passed on through generations, that separates today's political categories or whether these identities are constructed upon cultural signifiers that, over time, have been nationalized, signifiers that, with modernity's forces at work, are being singularized in meaning and appropriated by respective national narratives. In such a climate, providing for an understanding of the constructed nature of political identities paves the ground for humans to stay active in their interpretation processes in face of the downwards introduction of ideology with claims to the absolute knowledge of the self, the other and the so-called 'natural' borders of belonging.

REFERENCES

Alexandris, A., 1983, "Η απόπειρα δημιουργίας Τουρκορθόδοξης Εκκλησίας", Δελτίο: Κέντρου Μικρασιατικών Σπουδών, 4: 159-210.

Anagnostakis, I. and E. Balta, 1994, *La Découverte de la Cappadoce au Dix-Neuviéme Siécle*, Istanbul: Eren.

Anderson, B., 2000 (1983), *Imagined Communities: Reflections on the Origin and Spread of Nationalism*, 10th ed., London: Verso.

Anhegger, R., 1979-1980, "Hurufumuz Yunanca: Ein Beitrag zur Kenntniss der Karamanish-Türkischen Literatür", *Anatolica*, 7: 157-202.

—, 1983, "Nachtraege zu Hurufumuz Yunanca", *Anatolica*, 10: 149-164.

—, 1988, "Evangelinos Misaelidis ve Türkçe Konuşan Dindaşları", *Tarih ve Toplum*.

Anhegger, R. and V. Günyol, 1986, *Seyreyle Dünyayı: Temaşa-i Dünya ve Cefakâr-u Cefakeş*, Istanbul: Cem Yayınevi.

Arı, K., 2000, *Büyük Mübadele: Türkiye'ye Zorunlu Göç (1923-1925)*, Istanbul: Türkiye Ekonomik ve Toplumsal Tarih Vakfı Yayını.

Augé, M., 1995, *Non-Places: Introduction to the Anthropology of Supermodernity*, London: Verso.

Balta, E. (ed.), 1987a, *Karamanlidika XXe siècle: Bibliographie Analytique*, Athens: Centre d'Etudes d'Asie Mineure.

— (ed.), 1987b, *Karamanlidika: Additions (1584-1900): Bibliographie Analytique*, Athens: Centre d'Etudes d'Asie Mineure.

—, 1990, "Karamanlıca Kitapların Önsözleri", *Tarih ve Toplum*, 13: 18-21.

—, 1991, "Karamanlidika: Nouvelles Additions et Compléments I", *Deltio Kentrou Mikrasiatikon Spoudon* (Bulletin du Centre d'Etudes d'Asie Mineure), 8: 143-169.

— (ed.), 1997, *Karamanlidika: Nouvelles Additions et Compléments I*, Athens: Centre d'Etudés d'Asie Mineure.

—, 1998, "Périodisation et Typologie de la Production des Livres Karamanlis", Δελτίο: Κέυτρου Μικρασιατικώυ Σπουδώυ, 12: 129-153.

—, 2000, "Karamanlılar: The Turcophone Orthodox Population in Cappadocia" in K. Çiçek (ed.), *The Great Ottoman Turkish Civilization*, Volume 2, Ankara: Yeni Türkiye.

—, 2003, "Gerçi Rum İsek De Rumca Bilmez Türkçe Söyleriz: The Adventure of an Identity in the Triptych: Vatan, Religion and Language", *Türk Kültürü İncelemeleri Dergisi*, 8: 25-44.

Barutciski, M., 2004, "Lausanne Revisited: Population Exchanges in International Law and Policy" in R. Hirschon (ed.), *Crossing the Aegean: An Appraisal of the 1923 Compulsory Population Exchange between Greece and Turkey*, Oxford: Berghahn Books.

Baykurt, C., 1932, *Osmanlı Ülkesinde Hristiyanlaşan Türkler*, Istanbul: Sanayiienfise Matbaası.

Benlisoy, F., 2002, "Türk Milliyetçiliginde Katedilmemiş Bir Yol: Hristiyan Türkler" in M. Gültekingil and T. Bora (eds.), *Milliyetçilik*, Istanbul: İletişim Yayınları.

Braude, B., 1982, "Foundation Myths of the Millet System" in B. Braude and B. Lewis (eds.), *Christians and Jews in the Ottoman Empire: The Functioning of a Plural Society*, London: Holmes and Meier Publishers Inc.

Britannica, 1995, "Greece", Chicago: Encyclopaedia Britannica, Inc.

Bronner, S. E. (ed.), 1997, *Twentieth Century Political Theory: A Reader*, 1st ed., New York and London: Routledge.

Brubaker, R., 1996, *Nationalism Reframed: Nationhood and the National Question In the New Europe*, 1st ed, Cambridge: Cambridge University Press.

Cahen, C., 1994, *Osmanlılardan Önce Anadolu'da Türkler*, Istanbul: E Yayınları.

Cengizkan, A., 2004, *Mübadele Konut ve Yerleşimleri: Savaş Yıkımının, İç Göçün*

*ve Mübadelenin Doğurduğu Konut Sorununun Çözümünde 'İktisadi Hane'
Programı, 'Numune Köyler' ve 'Emval-i Metruke'nin Değerlendirilmesi İçin
Adımlar*, Ankara: Arkadaş Yayıncılık.

Chambers, I., 2005 (1994), *Göç, Kültür, Kimlik*, Istanbul: Ayrıntı.

Clifford, J., 1992, "Travelling Cultures" in C. Nelson and P. T. Grossberg (eds.),
Cultural Studies, New York: Routledge.

Clogg, R., 1999, "A Millet within a Millet: the Karamanlides" in D. Goodicas and
C. Isaawi (eds.), *Ottoman Greeks in the Age of Nationalism, Politics, Economy
and Society in the Nineteenth Century*, Princeton: The Darwin Press, Inc.

Colonas, V., 2004, "Housing and the Architectural Expression of Asia Minor
Greeks Before and after 1923" in R. Hirschon (ed.), *Crossing the Aegean: An
Appraisal of the 1923 Compulsory Population Exchange between Greece and
Turkey*, Oxford: Berghahn Books.

Copeaux, E., 1998, *Tarih Ders Kitaplarında (1931-1993): Türk Tarih Tezinden
Türk-İslam Sentezine*, Istanbul: Tarih Vakfı Yurt Yayınları.

De Planhol, X., 1958, *De la Plaine Pamphylienne aux Lacs Pisidieus: Nomadisme
et Vie Paysanne*, Paris: Institut Français d'Arcéologie d'Istanbul et Andrien
Maisonneuve.

Dernschwam, H., 1992, *Istanbul ve Anadolu'ya Seyahat Günlüğü*, Istanbul:
Kültür Bakanlığı Yayınları.

Drake, M., 2003, "Population: Patterns and Processes" in M. Pugh (ed.), *A
Companion to Modern European History: 1871-1945*, Oxford: Blackwell
Publishing Ltd.

Eckmann, J., 1964, "Die Karamanische Literatur", *Philolgiae Turcicae
Fundamenta*, 2: 819-835.

Ergene, T., 1951, *İstiklal Harbinde Türk Ortodoksları*, Istanbul: İ. P. Neşriyat Servisi.

Exertzoglou, H. 1999, "Shifting Boundaries: Language, Community and the 'non-
Greek-speaking Greeks'", *Historein: A Review of the Past and Other Stories*,
1: 75-92.

Eyice, S., 1962, "S. Salaville ve E. Dalleggio: Bibliographie Anaytique D'ouvrages en
Langue Turque Impremes en Characteres Greces I (1584-1850)", *Belleten*, 26.

Faroqhi, S., 2005 (1995), *Osmanlı Kültürü ve Gündelik Yaşam: Ortaçağdan
Yirminci Yüzyıla*, Istanbul: Tarih Vakfı.

Fırat, M., 2001, "Yunanistan'la İlişkiler" in B. Oran (ed.), *Türk Dış Politikası:
Kurtuluş Savaşından Bugüne Olgular, Belgeler, Yorumlar*, Istanbul: İletişim.

Gianaris, N. V., 1982, *The Economies of the Balkan Countries: Albania, Bulgaria,
Greece, Romania, Turkey, and Yugoslavia*, New York: Praeger Publishers.

Güresin, E., 1998, *31 Mart İsyanı*, Istanbul: Yeni Gün Haber Ajansı.

Hirschon, R., 1998, *Heirs of the Greek Catastrophe: The Social Life of Asia Minor
Refugees in Piraeus*, Oxford: Berghahn Books.

Hobsbawm, E., 1990, *Nations and Nationalism since 1780*, Cambridge: Cambridge University Press.

Jascke, G., 1964, "Die Türkisch-Orthodoxe Kirche", *Der Islam*, 39: 95-129.

Jusdanis, G., 1998, *Gecikmiş Modernlik ve Estetik Kültür: Milli Edebiyatın İcat Edilişi*, Istanbul: Metis.

Karpat, K., 1973, "An Inquiry to the Social Foundations of the Ottoman State: from Social Estates to Classes, from Millets to Nations", Center of International Studies Research Monograph No. 39, Princeton.

—, 2002, *Osmanlı Modernleşmesi: Toplum, Kurumsal Değişim ve Nüfus*, Istanbul: İmge Kitabevi Yayınları.

Keyder, Ç., 2000, "Arka Plan" in C. Keyder (ed.), *Istanbul: Küresel ile Yerel Arasında*, Istanbul: Metis.

Kitroeff, A., 1999, "Greek Nationhood and Modernity in the 19th Century", *Balkan Studies*, 40: 21-40.

Kitromilides, P., 1990, "'Imagined Communities' and the Origins of the National Question in the Balkans" in M. Blinkhorn and T. Veremis (eds.), *Modern Greece: Nationalism and Nationality*, Athens: Eliamep.

Kongar, E., 1995, *İmparatorluktan Günümüze: Türkiye'nin Toplumsal Yapısı*, Istanbul: Remzi Kitabevi.

Kushner, D., 1977, *The Rise of Turkish Nationalism 1876-1908*, London: Frank Cass.

Kut, T., 1987, "Temaşa-i Dünya ve Cefakar u Cefakeş'in Yazarı Evangelinos Misailidis Efendi", *Tarih ve Toplum*, 48: 342-346.

Kvale, S. T., 1996, *Interviews: An Introduction to Qualitative Research Interviewing*, Thousand Oaks, CA: Sage Publications.

Ladas, S., 1932, *The Exchange of Minorities: Bulgaria, Greece and Turkey*, New York: The Macmillan Company.

Mardin, Ş., 1991, "Türk Siyasasını Açıklayabilecek Bir Anahtar: Merkez-Çevre İlişkileri" in M. Türköne and T. Önder (eds.), *Türkiye'de Toplum ve Siyaset*, Makaleler-1, Istanbul: İletişim.

Meray, S. L. (ed.), 1972, *Lozan Barış Konferansı, Tutanaklar, Belgeler*, vol.8, Ankara: Ankara Üniversitesi Siyasal Bilgiler Fakültesi Yayınları.

Merlier, M., 1963, "Prologos", Μικρασιατικά Χρονικά, Κέντρο Μικρασιατικών Σπουδών.

Ortaylı, İ., 2003, *İmparatorluğun En Uzun Yüzyılı*, 16 ed., Istanbul: İletişim.

Özbaran, S., 2004, *Bir Osmanlı Kimliği: 14.-17. Yüzyıllarda Rum/Rumi Aidiyet ve İmgeleri*, Istanbul: Kitap Yayınevi.

Pentzopoulos, D., 1962, *The Balkan Exchange of Minorities and Its Impact Upon Greece*, Paris: Mouton & Co.

Petropoulu, I., 1993, "Cultural and Intellectual Life in 19th Century Cappadocia:

a Sketch" in L. Kipraiou (ed.), *Cappadocia a Travel in the Christian East*, Athens: Adam Editions.

Quataert, D., 2002, *Osmanlı İmparatorluğu: 1700-1922*, Istanbul: İletişim.

Salaville, S. and E. Dalleggio (ed.), 1958, *Karamanlidika I. Bibliographie Analytique des Ouvrages en Langue Turque Imprimés en Caractéres Grecs*, Athens: Institut Français d'Athènes.

— (ed.), 1966, *Karamanlidika II. Bibliographie Analytique des Ouvrages en Langue Turque Imprimés en Caractéres Grecs*, Athens: Institut Français d'Athènes.

—, 1974, *Karamanlidika III. Bibliographie Analytique des Ouvrages en Langue Turque Imprimés en Caractéres Grecs*, Athens: Institut Français d'Athènes.

Shils, E., 1975, *Center and Periphery: Essays in Macrosociology*, Chicago: The University of Chicago Press.

Smith, P., 2001, *Cultural Theory: An Introduction*, London: Blackwell.

Stelaku, V., 2004, "Space, Place and Identity: Memory and Religion in Two Cappodocian Greek Settlements" in R. Hirschon (ed.), *Crossing the Aegean: An Appraisal Of The 1923 Compulsory Population Exchange Between Greece and Turkey*, Oxford: Berghahn Books.

Swingewood, A., 1991, *Sosyolojik Düşüncenin Kısa Tarihi*, Ankara: Bilim ve Sanat Yayınları.

Şimşir, B. N. (ed.), 1990, *Lozan Telgrafları 1922-1923*, Ankara: T.T.K. Basımevi.

Topuz, H., 2003, *II. Mahmut'tan Holdinglere Türk Basın Tarihi*, Istanbul: Remzi Kitabevi.

Toynbee, A. J., 1922, *The Western Question In Greece and Turkey: A Study In the Contact of Civilizations*, London, Bombay, Sydney: Constable and Company Ltd.

Tökin, İ. H., 1984, "Grek Alfabesiyle Türkçe", *Tarih ve Toplum*, Haziran 1984.

Turner, V., 1969, *The Ritual Process: Structure and Anti-Structure*, New York: Aldine de Gruyter.

—, 1982, *From Ritual to Theatre: The Human Seriousness of Play*, New York: PAJ Publications.

Valavanis, I., 1891, *Mikrasyatika*, Athens.

Van Gennep, A., 1960, *The Rites of Passage*, London: Routledge and Kegan Paul.

Vryonis, S., 1971, *The Decline of Medivial Hellenism in Asia Minor and the Process of Islamisation from the 11th Through the 15th Century*, Los Angeles: University of California Press.

Yıldırım, O., 2002, "*Diplomats and Refugees: Mapping the Turco-Greek Exchange of Populations, 1922-1934*", Department of Near Eastern Studies, Michigan: Princeton University.

Zolberg, A. R., A. Shukre and S. Aguayo, 1989, *Escape from Violence*, Oxford: Oxford University Press.

2

Turkish Highly Skilled Migration to the United States: New Findings and Policy Recommendations

ŞEBNEM KÖŞER AKÇAPAR

INTRODUCTION AND LITERATURE REVIEW

The inscription on the Statue of Liberty on Liberty Island located in New York Harbor reads: "Give us your tired, your poor, your huddled masses yearning to breathe free." In order to keep up with the times, a more fitting inscription could be written as: "Give us your educated, your talented, your skilled masses yearning to earn more." In the age of globalisation, migration takes different forms as people are more mobile and as information spreads more easily. Moreover, international migration is increasingly becoming a matter of selection (Tanner, 2005: 12). Skilled migration in the form of 'brain drain' and the movement of professionals has become an important part of international migratory flows (Brandi, 2001: 102).

What is 'Brain Drain'?

Referring mainly to the emigration of skilled and professional people mainly from less developed regions to the most developed, the term 'brain drain' officially appeared in the 1960s to address skilled migration from Europe, especially from the United Kingdom (UK), to North

America (Salt, 1997). There is myriad terminology other than 'brain drain', including "brain exodus", "brain migration" or "brain emigration", "exodus of talent", and "brain export" (Khadria, 2001: 46; Tanner, 2005: 20-21). However, irrespective of the particular terminology, the concept is associated closely with the flight of brain power or "loss of human capital" (Meyer, 2001). Human capital is described as the stock of knowledge embedded in people and it is a key to economic growth in any country (Martin and Kuptsch, 2006). Accordingly, human capital theory is based on the concept that every human being is a single unit of human capital and is able to move his body, or rather his brain, which is regarded as his capital (Meyer, 2001: 95).

The emigration of the highly skilled[1] has been a concern for scholars and policymakers for many decades. Starting from the 1960's the term 'brain drain' gained wider usage as the issue itself fuelled many debates (Adams, 1968; Commander et al., 2003). Especially in the early 1970's, research on brain drain and the migration of professionals or highly qualified personnel from developing countries especially to the United States (US) highlighted this topic in the context of a dichotomy between the loss of sending countries and the substantial gain of the receiving ones (see Portes, 1976). At that time, the US was even accused of draining professionals from other countries, thereby saving lots of money by not training these people (Fortney, 1970: 231). Toward the end of the 1960's, for example, more than 15 percent of the physicians in the US were foreigners (quoted in Fortney, 1970: 223).

Early Literature on 'Brain Drain'

Not surprisingly, the negative consequences were much more visible if the sending country was a developing country, although the "highest

---

1   According to the OECD, highly skilled workers are defined as having a university degree or extensive experience in one field. It includes highly skilled specialists, independent executives and senior managers, specialized technicians or tradespersons, investors, businesspersons, etc. (Iredale, 2001: 8). For the purposes of this study, 'highly skilled' are defined as those who have either completed their tertiary education of 13 years or more and started working in the labor market or who are about to finish their doctoral or post-doctoral studies.

levels of professional emigration are not necessarily associated with lowest levels of economic development" (Portes, 1976: 496). Some of these negative outcomes of skilled migration from a developing country can be listed as follows:

i. Highly skilled people are net contributors to the government budget, and when they leave the country, there is a financial burden on the remaining population;

ii. Skilled labor and unskilled labor are complementary; thus, when there is a scarcity of skilled labor and abundant unskilled labor in a developing country, this has direct effects on the productivity;

iii. Losing human capital affects a country's growth prospects negatively; and,

iv. Highly skilled labor is needed to attract foreign direct investment (FDI) and to work on research and development (R&D) (Docquier and Rapoport, 2004).

The early literature on brain drain goes as far as proposing taxation; either in the form of a tax levied against the receiving country and transmitted to the sending country, of the brains lost (Bhagwati and Hamada, 1974), or through imposing restrictions on the mobility of the highly skilled. Taxing the skilled migrants in receiving countries did not work however as there were too many complications and blurred categories. Furthermore, developing countries characteristically face problems in taxing their own residents. Therefore, imposing a tax on emigrants and/or non-residents might be problematic. Restricting the mobility of the highly skilled is easier to do, but then countries "have the risk of decreasing the long-run level of their human capital stock, as the optimal migration rate of highly educated population is more likely to be positive in the long-run" (Docquier and Rapoport, 2004).

Recent Literature on Brain Drain

There is a renewed interest in skilled migration all around the world (Cheng and Yang, 1998). However, recently, the debate about brain drain and whether it is really negative for the sending countries has undergone some changes. Many developing countries have recognized that what they considered brain drain was in fact "brain overflow" (Ghosh, 1985; quoted in Williams and Balaz, 2005: 441), which can be considered as "the result of investing in education that exceeds the capacity of the economy to absorb skilled labor" (Weiner, 1995: 39). There are also some indications that when the number of university graduates exceeded the real recruitment needs, some developing countries favor brain drain as a cushion against lower salaries and unemployment among the young generation at home (See Ayubi, 1983).[2]

There has been growing recognition that the emigration of skilled labor may not be all that negative for the sending country (Commander et al., 2003; Beine, Docquier and Rappaport, 2001). Accordingly, some scholars even argue that skilled migration from a sending country might bring positive outcomes in the long run, because:

i. Emigration of skilled people may give a positive signal that motivates others in the sending country to acquire more education and at the end encouraging more human capital and economic growth;

ii. Emigrants may either return, send remittances, or invest in their home country through various ways;

iii. Skilled emigrants may promote knowledge and innovation flow from the destination country to the country of origin;

iv. Through the advances in communication technology and travel, skills of migrants are not lost forever. Creation of networks between the sending and receiving countries may facilitate trade, capital and knowledge flows;

v. Emigration of the highly skilled may reduce the immediate pressures on employment of the less skilled in developing countries (Commander et al., 2003; See also Docquier and Marfouk, 2006; Docquier and Rapoport, 2004; Lowell, 2002b).

---

2   Portes (1976) also suggests that the lack of capacity to absorb highly skilled in a country is one of the major push factors.

Along with this new more optimistic attitude towards skilled migration, the terminology has started to change as well into more positive connotations, and new paradigms appeared, like "brain circulation", "brain gain", and "brain exchange" (Lowell et al., 2004; Williams and Balaz, 2005). There is also increasing optimism that in time brain drain will turn into "brain exchange" (the two-way flow of skilled people between countries of origin and destination) or "brain gain" (the opposite situation of brain drain in which the highly skilled tend to return to the country of origin).

Persisting Skepticism on Skilled Migration

Other scholars, on the other hand, are still more skeptical about the positive effects of skills transfer, and they insist that emigration of the highly skilled from a country may or may not bring positive results for sending countries. Faini (2003) cautions that there has not been much evidence to support optimism regarding the benefits of skilled migration for the sending countries. Miyagiwa (1991) argues that the welfare of those citizens in the sending country would not be affected only if skilled emigration is small in numbers. Schiff (2006) gave warnings that "the size and the impact of brain gain are exaggerated". Tanner (2005) underlines the need to do more research on the long-term developmental effects of return migration, remittances, and diaspora networks in order to be able to evaluate critically the compensating measures for the outflow of skilled people from a country.

Apparently, there may be both negative and positive outcomes of skilled migration from any given country. Lowell and his colleagues (2004) therefore adopted the term "brain strain" to describe the positive and negative consequences of today's skilled migration.

New Trends in Skilled Migration

Although the phenomenon of skilled migration is far from being new, the numbers and trends are changing rapidly (Iredale, 2001: 8; Salt, 1997; Commander, 2003). First of all, the flow of the highly skilled represents an increasingly large component of global migration streams (see **Figure** 2.1 below). Today, the processes of globalisation, internationalization of education, changes in production, expansion of world trade, and the spread of multinational companies not only have increased the demand for skilled labor even more, but the well educated and highly skilled tend to be the most mobile, thanks to advances in communications and travel (Rudolph and Hillmann, 1998; Findlay, 1990; Salt, 1992; Iredale, 1997). Therefore, immigration of highly skilled people has become an "inseparable segment of national technology and economic development policies" (Mahroum, 2001: 27) and is certainly having its share in terms of the migration debate. It is estimated that there are 1.5 million professionals from developing countries in the industrial countries alone (Stalker, 2000; quoted in Iredale, 2001: 8). Studies indicate that "the number of migrants residing in OECD countries increased by 50 percent within the ten years between 1990 and 2000, and that the increase in the number of skilled migrants is equal to 2.5 times that of unskilled migrants" (Docquier and Rappoport, 2004; quoted in Schiff, 2006: 202). The US Census also revealed that in 1990, there were more than 2.5 million highly educated immigrants from developing countries above the age of 25 (Docquier and Rapoport, 2004: 5).[3] Especially migrants coming from Asia and the Middle East to the US tend to be more educated than the average person in the sending country (National Academies, 2005: 93).

Secondly, skilled migration is facilitated by the policies of receiving and developed countries (Stalker, 2000: 108; Castles, 2002: 1151; Pellegrino, 2001: 11). The United States is still number one in attracting human capital and the highly skilled (Cheng and Yang, 1998: 627). Professional migration and skilled migration is seen as an integral part of the US in order to maintain its economic and political position in the global markets (Iredale, 2001: 8).[4] Other countries, like

3   See **Figure** 2.1 on the emigration rate of the highly skilled people around the world.
4   In the US, since the Immigration Act of 1990 followed by the American Competitiveness and Work Force Improvement Act of 1998, more emphasis has been put on the intake of highly

Germany, France, the UK, Australia, New Zealand, Canada, and East Asian countries, have recently established certain programs to attract more skilled labor and to increase their participation and share in the labor markets (Lowell, 2002a; Findlay and Stam, 2006; DeVoretz, 2006; Martin and Kuptsch, 2006). For example, in France, a specific visa has been introduced to allow scientists from non-European countries into the country. In Germany, green cards have been introduced for IT specialists.[5] Outside the EU, Australia and Canada have started to implement new policies to attract highly skilled professionals (Mahroum, 2001: 28).

Thirdly, both skilled and unskilled migrants target developed countries, but for skilled migrants, distance seems to matter less. Last but not least, skilled migration involves a greater diversity of professions, from the health sector to information, communication, and technology (ICT) sectors. Mahroum (2000, 2001) argued that the dynamics of the migration of the highly skilled vary not only across types of professions but also with the type of work. He identifies five major groups (senior managers and executives, engineers and technicians, scientists, entrepreneurs, and students) for which the push and pull factors from one group are different from the other. For example, the motives for a scientist to find a job outside his native country might be scientific advancement and available funding for research and development (R&D), but for an engineer it might be salary conditions or the labor market situation (Mahroum, 2001: 29). It seems that personal reasons or micro-factors are important as well, such as marriage with a partner from a different national and ethnic back-

---

skilled workers. Moreover, a system of quotas favors those with academic degrees and with specific skills. Immediately after 9/11, there were problems with the issuing of visas to professionals and foreign students. Although the situation is getting better now in the U.S, there is still criticism that American immigration policy is not pursuing a skilled immigration, which is based mainly on H-1B program. Its competitors, Australia, Canada and some EU countries, follow a point-based system giving points to skilled immigrants.

5   Unlike the American green card allowing permanent residency, German green cards are issued temporarily for a maximum of five years.

ground, children's education, and dissatisfaction with the living standards in the home country.

FIGURE 2.1
Emigration Rates of the Highly Skilled Around the World

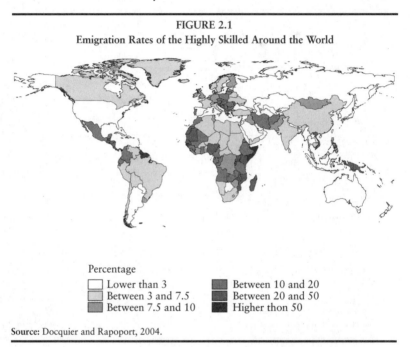

Percentage

☐ Lower than 3	▨ Between 10 and 20
▨ Between 3 and 7.5	▨ Between 20 and 50
▨ Between 7.5 and 10	■ Higher thon 50

Source: Docquier and Rapoport, 2004.

The Emigration of Highly Skilled People from Turkey to the US

The brain drain issue has started to attract growing attention in Turkey as well. Even before the foundation of the Turkish Republic, there had been flows from Ottoman territories to western Europe to receive education and professional training. Especially after the 1960's, there was an increase in the numbers of migrants from Turkey to the US. Concern about Turkish emigration of the highly skilled and brain drain was high on the agenda in the 1970's in Turkey, as an important part of that number implied brain drain or brain loss for Turkey (Kurtuluş, 1999: 54-55). Oğuzkan's survey (1975) based on 150 replies to a questionnaire carried out among the highly skilled

Turks with doctoral degrees working abroad in 1968 was very timely to explore the brain drain movement from Turkey.[6]

However, mass unskilled migration in the 1960's and the 1970's and the economic and political downturn in the 1980's gained much attention of both the Turkish public and policy circles. The Turkish academic world also followed suit in its lack of interest in highly skilled migration. One of the other reasons that the debate on skilled migration lost vigor in Turkey between the 1980's and the 1990's was that international migration topics at that time usually revolved around guest-worker programs and integration issues, asylum seekers, and Turkey's changing role from an emigrant country to a transit country.

For its part, the topic of brain drain has received greater attention from the Turkish media and is often portrayed as a serious socio-economic problem, especially in the wake of the 2001 economic crisis in Turkey. Many Turkish scientists, engineers, physicians, and other highly skilled professionals still live and work in the US. The success of Turkish engineers, doctors, and scientists attracts the attention of the Turkish media and is sometimes described as the "fetish of the successful Turk abroad".[7] More recently, a number of articles also appeared on the non-return of students and scholars, warning about a possible brain loss in the future unless serious measures were taken.[8]

---

6   In his article, Oğuzkan (1976) referred to other researches on brain drain from Turkey. One of them is on Turkish engineers and architects working in Europe and in the US carried out by Peter Goswyn Franck (1967), Committee on the International Migration of Talent, pp. 299-373. The others are on Turkish medical doctors a) carried out by Taylor, Dirican, and Deuschle (1968) entitled *Health Manpower Planning in Turkey*, published in Baltimore by Johns Hopkins Press; b) by Ferguson and Dirican (1966) entitled "The Turkish Medical Graduate in America, 1965: A Survey of Selected Characteristics," published in *The Turkish Journal of Pediatrics*, 8 (3): 176-190.

7   See the article on Doctor Mehmet Oz, who also became a popular figure in Turkey: "Doctor Oz Relates His Popularity With American-Like Team Work Formula", published in *Zaman USA*, Friday, July 22, 2005. Such articles abound. But more articles on successful Turkish scientists can be found in *Posta*, dated August 24, 2005, "Türk'ten müthiş buluş" (Brilliant discovery by a Turk); *Cumhuriyet*, Bilim Teknik, dated November 19, 2005, "Türk Bilimadamına ABD'den büyük ödül" (Grand prize given to a Turkish scientist in the USA).

8   See the article "Beyin Göçü Salgın Hastalık Oldu" (Brain drain has become an epidemic) in daily *Hürriyet*, July 18, 2004.

The issue of 'brain drain' has attracted more attention in recent years from Turkish scholars (Kurtulmuş, 1992; Gençer, 1998; Kurtuluş, 1999; Kaya, 1999; Işığıçok, 2002; Gençler and Çolak, 2003; Tansel and Güngör, 2003; Erdoğan, 2003; Çulpan, 2005; Gökbayrak, 2006).[9] While most of the recent research is lacking empirical data and is much more focused on developing strategies for Turkey in order to pave the way for brain gain, some depended on Internet surveys and conventional mail to reach respondents.[10] These studies also indicated that in Turkey's case there was a relationship between economic and political instability and the emigration of skilled people. Another problem was the slow absorption of young graduates into the Turkish labor force. Labor force participation rates have not kept up with the pace of growth of the young population in Turkey, leading to internal migration for the unskilled and international migration and brain drain for the skilled (Tansel and Güngör, 2003: 53-54; Kurtuluş, 1999: 24).

RESEARCH QUESTION AND METHODOLOGY

Theoretical Framework
For many years, highly skilled migrants were not visible,[11] and migration theories have not even considered the movement of the highly skilled as migration, as their movement may be relatively short-term, and because they are middle-class, well-paid, and definitely do not constitute a problem for the governments of receiving countries (Iredale,

---

9 One ongoing research is carried out by S.E. Esen as a policy analysis exercise to be submitted to the John F. Kennedy School of Government, Harvard University, titled "Policy Recommendation to Manage the Emigration of Highly Skilled Labor in Turkey". Another ongoing research is carried out by Uludağ University. It is a comparative study on Turkish skilled migrants living in Europe and the US.

10 Kurtuluş based her survey on 90 respondents, although she initially wanted to reach a number of 500 respondents. As she mainly depended on return of questionnaires by post, there were many unanswered or unreturned mail. Tansel and Güngör (2003) based their research on internet survey only, and this resulted many incomplete forms and less accuracy at the qualitative level. They included the universities located in the U.S., Canada, and the UK, but 85 percent of the data was collected from Turkish students in the U.S.

11 Findlay (1995; quoted in Iredale, 1997: 4) refers to skilled migrants as "invisible phenomenon".

1997: 4; Koser and Lutz, 1998: 7-8). In the past, movements of skilled migrants were regarded as "personal responses to individual life situations, and as migrants wanting to maximize the returns to their human capital investment or improve the life opportunities of themselves and their families" (Iredale, 1997: 2). Today, many of the highly skilled around the world have become even more mobile thanks to globalisation, advances in technology, and the creation of new cutting-edge jobs. This mobility is expected to increase in the years to come (Docquier and Marfouk, 2006: 151; Kapur and McHale, 2005: 209).

A theoretical framework for skilled migration needs to incorporate a mixture of micro- and macro-variables (Salt and Findlay, 1989; Iredale, 2001). According to human capital theory, which is constructed at the micro-level, people move to find more attractive and better-paid jobs in line with their education and training. The structuralist neo-Marxist theory at the macro-level, however, investigates the effects of gender and class together with the notions of core and periphery states (Iredale, 2001: 8-9). At the macro-level, the world systems theory, built on the work of Wallerstein (1974) also considers international migration as a natural outcome of economic globalisation and market penetration across national boundaries (Alarcon, 2000: 306; Quaked, 2002; Cheng and Yang, 1998). Nonetheless, there is no room in these two approaches for the important role played by various formal and informal institutions, ethnic and other networks. Therefore, it is important to include a "structuration" approach (Giddens, 1990; Goss and Linquist, 1995) or to add a "meso-level" (relational) (Faist, 2000) to the already existing micro (individual) and macro-levels (structural), thereby connecting individuals, institutions, and other organizational agents.

At the micro-level, the mobility for the highly skilled is still a strategic decision to have more professional opportunities, to attain additional qualifications, to work in a dynamic environment, and to accumulate more income as well as status. Age, gender, family obligations, marriage partners, nationalistic sentiments, homesickness, and the education of children are among other important criteria at the micro-level.

At the meso-level, institutions and expatriate networks are creating more skilled migrants and these networks, which mobilize more migrants, are considered as determinants of a migration process. In Turkey, the role of many private foundations such as the Fulbright, private counseling companies operating for universities abroad, formal and informal organizations in the United States, and other institutions such as YÖK and private universities – especially those offering education in English – in sending Turkish students abroad, directly or indirectly, should not be underestimated. The social capital theory[12] explains that international migration becomes self-perpetuating over time. It is documented that social networks facilitate the migration process. Connections with earlier migrants provide potential migrants with information and resources and eliminate the high costs of migration in the absence of supportive networks in countries of origin (Meyer, 2001: 93; Tanner, 2005: 27; Kapur and McHale, 2005: 125-128).

Social networks play a critical role in the migration of the highly skilled and Turkish students. The foreign-educated Turkish instructors and academicians are said to accelerate the tendency to go abroad for further study at the masters or doctoral level. Social networks not only facilitate migration but also channel it by choosing who gets to migrate to fill in jobs as research assistants. The highly skilled have the ability to mobilize their social capital in an even more effective way because they rely on more extensive and diverse networks, which consists of professional colleagues, fellow alumni, acquaintances, and friends (Meyer, 2001: 94). The creation of migrants' networks facilitates the movement of goods, people and ideas between host and home countries. The personal connections are important for Turkish

---

12 The concept of social capital was introduced into social science by the economist Glenn Loury (1977). The concept was later elaborated theoretically by the sociologists Bourdieu (1986) and Coleman (1988; 1990).

respondents in coming to the US, finding a proper job, or finding emotional support to ease initial settlement. Networks also facilitate trade, create business, foreign direct investment (FDI), and technology transfer. Moreover, they have the potential to turn brain drain into brain circulation. This can be also termed as the "diaspora effect" (Bhagwati, 2003; Barre et al., 2003; quoted in Lowell et al., 2004: 22). The Turkish-American Scientists and Scholars' Association (TASSA), which was founded by young Turkish-American professionals, established a visiting scientists program in 2004, enabling Turkish scientists and scholars working in the US to visit Turkey temporarily and share their research and experience with their colleagues in Turkey. TASSA also initiated a partnership program called TASTUB with the Scientific and Technical Research Council of Turkey (TÜBİTAK).[13]

At the macro-level, the process of skilled migration – like any other type of migration – goes hand in hand with the restrictions of states on mobility in general, institutions, multinational companies, internationalization of labor, and globalisation of human capital and markets. Skilled migration or so-called brain drain can also be seen within the context of transnational processes as this kind of migratory flow takes place in an environment of dense networks, and ever-increasing internationalization of higher education and labor markets (Pellegrino, 2001: 121). Transnationalism offers new perspectives for understanding the migration experiences of skilled migrants (Alarcon, 2000: 307). Nonini and Ong (1997) argue that the globalisation of the world economy has led to the appearance of transnational professionals with expertise in managerial, financial, legal, technical, and commercial services (quoted in Alarcon, 2000: 307). This is also called "transnationalism from below" emerging in parallel to "transnationalism from above" (Smith and Guarnizo, 1998).

Therefore, the phenomenon of brain drain, or the emigration of the highly skilled to the US from Turkey, was analyzed within this per-

---

[13] See website of TASSA: www.tassausa.org.

spective described above and an integrative approach was adopted to study these kinds of migratory flows.

Research Question and Objectives

As it would not suffice to deal with the causes of brain drain, this project further intends to elaborate on the consequences both in the countries of origin and destination. A thorough inquiry is also added to the project to discuss the economic, social, political, and cultural aspects of brain drain. In doing so, it seeks answers for both the reasons and consequences of skilled migration, such as:

- What are the push and pull factors?
- What are the most represented academic fields among Turkish students in the US?
- Why did they choose that specific institution/university for further study? Where did they get information?
- What are the prospects and future plans of respondents?
- What are the main reasons for non-return?
- What are the main criteria for migration to the US among the highly skilled?
- How important are the personal reasons for return to the homeland after the study/work period, and also for non-return?
- Do they see themselves as temporarily or permanently in the host country?
- How well do students and graduates who have started working in the US know of the job prospects in Turkey?
- Under which circumstances will they return to Turkey?
- How do they rebuild their sense of identity?
- What about their religious affinity? Have they become more observant Muslims after arrival or is there no change?
- Is there an intensive contact with the dominant culture or a limited one?
- Do they feel themselves as accepted and welcome?

The research project further aims to clarify:

• The gender, age, marital status, birthplace, parents' occupation, and visa status of the respondents.

• The social and economic status of their parents.

• Whether their education was financed by private means, by the Turkish state, or whether they earned a scholarship from the American institutions/universities.

• What are the employment rates among non-returnees? What are the job prospects?

• What are the main reasons they choose to come to the US?

• What are the main reasons they choose to stay in the US?

• Have they witnessed a change after 9/11 in the American labor market?

• Whether the students' bicultural and bilingual competence enables them to adapt themselves fully in the United States.

• How strong are their community ties?

• Do they form groups of same ethnic origin?

• If that is the case, do these groups offer some sense of solidarity and social safety?

• Do these groups also offer job opportunities in the US?

• How strong is their attachment to Turkey?

• What kind of relations do they have with the home country? How often do they call their homeland/send an e-mail/chat/ICQ/etc.?

• Do they send remittances to Turkey after completing their studies and finding a job? If so, to what extend? Are these remittances big enough to make Turkey gain something financially in return?

• Do non-returnees invest more in the host country or in Turkey?

• What are the generational differences between the three groups under focus?

• If students are sent by an official institution, are they willing to return to Turkey and serve in the country, or there is more of a tendency to stay regardless of the fines to be paid later on?

• If Turkey is successful in creating favorable economic conditions in line with the EU harmonization processes, will they choose to return home?

As mentioned earlier, there are only a few and limited studies previously carried out on brain drain and student flows from Turkey to the US (Tansel & Güngör, 2003; Kurtuluş, 1999; Oğuzkan, 1975). This project therefore seeks to construct a descriptive and an exploratory study on such issues. In addition to this, considering the complexities of such a social phenomenon, the study combines information of various types in order to gain access to and to gather information, which provides information necessary to develop a program in the future to ensure that both sending and receiving countries benefit from these flows. The project therefore includes not only qualitative data but also quantitative data from several resources in the US and in Turkey. It should be noted, however, that there is no available uniform statistical data on the exact number and characteristics of the highly skilled from Turkey. Therefore, it is difficult to measure precisely whether the emigration of the highly skilled is detrimental to the growth of Turkey. One other problem with the US Census data is that foreign-born individuals may not be immigrants, but either temporary workers or students.

In line with the findings, some suggestions regarding the migration policy of the Turkish government on the highly skilled were made in order to turn brain drain into brain exchange, and make it profitable for all parties involved: the individuals, the country of destination – in this case, the US – and the country of origin, Turkey.

Data Collection and Respondents
The information in this study was gathered by: (1) all available secondary data; (2) on-site observation and inquiry; (3) primary data from semi-structured and in-depth interviews with (a) doctoral students currently studying in different cities in the US, (b) former students who have finished their studies and started working in the US, and young professionals of 25 to 45 years old, (c) those who came to

the US 20 or 30 years ago and decided to stay for a number of reasons, (d) representatives of Turkish students' associations, (e) educational attaches and other government officials at the Turkish Embassy in Washington, DC, at the Turkish General Consulate in New York City; and also with the General Consuls of Houston and of Los Angeles; (4) interviews and meetings[14] with the US officials and scholars working on skilled migration; and, (5) data collection through an web survey. The e-mail addresses of doctoral students studying in the US and some Turkish scholars working at research centers and at universities were collected from various sources, including the directories of universities, the Institute for Turkish Studies at Georgetown University, as well as some Turkish student associations, especially the Intercollegiate Turkish Students Society (ITSS). After obtaining addresses of students meeting the criteria, the survey form consisting of close-ended and open-ended questions were distributed to at least 500 respondents; however, the rate of return for these kind of on-line interviews were very limited.

At one level, these five types of data collection will proceed in stages, collection of secondary data being first, and on-site observation being second, followed by interviews and the Internet survey. At another level, the secondary data collection and on-site observation continued over the period of primary data collection, which contains a considerable number of semi-structured and in-depth interviews with various actors. An anthropological research strategy was included in the project. For example, life histories were collected through repeated interviews and participant observation was conducted during reunions, association meetings, and gatherings. Qualitative and quantitative data were collected from selected study

---

14 Meetings attended: Center for Global Development on October 18, 2005 in Washington, DC about the global migration of talent; Institute for the Study of International Migration, at Georgetown University, on March 31, 2006 about the global competition for international students; the Heritage Foundation, "Dialogue, not Monologue: International Educational Exchange and Public Diplomacy," on November 16, 2005.

sites, i.e. multinational companies, some international Turkish companies operating both in the US and in Turkey, and the universities in the United States, mainly in New York City, Massachusetts, Virginia, Maryland, and Washington D.C, where a great number of universities are located.

The interviews formed the heart of the inquiry. Semi-structured and in-depth interviews were conducted with 140 persons selected on the basis of their departments and working sectors. In order to show the diversity and possible differences and similarities between respondents, 45 people who have completed studies and started working in the US and 50 people who are still studying at the graduate level, including the post-doctoral level, were interviewed. An additional 25 people who came to the US with the initial intention to study at least 20 or 30 years ago and who became successful in their fields were also interviewed to trace the motivations and reasons for the non-return of the so-called pioneer migrants. Interviews were conducted to supplement existing data pertaining to the dynamics under investigation. Ten interviews were also conducted in Turkey among those who have studied in the United States and returned to Turkey to assume high-end employment positions in the private sector in big cities, especially in Istanbul, and ten interviews were conducted with university students to assess their future intentions to emigrate to earn masters and/or PhD degrees abroad.

ANALYSIS

In the analytical part of this research, a brief history of Turkish migration to the US and information about the transnational role of Turkish-American associations linking the two countries is provided in order to see the changes in time in terms of identity and the skill formation of migrants. Moreover, the internationalization of higher education and the skilled migration policies of the US will be elaborated upon.

Patterns of Turkish Migration to the US

Immigration from Turkey to America can be classified under three groups. The first one is the early flows from the Ottoman Empire and from the subsequently established Turkish Republic. The first migratory flows included Turkish, but mostly non-Turkish citizens of the Empire, and happened largely due to economic and political problems (see McCarthy, 2001). There were also many draft-evaders at that time (Bali, 2004: 25).[15] According to the official American statistics, 93.51 percent of 22,085 immigrants registered as Turks between 1900 and 1925 were young and illiterate males (Bilge, 1997; quoted in Bali, 2004: 264). The First World War (WWI) and a number of laws restricting the entry of immigrants affected the flows negatively (Bali, 2004: 28).

The second wave of immigration took place between 1950 and 1980, and it was more of a highly skilled migration as many professionals and graduate students were involved. As opposed to the male-dominated first flows, there were many young women and accompanying families. The third wave covers a period after the 1980's until now, during which the flow of Turkish nationals to the US took many different forms – an increasing number of students, professionals, as well as clandestine migration, and unskilled and semi-skilled labor.

Early Flows from Turkey to the US (1820-1950)

Regardless of the long history of Turkish immigration to the US, Turkish immigration and integration in the US have not been documented thoroughly (Kaya, 2003: 4).[16] According to official American statistics, Turkish immigration to the US started around the turn of the

---

15 Non-Muslims in the Ottoman Empire were not required to be conscripted in the army as long as they paid a tax, named 'cizye'. However, the situation changed first in 1843 and then later in 1909 with the change in the Constitution, making army service compulsory for non-Muslims as well (Acehan, 2005).

16 Sedat İşçi, from Ege University in İzmir and Prof. John J. Grabowski, from Case Western Reserve University, have a long-standing project on first Turkish immigrants to the US: 1860-1924 (www.amerikadakiturkler.org).

twentieth century and was insignificant until 1900 (Reimers, 2005: 215).[17] In fact, a very small number of Turkish Muslims came to America between 1820 and 1860. By the early 1900's, larger numbers of Turks immigrated to the US and settled in New York City, Chicago, Detroit, Philadelphia, and San Francisco (Turner, 2003: 120).

During the last fifteen years of Sultan Abdul Hamid's rule (1876-1915), many immigrants whose last country of residence was recorded as Turkey came to US shores. By 1910, the number of immigrants from the Ottoman Empire was distributed between two categories: Turkey in Asia,[18] and Turkey in Europe (Schmidt, 1999: 40). By 1910, the number of Ottomans from Asia was given as 59,729 (Karpat, 1985: 181). These early immigrants were mostly non-Muslim Ottoman citizens carrying Ottoman passports, namely Sephardic Jews, Greeks, Armenians, Bosnians, Serbs, Assyrians and Bulgarians, and they identified themselves with their ethnicity and/or religion (Pultar, 2000: 131; Halman, 1980: 992; Haddad, 2004: 3).[19] Ahmed notes that that a conservative estimate of Muslim Turks entering the US between 1900 and 1920 is around 45,000 to 65,000 (1993: 11). It is suggested that the first American encounter with Islam took place through Muslim Turkish immigrants in this early period (Grabowski, 2005: 86).

The early Turkish immigrants to the US were mainly from southeastern Anatolia and from the lower socio-economic classes (Karpat, 1985). There were also reports on a considerable number of illegal migrants from Anatolia, as young men were trying to escape military service as well as poverty (Karpat, 1985: 182). Emigration from the Ottoman Empire was forbidden, and most of the time pass-

---

17 See **Table 2.1** for more details.
18 Karpat states that although statistics on immigration from Turkey in Asia started to be kept as of 1869, they were most of the time unreliable and a very limited number of people were recorded. For example, it was recorded that between 1867 and 1881, only 74 Asian Ottomans entered the US and no information was provided for the ten-year period after 1885 (Karpat, 1985: 181).
19 See Daniels (2002) for more information on Greeks, Armenians, and Arabs coming from the territory of the Ottoman Empire in the 1800s and early 1900s.

ports were denied to citizens (Karpat, 1985: 187). Some of the reasons for this exit prohibition might be explained as: 1) a lack of desire to lose young men and tax income; and, 2) a fear of damaging Ottoman prestige abroad, as most of the would-be emigrants were poor and uneducated (Karpat, 1985: 186). Because of two different approaches to citizenship in the Ottoman Empire and in the United States,[20] the relations between the two countries were negatively affected until the beginning of the twentieth century (Karpat, 1985: 189). Problems arose especially when naturalized former Ottoman citizens returned to their homeland and claimed property and inheritance, as they were neither recognized as foreign subjects nor as Ottoman citizens (Karpat, 1985: 189-191). Nevertheless, almost 70,000 former citizens of the Ottoman Empire returned to their homeland after acquiring American citizenship within the first quarter of the 20th century (Leland, 1932; quoted in Bali, 2004: 31). The American government then issued decrees warning its naturalized citizens of the problems (Bali, 2004: 31). Another reason why Ottoman officials did not want to admit its former citizens from the US was due to the concern about a possible Armenian uprising and remittances brought back to buy firearms (Mirak, 1983: 207; quoted in Acehan, 2005).

The flow of immigration to the US was interrupted first by the Act of 1917, which was based on literacy (Schmidt, 1999: 40), and then by WWI (Haddad, 2004: 4). Subsequently, the Johnson-Reed Quota Act of 1924 restricted large-scale Turkish immigration to the US.[21] Between 1931 and 1940, the immigration from Turkey to the US

---

20 Ottoman Empire followed the principle of 'jus sanguinis' whereas the United Stated adhered to the 'jus soli' principle.

21 The U.S. Immigration Act of 1924, also known as the National Origins Act or the Johnson-Reed Act, limited the number of immigrants who could be admitted from any country to two percent of the number of people from that country who were already living in the United States in 1890 according to the census of 1890. The number of immigrants from the Middle East was restricted to 100 per annum. This law severely restricted immigration by establishing a system of national quotas that blatantly discriminated against immigrants from southern and eastern Europe and virtually excluded Asians. The policy stayed in effect until the 1960's.

decreased tremendously to a low of 1,065, mainly due to restrictions in American immigration law, the Great Depression, and the pull effect of the new Turkish Republic (Kaya, 2003: 51).

A majority of Turks entered the US via the Port of Providence Rhode Island, Portland, Maine, and through Ellis Island (Ahmed, 1993: 14; Bilge, 1994: 386). French shipping agents, the missionary American college in Harput,[22] French and German schools, and word of mouth from former Armenian migrants, were major sources of information about the new world for those who wished to emigrate (Kaya, 2003: 48-49; Bali, 2004: 339).

Although some figures on early migration from Turkey were made available, they do not accurately reflect the whole Turkish population. Some of the reasons for the lack of accuracy of the data are that many of the immigrants were registered by American authorities under ethnic and/or religious affiliation. Therefore, it was impossible to differentiate who was Turkish. Some immigrants also anglicized their names and declared themselves as Armenians or Christians to have easy access to the US (Kaya, 2003: 49; Bilge, 1994: 385; Karpat, 1985: 182). It is estimated that less than 10 percent of all people who emigrated from Turkey between 1820 and 1950 were Turks (Kurtuluş, 1999: 53).

In 1940, there were 104,201 Turks in the US. The majority of them, or 52,950 native Turks (93.05 percent), lived in urban areas, whereas 2,603 (4.6 percent) lived in rural non-farm areas, and 1,338 (2.35 percent) lived in rural farm areas (Ahmed, 1993: 95). Their geographical distribution in the same year was as follows: 47,011 (82.6 percent) were living in the northern part; with over 20,000 were living in the northeast, notably in New York City, whereas 5.2 percent were living in the south, and 12.2 percent were living in the west (Ahmed, 1993: 95).

Most of these early Turkish Muslim immigrants had difficulties in adjusting to American society. First of all, more than half of the

---

22 See Acehan (2005) on the role of American consulate in Harput and American missionaries there in the increased number of Armenians and Muslims alike at that time.

TABLE 2.1
Turkish Immigration to the US (1820-1950)*

Years	Number of Immigrants
1820	1
1821-1830	20
1831-1840	7
1841-1850	59
1851-1860	83
1961-1870	131
1871-1880	404
1881-1890	3,782
1891-1900	30,425
1901-1910	157,369
1911-1920	134,066
1921-1930	33,824
1931-1940	1,065
1941-1950	798
Total	362,034

(*) Region and Selected Country of Last Residence.
Source: 2004 Yearbook of Immigration Statistics, Office of Immigration Statistics, US Department of Homeland Security.

Turkish immigrants were illiterate and they did not know English. The majority of them were farmers and shepherds who had never seen a big city in their lives, and they came from the villages and towns of Harput, Dersim, Capakcur, Siverek, Rize, Samsun, Trabzon, Giresun, Antep, and Elazığ (Ahmed, 1993: 10-11; Kaya, 2003: 48). Secondly, as they regarded themselves temporary migrants and, they often had little or no interest in adaptation to American society. The main concern among this wave of male-dominated economic migrants was to save enough money and to return to their homeland; therefore, they worked in the factories along the east coast, especially in New England, New York, Detroit, and Chicago (Ahmed, 1993: 12). Moreover, their numbers were not sufficient to establish ethnic communities, although they maintained their linguistic and religious iden-

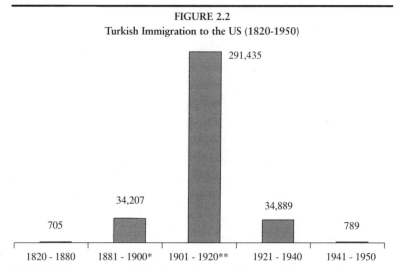

FIGURE 2.2
Turkish Immigration to the US (1820-1950)

(*) 29,019 of them were from Turkey in Asia (Karpat, 1985, Appendix I).
(**) 156,782 of them from Turkey in Asia) (Karpat, 1985: Appendix IX) (Peak immigration years were 1904-1908; 1910-1914).
Source: US Immigration and Naturalization Service Statistical Yearbook (2004).

tity (Halman, 1980: 993). Among the first-comers, Islam was one of the most powerful elements in their identity and communal life in America (Ahmed, 1993: 75; Bilge, 1994: 381).

The first Turkish Muslim immigrants mainly settled into urban areas and worked in the industrial sector. They trusted each other to find jobs and a place to stay. Many of them stayed in boarding houses. They also established their own communities and coffeehouses[23] and felt insecure outside of their own re-created environment (Ahmed, 1993: 41-44). The ethnic conflicts were carried to some parts of the

---

23　Ahmed notes that coffeehouses were strange to the American culture until the arrival of Turks and the highest concentration of coffeehouses in New England were along the Walnut Street in Peabody (1986: 66). However, coffeehouses did not only function as 'clubhouses' for men, but they were also used as informal employment agencies, charity organizations, and public places where people used to meet to celebrate religious holidays (Bilge, 1994: 392-393).

country, like Peabody, Massachusetts, where there was tension between Greeks, Armenians, and Turks, all coming from the Ottoman Empire (Acehan, 2005; Ahmed, 1993). There is evidence, however, that there was also solidarity between the Muslim Turks and other ethnic and religious groups of the Ottoman Empire.[24]

The rate of return migration was exceptionally high among Turkish Muslims after the establishment of the Turkish Republic in 1923 (Halman, 1980: 993; Ipek and Caglayan, 2006: 36).[25] Ahmed states that Atatürk sent Turkish ships, such as the *Gülcemal*, to the US to take these men back to Turkey without any charge (1993: 81). Interestingly enough, the *Gülcemal* was the first ship that carried people and cargo between Istanbul and New York as of 1920 (Bali, 2004: 36). Well-educated Turks were offered jobs in the newly-created Turkish Republic, whereas other unskilled workers were encouraged to return as the male population was depleted due to WWI and the Turkish Independence War (Halman, 1980: 993). Those who stayed in America married native-born Americans of European heritage. Although they were said to retain their cultural and religious beliefs to a certain extent (Ahmed, 1993: 15), many of them or their children converted to Christianity, changed their names, and assimilated into the mainstream of the society.

Flows of Professionals (1951-1980)

After the Second World War, immigration from Turkey resumed and more than 3,500 persons came to the US between 1951 and 1960. In the 1960's, 10,000 persons entered the US from Turkey, and another 13,000 in the 1970's (See also Remiers, 2005: 216). According to research carried out by the National Science Foundation (NSF),

---

24 For example, Turks in Peabody turned to Sephardic Jews for kosher meat and circumcisions (Acehan, 2005; Grabowski, 2005: 89), and Turks in Worchester turned to Armenians for translation (Ekinci, 2006: 49).

25 Halman states that almost 86 percent of 22,000 Turks who came to the United States between 1899 and 1924 returned to Turkey (1980: 993). Ahmed also confirms that only less than 20 percent stayed after 1923 (1986: 80).

between 1956 and 1970, 907 Turkish engineers and 594 Turkish medical doctors came to the US (Oğuzkan, 1976).

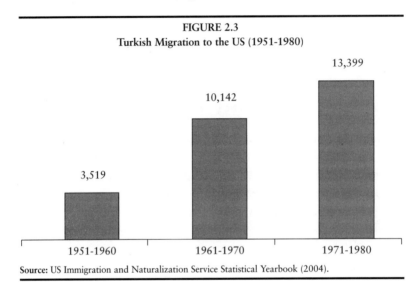

FIGURE 2.3
Turkish Migration to the US (1951-1980)

Source: US Immigration and Naturalization Service Statistical Yearbook (2004).

As of the late 1940's, but especially in the 1960's and 1970's, Turkish immigration changed its nature from one of unskilled flows to skilled migration. It is estimated that at least 2,000 engineers and 1,500 physicians have come to the US between these years (Halman, 1980: 993). If it had not been for the annual quota allowed for Turkish immigrants, the numbers could have been much higher (Halman, 1980: 994). In other words, the migratory flows in this period were largely motivated by educational and professional reasons as well as economic considerations (Halman, 1980: 994), and the skills of Turkish immigrants increased to a large extent during this period. Most Turkish people coming to the US at that time were owners of small- to medium-scale businesses, physicians, engineers, and scientists. In the 1950's, many graduates of Istanbul Robert College came to have further education (Ahmed, 1993: 84). The general profile of Turkish men and women coming to the US in the 1950's and 1960's were young, college educated, with a good knowledge of English and careers in medicine, engineering, or another profession in science or the arts (Ahmed, 1993: 85). Hand in hand with this skilled migration, several hundred semi-skilled workers, especially tailors, came from Turkey with their families to work in the Bond Clothing Company in Rochester, NY, in the late 1960's and early 1980's (Ahmed, 1993: 86).[26]

Until 1965, the number of Turkish immigrants was quite low as a result of US immigration laws. The rate for Turkish immigration between 1940 and 1950 was around 100 a year; however, the number of Turkish immigrants to the US increased to 2,000 to 3,000 a year after 1965 due to the liberalization of American immigration laws (Kaya, 2003: 2). After the more liberal 1965 Immigration Act, there was a substantial increase in the number of specialists and professionals migrating to the US from Turkey, and the number of people from Turkey increased by more than threefold during the period between 1961-1970 (See **Figure 2.3** for more details). Halman notes that there has been no substantial increase in the number of Turkish engineers and physicians in the 1970's, mainly due to economic setbacks in the US and difficulty in obtaining licenses for foreign medical doctors (1980: 994). During this period, Turks left mainly because they did not have enough supportive networks to build and use their skills in Turkey.

Apart from the skills of incoming Turkish people to the U.S, another characteristic differentiating the earlier flows from the second wave was that the return migration was minimal (Halman, 1980: 994). They mainly stayed in the country and integrated into the larger society. Despite the lack of reliable figures, it is estimated that in the late 1970's, there were less than 100,000 Turks in the US. This group included naturalized citizens, permanent residents, long-term illegal aliens, and some members of the second and third generations. In 1970, the US Census reported 54,534 foreign-born and American-born people of foreign and mixed parentage from Turkey. In the same cen-

---

26 According to Sonn (1994: 280), some 200 – 300 Turkish families immigrated to Rochester in the late 1960's, and even established their own ethnic associations and mosques.

sus, 24,000 listed Turkish as their mother tongue (Halman, 1980: 992). They settled mainly in urban areas, like New York City, Chicago, Detroit,[27] Los Angeles, Philadelphia, San Francisco, Maryland, Virginia, and Connecticut (Halman, 1980: 994; Kurtuluş, 1999: 55).

Immigration of Different Groups: Professionals, More Student Flows, and Semi-skilled/Unskilled Workers (1980-2004)

After the 1980's, there was an increase in the number of temporary skilled migrants, as students, scholars, and professionals coming from Turkey to the US (See **Tables 2.2** and **2.3** and **Figure 2.4** below).

TABLE 2.2

Turkish Citizens Admitted Into the US by Selected Class of Admission (2004)

Selected Class of Admission	Numbers
All classes (including tourists, international representatives, spouses and children of all classes)	106,338
All temporary workers, exchange visitors, intra-company transferees	10,831
Exchange Visitors (J-1)	4,470
Workers with specialty occupations (H-1B & H-1B1)	5,195
Non-agricultural temporary workers (H-2B)	27
Industrial trainees (H-3)	7
Intra-company transferees (L-1)	760
Workers with extraordinary ability (O-1)	176
Internationally recognized athletes and entertainers (P-1)	50
Artists and entertainers in reciprocal exchange programs (P-2)	16
Artists and entertainers in culturally unique programs (P-3)	77
Workers in religious occupations (R-1)	45

Source: 2004 Yearbook of Immigration Statistics, US Department of Homeland Security.

The highly skilled and educated profile of the Turkish-American community has changed in recent years, as another group of Turkish immigrants includes unskilled or semi-skilled Turkish labor workers.

---

27 See Bilge's article (1996) on the Turkish community of metropolitan Detroit and adjacent Ontario and patterns of intermarriages between Turkish and Americans.

FIGURE 2.4
Turkish Non-immigrants (All Categories) Admitted to the US by age (2004)

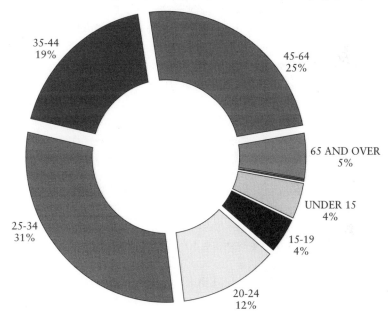

Total (all ages) = 106,338
Source: 2004 Yearbook of Immigration Statistics, US Department of Homeland Security.

They usually work in restaurants, gas stations, construction sites, grocery stores, and as hairdressers, although some of them obtained American citizenship or green cards and opened their own ethnic businesses (Kaya, 2003: 58). It is reported that some of these workers arrived in the US in cargo ships and then left their ships illegally, whereas some others overstayed their visas. It is also difficult to estimate the number of undocumented Turkish immigrants in the US who overstayed their visas or jumped ship.[28] This trend in migration to the US is called the "Germanification" of Turkish-Americans because of their

---

28 In 1996, the INS estimated that their numbers were fewer than 30,000 (Reimers, 2005: 216).

resemblance in many ways to Turkish guest-workers in Germany (Akıncı, 2002; quoted in Kaya, 2003: 58; also quoted in Micallef, 2004: 240). Today, more than 20,000 Turks are living in Passaic County, New Jersey, with the largest community settled in Paterson (Reimers, 2005: 217). Paterson is likened to Berlin's Kreuzberg or Brussel's Schaarbeek, where large numbers of Turkish immigrants live.

With the US lottery system (Diversity Immigration Visa Program) giving permanent residency in the United States, there is more social and economic diversity among Turkish immigrants as they come from all socio-economic and educational backgrounds. Although there has not been a specific study for this type of migratory flow into the US, many of them were only able to find work well below their educational level – at least during the initial years of their residency.

TABLE 2.3
Turkish Immigration to the US (1987-2004)

Years	Numbers
1987	1596
1988	1642
1989	2007
1990	2468
1991	2528
1992	2488
1993	2204
1994	1840
1995	2947
1996	3657
1997	3145
1998	2682
1999	2219
2000	2613
2001	3229
2002	3400
2003	3040
2004	3833

Source: 2004 Yearbook of Immigration Statistics, US Dpt of Homeland Security.

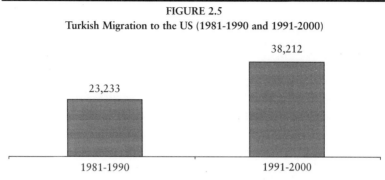

FIGURE 2.5
Turkish Migration to the US (1981-1990 and 1991-2000)

Source: 2004 Yearbook of Immigration Statistics, US Dpt of Homeland Security.

The Foreign-Born from Turkey and Naturalized Turkish People in the US

According to the 2004 American Community Survey by the US Census Bureau, 149,556 people reported their ancestry as Turkish. Since many Turkish-Americans do not participate in census surveys or those who participate often identify themselves as white rather than as Turkish-Americans, it is difficult to give an exact number of Turkish-Americans (Kaya, 2003: 60).

Results from the 2000 US Census show that there were 78,378 foreign-born[29] from Turkey in the United States. The foreign-born from Turkey represented 0.3 percent of the US total foreign-born population of 31.1 million. Of the 281.4 million people in the US, the foreign-born from Turkey accounted for less than 0.1 percent of the total population. According to the same census, the profile of Turkish people born in Turkey and living in the US is as follows: 35,025 (44.7 percent) of them were naturalized citizens with more than half (21,080) having entered the country before 1980; whereas the majority of them (33,030) entered the US between 1990 and 2000. Another 43,350

---

29 The term *foreign-born* refers to people residing in the United States on census day who were not United States citizens at birth. The foreign-born population includes immigrants, legal non-immigrants (e.g., refugees and persons on student or work visas), and persons illegally residing in the United States.

(55.3 percent) were not American citizens. The gender distribution was 54.7 percent male (42,880) and 45.3 percent (35,500) female. As for ages of the sample data, the majority of them, 19,480 people (24.9 percent) were between 25 and 34 years old. As for educational attainment, an overall 42.7 percent had a bachelor's degree or higher, and 14, 935 (23.1 percent) of them were holding graduate or professional degrees.

Relying on the 2000 census, the National Science Foundation (NSF) carried out a survey on college graduates in the US, the National Survey of College Graduates (NSCG), in 2003. The survey does not count, however, incoming and departing people between the years of 2000 and 2003. According to this survey, there are 24,604 college graduates of Turkish origins living in the US. The majority of them are between 40 and 44 years old (6,937), and male (14,979). The most important reason for coming to the US cited most often was for educational opportunities (9,665). Almost half of the respondents obtained a bachelor's degree (11,399), whereas the number of those holding masters degrees was 7,977; of those awarded with PhDs were 3,797, and the number of professionals was only 1,430. The majority of them had full-time jobs (17,244), and they were mostly employed in non-science and engineering occupations (9,338).[30]

In the 2000 US Census, the five states with the largest foreign-born populations from Turkey were New York, California, New Jersey, Florida, and Massachusetts. Combined, these five states constituted 60.7 percent of the total foreign-born population from Turkey in the US. There is also a fast-growing Turkish population in Philadelphia (Remiers, 2005: 216).

Based on informal estimates by the Voice of America – Turk, Micallef states that there are approximately 200,000 Turkish-Americans (2004: 233). According to the SOPEMI Report on Turkey (İçduygu, 2004), the number of Turkish people in the US was estimat-

---

30 Some of the non-science and engineering occupations are managerial and administrative jobs, health-related occupations, technologists and technicians, and sales and marketing occupations.

TABLE 2.4

Ten States With the Largest Foreign-Born Population from Turkey (2000)

Area	Number	Percentage
United States	78,378	100
New York	16,228	20.7
California	13,438	17.1
New Jersey	9,606	12.3
Florida	4,744	6.1
Massachusetts	3,525	4.5
Virginia	3,059	3.9
Illinois	3,038	3.9
Texas	2,943	3.8
Pennsylvania	2,237	2.9
Maryland	2,147	2.7

Source: U.S. Census 2000, quoted in MPI (www.migrationpolicy.org)

FIGURE 2.6

Naturalized Turkish People in the US (1994-2004)

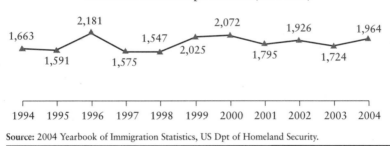

Source: 2004 Yearbook of Immigration Statistics, US Dpt of Homeland Security.

ed as 220,000 in 2003 (see **Table 2.5** below). The Assembly of Turkish-American Association's (ATAA) vice-president's estimates are around 300,000 – of which 15,000 to 20,000 live in the greater District of Columbia area, 100,000 live around New York City, and large numbers reside in Texas, Chicago, and California. The Turkish Foreign Ministry has no precise figures for the total number of Turkish people living in the US. However, Turkish consular offices in Washington, DC, New York City, Los Angeles, Houston, and Chicago estimated that there were around 350,000 Turks living in the United

States in 2006. This number includes immigrants and non-immigrants. According to the US Immigration and Naturalization Service (INS), 465,771 Turkish immigrants have come to the United States between 1820 and 2004. As noted earlier, these figures may include those ethnic and religious minorities of the Ottoman Empire.

TABLE 2.5
Stocks of Turkish Nationals Abroad (in thousands)

Host Country	2000	2001	2002	2003
Europe	3,191	3,125	3,086	3,063
of which: EU	3,086	3,015	3,019	2,958
USA	130	220	220	220
Australia	51	54	54	56
Canada	35	40	40	40
CIS	52	42	36	40
Others	144	138	153	157
Total	3,603	3,619	3,574	3,576

Source: Icduygu, SOPEMI, 2004.

From Temporary Migration to Permanent Residency

Most of the time, the admission conditions of skilled people are temporary, but temporary may lead to permanent migration if the conditions are conducive. A high number of foreign students move from temporary status to a permanent one.[31] H-1B visas are also considered as a feeder program leading to permanent status (Lowell, 2001: 148). Therefore, it is important to look at non-immigrants as well as immigrants when trying to assess the size and development of migration flows from a certain country (Diehl, 2005). According to the Migration Policy Institute (MPI), in 2000, 13 percent of all college graduates in the civilian labor force (33.2 million aged between 25 and 64) were foreign born. Of the 4.3 million college-educated foreign-

---

31 Batalova (2006) states that foreign students move from F visas to H-1B, and then from H-1B to permanent status, although their initial admission to the United States depends on their will to return to country of origin.

born, over one-third arrived between 1990 and 2000. The two largest sending countries are India and China. California, New York, Florida, Hawaii, and New Jersey have the highest share of college-educated foreign workers. Among the college-educated foreign-born, 43.6 percent hold masters, professional, and doctoral degrees, compared to 35.2 percent of native-born workers.[32] Research and development (R&D) in science and engineering, and the information technology (IT) industry depends on foreign-born highly skilled professionals. They are more likely to be employed in either high-tech, computer-related jobs or to have science and engineering occupations (Jachimowicz and Meyers, 2002). It is suggested that Silicon Valley, the leading centre of innovation and entrepreneurship in the electronics sector in California, would not be the same without the contribution of skilled temporary and permanent migrants (Paisley, 1998; Fink, 1999; quoted in Benson-Rea and Rawlinson, 2003: 64).

It is difficult to determine how large the Turkish skilled migration flows are. For one thing, the statistics on skilled migration are scarce, and secondly, skilled people use different channels to reach their destinations and the status between temporary and permanent is usually blurred. The temporary visa program – H-1B[33] – enables US employers to hire foreign professionals for a period of three years, which is extendable for another three years. The H-1B visa requires that the foreign worker should have at least a bachelor's degree, and half of them apply for permanent residency or green cards (Martin, 2006). H-1B visa holders may change employers during this time, but in order to stay on in the US, their companies must sponsor green cards. In order to prevent exploitation and to eliminate the possibility of depressing the wages, US law requires that the H-1B holders are

---

32 See Jeanne Batalova's article entitled "College-Educated Foreign Born in the US Labor Force" for more details (www.migrationinformation.org/USFocus/display.cfm?ID=285).

33 The H-1 visa system dates back 1952 Immigration and Nationality Act and was broken up to H-1A (for nurses) and H-1B (for temporary workers of distinguished merit and ability) (Rosenblum, 2001: 388).

either paid the same rate as other employees with similar skills or the prevailing wage (Miano, 2005).

With the Immigration Act of 1990, the US Congress gave its open support for a more "skills-based" immigration policy, and in 2000 there were 4.3 million college-educated foreign-born in the US working mainly in high-tech jobs or in fields such as science and engineering (Batalova, 2005). The 1990 Immigration Act also established an annual cap[34] of 65,000 on H-1B visas.[35] The annual cap was increased from 65,000 to 115,000 in 1999 and in 2000 was expanded to 195,000 per year between 2001 and 2003, but it returned to 65,000 in 2004. In November 2005, the US Senate voted to increase the cap on H-1B visas from 65,000 to 95,000 per year as the 2006 quota had already been reached in August 2005 (USCIS, 2005). H-1B holders depend on employers to sponsor them to stay in the US and they are supposed to be paid a prevailing wage but it is reported that they are working longer hours for lower pay.[36]

Of the 30.8 million nonimmigrant[37] admissions recorded by the Nonimmigrant Information System (NIIS) of the Department of Homeland Security (DHS) in 2004, 22.8 million entered as tourists, with an additional 4.6 million entering as business travelers. Combined, tourists and business travelers accounted for 89 percent of all arrivals for 2004. Five additional classes accounted for more than one percent each of all arrivals. These are: 1) Temporary

---

34 The word "Cap" refers to annual numerical limitations set by Congress on the numbers of workers authorized to be admitted on different types of visas or authorized to change status if already in the United States.

35 See Usdansky and Espenshade (2001) for more details on the evolution of US immigration policy towards skilled migrants.

36 See article in *New York Times* titled "How to Lose the Brain Race" by S. Clemons and M. Lind dated April 10, 2006; see also the article "The H-1B Equation" in *Computerworld*, published February, 28, 2005.

37 A nonimmigrant is a foreign national seeking to enter the United States temporarily for a specific purpose. Nonimmigrants are admitted for a temporary period of time and, once in the country, are restricted to the activity or reason for which their visa was issued. They may have more than one type of nonimmigrant visa but are admitted in only one status.

FIGURE 2.7
Top Thirty Skilled Emigration Countries, 2000

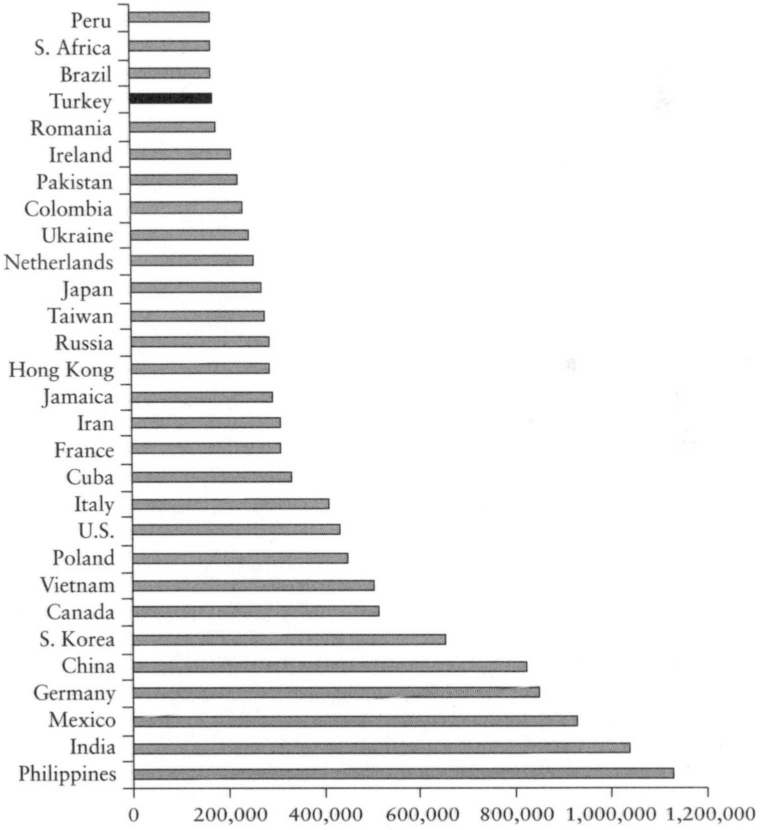

Source: Docquier and Marfouk (2006: 175-176).

workers/trainees and their families (H visas)[38] (which amounted to 2.7 percent with 839,510), 2) Students and their families (F and M visas) (which amounted to 2.1 percent with 656,373), 3) Intracompany transferees and their families (L visas) (1.5 percent with 456,583), and

---

38 Under H category, Turkish nationals usually enter the USA with H-1B visas and the total number of people holding H-1B visas was 386,821.

FIGURE 2.8

Selection Rate of the Highly Skilled Labor Force Living Abroad

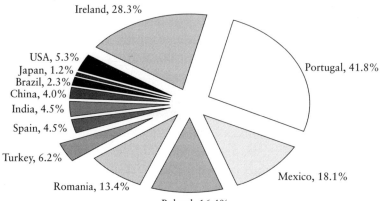

Source: Docquier and Rapoport, 2005.

TABLE 2.6

Number of Turkish Immigrants to the US by Educational Attainment (1990)

Total	Primary	Secondary	Tertiary
	OR LESS		
43,605	2,780	21,540	19,285

Source: Carrington and Detragiache, 1998.

4) Exchange visitors and families (J-visas) (1.2 percent with 360,777).[39]

Turkish Students in the US and the Internationalization of Higher Education

A significant component of skilled migration is now accounted for by foreign students who stay on after completion of degrees (Commander et al., 2003). Therefore, it will not be wrong to call international students another group of professional migrants (Alberts and Hazen,

---

[39] See Grieco, E. M. "Temporary Admissions of Nonimmigrants to the US in 2004," released in May 2005. Available at: www.uscis.gov/graphics/shared/statistics.

2005). In the near future, we can anticipate the increasing mobility of skilled people with the emergence of more international professional markets and a growing internationalization of higher education (Iredale and Appleyard, 2001: 6). The internationalization of higher education occurs for different reasons (Iredale, 2001: 9-10). First, as knowledge can be sold to individuals, developed countries earn a great deal of money as a result of "educational exports". Secondly, young scholars or students, parents, as well as employers in countries of origin consider education in the US very highly, and there is a common perception in Turkey that those who have studied overseas can find employment at home much more easily than the ones who stayed.

Growing competition for skilled workers and foreign students were cited as one of the top ten migration issues of 2005.[40] The International Institute of Education (IIE) database indicates that in the 2004-2005 academic year, international students enrolled in American universities and colleges, comprising four percent of the total enrollment (13,994,869) at American universities and colleges. International education is no doubt making a significant contribution to the American economy. According to the Association of International Educators (NAFSA), it is estimated that foreign students and their families contributed more than 13 billion USD to the US economy in the 2004-2005 academic year alone.[41] Based on information gathered from campuses all around the US, Open Doors 2004/05 data published by the IIE indicated that nearly 72 percent of all international students reported that their primary source of funding came from personal and family sources or other sources outside of the US.

In Louscher and Cook's study sponsored by the American Turkish Council, the American Friends of Turkey, the Turkish Industrialists' and Businessman's Association of the United States

---

40 See MPI's website under Top 10 Migration Issues of 2005. Competition for Skilled Workers and Foreign Students was cited as migration issue number 8 (www.migrationinformation.org).

41 This figure is based on tuition and enrollment fees plus living expenses of foreign students and their dependents.

(TÜSIAD-US), the Turkish-American Business Forum, and the Turkish–US Business Council of the Foreign Economic Relations Board of Turkey (DEIK), they assessed the American domestic economic benefit from Turkish graduate and undergraduate students, and noted that each Turkish student in the US is estimated to spend more than $28,000 USD per year.[42] According to their calculations, the impact of the total annual income[43] of Turkish students' attendance at American universities is $836 million USD, whereas the tax revenue that may result from Turkish students amounts to $209 million USD.[44]

International students are also believed to bring educational benefits to American higher education by enriching American culture and by making significant contributions to teaching and research.[45] Out of 565,039 active international students during the 2004/05 academic years, 47 percent of all (264,410) were graduate students and 38 percent of all graduate students were international students. **Table 2.7** shows the leading ten places of origin of international students in the United States. Between 2005 and 2006, the top ten countries of origin of foreign students studying in the US at the university level were (in descending order): India, China, the Republic of Korea, Japan, Canada, Taiwan, Mexico, Turkey, Germany, and Thailand.

We have to note however that the statistics on the number of Turkish students in the US are contradictory. According to the IIE Reports, in 2005 there were 12,474 Turkish students in the US, out of

---

42 Although this is a conservative estimate and the tuition, fees, room and board of some American universities are much higher, the researchers did not take into consideration the number of Turkish students sent by the Turkish government as well as those who received scholarship and research assistantship from individual universities.

43 Total annual income is the sum of direct (income generated by an educational institution providing services and goods) and indirect income (income generated in the community as a result of expenditures other than education) (Louscher and Cook, 2001).

44 Overall contribution of foreign students to the US economy is estimated to be around 13.3 billion USD (www.iie.org).

45 For more details see NAFSA's report (2005) prepared by the Strategic Task Force on International Students in which the importance of international students was underlined and a strategic approach was recommended to policy-makers in order to promote easier access of international students to US educational institutions.

TABLE 2.7
Leading Twenty Places of Origin of International Students

Rank	Origin	2004/2005	2005-2006	% Total Student Total	% Change
1	India	80,466	76,503	13.5	-0.05
2	China	62,523	62,582	11.1	0.1
3	Korea	53.358	58,847	10.4	10.3
4	Japan	42,215	38,712	6.9	-8.3
5	Canada	28,140	28,202	5	0.2
6	Taiwan	25,914	27,876	4.9	7.6
7	Mexico	13,063	13,931	2.5	6.6
8	Turkey	12,474	11,622	2.1	-6.8
9	Germany	8,640	8,829	1.6	2.2
10	Thailand	8,637	8,765	1.6	1.5

Source: Open Doors 2005, Report on International Educational Exchange

which 6,486 were graduate students, whereas 5,114 of them were undergraduate students and 874 of them were other students coming for language courses and vocational schools. **Table 2.8** below shows the changes in the number of Turkish students in the US between 1999 and 2006. Especially between 2000-2001 and 2001-2002, we see a 10.1 percent increase in the number of Turkish students at American universities and colleges. After that, there was a 4.1 percent decrease in the 2002-2003 academic year. The declining trend also continued in the 2003-2004 academic year with a 1.7 percent change. In the same year, the overall number of international students also decreased by 2.4 percent. In the 2004-2005 academic year the number of Turkish students increased again by 9.4 percent when compared to the previous academic year. Within the same period, Turkey (number eight with 12,474) experienced the highest rate of growth among the top senders, with an increase of 9 percent. Within the same period, the total number of students from the Middle East continued to decline, although at a much-reduced rate (down 2 percent, as compared to a 9 percent decline in the previous year). However, there was a slight decrease by almost 7 percent in the number of Turkish students in the US between 2005 and 2006. This may be due to rising costs of American universities and growing competition in the international education sector.

TABLE 2.8
Turkish Students in the US (1999-2006)

Rank	Academic Years	Turkish Students International Students	Total
#9	1999-2000	10,100	514,723
#8	2000-2001	10,983	547,867
#8	2001-2002	12,091 (+10.1 %)	582,996
#8	2002-2003	11,601 (-4.1 %)	586,323
#8	2003-2004	11,398 (-1.7 %)	572,509
#8	2004-2005	12,474 (+9.4 %)	565,039
#8	2005-2006	11,622 (-6.8 %)	564,766

Source: Open Doors 2000-2006 Data Sets, Report on International Educational Exchange

Although the IIE is one of the most reliable sources, Louscher and Cook (2001) estimate that the number of Turkish students in the US is much higher: around 15,000 Turkish students are attending American educational institutions, including language institutes and other technical schools.[46] According to the 2004 Yearbook of Immigration Statistics released in January 2006 by the US Department of Homeland Security, the number of Turkish students reached 14,518[47] and the number of their spouses and children was given as 611. The statistics provided by the US Immigration and

---

46 It should be noted that their estimate is much larger than IIE's annual reports, namely Open Doors Report on International Educational Exchange, on the number of Turkish students. This difference may partly be explained by the fact that small colleges, business schools, language institutes, and other technical schools are not always listed in the IIE's survey.

47 The term "student" was described as a nonimmigrant class of admission, an alien coming temporarily to the US to pursue a course of study in either an academic (college, university, seminary, conservatory, high school, elementary school, other institution, or language training program) or a vocational or other recognized nonacademic institution.

Customs Enforcement (ICE) Student and Exchange Visitor Program, as of April 24, 2006 indicate that there are a total of 13,923 Turkish students in the US out of which 11,905 hold F-1 (academic) visas, 18 of them with M-1 (vocational visas), and 2000 with J-1 (exchange visitor) visas. The statistics also indicate that 35.7 percent of all Turkish students are females, whereas 64.3 percent are males. Education levels of the Turkish students are shown in the **Table 2.9** below:

TABLE 2.9
Education Levels of Turkish Students in the US

Doctorate	3,393
Bachelor's Degree	2,858
Master's Degree	2,744
LanguageTraining	1,575
Associate	826
Other	527
Total	11,923

Source: ICE, Student and Exchange Visitor Program.

Tables 2.10 and **2.11** indicate the top five schools by number of Turkish students.

TABLE 2.10
Top Five Schools by Number of Turkish Students

School Name	Number of Students
1. The City University of New York	421
2. State University of New York at Binghamton	193
3. Kaplan Test Prep, Inc	188
4. Georgia Institute of Technology	150
5. State University of New York	140

Source: ICE, Student and Exchange Visitor Program.

Tables 2.12 and **2.13** indicate the top twenty-five schools by Turkish students and by Turkish graduate students respectively.

TABLE 2.11

Top Five Courses of Study by Number of Active Students

Course of Study	Number of Students
1. Business Administration and Management	1,598
2. Second Language Learning (NEW)	1,382
3. Economics, General	630
4. Electrical, Electronics and Communications Engineering	458
5. Computer Science	333

Source: ICE, Student and Exchange Visitor Program.

TABLE 2.12

Top Twenty-five Schools by Number of Turkish Students

School Name	Number of Active Students
The City University of New York	421
State University of New York at Binghamton	193
Kaplan Test Prep, a division of Kaplan, Inc.	188
Georgia Institute of Technology	150
State University of New York	140
The Pennsylvania State University	127
Columbia University in the City of New York	125
University of Connecticut	119
Strayer University	115
Boston University	112
University of Illinois	109
New York Institute of Technology	106
University of Florida	101
Purdue University	99
Rutgers, the State University of New Jersey	95
The Ohio State University	95
University of North Alabama	93
Northeastern University	91
New York University	90
Cornell University	85
University of Texas at Austin	79
University of California, Los Angeles	78
University of Southern California	78
University of Michigan	77
University of Virginia	76

Source: ICE, Student and Exchange Visitor Program

TABLE 2.13

Top Twenty-five Schools by Number of Turkish Graduate Students

School Name	Number of Active Students
The City University of New York	179
Georgia Institute of Technology	125
University of Illinois	103
University of Florida	91
Columbia University in the City of New York	90
The Pennsylvania State University	89
New York Institute of Technology	85
The Ohio State University	84
Rutgers, the State University of New Jersey	80
Boston University	78
Texas A&M University	70
University of Texas at Austin	70
Purdue University	68
New York University	64
Stanford University	62
University of Michigan	61
University of Southern California	61
University of Minnesota	60
Northeastern University	58
State University of New York at Binghamton	58
Strayer University	58
University of Pittsburgh	58
Cornell University	57
University of Maryland	57
University of Houston-System	56

Source: ICE, Student and Exchange Visitor Program, 2006.

Tables 2.14 and 2.15 show the top twenty-five courses of study by Turkish students in the US and their numbers by state. Business administration and management, second language learning, and engineering are by far the most attractive courses of study.

The 1982 Constitution of Turkey paved the way for non-profit foundations to establish higher education institutions, which marked the beginning of private universities in Turkey. At the same

TABLE 2.14

Top Twenty-five Courses of Study by Number of Turkish Students

Courses of Study	Number of Active Students
Business Administration and Management, General	1,598
Second Language Learning (NEW)	1,382
Economics, General	630
Electrical, Electronics and Communications Engineering	458
Computer Science	333
Industrial Engineering (NEW)	277
International Business/Trade/Commerce	269
Mechanical Engineering	233
Civil Engineering, General	231
Computer and Information Sciences, General	213
English Language and Literature, General	193
Political Science and Government, General	192
Chemistry, General	191
Liberal Arts and Sciences, General Studies and Humanities, Other	185
Liberal Arts and Sciences/Liberal Studies	175
Physics, General	175
Mathematics, General	167
Business Administration, Management and Operations, Other	151
Marketing/Marketing Management, General	145
General Studies	135
Finance, General	133
Engineering, General	130
Business/Commerce, General	107
International Relations and Affairs	99
Chemical Engineering	93

Source: ICE, Student and Exchange Visitor Program.

time, several new state universities were opened in many parts of Turkey as well. Today, there are 24 private and 53 state universities throughout Turkey. Although the high numbers of Turkish students in the US given above might prove otherwise, it is suggested that the private universities have reversed the brain drain to a certain extent (Tansel and Güngör, 2003: 54), especially at the undergraduate level.

TABLE 2.15
Number of Turkish Students by State

State	Number of Active Students
New York	2,286
California	1,390
Massachusetts	980
Texas	699
Pennsylvania	670
Florida	541
Illinois	524
New Jersey	462
Virginia	436
Ohio	349
Connecticut	315
Georgia	311
District of Columbia	299
Maryland	229
Michigan	227
Alabama	206
Indiana	195
North Carolina	193
Rhode Island	141
Missouri	121
Washington	101
Louisiana	98
Minnesota	96
Arizona	94
Delaware	87
Iowa	87
Tennessee	71
Wisconsin	66
Oregon	59
Kentucky	54
Arkansas	51
Oklahoma	51
New Hampshire	50
Colorado	43
Kansas	43
South Carolina	41

TABLE 2.15 (continued)
Number of Turkish Students by State

State	Number of Active Students
Mississippi	39
Nevada	37
West Virginia	33
Nebraska	32
Utah	30
Maine	21
New Mexico	19
Vermont	13
North Dakota	7
Wyoming	6
Idaho	4
Puerto Rico	4
South Dakota	4
Hawaii	3
Montana	3
Alaska	2

Source: ICE, Student and Exchange Visitor Program.

Since September 11, 2001, there have been notable downturns in the number of foreign students applying to and attending American institutions of higher education (Lindsay, 2005: 155). There are many reasons for this decline. First of all, the US has become less hospitable in the wake of 9/11, and, because of changes in immigration policy, the number of foreign students and workers declined as well (Lindsay, 2005: 156; Martin and Kuptsch, 2006).

Secondly, discouraging labor market conditions in the US between 2001 and 2004 for both foreigner and native populations alike was another factor (Lindsay, 2005: 157). Third, global competition for both international students and skilled workers has increased in recent years. European countries like Germany, the UK, France, and the Netherlands have adjusted their immigration policies in order to attract more skilled workers and graduate students. Australia, New

Zealand, and Canada also encouraged skilled migration and foreign student flows into their countries.[48]

In 2004-2005, the overall number of international students enrolled in US higher education institutions remained fairly steady at 565,039, off about one percent from the previous year's totals, according to the annual report on international academic mobility published by the Institute of International Education (IIE), with support from the US Department of State's Bureau of Educational and Cultural Affairs. This marked the sixth year in a row that America has hosted more than half a million foreign students. This year's numbers indicate a leveling off of enrollments, after last year's decline of 2.4 percent. Some campuses reported significant increases in enrollments, while other campuses reported declines.

It seems that the main problem lies in the number of science and engineering students at the graduate level.[49] The United States is faced with declining rates of participation by native-born students in graduate science and engineering educations, and therefore relies heavily on the participation of foreign students and skilled workers, as the potential of any given country for growth and innovation is determined by the highly-skilled such as scientists, managers, and entrepreneurs (Gilles, 2004).[50] According to the National Science Foundation, for-

---

48 Migration Policy Institute, top migration issues of 2005, issue number 8. Available at: www.migrationinformation.org.

49 See e.g. the article in *The Economist* under the catchy title "Land of the Freeze", Special Issue: The World in 2005, p. 32, published in December 2004. It is noted that each year fewer and fewer American students apply for graduate degrees in science and engineering and American companies are increasingly dependent on foreign nationals who earned advanced degrees from American universities despite the limited quotas.

50 NSF report suggests that US employers have grown increasingly dependent on the global S&E workforce to meet needs in industry, government, and academia. For example, in 1999, one-third of all S&E PhD-holders working in industry were born abroad. Among computer scientists, the proportion was half, and among engineers it was more than half. For the Federal Government workforce, 16 percent of PhD holders in 1999 were born abroad. In academia, about 20 percent of the yearly job openings for college and university faculty in S&E are being filled by permanent residents or temporary visa holders. Available at: www.nsf.gov/nsb/documents/2003/nsb0369/nsb0369.pdf

eign students made up 41 percent of the science and engineering doctoral graduates in 2001. **Table 2.16** below shows the number of foreign students who earned science and engineering doctorates in the US between the years of 1983-2003.

TABLE 2.16
Foreign Recipients of US Science and Engineering Doctorates by
Country of Origin: 1983-2003*

Country	Number	Percent
All foreign recipients	176,019	100
Top 10 total	111,959	63,6
China	35,321	20,1
Taiwan	19,711	11,2
India	17,515	10
South Korea	17,112	9,7
Canada	5,832	3,3
Iran	3,807	2,2
Turkey	3,413	1,9
Thailand	3,102	1,8
Japan	3,100	1,8
Mexico	3,046	1,7
All others	64,060	36,4

(*) Including permanent and temporary residents.
Source: National Science Foundation, Division of Science Resources Statistics, Survey of Earned Doctorates (www.nsf.gov.statistics/seind06/c2/tt02-03.htm).

The leadership of American universities in international education and especially in science and engineering (S&E) is an important component of US strength in drawing the best students and scholars to study and work in the US (See **Figure 2.9** for the number of Turkish S&E doctorates in the US between 1995-2004). Since September 11, 2001, however, security-motivated policies, visa requirements, as well as the Student and Exchange Visitor Information System (SEVIS)[51]

---

[51] SEVIS is a student tracking system implemented by the US Department of Homeland Security. It requires all schools and related academic institutions to enter and regularly update student information electronically into a central database that can be accessed by the government.

and the Mantis program,[52] not only affected the nationals of some
countries negatively, but also have changed the climate for foreign
graduate students and scholars who wish to come to the US, which
was the most popular destination for many scientists and engineers
since WWII (The National Academies, 2005). According to the
National Science Foundation, there are also increasing rates of return
to countries of origin by foreign students after completing their
degrees due to personal reasons, as well as inconsistencies among policies related to the recruitment and treatment of foreign scientists.[53]
This is followed by concerns about enrollment declines by foreign students in the US and the international competition to recruit the best
foreign students. As domestic students show less interest in pursuing
careers in science and engineering,[54] the US academic research enterprise depends heavily on non-American students and scholars
(Institute of Electrical and Electronics Engineers, 2004; quoted in
Lindsay, 2005: 156).

The internationalization of higher education owes a great deal
to the institutional collaboration between universities in countries of
origin and destination (Iredale, 2001: 9). Although nowadays the
majority of Turkish students are private students financing their own
means, there are also those holding scholarships – especially at the
doctoral level – from the Turkish Ministry of Education (MEB), the
Turkish Board of Higher Education (YÖK), the Turkish Academy of
Sciences (TÜBA), and the Scientific and Technological Research

---

SEVIS was mandated in the Illegal Immigration Reform and Immigrant Responsibility Act of
1996, and the full implementation date of August 1, 2003 was set forth in the Patriot Act of
2001 and the Enhanced Border Security and Visa Entry Reform Act of 2002.

52 The MANTIS program aims at imposing restrictions on foreign scholars and scientists who
work in so-called 'sensitive' fields, such as nuclear engineering.

53 Quoted from the National Science Foundation's report entitled "The Science and Engineering
Workforce: Realizing America's Potential" published on August 14, 2003. Available at: www.
nsf.gov/nsb/documents/2003/nsb0369/nsb0369.pdf.

54 Some of the reasons influencing US-born students lack of interest in pursuing a graduate work
in S&E are cites as less economic rewards compared to the private sector, decreased availability
of tenure-track positions, and discouragement of faculty (The National Academies, 2005: 106).

FIGURE 2.9
Turkish Citizens Awarded Science and Engineering Doctorates (1995-2004)

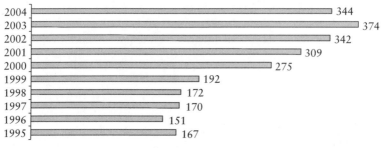

Year	
2004	344
2003	374
2002	342
2001	309
2000	275
1999	192
1998	172
1997	170
1996	151
1995	167

Source: www.nsf.gov/statistics/nsf06308/pdf/nsf06308.pdf.

TABLE 2.17
Top Ten Countries of Origin of non-US Citizens Earning Doctorates at
American Colleges and Universities (YEAR 2004), all Fields of Study

Rank	Country	Number of PhD Recipients
1	China	3,209
2	Korea	1,448
3	India	1,007
4	Taiwan	703
5	Canada	601
6	Turkey	430
7	Thailand	363
8	Japan	278
9	Germany	249
10	Mexico	231

Source: NSF/NIH/USED/NEH/USDA/NASA, 2004 Survey of Earned Doctorates.
(www.norc.uchicago.edu/issues/sed-2004.pdf)

Council of Turkey (TÜBİTAK). Currently, there are several thousand government-sponsored Turkish students in the US. The reason behind sending these students is mainly to train academics to fill positions in state universities.

Every year, the MEB sends students abroad to receive mostly graduate education in order to meet the instructor requirements of universities and the requirements of other institutions and organizations for qualified personnel educated abroad.[55] In the academic year 2000-2001, 20,400 students (private and public) were being educated abroad, 15,100 of which were in undergraduate programs, 3,200 in graduate programs and 2,100 in doctorate programs. Most of them are studying in the US. Of the students being educated abroad, 19,400 had private and 1,000 of them had public status. Of the students being educated abroad, 74 percent were in undergraduate programs, 16 percent in graduate programs and 10 percent in doctorate programs, and 44 percent were in the science area and 56 percent in the social area. In the academic year 2000-2001, three of the 1,014 students being educated abroad with formal scholarship were receiving language education, 25 were in undergraduate, 258 in graduate, and 728 in doctorate programs.[56] Most students who obtained scholarships from the MEB are sent to the US; however, without sufficient knowledge of English, they are expected to learn English within a year before they can follow their studies.

Another institution in Turkey sending students and young scholars abroad on scholarship is the Council of Higher Education of the Republic of Turkey (YÖK). The Vice-President of the YÖK, Professor Aybar Ertepınar, stated that there was no institutional opinion on brain drain, although the rate of non-return is a major concern, as this situation causes problems in the planning of human capital in the universities. To date, 167 research assistants who got scholarships from the YÖK resigned from their positions and did not return to Turkey, whereas 352 of them are considered to have resigned, as they were unsuccessful in completing their studies on time. If the education of the non-returning highly skilled is funded by the sending state from taxes on residents, then the skilled migration can be harmful for the sending country. He also said that he held the view that emigration of

---

55 Law no. 1416 on the students to be sent to foreign countries, and the Law no. 4307 amending Article 19 of the law on the organization and duties of the Turkish Ministry of National Education.

56 MEB website: www.meb.gov.tr/english/indexeng.htm.

the highly skilled from Turkey was not a loss but a gain, and added that this phenomenon could best be described as brain network, signifying more collaboration between Turkish scientists in Turkey and in the US.[57] The YÖK sent a total of 3,694 research assistants on scholarships abroad between 1987 and 2003, out of which 20 percent (730) still continue their education. Half of them chose the US as the destination for their further studies.[58] However, due to increasing numbers of non-return, the YÖK not only decreased the number of scholarships significantly but also raised the bar to get one.

The number of scholarships allocated to the institution decreased significantly in 1996, and this number dropped to 80 in 2004. Only doctoral students have been sent abroad in recent years, and it is expected that the applicants should have high scores on the Test of English as a Foreign Language (TOEFL) and the Graduate Record Examination/Graduate Management Admission Test (GRE/GMAT).

There are two Turkish educational attachés in the US: one in New York and one in Los Angeles. There is also an acting educational counselor in Washington, DC. The acting counselor in Washington, DC is responsible for both private and YÖK-sponsored students in North America. The attaché in Los Angeles is responsible for private students only, and the attaché in New York handles the MEB-sponsored and private Turkish students as well. According to the office of the Counselor for Education at the Turkish Embassy in Washington, D.C., the number of Turkish students registered is 3,303. This number includes both private students (2,840) at undergrad (46.6 percent), masters (31.5 percent), and doctoral (21.9 percent) levels, and those who are sent by YÖK scholarships (463) for graduate studies.[59] The ratio of female private students registered with the Counselor for Education is as low as 2.4 percent, as male students have to register in

---

57 Personal communication, February 2005.
58 Between 1987 and 2003, 1,835 of them were sent to the US.
59 Personal communication with the acting Educational Counselor, Ms. Güldan Kalem, April 2005.

order to delay their military service. Private students usually prefer to study business administration, computers, economics, electrical engineering, and mechanical engineering, and they are heavily concentrated in the states of New York, Massachusetts, Pennsylvania, Florida, Virginia and Georgia. By the end of 2004, the number of private students registered in the Office of Educational Attaché in Los Angeles was 1,709. In the 2005-2006 academic year, the number of students with MEB scholarships was 330 – 10 of them at the undergraduate level, whereas the rest were in the masters and PhD programs of selected universities, most of them are working on education issues.[60] Universities that attract MEB-sponsored students at the PhD level are Indiana-Bloomington, Florida State, Syracuse, Ohio State, Florida-Gainesville, Wisconsin-Madison, Pittsburgh, Clemson, Illinois State, and Arizona State (www.yogm.meb.gov.tr/SUNU.htm).

The Role of Turkish-American Organizations in Creating a Transnational Identity

Nowadays, there is a renowned [Editorial suggestion: replace "renowned" with "popular".] interest in immigrant organizations among migration scholars. Such organizations help us better understand the dynamics within the immigrant communities (Schrover and Vermeulen, 2005: 823). Governments of host countries have a great impact on the establishment of such ethnic organizations, as they may choose to prohibit, ignore, or encourage immigrant organizations or parts of their activities (Shrover and Vermeulen, 2005: 828). Migrant associations have always been an important feature of migrant communities in the US (Babcock, 2006). Immigrant organizations assume a significant role in integration, by increasing the contact among its members, thereby providing a form of 'social capital' facilitating adaptation and assistance (Massey et. al, 1987; quoted in Cordero-Guzman, 2005: 890). They also create or re-create a national/ethnic

---

60 Personal communication with the Educational Attaché in New York, March 2006.

identity, often above nation-states, and establish a link between the two countries. In that sense, they may even attempt to influence the foreign policy of the host country toward the home country (Cordero-Guzman, 2005: 907). In the pages that follow, some information is provided on early Turkish Associations in the US, and the evolution of Turkish-American organizations over the years.[61]

Early Turkish Associations in the United States

Between 1860 and 1924, approximately 60,000 Muslim Turks immigrated to the US. The first Muslim housing cooperatives and associations were founded by these early-comers to America in Chicago (IL), Worcester (MA), and Detroit (MI) between 1909 and 1914. They established more than 25 associations and published newsletters called *Hemşehri* (Fellow Townsman), *Sedai-Vatan* (Native Country), and *Birlik* (Unity). It was also documented that there was cooperation between these first Turkish associations and Sephardic Jewish associations in New York and Chicago.[62]

Although in the wake of WWI the number of Turks in the US decreased by half, the ones who stayed became more organized (Ahmed, 1993: 65). In the 1930's, the Turks in the US established the Cultural Alliance of New York, the Turkish Orphans' Association, and gathered to collect money for Turkish orphans in Turkey. They also channeled money and materials back to Turkey through the Red Cross, who turned it over to the Red Crescent, their Muslim organization to help victims of earthquakes and floods (Ahmed, 1993: 60-61).[63] In Chicago, Detroit, New York,[64] Worchester, and Peabody,

---

61 See Appendix for a detailed list of Turkish-American Associations and Organizations in the USA.

62 Sedat İşçi's paper presented on the occasion of ATAA's 25th Annual Convention in Washington, DC on December 10, 2004.

63 Apart from such Turkish organizations, the Sephardic Jews immigrated to the US from Turkey established the American Sephardic Committee for the Turkish Earthquakes' Relief in the 1940s and collected money to be sent to Turkey (Papo, 1987; quoted in Bali, 2004: 98).

64 Micallef notes that Cultural Alliance of New York, which was the oldest Turkish-American association, established in 1933.

they established clubs and convened once a week (Ahmed, 1993: 65). But neither the second generation nor the newcomers in the 1950's and 1960's were as eager to continue the ethnic associations established by the first generation (Bilge, 1994: 400).

In the late 1950's, many Turkish associations sporadically published their own periodicals, like *Yanki* (Echo), *Türk Dünyası* (Turkish Planet) and *Anavatan* (Homeland). *Türk Evi*, a monthly in English and Turkish, was published between 1970 and 1978 (Halman, 1980: 995). The early Turkish associations in the US reflected the first generation's lack of desire to integrate fully into American society. As Bilge notes:

> The type of voluntary associations they (earlier immigrants) established not only reflected their preference for insulation against outsiders, but also actively served to thwart their acculturation and assimilation into the American mainstream (1994: 400).

Halman mentions that although there were nearly 100 Turkish-American clubs and organizations in the late 1970's, including university student associations, they were either not well organized or they had just a few active members (1980: 994).

Turkish-American Associations Today

Immigrant organizations do not only form a transnational space, linking the countries of origin to destination, but also become places of belonging, strengthening solidarity among its members, and relating the first generation with the newly arrived (see also Moya, 2005: 849). The early Turkish-American associations were founded mainly for cultural reasons, like celebrating *bayrams* (religious festivals) and national holidays. As the Turkish community grows and diversifies in time, it also has the capacity to generate a more "differentiated organizational structure" (see e.g. Vermeulen, 2005: 959; Moya, 2005: 852). Today, there are more than 200 Turkish associations all around the US, including those of the ethnic Turks. Through

the extensive use of the Internet,[65] Turkish-Americans are also creating "virtual communities", and through naturalization and double citizenship they have become one of the other hyphenated groups in the
US (Micallef, 2004: 240).

Some of the earlier Turkish-American associations changed
names, status and the profile of membership.[66] There are still many cultural organizations, mainly involved in organizing parties and events for
their members, but some of them are only involved in development projects in Turkey.[67] Migrant communities are a source of remittances, and
migrant remittances constitute another channel through which the
skilled migration may generate positive impacts for Turkey (see Tanner,
2005: 28). There is much evidence that lower-skilled migrants send
more money to relatives or save enough to start small businesses. Skilled
migrants, on the other hand, integrate into the host society much more
easily and usually invest in the country of settlement (Lowell et al.,
2004). Faini also (2002; quoted in Docquier and Rapoport, 2005)
states that skilled migrants tend to send fewer remittances over time,
and therefore the negative effects of brain drain cannot be counterbal-
anced by higher remittances to the country of origin.[68] However, the
higher skilled immigrants tend to invest directly or indirectly in health

---

65 At the moment, Turkish-Americans are quite active in the Internet and they have different pub-
    lications (See Appendix for the list of journals, periodicals, and internet portals by Turkish-
    Americans).

66 For example, the Anadolu Club that was established in Long Island mostly by doctors and engi-
    neers as a professional society is now located in New Jersey and has a wide range of members,
    from white-collar to blue-collar workers, and a wide range of activities, from cultural gathering
    to social aid and fostering U.S-Turkey relations. The FTAA is now an umbrella organization
    consisting of over 40 member associations. The ATAA started with two associations – The ATA-
    DC and MATA – but now it has over 50 component associations and over 8,000 members.

67 HasNa works on development projects in Turkey and in Turkish Republic of Cyprus and on the
    Greek side. Another organization, ATS, invests in Turkey and supports projects in collaboration
    with NGOs in Turkey. ATS initiated a teacher exchange program and a fellowship for the train-
    ing of young Turkish physicians in the US Anatolian Artisans, Bridges of Hope Project, Turkish
    Children Foster Care, Washington Turkish Women's Association also collect money from their
    members and sent to Turkey to be used in education and building of schools in underprivileged
    regions in Turkey. See Appendix I for a complete list of Turkish-American associations in the US.

68 See also Straubhaar and Wolburg (1999) for a similar discussion.

and education services in the source country through associations. Some Turkish associations send remittances which are used to finance community projects such as hospitals and schools, and may reduce poverty and initiate development in certain areas.

"Social remittances" (Levitt, 1996, 2003; see also Kapur, 2003, quoted in Tanner, 2005: 70) are also important in the sense that closer contacts with Turkish people settled in the US could help Turkey to benefit from a flow of ideas, know-how, etc. Another huge potential for development is through transnational business networks, which still need to be explored. As the members of the Turkish-American community who work as investors and entrepreneurs have the knowledge of both countries, they can either significantly contribute to private sector developments in Turkey, either directly by engaging business ventures and investments themselves, or they can establish a link between companies and facilitate trade.

Religion incites the formation of separate associations within the same national group (Moya, 2005: 846). Within the last several years, many different local-cultural associations as well as religious organizations were founded (see Appendix 2.1), serving the needs of Turkish people with even more diverse backgrounds living in the US. One of the most influential associations belonged to the Fethullah Gülen's followers, named the American Turkish Friendship Association (ATFA). The members of ATFA are a mixed group, with blue-collar and white-collar workers, and they are sometimes described as the "other" among highly skilled and secular Turkish-Americans. As in Central Asia, Fethullah Gülen has also opened several private schools in the US with good reputations in the communities, like the Amity School and the Pioneer School.

Some of the Turkish-American associations have assumed a bigger political role in American society, representing the political views of the Turkish-American community vis-à-vis the Greek and Armenian lobby. The turning point for the politicization of Turkish-American associations was other ethnic groups, especially Greeks and

Armenians, over the need to defend the homeland and to build a transnational identity in the 1970's.[69] After the mid-1970's, due to a series of events, like the Turkish intervention in Cyprus, the American military embargo, the Greek and Armenian lobby, and the Armenian Secret Army for the Liberation of Armenia's (ASALA) massacres targeting Turkish diplomats in the US and elsewhere, Turks living in the US felt for the first time the need to mobilize politically. The Vice-President of the Assembly of Turkish-American Associations (ATAA), Dr. Oya Bain, stated that the turning point for the Turkish-American community was 1974, as the hostilities against Turks started at that time with the Cyprus intervention. She further stated that:

> At that time, in the mid-1970s, there was much negative news in the media about Turkey. That kind of hostility made the Turkish community proactive and we became sensitive to the issues. But even then we had a cultural association and the understanding was that since the charter was a non-profit and non-political association, we did not touch political issues. At that time, there were many Turkish cultural organizations in the US. Every city has formed a cultural association. Religious issues were not important. Everybody was united but there was a lot of shyness and fear in the Turkish community. But we became sensitive to the political issues. We started to respond by writing letters at that time but politically we were very weak. Then the movie *Midnight Express* came out and it did huge damage to the Turkish image in the US and we started to be on the defensive. We were also attacked by Greeks and Armenians and they accused us of committing genocides. Greeks victimized themselves as a result of our Independence War. In 1979, the Armenian terrorism started. The Turkish community in the US wanted to be out of any political involvement, especially during the terrorism. ASALA was killing people all throughout the world. But the media response was very lukewarm. For a while, even the founders of the Assembly were under FBI protection, we

---

69 See Karpathakis (1999) for a discussion that Greek immigrant incorporation into the American political system and the "Americanization process" among Greek migrants were brought about by political concerns in the home country through migrant organizations.

were being threatened. We are still at the very early stages and far from being the Armenian organization, ANKA, and the Greek organizations. They have lot of members. But the diaspora numbers are big too. I think a million Armenians and a million and a half Greeks" (personal communication, October 2005).

The Assembly of Turkish-American Associations (ATAA) is totally oriented to increasing political awareness in the US, was established in Washington, DC in 1979 and closely follows the politics of both the home country and the host country. The membership of ATAA can be described as more elitist and highly skilled, whereas the Federation of Turkish-American Associations (FTAA) can be considered a migrant organization combining members with different profiles and worldviews. The founding principle and main objectives of ATAA are described as follows:

> The founding principle of ATAA was to create cohesion and cooperation between social/cultural Turkish-American organizations around the US. Main objectives of ATAA are two-fold: One is to create an informed national Turkish community that can help foster US-Turkish relations and take an active part in promoting a balanced and truthful picture of Turkey in the US. The other is to educate Americans in government, the media, and the public at large about Turkey and issues that concern us as Turkish-Americans. (www.ataa.org).

The other politically motivated Turkish Association, the FTAA, is located in New York City,[70] and it was established in 1956 by the Turkish Cypriot Aid Society and the Turkish Hars Society to unite and support the Turkish community living in the US. It is operating especially in the New York City area, New Jersey, and Connecticut. It was established with the aim of being the umbrella organization for small-

---

70 The Turkish House which is situated at 46th Street and First Avenue in NYC was bought by the Turkish Government in 1977 and serves as a center for cultural activities, Saturday school for Turkish-American children and it houses the FTAA and Turkish Women's League of America.

er Turkish associations. It now has 44 member associations, with only 31 of them paying their dues. They bring together different groups of people from different backgrounds – educated, less educated, secular, and religious. The President of the FTAA, Mr. Atilla Pak, claimed that they are the only grassroots organization among Turkish-Americans and stated that they did not pay attention to socio-economic and cultural differences, as the most important thing was serving the national interest and working towards a common objective, which is working against the Greek and Armenian lobby and to make the Turkish-American voice heard by the American authorities (personal communication, April 2006).

The evolution of Turkish-American organizations was quite different than those established in western Europe. Many Turkish associations in western Europe were initially oriented only towards Turkey and Turkish political parties for many years, although after the 1980's some associations raised their voices to address the issues in the host country (Gitmez and Wilpert, 1987: 107-111; Vermeulen, 2005: 956). As Turkish immigrants in western Europe become much more involved with the politics in the host country after gaining the rights to vote and to be elected, they assume a bi-national identity. Turkish immigrants in the US, on the other hand, are much more integrated, skilled, and have the advantage of getting citizenship earlier than those in Europe. Although they are establishing a Turkey caucus in the US Senate, they are keeping behind in the main decision-making processes, as there are not any Turkish-origin politicians up to this date in the Senate.[71] Policies of the host country towards ethnic organizations, the objectives of the sending country, group characteristics (skilled vs. unskilled and semi-skilled; legal, educational, socio-economic positions of its members; gender, religious observance, etc.), and patterns of migration (temporary vs. permanent) (Schrover and Vermeulen, 2005: 825-830),

---

71 Osman (Oz) Bengur, is the first candidate of Turkish origin to run for Congress in US history and he is the Democratic Party candidate from Maryland in the upcoming September elections in the United States.

also play an important role in the differences between the formation of Turkish associations in western Europe and in the US.

Although Turkish-American associations grew larger in size by attracting more members and have become more diverse over the years, they still had limited financial resources and the political, socio-cultural and even personal divisions within the larger Turkish-American community continued to be a major obstacle in raising a stronger voice. Instead of uniting their forces, heads of two umbrella associations, the Federation of Turkish-American Associations (FTAA) and the Assembly of Turkish-American Associations (ATAA), complain that membership is not large. Nevertheless, the Turkish-American community is a dynamic group. Turks arriving from Turkey – recently blue-collar as well as white-collar workers – are now changing the demographics. Although they may not speak the language well, or be graduates of Robert College and other elite schools, they are quite expressive and assertive. Some of them started their own small businesses and became very successful businessmen in no time. The Turkish- American community has started to become much more involved politically and to make an impact as a group both in the US and in Turkey (Micallef, 2004). As the Turkish- American second generation became more involved, Turks became more assertive.

RESEARCH RESULTS AND THE FINDINGS

According to Iredale, there are six – often-overlapping – typologies of categorizing professional migrants: 1) by motivation (forced exodus, government induced, industry led); 2) by nature of source and destination countries (lack of economic opportunities, poor working and intellectual environments in the country of origin); 3) by channel or mechanism (recruitment agents, ethnic networks, multinational companies); 4) by length of stay (permanent or temporary); 5) by mode of incorporation to the host society (disadvantaged, neutral, advantaged); and, 6) by nature of profession (the extent of internationalization varies with professions) (2001: 16).

The three major groups that will be analyzed in this chapter fall under these typologies as well. These are graduate students, who are motivated to go to the US because of more opportunities in research and education; young professionals who decide to stay on in the host country usually after their studies because of the nature of global markets, wage differentials, differences in living conditions between the two countries, and the education of their children; and pioneer skilled migrants or first-comers who arrived in the US in the 1960's and 1970's due to economic, social, professional and political conditions in Turkey at that time. This latter group is the most integrated in the host country but also the most active in the philanthropic activities through associations between Turkey and the US. Two other groups are the returnees, who have gone back to Turkey because of a combination of personal and professional reasons, and undergraduate students, who are still in Turkey, but who would like to do further studies abroad in the near future.

Turkish Graduate Students
This first group of respondents mainly included (with one exception who was born in the UK) adult foreign-born persons who initially came to the United States from Turkey to pursue graduate studies.

The ages of the respondents ranged from 25 to 36, with a mean age of (n=50) 28 years. At the time of the interview, 11 of them (22 percent) were married. Out of 11 married respondents, 3 were married to American and/or foreign nationals. Of the respondents, 13 were females (26 percent) and the remaining 37 of them were males (74 percent). The majority of the graduate student respondents (19 of them) in the US were studying engineering (38 percent), with 12 of them majoring in finance, business administration, economics, and management, 8 of them in the basic sciences, like physics, mathematics, chemistry, and biology; 7 of them in the social sciences, like political science, international relations, and international law; three of them (all National Education Ministry – MEB – students) in the edu-

TABLE 2.18
Information on Turkish Student Respondents

Age	Gender	Place of Birth	University in the US	University in Turkey	Financing
25	M	Adana	Economics/ Yale University	Economics/Boğaziçi University (BU)	Scholarship from the university (S)
28	M	Manisa	Mechanical Engineering/West Virginia University	Chemical Engineering/Middle East Technical University (ODTÜ)	S
36	M	Istanbul	International Relations (IR) and Conflict Resolution/ George Mason University	Political Science (PS) and IR/BU	S
33	F	Ankara	Public and International Affairs/ University of Pittsburg	IR/ODTÜ	S
26	M	Trabzon	International Law/ Georgetown University	Engineering/Marmara University	Private funding and S
28	M	Istanbul	Biomedical Engineering/Drexel University	Mechanical Engineering/BU	Private sponsor/RA*
27	F	Istanbul	International Law/ Georgetown University	Studied in Cornell University	S
25	M	Ankara	Electrical Engineering/ Stanford University	Electrical Engineering/Bilkent University (BİL)	S
31	F	Ankara	PS and IR/University of Massachusetts – Amherst	PS/BU	YÖK
28	M	Antalya	Design/North Carolina State University	Graphic Design/BİL	S

TABLE 2.18 (continued)
Information on Turkish Student Respondents

Age	Gender	Place of Birth	University in the US	University in Turkey	Financing
28	M	Ankara	Civil and Environmental Engineering/ Georgia Tech.	Civil Engineering/ ODTÜ	S
26	M	Istanbul	Resource Economics/ West Virginia University	Economics/ Istanbul University	RA
27	M	Ankara	Electrical and Computer Engineering/ University of Rochester	Electrical Engineering/ Sabancı University	S
26	M	Ankara	Mathematics/University of Maryland	College of Arts and Sciences/Koc University	TA**
27	M	Ankara	Civil Engineering/ University of Maryland at College Park	Civil Engineering/ ODTÜ	RA
30	M	Istanbul	Economics/University of Rochester	Economics/BU	S
25	M	Ankara	Electrical and Computer Engineering/ University of Rochester	Electrical Engineering/ODTÜ	S and RA
31	M	Izmir	Finance/University of Florida	Finance/Istanbul Technical University (ITÜ)	S
29	F	Manisa	Education/University of Illinois at Urbana-Champaign	Education/Dokuz Eylül University	MEB
25	M	Bursa	Physics/Auburn University	Physics/Marmara University	RA
26	M	Konya	Electrical and Computer Engineering/ Georgia Institute of Technology	Electrical Engineering/ BİL	RA

TABLE 2.18 (continued)
Information on Turkish Student Respondents

Age	Gender	Place of Birth	University in the US	University in Turkey	Financing
27	M	Istanbul	Economics/University of Virginia	Economics/ Koc University	S
28	M	Istanbul	Chemistry/University of Massachusetts	Chemistry/BU	RA/TA
31	M	Adana	Electrical and Computer Engineering/ Georgia Tech	Electrical Engineering/BU	TA
31	M	Izmir	Mechanical and Nuclear Engineering/ University of Pennsylvania	Mechanical Engineering/ Hacettepe University	RA
32	M	Istanbul	Ecology and Evolutionary Biology/ University of Connecticut	Biology/ODTU	RA
25	F	Kircali	Electrical and Computer Engineering/ Boston University	Electrical Engineering/ ODTU	S
26	M	Izmir	Mechanical Engineering/Louisiana State University	Mechanical Engineering/ODTU	RA
26	M	Chertsey, UK	Electrical Engineering/ Princeton University	Electrical Engineering/ ODTÜ	S and TA
30	M	Bursa	Physics/University of Massachusetts – Amherst	Physics/BU	RA
25	F	Istanbul	PS/Rice University	PS/BU	S
25	M	Ankara	Operations/ Weatherhead School of Management/Case Western Reserve University	Industrial Engineering/ ODTÜ	S

TABLE 2.18 (continued)
Information on Turkish Student Respondents

Age	Gender	Place of Birth	University in the US	University in Turkey	Financing
30	M	Kars	Civil Engineering/ George Washington University	Civil Engineering/ ODTÜ	S and TA
29	M	Ankara	Science and Engineering/Rutgers University	Mechanical Engineering/ ODTÜ	RA
25	M	Istanbul	Business Administration (BA)/American University	BA/Istanbul University	Private
25	F	Istanbul	Economy/American University	Economy/BU	S and TA
25	F	Istanbul	PS/Yale University	PS and Sociology/BU	S
26	F	Ankara	Economics/Yale University	Economics/BU	Jean Monnet –Fulbright
26	F	Istanbul	Economics/University of Illinois at Chicago	Economics/BU	TA
28	F	Ankara	BA/University of Illinois at Chicago	Law/Ankara University/MA in BA in Warwick University, UK	S
26	M	Kayseri	Physics, Molecular Science/California University	Physics/BU	S and RA
28	F	Ankara	Genetics/Harvard University	Biology and Chemistry/MIT	S
27	F	Istanbul	Economy/Cornell University	Economy/Koc University	S and part-time job
29	M	Istanbul	Mathematics/Princeton University	Mathematics/BU	S and RA
25	M	Izmir	Biomedical Engineering/Drexel University	Engineering/BU	S and TA

TABLE 2.18 (continued)
Information on Turkish Student Respondents

Age	Gender	Place of Birth	University in the US	University in Turkey	Financing
32	M	Adana	Education/Florida State	Education/Ankara University	MEB
34	M	Manisa	Education/Florida State	Education/Hacettepe University	MEB
31	M	Ankara	Materials Engineering/ Drexel University	Metallurgical and Materials Engineering/ ODTÜ	S
30	M	Istanbul	Electrical Engineering/ Yale University	Electrical Engineering/ITÜ	S
35	M	Adana	Electrical Engineering/ George Washington University	Physics/Çukurova University	YÖK

cation departments; and one of them was going to a college of design. They were coming mainly from universities in Istanbul and Ankara. Of the respondents, 16 were graduates of Boğaziçi University, 13 of them had undergraduate studies in Middle Eastern Technical University (ODTÜ), and 3 of them completed undergraduate studies at Bilkent University, whereas 3 of them had diplomas from Koc University. Two of them were from Marmara University, 2 from Istanbul University, 2 from Hacettepe, 2 from Ankara University, 2 from Istanbul Technical University, and 1 from Sabancı University. Apart from universities located in Ankara and Istanbul, one of the respondents came from Dokuz Eylül University in İzmir, and the other one from Çukurova University in Adana. Two of the respondents, on the other hand, came to the US for undergraduate studies after finishing Robert College in Istanbul.

Two of the respondents were on YÖK scholarships, three of them were on MEB scholarships, and one of the students received Jean-Monnet/Fulbright scholarship, whereas another one financed his studies through private funding (his family). One of them depended on his family (private) and a scholarship he received from the university in the US. The majority and the rest of the respondents (90 percent) got full scholarships from American universities, while some also worked as teacher's assistants and research assistants.

As for the professions of parents, most of the respondents reported that they came from educated and middle or upper-middle class families. Their parents were either retired or working as engineers, lawyers, university professors, businessmen, physicians, contractors, pharmacists, economists, and teachers. In fact, only two respondents said that their parents did not receive any university education: one of the fathers was a truck driver and the other one a farmer with primary school education. Mothers of nine respondents were housewives with university or at least high school education, and their husbands had well-earning jobs. Only one of the respondents stated that his mother was deceased, and one of them reported that his mother was illiterate.

Before coming to the United States, the respondents got information about the department and educational institution through their friends, family members, the Internet, and professors either in Turkey, who studied in the US, or those who came to Turkey for a conference or for scholarly exchange. As for reasons that led them to seek further education in the US, most of them stated that the main pull factor was better research facilities and higher quality education in the US; whereas a number of them reported that it was necessary for them to come to the US in order to become self-sufficient academics. An equal number said that expectation of more employment opportunities after graduation was an important factor. They also mentioned the opportunity to live and work in a multi-cultural environment, and only one brought up human rights violations, especially violation of religious rights in Turkey, as a reason to come to the US (see **Figure 2.10** below).

The amount of time the respondents in this group had been living in the US ranged from a minimum of one year to a maximum of

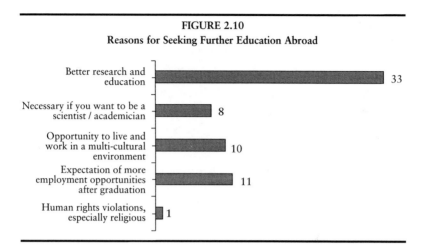

FIGURE 2.10
Reasons for Seeking Further Education Abroad

eleven years (for the respondent who came for undergraduate studies and stayed on for post-graduate as well), with a mean of 4.16 years. It seems that the perceptions of individuals, extensive use of media and the Internet, private recruitment agencies, socio-cultural influences, like knowledge of English and familiarity with American culture, and social networks, play an important role in choosing the US as a destination country for further study among Turkish graduate students. There are other pull factors as well, like the superiority of education at some US universities, and the availability of research and funds. They often see a western degree as a ticket to employment in the industrialized countries or to find a better-paying job in the home country.

Some students of engineering, economics, and basic sciences also mentioned that there were no better alternatives in Turkey if they wanted to have a PhD in their fields. As some examples below illustrate, some also underlined that although education in Turkey is good, research opportunities are very limited:

> The United States is the best country that can provide me with skills and vision to be a global actor in global policy making (26 year-old international law student at Georgetown University).

You cannot possibly get a job in a respectable university in Turkey without a PhD from the US. Also, given the limited research opportunities in Turkish higher education institutions — like poor libraries, no research money, primitive labs, etc. — you cannot realistically get cutting-edge knowledge in advanced degrees in Turkey (31 year-old political science student).

Boğaziçi University was very good in undergraduate studies but for the graduate level, if you want to become a scientist, your options are very limited and no grants for research and lab. I was given awards for my PhD research in the US but still nobody from YÖK or TÜBİTAK called me to congratulate. In the last years, many private universities were opened but in my field (molecular science) the research is still limited (26 year-old physics student).

Main Problems while Studying Abroad

Adaptation problems due to cultural differences, missing Turkish food, loneliness, homesickness, being away from family and loved ones, F1 visa problems, racism and discrimination in some cities, and some financial problems were cited as the main problems of student respondents.

At first it was difficult to adapt to the social environment. Americans are different from us – they have a different concept of friendship, for example. They are individualistic. You have to have an appointment from your American friends to have a cup of coffee together. Everything is different, but then you get used to it – whether you like it or not (25 year-old political science student).

I also got [an] acceptance from German universities. But at the end, I chose [the] US, because the image of the US in Turkey was more democratic and more egalitarian as opposed to a more homogeneous and nationalistic German society. There is also a prejudice against Turks in Germany. But after I came to the US, I changed my mind about the American image, because I feel that I was a foreigner here in the US. First of all, human relations are difficult. If you are Turkish, you are treated differently. International students and American students do not really mingle. You are not consid-

> ered as 'one of them'. One professor told me jokingly that I come from the third world! Work permits for foreign students are also restricted. Americans also tax foreign students from fellowships they earn (25 year-old economics student).

> I had so many problems. 9/11 has been the major problem for foreign students. It limited everything. I cannot digest the way people's perceptions changed towards students overnight. We are talking about a 13-billion dollar industry and [a] very well educated group of individuals. Yet, it is not peculiar to find people who see foreign students as potential terrorists. I have not visited my family for three years in fear of losing my right to return to the US and jeopardizing my degree (31-year old engineering student).

Compulsory military service is another reason among young males for not returning to Turkey immediately after the completion of studies. Two of the male respondents stated that military service in Turkey was a major obstacle for Turkish young men. If they work for a period of three years abroad, then they are exempt from long-term military service and have the option of doing one-month of basic military training in return for $6,048 USD in Burdur, Turkey.

State-sponsored respondents mentioned the pressure to finish studies on time, and they were also concerned as to whether they could find a similar work and research environment in Turkey:[72]

> I did not know much English before coming to [the] US In 1995 when I got the YÖK scholarship, the exam was more science-oriented, and it was not obligatory to have a high score in TOEFL, as it is now. So, a lot of young students from small cities who had no prior knowledge of English were able to get the scholarship at that time. We went to a language course for six months. This was criticized publicly at that time. In 1999, when the President of YÖK was replaced, YÖK students with GPAs lower than 3.5 and those

---

[72] Poyrazlı et al. (2001) also indicated that the Turkish students in the US who received state-scholarship had more adjustment problems due to the bureaucracy the students needed to deal with and the pressure to do well academically in order to keep their scholarships.

who could not get acceptance for [a] PhD from top-50 universities in the US called back to Turkey and they were considered 'unsuccessful'. The requirement to finish a PhD in four years put lots of stress on everyone as well. It is not very common to finish a doctoral study in engineering within four years. As I could not finish my PhD in four years, YÖK suspended my scholarship. I still continue my studies and I got [a] research scholarship from the university (33 year-old engineering student).

MEB-sponsored students especially complained about language problems and lack of communication with their professors. At the moment, in order to get MEB scholarships, students only enter [write?] the Graduate Entrance Exam (LES) in Turkey. Their Grade Point Averages (GPA) at the undergraduate level is also considered. There was no foreign language requirement before leaving Turkey. Instead, they take intensive English lessons after their arrival in the US. Another challenge is that the students with no command of English have to choose on their own and get acceptance from one of the top-50 universities in the US without any consultation from the Ministry of National Education. After getting the acceptance letter from a university, the ministry then sends an authorization form, and is responsible to pay the full tuition and cover the health insurance of the students. The MEB spends $10 million USD per year on the students sent to the US (personal communication with the educational attaché in New York, March 2006).

We did not know any word in English. After we got [the] scholarship from [the] MEB, they sent us to ODTÜ for seven months to learn English. We were the lucky ones. [The] MEB did not send anyone to English language courses in Turkey anymore. They learn it when they come to the US and they are really struggling with it. We learned enough English to pass the TOEFL test but when I came here, I realized that it was not enough at all. I was not able to communicate with my advisor. I still make grammar mistakes when I write papers (32 year-old student).

Almost half of the respondents (46 percent), however, said that they had either not encountered any problems in the US at all, or had to face minor problems at the beginning, and that the environment was so civilized and that they did not feel that they were foreigners in the US. Most of them had international friends and a small cluster of Turkish friends. Of them, 58 percent stated that they visit their homeland once a year, 22 percent twice a year, and 20 percent once in every two or three years. They usually read Turkish newspapers, like *Milliyet* (Nationality), *Hürriyet* (Liberty), *Radikal* (Radical), and *Sabah* (Morning) online, and the majority of them had contacts with Turkey through telephone and e-mail twice or three times a week.

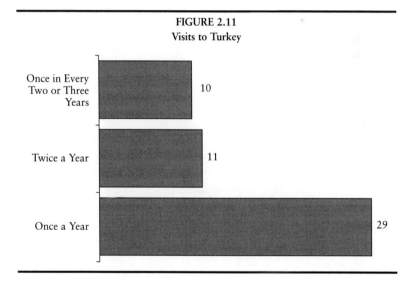

FIGURE 2.11
Visits to Turkey

Figures **2.12** and **2.13** below illustrate the relations of the respondents between the Turkish community and American society.

Many respondents underlined the differences between Turkish and American culture, and their limited relations with American society in general. Often, their workload as graduate students is given as an excuse not to get involved with the dominant culture other than

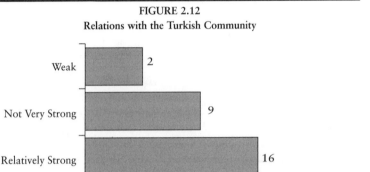

FIGURE 2.12
Relations with the Turkish Community

Weak	2
Not Very Strong	9
Relatively Strong	16
Strong	23

FIGURE 2.13
Relations with American Society

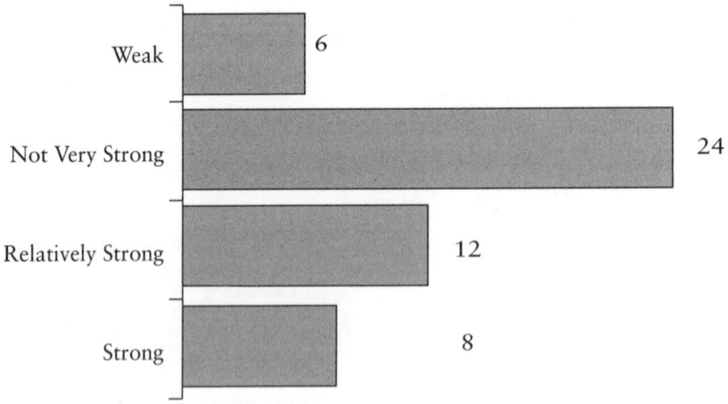

Weak	6
Not Very Strong	24
Relatively Strong	12
Strong	8

professional ties. Despite the perceived cultural differences, some respondents affirmed the positive qualities of American society:

> American society is more individualistic and not very warm compared to Turkish people. But, sadly for us, I find Americans more ethical in their actions and in daily life than the Turkish people.

> When doing business, they will not give you good bargains, but they are fair and will not rip you off either (31 year-old engineering student).

As for the information on the labor market and job opportunities in Turkey, a great majority of respondents reported that they did not know much about job opportunities in Turkey (see **Figure 2.14** below).

> I think we don't know much about the job prospects in Turkey. The degrees earned in the US worked in favor of some of my friends who returned, whereas in some other cases, it did not make a huge difference. Finding a good job depends on people you know and on the conditions of Turkey. It does not matter anymore to have a masters degree in the US or to have a good command of English. Networks are still important. But in the recent years, many foreign companies have opened branches in Turkey. My friends say that it is getting better (26 year-old economics student).

Although the number of universities in Turkey has increased in recent years, similarly there is an increase in the demand for universities offering better education, especially in a foreign language, thereby widening the uneven gap in the educational system. Therefore, only the diplomas of certain universities are valued in the labor market after graduation and many university graduates are either left without a job or have to accept jobs way below their skills and training. This shows that most young people are trained not in accordance with the expectations of the job market in Turkey.

Kwok and Leland (1982) suggested that "asymmetric information in the labor market" is another cause for the non-return of students trained abroad. According to their argument, employers in the country of origin usually have limited information about the skills of foreign-trained students and can only offer wages based on the average quality of returned students. Employers in the host country, on the other hand, are more advantaged in recognizing the true abilities and offer better wages in line with their skills and education. The National

Science Foundation (NSF) indicates that between 1990 and 2001, almost half of the Turkish science and engineering doctoral students stayed in the US.[73]

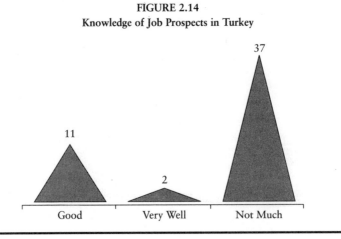

FIGURE 2.14
Knowledge of Job Prospects in Turkey

Future Plans (Temporary or Permanent)

Even though the future intentions of student respondents are not a perfect measure of the actual number of those who stay in America or go back to Turkey, they still can be a useful indicator (See also Li et al. 1996; quoted in Alberts and Hazen, 2005: 133). Twenty-one respondents (42 percent) regarded themselves as temporarily in the US, although except for those who were sent on state scholarships, they all said they would like to work for a couple of years to gain some experience.

> I don't plan to stay in the US after graduation. I hope I can be useful to my own country. If someone is good enough to find employment and education opportunities in the US, then he will find

---

73 Information gathered from NSF, Division of Science Resources Statistics, Survey of Earned Doctorates, 2003.

employment in his own country too. There should be no excuses (30 year-old engineering student).

Only 16 percent of the respondents expressed that they would like to stay on a permanent basis in the US. An equal number of respondents (42 percent) did not have any idea, however, what they would like to do after completing their studies (see **Figure 2.15** below):

> I don't know what the future will bring. I want to return to Turkey eventually but I don't know the realities and challenges of academia in Turkey. I don't think I can be a part of American society but I don't think I am a part of overall Turkish society either. I see myself more as a global citizen, mobile and intellectual. I may go and work in other countries as well (25 year-old political science student).

> After 9/11, it is more difficult to find a job if you do not have a green card or citizenship. Nobody wants to sponsor you. I think job opportunities in social sciences might be even better in Turkey (33 year-old student of public and international affairs).

> In the short-run, I will go where I find a good job and where I think I will be more productive academically. The long-run is the series of short runs (quoted from Keynes)! So, time will show. If I can get a job in Koc University after [my] PhD, I will be really pleased. Koc University is better than most universities in the US." (26 year-old mathematics student).

I don't have a definite future plan. I have seen so many people who wanted to go back to Turkey and stayed. I have known many people, on the other hand, who wanted to stay in the US but who returned. I would willingly consider staying in the US. But it is difficult to say anything at this moment. There are too many things to consider and this is a decision that you cannot come up with on your own. There are many jobs in Turkey but lots of young people are looking for jobs and salaries are really low. I don't feel I would have [a] financial security if I go back to Turkey. As for the political environment, it is getting worse every day. I hesitate to go out sometimes. One time, they threw a burning cigarette towards my legs, just because I had a medium-length skirt and no socks! There are so many fundamentalists even in Istanbul. They complain so much about lack of religious freedoms but I don't have religious freedom as well (25 year-old economics student).

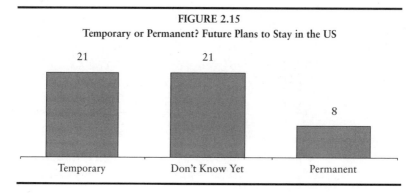

FIGURE 2.15
Temporary or Permanent? Future Plans to Stay in the US

In answering the question as to whether they believed that Turkey would be an EU member state eventually, 54 percent (27 respondents) said that they did, whereas 46 percent (23 respondents) said that they did not. In answering a question as to whether Turkey's success in creating favorable economic conditions in line with the harmonization process with the EU would affect their decisions to return home after completing studies in the US, 62 percent said that it would, 26 percent said maybe, and 12 percent said that it would not affect them in any case, either because they were planning to return anyway, or they had made up their minds not to return.

> It would be a very good reason to return for me and for most people I know. Turkish students here are mostly scared about losing their liberties and personal improvement opportunities given to them in the US and therefore they are reluctant to return. If the obstructions are removed, then it will be more favorable for young and skilled people like us to return in large numbers (31 year-old engineering student).

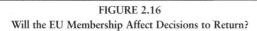

FIGURE 2.16
Will the EU Membership Affect Decisions to Return?

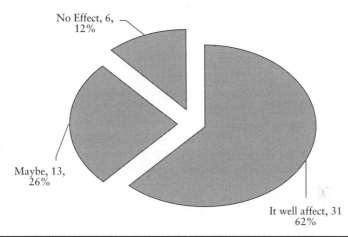

No Effect, 6,
12%

Maybe, 13,
26%

It well affect, 31
62%

Some students do not want to return to their homeland if they cannot find a way to implement their training in Turkey, either because of unemployment and underemployment, or lack of equipment and resources.

> Yes, I feel that I am a part of the 'brain drain'. It is hard to reverse the tide when the US offers so much in terms of research opportunities. [The] economy and the way people think about research needs to change. We really need to boost the money and energy allocated for R&D. Ideally I would like to have a dual position between the US and Turkey. But biology/genetics is a very expensive field. Turkey does not spend much money on research (28 year-old post-doc student in the Department of Genetics).

> I think Turkey should emphasize building more opportunities for young and capable individuals and this would help building [a] better economy and prosperity. (25 year-old engineering student.)

> Even if I decide to stay in the US, I might serve my country. There are many examples. Turkish professors at NYU helped me a lot (26 year-old economics student).

Job prospects in Turkey should be more available to students living abroad like me. Faculty in Turkey should also keep in touch with graduate students that they have helped in sending to the US. But in general, [the] salary of the faculty in Turkey should be more reasonable. There should be more funding allocated to academic research from private agencies and businesses (25 year-old political science student).

I don't believe in brain drain. I think it is a complicated issue and there is no right answer. I think you should not ignore the remittances sent back to Turkey and the image of our country created by respected scientists/researchers/business people in the US. I am not convinced that by bringing back all these people, Turkey has much to gain (26 year-old engineering student).

It is not a matter of brain drain vs. brain gain. Rather, it is brain-use vs. brain-waste. As a result of globalisation, digital technology, removal of borders, 'brains' that could benefit Turkey do not necessarily have to be in Turkey in order to serve the interests of Turkey. Turkey could and should take advantage of its 'brains' abroad in order to transfer technology to Turkey and promote its culture through these 'brains' abroad (26 year-old international law student).

It is a long-term project that needs to be engineered starting immediately. Foreign students in the US usually feel second-class. Especially after 9/11, they are usually not allowed high-level positions for security reasons and compelled to accept mediocre career paths notwithstanding their performances and successes. When they are left with a limited number of career opportunities and lack of resources, they would also feel outside the system in their own country. This is not healthy planning (31 year-old engineering student).

The US provides better means to improve ourselves. Turkey needs to establish a fair and effective legal system and reduce corruption first. [The] economy will not improve without justice. People who are highly skilled and able to perform certain jobs should be employed rather than the relatives/friends of people in certain positions. There should be more support for small and medium scale businesses so that there will be room for brains who can consider returning. Our economy will benefit more and quality will rise higher if we have more businesses focusing on high tech products and design centers. This will also make Turkey more attractive for people who have gained some experience and capital by working in high-tech companies abroad (31 year-old engineering student).

Turkey should develop strategies to attract some of the graduates. They don't have to bring everyone back. Turkey should decide what it needs and provide opportunities for them. But the returnees should be respected and provided [for] and open-minded and [in a] modern atmosphere as well (26 year-old economics student).

Young Professionals

The second group of respondents mainly consisted of young professionals who are still working in the US with visas such as the H-1B after completing their studies in the US (with three exceptions: one respondent had L-1 visa, another had a *laissez-passer* as she was working at the World Bank, and another was born in the US), and those who have obtained green cards or who have become naturalized American citizens.

The ages of the respondents ranged from 27 to 45, with a mean age of (n=45) 35.33 years. The gender distribution of the respondents was 16 females (35 percent) and 29 males (65 percent). Twenty-five of the respondents (55 percent) were married (four of them married to Americans and one married to a Chilean), 15 of them were single (33 percent), four of them were engaged, and one was divorced. Twenty-eight of the respondents (62 percent) were born in three major cities in Turkey – Istanbul, İzmir, and Ankara. Three of the respondents reported that they were born in the US, as their parents were working in the US as non-immigrants at that time. Including these three respondents born in the US, there were a total of 15 people with dual nationality, another 15 with green cards, nine with H-1B visas awaiting green cards, three with H-1B visas, one with an L-1 visa, one Turkish citizen working in the World Bank, and one American citizen (1,5 generation [unclear] – born in Turkey but the son of a skilled immigrant).

TABLE 2.19
Information on Young Professional Respondents

Age	Gender	Place of Birth	Marital Status/ Children/ Partner's Nationality	Visa Type/ Nationality	Occupation	Education
29	M	Istanbul	Engaged/ none/Tur- kish Cypriot	H-1B/Green card pending	Marketing Manager	MBA, New Haven University
35	M	Istanbul	Married/one/ Turkish	Dual nationality	IBM Research Center in San Jose, CAL.	PhD, University of Columbia, Computer Sciences
40	F	Ankara	Married/two/ Turkish	Dual nationality	Has her own private firm	BA, Economics, Yale University
33	M	Nort- hampton, US	Single	Dual nationality	Physician, University of Southern California, Dep. Of Obstetrics and Gynecology	Ankara University, Medical School, New York University
28	M	Istanbul	Single	L1/Turkish	Banking/Risk Management	MBA, University of Northern Carolina
36	M	Erzurum	Married/ two/ American	Green card	World Bank/ head of research	PhD, economy, Stanford University
40	M	Diyar- bakır	Married/ one/ Turkish	Green card	Physician, Pittsburg University	Ankara University, Pittsburg University
42	M	Malatya	Married/ two/ Turkish	H-1B/ Green Card pending	Physician, Epidemiologist, Center for Disease Control, NIH	Ege University Medical School, Dokuz Eylül University

TABLE 2.19 (continued)
Information on Young Professional Respondents

Age	Gender	Place of Birth	Marital Status/ Children/ Partner's Nationality	Visa Type/ Nationality	Occupation	Education
30	M	Ankara	Single	H-1B/ Green Card pending	Marketing manager in a music company	ITÜ, Electrical Engineering, NYU MA in Music Business
35	F	Chicago, IL	Single	Dual nationality	Global Marketing Programs Manager	Boğaziçi University, BA/Babson Graduate School of Business (MBA)
45	F	Istanbul	Married/one/ Turkish	Dual nationality	President of an NGO	Economics, Baltimore University
31	F	Tekirdağ	Single	Turkish	World Bank	ITU, computer engineering George Washington University, finance
40	M	Ankara	Married/one/ Turkish	American citizen	Lawyer, has his own law firm	PS, University of California, Davis /Jr.Dr. Washington& Lee University, School of Law, VA
29	M	Istanbul	Single	Green card	Professor, Electrical Engineer/Yale	PhD, at MIT, EEC
35	F	Denizli	Married/ two/Turkish	Dual nationality	Ass. Prof., University of Massachusetts	Bogazici University/Southern Connecticut State University, PhD

TABLE 2.19 (continued)
Information on Young Professional Respondents

Age	Gender	Place of Birth	Marital Status/ Children/ Partner's Nationality	Visa Type/ Nationality	Occupation	Education
27	M	Istanbul	Single	H-1B/green card pending	Demand Planning Analyst, Schweppes	ITU Electrical Engineering, MBA, Syracuse University
29	M	Mersin	Married/ none/ Turkish	H-1B/green card pending	Businessman, owns his own firm	Bilkent University, A/University of Hartford, MBA
28	M	Erzurum	Engaged/ Turkish	H-1B	Financial Analyst, S&P Finance	Hacettepe, Economics/Pace University, MBA in Marketing and Finance
45	M	Istanbul	Married/ two/ Turkish	Dual nationality	Scholar, French Language Program Director	University of Iowa/BA, SUNY-Buffalo (Economics, French).
28	M	Kayseri	Single	H-1B	Scholar, University of Chicago	Bilkent University/PhD in math at the University of Chicago.
45	F	Afyon	Married/ one/ Turkish	Dual Nationality	Professor of German Studies, Pennsylvania State University	Hacettepe University, Germanic Languages/University of Michigan, PhD, Germanic Languages and Literature

TABLE 2.19 (continued)
Information on Young Professional Respondents

Age	Gender	Place of Birth	Marital Status/ Children/ Partner's Nationality	Visa Type/ Nationality	Occupation	Education
38	M	Ankara	Married/two/ American	Dual Nationality	Professor, Texas A&M University	ODTU, BSME/ PhD, Princeton University, Mechanical Engineering
35	F	Ankara	Married/one/ American	Green card	Professor of math, University of Texas	Oklahoma University, PhD in math
41	M	Mersin	Married/ one/ Turkish	Green card	Physician, Assistant Prof. of Anesthesiology and Preoperative Medicine, University of Louisville	Istanbul University, School of Medicine, did not study in the US but research fellowships in Austria and in the US
36	M	Izmir	Married/ none/ Turkish	Green card	Ass. Prof. at Robins school of Business (University of Richmond)	Boğaziçi University, BS/MBA, University of Texas-Pan American, PhD, Texas A&M University
29	F	Sinop	Single	H-1B	Project manager, private company	Yıldız Teknik, Industrial Engineering, University of California, MBA
34	F	Istanbul	Married/ one/ Chilean	H-1B, green card pending	Scholar at the American University, PS Department	PhD in PS at the American University

TABLE 2.19 (continued)
Information on Young Professional Respondents

Age	Gender	Place of Birth	Marital Status/ Children/ Partner's Nationality	Visa Type/ Nationality	Occupation	Education
29	M	Istanbul	Engaged/ Turkish	H-1B, green card pending	Private sub-ontracting company working on electrical and signal systems of NYC underground.	ITU, EEC/New Orleans University, MS in EEC.
34	F	Izmir	Married/one/ American	Dual Nationality	Investor at a private company	Ege University, English Language, Alaska University, Finance.
39	M	Izmir	Married/two/ Turkish	Dual Nationality	Physician and Researcher, Molecular Genetics, Harvard School of Public Health	Hacettepe Medical School, Harvard Medical School.
31	F	Istanbul	Single	Green card	Educational media and Management/ private firm	Ankara University, College of Communication/ Boston Univerrsity, College of Communiciation

TABLE 2.19 (continued)
Information on Young Professional Respondents

Age	Gender	Place of Birth	Marital Status/ Children/ Partner's Nationality	Visa Type/ Nationality	Occupation	Education
29	F	Istanbul	Engaged/ Turkish	H-1B, green card pending	Multinational Import-Export Firm	Bilkent University Economics/ Johnson and Wales University in Rhode Island, MBA
29	M	Istanbul	Single	Green card	Works in a law firm, President of a non-profit organization	Marmara University, School of Law/New Orleans, Tulane Law School, LL.M
36	F	Istanbul	Divorced	Green card	Lawyer	Princeton University, economics/ Boston University Law School.
37	M	Istanbul	Single	Green card	Scholar and senior policy analyst in a think-tank	Marmara University, IR/Bilkent University, MA/ Yale University, PhD, History
41	F	Ankara	Married/ one/ Turkish	Green card	Artist, wife of a famous performer.	Mimar Sinan University, Istanbul State Conservatory, Theatre.
45	M	Ankara	Married/ two/ Turkish	Dual nationality	Mechanical engineer	ITU, Mechanical Engineering/MIT

TABLE 2.19 (continued)
Information on Young Professional Respondents

Age	Gender	Place of Birth	Marital Status/ Children/ Partner's Nationality	Visa Type/ Nationality	Occupation	Education
43	M	Elazig	Married/ two/ Turkish	Green card	Manager in a private finance company	Bogazici University, Business Administration, MBA.
33	M	Adana	Married/ one/ Turkish	Green card	Has his own private firm in computer programming	ODTU, EEC/PhD George Washington University, EEC
36	M	Istanbul	Single	Green card	Neurosurgeon	Istanbul School of Medicine/ Intern: Yale University School of Medicine
42	F	Istanbul	Married/ one/ Turkish	Dual Nationality	Architect, has her own firm	Mimar Sinan University/ University of Wisconsin, School of Architecture and Design
41	M	Bursa	Single	Dual Nationality	Financial Planner, has his own firm	Uludağ University, BA/University of Baltimore, MBA
32	M	Istanbul	Single	H-1B, green card pending	Electrical and Computer Engineer, Carnegie Melon	Bilkent University, Stanford University, ECE

TABLE 2.19 (continued)
Information on Young Professional Respondents

Age	Gender	Place of Birth	Marital Status/ Children/ Partner's Nationality	Visa Type/ Nationality	Occupation	Education
34	M	Washing- ton, DC	Married/ two/ Turkish	Dual Nationality	Works in a private software company	Boğazici University, ECE/PhD at University of West Virginia
36	F	Istanbul	Married/ one/ Turkish	Green card	Ass. Prof. At the Catholic University of America	Boğazici University/PhD George Washington University

They have diverse occupations, ranging from medical doctors to artists, from managers to scholars, from architects to information technology specialists, from artists to businessmen. Almost half of the respondents (including lawyers and medical doctors) have PhDs. They have spent a minimum of three years to a maximum of seventeen years in the US. Although there were a couple of exceptions, one general characteristic of this group of young professionals was that they usually had a small group of Turkish friends with whom they met on a regular basis, and they did not have much time to be actively involved in the Turkish-American associations.

> I have a small circle of Turkish friends which we meet on a more regular basis. As a working woman with small kids, I have no time at all for such gatherings and socialization. This socializing with friends can be an important necessity and a luxury at the same time. You cannot afford to spend time in this system. You only have time for your family and your job and that is it! But when you don't have time to call friends over, then you suffer because you need that as well (40 year-old businesswoman).

Among those interviewed, no professional complained about receiving lower wages than native-born professionals holding similar positions. What they complained about is the existence of a glass ceiling (see also Alarcon, 2000: 318), and the difficulty of finding jobs as easily as they used to before 9/11. Some of them also mentioned that they did not get any raise or promotion while their companies applied for the green card on their behalf.

Que Sera, Sera? Return Intentions of Young Professionals From Turkey to the US

The main reasons for coming to the US were cited as further training in their field of study and to get a masters or doctoral degree from one of the educational institutions in the US. Most of the respondents (93 percent) were temporarily in the US at first with the academic student visa F-1, and then with the non-immigrant visa H-1B. Some acquired citizenship through marriages or obtained green cards, allowing permanent residence in the US. As noted earlier, three respondents were born in the US. Many young Turkish professionals decided to stay on after their graduate studies. This is a clear evidence that globalisation of higher education is the first step in a skilled international migration path.

The distinction between permanent and temporary residency, which once separated the two categories of migration (professionals and students), has lost its prominence (Khadria, 2001: 48). Likewise, many Turkish students do not return immediately after the completion of studies, but instead they choose to stay and work in the host country. Earlier studies also point out the fact that many students from developing countries fail to return to their home countries upon completion of their studies in the US by changing their immigration status after graduation (Fortney, 1970: 220).

A total of twenty-one respondents considered themselves permanent in the US, whereas sixteen of them were not sure, and eight reported that they would definitely return within a couple of years.

For some respondents, returning may become especially difficult when it means terminating some established relations while building up new ones, and also when the economic conditions in Turkey remain uncertain. Some of the reasons for non-return were cited as: 1) economic reasons (wage differentials, higher living standards, unemployment, underemployment); 2) personal reasons (anxiety about the future, children's education);[74] 3) political reasons (political instability, bureaucratic obstacles, corruption); and, 4) professional reasons (not enough R&D, lack of scientific research at universities, lack of opportunities for highly skilled). After a cost-benefit analysis, there was a tendency to stay in the US for almost half of the respondents, especially for those who have children of school age, and for certain professions, such as researchers and scientists.

> My initial plan was to finish my fellowship in two years and go back to my university where I was a faculty member at that time. But now they are giving me permanent residence under the 'outstanding researcher category' and my plan is to settle down here and give my children an advantage at start-up to prevent them struggling as I did. The Turkish state and the society should value individual talents, potentials, and create more opportunities (42 year-old epidemiologist).

> I am here in the US to do research and to be a scientist. I can go to any international conference around the world. I have my own lab and freedom of work. I had the opportunity to collaborate with qualified scientists in the field... If my own country could give me these opportunities, I would have stayed there. Private universities in Turkey give satisfactory salaries maybe but there is no money for research. Those who return after graduation cannot find jobs easily. Engineers work in the marketing sector in Turkey for foreign companies. They are not doing R&D." (29 year-old electrical engineer.)

---

74 There is evidence from fieldwork that children influence return plans of their parents (See Dustmann, 2003 for a similar discussion).

Those who were not sure about their future plans and returning to Turkey stated that they could move elsewhere other than the US or Turkey and make a living as global workers. Some indecisive others were concerned about where Turkey was heading.

> I always wanted to go back to Turkey after my PhD. Koc University made me an offer after graduation. But I chose to stay in the US for now. I don't know what the future will bring. We are open to go elsewhere. I don't want my children to be exposed to American culture only (36 year-old economist).

> There are some positive developments in Turkey thanks to the EU process. But whenever we go to Turkey, we don't see much positive change. The mentality of the people in the streets is the same. It is uncertain where Turkey is going. I am afraid that if I return to Turkey, I would be nobody. I am afraid that I will not have life security. But I know that criticizing from afar is not enough. At the end, if we want to change something in Turkey, these changes will be done by people like us (29 year-old junior manager at a multinational firm).

Return Trends

While some respondents believed that there is still brain drain or brain migration from Turkey to the United States in certain fields and professions, some others indicated the recent return trends of their close friends (see also the returnees in the coming pages).

> I used to believe that there is brain drain. There was brain drain in the 1970s. But as of 1990s, and especially now, there is a return trend. Some of our friends returned and they found what they deserved in telecommucations sector and management. Financial terms are a critical factor but not always a determining factor in facilitating return of skilled people. Family unity is also important. Some people return to be close to their aging parents and loved ones (40 year-old lawyer).

> I believe that there is less brain drain from Turkey to the US. There was more brain drain in the past. But now, people want to work

here for a while and then trying to find opportunities how to go back or how they can take the American company to Turkey. They usually return to Istanbul because it is the business center. There is a trend for return. Turkey is more desirable. If you are successful in the US, then you can be successful in Turkey. Besides, the US has become a difficult place after 9/11. It is difficult to live in certain states" (40 year-old businesswoman).

Recently, more and more people are returning to Turkey. I believe that the US is harming itself by its foreign policy and made productive people run away. Those qualified people who want to come to the US are now thinking twice. There are visa problems. If there is reverse brain drain, then America will lose its technical advantage. There is already a significant amount of out-resourcing in India and China. Maybe this generation will not lose but the next generation certainly will. The number of Americans who are studying at technical schools dropped. But Americans are aware that they are about to lose the technical leading edge (29 year-old engineer).

'Pioneer' Highly Skilled from Turkey

This group of respondents included those who have been in the US for at least 20 years, and who have either become American citizens or dual citizens (with the exception of one respondent working with the World Bank).

The ages of the respondents ranged from 47 to 77, with a mean age of (n=25) 62.52 years. The gender distribution of the respondents was 10 females (40 percent) and 15 males (60 percent). Of the respondents 23 (92 percent) were married, 8 of them had American partners, and 2 of them were divorced from their American partners. Their arrival dates in the US varied. Seven of them arrived in the US in the 1950's, five arrived in the 1960's, ten came in the 1970's, whereas three of them came in early 1980's. All respondents except one arrived in the US as young adults to have further education and training or to work. In fact, all of the respondents had very high educational levels: five of them had masters degrees, nineteen had PhDs, and only one of

TABLE 2.20

Information on Turkish 'Pioneer' Skilled Migrants

Case	Age	Gender	Arrival Date in the US	Birthplace	Citizenship	Marriage Partner	Profession
1	77	M	1959	Istanbul	Dual citizen	Turkish-American	Architect
2	65	M	1962	Ankara	Dual citizen	American	Engineer
3	75	M	1951	Istanbul	Dual citizen	Turkish-American	Engineer
4	73	M	1957	Ankara	Dual citizen	Turkish-American	Physician
5	68	M	1958	Istanbul	Dual citizen	Turkish American	Businessman
6	72	F	1970	Istanbul	Dual citizen	Turkish-American (Jewish origin)	Business-woman
7	66	F	1960	Istanbul	Dual citizen	American	Bio-chemist
8	56	F	1972	Istanbul	Dual citizen	American	Chemist
9	65	M	1974	Istanbul	Dual citizen	American	Economist
10	61	F	1970	Izmir	Dual citizen	Turkish-American	Physician
11	67	F	1958	Istanbul	Dual citizen	American	Director of an NGO
12	55	F	When she was 3 years old, 1954	Istanbul	Dual citizen	Turkish-American	Architect, business-woman
13	47	F	1982	Artvin	Dual citizen	Turkish-American	Administ-rator
14	58	M	1971	Erzincan	Dual citizen	American	Electrical Engineer
15	55	M	1971	Izmir	Dual citizen	American	Professor of PS

TABLE 2.20 (continued)
Information on Turkish 'Pioneer' Skilled Migrants

Case	Age	Gender	Arrival Date in the US	Birthplace	Citizenship	Marriage Partner	Profession
16	68	M	1958	Izmir	Dual citizen	Turkish-American	Engineering Consultant
17	57	M	1976	Malatya	American citizen	Turkish-American	Professor and Chair, Materials Engineering
18	50	M	1981	Diyarbakır	Dual citizen	Turkish-American	Full-time researcher on x-ray metrology
19	62	M	1974	Tokat	American citizen	American	Professor of Electrical Engineering
20	48	F	1981	Istanbul	Dual citizen	American	Professor of Sociology
21	65	F	1963	Istanbul	Dual citizen	Turkish-American	Professor of Art and History
22	60	M	1975	Ankara	Dual citizen	Divorced	Professor of Civil and Environmental Engineering
23	63	M	1966	Kütahya	Turkish citizen	Turkish-American	Consultant at the World Bank
24	70	F	1962	Istanbul	Dual citizen	Turkish	Physician
25	60	M	1977	Adana	Dual citizen	Divorced	Physician

them had a high school diploma. There were eight engineers, four physicians, three full professors of social sciences, two architects, two self-employed businesspersons, one World Bank consultant, one director of an NGO, one chemist, one biochemist, one economist, and one administrator at a well-renowned university. Of the respondents, 72 percent came from big, urban centers in Turkey, like Izmir, Ankara and Istanbul.

Unlike the other groups of respondents who had intense contacts with Turkey, this group reported that their communications with homeland and families were quite restricted during the initial years of their stay in the US, as phoning was very expensive at that time, and there was no Internet. The best thing they could do then was to write letters once a month, and, if available, to read old Turkish newspapers in the libraries of the universities. They were all thinking of themselves as temporary when they first came to the United States. At the moment, however, only two respondents said that they were still not sure, and the rest (92 percent) acknowledged that they regarded themselves as permanently in the US.

> It took us a while to get used to our new 'immigrant' identity, but we are permanent in the US now. Living here took lots of things away from us but it has brought lots of positive things as well. Diplomats come and go but we are always here to represent Turkey in America (47 year-old administrator).

> Our children are here. We spent more time in the US than we did in Turkey. One of the best things of living in America is that we could follow[the] latest innovations. Because of my interest in technology, it is important to me to see where science and technology is going. If we had stayed in Turkey, we could have only followed from far away. Here, in the US you are living in it (63 year-old consultant).

After completing their graduate studies, ten of the respondents returned to Turkey for some time, but then they felt that they were compelled to go back to the US due to a combination of reasons, such as political instability (especially in the late 1970's), corruption, lack of resources, weakness of infrastructure, lack of available jobs, lack of opportunity for professional advancement, lack of appreciation for work and qualifications earned, the huge differences in living standards and wages between the two countries at that time, and the education of children. Some others changed their minds about returning to Turkey because of the negative political and economic environment.

> I returned to Turkey after my PhD but the political climate, anarchy, and the economic conditions in the 1970s were not bearable at that time to continue further (60 year-old engineer).

> I went back for good in 1968, first for my military service and then to stay in teaching. Unfortunately, the situation in the universities in Turkey in the 1960s and 1970s was not very attractive due to student unrest, jealousy among faculty, and very unattractive working conditions (68 year-old engineering consultant).

> I went back to Turkey and worked for two years between 1974 to 1976 in the industry. But seeing [that] how corruption had permeated into every layer of government bureaucracy, I decided to quit and came back to the US (58 year-old engineer).

> In 1980, I went to Turkey to do my military service. Then there was the military coup. I could not get along with the communists, as I came from the US. The rightists did not think I was good enough for them either. I worked in Gülhane for a while. I gave [had] a struggle in Turkey. All the doctors were going to lunch at the same time, and then there was nobody left to take care with [of] the patients. But you could not do this in our profession. Finally, they accepted. I wanted to work on microsurgery. Unfortunately, there were no options for me in that field in Turkey, so I came back to the US in 1983. Later on, I wanted to go back but once you get settled, it becomes even more difficult, especially when you have kids (60 year-old medical doctor).

> When I first arrived in the US in 1981 for PhD, my initial plan was to get my degree and go back to Boğaziçi University and teach. Then YÖK took over the universities and did away with whatever little freedom they used to have. My professors even changed their line from asking me to come back to telling me to stay put and invite them over to come to the US (48 year-old sociology professor).

Back in the 1970's, with the exception of Turkish physicians who were mostly naturalized in order to meet legal requirements, many first-generation Turks retained their Turkish citizenship even after they were allowed to acquire American citizenship after several years of stay in the country (Halman, 1980: 995). Change of citizenship and denouncing Turkish nationality was severely criticized then by the Turkish media (Halman, 1980: 995) and probably by some circles inside the Turkish community living in the US. When the dual citizenship became law and was adopted by the Turkish Parliament in the 1980's, many of the respondents became naturalized American citizens. As this group felt very close to Turkey despite their long years of voluntary separation, most of them retained their Turkish citizenship.

> I became an American citizen when the law allowing double citizenship passed in Turkey. It was important for me not to lose Turkish citizenship (77 year-old architect).

> I am sentimental about leaving [my] Turkish passport. I think I have a fear of losing my Turkish identity. We were raised with nationalist values. My father used to say that the aim of every good Turkish citizen is to become useful for his own country. If I get an American passport, would it be treason against Turkey? Of course not and I will eventually get an American passport like a *laissez-passer* – to make things easier. This is a global village; you can feel it more and more nowadays. We happen to live in the US, but we have a base in Istanbul. We could well have a base elsewhere in the future (63 year-old World Bank consultant).

> We kept our Turkish nationality for 10 years. But whenever we decided to go to abroad with relatives/friends from the US, it was difficult to get a visa. Customs officials were stopping my husband every time, because people would automatically associate opium and drugs when they saw a Turkish man at the border. So, my husband said that it was time to get American passports (72 year-old businesswoman).

Identity Re-formation and Transnationalism
Among Turkish-Americans

Most professional and first-generation Turkish-Americans who came to the US in the 1960's were raised and educated in secular Turkey; therefore, religious observance seems to be a minor factor in their identity. In time, most of those highly skilled Turkish immigrants who came to the US after 1950 until the early 1980's have established their own communities and groups of Turkish friends. They also kept close ties with Turkey. As noted by Portes and Rumbaut:

> In general, professional immigrants are among the most rapidly assimilated – first because of their occupational success and second because of the absence of strong ethnic networks that reinforce the culture of origin. However, assimilation in this case does not mean severing relations with the home country. On the contrary, because successful immigrants have the means to do so, they attempt to bridge the gap between past and present through periodic visits and cultivating family and friends left behind (1990: 20).

This generation of Turkish highly skilled immigrants is an excellent example of a "transmigrant" (Glick Schiller and Basch, 1995). In other words, they are able to "cross cultural boundaries and build multiple or hybrid identities" (Castles, 2002: 1158), but they feel solidarity with co-ethnics in the US. Within the walls of their houses or cultural associations, they establish their own states.

> We have a small circle of Turkish friends. We are each other's 'Turkey' in a sense. We come together, talk in Turkish, eat Turkish food, and our children get together (66 year-old bio-chemist).

They also find creative ways of changing and adapting to their social environments. This can be described as "code-switching" and "negotiating identity" (Kastaryano, 1996; quoted in Castles, 1160).

> Some of my friends could not integrate and returned to Turkey. Then they could not make it in Turkey and came back to the US again. Many Turks have their own Turkish friends and they do not socialize with Americans. They are not into the fabric of the society. It is important to be an American in the US and to be a Turk in Turkey. I have a switch, for example (60 year-old medical doctor).

According to Portes and his colleagues: "Immigrant communities with greater average economic resources and human capital (education and social skills) should register higher levels of transnationalism because of their superior access to the infrastructure that makes these activities possible". [Reference date required.] Not all activities of the respondents consist of establishing businesses linking the two countries, or sending money for those left behind. More often, their transnational activities are quite modest, like reading the Turkish newspapers online, going to Turkey once a year, buying summer houses if they are retired, and calling friends and other family members in Turkey once a week. However, as Phizacklea suggested, these modest activities are "no less transnational in form" (2004: 129).

All the respondents stated that they were pretty much integrated into American society. Integration into American society is very much determined by the host country, their socio-economic status, and high educational levels. The knowledge of English language prior to coming to US, being familiar with the ways of living, and the long number of years spent in what they call 'our second home' are important factors facilitating easy integration. As Halman observes:

> Although a very high percentage of the educated and well-to-do Turkish-Americans retain strong emotional and intellectual ties with Turkey, they tend to adopt an American way of life with a great deal of ease, whereas Turks at lower income levels are more apt to maintain a Turkish style of living. Contact between the upper and the lower classes is limited – which is similar to patterns that prevail in Turkey (Halman, 1980: 994).

In answering a question about whether they feel their place of belonging is Turkey or the US, eighty percent of them (twenty respondents) said both, eight percent (two respondents) said the US, eight percent (two respondents) said Turkey, and one said none. When they retire, they start to live more in Turkey and become more involved in Turkey than ever before:

> If you had asked me this question about belonging five or six years ago, I would have said 'US'. My family is here. I spent most of my life here. But this is changed in the last years. After my retirement 4 years ago, we started to spend 6 months here, and 6 months in Turkey. Now partly because of my age, I think of Turkey a lot. There are also still too many things to do in Turkey. During summers, we are in Bodrum and I write in a local newspaper. I have the ambition of changing the neighborhood that I live at least (77 year-old architect).

> At this point I feel I do not belong to either society and I try to rise above them both: I try to use the tension between belonging to either one in a constructive manner to trespass national boundaries. I feel fully accepted and welcome and most importantly, appreciated for the work I do and rewarded in the US, rather than put upon (48 year-old sociology professor).

> I have multiple identities. I am a Turkish-American Jew. I feel that one part of me belongs to America and one part of me belongs to Turkey. I like America a lot, but my Turkish Muslim friends say that I love Turkey even more than they do. I still invoke the memory of our people and remember how Ottomans welcomed us when no other nation wanted us. When there were attacks on synagogues in Turkey, I gave a speech to [a] local television. Some American people think that there is anti-Semitism in Turkey. They think that we ran away from Turkey to save our lives (72 year-old businesswoman).

Generational Changes

The first generation usually maintains much stronger ties with the country of origin. They are also the ones who are most involved in Turkish-American associations. Children of first-comers who were born and raised in Turkey until a certain age, i.e. a "1.5 generation" (Rumbaut, 1997) or the second generation, who were born in the US, on the other hand, are much more aware of their American identity with Turkish heritage. The children of the 'pioneer' skilled migrants reported that they feel more attached to the US than Turkey although they are proud of their Turkish heritage. In this respect, it is the children of the respondents who have the common ground with most of the Americans. As Halman states: "This predominantly non-Turkish speaking group may form a core that will exert change upon Turkish-American ethnicity through patterns of participation and achievement that have been characteristic of other ethnic groups in the US" (1980: 996).

As one second-generation Turkish-American woman nicely put it, they are re-claiming their Turkish identity mainly due to the changing demographics and attitudes due to globalisation and immigration:

> When I was growing up, my parents had Turkish friends and they were socializing with them. So, as children we socialize with their children. At that time, I remember that nobody was happy [of] being Turkish. We wanted to be as much [as] American as possible. We did not want to say that our parents come from another country. One reason for that was at that time; there were not many foreigners around. People around us were all white Americans. Now it is a different atmosphere. Everybody is proud of his or her own heritage and they speak different languages. Other children at school used to tease me saying "turkey, turkey" and beat me up. But I never said a word to my mom. It was a bigger embarrassment that she comes and talks with school authorities and with my teacher with her broken accent. Now I am happy about being Turkish and we go to Turkey for the summer holidays. My children could understand but not really speak Turkish that well. But they cherish their Turkishness, and they want to learn more about Turkey (Second generation Turkish-American, daughter of a medical doctor).

Returnees

This group consists of people who have returned to Turkey after studying and working in the US.

TABLE 2.21
Information on Returnees

Age	Gender	Birthplace	Marital Status	Education	Time Spent in the US	Profession
42	M	Istanbul	Divorced	American School of International Management, MS in Int. Business	10 years	Manager in a private firm, Istanbul
55	M	Konya	Married	University of Southern California, PhD, Computer Engineering	20 years	Computer Engineer, Visiting Professor at Bilkent University
32	M	Ankara	Single	Electrical and Computer Engineering	8 years	Head of a private software company in Istanbul
31	M	Ankara	Single	MA in Human Resources Development, Towson University	7 years	Human Resources, Private Firm, Istanbul
30	M	Istanbul	Single	MBA, Johns Hopkins University	6 years	Regional Manager, Foreign company, Istanbul
34	M	Ankara	Single	MBA, New Jersey City University	11 years	Marketing Manager in a private company, Istanbul

TABLE 2.21 (continued)
Information on Returnees

Age	Gender	Birthplace	Marital Status	Education	Time Spent in the US	Profession
62	M	Istanbul	Single	PhD, Columbia University, PS	20 years	Professor at Sabancı University
35	F	Ankara	Single	MSc, Northeastern University	12 years	Sales Manager, IT firm in Istanbul
31	F	Istanbul	Single	The City University of New York, Baruch College, MBA	10 years	Marketing Manager in a foreign company in Istanbul
35	M	Istanbul	Married	Computer Engineering, Georgia Tech.	9 years	Business Development Director, in a US-based telecommunications company

The ages of the respondents ranged from 30 to 62, with a mean age of (n=10) 38.7 years. Of the returnees, two were married, whereas one of them was divorced and the rest were single. They were born in big cities in Turkey, like Istanbul, Ankara and Konya. They spent a minimum of six years and up to twenty years in the US (the mean is 11.3 years). The gender distribution was two females and eight males.

The main reasons that led to their return to Turkey from the US are a combination of personal and professional choices. The developments and economic impetus Turkey has undergone in the last years was also cited as an important factor. The respondents also mentioned that it was getting harder to find suitable jobs in the US, and there were discriminatory attitudes towards foreigners after 9/11.

Interestingly enough, except for two respondents – one is a temporary returnee, and another is a professor of political science – all of the others were working in the private sector in Istanbul.

> After having lived in the US for 10 years, I felt it had offered all it had to give. I did not want to start up a new life in a new city after grad school. Turkey had developed quite a bit since when I had left it and I had a concentrated group of friends and acquaintances in Istanbul, most of whom had returned from the US (42 year-old manager).

> We returned to Turkey for a year. We wanted to be in our country for a while. We also thought about our children, this gives them opportunity to practice their mother tongue. I am very satisfied with the work conditions in Bilkent (55 year-old visiting professor of computer engineering).

> The company I was working for is opening a branch in Istanbul and I am transferred to Turkey. I believe I will have [made a] more significant contribution if I go to Turkey. I might also teach part time at a university. Going to America is a dream. That's why skilled migration from Turkey to the US will not end. But return migration has started thanks to the improved conditions of [in] Turkey (32 year-old software company director).

> If you are doing scientific research, then you are happy to be in the US but for business people like us, there is not much life. Americans are not social people. They help but they are distant. They are very individualistic. There is too much emphasis on how much you make, rather than who you are. The concept of 'friendship' is very different here in the US. People are egoistic. The system requires that in a way. I have two aunts. One of them lives in America and the other lives in Turkey. They are way different from each other. My aunt who has been living in the US for some time now has become 'Americanized' (34 year-old marketing manager).

> After 9/11, the attitudes of Americans towards foreigners have changed completely though it is still better than in Europe. At least, they don't turn their backs when you say that you are Turkish. The

Turkish people who come to the US are ambitious, hard working, and mostly educated. After I had my masters degree, I worked in a company. I had plans to stay for another two years. But I got an offer from a foreign company in Istanbul, so I will go back and try my luck. I wanted to return to Turkey anyway. Money is not everything to me. Besides, I have a girlfriend in Istanbul and it is where I want to live. If it does not work out, I can come back (30 year-old regional manager in a private company).

One respondent who was about to leave for Sabancı University at the time of the interview said that he went back to Turkey in the 1970's, but had to go back to the US in order to pursue a better professional career because there were many problems at that time.

I always wanted to go back to Turkey after my PhD. But then I was offered a job at Rutgers University and I accepted. In 1974, Şerif Mardin was at the Boğaziçi University and he invited me. In those years, many good young Turkish professors from the US were recruited for the Boğaziçi University. Although life was very good, academic life was not very stimulating in Turkey. The working pace is very different in the US. I only published in the US for example. Then there were other problems, like inflation, money, YÖK, the political environment, etc. So, in 1982, I went to Denmark. In 1984, I came back to the US to work at the Rand Corporation. I also worked at the National Academy of Science for two years and at different universities. When compared to the 1970s, the academic environment is much better in Turkey now. In 1996, I got an offer from Koc University but I could not go. I always kept my friendships alive in Turkey. I invited colleagues from Turkey for conferences (62 year-old professor).

In answering a question about their place of belonging, unlike the 'pioneer' skilled migrants who had been living in the US for more than 20 years, all of them said that it was Turkey.

I feel my belonging is in Turkey, but much more as an American who chose to live in Turkey. I travel a lot, have foreign friends in Istanbul, hardly watch Turkish TV, read in English, etc... I felt very accepted and welcome while in the US. I do not feel like a stranger in Istanbul, but I do not relate to cultural values and social expectations at times. I feel I am much more liberal-minded then most people I meet (42 year-old manager).

I feel that my place of belonging is Turkey of course. Yes I did not have any problems and felt accepted. While my wife feels her place of belonging is Turkey, my children seem to be confused about it (55 year-old visiting professor).

I feel my belonging is in Turkey. The US welcomes everyone, but at the beginning it was hard to be accepted. But after a while, I realized that I would be happier to continue living in Turkey with the things I have grown accustomed to – rather than trying to adjust to things I was not so used to (31 year-old marketing manager).

I definitely belong in Turkey – or Anatolia, and not in these lands inherited from Native Indians by WASPs. Therefore, I will do my best to help my country improve economic conditions and to secure a better future for the future generation – just as Americans say, "Ask not what your country can do for you, but what you can do for your country (35 year-old sales manager).

Undergraduate Students in Turkey with Intentions to go abroad

Ten undergraduate students from different fields in Turkey were interviewed to learn more about their future intentions of going abroad for a masters and/or doctoral study. The students were from the departments of management (22 year-old, male), international relations (23 year-old, male and 24 year-old female), graphic design, (24 year-old, male), mathematics (23 year-old, female), political science (23 year-old, male), molecular biology and genetics (24 year-old, female), chemistry (24 year-old, male), and electrical and electronics engineering (23 year-old, female and 23 year-old, male). The main reasons for further education abroad are cited as: the opportunity to have a totally different experience in a different country with different customs and values; the perception that universities in the US provide high quality education and that they have more research possibilities; and the common view that people who study abroad are more preferred by employers or it is necessary to have an experience in the US to pursue a successful academic career in Turkey; and, to obtain a wider perspective on the profession and to have professional advancement which would lead to a better career.

The Internet, professors in Turkey who have completed their studies abroad, and friends or relatives in the United States already doing their graduate studies are the main sources of information among students in Turkey who would like to go abroad for further study.

> My friend informs me about the quality of the social science departments in Canada and the US. He also tells me that in order to find a good job in a Turkish university, I should go abroad. So, my first aim is to attend my further education in the US then in Britain or in Canada (24 year-old international relations student in Turkey).

> Firstly, in my department it is more prestigious to study abroad than studying in Turkey. Secondly, it will be a great experience for me both academically and personally; I will have the chance to be informed[as to] how the people in other countries see international relations and the role of Turkey and additionally I will test myself whether I can live abroad or not. Thirdly, it would be a bit easier for me to study in the US because my sister is also there (23 year-old international relations student in Turkey).

The main destination country is the US, whereas four of the respondents mentioned that they would also consider going elsewhere, like Australia, Canada, the UK or Germany. The respondents plan to finance their education through a scholarship from the university they would like to attend and try to get a teacher's assistantship or research assistantship. They all want to return to Turkey after completing their graduate studies and pursue careers in Turkey. Male respondents mentioned that they would look for working opportunities to have the option of short-term military service upon return. One of the respondents mentioned the negative consequences of brain drain and he said he would return to Turkey in any case. Another had expectations that there would be more research possibilities in Turkey within five to ten years.

> I am going to return to Turkey under *any* circumstance. Too many educated individuals from Turkey are settling abroad. For Turkey to develop at the needed rate, no matter how difficult the situation is, the educated people must stay in Turkey (23 year-old political science student).

> We do not have many job opportunities right now, and the ones available are not satisfactory in terms of salary and amount of research funding. But I expect that new research centers in Turkey will be established in 5-10 years. I plan to come back to Turkey as an independent investigator (24 year-old biology and genetics student).

In the cases of students with backgrounds in basic sciences such as biology, chemistry, mathematics and engineering, return to the country of origin after completion of studies abroad are mostly determined by the ability to find related employment and funding for their research. They also said that if they could find a better position abroad, they would stay.

CONCLUSIONS AND POLICY RECOMMENDATIONS

This research sheds light on the debate about brain drain and brain gain. The key question is whether the emigration of skilled people, including graduate students, or the so-called brain drain phenomenon is detrimental to Turkey, and what the costs and benefits are of this process. Lowell (2003) says that two conditions are necessary for the brain drain to occur. First, there must be a significant loss of the highly educated population. Second, adverse economic consequences must follow, as the loss of human capital – acting like financial capital – affects economic growth negatively. The direction of flows might be added as a third condition, as brain drain usually refers to a one-way flow of the highly skilled. Moreover, in order to assess the impact of brain drain and brain gain on any sending country, apart from the selection of emigrants, the net migration rate, long-term effects on economic growth, duration and direction of migration as stated above, there should be certain criteria taken into consideration, like the size (population) and the wealth of the sending country,[75] the diaspora effect (Docquier and Marfouk, 2006), and the pull factors to attract the highly skilled back to the country of origin.

Although it is difficult to assess the brain drain-induced losses caused by skilled migration and the long-term effects of brain drain on economic growth, in line with the criteria given here, we have come to the conclusion that the flow of Turkish highly skilled people to the US should not be seen as a great loss of human capital. First of all, the numbers leaving Turkey are not that high, and therefore do not pose an immediate threat to the country's economic, scientific, social, and cultural development. Describing the loss of skilled workers in both developing and developed countries, Docquier and Marfouk (2006) underline that the "selection rate" or the proportion of skilled emigrants in the total emigration stock from Turkey is rather low, and the brain drain is particularly overestimated in Turkey when compared with the previous study by Carrington and Detragiache (1998).[76] This becomes more evident when one considers the low levels of education among the majority of Turkish immigrants who live mainly in Europe.

---

[75] In countries as big as China and India, although they have the highest number of skilled migrants in the USA, 'brain drain' is not a concern anymore, as they still have a significant share of skilled and educated workers and low emigration rates when compared to the size of the population. But if small countries with less educated labor force and less income levels have high emigration rates, then they are the hardest hit (like Jamaica, Gambia and Ghana) (Commander et al., 2003; see also Docquier and Marfouk, 2006).

[76] Carrington and Detragiache (1998) generalizes that migrants tend to be much better educated than the rest of the population in their country of origin, which does not hold true for the vast majority of Turkish immigrants in Western Europe.

Secondly, most of the highly-skilled establish strong bonds with the country of origin, visiting Turkey at least once a year, teaching Turkish, and passing on the values of Turkish society to their children born in the US. Therefore, the presence of the highly skilled and the emergence of a Turkish diaspora in the US is an asset for Turkey, which could be mobilized both for the benefit of the home country and to foster relations between Turkey and the US.

Iredale and Appleyard state that there are three stages with brain drain: 1) little or no benefit from skilled migrants for the sending country; 2) some benefits accrued from returned skilled people and investments made in the sending country; and, 3) return skilled migration and temporary or permanent return of talent and capital (2001: 5-6). This research confirms that Turkey is now more or less in the second stage, as the face-to-face interviews with the young professionals and pioneer skilled migrants suggest that brain circulation is on the rise with the intensive contacts between the countries of origin and destination. A large number of Turkish origin people in the US are involved in transnational activities, such as information transfer, charity work, and investments. At the same time, there is a certain flow of social and economic remittances. However, if the major determinants of skilled migration remain and get even worse in Turkey, such as differences in living, working, and research conditions, lack of technological resources, and the absence of professional employment opportunities, many Turkish scientists and engineers working and studying in the United States will be more reluctant to circulate, let alone return for good.

In the past, there were either no policies in Turkey dealing with so-called brain drain or some limited policies were put into force. In 2000, however, the Turkish government initiated a task force to prevent brain drain together with experts from YÖK (the Turkish Board of Higher Education), TÜBA (Turkish Academy of Sciences), the Atomic Energy Agency, and the Scientific and Technological Research Council of Turkey (TÜBİTAK) (Tansel and Güngör, 2003: 53). Yet, there are still a number of steps to be taken to prevent brain drain or brain exchange, including technology transfer and increased trade. Therefore, it is high time to come up with short, medium, or long-term policies to tackle with this phenomenon. There are six policy responses to high skilled emigration, which Lowell (2002b) identifies as the six R's. These are return of migrants to their country of origin, restriction of international mobility, recruitment of international migrants, reparation for loss of human capital by taxing, resourcing expatriates and using diaspora options, and retention through educational sector policies as well as by economic development. As stated by Meyer: "Thinking in terms of policy options to monitor and manage highly-skilled mobility has definitely changed, and traditional brain drain/human-capital based approaches (restriction, repatriation, compensation by taxing) are losing ground" (2001: 104). Although mobility of the highly skilled posit challenges for the formation of human capital in a developing country, the increased mobility of skilled people means greater integration in the global markets (Mahroum, 2001: 27). However, instead of imposing restrictions or limiting possibilities, the temporary movement of the highly skilled could be encouraged. It has also become clear that the permanent return of the highly skilled from abroad is no longer effective without providing attractive conditions and infrastructure development. It should also cautiously be noted that returned skilled migrants alone cannot trigger economic, political, and social change on their own, rather what is needed is the sound policies initiated by the governments, international organizations, and non-governmental organizations (Iredale and Appleyard, 2001: 6).

In terms of research and education, it is recommended that Turkey should act immediately upon the need for improvement of the overall research environment in Turkey. There is an urgent need to follow the YÖK example and re-evaluate the scholarships given by MEB to students without any knowledge of English. Most of the time, students on a MEB scholarship complain that they cannot finish their studies within the given period, as they need more time to integrate into the linguistic, social and educational environment of the US.

It is also necessary to build a close scientific collaboration between the US and Turkey. Institutional relationships are very important, and the bilateral agreement between NSF and TÜBİTAK[77] is a good step forward. There are other initiatives run by TÜBİTAK as well: One is the EU-oriented Turkish Research and Business Organizations (TURBO) program located in Brussels; the other ones are the Universal Researcher Program (EVRENA),[78] the Turkish Research Area (TARAL),[79] and the Researcher Information SystemARBIS.[80] Some other recommendations on education and research are listed below:

• Increase the number of scientific research studies carried out with international and intergovernmental organizations, like NATO, UNESCO, WHO, World Bank, and others.

• Facilitate the international movement of scholars and researchers and encourage academic and sectoral cooperation at an international level. Universities in Turkey do not put any restrictions on the academic staff and students who want to go abroad to participate in exchange programs and international conferences, but because of very limited funding especially in state universities, mobility of researchers has been a problem.

• Taking from the US example of Silicon Valley in California, Route 128 near Boston, Massachusetts, and the Research Triangle near North Carolina, encourage the partnership of universities with the private sector.

---

[77] The aim of TÜBİTAK is to increase public awareness for science and technology, increase the number of researchers, and to improve research infrastructure and environment.

[78] The Universal Researcher Program (EVRENA) aims at temporary return of Turkish researchers abroad and to facilitate knowledge exchange and technology transfer.

[79] Turkish Research Area (TARAL) aims corporation in the field of R&D, between universities, public agencies, private sector and NGOS.

[80] Researcher Information System (ARBIS) has been designed as a system for the research personnel in universities, public and private sector establishments in Turkey and the Turkish researchers serving abroad. ARBIS is a dynamic system, which provides for collection of researcher information, updating of collected data and evaluation of said data by different establishments for different purposes.

• Try to attract more skilled labor and foreign students into Turkey from Central Asia and former Soviet Republics to increase brain gain.

• Invest more in quality education in cutting-edge professions, and set up departments/research centers/labs that focus on ICT, nanotechnology, biotechnology, energy, and environmental technologies, etc.

• In order to transfer technology and knowledge from the US to Turkey, it is necessary to develop and invest in the science and technology sector as well as allocating more resources to research and development (R&D). More involvement by industry is needed on R&D. Techno-parks in Middle East Technical University (ODTÜ) and Istanbul Technical University (ITÜ) are good examples to build a strong relation between universities and industry. In Turkey, the percentage of R&D performed by industry was 28.7 percent, by higher education 64.3 percent, and 7 percent by government in 2004 (See Appendix 2.4). Comparatively, the percentage of R&D performed by American industry was 70.1 percent, by higher education 13.6 percent, and 12.2 percent by the government in the same year.[81] As Alarcon rightly states: "Education is a crucial factor in high technology because it is a knowledge-based industry, and R&D is therefore one of its major components" (2000: 308).

• In order to realize a creative environment, there should be tripartite collaboration among universities, the private sector, and the state. The Turkish government agencies should also work closely with the private sector to make available the benefits of new technologies, especially information and communications (Target 18, Goal 8 of the Millennium Development Goals).

• Promote international cooperation aiming at more brain circulation.

Like many developing as well as developed countries in the

---

[81] See OECD's Main Science and Technology Indicators, November 2005 for more details on other OECD member and non-member countries.

world, Turkey must be prepared to address the challenges by the globalisation of the labor market and the increased mobility of its highly skilled nationals. A well-managed skilled migration policy should be developed in Turkey to secure brain gain. By following the Indian example, Turkey can attract R&D and technology transfer in the long run (many Indians who have studied in the United States returned home and establish their own companies with close links to the American firms). Therefore, Turkey should also:

• Address structural problems, like corruption, low wages, unattractive working conditions, etc.

• Provide a sound and favorable economic environment to pave the way for more investments in business, and reduce the major determinants of out-migration for skilled people.

• Try to eliminate frustration associated with doing business with Turkey, and fight vigorously against corruption and further develop an open, rule-based, trustworthy trading and financial system (Target 12 of Goal 8 of the Millennium Development Goals).

• Continue reforms in the labor markets and attract more foreign direct investment (FDI), as FDI will also accelerate reverse brain drain as in the case of China, India, and Korea (See Stalker, 2000: 111-112).

• Wages of highly skilled public employees and those working in the state universities should be bettered.

Another policy approach is to ensure that highly skilled immigrants and temporary migrants stay connected to the country of origin. Therefore, Turkey should also:

• Assist the Turkish-American community in maintaining its cultural identity and strengthening relations with the country of origin. This is especially important in second or third generations, who are much more integrated in the US in social terms and might tend to speak Turkish less frequently.

• Turkey should establish policies to strengthen the involvement of the diaspora in national development processes. As stated in the Millennium Development Goals (Goal # 8),[82] Turkish-origin people can assume even a greater responsibility in the creation of global partnerships for development and create programs of temporary return to work and train professionals in the country of origin to allow more skills and knowledge transfer from the US to Turkey. Although it is not a fundamental solution for the brain drain, using international programs in order to bring back highly skilled persons for a short period will be one of the most effective ways. One of such programs implemented in Turkey as well as other developing countries is called TOKTEN (Transfer of Knowledge through Expatriate Nationals). This program was initiated in 1976 by the United Nations Development Program (UNDP) and the Turkish government and was originally called "Retransfer of Technology to Turkey". The main objective of the project was to supply Turkey with short-term expertise not immediately available in scientific, technological, and socioeconomic fields through high-level expatriate specialists of Turkish origin, and thus contribute to the development of the country in the long-term. The activities of TOKTEN in Turkey have mainly been academic and the assignments vary from one to twelve weeks. The program has been running by a committee composed of representatives of UNDP, TÜBITAK and the State Planning Organization (SPO).

• Mitigate any negative impact on return migration by providing training and capacity-building in Turkey.

• Attract those living in the US into general business and industry and make favorable conditions with lower taxes if they want to send remittances or invest in Turkey.

• Support dialogue and coordination among the highly-skilled

---

82 Goal 8: The aim of developing a global partnership for development needs to take into account the importance of facilitating financial transfer costs for migrant remittances, the liberalization of the movement of people and the importance of transferring skills and knowledge between countries of destination and origin. The potential for development through global diaspora networks and transnationalism should be explored further in for such as regional consultative processes. (IOM, Millennium Development Goals, www.iom.int/DOCUMENTS/PUBLICATION/MRS20.eBOOK.pdf.

Turks living abroad as well and between them and those who work in Turkey.

• Prepare the ground for the prospect of skilled emigrants becoming agents of positive change and development.

Today, as we are living in a more globalized and smaller world, there is an urgent need for Turkey to come up with solid decisions to catch up with the developed nations. This is more apparent after the EU bid of Turkey and the overall desire to be a part of the 'western' world while preserving its own local values. In the future, student flows from Turkey as well as highly skilled migration are likely to increase. If the EU accession process continues without interruption, the flows of students and skilled professionals may chose to go to the EU countries rather than the US. Furthermore, if the economic down-turn in the US persists, and if the job opportunities become scarce for the foreign-born, if the wage differentials between foreign-born and native-born continue to grow, and if the public attitudes towards Islam and Turkey deteriorate in general, then more return migration to Turkey may be expected. In the future, it is more likely that there will be even more selective procedures for the skills of those who want to stay in the US. At the same time, this of course depends heavily on whether Turkey can realize economic and social reforms to attract temporary and permanent highly skilled emigrants back to the country. The success of this challenging task will also encourage more investment from overseas.

There is anecdotal but limited evidence that return migration is on the rise from the US to Turkey.[83] Some scholars (Faini, 2003; Kwok and Leland, 1982) argue that the returnees are usually those with fewer skills and less productivity. Among the whole respondent group, the returnees constitute only a minor part and they returned to the private sector mainly in Istanbul. There is, however, no evidence in this

---

83 See for example Can Dündar's article "Dönüyorlar" (They are Returning) in *Milliyet* on October 3, 2004 or Kaan Okurer's article "Kesin Dönüş or Returning for Good" in *Robert College Quarterly*, Winter 2005.

research suggesting that return migration to Turkey is characterized by negative self-selection. Although it will be difficult to assess the negative selection, more comprehensive research is needed on the returned migrants in different sectors. It will also be interesting to compare Turkish skilled migration to other countries, especially to major Western European countries, like Germany and the UK.

REFERENCES

Acehan, I., 2005, "Outposts of an Empire: Early Turkish Migration to Peabody, Massachusetts", unpublished masters thesis, Ankara: Bilkent University.

Adams, W. (ed.), 1968, *The Brain Drain*, New York: Macmillan.

Ahmed, F., 1993, *Turks in America: The Ottoman Turk's Immigrant Experience*, Greenwich, Connecticut: Columbia International Press.

Alarcon, R., 2000, "Skilled Immigrants and Cerebros: Foreign-Born Engineers and Scientists in the High-Technology Industry of Silicon Valley" in N. Foner, R.G. Rumbaut, and S.J. Gold (eds.), *Immigration Research for a New Century: Multidisciplinary Perspectives*, New York: Russell Sage Foundation.

Alberts, H. C. and H. D. Hazen, 2005, "There Are Always Two Voices...: International Students' Intentions to Stay in the United States or Return to their Home Countries", *International Migration*, 43(3): 131-152.

Balaz, V., A. M. Williams, and D. Kollar, 2004, "Temporary versus Permanent Youth Brain Drain: Economic Implications", *International Migration*, 42(4): 3-29.

Bali, R. N., 2004, *Anadolu'dan Yeni Dünyaya: Amerika'ya İlk Göç Eden Türklerin Yaşam Öyküleri*, Istanbul: İletişim.

Batalova, J., 2005, "College-Educated Foreign Born in the US Labor Force", Washington, DC: Migration Policy Institute, available at (http://www.migrationinformation.org/USFocus/display.cfm?ID=285.html).

—, 2006, "The Growing Connection between Temporary and Permanent Immigration Systems", *Insight*, Washington, DC: Migration Policy Institute, 6(14).

Beine, M., F. Docquier, and H. Rappaport, 2001, "Brain Drain and Economic Growth: Theory and Evidence", *Journal of Development Economics*, 64(1): 275-289.

Benson-Rea, M. and S. Rawlinson, 2003, "Highly Skilled and Business Migrants: Information Processes and Settlement Outcomes", *International Migration*, 41(2): 59-77.

Bhagwati, J. N. and M. Partington, 1976, *Taxing the Brain Drain: A Proposal*, Amsterdam: North-Holland.

Bilge, B., 1994, "Voluntary Associations in the Old Turkish Community of Metropolitan Detroit" in Y. Y. Haddad and J. I. Smith (eds.), *Muslim Communities in North America*, Albany: State University of New York Press.

—, 1996, "Turkish-American Patterns of Intermarriage" in B. C. Aswad and B. Bilge (eds.), *Family and Gender among American Muslims: Issues Facing Middle Eastern Immigrants and their Descendants*, Philadelphia: Temple University Press.

Brandi, M. C., 2001, "Skilled Immigrants in Rome", *International Migration*, 39(4): 101-131.

Carrington, W. J. and E. Detragiache, 1998, "How Big is the Brain Drain?", International Monetary Fund Working Paper, Washington, DC.

Castles, S., 2002, "Migration and Community Formation under Conditions of Globalisation", *International Migration Review*, 36(4): 1143-1168.

Cheng, L. and P. Q. Yang, 1998, "Global Interaction, Global Inequality, and Migration of the Highly Trained to the United States", *International Migration Review*, 32(3): 626-653.

Cordero-Guzman, H. R., 2005, "Community-Based Organizations and Migration in New York City", *Journal of Ethnic and Migration Studies*, 31(5): 889-909.

Culpan, R., 2005, "Turning Brain Drain into Brain Gain: Some Suggestions for Turkey", poster presentation at the First Turkish-American Scientists and Scholars Association Conference in Washington, DC, February 19-20.

Daniels, R., 2002, *Coming to America: A History of Immigration and Ethnicity in American Life*, 2nd edition, New York: Perennial.

DeVoretz, D., 2006, "Global Competition for International Students: The Case of Canada", paper prepared for a meeting on the "International Competition for Science and Engineering Students and Workers", Institute for the Study of International Migration, Georgetown University, Washington, DC, March 30-31.

Diehl, C., 2005, "New Research Challenges Notion of German "Brain Drain", Washington, DC: Migration Policy Institute, available at (http://www.migrationinformation.org/Feature/display.cfm?ID=328.html).

Docquier, F. and A. Marfouk, 2006, "International Migration by Education Attainment, 1990-2000" in Ç. Özden and M. Schiff (eds.), *International Migration, Remittances and the Brain Drain*, New York and Washington, DC: A co-publication of the World Bank and Palgrave Macmillan.

Docquier, F. and H. Rapoport, 2004, "Skilled Migration: The Perspective of Developing Countries", World Bank Policy Research Working Paper Series No.3382.

—, 2005, "Skilled Migration: the Perspective of Developing Countries" (revised version), paper submitted at the Conference on "Skilled Migration Today: Prospects, Problems, Policies" held in New York, March 4-5, 2005.

Dustmann, C., 2003, "Children and Return Migration", *Journal of Population Economics*, 16(4): 815-830.

Ekinci, M. U., 2006, "Reflections of the First Muslim Immigration", *International Journal of Turkish Studies*, 12(1&2): 45-51.

Esen, S. E. 2006, "Policy Recommendation to Manage the Emigration of Highly Skilled Labor in Turkey", ongoing policy analysis exercise to be submitted to the John F. Kennedy School of Government, Harvard University.

Erdoğan, İ., 2003, "Brain Drain and Turkey", *Educational Sciences: Theory and Practice*, 3(1): 96-100.

Faini, R., 2003, "The Brain Drain: An Unmitigated blessing?", available at (www.economia.unimi.it/pubb/sem31.pdf).

Findlay, A. M., 1990, "A Migration Channels Approach to the Study of High-Level Manpower Movements: A Theoretical Perspective", *International Migration*, 28(1): 15-22.

Findlay, A. M. and A. Stam, 2006, "International Student Migration to the UK: Training for the Global Economy or Simply Another Form of Global Talent Recruitment?", paper prepared for a meeting on "International competition for S&E students and workers", Institute for the Study of International Migration, Georgetown University, Washington, DC, 30-31 March.

Fortney, J. A., 1970, "International Migration of Professionals", *Population Studies*, 24(2): 217-237.

Gençer, A. H., 1998, "Turkish Engineers in the US Labor Market: Characteristics, Perspectives and Wages", *Sosyal Bilimler Dergisi*, 3(3).

Gençler, A. and A. Çolak, 2003, "Türkiye'den Yurtdışına Beyin Göçü Ekonomik ve Sosyal Etkileri", available at (www.bilgiyonetimi.org/cm/pages/mkl_gos.php?nt=179).

Gilles, S., 2004, "The Brain Drain: Some Evidence from European Expatriates in the United States", IZA Discussion Paper Series No.1310, Forschungsinstitut zur Zukunft der Arbeit, available at (www.idei.fr/doc/wp/2004/braindrain_abs.pdf).

Gitmez, A. and C. Wilpert, 1987, "A Micro-Society or an Ethnic Community? Social Organization and Ethnicity amongst Turkish Migrants in Berlin" in J. Rex, D. Joly and C. Wilpert (eds.), *Immigrant Associations in Europe*, Aldershot: Gower. Glick Schiller, N. and L. Basch, 1995, "From Immigrant to Transmigrant: Theorizing Transnational Migration", *Anthropological Quarterly*, 68(1): 48-63.

Gökbayrak, Ş., 2006, "The Conditions of Brain Gain Strategies", poster presentation at the Second TASSA Annual Conference, 25-26 March, Drexel University, PA.

Grabowski, J. J., 2005, "Prospects and Challenges: The Study of Early Turkish Immigration to the United States", *Journal of American Ethnic History*, 25(1): 85-100.

Haddad, Y. Y., 2004, *Not Quite American? The Shaping of Arab and Muslim Identity in the United States,* Waco, TX: Baylor University Press.

Halman, T. S., 1980, "Turks" in S. Thernstrom (ed.), *Harvard Encyclopedia of American Ethnic Groups*, Cambridge, MA: The Belknap Press of Harvard University Press.

Iredale, R. R., 1997, *Skills Transfer: International Migration and Accreditation Issues*, Australia: University of Wollongong Press.

—, 2001, "The Migration of Professionals: Theories and Typologies", *International Migration* (Special Issue: International Migration of the Highly Skilled), 39(5): 7-26.

Iredale, R. R. and R. Appleyard, 2001, "Introduction", *International Migration* (Special Issue: International Migration of the Highly Skilled), 39(5): 3-6.

Işığıçok, Ö., 2002, "Türkiye'de Yaşanan Son Ekonomik Krizlerin Sosyo-Ekonomik Sonuçları: Kriz İşsizliği ve Beyin Göçü", available at (www.isguc.org/calhay_beyingocu.php).

Ipek, N. and K. T. Çağlayan, 2006, "The Emigration from the Ottoman Empire to America", *International Journal of Turkish Studies*, 12(1&2): 29-43.

Jachimowicz, M. and D. W. Meyers, 2002, "Temporary High Skilled Migration", Migration Policy Institute, available at (www.migrationinformation. org/ Feature/display.cfm?ID=69).

Karpat, K. H., 1985, "The Ottoman Emigration to America, 1860-1914", *International Journal of Middle East Studies*, 17(2): 175-209.

Karpathakis, A., 1999, "Home Society Politics and Immigrant Political Incorporation: The Case of Greek Immigrants in New York City," *International Migration Review*, 33(1): 55-78.

Kaya, İ., 2003, *Shifting Turkish-American Identity Formations in the United States*, unpublished PhD dissertation submitted to the Florida State University, College of Social Sciences.

Kaya, M., 1999, "Beyin Göçü/Erozyonu", *Popüler Medikal*, available at (www.populermedikal.com/beyingoc.htm).

Khadria, B., 2001, "Shifting Paradigms of Globalisation: The Twenty-first Century Transition towards Generics in Skilled Migration from India", *International Migration*, 39(5): 45-71.

Koser, K. and H. Lutz, 1998, "The New Migration in Europe: Contexts, Constructions and Realities" in K. Koser and H. Lutz (eds.), *The New*

Migration in Europe: Social Constructions and Social Realities, London: Macmillan Press.

Kurtulmuş, N., 1992, "Gelişmekte Olan Ülkeler Açısından Stratejik İnsan Sermayesi Kaybı: Beyin Göçü", *Sosyal Siyaset Konferansları*, 37-38, Istanbul: Istanbul Üniversitesi Yayın No.3662.

Kurtuluş, B., 1999, *Amerika Birleşik Devletleri'ne Türk Beyin Göçü*, Istanbul: Alfa.

Kwok, V. and H. Leland, 1982, "An Economic Model of the Brain Drain", *The American Economic Review*, 72(1): 91-100.

Levitt, P., 1996, "Social Remittances: A Conceptual Tool for Understanding Migration for Development", Working Paper No.96.04, Cambridge: Harvard Center for Population and Development Studies.

—, 2003, "You Know, Abraham Was Really the First Immigrant: Religion and Transnational Migration", *International Migration Review* (Special Issue: Transnational Migration, International Perspectives), 37(3): 847-873.

Lowell, L. B., 2001, "The Foreign Temporary Workforce and Shortages in Information Technology" in W. A. Cornelius et al. (eds.), *The International Migration of the Highly Skilled: Demand, Supply, and Development Consequences in Sending and Receiving Countries*, San Diego: Center for Comparative Immigration Studies, University of California Press.

—, 2002a, "Some Developmental Effects of the International Migration of Highly Skilled Persons", ILO International Migration Papers No.46, Geneva: ILO.

—, 2002b, "Policy Responses to the International Mobility of Skilled Labor", International Migration Papers No.45, Geneva: ILO, also available at (www.ilo.org/public/english/protection/migrant/download/imp/imp45.pdf).

—, 2003, "Skilled Migration Abroad or Human Capital Flight?", Migration Policy Institute, available at (www.migrationinformation.org/Feature/display.cfm?ID=135).

—, 2005, "Declining Numbers of Foreign Students and America's Science and Engineering Enterprise", *International Migration*, 43(3): 155-160.

Lowell, L. B., A. Findlay and E. Stewart, 2004, "Brain Strain: Optimizing Highly Skilled Migration from Developing Countries", Asylum and Migration Working Paper No.3, London: Institute for Public Policy Research.

Mahroum, S., 2001, "Europe and the Immigration of Highly Skilled Labor", *International Migration* (Special Issue: International Migration of the Highly Skilled), 39(5): 27-43.

Martin, P. and C. Kuptsch, 2006, "Foreign S&E Students in France and Germany", paper prepared for a meeting on "International competition for S&E students and workers", Institute for the Study of International Migration, Georgetown University, Washington, DC, 30-31 March.

Martin, S., 2006, "US Employment-Based Admissions: Permanent and Temporary", policy brief, Washington, DC: Migration Policy Institute.

Mattoo, A., I. C. Neagu and Ç. Özden, 2005, "Brain Waste? Educated Immigrants in the US Labor Market", World Bank Policy Research Working Paper No.3581.

McCarthy, J., 2001, *The Ottoman Peoples and the End of the Empire*, New York: Oxford.

Meyer, J. B., 2001, "Network Approach versus Brain-Drain: Lessons from the Diaspora", *International Migration* (Special Issue: International Migration of the Highly Skilled), 39(5): 91-110.

Miano, J., 2005, "The Bottom of the Pay Scale: Wages for H-1B Computer Programmers", Center for Immigration Studies, available at (www.cis.org/articles/2005/back1305.html).

Micallef, R., 2004, "Turkish-Americans: Performing Identities in a Transnational Setting", *Journal of Muslim Minority Affairs*, 24(2): 233-241.

Miyagiwa, K., 1991, "Scale Economies in Education and the Brain Drain Problem", *International Economic Review*, 32(3): 743-759.

Moya, J. C., 2005, "Immigrants and Associations: A Global and Historical Perspective", *Journal of Ethnic and Migration Studies*, 31(5): 833-864.

National Academies, 2005, *Policy Implications of International Graduate Students and Postdoctoral Scholars in the United States*, Washington, DC: The National Academies Press.

Oğuzkan, T., 1975, "The Turkish Brain Drain: Migration of Tendencies among Doctoral Level Manpower" in R. E. Krane (ed.), *Manpower Mobility across Cultural Boundaries: Social, Economic and Legal Aspects, the Case of Turkey and West Germany*, Leiden, Netherlands: E.J. Brill.

—, 1976, "The Scope and Nature of Turkish Brain Drain" in N. Abadan-Unat (ed.), *Turkish Workers in Europe, 1960-1975: A Socio-Economic Reappraisal*, Leiden: E.J. Brill.

Peixoto, J., 2001, "Migration and Policies in the European Union: Highly Skilled Mobility, Free Movement of Labor and Recognition of Diplomas", *International Migration*, 39(1): 33-61.

Pellegrino, A., 2001, "Trends in Latin American Skilled Migration: "Brain Drain" or "Brain Exchange?", *International Migration* (Special Issue: International Migration of the Highly Skilled), 39(5): 111-132.

Phizacklea, A., 2004, "Migration Theory and Migratory Realities: a Gendered Perspective?" in D. Joly (ed.), *International Migration in the New Millennium: Global Movement and Settlement*, Aldershot: Ashgate.

Portes, A., 1976, "Determinants of the Brain Drain", *International Migration Review*, 10(4): 489-508.

Portes, A. et al., 1999, "The Study of Transnational Communities: Pitfalls and Promise of an Emergent Field", *Ethnic and Racial Studies*, 22(2): 217-237.

Portes, A. and R. G. Rumbaut, 1990, *Immigrant America: A Portrait*, Berkeley: University of California Press.

Poyrazlı, Ş. et al., 2001, "Adjustment Issues of Turkish College Students Studying in the United States", *College Student Journal*, 35(1): 52-63.

Pultar, G., 2000, "Shadows of Cultural Identity: Issues of Biculturalism Rised by the Turkish-American Poetry of Talat Sait Halman" in R. Hsu et al. (eds.), *Replacing America: Conversations and Contestations*, Honolulu: University of Hawaii and the East-West Center.

Rosenblum, M., 2001, "High Skilled Immigration and the US National Interest" in W. A. Cornelius et al. (eds.), *The International Migration of the Highly Skilled: Demand, Supply, and Development Consequences in Sending and Receiving Countries*, San Diego: Center for Comparative Immigration Studies, University of California Press.

Quaked, S., 2002, "Transatlantic Roundtable on High-skilled Migration and Sending Countries Issues", *International Migration*, 40(4): 153-166.

Reimers, D. M., 2005, *Other Immigrants: The Global Origins of the American People*, New York: New York University Press.

Richmond, A. H., 2005, "Globalisation: Implications for Immigrants and Refugees" in K. Slany (ed.), *International Migration: A Multidimensional Analysis*, Cracow: AGH University of Science and Technology Press.

Rudolph, H. and F. Hillmann, 1998, "The Invisible Hand Needs Visible Heads: Managers, Experts, and Professionals from Western Countries in Poland" in K. Koser and H. Lutz (eds.), *The New Migration in Europe: Social Constructions and Social Realities*, London: Macmillan Press.

Rumbaut, R., 1997, "Assimilation and Its Discontents: Between Rhetoric and Reality", *International Migration Review*, 31(4): 923-960.

Salt, J., 1992, "Migration Process among the Highly-Skilled in Europe," *International Migration Review*, 26(2): 484-505.

—, 1997, "International Movements of the Highly Skilled", OECD Occasional Paper No.3, International Migration Unit.

Schiff, M., 2006, "Brain Gain: Claims about Its Size and Impact on Welfare and Growth are Greatly Exaggerated" in Ç. Özden and M. Schiff (eds.), *International Migration, Remittances and the Brain Drain,* New York and Washington, DC: A copublication of the World Bank and Palgrave Macmillan.

Schmidt, G., 1999, *American Medina: A Study of the Sunni Muslim Immigrant Communities in Chicago*, Lund, Sweden: University of Lund, Department of History of Religions, vol.8.

Schrover, M., and F. Vermeulen, 2005, "Immigrant Organizations", *Journal of*

Ethnic and Migration Studies, 31(5): 823-832.

Smith, M. P. and L. E. Guarnizo (eds.), 1998, *Transnationalism From Below*, New Jersey: Transaction Publishers.

Sonn, T., 1994, "Diversity in Rochester's Islamic Community" in Y. Y. Haddad and J. I. Smith (eds.), *Muslim Communities in North America*, Albany: State University of New York Press.

Stalker, P., 2000, *Workers without Frontiers: The Impact of Globalisation on International Migration*, Colorado: Lynne Rienner Publishers.

Straubhaar, T. and M. R. Wolburg, 1999, "Brain Drain and Brain Gain in Europe: An Evaluation of the East European Migration to Germany", *Jahrbücher für Nationalokonomie und Statistik*, 218(5/6): 574-604.

Tanner, A., 2005, *Emigration, Brain Drain and Development: The Case of Sub-Saharan Africa*, Helsinki, Finland: East-West Books and Washington, DC: Migration Policy Institute.

Tansel, A. and N. D. Güngör, 2003, "Brain Drain from Turkey: Survey Evidence of Student Non-Return", *Career Development International*, 8(2): 52-69, available at (http://www.yogm.meb.tr/BrainDrain.htm).

Turner, R. B., 2003, *Islam in the African-American Experience*, 2nd edition, Bloomington: Indiana University Press.

US Citizen and Immigration Services (USCIS), 2005, "Allocation of Additional H-1B visas Created by the H-1B Reform Act of 2004", *Federal Register* 20 No.86, Washington, DC: Department of Homeland Security.

Usdansky, M. L. and T. J. Espenshade, 2001, "The Evolution of US Policy toward Employment-Based Immigrants and Temporary Workers: The H-1B Debate in Historical Perspective" in W. A. Cornelius et al. (eds.), *The International Migration of the Highly Skilled: Demand, Supply, and Development Consequences in Sending and Receiving Countries*, San Diego: Center for Comparative Immigration Studies, University of California Press.

Vermeulen, F., 2005, "Organizational Patterns: Surinamese and Turkish Associations in Amsterdam, 1960-1990", *Journal of Ethnic and Migration Studies*, 31(5): 951-973.

Weiner, M., 1995, *The Global Migration Crisis: Challenge to States and to Human Rights*, New York: Harper Collins College Publishers.

Williams, A. M. and V. Balaz, 2005, "What Human Capital, Which Migrants? Returned Skilled Migration to Slovakia from the UK", *International Migration Review*, 39(2): 439-468.

Xiang, B., 2001, "Structuration of Indian Information Technology Professionals' Migration to Australia: An Ethnographic Study", *International Migration* (Special Issue: International Migration of the Highly Skilled), 39(5): 73-90.

Appendices

Formal associations
- American Turkish Society (ATS) (www.americanturkishsociety.org)
- Turkish-American Business Forum (FORUM) (www.forum.org)
- Federation of Turkish-American Associations (FTAA) (www.ftaa.org)
- Assembly of Turkish-American Associations (ATAA) (www.ataa.org)
- American Turkish Council (ATC) in Washington, DC (www.americanturkishcouncil.org)
- Ataturk Society of America (ASA) in Washington, DC (www.ataturksociety.org)
- Institute of Turkish Studies (ITS) at Georgetown University
- Turkish-American Scientists and Scholars Association (TASSA) (www.tassausa.org)
- Ari Foundation (www.ari-us.org)
- Turkish Industrialists' and Businessmen's Association (TÜSİAD) USA (www.tusiad-us.org)
- Turkish-US Business Council of DEIK in Washington, DC (www.deik.org.tr)
- Turkish-Americans for Informed Policy (TAFIP) (www.tafip.org)

Other Associations and NGOs working on Development Projects, Education and Arts
- Bridges of Hope Project (www.bridgesofhopeproject.org)
- Friends of Anatolia (www.friendsofanatolia.org)
- Turkish Fine Arts Ensemble
- Anatolian Artisans (www.anatolianartisans.org)
- Turkish Children Foster Care (TCFC) (www.turkishchildren.org)
- Turkish Folk Dance Troupe (www.turkfolkdc.org)
- Moon and Stars Project (www.moonandstarsproject.org)
- Bosphorus Art Project (www.bosphorusartproject.org)
- HasNa (www.hasna.org)

Youth/student/alumni associations
- Intercollegiate Turkish Student Society (ITTS) (www.itts.org)
- Turkish-American Youth Association

- Assembly of Turkish Student Associations in Washington, DC (www.atsadc.org)
- Istanbul Technical University Alumni Association Intl, Inc. (www.itumuk.com).
- Middle East Technical University Alumni Association
- Boğaziçi University Alumni Association
- Robert College Alumni Association
- Istanbul University Alumni Association of USA (www.iumezusa.org)

Local cultural associations
- Turkish-American Cultural Association of Alabama (TACA-AL)
- Turkish-American Association of Arizona (TAA-AZ) (website: www.taaaz.org).
- Turkish-American Cultural Association of Southern New England (TACA-SNE)
- Turkish-American Cultural Society of Colorado (TASCO) (www.tacsso.org).
- Turkish-American Association of Southern California (ATA-SC) (www.atasc.org).
- Turkish-American Association of California (TAAC) (www.taaca.org).
- Florida Turkish-American Association (FTAA)
- Turkish-American Cultural Association of Florida (TACAF) (www.tacaf.org)
- Turkish-American Cultural Association of Georgia (TACA – GA) (www.tacaga.org)
- Turkish-American Society of Georgia
- Turkish-American Friendship Association of Hawaii (TAFA – HI)
- Turkish-American Cultural Association (TACA – Chicago) (www.tacaonline.org)
- Turkish-American Association of Greater Kansas City (www.taako.org)
- Turkish-American Association of Louisiana (TAAL)
- Turkish-American Cultural Society of New England (TACS – NE) (www.tacsne.org)
- Maryland American Turkish Association (MATA) (www.atamd.org)
- Turkish-American Cultural Association of Michigan (TACAM) (www.tacam.org)
- Turkish-American Association of Minnesota (TAAM) (www.taam.org)
- Turkish-American Cultural Alliance of St. Louis (TACA – St. Louis) (www.tacastl.org)
- American Turkish Association of North Carolina (ATA – NC) (www.ata-nc.org)
- Turkish-American Association of New Jersey (Turk Ocagi)
- Turkish-American Community Center in New Jersey (www.taccusa.com)
- Turkish Society of Rochester (TSR) (www.tsor.org)
- Syracuse Turkish Association
- Anadolu Club (www.anadoluclub.org)
- Young Turks Cultural Aid Society in New Jersey (www.youngturks.org)
- Young Turks of America Cultural Aid Society in NYC
- Turkish-American Association of Central Ohio (TAACO) (www.taaco.org)

- Turkish-American Society of Northeastern Ohio (TASNO)
- Turkish-American Association in Ohio
- Turkish-American Association of Oklahoma (TAA – OK)
- Pittsburgh Turkish-American Association (PTAA) (www.ptaa.org)
- Turkish-American Friendship Society of the United States (TAFSUS) (www.tafsus.org)
- American Turkish Association of Houston – (ATA – Houston) (www.atahouston.org)
- Turkish-American Association of Northern Texas (TURANT) (www.turant.org)
- Turkish-American Cultural Association of Washington (TACAWA) (www.tacawa.org)
- American Turkish Association of Washington DC (ATA-DC) (www.atadc.org)
- Turkish-American Association of Milwaukee (TAAM)
- American Turkish Association of Milwaukee in Wisconsin
- Turkish-American Association for Cultural Exchange (www.taace.org)
- Turkish-American Cultural Association of Long Island (TACA – LI) (www.tacali.org)
- Turkish-American Cultural Alliance of Chicago (www.tacaonline.org)
- Turkish Cultural Foundation (www.turkishculture.org)
- Orange County Turkish-American Association (OCTAA)
- American Turkish Association of San Diego (ATA – SD)
- Turkish-American Association of San Antonio (www.taa-sa.org)
- Istanbul Sports, Cultural and Educational Association (www.istanbulspor.net)
- American Turkish Friendship Association (ATFA) (www.atfa.us)
- Turkish Hars Society
- Maryland Turkish Inhabitants (MARTI) (www.themarti.org)
- International Turkish Society Federation (ITSF)
- American Turkish Veterans Association (ATVA) (www.atvets.org)
- Turkish-American Alliance for Fairness (TAAF) (www.taaf-org.net)
- Hudson Turkish-American Cultural Association (HUTACA) (www.hutaca.org)

Religious Organizations
- Connecticut Turkish Islamic Cultural Association (Mevlana Camii Connecticut Turk-Islam Kültür Derneği)
- Delaware Valley Muslim Associations – Selimiye Mosque
- American Turkish Islamic and Cultural Center in Forest Hills, NY
- United American Muslim Association in Brooklyn, NYC (www.fatihcami.org)
- Turkish-American Eyüp Sultan Islamic Center in Brooklyn, NYC
- Turkish-American Muslims Cultural Association in Levittown, PA (TAMCA)
- Turkish-American Islamic Foundation in Lanham, MD

Professional associations
- Turkish-American Physicians Association (TAPA)
- Turkish-American Medical Association (TAMA)
- Association of Turkish-American Scientists (ATAS) (www.atas.org)
- Turkish-American Neuropsychiatric Association (TANPA)
- Turkish-American Chamber of Commerce, Industry and Maritime (TACCIM) (www.taccim.org)
- ITKIP Association USA (Istanbul Textile and Apparels' Exporters' Association in NY) (www.itkibusa.org)
- The Society of Turkish-American Architects, Engineers, and Scientists (MIM)
- (www.m-i-m.org)
- Turkish-American Physicians Association
- Turkish-American Chamber of Commerce (TACCOM) (www.taccom.org)
- Turkish-American Chamber of Commerce and Industry (TACCI) (www.turkishuschamber.org)
- American Association of Teachers of Turkic Languages (AATT) (www.princeton.edu/~turkish/aatt)

Women's groups
- Florida Turkish-American Association, Women's Club
- Washington Turkish Women's Association (WTWA)
- Turkish Women's League of America (TWLA)
- Boston Anneleri (www.angelfire.com/ab7/bostonanneleri)
- Daughters of Ataturk (www.DofA.org)
- Turkish-American Women Scholarship Fund (TAWSF) (www.tawsf.org)
- Turkish-American Ladies League (TALL)

Turkic Associations
- Azerbaijan Society of America (www.usa.azeris.org)
- Karacay Turks Mosque and Cultural Association
- Solidarity of Balkan Turks of America
- US Council for Human Rights in the Balkans, Inc.
- Turkestanian American Association
- Uyghur American Association
- Kazak-Tatar Association
- Turkish Cypriot Cultural and Educational Association in New Jersey
- Turkish Cypriot Aid Society
- Association of Balkan Turks of America (Brooklyn, NYC)
- American Association of Crimean Turks (Brooklyn, NYC)
- The Melungeon Heritage Association in Virginia (www.melungeon.org)

Turkish-American Media Organizations, Newspapers, Periodicals and Internet Portals

- The Turkish Times (ATAA's newspaper published bi-weekly in English)
- USA Turkish Times (first weekly Turkish newspaper in the USA)
- Zaman America
- Hürriyet America (www.hurriyetusa.org)
- Turk of America (www.turkofamerica.com)
- Mezun Life (monthly magazine from mezun.com)
- Turkuaz Magazine (www.turkuaz.us)
- The Turkish-American (quarterly magazine of ATAA)
  (www.ataa.org/magazine/tta_summer05/pdf).
- Voice of Ataturk
- Turkish Hour (weekly Turkish TV show) (www.turkishamericanhour.org)
- Bonbon (monthly magazine for Turkish-American children)
  (www.bonbonkids.com)
- Mezun (www.mezunusa.com)
- Tulumba (www.tulumba.com)
- Laz Bakkal (www.LazBakkal.com) (online Turkish superstore)
- Taste of Turkey (www.tasteofturkey.com) (online Turkish superstore)
- Turk North America (www.turknorthamerica.com)

Turkish Radio and TV Broadcasts in the US.

Weekly radio programs in Turkish broadcasted in NYC, Chicago and Boston between 1950 and 1980, weekly one-hour TV program "Turkish Hour" was aired between 1975 and 1980. On September 2005, a new half-hour TV show called Turkish-American Hour started airing at the Fairfax Public Access Channel in Northern Virginia. All-volunteer production team's mission is to inform the Greater Washington DC community about events and activities related to Turkish-American life, art, and culture. Currently, the programs are aired on Channel 10, Cox Cable of Fairfax County, Virginia. Turkish-American Hour is making arrangements to show its programs at Montgomery Community Television, Arlington Independent Media, Community Television of Prince George's County, and Public Access Corporation of the District of Columbia. (The link below provides a question and answer session with an Immigration Attorney broadcasted on the Turkish-American Hour:
   www.turkishamericanhour.org/e107_plugins/content/content.php?content.16).

Local Television Broadcasts and Cable Video Channels

- Voice of Anatolia TV – WNYE Channel 25, Sundays at 3: 30 PM to 4PM (Can be received off the air in the NYC metropolitan area, also everyday from 7: 30 to 8 PM on cable Channel 57 in some NYC boroughs).

- ATV News – *SCOLA* channel cable TV, Monday-Friday 11 to 12 AM EDT, Saturdays 7 to 8 PM EDT (taped).
- Turkish Hour – Broadcasted three times a week on Cultural Cable Channel, Ch. 50 on Cox Cable in New Orleans, Louisiana.
- Turkish Hour – Broadcasted on Channels 7 & 10 on Warner Cable System, Cincinnati, OH. Sponsored by Tri-State Turkish-American Association.
- Voice of Turkey – Broadcasted twice a week on ICAT Channel 15 (Cable) in Rochester, NY.

FM and AM Band Local Broadcasts
- Voice of Anatolia Radio – Mondays 10 to 11 PM (Can be heard in the NYC metropolitan area.)
- The Turkish Voice – Mondays 8 to 8: 30 PM (Can be heard in the NYC metropolitan area).
- Rutgers University Radio – Sundays at noon to 1 PM. (Can be heard in a 30-mile radius around *New Brunswick, NJ*).
- Turkish Voice – Tuesdays at 9: 30 to 10: 30 PM. (Can be heard in the NYC metropolitan area).
- Turkish Cultural Hour – KUSF FM 90.3 MHz, Saturdays at 5 to 7 PM. (Can be heard in the Northern San Francisco Bay Area).
- Turkish Music Hour – Saturdays at 1 to 3 PM. (Can be heard in the *Southwestern Virginia Area*).
- Turkish Rainbow – Saturdays at 11: 30 AM to 1 PM. Music and special programs (Can be listened in a 50 mile radius of Troy, NY, including Albany, Schenectady, and small towns in MA and VT near the NY state border).
- Orient Express – 3rd Saturday of each month at 6 PM to 9 PM (Can be heard in the Southern San Francisco Bay Area, Monterey and Santa Cruz).
- The Turkish Delight Radio Show – Sundays at 10 to 11 AM by The Campus Broadcasting Network of The University of Michigan.
- Turkish Hour – (www.tsor.org/radio.html). Sundays, 11:00 a.m. to noon in *Rochester, NY*.

Short-Wave Broadcasts
Türkiye'nin Sesi (Voice of Turkey) broadcasted in English and in Turkish

APPENDIX 2.2
QUESTIONNAIRE

Background Information
1. Name and current e-mail:
2. Telephone number:
3. Age:
4. Gender:
5. Date and Place of Birth (city/town/village):
6. Marital Status/nationality or ethnic origin of partner:
7. Social and economic status:
8. Children:
9. Professions of Parents:
10. Job and Department he/she is currently working:
11. Education (universities attended and the diplomas received):
12. Visa Type/Nationality:
13. Whether she/he has obtained green card or become a US citizen? Why?
14. For how long you have stayed in the US altogether? In which cities? Specify. Why did you change places?

Education in the States
15. When/Where did you go abroad for further education after graduation? Which state?
16. Why did you choose that university?
17. Did you get information about the country/department prior to further study?
18. What were the main reasons that led you seek further education or job abroad?
19. Why did you choose US and not any other country?
20. How did you plan to finance education abroad? (If through YÖK and other state funds, did he/she return to Turkey for compulsory service?)
21. What were the main problems for you while studying/living abroad?
22. What were the nationalities of your friends at the university/outside the university/at the workplace?
23. Compare the universities in Turkey and in the States.

Living Conditions and Social Life
24. When you were a student/younger, how often did you have contacts with Turkey? (via telephone, e-mail, letters, visits, etc.).
25. What about after graduation/retirement?
26. How often do you visit Turkey?

27. When you were a student, how often did you read Turkish newspapers and magazines? Which ones?
28. What about after graduation?
29. How would you describe ties among the Turkish community in the places where you have lived in the US?
30. How strong are your ties at the moment with the Turkish community?
31. Are you a member of any Turkish-American associations? Which ones?
32. Do you have small circle of Turkish friends? Where did you meet them? For how long you have come to know each other? How often do you see them?
33. When you first arrived in the US for study or for work, what were your initial plans? What made you come to that decision?
34. Why did you choose to stay in the US?
35. Towards the end of your study, did you see yourself temporary or permanent in the US? What about now? When did you start to see yourself permanent in the US?
36. To what extend do you think students and graduates who have started working in the US know about the job prospects in Turkey?
37. Compare the job opportunities in Turkey and abroad.
38. Do you have relatives/close friends/Turkish colleagues living abroad? If so, in which country/state?
39. Would your familial and close relationships affect your return/non-return? If so, how?
40. While working abroad, did you rather make investments in Turkey or in the US? What kind of investments?
41. Do you send remittances to Turkey? Do you invest here and/or in Turkey?
42. Do you feel that your place of belonging is Turkey or the US? Why? Do you also feel accepted and welcome in the US?
43. How do you achieve contact with the dominant culture? How would you describe your relations with Americans?
44. What are main differences between American and Turkish society?
45. What do your family and children feel about their place of belonging? Do you see any generational differences?
46. Do you feel that you are exposed to "brain drain"? What should be done to reverse the tide and make it "brain gain"?

Future Plans
47. What are your plans in the future? Any plans to return to Turkey/to change your job? Why?
48. (When applicable) Why would you consider staying abroad?

49. Have you noticed/witnessed any changes in the job market in the US after 9/11? What kind of implications does this have on your career?
50. Under what circumstances would you return to Turkey for good?
51. What do you think about the prospective job opportunities in your field in Turkey?
52. Have you ever considered returning to Turkey for short-term? If you have done it before, were you satisfied with the work conditions in Turkey?
53. Do you believe that Turkey would be a EU member state eventually? What are differences in Turkey's economic, social and political conditions now and when you just left Turkey?
54. If Turkey is successful to create favorable economic conditions in line with the harmonization process with the EU, will it affect your position to homeland and choose to return home?

APPENDIX 2.3

TABLE 2.22: Nonimmigrant Visa Reference Chart

A-1	Diplomatic personnel, including ambassadors, public ministers, career diplomatic officers or consular officers, and members of their immediate families.
A-2	Other foreign government officials or employees, and spouses and children.
A-3	Personal employees, attendants and servants of A-1 and A-2.
B-1	Temporary business visitors
B-2	Temporary visitors for pleasure
C-1	Aliens in transit through the U.S. to a third country
D	Crewmen of aircraft or sea vessels
E-1	Those creating substantial trade between the U.S. and a country with which the U.S. maintains an appropriate treaty, and members of their immediate families.
E-2	Those who have invested a substantial amount of capital to develop and direct the operation of an enterprise in the U.S. and members of their immediate families.
F-1	Students pursing academic courses of study
F-2	Spouse and minor children of F-1
G-1 to G-5	Representatives of international organizations like the United Nations and the World Bank, their family, staff and servants
H-1A	Registered nurses
H-1B	Workers in specialty occupations. Initial admission for 3 years (renewable once and with the possibility of changing status)
H-1B exempt	Workers in specialty occupations who are not subject to the U.S. government's cap on H-1B workers. This includes employees of higher education institutions and non-profit and government research organizations.
H-2A	Agricultural temporary workers
H-2B	Non-agricultural temporary workers
H-3	Temporary industrial trainees, special education
H-4	Spouse and minor children of H-1, H-2 and H-3 visa holders
I	Representatives of foreign information media, and their family
J-1	Exchange visitors (this visa requires a 2-year return to the country of origin before applying for another type of visa).
J-2	Spouse and minor children of J-1 visa holders.
K-1	Alien fiancé or fiancé of U.S. citizen and minor children.

K-2	Children of fiancés (ees) of U.S. citizens.
K-3	Alien spouse of U.S. citizen.
K-4	Alien child of U.S. citizen.
L-1	Temporary intra-company transferees.
L-2	Spouse and minor children of L-1 visa holder.
M-1	Students enrolled in vocational educational programs.
M-2	Spouse and minor children of M-1 visa holders
N-1 to N-7	NATO visa holders
O-1	Those with extraordinary ability in the sciences, arts, education, business, or athletics, or with a record of extraordinary achievement in television or motion pictures. Initial admission up to 10 years with the possibility of changing status.
O-2	Those who accompany or assist an O-1 visa holder
O-3	Spouse and children of O-1 and O-2.
P-1	Members of entertainment groups, individual athletes, and members of athletic teams.
P-2	Entertainers who are a part of reciprocal international exchanges.
P-3	Performers in culturally unique programs.
P-4	Spouses and children of P-1, P-2, and P-3 visa holders.
Q	Participants in an international cultural exchange program in the U.S.
R-1	Religious workers coming to the U.S. temporarily.
R-2	Spouse and minor children of religious workers.
T-1 to T-4	Victims of severe form of trafficking (and spouses, children, and parents).
U-1 to U-4	Aliens suffering physical and mental abuse (and spouses, children, and parents).
V-1 to V-3	Spouse or child of a lawful permanent resident who has been waiting three years or more for an immigrant visa (and dependent children).

APPENDIX 2.4

FIGURE 2.17: R&D expenditures as a percentage of GDP

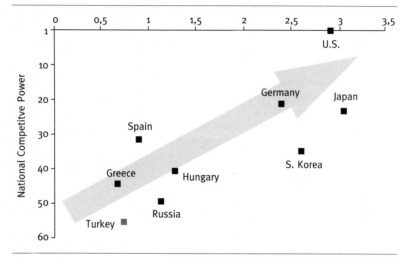

Source: TÜBİTAK.

TABLE 2.23: Science and Technology Indicators in Turkey and in the US

Researchers per 1,000,000 inhabitants in TR	345
Expenditure on R&D as a % of GDP	0.7
Researchers per 1,000,000 inhabitants in the US	4,526
Expenditure on R&D as a % of GDP	2.7

Source: UNESCO, Institute for Statistics, www.uis.unesco.org/profiles/selectCountry_en.aspx

APPENDIX 2.5
ABBREVIATIONS

ATAA	Assembly of Turkish-American Associations
DEİK	Dış Ekonomik İlişkiler Kurulu (in Turkish) Foreign Economic Relations Board
FTAA	Federation of Turkish-American Associations
IIE	Institute of International Education
IL	Illinois
INS	Immigration and Naturalization Service
IT	Information Technology
MA	Massachusetts
MEB	Turkish Ministry of National Education
MI	Michigan
MPI	Migration Policy Institute
NAFSA	Association of International Educators
NSF	(US) National Science Foundation
NYC	New York City
OECD	Organization for Economic Cooperation and Development
OIC	Organization of Islamic Conference
R&D	Research and Development
S&E	Science and Engineering
SEVIS	Student and Exchange Visitor Information System
SPO	State Planning Organization (or DPT in Turkish)
TASSA	Turkish-American Scientists and Scholars' Association
TOKTEN	Transfer of Knowledge Through Expatriate Nationals
TÜBA	Turkish Academy of Sciences
TÜBİTAK	Scientific and Technical Research Council of Turkey
TÜSİAD	Turkish Industrialists' and Businessmen's Association
UNDP	United Nations Development Program
UNESCO	United Nations Educational, Scientific and Cultural Organization
US	United States
USA	United States of America
USD	US dollars
WWI	First World War
WWII	Second World War
YÖK	Turkish Higher Board of Education

3

World City Berlin and the Spectacles of Identity: Public Events, Immigrants and the Politics of Performance

LEVENT SOYSAL

INTRODUCTION

This research is part of a larger project I have been carrying out in Berlin. The larger research expands on my dissertation work and prior research in Berlin, where I have been conducting fieldwork since 1990. The project concerns the changing meaning and constitution of public events and the politics and performance of identity in the contemporary metropolitan centers of Europe, in particular in Berlin. It is an attempt to map and gather an inventory of the changing landscape of culture in what I designate as the newly emerging WorldCities.

By public events, I mean formally organized cultural, social, and political activities which aim to facilitate formations of community and solidarity and to expedite participation in local, national, and transnational social spaces. The events I include under this rather broad definition range from political meetings and rallies to concerts and festivals, and from panels and workshops to international conferences and fairs. Large and small, these events constitute the cultural fabric of the city and provide the metropolis with an aura of cultural creativity and finesse. Moreover, with the intensification of media

attention and the global explosion of travel, public events, particular-
ly those that realize dimensions of grandeur, have become indispens-
able and identifying features of the contemporary metropolitan order.
I have launched this project during my tenure in Berlin as a Research
Fellow at the Berlin Program for Advanced German and European
Studies, Free University in the academic years 2001-2003.

The research site I have chosen for the project, the city of Berlin,
is a self-designated multicultural "Open City", exhibiting a myriad of
public events and the home to the largest immigrant population in
Germany. Among the multitude of public events staged annually in
Berlin, for instance, certain mega events capture the public imagination: the Love Parade (the largest public parade in Europe, recently
moved to Essen, Germany), the Christopher Street Day Parade (one of
the most important gay celebrations in Europe), the May Day Parade
(an annual demonstration of multi-ethnic worker solidarity), and the
Carnival of Cultures (a multicultural display of diversity). Migrants in
Berlin are especially visible as participants and audiences of the mega
events that characterize the cultural scenery of Berlin's urban landscape – though the degree of their participation significantly varies
from one event to another. While the Love Parade hardly attracts the
attention of the immigrant youth of Berlin, the May Day Parade and
the Carnival of Cultures are unthinkable without large contingents of
immigrant performers and participants, and the Christopher Street
Day Parade provides a forum for the increasing presence of gay immigrants in the public spaces of Berlin. In 2002, at the 40th anniversary
of Turkish immigration to Germany, Berlin had its first "Annual
Turkish Day" parade, gathering close to 50,000 participants from all
corners of Germany.

Is organizing Turkish Day in Berlin a sign of displacement and
dislocation, and a marker of nostalgic orientation to homes elsewhere?
Or does it implicate salient movements between Turkey and Germany,
places of origin and destination, and the margins and the core of
Europe? What do public festivals, May Day and the Carnival of

Cultures, for instance, reveal about the relation of immigrants to Berlin and the degree of their participation in the economies and social and cultural life of the city? What are the cultural properties and confines of the public displays of identity and diversity? What is the significance of the new styles of performance and diversity for our understandings of and engagements in public life? How do undercurrents of Europeanization, national configurations of culture, and the transnational connections of immigrants figure into the project of making Berlin once again a cosmopolitan metropolis?

This research seeks to delineate the consequential affinities between public events, identity, and metropolis, and to locate the contemporary transformations in public performance and civic participation within a framework, which exposes Berlin's cultural connections to transnational social spaces emerging within and without Europe. Concurrently, through the investigation of the modes of immigrant participation in public events, the research aims to disclose the elaborate connections that are emerging between the social and cultural spaces of host and home countries.

LITERATURE REVIEW

In the following I provide brief and selective accounts of:

(1) A history of Turkish migration to Europe, with specific references to Germany,

(2) Three major turns in scholarly narratives, public opinion, and policy with respect to European immigration, specifically labor, culture, and transnationalism,

(3) The "integration question," specifically as it pertains to the perceptions of Islam and women—thus culture and tradition, and

(4) Finally, an assessment of the current standing of immigrants as "symbolic foreigners."

This account is not a literature review in the strict sense of the word. It is intended to contextualize the research at hand and frame its premises.

From Turkey to Europe-A Brief History

Turkish migration to Europe begins in 1963, with the signing of bilateral agreements with Germany (and various European states), giving way to what is called the *Guestworker* programs. The official story is an exercise in statistics, registering who entered and left and keeping account of the difference; as it is called, the net migration. Europewide, the hero in this migration history is the categorical international migrant worker, primarily taking part in institutionalized worker exchanges.

In this migration, the movement of labor is between countries at the industrialized center of Europe, (i.e., Austria, Belgium, Germany, France, the Netherlands, Sweden, and Switzerland), and the countries at Europe's southern periphery, (not only Turkey but also Italy, Spain, Portugal, Greece, the former Yugoslavia, Algeria and Morocco). The direction of the movement is from the latter to the former, from the periphery to the center. Also in movement toward the center, (Britain, France, and the Netherlands), are migrants from former colonies, (India, Pakistan, the Caribbean, Algeria, Suriname, and Indonesia).

The formal policies of labor recruitment in Europe ended in the mid-1970s (in Germany in 1973). By this time, the presence of foreign populations in Europe had risen substantially.[1] In 1976, there were about 12 million foreigners in the above-mentioned European countries, whereas in 1960 this number had been only 5 million. Germany's share in the number of foreigners in 1976 was close to 4 million, about 6.4 percent of the total population of the then Federal Republic (Soysal Nuhoğlu, 1994: 22).

The end of formal recruitment did not mean the end of migration. Mainly through family reunification programs and political asy-

---

1   The term "foreigner" refers to persons belonging to a wide array of differentially organized membership categories, including third-country (non-European Union) citizens, European citizens (holding citizenship in a country other than their host country), asylum seekers, dual citizens, holders of various temporary and permanent residency permits, and illegal aliens. Surely, not all foreigners are equal.

lum, the influx of foreign populations, Turks included, continued throughout the 1980s and 1990s, with occasional drops fuelled by restrictive legislation and the promotion of return migration. By 1990, the foreign population in Europe had reached 14.5 million (Soysal Nuhoğlu, 1994: 23). In Germany, the number of foreigners amounted to 7 million in 1994, 2 million of which were from Turkey (Muenz and Ulrich, 1997: 84, 93). Since then, the number of foreigners in Germany has remained stable at around 7.3 million (SOPEMI, 2004).

Today, according to the latest statistics published by the Turkish Ministry of Labor about 3.5 million Turkish citizens live and work abroad; about 3 million in Europe, with the largest contingent in Germany with 1.9 million, followed by 220,000 in the US, 100,000 in Saudi Arabia, and last but not least 2,424 in Japan.[2]

Labor, Culture, and Transnationalism

In scholarly writing, public policy, and popular culture, migration stories unfold in three distinct stages: labor, culture, and transnationalism. In the first stage, the categorical migrant is a worker and is male. He is a breadwinner. Having left behind a family, homeland and roots, he is condemned to silence and exploitation, living in *Heims* (homes) in the *Heimats* (countrie s) of Others. He is the villager in *Die Bauern von Subay*, a hypothetical town in Anatolia, in Werner Schiffauer's sensitive ethnographic account of migration (1987) and the struggling worker cited in the classics of immigration literature, such as Castell's and Kosack's *Immigrant Workers and Class Structure in Western Europe* (1973).

In Günter Wallraff's best-selling story of exploitation and survival, *Ganz unten* (1985, in its English reincarnation, *Lowest of the Low*; in its Turkish, *En Alttakiler*), the immigrant takes the persona of Ali, stressed at the bottom of the German social ladder. In the story, Ali frequently changes jobs, one day a construction worker, the next

---

2   See the official website of Turkish Ministry of Labor at http://www.csgb.gov.tr/birimler/yih/istatistik/sayisal_bilgiler.htm

day a part-time cleaning person at McDonald's, and expectedly gets exploited. He lives in dire conditions, experiences oppression, and feels discrimination in the lowest of the segregated echelons of Germany.

Ali's picture and story convey a starkly different impression than the solemn images of absence inscribed into the migrant photos that beautify the artful pages of *A Seventh Man*. There, John Berger's lyrical gaze marks the migrant in disturbing absences of speech and gesture. There, the migrant is not heard or seen, remaining invisible beyond walls that separate him from European imagination. In Wallraff's story, the migrant enters the world of the German economy and imagination. The Turkish *Gastarbeiter* now has a face, dark hair, dark eyes and moustache, as well as a place, at the bottom of society, and he speaks as a member of the dispossessed and underprivileged. The story of Wallraff's Ali identifies a presence, reconfigures statistical evidence as experiential narrative, and accords a blueprint for the habitual stories of the Turkish *Gastarbeiter* experience to come, *ganz unten* and with nowhere to go.

In the two decades following the end of labor recruitment, the foreigners in Europe have been solidly "*incorporated*" into the available legal, political, economic, and social structures and institutions in their countries of residence.[3] They have become part of the labor and investment markets, education and welfare systems, policy discourses and regimes. They have attained and exercised, *as foreigners*, rights and privileges that are conventionally reserved for *national* citizens. They have been extensively involved in public life through associa-

---

3 In her *Limits of Citizenship,* Soysal Nuhoğlu defines incorporation as "a process whereby a guestworker population becomes a part of the polity of the host country," independent of the degree of the individual migrant's adaptation "to the life patterns of the host society" (1994: 30). In this sense, incorporation is different than integration and assimilation—the other two terms widely used in immigration debates and research. Furthermore, the incorporation of migrants is primarily dependent on host country structures and institutions and world-level universalistic discourses of personhood and human rights—not to "home" country culture and traditions as commonly asserted.

tional activity, union membership, party politics, electoral practices, and arts and literary production. They also have been part of existing regimes of income inequity, social differentiation, and ethnic and racial discrimination. In short, the foreigners have become *subjects* in a complex terrain of exclusions and inclusions, contention and accommodation, and disenfranchisement and membership.

In the mid-eighties, Europe enters the world of "multiculturalism" and the predominant mode of thinking about migration becomes centered on culture and identity. With cultural change, the *Gastarbeiter* gets re-signified as a *person*, a total being with feelings and culture—not simply a worker and no longer a guest. The protagonist of the story is the Turk, (the Other), whose identity is analyzed *vis-à-vis* the German, (the native) – within the conventions of cultural otherness and difference. Labor statistics no longer dominate the migration texts but attribute credence to identity stories.

In the same period, policy debates move away from the economics and logistics of labor importation and focus on nebulously defined integration and border controls. While integration involves the "adjustment" of those who are already in, border controls regressively concern limiting further *im*migration into the nation-states that comprise Europe. The integration policies, if they do exist, reify supposed "integration problems," which are never defined but circularly deployed as proof for the need to integrate migrants in their new society – seasoned with occasional statistics about the number of German friends a migrant has, and the obligatory recitation of cultural differences such as being Muslim or Turkish.

As for disciplinary prowess, anthropology and literary/cultural studies take over the task of writing on migration, which thus far has been a proper subject matter for sociology and economics. Their disciplinary trademark being culture, both anthropology and cultural studies emerge as natural candidates for documenting the new migration stories. Relieved from the social analysis of labor markets, sociology revives studies of citizenship, an historical concern of the discipline, which is apparently amplified by massive migrations and foreignness within nation-states.[4]

It is crucial to note that the cultural version of the migration story differentiates its subject, *the migrant*, along gender lines and that women become legitimate topics of inquiry in their own right. At the earlier stages of migration, the proportion of women to male migrants was significantly low, for migration meant recruitment of male factory workers. Later however, the numbers of female immigrants have reached considerable parity with men, mostly due to women-only recruitment policies and family reunifications. Despite this, the women immigrants remained simply invisible. Migration was perceived as a matter of labor importation — and temporary — while women hardly made the public agenda.

In her introduction to the landmark issue of the *International Migration Review*, the first-ever special volume devoted to the female migrant, Mirjana Morokvasic rightly remarks:

> Rather than "discovering" that female migration is an understudied phenomenon, it is more important to stress that the already existing literature has had little impact on policy-making, on mass media presentation of migrant women, but also on the main body of migration literature, where male bias has continued to persist into the late seventies and eighties in spite of growing evidence of women's overwhelming participation in migratory movements (1984: 899).

With the cultural turn in migration, that is, with the increased emphasis on culture in terms of rights, duties, and membership of immigrants, it is safe to state that women, and the "woman question",

---

4   In the last two decades, there has been an explosion in migration studies covering all continents of the world and focusing on numerous ethnic groups, their movements and cultures. Among this corpus, the literature devoted to studying Turks in Europe is rather significant – both in terms of its topical and theoretical expanse and representativeness of the field. See the selected bibliography for a sample of studies on migration, culture, and identity regarding Turks in Europe, with varying degrees of emphasis on, and analytical significance attributed to, culture.

have come to the fore of the immigration question. In the cultural story, the immigrant is no longer male and women have a role to play —but not always following leads suggested in the interventions such as the one in the *International Migration Review* (1984). As categorical Muslims, immigrant women from diverse places (such as Turkey, Pakistan, Morocco, and Suriname), and with different social, educational, and cultural backgrounds, have become subjects of *foulard* affairs, or headscarf debates. In media representations, they have been immanently portrayed as "beyond the veil", thus silent. Their presumed invisibility, and patriarchal oppression under Islamic traditions have led to, in the words of Stanley Cohen (1980), unremitting "moral panics", especially after the indiscriminate attacks perpetuated by radical Islamist groups and organizations in Europe and elsewhere.

The last episode in the immigration story is that of transnationalism. In the late nineties, it had become obvious that in the face of the extensive movement of goods, labor, and capital worldwide, not only was the cultural story of migration limiting, but also the delimitation of migration by 'nation' was no longer sustainable. Turks in Germany occupy and traverse spaces that defy conventional distinctions of home and host country cultures and economies. A fashion trend in Turkey abruptly travels to Germany. Major Turkish movies have their gala openings simultaneously in Berlin and Istanbul. The staging of a concert, reading, exhibition, or play by (famous and not so famous) Turkish artists in Germany is only a commonplace act of culture. Important Turkish rappers in Istanbul cite their birthplaces as somewhere in Germany.

In the realm of politics, quests for recognition by minority ethnic and religious groups (i.e., Alevites and Kurds) in Turkey and Germany condition the shape of politics and claims making in both countries by way of the diffusion of organizational know-how, political activism, and discursive strategies. Islamic politics in Germany engenders activism in Turkey and vice versa. The German Parliament's decision to condemn the Armenian massacre creates the grounds for a political rally staged in Berlin by a variety of Turkish political organizations, with left and right leanings, and both from Germany and Turkey.

As Germany becomes an attractive market for accomplished artists from Turkey, young Turkish professionals from Germany seek jobs and fortunes in Turkey. The immigrants who have led the way to Germany now retire in two countries —six months in Turkey, six months in Germany. The return to Turkey is neither the ideal corrective to the disruptive forces of migration (as in going back home) nor the disruption of a life built in Germany. Return is only temporary in a world that permanently connects Turkey and Germany in more ways than those depicted in linear narratives of leaving home and settling in foreign places.

Last but not least, Turkey's candidacy for the European Union, and the consequent negotiation process, affectively reconfigures the political landscapes, cultural debates, and economic ventures in both countries. Turkey and Germany are now more imminently connected than being two nation-states with historical ties, cultural links, and migration stories.

Coined and advocated by Nina Glick-Schiller and her colleagues (1994), "transnational migration" is the new name given to the story of migration, after the discovery of manifold border crossings and excessive movement of goods, peoples, information, and capital. The new story is more demanding than the prosaic labor-culture stories. For we encounter stories of migration in unlikely places, the places which we hardly associate with migration —Pakistanis and Turks in Japan, for instance. The new migration numbers overburden inter-*national* statistical exercises beyond recognition and the extant of contemporary movement confuse migration geographies that are mapped into *nation*-states. Transnationalism promises to capture this emergent new narrative in the stories of migrants who traverse the world in inordinate numbers, as illegal and legal aliens, burdened with inequities of travel regulations, market demands, and fortunes and desires. However, a word of caution is necessary: "migration studies", and migration policies, tend to "stay stubbornly loyal to the old dichotomies of homes and host countries, tradition and modernity, Turkey and Germany. The old stories have yet to release their intractable hold on new paradigms" (Çağlar and Soysal, 2003).

Integration Question

Religion is conceivably the most contentious issue with respect to the "integration" of immigrants. In policy and academic debates, religious orientation categorically serves as the measure against which integration should be judged. Compounding the problem, there has been heightened sensitivity towards "Islamic" inclinations of Turks and Arabs in Europe in the aftermath of the incident of September 11. Revived debates on the "veil", and newly invented ones on "parallel societies" (read as segregated ethnic enclaves), and the proclivity of Muslim youths to "terrorism", bring to fore an underlying anxiety about the potential of Muslims to integrate into "European" societies and values, as well as the civilizational incommensurability of Islam and the West.

The state authorities in Germany—and Europe—are surely in an uneasy relationship with Islam. The inflammatory emphasis on religious orientation as an indicator of "*dis*-integration" seriously contradicts the discursive emphasis on diversity and cultural rights on the part of European courts and state agencies. While the "security" concerns lead to measures that constrain the activity realm of immigrants, by designating them *de facto* Muslims, and dangerous at that, discourses of diversity promote religion as a cultural right and facilitate provisions for realizing this right.

The state of Berlin, and many other states in Germany, pursues a concerted policy of multiculturalism, relentlessly expressing their support for cultural diversity and funding projects to that end. Multiculturalism, at work in Berlin since early 1990's, hardly amounts to an unambiguous conceptual framework and coherent policy agenda. At times the acts of multiculturalism stop short of being a feel-good discursive practice on the part of state officials and immigrant activists. Nonetheless, as a discursive instrument and policy tool it is shared across the political spectrum, even by certain factions of conservative parties. As it is practiced in Berlin multiculturalism is rather consequential.

A case in point is the teaching of religion in schools. In a recent court case, for instance, the Islamic Federation in Berlin won the right to provide religious education in Berlin's schools, establishing parity between Islam and formally accepted Protestant and Catholic churches. The major Alevite association in Berlin, claiming their religious and cultural difference from the Sunnite Islamic Federation, appealed to Berlin State and was granted the right to teach its own religion classes. Now there are after-school courses on the teachings and rituals of the Alevite persuasion, offered in a number of schools in Berlin and taught by educators on the state payroll. In addition, the Foreigners' Office, recently renamed as the Directorate for Integration and Migration, as part of its effort to publicize the cultural diversity of the city, published a booklet on Alevite culture, adding another entry to the series of forty-plus booklets produced under the generic title of *Miteinander Leben* [Living Together].

Another field of government action where multiculturalism brings about substantial results is youth work. Berlin, for instance, is the *Holy City* of youth organizations. These organizations display a spectrum of orientations and attract representative cross-sections of Berlin's migrant youth. In Kreuzberg, NaunynRitze, a youth center operating under the auspices of Kreuzberg's municipal government, operates as the headquarters for hip-hop. In the early 1990s, NaunynRitze was home to one of the most successful and long-lasting hip-hop posses, *To Stay Here is My Right*. Under the approving supervision of NaunynRitze's social-worker team, the posse flourished into a successful "hip-hop community" and attracted the prospective stars and hip-hop hopefuls to NaunynRitze. Graffiti writing sessions, break dance practices, rap courses, and hip-hop parties promptly dominated the cultural agenda of the "ghetto" youth attending NaunynRitze. Throughout the 1990s, the hip-hop scene in Kreuzberg produced its prominent names, MC Gio, writer Neco and Sony, DJ Derezon, dancer Storm, and rapper Boe B. Like Neco, who has become an important director with three films to his credit, many of these young artists have found themselves niches in the art scene of Berlin.

Though prominent, hip-hop of course does not exhaust the range of creative cultural projects migrant youths of Berlin produce and consume. They stage concerts, poetry readings, parties, dance performances, and plays. They dance through the streets of Berlin the entire day in the Carnival of Cultures, print poems on love and justice in short-lived literary periodicals they publish, write articles on bilingualism, and take part in rallies to protest the drastic budget cuts proposed by the state. In turn, their pictures and words are eminently featured in the stylish pages of cosmopolitan Berlin bi-weeklies and their stories and art are interpreted, and amplified, as the necessary condition for social harmony and the multicultural unison of Berlin.

This does not preclude the intensive — and increasingly contentious — debate over Turks and Islam and the prospects of a multicultural society. The cover of a recent issue of the journal *Focus*, which styles itself as 'the modern news magazine', was headlined '*Die Multikulti-Lüge* [The Multiculti-Lie] against a stenciled figure of a woman in headscarf (10 April, 2006). *Focus* was not alone in spotlighting 'multikulti' as *the* problem of Germany. It was simply following suit and highlighting the usual stories: headscarves, youth gangs, segregated men's coffee houses, segregated high-rises with seventy percent immigrant inhabitants, soaring crime figures, low language skills, unemployment, and extremism of various kinds — indeed a bleak picture.

What ignited the latest integration debate was the brutal murder of Hatun Sürücü, a young twenty-three year-old Turkish woman, by her brothers for disgracing her family. Hatun's guilt was to leave her husband and attempt to raise her child as a single mother —hence bringing shame to her family. The murder of Hatun Sürücü galvanized the long entrenched doubts and questions about the compatibility of Turkish (or Muslim) traditions with western norms, and western ways of life, particularly with regards to the place of women in Muslim societies and culture. The debate did not simply bring Germans against Turks, but generated a multi-vocal questioning. Turkish feminist activist, Necla Kelek, for instance, condemned honor-killings in an article published in the pages of the renowned intellectual weekly, *Die Zeit*, and made a plea to the Muslims to question their traditions and change.[5] Her call for reform in Islam was answered in the same newspaper with a strongly worded rejoinder from sixty prominent German and Turkish ethnographers, intellectuals, immigration researchers and activists, mainly calling attention to the complexity of the debate and the dangers of blanket condemnation of immigrants (as Muslims) at a time when there is an increasing anti-immigrant sentiment, both among the populace and the policy-makers.

Without going further into the details and merits of such polemics, it is necessary to assert that what lies at the locus of all this debate on integration –and divergent positions as regards to gender equality and culture– is the woman question. In the post-Nine-Eleven era, the term "Muslim" has attained a status of unqualified infamy, making every Muslim person perceived as no less than an adherent of uncivilized, non-modern culture, if not a terrorist. Muslim women, not coincidentally, have always been at the center of the debates on Islam and its place in European social spaces.

In Europe today, imprinted on the female body, the headscarf empirically discriminates foreignness (as in being non-Western) and authenticates it, mostly as Islamic. When the subject matter is immigration or Islam, pictures of women with headscarves invariably accompany newspaper articles, television coverage, and academic

---

5   For the debate between Kelek and her adversaries, see Terkessidis, Mark and Yasemin Karakasoglu, *"Gerechtigkeit für die Muslime!,"* Die Zeit, 01 February 2006, Nr. 6, and Kelek, Necla, *"Sie haben das Leid anderer zugelassen!,"* Die Zeit, 09 February 2006, Nr. 7.

works. The image provides the necessary visual accreditation to the written and spoken word.

Though intuitive, this cultural take and undue emphasis on the headscarf –thus on Islam– renders invisible the extensive participation of immigrant women in the social, cultural, and the economic life of the countries in which they reside. Their accomplishments and their resilience, inventiveness, and activism since they have surfaced in the imagery of the European mind, become captive to reified categorical identities (Turkishness and Islam).

Germany and Europe at this juncture in the history of migration seek to reconcile managing diversity with achieving security, both of which are highly charged discursive policy agendas. The apparent conflict between these two agendas seems to stay with us for sometime to come and will afford grounds for a continuing debate on the potential integration of immigrants in Europe.

Symbolic Foreigners

The incorporation of immigrants in Germany has proceeded rather rapidly and without exceptional controversy. The amplified talk of integration today is more about maintaining the categorical integrity of national order and fighting the ghost of a civilizational enemy rather than remedying empirical inequalities, which are more often than not subsumed under the foreignness of migrants and erased from social agendas. In other words, heightened but undue attention to the cultural "problems" associated with migration disregards the processes of incorporation and the difficulties of maintaining foreignness in a globalizing world.

What we end up having is an elementary story of integration, in which the parameters that make difference and identity are taken to be national/ethnic – Turkishness, Germanness, and Islam being three principal ones. Rather than attending the complex layering of inequities and affinities within and without the nation-state, the incessant talk on integration concerns itself with apocalyptic cultural fragmentations, parallel societies, and ghetto narratives. In the end, "iron-ically, as immigrants are increasingly incorporated into the member-ship schemes of European host polities, the debate over how well they 'adjust' intensifies, and their cultural otherness is accentuated. Guestworkers become *symbolic* foreigners" in Europe (Soysal Nuhoğlu 1994: 135).

As symbolic foreigners, (Turks in Germany, Indians in Britain, Arabs in France), the contemporary immigrants are confined to an unyielding past –the past of their home and culture– and a persistent present –the present of their host country and their Otherness. They are considered to be bounded by their nation (or religion) in nations of others and thus bound, they live in permanent diasporas. Lost are *futures, dreams, and competencies*, along with possibilities for achiev-ing more homes than one, and living without nations. All stories of migration turn into stories about homes, pasts, and tedious repetitions of the present. Contemporary migration simply becomes a cultural economy of movement between peripheries with Edenic pasts and cen-ters with affluent presents, or between the nothingness of underdevel-opment and the wealth of advancement.

Europeanization, that is Turkey's accession to the European Union, only complicates the story of migration. This is a hotly debat-ed issue in Europe today –and perhaps for years to come. On December 17, 2004, the current leaders of the Union decided on the future of European Union-Turkey relations and agreed to initiate for-mal negotiation talks on Turkey's accession. The public imagination in Europe is already saturated with a heightened debate on the Europeanness of Turks and Turkey. Although where the Turks belong culturally is the question, (possibly an unanswerable question because it is a political rather than an empirical matter), the real pressing item is migration –the potential flood of Turks overburdening Europe's stagnant labor markets and welfare institutions. The expert opinion on this is divided. While the opponents of Turkish accession forecast an eminent disaster, those who favor accession draw attention to the decreasing and aging population of Europe and welcome the promise of a young labor force as fresh blood.

The question that needs to be posed is a slightly different one: What will happen to our understanding of migration when Turkey becomes a member of the Union? With the Union, in effect with Turkey's accession talks, comes the "free movement of people" and with the "free movement" the term "immigrant" becomes redundant. The matter for negotiation is not the number of Turks who could migrate, but when Turkish citizens –then also European citizens– would be allowed to move freely in Europe in search of their fortunes and futures. Aren't we witnessing a superfluous debate on the immigration and integration of Turks in Europe? This question anticipates the end of the migration story of Turks in Germany and Europe.

RESEARCH DESIGN

Questions and Premises
What drives this research is a general interest in the formations of identity and politics of performance, particularly among immigrant groups in Europe. The new Europe to which I refer includes, but is not exclusive to, the European Union. I take Europe not as a unit of analysis in and of itself but as a social, institutional, and cultural formation in the making and conclusively connected to the Middle East. In this process, Germany, a "central" European nation-state which is undergoing a unification process of its own former East and West, and Turkey, a Middle Eastern nation-state about to become a formal member of the European Union, comprise the two nodes in a complex set of transformations unfolding in Europe and the Middle East. At these restive sites of ethnography, with their precarious and difficult affinities and connections, it is viable to capture the simultaneous processes of consolidation and the unsettling of Europe and the Middle East, both as supranational political and economic entities, and as emerging cultural formations and identities.

My prior work has focused on the cultural projects of Turkish migrants –and youths in particular– in Berlin, Germany, their responses to social change, and their reactions to the discourses of "in-betweenness". Although the prevalent discourse of in-betweenness fixes Turkish migrants on a bipolar axis of the modern and traditional, they are not simply passive recipients of change in an alien landscape. Their cultural projects are not simply revivals of an essential Turkishness (or Islam) in response to alien formations of modernity. Rather, as active participants at several social and cultural borders, they cultivate their projects and engender spaces of self and belonging, drawing on a repertoire of contemporary discourses and signs of identity through processes of selection, modification, and enactment. As actors at the intersections of local, national, and transnational environs, (Kreuzberg, Berlin, Germany, Turkey, and Europe), they partake in the construction of the social and cultural landscape of the new Europe and enter into dialogues with global flows of youth culture. In my work and publications, I argue and show that these connections and competencies condition their productions of culture and provide them with the means to conceive and cross boundaries –thus unsettling national configurations of belonging and conventional conceptions of Otherness.

In my new research, of which the MiReKoc-funded project is an integral component, I focus on public events and their role in the making of WorldCities. The compelling characteristic of public events staged in Berlin, as well as in other metropolitan centers of Europe, is that they predominantly aim to cultivate a civic sense of plurality and advocate tolerance, multiculturalism, and diversity. Employing markers of ethnicity, culture, gender, youthfulness, hip and coolness, such public events delimit and present identities and celebrate cultural particularisms within an imagery of diversity. In other words, metropolitan public places become stages for what I call the *Spectacles of Identity*. I argue that this emergent genre is a symptom of the identifiable shifts in the conceptualization and performance of identity, in public manifestations of expressive culture, and in the definitions and practice of urban experience. The new spectacle is profoundly animated by the pervasive amplification of culture and identity discourses, and follows the transformation of city space into a stage for the production and performance of global spectacles, and is facilitated by the dialectical impact of global cultural flows on local expressions of culture. In this sense, the new spectacle and its permutations are responses to transnational processes in as much as they are reflections of local, regional, or nationally situated specificities.

More specifically, the inventory and analysis of spectacles of identity, on the one hand, afford a way to assess the scope and content of the social and cultural spaces occupied by and designated for migrants, youth, and other identity groups and collectivities in the city. The presence or absence of migrants and minorities in these public spectacles are signs of their responses to the discourses on and about them. Their protests and participation reveal the politics and policies of inclusion and exclusion. On the other hand, the inventory and typology of public performance, particularly the manifestations of spectacular mega-events, serves to certify the City's standing or self-image as a global and ordered metropolis, inhabited by cosmopolitan natives and catering to transnational *flâneurs*. The contemporary topography of public events allows us to understand the relationship between these two constitutive but apparently incommensurate facets of the new spectacle.

To this end, I seek to discern:

• Parameters of legitimate collective action in public spaces (which collectivities and performances are celebrated, authorized, or repudiated; what characteristics make a proper spectacle),

• Prerequisites of patronage for public events (who promotes, underwrites, and manages the spectacle; the extent to which public and/or private funds are allocated; which spectacles draw preferable funding and support),

• Cultural and political articulation of identity (what are the content and limits of the sayable, creative, and defiant; which signs and artifacts constitute the expressive repertoire of identity), and,

• Changing modulations of the local, national, and global (to which extent the new public spectacle departs from being national in content and local in form; to whom the spectacle caters; who are its audiences and participants; what are the markers of diasporic or cosmopolitan projections in the new spectacle).

A Note on Methodology

As I have indicated, this project was launched during my tenure in Berlin as a Research Fellow at the Berlin Program for Advanced German and European Studies, Free University in the academic years 2001-2003 (funded by the Social Science Research Council and Free University). The larger research is designed as an ethnographic inquiry, with participant observation as the primary research method. During my residency in Berlin, I devoted my time to observing the preparatory stages of the festivals and drawing up an inventory of minority groups, governmental offices, and private and corporate concerns involved in the process – at the local, national, and European levels. Starting with the May Day Parade in the spring of 2002, I have participated in public festivals taking place in Berlin, including the Carnival of Cultures, the Turkish Day Parade, the Christopher Street Day Parade, and the Love Parade.

The episodic nature of the spectacles has allowed me to carry out the participatory and observational tasks of the research and simultaneously devote substantial time to taking inventories and documenting the landscape of public performance in Berlin. I have recorded my participation by writing field notes, taking pictures and slides, and, most importantly, videotaping the events. I have used video extensively as an instrument of note taking and I have accumulated substantial film footage covering a variety of public events.

An important part of the research design involves conducting open-ended, in-depth interviews with the leaders of the formal associations or collectivities which organize the spectacles, members of various groups performing in the festivals, officials from governmental bodies providing resources and services, leaders of immigrant and minority associations, and officials of governmental and private cultural organizations, media outlets, and sponsoring agencies and corporations. With a MiReKoc grant, I carried out the interviews included in the roster of officials responsible for organizing, managing, and sponsoring the events, as well as representatives of immigrant groups taking part in the events. I also followed some of the major public events that coincided with the grant period.

Another important aspect of this research is its reliance on public debates on a variety of topics regarding immigrants, city, and culture. Public debate is not taken simply as a contextual element of the research, but as its primary material. To this end, I have extensively followed the media, both print and visual, and assembled and utilized large collections of data on public debates over the place of immigrants in Berlin, Germany, and Europe, the prospects of Berlin as a WorldCity, and major European and German political controversies and performances.

ANALYSIS

With its methodological emphasis on visual material and media, and public debate as primary data, this research abides by the dicta of "thin ethnography" (Marcus, 1998). It also differs from conventional migration studies in its utilization of experimental presentation techniques (Marcus and Fischer, 1986). In so doing, it follows recent trends in conducting and writing ethnography. Accordingly, in this section I first present the findings and results of the research I carried out during my tenure as the recipient of the MiReKoc fellowship and then present a discussion based not only on the current findings, but also on the results of larger research I have been carrying out.

Findings and Results

Under the MiReKoc funded part of this research, I made various trips to Berlin, during which I conducted interviews, followed spectacles staged in the city, and organized and attended a conference on spectacle at Humboldt University. In this section I provide an account of my findings in the order in which I carried out the research, starting with the conference on spectacle. I will also give a brief account of the classification exercise I have taken up as part of this research.

Theory and Practice of Spectacle and Plurality in Europe

The primary purpose of my research trip in May 2005 was to participate in the symposium on the new European carnivals, which I had been co-organizing with Michi Knecht of Humboldt University and our research team at the Department of European Ethnology (funding for the symposium was granted by the Fritz Thyssen Foundation). The title of the symposium, which took place at Humboldt University between May 13th and 15th, was *"Performing Policy –Enacting Diversity: European Summer Carnivals in Comparative Perspective."* Conceptually, the symposium was designed to inquire into the contemporary urban summer carnivals –the new urban spectacles of diversity and identity– in different European cities and in the context of new forms of political regulation, changing migratory regimes and progressive processes of Europeanization. The symposium provided an opportunity to observe the limits of the scholarly work on the new spectacles in Europe and to learn from the major practitioners/organizers of multicultural festivals in London, Bremen, Brussels, and Rotterdam.

The first panel opened the conference with inter-temporal as well as intercultural comparative analyses. In the second panel, the notion of *Spectacles of Identity* was at the center of discussion. Following Levent Soysal's interpretation (n.d.) of these spectacles as a symptom of the remarkable shifts in the conceptualization and performance of identity, as well as the changes in the public manifestation of expressive culture and urban experience, the panel focused on subject positions, participation structures, and displays of citizenship. The third panel discussed interconnections and relations between summer carnivals and processes of Europeanization, seeking answers to the question of how political programs for recognition of "unity in diversity" get converted into structures of urban events, into specific cultural practices, emotions, identifications, and strategies of inclusion and exclusion. The final session was an open forum in which the conference revisited the questions of "Comparison and Transfer."

The most important aspect of the conference was the participation of practitioners/organizers of carnivals: *Notting Hill Carnival* in London, *Zineke* Festival in Brussels, *Sommer Carnival* in Rotterdam, and *Carnival of Cultures* in Bremen. Carnival practitioners included Marcel De Munnynck (Zinneke Parade Brüssel), Ruth Tompsett (Notting Hill Carnival, Middlesex University of London), Gré Ploeg (Zomercarnaval Rotterdam), Paul McLaren (Carnival of Cultures-Bremen, Shademakers Carnival Club), and Patricia Alleyne-Dettmers (Notting Hill Carnival, Universität Hamburg). The organizers of the *Carnival of Cultures* in Berlin did not attend the conference because of their involvement with the daily tasks of the Carnival of Cultures, taking place in the streets of Berlin that weekend. It is crucial to note that all the cities represented at the conference have large and established immigrant populations and vibrant immigrant economies.

It became clear from the discussions at the conference that diversity was the driving concept behind all the carnivals in question. According to the organizers, the carnivals were showcases for the diversity of their cities, contributing to tolerance and enriching the city life. What was being understood by diversity and what kind of diversity was being promoted, however, significantly differed from carnival to carnival:

• In Bremen, the emphasis was placed on artistic merit and the carnival of cultures was seen as a showcase of the aesthetic accomplishments of individual artists –not necessarily of ethnic origin but surely creating works that derive their inspiration from carnival arts and performances.

• In Brussels, while the artistic aspect of the carnival was at the fore and promoted, the emphasis was placed on the creative potential of the *citizens* and educational value of the festival event, inculcating a secular and universal understanding of *citizenship*.

• As expected, London's Notting Hill Carnival was understood as an alternative event launched by the Afro-Caribbean British communities within the context of anti-racial politics and policies in Britain — though, it was argued, the carnival has been turning into a stage for entertainment, rather than resistance, in the last decade or so.

• In Rotterdam, Carnival, being one of the many summer events, was partly taken as a festival for attracting tourists to the city and partly as a stage for the Caribbean community for forging transnational ties to the Islands.

• In Berlin, the organizers of the Carnival of Cultures were placing the emphasis on the community participation and self-organization — even though this was seen as the reason for the amateurish floats and performances abundantly present at the carnival. It was also the case that Berlin Carnival was consciously staged as a policy instrument to further tolerance and multiculturalism.

Spectacular Events, Events on Spectacle

In the month of May, with the help of my research assistant, Martina Klausner, I followed several public events, which took place in Berlin. Among them, three were important for the purposes of this project: the Turkish Day Parade, the Walk-of-Islam Fashion Show, and the conference on the myth of Kreuzberg, called Mythos Kreuzberg.

Turkish Day

Turkish Day was the fourth instance of the event since its inaugural in 2002 to celebrate the 40th year of Turkish immigration to Germany. As on the previous occasions, immigrants from various parts of Germany gathered in Berlin for the event. A citizens' committee, comprising of immigrants who represent various cities in Germany, organizes Turkish Day. However they receive support from DITIB (*Diyanet İşleri Türk İslam Birliği*/Turkish Islamic Union of Religious Affairs), a union of mosque organizations in Germany associated with the Office of Religious Affairs in Turkey. DITIB is organized and has branches throughout Germany. In fact, mosque organizations of DITIB hire buses and bring Turkish immigrants to Berlin. They walk under DITIB banners representing their cities. Although the DITIB is the major sponsor of the event, as the years pass, other organizations, for instance *Atatürkçü Düşünce Derneği* (Association for Ataturkist Thought) have begun to participate in the parade, as well as independent citizens.

The Turkish Embassy in Berlin supports the parade, although it does not take part in the actual organization. The Ambassador or Council General of Berlin always delivers a speech to the participants, mostly celebrating multiplicity of cultures and urging immigrants take German citizenship — thus becoming citizen ambassadors of their country of origin. German politicians also attend Turkish Day. Aside from the Director of the Foreigners' Office, many high-level politicians appear on the stage and welcome the contribution of immigrants to German society, praise diversity, and call for tolerance and understanding. Inviting Turkish immigrants to take up German citizenship is their message, too. At the parade of 2005 there was a larger contingent of politicians, anticipating the important role the Turkish vote would play in the upcoming elections in September.

As in the previous years, the participants carried Turkish flags in abundance, along with German and EU flags. In numbers there was no comparison: German and EU flags stood isolated within a red-and-white sea of flags carried and t-shirts worn by the participants. Again as expected, this emphasis on the Turkish flag raised concerns among the politicians present at the event over the integration of the Turkish community. Regardless of their political orientation and ethnic background, all the politicians and activists with whom I talked shared this concern. However, when examined as a whole, the flags signify less of an isolationist and national attitude but more of a multicultural twist. Flags come as the only apparent and respectable sign of Turkishness. Moreover the flag is not the only sign exhibited. Flags accompany the Mehter band of the Ottoman army, Turkish pop music, and folk dances; all read as the customary signs of cultural difference.

The most anticipated part of Turkish Day is the popular concert staged at the end. It is what the young people wait for –seeing their most celebrated singers on stage. Over the years, major pop stars like Sevtab Erener and Kenan Doğulu took the stage to the cheers of their audiences. The Turkish Day stage is also a stage for dance and music groups from Berlin and other cities of Germany, at times displaying modernized folkdances and the folk music of Turkey, at times doing modern dance to the tunes of arranged Turkish melodies. More often than not, these are amateur performances but semi-professional acts also take the stage. The concert is fast becoming the most important element of Turkish Day, with its audiences growing every year. After the concert, the participants of Turkish Day, particularly those who come from afar, wander in the streets of Berlin, mostly in Unter den Linden, and do things customarily done by tourists in the area –visiting landmark historical sites, buying Berlin curios, and drinking coffee and having ice cream. Having done the tourist things, they embark the buses that brought them to Berlin and return to their own cities.

As such, Turkish Day is a replica of other multicultural festivals staged in the public places of Berlin. Turkish Day adds a New York style parade to Berlin's repertoire of festivals, celebrating Turkishness as a color added to the multicultural richness of the city. This is the attraction of the parade for the organizers, politicians, and activists. This is what they revel in their speeches and interviews that they give to the media.

Walk-of-Islam

The Walk-of-Islam is a fashion show launched by an entrepreneurial Turkish youth interested in pursuing a career as a designer. In 2005, the event, a small-scale happening in its second installment, was far from meeting the expectations its name and flyers had generated (a woman in headscarf walking the catwalk). The organizers intended to launch the event as a multicultural design show but failed to attract customers. Despite the disappointing turn-out, when seen through the lens of the arguments made in this research, the event signifies the extent to which multiculturalism has become an organizing and inspiring feature of social and economic life in Berlin. (Unfortunately we were not successful in arranging an interview with the organizers in order to get their assessment. This interview will be carried out during a future trip to Berlin.)

Mythos Kreuzberg

The conference "*Mythos Kreuzberg*" was organized by the Kreuzberg Municipality and *Heinrich Böll Stiftung*, both committed to diversity and multiculturalism. The goal was to assess and celebrate Kreuzberg's claims of diversity and alternative lifestyles. Not surprisingly the outcome was less of a critical appraisal, but enshrining the reputation of Kreuzberg as *the* multicultural district in Berlin. The pamphlets distributed in a bag under the apt title of *Mythen in Tüten* [Myths in a Bag] exemplified all the usual suspects: multicultural youth centers, the Kreuzberg Museum, social work organizations, Kreuzberg branches of the Greens, the Social Democrats, the Left Party (as it is now called), Turkish associations, art galleries, theaters and alternative music and dance venues. The message was that Kreuzberg was alive and well, and committed to diversity. The conference rendered visible (once again) the willingness of the political actors in Berlin to promote diversity and the extent of institutional and discursive resources devoted to its advancement.

What is important for the purposes of this research is the self-awareness and self-reflexivity on the part of the organizers as to the mythical place and essence of Kreuzberg for Berlin and its diversity. Although as it appears on the title of the conference, mythos suggests a critical stance, the participants of the conference were busy and content with affirming the mythos. Nonetheless, whether affirmative or critical, this conference highlights the fact that even for its proponents, a multicultural mythos of Kreuzberg cannot be taken for granted, but needs reaffirmation in order to be realized and continued.

Prime Institutional Players

During this phase of my research, one of my major goals was to conduct formal interviews with the prime players in the reconfiguration of the cultural topography of Berlin after Berlin's, and Germany's, unification. In this period, new semi-private, semi-autonomous funding institutions have been founded and they have been instrumental in shaping Berlin's cultural policies and re-establishing funding priorities according to what they see as fit for advancing a new profile for the up-and-coming WorldCity Berlin.

Among others, three institutions stand out as the "prime players" in Berlin's new cultural landscape: *Haupstadt Kulturfonds*, *Berlin Tourismus Marketing*, and *Berlin Partners*. With their funding and advisory powers, they effectively determine the parameters of what counts as legitimate, useful, and appropriate cultural events. With my research assistant Martina Klausner we carried out interviews with the directors of each organization. In the case of Berlin Partners, the director responsible for funding cultural events and devising cultural policy sent her assistant as her replacement at the last minute. This interview took place, though it did not reveal any substantive insight to the workings and policies of the institution. This interview will be attempted again in the future.

Hauptstadt Kulturfonds

As it is apparent from its name, Hauptstadt Kulturfonds funds the cultural event scene of Berlin as they see fit in a capital city. Its outgoing director, Adrienne Goehler, has been a very controversial figure. Her decision to fund an exhibition on RAF (Red Army Fraction) as a means to shed light on Germany's recent past –and her determination not to back off in the face of wide-spread criticism from all circles– made her a celebrity in her own right. She also opposed the destruction of the Palace of the Republic, East Germany's seat of Government and Parliament, against the greater opinion favoring getting rid of this prominent sign of Germany's socialist experience from the center of the city. This didn't earn her any credits. She recently published a book entitled *Verfluessigugingen* (2006), in which she shares her experiences as one of Berlin's cultural movers, and advances her ideas on how to revive the capital and its art scene as Berlin moves from Welfare State to Culture Society.

The money for the Hauptstadt Kulturfonds has two sources: the Federal Government and the Berlin City State, for a combined total of approximately ten million Euros in 2007. When compared to Berlin's debt, somewhere in the neighborhood of 60 million Euros, this is a substantive amount –though within the larger city and national budget, the amount is merely negligible. The final decisions on which projects to fund are made by a committee of two representatives from the Federal level and two from Berlin. Funding is project-based and distributed through competitions held twice a year.

According to the director we interviewed at the offices of the Hauptstadt Kulturfonds, Berlin's budgetary problems meant trouble for Berlin's art and culture scene, and hardship for the thriving artist community. Consequently, for the director, the lack of funding monies would gravely damage the image of Berlin as the scene of artistic innovation and creativity. In order to compensate for this situation, she made her priority to subsidize and fund projects coming from young artists who constitute the "informal" art scene in Berlin. For her, "the unofficial Berlin was alive and represented the future." She made clear they were funding mega projects but only reluctantly. Funding priority was to support projects by young artists, who have an "innovative" edge and the potential for "national and international influence." In a sense, funding was seen as a mechanism to supplant the disappearing welfare instruments, and to create the necessary environment for the survival of young artists — thus, to further the image of Berlin as a creative city and a city of creativity.

Among the mega art events sponsored and funded by the Hauptstadt Kulturfonds on a continuing basis are *Tanz im August* (Dance in August), an annual international dance festival during the month of August, and *Karneval der Kulturen* (Carnival of Cultures), the major venue for displaying the multicultural facets of Berlin. The reasoning behind funding this dance event was explained as a means to make Berlin a center for modern dance in the next three years. The second event, initiated by the *Werkstatt der Kulturen*, a cultural center founded by Berlin's Directorate of Foreigners' Office, recently renamed as Directorate for Immigration and Integration, was first launched in 1996 and celebrated its tenth anniversary in 2005. Both events, plus a number of smaller events supported on a regular basis, seemed to receive the lion's share of the funding budget of the Kulturfonds; about 2 million euros, or one-fifth of the budget.

Karneval der Kulturen is the sign of the city's and Kulturfonds' commitment to diversity. Steadily growing each year, both in terms of participant organizations and audiences, Karneval gathers together community associations, youth centers, cultural centers, social work and help organizations, youth, women, and gay groups with social messages, into the fold of a three-day carnival, with food and artwork stands, music and dance stages, a night for sound-systems, and a parade with floats displaying the diversity of cultures in Berlin. Diversity here means many things, not at all homogeneously defined, and ranges from strictly folkloristic depictions (Kurdish or Bolivian folk dance groups), to ironic takes on culture (Soviet or German culture on floats), and from strictly carnival acts *a la* Brazilian carnival, (at times represented by actual Brazilian Carnival groups), to sound-systems and DJs on floats.

To the disappointment of its organizers, Karneval does not attract many participants from organized Turkish groups. They attend the Karneval as spectators in large numbers (after all, Karneval takes place in Kreuzberg where they live), sell food and artwork and perform on the Oriental Stage, one of the four stages reserved for the dance and music performances (the other three stages thematically represent Asian, European, and Latin American culture). When it comes to representing "Turkish culture" in the parade, they scarcely come with a float of their own –and if they do, with a very mediocre one, at that. Over the years, there have been only a few Turkish floats in the parade. Some Kurdish organizations participate with a float each year but their acts do not come close to anything spectacular, either. When the Turks appear in the floats they do so by participating in the success of the floats of organizations with which they are associated, such as youth centers, sound mobiles, and gay self-help organizations.

In short, Turks in Berlin, as well as the Kurds from Turkey, do not respond to what is expected of them: appearing at the parade as proper "cultures" within the diversity display that is the Karneval der Kulturen. This is variously interpreted as an unwillingness of Turks to participate in Berlin's multiculturalism, but this interpretation ignores the fact that the major constituency of the Karneval is in fact the Turkish residents of Berlin. Their participation as spectators, artists, and entrepreneurs is essential to the Karneval, but they refrain from taking part in the diversity display. They prefer to be present in the carnival stage as citizens of Berlin.

Berlin Tourismus Marketing

Berlin Tourismus Marketing is new among the influential institutions of culture makers in Berlin. Their influence comes from the place assigned to tourism in creating the future of Berlin as a seat of creativity and culture –thus as a place of attraction for capital, creative industries, and talent– in Europe and in the world. The office is not new in the sense that it had a predecessor organization, which was organizationally located under Berlin's Public Transportation Office (*Verkehrsamt*). In 1994 the tasks that were carried out by the Transportation Office were transferred to the newly created, semi-private Berlin Tourismus Marketing.

The office sees itself as a Public-Private Partnership (PPP). Its primary partners come from the tourism sector. These are the Association of Berlin Hotels, with a 40 percent share, KaDeWe, the major department store in Berlin (in the order of Harrods in London, La Fayette in Paris, and Saks Fifth Avenue in New York), and by itself a tourist destination, with a 10 percent share, and *Messe Berlin*, the city's fair and trade centers, with a 5 percent share. The remaining 15 percent share belongs to the Berlin Senate. The annual budget of the organization is about 10 million euros, with 2 million coming from the Senate. Of the budget, 20 percent covers the overhead and 80 percent goes to operational items.[6]

The Director of Culture of Berlin Tourismus Marketing imagines Berlin as an international city, not particularly as a national city –though he admits at present that the major portion of tourists in Berlin arrive from national destinations. For him, "tourist" is a universal category. His eyes are on the mega events, the likes of the Love Parade, *Berlinale* (Berlin Film Festival), the Berlin Marathon, *Festtage* (Festival Days) at the Opera, special exhibitions such as the MOMA in Berlin and the Goya Exhibit, and various international trade shows such as the ITB (International Tourism Bourse), the IFA (International Electronics Show), and the ILA (International Airplane Show), and last but not least the WM (World Football Championship). The

---

6 Even though the *Haupstadt Kulturfonds* is branded as a PPP organization, its director was very dismissive of the idea, stating that "PPT does not make sense when the only private partner was Schering," the chemical conglomerate.

Karneval der Kulturen does not make the director's initial list, but was confirmed as important when specifically asked.

The Director's list of events considered important for Berlin is almost endless. According to him, about 14 to 15 hundred events take place every day in Berlin. Winter is the dead season and things pick up in the summer. February is the time for the Berlin Film Festival; March is for the International Tourism Bourse. The Director firmly indicates that they do not believe in branding the city. For them, Berlin is already a brand, if anything.

It was evident from the interview that the vision of Berlin upheld by the institution –that is the vision of what makes Berlin significant and hence attractive– was rather academic. Put differently, and perhaps not surprisingly, the vision outlined by the Director of Culture at the Tourismus Marketing is no different than the depictions of Berlin's significance as a WorldCity in the works of Jane Kramer, Brian Ladd, Levent Soysal, and others. For the director, there are three elements that make and should make Berlin a point of attraction on a world scale. The first element is Berlin's lively cultural scene, itself a tradition. The second is Berlin's history: Weimar's cultural capital in the 1920s, the capital of the Third Reich and the Holocaust, the divided city of the Cold War, the frontier of the East-West conflict, the capital city of Unified Germany; and finally the modern metropolis. For him, this history is neither unified nor can be unified as German history; it comprises not only German but also world history. It is controversial, and therein lays its attraction. The third element is Berlin's tradition as a trendsetting city for design, music, and clubs, and with the potential for becoming a center in an international creative network.

As for the multicultural potential of Berlin, the Director volunteers the following when asked: "Berlin is surely a multicultural city and this is an asset but only within Germany. When considered worldwide, there are other cities that fit the description much more than Berlin." The conclusion the Director draws from this is that though multiculturalism is an asset of Berlin, it is not something to build upon on a world scale; there exists "more multicultural cities in other countries."

Classifying the Spectacle

In Istanbul, together with my research assistant Özlem Aslan, we had undertaken the classification of the newspaper archive I had had assembled on Carnival, immigrants, and the city. In this exercise, we essentially utilized the new classification scheme I had been crafting –namely, *Spectacles of Identity*, *Spectacles of Migration*, *Spectacles of State*, *Spectacles of Dissent*, and so on. It has become apparent during the exercise that this new classification scheme is more reflective of the changes and shifts in the form and content of spectacles under the new regimes of diversity, multiculturalism, and Europeanization.

We have also carried out the codification of the visual and textual material collected so far, using the same classificatory scheme as the basis. Here we primarily focused on what constitutes a legitimate collective action in public spaces, (which collectivities and performances are celebrated, authorized, or repudiated; what characteristics make a proper spectacle), who promotes, underwrites, and manages the spectacle; the extent to which public and/or private funds are allocated; which spectacles draw preferential funding and support, the specific ways in which identity is articulated, which signs constitute the expressive repertoire of identity, and the ways in which the new public spectacle departs from being national in content and local in form.

A preliminary analysis of the event scene in Berlin and visual material collected indicate the following:

• The two main key words that organize and authorize the new spectacle emerge as *diversity* and *creativity*. The first implies and legitimizes the social and moral good of the spectacle, while the second marks its individual and commercial potential.

• Any spectacle which makes the grade in terms of its diversity and creativity potential receives a welcome from governmental and funding organizations, and finds itself a space within the cultural scene that is Berlin. Any sign that implies *conflict* is strictly avoided –though Berlin is a city of controversies.

• Identity, as it plays out in the spectacles, more often than not, is understood and represented as cultural identity –ethnic, religious, or otherwise. This does not mean that the politics of identity is the only formal playing field. Various forms of cosmopolitanisms weaken the premium placed on cultural identities.

• *National* is simply out, although the city is the capital of the Unified Germany. All events embrace a vision of the city as a world-level metropolis and aim for approximating world-level standards and ideals. In this respect, any act that recalls national signs and ideals on the part of immigrant populations (such as in Turkish Day) is seen as suspect, even though the very emphasis on cultural identities facilitate the branding of ethnic, religious, and national repertoires of signs and signatures, flags being the most important ones.

• Mega events are becoming the norm because of the economies of scale and because of the budgetary troubles of Berlin as a city and a state.

Discussion

As indicated before, the discussion that follows draws upon not only the empirical research carried out under the grant provided by MiReKoc, but also benefits from the material collected and the analyses carried out over the years that I have undertaken this research. I start with the identities of Berlin, continue with the content and politics of the new spectacle in relation to the city, and end with the place of migrants in the city.

Identities of Berlin and Kreuzberg

In the short time span between the emblematic fall of the Berlin Wall in 1989 and the official unification of the two Berlins and the two Germanies in October of 1990, more than the physical impediments that had divided the city had disappeared. Also gone was the narrative of the Divided City that had organized the lives of Berliners for more than four decades. On October 3rd, Berlin was figuratively inaugurated as a WorldCity. As the re-unified Berlin has adapted to the narrative of the metropolis and underwent reconstruction at an extraordinary scale, it has been re-mapped in the image of a *Hauptstadt* (Capital City) of the unified Germany, *Kulturstadt* (Culture City) in a unified Europe, and *Weltstadt* (WorldCity) in a cosmopolitan world. New identifications have replaced the old idiosyncratic Berlin stories of a Divided City.

In the new spatial and narrative configuration of the city, Kreuzberg was no longer a desolate margin next to the Wall – a *Gastarbeiter* quarter, where the (Western) city literally met its borders. It has suddenly moved to the center, neighboring the historic *Mitte* (the mid-city) and the Government and Business Centers, under construction along the axis of the new Potsdamer Platz and Reichstag. With this move, Kreuzberg has become the ceremonial ghetto for the metropolis.

Note that Berlin's current population is about 3.2 million, of which approximately 12 percent are foreigners. Migrants from Turkey comprise the largest and the most visible minority group, nearly 4 percent. Of the Turks in Berlin, 36 percent are between the ages of 10 and 20; a fairly young population, crowding schools, streets, youth centers, and work places, as well as unemployment and drop-out statistics. While Turks live and work in other parts of Berlin almost in equal numbers, Kreuzberg is known variously as the "Turkish ghetto" or "Little Istanbul."

In its ghetto guise, Kreuzberg is cast not as a zone of excessive criminality and utmost poverty, but one of cultural pluralism and alternative lifestyles. Among others the widely available youth guide, *Berlin for Young People* (1992), describes the district as a "multicultural mix of peoples, Turks [living] along with students, 'alternatives,' punks, and perfectly normal Berlin families," and "off-movie houses and theaters, wonderfully dingy bars, affordable restaurants and second-hand shops." This vision of Kreuzberg is extremely popular and quasi-official.

Parallel to the reconstruction of Berlin, Kreuzberg has also undergone gentrification and is now facing competition from the "newly" discovered alternative neighborhoods, such as Prenzlauer Berg of the former "East." Nonetheless, Kreuzberg remains in the self-portrayal of the city as the locus of hipness and diversity. What is significant – and consequential – for our purposes is that in the intervening years hipness and diversity have come to identify and edify not just Kreuzberg but the whole of Berlin.

Conjecture 1) In the process, Kreuzberg — and the ghetto narrative — has lost its singular place in the imagery of the city and become normalized. Now Berlin aspires to be a WorldCity, and compete and forge alliances with other WorldCities such as London, New York, and Tokyo. Kreuzberg is its stage for displaying diversity and multicultural flavor and color. Immigrants do have a prominent place in the staging of diversity — hence the charisma and allure of Kreuzberg.

Calendar of Spectacles in Berlin

The Carnival of Cultures, (the multicultural display of diversity), is by all means not the end of the Carnival season for Berlin but signals a beginning. May Day, the annual celebration of working people — and the annual day of ritualized fights between the *antifa* (short for anti-fascist) youths and the police — precedes the Carnival, and in a way opens the carnival season. Then come the Christopher Street Day Parade, (one of the earliest and most important gay celebrations in Europe), and the Love Parade (claiming to be the largest public parade in Europe — now defunct), along with a variety of neighborhood and street festivals, and occasional shopping and fashion festivals on major avenues such as Ku'Damm.

Every summer for two months Berlin puts itself on display (*Schaustelle Berlin*) as a self-designated *öffene Stadt* (Open City) and offers cosmopolitan ambience to its blasé natives and curious visitors. As such, the city itself emulates spectacle and competes with the spectacular performances taking place on its terrain. *Museum Insel Festival* (Museum Island Festival) brings together music stars from around the world to stages set in the space between *Alte Museum* (Old Museum), History Museum, and Pergamon Museum, while *Heimetklaenge* (Voices from Home), becomes a stage for world music during the summer months.

The fall and winter have their fair share of festivals. First there is the official Day of Unification celebration which has been taking place on the 3rd of October every year since 1991. Halloween and "traditional" pumpkin fests merge into each other towards the end of October. Come November, the Christmas season starts with Christmas markets and ends with the climactic fireworks; both official in the shadow of Brandenburg Gate, and unofficial on every street corner. February is the time of Berlinale, an annual movie spectacle with celebrities, prizes, and parties. Berlin's traditional Carnival in February, is a "tradition which has become livelier, with the moving of Germany's capital and bureaucratic classes from Bonn to Berlin.

Conjecture 2) As one character says in Tom Schreiber's film *Narren* (2002), a poignant reflection on Kölln carnival, there is no end to the carnival, "Now life in Berlin is a year-around, non-stop event. The Turkish Day Parade is a newly added item to the Parade list, commemorating migration and migrants, and celebrating the friendship of the natives and foreigners."

Spectacle is No Longer Unique
The fact that it is difficult to distinguish festivals from each other is not just a case of a naming practice perpetuated by travel inserts. Berlin's contemporary carnivals are hardly local or particular. As the presentations of scholars and practitioners of carnival testify in the symposium on European carnivals, the new spectacles borrow from each other, they mimic each other, and they approximate each

other. Unlike performance genres that come to world attention at the time of nation building, the carnivals of today attract attention inasmuch as they resemble other events of their kind in content and form. Nations want their festivals to be unique; in a globalizing world claim to uniqueness does not necessarily amount to capital — of the monetary and the symbolic kinds.

Conjecture 3) Today it is possible to assemble these diverse and dissimilar events under the same category, speak of them with the same vocabulary, bring them together in the same imagery of the spectacle — as shown by the calendar of events assembled above and as undertaken by our interviewees in Berlin. The aforementioned Carnival of Cultures, the Notting Hill Carnival, the Zineke Festival, and Sommer Carnival all operate with the same premises of diversity and pluralism. In the same vein, Turkish Day is no different than its counterpart in New York, from which the organizers borrowed the form and content from the Berlin version. Lacking uniqueness, Turkish Day does not stand out as a national celebration but falls under the fold of multicultural spectacles.

The Politics of Spectacle

Carnival theory, more often than not, locates the politics of performance in the constitutional elements of the spectacle: Politics emanates from the practice of the grotesque, inversion, and wonder. Contemporary spectacle, on the other hand, is successfully elusive in this respect. Its politics is proclaimed as lacking from the outset or reduced to a plasticity that can only be experienced or practiced as an aestheticized cliché.

This new politics of the spectacle is tightly connected to the process of Europeanization. Here Europe is taken as a supranational cultural and political entity, taking shape in the general geography of the European Union –and beyond– and shaped by the enfolding realities of regional, national, and global order. As Europe becomes a supranational entity, existing national identities are increasingly contested and "normalized" (Soysal Nuhoğlu 2002) both by emerging notions of "Europeanness" and by the proliferation of regional and minority identities. While European identity claims an encompassing, inclusive formation, regional and minority identities project cultural pluralism within the boundaries of the newly imagined Europe.

It is in this Europe that the new spectacle, and its ephemeral politics, is taking shape. It is no coincidence that the goals stated by organizers of new festivals and conveyed to the public through carnival slogans and publicity material correlate with the civic virtues and tales of morality that the new Europe desires to foster: understanding, tolerance, and cooperation among peoples within and without Europe. In this sense, the new spectacle becomes an instrument of making the new Europe, contributing to the production of what Chris Shore (2000) identifies as a "'European' sense and sensibility of self" and Yasemin Nuhoğlu Soysal (2002) terms as *"affective Europeanness"*. Like cultural policy and education, respectively the sites of realizing Europe in Shore's and Soysal Nuhoğlu's work, the space of spectacle is yet another site for contention and affirmation of "multi-cultural", "diverse" Europe. Here on the site of carnival –the site of food, dance, music, and togetherness– the "diverse" peoples of Europe are expected to share and enjoy culture, forge bonds with each other, and "imagine" (Anderson, 1991) a new Europe.

Conjecture 4) In the aestheticized politics of European festivals we discover the longings of Europe for identity, and the banishment of particularisms, (Europe's own particularity included), into the hegemonic realm of the spectacle, (form, so to speak), morality, and universalism. Berlin's spectacles are part of the repertoire of the new spectacles in Europe. The exhibition of immigrant particularities –food, dance, and arts– at the Turkish Day or Carnival of Cultures serve to exemplify diversity and affirm multiculturalism, rather than being signs of national displacement or isolation. With their festivals, the immigrants join the ranks of the new Europe.

Spectacle is What Makes a City a City

Since Saskia Sassen's *Global City* (1991), we are more attentive to the fact that the global character of metropolitan centers intensifies at the expense of national configurations. Berlin, London, Rotterdam, Istanbul, and other major urban centers project themselves beyond the nation-state within which they are located. The cities less and less come to prominence by being the capital or industrial hub of a nation-state, say of Germany, the United Kingdom, or the Netherlands, and seek their fortunes and fame elsewhere. More and more they fashion themselves as "world" or "global" cities and under the tutelage of marketing companies they strive to develop themselves as "brands," as cities of culture, art, fashion, science, sports, and various other forms of entertainment. The brand "European (Culture) City" is one instance of being and projecting an image of a city beyond the conventional geography of local or national import, and achieving global stature.

At this juncture, we observe the reorganization of public spaces and the proliferation of carnivals and public spectacles of all sorts in metropolitan centers. Ranging from street festivals, carnivals, and concerts to international conferences, fairs, and sports gatherings, these events have become the identifying features of the contemporary metropolitan order and provide the metropolis with an aura of cultural grandeur and finesse. Olympic Games, for instance, are no longer an arena for "national" (or cold war) rivalry but a stage for literally and figuratively remaking a city as a WorldCity.

Conjecture 5) Spectacles provide the raw material for creating a brand name for the city by catering to contemporary "life styles" and to the demands of media and global travel. At the same time, they aim to facilitate formations of community and solidarity and allow for participation in local, national, and transnational social spaces. Politics and economies of launching public events do not oppose but compliment each other. Immigrant spectacles have become indispensable instruments for making a city worthy of branding itself

"WorldCity",for the immigrant is categorically the sign of diversity and cosmopolitanism.

Where Have All the Immigrants Gone?

Spectacles such as the Carnival of Cultures, the Love Parade, the Christopher Day Parade, and the Turkish Parade, if we take Berlin as our case, signal the advent of a new performance genre, which I referentially call *spectacles of identity*. Employing markers of ethnicity, race, culture, gender, and other particularisms, the spectacles of identity delimit and present *identity groups*, and perform and celebrate *in public* their *cultural specificity* within an imagery of *diversity*.

The discourses of plurality, on the other hand, intensify the pronunciation and delineation of cultural particularities and ensure the public visibility of the genre. The legitimacy of claims for a distinct cultural identity – and, therefore, the right to be recognized as an identifiably discrete group – lies with the existence and ownership of marked domains of customs, traditions, food, rituals, dances, music, costumes, and other cultural artifacts. Once an identity is legitimated and formalized as distinct, its public performance becomes integral to the social movement(s) that embraces and cultivates that particular identity. The vocabulary and activity routines of the social movement(s), in turn, put the identity spectacle on public stages, progressively magnifying its visibility and negotiating its cultural content.

Thus, we have Turkish culture and its performances by Turkish immigrants reigning on the stages of multiculturalism in Berlin. However, once they reach the stage and multiply, they become normalized within the elusive discursive spaces of Europeanness. The signs and signatures of uniqueness become captivated in the sameness of the spectacles that celebrate universalized diversities.

Conjecture 6) Immigrant cultures — performed as identity spectacles — are not absent from the social and cultural spaces of diversity in Berlin. Nor are they sanctioned to be visible as distinctly different. This seeming paradox is ingrained in the working definition and

moral content of diversity displays, as universally imagined and performed today.

CONCLUSION AND POLICY IMPLICATIONS

I have taken up this research because of an interest in the participation
of immigrants in their countries of residence. At the early stages of the
immigration to Europe, emphasis on matters of labor overshadowed
any concern –scientific or otherwise– regarding the daily lives of
immigrants. With the cultural turn, the immigrant has entered the
imagery of Europe as a human being with cultural needs and rights.
Even then, under the clouds of raging integration debates, the participation of immigrants in the everyday economies and politics has been
largely overlooked, if not ignored.

      The findings of this research clearly show that immigrants have
long been participants in the public spaces of Berlin, the self-designated Open City, with a large Turkish population and a self-declared policy of multiculturalism. At the Carnival of Cultures and the May Day
Parade, immigrants have been regular participants as audiences and
performers. It is impossible to think of the May Day Parade and the
Carnival of Cultures without the involvement and contribution of sub-
stantively large groups of immigrants. Then, there are numerous small
events and performances staged by immigrants in the informal cultural scenes of Berlin. With the now annual Turkish Day parade, Turkish
immigrants have managed to produce their own spectacles, however
small and unprofessional, in the likeness of ethnic parades staged in
other metropolitan centers such as New York. They are requisite fix-
tures of –and immanently featured on– the stages of diversity, tolerance, and solidarity in the WorldCity Berlin.

      This project has also emerged from a concern regarding the
changing meanings of public spectacles and the performance of identity within the new cultural topography of the metropolis. The task
has been to delineate the affinities of Europeanization with the burgeoning urban festivals and carnivals, interrogate the policies and

processes that lead to the proliferation of urban spectacle, and map out the contours of the newly emerging expressive culture of the contemporary metropolis.

The larger research I have undertaken firmly indicates that public spectacle underwrites the re-organization of public spaces and the metropolitan order. Cities are now unthinkable without a large repertoire of spectacles. The totality of these events constitutes the cultural fabric of the contemporary metropolis, set the stage for many creative industries, and further solidarity within the framework of diversity. In this process the city has become a novel spectacle in its own right. In the new design of the metropolis, the city is *in and of itself* a spectacle. With its stupendous architectural monuments designed by brand name architects, diversity displays that duly commemorate metropolitan plurality. Combined with renovated (and scaled up) living spaces and designer lifestyles, the city fosters and intensifies the spectacular performances of urban living.

In this city, organizing a Turkish Day in Berlin is not a sign of displacement but of civic participation. For the norm for participation is the spectacle, and the contemporary urban spectacle articulates the commanding discourses of our times. Hence, in the new city what is expected of the citizen is to take part in the spectacle, contribute to it by displaying his or her culture, and enjoy the cultural proceeds that materialize. Through Turkish Day, and various public spectacles they stage and take part in, Turkish immigrants do exactly that: contribute to the new formations of culture in the metropolis. Whether they are audiences in Karneval der Kulturen or active participants in Turkish Day, their presence on the city stages is an asset for diversity displays that make the city a proper city. In other words, their involvement contributes to the making of Berlin a cosmopolitan metropolis and WorldCity.

These findings have serious implications for the ways the local or national governments approach integration. Still under the spell of conventional immigration models that take the national as the primary determinant, officials, activists, and social workers responsible for devising immigration and integration policies dutifully search for immigrant cultures that lie elsewhere, in home countries and villages located away from the amenities and imagery of modernity. They do not entertain the idea that immigrants may very well be adjusted to living in and have the competencies for shaping the life of a contemporary metropolis after four decades of praxis as residents of Berlin, Germany.

Consequently, policies devised for integration ignore the already existing integration and get embroiled in heated debates on superfluous parallel societies, and immigrant ghettos. The time is ripe for new beginnings and recognizing immigrant populations for what they are: civic participants in the everyday economies, politics, and public stages of the new metropolis.

WorldCity is inconceivable without their presence and participation. Only then does immigrant integration become a policy field for advancing the immigrants' quality of life with novel approaches, rather than a quagmire of endless argumentation over abstract, categorical differences between East and West, tradition and modernity, and Turkishness and Germanness.

Select Bibliography

The larger research is interdisciplinary in nature and derives its theoretical inspiration from recent scholarship spanning many disciplines, in particular work on globalisation, performance and expressive cultures, immigration, and space and urban theory. The following list includes a select bibliography of works that frame the theoretical premises of the larger research, a representative sample of the literature on Turkish immigration to Germany, as well as references cited in the report.

REFERENCES

Abadan-Unat, N. (ed.), 1975, *Turkish Workers in Europe, 1960-1975: A Socio-Economic Reappraisal*, Leiden: E. J. Brill.

Adelson, L., 2005, *The Turkish Turn in Contemporary German Literature: Toward a New Critical Grammar of Migration*, London: Palgrave Macmillan.

Anderson, B., 1991, *Imagined Communities*, London: Verso.

Appadurai, A., 1996, *Modernity at Large: Cultural Dimensions of Globalisation*, Minneapolis: University of Minnesota Press.

Argun, B. E., 2003, *Turkey in Germany: The Transnational Sphere of Deutschkei*, New York: Routledge.

Bade, K. and M. Weiner (eds.), 1997, *Migration Past, Migration Future: Germany and the United States*, Providence: Berghahn Books.

Basch, L., N. G. Schiller and C. S. Blanc, 1994, *Nations Unbound: Trans national Projects, Postcolonial Predicaments, and Deterritorialized Nation-States*, Langhorne, Pennsylvania: Gordon and Breach.

Bauman, Z., 1998, *Globalisation: The Human Consequences*, New York: Columbia University Press.

Beeman, W. O., 1993, "The Anthropology of Theater and Spectacle", *Annual Review of Anthropology*, 22: 369-393.

Benhabib, S., 2002, *The Claims of Culture: Equality and Diversity in the Global Era*, New Jersey: Princeton University Press.

—, 2004, *The Rights of Others: Aliens, Residents, and Citizens*, Cambridge: Cambridge University Press.

Berger, J., 1975, *A Seventh Man: A Book of Images and Words about the Experience of Migrant Workers in Europe*, Baltimore: Penguin.

Boissevain, J. (ed.), 1992, *Revitalizing European Rituals*, London: Routledge.

Borneman, J. and N. Fowler, 1997, "Europeanization", *Annual Review of Anthropology*, 26: 487-514.

Brubaker, W. R. (ed.), 1989, *Immigration and the Politics of Citizenship in Europe and North America*, Lanham, Maryland: University Press of America.

Çağlar, A. S. and L. Soysal, 2003, "Introduction: Turkish Migration to Germany—Forty Years After", *New Perspectives on Turkey*, 28-29: 1-18.

Carter, D. M., 1997, *States of Grace: Senegalese in Italy and the New European Immigration*, Minneapolis: University of Minnesota Press.

Castles, S. and G. Kosack, 1973, *Immigrant Workers and Class Structure in Western Europe*, London: Oxford University Press.

Castles, S. and M. J. Miller, 1998, *The Age of Migration: International Population Movements in the Modern World*, 2nd ed., New York: The Guilford Press.

Chambers, I., 1994, *Migrancy, Culture, Identity*, London: Routledge.

Chaney, D., 1993, *Fictions of Collective Life: Public Drama in Late Modern Culture*, London: Routledge.

Cohen, S., 1980, *Folk Devils and Moral Panics: The Creation of Mods and Rockers*, New York: St. Martin's Press.

Cohen, A., 1993, *Masquerade Politics: Explorations in the Structure of Urban Cultural Movements*, Berkeley: University of California Press.

de Certeau, M., 1984, *The Practice of Everyday Life*, Berkeley: University of California Press.

Eickelman, D. F. and J. Piscatori (eds.), 1990, *Muslim Travelers: Pilgrimage, Migration, and the Religious Imagination*, Berkeley: University of California Press.

George, K. M., 1996, *Showing the Signs of Violence: The Cultural Politics of a Twentieth-Century Headhunting Ritual*, Berkeley: University of California Press.

Goddard, V. A., J. R. Llobera, and C. Shore (eds.), 1994, *The Anthropology of Europe: Identity and Boundaries in Conflict*, Oxford: Berg Publishers.

Goehler, A., 2006, *Verfluessigungen: Wege und Umwege vom Sozialstaat zur Kulturgesellscahft*, Frankfurt: Campus Verlag.

Gupta, A. and J. Ferguson (eds.), 1997, *Anthropological Locations: Boundaries and Grounds of a Field Science*, Berkeley: University of California Press.

Handelman, D., 1990, *Models and Mirrors: Toward and Anthropology of Public Events*, Cambridge: University of Cambridge Press.

Hannerz, U., 1996, *Transnational Connections: Culture, People, Places*, New York: Routledge.

Herzfeld, M., 1987, *Anthropology through the Looking-Glass: Critical Ethnography in the Margins of Europe*, Cambridge: Cambridge University Press.

Horrocks, D. and E. Kolinsky (eds.), 1996, *Turkish Culture in German Society Today, Providence*, Rhode Island: Berghahn Books.

Jelavich, P., 1993, *Berlin Cabaret*, Cambridge: Harvard University Press.

Kaplan, T., 1992, *Red City, Blue Period: Social Movements in Picasso's Barcelona*, Berkeley: University of California Press.

Kastoryano, R., 1986, *Être Turc en France: Réflexions et Communauté*, Paris: Editions L'Harmattan.

—, 2003, *Negotiating Identities: States and Immigrants in France and Germany*, New Jersey: Princeton University Press.

Kaya, A., 2001, *"Sicher in Kreuzberg": Constructing Diasporas. Turkish Hip-Hop Youth in Berlin*, Berlin: Transcript Verlag.

Klopp, B., 2002, *German Multiculturalism: Immigrant Integration and the Transformation of Citizenship*, London: Praeger.

Kramer, J., 1996, *The Politics of Memory: Looking for Germany in the New Germany*, New York: Random House.

Ladd, B., 1997, *The Ghosts of Berlin: Confronting German History in the Urban Landscape*, Chicago: University of Chicago Press.

Mandel, R., 1996, "A Place of Their Own: Contesting Spaces and Defining Places in Berlin's Migrant Community" in B. D. Metcalf (ed.), *Making Muslim Space in North America and Europe*, Berkeley: University of California Press.

Marcus, G. E., 1998, *Ethnography through Thick and Thin*, NJ: Princeton University Press.

Marcus, G. E. and M. M. J. Fischer, 1986, *Anthropology as a Cultural Critique: An Experimental Moment in the Human Sciences*, Chicago: University of Chicago Press.

Moore, S. F. and B. G. Myerhoff (eds.), 1977, *Secular Ritual*, Amsterdam: Van Gorcum.

Morokvasic, M., 1984, "Birds of Passage Are Also Women . . .", *International Migration Review*, 18(4): 886-907.

Muenz, R. and R. Ulrich, 1997, "Changing Patterns of Immigration to Germany, 1945-1995" in R. Muenz and M. Weiner (eds.), *Migrants, Refugees, and Foreign Policy: U.S. and German Policies toward Countries of Origin*, Providence: Berghahn Books.

Richie, A., 1998, *Faust's Metropolis: A History of Berlin*, New York: Carroll and Graf Publishers.

Robertson, R., 1992, *Globalisation: Social Theory and Global Culture*, London: Sage Publications.

Sassen, S., 1991, *The Global City: New York, London, Tokyo*, New Jersey: Princeton University Press.

—, 1998, *Globalisation and Its Discontents*, New York: New Press.

Schiffauer, W., 1987, *Die Bauern von Subay: das Leben in einem Türkischen Dorf*, Stuttgart: Kleff-Cotta.

Schiffauer, W., G. Bauman, R. Kastoryano and S. Vertovec (eds.), 2004, *Civil Enculturation: Nation-State, School and Ethnic Difference in the Netherlands, Britain, Germany and France*, New York: Berghahn Books.

Shore, C., 2000, *Building Europe: The Cultural Politics of European Integration*, London: Routledge.

Soekefeld, M. (ed.), 2004, *Jenseits des Paradigmas kultureller Differenz: Neue Perspektiven auf Einwanderer aus der Türkei*, Bielefeld: transcript Verlag.

SOPEMI, 2004, "German Report on International Migration", written by Barbara Froechich.

Soysal Nuhoğlu, Y., 1994, *Limits of Citizenship: Migrants and Postnational Membership in Europe*, Chicago: University of Chicago Press.

—, 1997, "Changing Parameters of Citizenship and Claims-Making: Organized Islam in European Public Spheres", *Theory and Society*, 26: 509-527.

—, 2000, "Citizenship and Identity: Living in Diasporas in Post-war Europe?", *Ethnic and Racial Studies*, 1: 1-15.

—, 2002, "Locating Europe", *European Societies*, 4(3): 265-284.

Soysal, L., 2001, "Diversity of Experience, Experience of Diversity: Turkish Migrant Youth Culture in Berlin", *Cultural Dynamics*, 13(1): 5-28.

—, 2002, "Beyond 'Second Generation': Rethinking the Place of Migrant Youth Culture in Berlin" in D. Levy and Y. Weiss (eds.), *Challenging Ethnic Citizenship: German and Israeli Perspectives on Immigration*, New York: Berghahn Books.

—, 2004, "Rap, HipHop, and Kreuzberg: The Institutional Topography of Migrant Youth Culture in the WorldCity Berlin", *New German Critique*, 92: 62-81.

Sen, F. and A. Goldberg, 1994, *Türken in Deutschland: Leben zwischen zwei Kulturen*, München: Verlag C.H. Beck.

Tertilt, H., 1996, *Turkish Power Boys: Ethnographie einer Jugenbande*, Frankfurt am Main: Suhrkamp.

Turner, V. W., 1987, *The Anthropology of Performance*, New York: PAJ Publications.

Wallraff, G., 1985, *Ganz unten*, Koeln: Verlag Kiepenheuer and Witsch.

Werbner, P. and T. Modood (eds.), 1997, *The Politics of Multiculturalism in the New Europe: Racism, Identity and Community*, London: Zen Books.

White, J., 1997, "Turks in the New Germany", *American Anthropologist*, 99: 754-769.

Wikan, U., 2002, *Generous Betrayal: Politics of Culture in the New Europe*, Chicago: University of Chicago Press.

Willis, P., 1990, *Common Culture: Symbolic Work at Play in Everyday Cultures of the Young*, Boulder: Westview Press.

Wolbert, B., 1995, *Der getötete Pass: Rückkehr in die Türkei*, Berlin: Akademia Verlag.

4

Culture and Migration: A Comparison of Turkish Migrant and Non-Migrant Mother's Long-term Socialization Goals

Bilge Yağmurlu

INTRODUCTION

In addition to the importance of the early environment, early relationships are crucial in every aspect of human development and functioning. The growing rate of divorce, working mothers and the issues related to abuse and adverse child outcomes, such as behavioral problems (e.g., aggression), has led to a growing recognition of the importance of parent-child interaction (Abidin, 1992). In consequence, the impact of parenting on children's development has been examined widely in an attempt to understand the ways we can improve child outcomes (Kağıtçıbaşı et al., 2001).

For a long time, general parenting styles and parenting practices have been the only focus in the parenting literature. It is now generally recognized that an appropriate model of parenting must involve not only child-rearing practices but also underlying factors, such as parental cognitions (Abidin, 1992; Goodnow, 1988). Examining parental behaviors without paying attention to the goals they set for their children will not allow us to thoroughly comprehend 'parental socialization'. Hence, in the last decade, studies on parenting have not solely focused on parents' behaviors, but also on their ideas (Dix et al, 1986; Goodnow, 1988), values (Harwood, 1992), and goals (Hastings & Grusec, 1998; Kuczynski, 1984), which shape their child-rearing behaviors. It is also true that aspects of the social context (Vandell, 2000), particularly parents' education and family structure, are closely related to parenting (Cowan et al., 1998). It can thus be assumed that parenting influences are influenced by, several forces and that these factors shape child outcomes.

As is usually the case, most of our knowledge on parental socialization by and large, comes from studies of Western families. However, socialization is culture-bound (Ambert, 1994). The cultural context includes norms that shape the child's interaction with family members and the wider society (Clausen, 1966; Georgas et al., 1997; Slaughter-Defoe, 1995). The unique characteristics (e.g., rules, traditions) of each culture also shape the functions and impact of particular values, beliefs and behaviors of parents (Stevenson-Hinde, 1998). This implies that the pattern of relations between parent and child characteristics in a particular culture may not be generalized across cultures; hence, there is a need to examine parenting separately for different cultural groups. This brief introduction suggests that we need to examine the socialization goals of mothers in Turkey to have a better understanding of their child-rearing practices and interaction with children. Exploring the role of education in Turkish mothers' long-term socialization goals provides us further information on within-culture variations.

The following sections of the paper review the literature on parenting and summarize theoretical and empirical studies on parenting and the relations between social context and parenting. It starts with an exploration of the relationship between parenting style, ideas, values and behaviors. Socioeconomic background is proposed to be an important determinant of parenting, so the association between socioeconomic status and parenting is examined. In the subsequent sections, the aims and hypotheses of the study are presented in the light of the findings reviewed; characteristics of the participants in the study and the measures used to assess the variables are given. Then, a detailed report of the results of statistical analyses is presented. More peripheral information concerning the procedure and data is presented in the Appendices. The final section interprets the findings of the present study and discusses them in relation to the literature.

PARENTING STYLES, IDEAS, VALUES AND BEHAVIORS

There are several socializing influences on child development. Although some researchers (Harris, 1995, 2000) propose that the impact of peers, teachers, and school context can be more significant than that of parents, it is mostly agreed that parents and the family context influence child outcomes dramatically across development. Different models have been suggested to explain the process through which parents affect child development. Here, the focus is on theories and empirical findings related to parenting styles, behaviors, and cognitions.

Darling and Steinberg (1993: 493) define parenting style as "a constellation of attitudes toward the child that are communicated to the child and create an emotional climate in which the parent's behaviors are expressed." Baumrind (1973), whose typology of parenting styles has been influential in the field, suggests two dimensions: warmth/responsiveness and control, and three basic types of parental styles: permissive, authoritarian and authoritative. Permissive parents are warm but fail to set limits and provide a structure for the child. These parents do not take an active role in shaping their child's development (Baumrind, 1978). On the other hand, authoritarian parents highly value obedience. They exert firm control, but their rules can be arbitrary. Authoritarian parents are less affectionate and sensitive to the child's needs, and they do not communicate their expectations effectively. They use less verbalization (e.g., explanation) and do not aim to promote verbalization in the child. The third parenting style, authoritative parenting, includes affection, attention to the child's needs and parental reinforcement of positive behavior with clear requirements for desired behaviors. Firm control is also present in this type of parenting, but the parent also values autonomy in the child. Authoritative parents display a flexible orientation to parenting where they aim to explain to the child the reasons behind rules (Baumrind, 1973). Hence, authoritative parents display reasoning, reinforcement, warmth, and control and, as elaborated in the following sections, this is the parenting style which is assumed to best foster social competence in the child (Baumrind, 1978).

Darling and Steinberg (1993) emphasize the need to differentiate between parenting style and parenting behaviors. It has been suggested that 'parenting style' refers to the quality, and 'parenting behaviors' refers to the content and frequency, of practices (Stevenson-Hinde, 1998). Inductive reasoning (e.g., providing explanations), warmth (e.g., nurturance, affection, support), and power assertion (e.g., punishment, restriction, obedience-demanding behavior) are some of the most examined parenting behaviors in relation to child outcomes. As described in the preceding paragraphs, parenting behaviors are observed in varying degrees in each parenting style (e.g., inductive reasoning is a significant component of authoritative parenting). Thus, parenting style reflects a general attitude toward the child, and its influence on child outcomes is more indirect. It moderates the impact of parenting practices through affecting the parent-child interaction and the child's perception of the parents' behaviors. For example, the child's compliance with the parents' request or internalization of the parents' values is more likely in the context of an authoritative style of parenting.

It has also been shown that parenting styles might be structured differently in different cultures. For instance, Kağıtçıbaşı (1970) found that authoritarian parenting was associated with control and lack of affection in American families, while it was related to parental control but not to lack of affection in Turkish families. This finding suggests that Baumrind's (1973) descriptions of parenting styles are based on conceptualizations of family in "Western", English-speaking societies, and they may involve different parenting patterns across cultures.

Apart from parenting styles, parental cognitions have also been related to child-rearing behaviors (Abidin, 1992). Darling and Steinberg (1993) provided a distinction between thoughts and actions, and suggested that parenting styles and behaviors are both influenced by parenting ideas and goals. Similarly, Goodnow (1988) suggested that parents' ideas and emotions concerning the child are not only related to each other, but they also influence parenting practices and child outcomes.

Child-rearing behaviors are also related to parenting goals which are described as the attributes parents value and want their children to attain (Hastings & Grusec, 1998). Kuczynski (1984) described two types of parental socialization goals, long-term and short-term compliance goals. In short-term goals, the parent aims to acquire immediate compliance from the child. In long-term goals, the aim of the parent is to achieve the desired behaviors in other times and situations. Kuczynski's (1984) study revealed that mothers who endorsed long-term goals, rather than expecting immediate obedient behaviors from the child, displayed higher levels of nurturing and reasoning behaviors, and attributed more positive behaviors to their child. However, short-term goals were not significantly associated with power-assertive behavior.

Hastings and Grusec (1998) described parenting goals in terms of their target, and suggested three main types: parent-centered, child-centered and relationship-centered. They also showed that reported parenting goals were consistent with reported parenting behaviors. Adults who valued parent-centered goals which prioritized parents' wishes and needs reported higher levels of power-assertive behavior. On the other hand, child-centered goals and relationship-centered goals were related to more verbal reasoning and warmth, respectively. This study also revealed that parental attributions were related to their goals and they mediated the relation between goals and behaviors. For example, adults attributed more intentional and dispositional causes to the child's misbehaviors if they held parent-centered goals. They were also more disappointed with the child's misbehavior and reported less sympathy. On the other hand, parental empathy was positively related to child-centered and relationship-centered goals (Hastings & Grusec, 1998).

This review shows that parenting style, ideas and practices are closely related to each other, at least for "Western" societies. Although parental cognitions have been studied much less than parenting styles or practices, they have lately become an integral part of models of parental socialization (Abidin, 1992; Goodnow, 1988).

PARENTING AND CHILD CHARACTERISTICS

It has been suggested that child characteristics such as gender and age affect parenting. In terms of the child's gender, studies indicate mixed evidence and small effects but usually more positive parenting toward girls. For example, Kuczynski (1984) found that mothers used more power assertion for boys compared to girls. Leaper, Anderson and Sanders (1998) showed that mothers talked more and used more supportive speech with their daughters than sons, regardless of the child's age. Italian mothers also reported lower levels of power assertion in response to socially withdrawing behaviors of their daughters than of their sons (Schneider et al., 1997).

Parental cognitions and behaviors, as well as the effectiveness of these behaviors, are affected by the child's developmental level (Clausen, 1966). Findings suggest that authoritarian parenting behaviors generally decrease with increasing child age (Ross, 1984). Dix and colleagues (1986) found that parents reported more negative affect and behaviors to children's misconduct if the child was younger. This finding indicated that parents' conceptions about age-appropriate abilities and limitations of the child shape their parenting behaviors. McNally, Eisenberg and Harris (1991) investigated the changes in mothers' parenting values and beliefs over five time points from 7-8 to

13-14 years of age. Results of this study showed that maternal control did not significantly change during primary school years but did decrease over the middle-adolescence period. Maternal warmth (e.g., expressing affection by hugging and kissing) and isolating the child as a way of punishment (e.g., sending him/her off somewhere to be by himself/herself) decreased, while emphasizing achievement and deprivation of privileges increased with the child's age. McNally and colleagues argued that although maternal goals may not vary much with time, the behaviors mothers engage in to achieve these goals may display more change with age.

These studies emphasize the bidirectional nature of the parent-child interaction, in that child attributes (e.g., age, developmental level) are related to parenting goals and practices.

PARENTING AND CULTURE

Culture influences all processes that affect developmental outcomes. It does not simply affect parental values or behaviors, but it is at the core of them (Garcia Coll et al., 2000). Several researchers (Greenfield & Suzuki, 1998; Kağıtçıbaşı, 1984; Stevenson-Hinde, 1998) have emphasized that culture is a critical element that needs to be paid significant attention in developmental studies.

Children actively learn values and rules in a cultural context. Cultural values are transmitted to them as they are socialized by parents, family and other agents in the larger society. Hence, individuals must be understood in the context of family and the family in the culture. This is the basic assumption of contextualism which Szapocznik & Kurtines (1993: 400) described as:

> ...the view that behavior cannot be understood outside of the context in which it occurs. Contextualism is concerned with the interaction between the organism and its environment – explaining and understanding the changing individual in a changing world.

Although there is no firm consensus on the definition of the terms 'individualism' and 'collectivism' (Oyserman et al., 2002), they can be used to indicate cultures' different approaches to socialization. A person in a collectivistic culture defines his/herself in terms of membership of an in-group (Triandis, 1994). Strong family ties, dependence and obedience are valued in such a culture (Kağıtçıbaşı, 1996), and an authoritarian parenting style is often observed, aimed at achieving a compliant child who gives priority to group needs. On the other hand, an individualistic culture values personal needs and aims to achieve autonomy and assertiveness in the child (Triandis, 1994). Authoritative parenting is suggested to be the ideal parenting style to reinforce autonomy, self-reliance, exploration and self-control in the child (Baumrind, 1973), characteristics which are highly valued in individualistic societies (Greenfield & Suzuki, 1998). Kağıtçıbaşı (1984) questions the universality of this assumption and says that it is not appropriate to presume that autonomy is a desired and functional characteristic in a traditional society. Kağıtçıbaşı (1996, 2005) suggests that 'relatedness' is another significant need and is not incompatible with the need for autonomy.

In her Family Change Model, Kağıtçıbaşı (1996, 2005) reformulates the relationship between the autonomy and relatedness dimensions which are theorized as separate and mutually exclusive dimensions in the individualism-collectivism construal. Kağıtçıbaşı (1996, 2005) argues for the possibility of being both autonomous and related and also elaborates on the familial and socioeconomical contexts that foster autonomy, relatedness or the synthesis of both autonomy and relatedness in an individual. The Family Change Model (Kağıtçıbaşı, 1996, 2005) explains the relative salience of autonomy and/or relatedness in child-rearing orientations as a function of the family patterns which are formed in the dimensions of material independence and emotional interdependence across generations within the context of urbanization. Kağıtçıbaşı (1996, 2005) suggests three family models which are conducive to different levels of autonomy and relatedness.

The first one is the *family model of interdependence*, which is mostly seen in traditional families in the rural context. The family pattern in this model is characterized by overall material and emotional interdependence. In the family model of interdependence, the child has an economic and utilitarian value, thus the obedience of the child is functional and valued, while autonomy of the child is dysfunctional and is not fostered. Thus, the parenting style in this model exhibits an authoritarian, obedience-demanding pattern and the self-developing in this family is described as the 'relational self'. The second type of family model displays an individualistic pattern which involves independence.

The second model, the *family model of independence*, is characteristic of the Western middle-class nuclear family where intergenerational independence is valued. In this family model, permissive and self-reliance-oriented parenting is more common since individuation and separation are considered to be prerequisites of healthy development. The appearance of self in the family model of independence is the 'separated self'.

The third family type shows material independence and emotional interdependence among members. Thus, the *family model of emotional interdependence* is conceptualized as the dialectical synthesis of the other two models. Economic independence and an increase in the need for the skills that require individuals to take individual responsibility in the urbanization context give rise to autonomy, but the family still values close familial ties. Hence, the self-development here is the 'autonomous-relational self'. Kağıtçıbaşı (1996) suggests that an authoritative parenting style may help to achieve an autonomous-relational self through both control and encouraging autonomy.

It has been emphasized (Kağıtçıbaşı, 1996; Triandis, 1994) that cross-cultural psychology needs to go beyond simple descriptions of cultural differences, and to attempt to interpret them. Researchers have investigated the circumstances associated with the valued child behaviors and common socialization practices in different cultures. It appears that independence is valued more highly in industrialized, developed, "Western" countries, and financial independence is an important condition for social independence (Triandis, 1994). On the other hand, interdependence is valued more in underdeveloped societies, where the social system does not provide extensive institutions to take responsibility for its dependent people, such as the elderly and sick, the orphans, and the disabled. Hence, valuing needs of family members over personal needs, interdependence, and self-sacrifice are reinforced rather than self-reliance and autonomy. Kağıtçıbaşı (1996) calls this a 'functionally extended family' and suggests that an important duty of the family members in these societies is to take care of its elderly vulnerable members. In addition, Kağıtçıbaşı (1996, 2005) notes that a move towards urbanization and economic advancement does not necessarily encourage individualism in traditional societies. For example, the family type which is more conducive to the 'autonomous-relational self' may be observed among families with educated parents living in urbanized, collectivistic contexts (i.e., material independence and emotional interdependence).

Consistent with the assumption that economic difficulties influence mutual support in traditional societies, findings in the 'Value of Children' study (Kağıtçıbaşı, 1982b) indicated that obedience was the most valued child characteristic, and independence and self-reliance were the least valued two features in Indonesia, the Philippines, Turkey, and Thailand. 'Being close, loyal and faithful to parents' was another attribute valued in adult children. Old-age security value (being seen as a source of economic and psychological security in old age) was highly valued in Singapore, the Republic of Korea, Turkey, and Taiwan. This value was not endorsed much in industrialized countries such as Germany, showing that children were raised to become independently functioning adults and were not expected to support their elderly parents. Lower education, lower income and lack of social security were related to the old-age security value and fertility rates (Kağıtçıbaşı, 1982a).

Another research investigating parental values in Turkish families showed that Turkish parents coming from a lower SES expect their children to be grateful to them; whereas, high SES families value autonomy and do not expect gratitude, yet they wish their children to be close to them (İmamoğlu, 1987).

A recent replication of the "Value of Children" study across three generations in Turkey (Kağıtçıbaşı & Ataca, 2005) supported the framework provided by the Family Change Model. Findings of this study revealed that rural and urban low SES mothers valued "minding parents" more than urban high SES mothers, but did not endorse independence and self-reliance. Kağıtçıbaşı and Ataca (2005) showed that material expectations from children declined with socioeconomic development, whereas no such decline was observed for emotional (psychological) dependence.

It might thus be suggested that the same cultural group may display different tendencies depending on the context (e.g., sociodemographic variables) (Göregenli, 1997). Cultural and cross-cultural studies provide some support for this suggestion by revealing that parenting values and practices that are associated with different tendencies (individualism and collectivism) may co-occur in the same culture (Kağıtçıbaşı, 1973; Kashima, 1987). One's socioeconomic background appears to have a central role in this variance.

PARENTING AND SOCIOECONOMIC BACKGROUND

As suggested in the earlier sections, parents' child-rearing styles or practices cannot be understood in isolation from the context in which they take place. The family is the child's most immediate environment and has been widely investigated in developmental psychology. It is conceptualized not simply as a constellation of members but as a context which significantly contributes to socialization of the child, and where parents directly or indirectly teach the child social and cultural norms and rules (Slaughter-Defoe, 1995). Parents sometimes transmit their child-rearing attitudes and behaviors from their own parents in this family context (Covell et al., 1995). Structure of the family (e.g., age, number and sex composition of members) and parent-child interaction are assumed to be closely related to socioeconomic status as well as other factors (e.g., culture) (Clausen, 1966; Cowan et al., 1998).

Kohn's (1963) theory examines the interaction between social class and parent-child relationships from a sociological perspective. Kohn (1963: 472) suggests that social class, described as "aggregates of individuals who occupy broadly similar positions in the scale of prestige", shapes a person's life perspective. Life perspective has an impact on which personal characteristics are perceived as desirable, influencing parenting goals and disciplinary behaviors. For example, working-class occupations require the person to obey directives of those in authority. Accordingly, working-class parents want their children to be obedient and respectful and they employ power assertion to achieve these functional behaviors. On the other hand, middle-class jobs emphasize self-direction rather than direct supervision, which affects middle-class parents' life perspectives and approaches to child rearing. Kohn emphasizes that this is not a conscious effort on the part of the parent and not related to a person's culture or religion.

Subsequent studies provided some support for Kohn's (1963) theory by indicating a relation between social class and parenting. Ellis, Lee and Petersen's (1978) study showed that parental emphasis on conformity over self-reliance in socializing children was related to economic and political conditions where adults were required to conform to other authority figures. Jobs that prevented self-direction in the person were related to a less flexible social attitude and a more rigid approach (Miller et al., 1979). Another study (Tudge et al., 1999) revealed that American, Korean, Russian and Estonian parents did not differ in their self-direction goals, but this value was endorsed more highly by middle-class parents. Furthermore, control and discipline were valued more by working-class parents. In accord with this, middle-class children displayed more self-initiation in their activities, which was argued to be related to their mothers' goals for self-direction. Eisenberg (1996) further indicated that working-class mothers in both Hispanic-American and Anglo-American families displayed less verbalization and more aversion (e.g., negative affect) in conflict situations than middle-class mothers, but no significant cultural difference was reported.

Luster, Rhoades and Haas (1989) investigated American mothers with children 9 to 23 months old and have found consistent results with Kohn's hypothesis regarding SES and parental values: social class was positively associated with parents' valuing self-direction (e.g., to think for him/herself, to be curious about many things) and negatively associated with valuing conformity (e.g., to keep him/herself and his/her clothes clean, to be polite to adults).

However, there are other findings (Abell et al., 1996) that contradict Kohn's (1963) assumption of linearity between parenting and social class. Harwood, Schoelmerich, Ventura-Cook, Schulze and Wilson (1996) found that although European American mothers coming from a lower socioeconomic background were more concerned with proper demeanor, as opposed to their high SES counterparts, who emphasized self-actualization, Puerto-Rican mothers coming from both middle and lower socioeconomic backgrounds endorsed goals for proper demeanor highly.

These studies suggest that parents in varying social classes may display a range of attitudes and behaviors, and constituents of SES (e.g., education, occupation) might be better indicators of parenting ideas, goals, and behaviors compared to this broad concept (Goodnow, 1988).

MATERNAL EDUCATION, PARENTING AND CHILD OUTCOMES

As stated earlier in this paper, the present study aims to reveal the effect of *education* on mothers' long-term socialization goals. There are several reasons for giving preferentiality to maternal education over a holistic approach to socioeconomic status.

The construct 'socioeconomic status' has been defined as the ranking of individuals, families, or groups on a hierarchy according to their access to or control over some valued commodities such as wealth, power and status (Mueller & Parcel, 1981). However, social scientists do not have a consensus over the definition of SES, the best way to measure it and the processes by which SES influences child development. In the recent years, developmental scientists display an inclination to focus on different aspects of SES, like education, occupation and economic resources, rather than adopting a holistic approach (Bornstein & Bradley, 2003). Especially, education has been examined increasingly in the literature on child and adolescent development. A review of relevant studies (Ensminger & Fothergill, 2003) showed that maternal education (45%) is the most commonly used indicator of socioeconomic background, which is followed by income (28%) and occupation (14%), respectively.

The preference for using maternal education as an indicator over other components of SES is related to its link to some important aspects of parental behavior and child outcomes. Bornstein, Hahn, Suwalsky and Haynes (2003) studied the link between two major SES composite indices, the Hollingshead Four-Factor Index and the Duncan Socioeconomic Index, by analyzing each composite of SES (education, occupation, income) separately with respect to six maternal behaviors (nurture, physical and verbal encouragement of gross motor skills, social exchange, didactic interaction, provision of the maternal environment, and speech to child) and child-related outcomes (physical development, social interaction, exploration, nondistress vocalization, and distress communication). The researchers showed that maternal education was the best predictor of mother and infant behavior as compared to SES as a composite index and its other components. The work of Von der Lippe (1999) is an example to research studies which investigate mother's education level in relation to her interaction with the child. Findings of this study indicated that better educated Egyptian mothers had more interactive and stimulating interaction with their children and were more authoritative than their less educated counterparts.

Examining maternal education is plausible also because it is less likely to change over time, as opposed to income (McLoyd, 1998). What is more, using a composite measure of SES as a general indicator of social context can hide some important variances that might arise from one's education level. This argument may hold true especially for countries like Turkey, where education and income level of an individual may not be highly compatible.

TURKISH FAMILIAL PATTERNS

Turkish family structure and interactions have undergone remarkable changes and reveal much diversity due to the fast and significant social changes that have taken place in the last few decades. In urban parts of Turkey, while there is more than one type of family, the nuclear family is the most common one. As put by Kağıtçıbaşı (1985), looking at 'traditional' familial interactions as a reference point is a way of dealing with the 'various family types' problem in studying family socialization. Two social norms, patriotism and respect for authority, are strong in the traditional Turkish family (Kağıtçıbaşı, 1970). Cultural values indicate a high valuing of sons and a clear differentiation in attitudes towards girls and boys. Girls are more directed and restricted than boys, and they are also expected to learn skills to keep house and to help mothers in housework (Kıray, 1976; Lloyd & Fallers, 1976). The traditions of hospitality and sharing are highly valued and reinforced by the family and the society (Göregenli, 1997). Mutual help (UNICEF, 1991) and assisting others, especially strangers, are observed more widely in families coming from rural backgrounds (Korte, 1984).

Although social change has resulted in more material independence among family members, 'emotional interdependence' is still a prominent aspect of the Turkish family. Interdependence is observed widely among families with different social backgrounds; even within upper class families there are strong and close ties between family members. Kağıtçıbaşı (1989) suggests that support is one of the positive features of this 'culture of relatedness' but it also reinforces dependency and obedience to parents. In this culture, similar to many other Third World countries and rural-agricultural families, children are dependent on their parents till their parents get old, when parents in turn depend on their children (Kağıtçıbaşı, 1987). The expectation of being looked after by children decreases from underdeveloped to more developed areas and with higher SES families, but some aspects of parenting such as obedience-demanding behavior may persist due to strong cultural traditions (Kağıtçıbaşı, 2007; Smith et al., 2006). On the other hand, the psychological value (providing companionship, love and joy and strengthening the marital bond) of children is emphasized more in higher SES families.

However, Turkish parents living in rural areas, small towns and metropolitan cities may display different parenting values and behaviors. To generalize, the rural father holds traditional values; although he is proud of his children, especially his sons, he keeps a distance from them to maintain authority and respect. Fathers in small towns are also conservative and authoritarian but they are not as traditional as the rural fathers. Fathers in the big cities tend to be well-educated and hold "modern views" and values similar to those endorsed by "Western" fathers. These fathers are aware of and accept parenting responsibilities (Volkan & Çevik, 1989).

Turkish parents' social background (e.g., education level) is also suggested to be a significant indicator of developmental outcomes for children (e.g., health, academic and social competence), which is mediated by child-rearing behaviors (Akşit & Akşit, 1989; Hortaçsu et al., 1990). The home environment in lower SES and rural areas is usually described as poor, where the number of toys, games, and books are insufficient for optimal stimulation. Although a positive value is attributed to play, Turkish parents coming from a lower social background do not tend to play with their children (Göncü et al., 1999).

There is little verbal communication between parents and children in these contexts.

Punishment-oriented control appears to be the most common method of control employed by Turkish parents, while verbal reasoning is rarely used. Parents are authoritarian (Taylor & Oskay, 1995) and interfere with the child's choice of occupation and friends (Kongar, 1976). Such parenting behaviors encourage dependency, and do not encourage autonomous decision-making (Kağıtçıbaşı, 1989). Kağıtçıbaşı (1973) showed that families coming from a rural or lower social background endorsed more control, which influenced children's attitudes. For instance, adolescents in these families displayed a more authoritarian, pessimistic and religious attitude, and believed in external control more highly. On the other hand, upper SES families were characterized more by affection, and children in these families were more optimistic, achievement oriented and believed in internal control. As the indices of socioeconomic development increase, the tendency of Turkish mothers to establish a closer relationship with the child, be more tolerant toward the child, support the child for being independent and encourage the child to make his or her own decisions, and adopt a more democratic parenting style increases.

The findings reviewed in the last three sections reveal that aspects of social background, particularly education level, may significantly affect parental cognitions and practices. Therefore, it is important to include these variables in developmental studies to elucidate within-culture differences in parenting.

THE PRESENT STUDY

In the literature, the socialization goals of mothers have been widely studied in research focusing on the cross-cultural differences in parenting (Harwood 1992; Harwood et al., 1995; Harwood et al., 1996; Harwood et al., 1999; Leyendecker et al., 2002). While the main concern of these studies is to explicate cultural differences in maternal socialization goals, some researchers emphasized the importance of studying within-culture heterogeneity (Harwood et al., 1996; Leyendecker et al., 2002).

Previous research on socialization goals (Harwood 1992; Harwood et al., 1996; Harwood et al., 1999; Leyendecker et al., 2002) suggests individualism and collectivism heuristics as useful tools to explain cultural differences. The present study was based on the theoretical framework provided by the Family Change Model (Kağıtçıbaşı, 1996). As explained beforehand, this model conceptualizes autonomy and relatedness as compatible orientations, rather than as two mutually exclusive categories, and provides a useful framework to understand variation in parenting goals and practices in terms of family patterns that are conducive to different levels of autonomy and relatedness in different socioeconomic contexts.

Given the established relations between socioeconomic background and parenting, the present study aimed to examine differences and similarities in the socialization goals of low- and high-educated Turkish mothers. In this regard, *how differences in education account for the variation in long-term socialization goals of mothers in the Turkish society* was the main research concern. Guided by previous research (Harwood et al., 1996; İmamoğlu, 1987; Kağıtçıbaşı & Ataca, 2005), it was predicted that high-educated mothers would value the goals that are consistent with autonomy orientation and would emphasize 'self-maximization goals' more. On the other hand, low-educated mothers were expected to endorse goals that are consistent with relatedness orientation, in particular 'proper demeanor goals'. In congruence with the framework provided by the Family Change Model (Kağıtçıbaşı, 1996, 2005), two groups of mothers were not expected to differ in their relationship-centered goals (i.e., 'lovingness goals' that emphasize close relationships within the family and interpersonal warmth).

METHOD

Participants

Constitution of two Groups of Mothers in Terms of Their Educational Status

The sample of the study was comprised of mothers living in Istanbul, Turkey. Forty mothers participated in the study as paid volunteers, and they formed two groups, as high-educated and low-educated (Descriptive statistics for demographic data for the Australian and Turkish samples are given in **Table 4.1**). These two categories were created with regard to years of formal schooling. Accordingly, mothers who had at most six years of education were classified as low-educated ($n = 20$, $M_{education} = 4.9$, $SD = 0.5$),[1] and those mothers who had at least two years of college education were classified as high-educated mothers ($n = 20$, $M_{education} = 15.5$, $SD = 1.7$).

The age of mothers in the two groups ranged between 24-39 years. According to the results of the 2000 Census of Population in Turkey, primary school graduates constituted 55% of the female population, and college graduates constituted 13% of the female population that fall under the specified age interval (i.e., 24-39 years). Participants of this study were recruited from Istanbul, which is representative of the whole country with respect to the distribution of female population in terms of the years of schooling. According to the results of the 2000 Census of Population in Turkey, among women whose age ranged between 24-39 years, primary school graduates constituted 57% of the female population of the specified age range in Istanbul, while college graduates constituted only 12.9% of that population in Istanbul. These data reveal that about half of the female population in Turkey in general, and in Istanbul in particular, had a primary school degree or five years of

---

1   *N* or *n* symbolizes 'sample size', *M* symbolizes 'arithmetic mean', and *SD* stands for 'standard deviation'.

TABLE 4.1

Statistics for Demographic Characteristics of the Participants (N = 40)

	Low-educated mothers		High-educated mothers		
	n = 20		n = 20		
	M	SD	M	SD	p
Mother's age	29.4	3.1	31.9	2.8	*
Minimum-maximum	24-37		25-39		
Mother's age when she give birth to her first child	24.6	2.3	28.4	2.2	*
Minimum-maximum	22-32		24-34		
Mother's education (in years)	4.9	0.5	15.5	1.7	***
Minimum-maximum	3.0-6.0		13-21		
Mother's attendance to programs for parents and children (in percentages)	5			35	*
Percent of mothers employed	25		75		**
Occupational prestige of mothers (including unemployed mothers)	5.5	0.5	3.7	1	***
Minimum-maximum	5.3-6.9		2.2-5.3		
Maternal work hours/week	8.8	18.6	31	18.7	**
Minimum-maximum	0-60		0-45		
Education of mother's mother	1.9	2.4	7.7	4.6	***
Minimum-maximum	0-5		0-15		
Education of mother's father	3.5	2.5	9.4	4.6	***
Minimum-maximum	0-8		0-16		
Occupational prestige of mother's mother	5.3	0	4.8	0.9	*
Minimum-maximum	5.3-5.3		2.4-5.3		
Occupational prestige of mother's father	5.5	1	4.6	1.3	*
Maximum-minimum	4.0-6.6		2.2-6.4		
Child's age (in months)	20.9	9.7	22.7	7.8	
Minimum-maximum	6.5-39		9.5-35		
Birth order of the target child (first born in percentages)	50		75		
Percent of fathers employed	100		95		
Father's age	33.9	4.5	35.2	3.9	
Minimum-maximum	26-42		26-41		
Father's education (in years)	6.8	2.3	15.2	3.4	***
Minimum-maximum	5.0-11		8.0-23		
Father's occupational prestige	5.8	0.8	3.5	1.2	***
Minimum-maximum	3.9-6.7		1.5-5.0		
Father's work hours/week	60.5	18.1	50.2	17.2	
Minimum-maximum	37-105		0-80		

"* p < .05; **p < .01; ***p < .001."

formal schooling. In this respect, the level of schooling for the low-educated category was restricted to at most six years of education in this study.

To see the role of education in long-term socialization goals of mothers and to eliminate the possibility of a merging of differences between these two education status categories, middle school and high school graduates were excluded from the sample in this study. Moreover, thirteen years of education, which is equal to two years of college education, was set as the lowest limit for the high-educated category.

Finally, formal schooling time ranged between 3-6 years for low-educated mothers (*Meducation* = 4.9, *SD* = 0.5), and between 13-21 years for high-educated mothers (*Meducation* = 15.5; *SD* = 1.7). Analysis showed that there was a statistically significant difference between the two groups in terms of formal schooling in years (F (1, 38) = 668.1, $p < .001$).

In the background information form, mothers were also asked whether they had attended seminars or educational activities related to children and mothers (e.g., workshops/seminars on parenting and/or child development offered by NGO's or governmental organizations). Analysis showed that a higher percentage of high-educated mothers (35%) attended such activities than low-educated mothers (5 %), $X2$ (1) = 5.6, $p < .05$.

A comparison of the high-educated and low-educated mothers further showed that the two groups differed significantly on a variety of demographic variables. Accordingly, with regard to age, high-educated mothers (M = 31.9, SD = 2.8) were found to be older than low-educated mothers (M = 29.4, SD = 3.1) (F (1, 38) = 6.8, $p < .05$).

Other Recruitment Criteria

As stated beforehand, the goal of the present study was to compare low and high-educated mothers in terms of their long-term socialization goals. Therefore, the educational status of the participants,

defined in terms of the years of formal schooling, was the major criterion on the basis of which two groups of participants were recruited.
Additional criteria used in the study included the following: a) maternal age at the time when the mother gave birth to her first child; b) age
of the target child; c) language that the mother speaks, and the country
in which she was brought up; d) number of children the mother has.

a) The age of the mothers at the time they gave birth to their
first children was one of the criteria in the recruitment of the participants. In this respect, the age range of participants was restricted to
include only mothers who were between 22 and 32 years of age at the
time when their first child was born. Accordingly, high-educated
mothers ($M = 28.4$, $SD = 2.2$) were older than the low-educated mothers ($M = 24.6$, $SD = 2.3$) when their first child was born ($F (1, 38) =$
26.4, $p < .001$).

b) The target child's age was another sampling criterion in the
study. Target child was defined in terms of his/her age and mothers
who had at least one child aged between 6 and 39 months were
recruited for the study. Mothers who had more than one child in this
age range were also allowed to participate but asked to think about
one of them (target child) as she answered the questions in the interview. If the mother had a child/children older than the target child, she
was asked to think about her socialization goals regarding the target
child only. It was assumed that the age of the child may have some
effects on long-term socialization goals of mother which are not related to educational status. The limitation of the target child's age was
expected to reduce age-related perspectives as a significant source of
variation in the mothers' socialization goals.

No limitation was set as a criterion in terms of the number of
children the participant mothers had, provided that they satisfied the
recruitment criteria given above. Descriptive analysis showed that the
two groups were similar in terms of the number of children the mothers had (high-educated mothers: $M = 1.3$, $SD = .4$; low-educated
mothers: $M = 1.7$; $SD = .7$).

c) Participant mothers were also expected to satisfy the criterion 'not to have been abroad more than a whole year' to eliminate influences on socialization goals that could be imported from other cultures. In this respect, participants were all born and brought up in Turkey and had not been abroad more than a year in their lifetime. Mothers also spoke Turkish as their first language.

Demographic Characteristics of Participants

Characteristics of Mothers

Employment Status
Regarding the employment status (being employed or not), a higher percentage of high educated mothers (75%) were employed outside home than the low-educated mothers (25%), $(X2(1) =10, p < .05)$. In addition, mothers in the low-educated and high-educated groups displayed a significant difference in terms of occupational prestige $(F (1, 38) = 45.5, p < .001)$. Mothers in the high-educated group $(M = 3.7, SD = 1.0)^2$ were likely to work in more prestigious jobs than mothers in the low-educated group $(M = 5.5, SD = 0.5)$.

Average Weekly Work Hours
There was also a significant difference in the average weekly work hours of high-educated $(M = 31, SD = 18.7)$ and low-educated mothers $(M = 8.8, SD = 18.6)$ $(F (1, 38) =14.1, p < .05)$. All of the employed high-educated mothers had jobs that required them to work as registered workers (e.g., teacher in public/private secondary schools, accountant in a firm, bank manager, engineer in a firm), whereas employed low-educated mothers were more likely to work as unregistered workers since most of them were doing house-cleaning without having formal connections with a cleaning firm and social security.

Marital Status

Mothers in the two groups were similar with regard to their marital status; they were all married and living with the father of their child(ren).

Characteristics of Parents of Participant Mothers

Formal Schooling in Years

Low and high-educated mothers were also found to differ in terms of the formal schooling level of their mothers (F (1, 38) = 25, p < .001) and fathers (F (1, 38) = 21.7, p < .001). Accordingly, mothers of high-educated participants (M = 7.7, SD = 4.6) attended school longer than mothers of low-educated participants (M = 1.9, SD = 2.4). Similarly, fathers of high-educated participants (M = 9.4, SD = 4.6) attended school longer than fathers of low-educated participants (M = 3.5, SD = 2.5).

Occupational Prestige

There was also a significant difference between the occupational prestige of mothers of high-educated (M = 4.8, SD = .9) and low-educated mothers (M = 5.3, SD = .0) (F (1, 38) = 5.6, p < .05) and fathers of high-educated (M = 4.6, SD = 1.3) and low-educated mothers (M = 5.5, SD = 1.0) (F (1, 38) = 6.1, p < .05).

Characteristics of the Target Child

Age, Gender and Birth Order

With regard to the age of the target child, there was no significant difference between low-educated (Mage = 20.9 in months, SD = 9.7) and high-educated (Mage = 22.7 in months, SD = 7.8) groups. Chi-square analysis showed that the two groups of mothers were similar in terms of gender distribution of the target child (low-educated mothers had 9 girls and 11 boys; high-educated mothers had 10 girls and 10 boys) and his/her birth order (50% of children in the low-educated group and 75% of children in the high-educated group were firstborns).

Characteristics of the Father of the Target Child

Formal Schooling in Years
The formal schooling of fathers in the high-educated group ($M = 15.2$, $SD = 3.4$) was significantly longer in years than the fathers in the low-educated group ($M = 6.7$, $SD = 2.3$) ($F (1, 38) = 81$, $p < .001$).

Employment Status and Occupational Prestige
Chi-square analysis indicated that the employment status was similar for fathers in the high-educated group (95% were employed) and low-educated group (100% were employed). However, fathers in the two groups significantly differed in terms of their occupational prestige ($M = 3.5$, $SD = 1.2$ and $M = 5.8$, $SD = .8$, for high- and low-educated groups respectively) ($F (1, 38) = 46$, $p < .001$).

Age
The two groups were similar in terms of the age of the child's father ($M = 35.2$, $SD = 3.9$ and $M = 33.9$, $SD = 4.4$, respectively, for spouses of high- and low-educated mothers).

Average Weekly Work Hours
No significant difference was found in the weekly work hours of fathers between the two groups ($M = 50.2$, $SD = 17.2$ and $M = 60.5$, $SD = 18.1$, for high- and low-educated groups, respectively).

Country of Origin and Native Language
Just like mothers, all of the fathers were born and grew up in Turkey, and their native language was Turkish.

Household Composition

There were no group differences in terms of the total number of people in the household ($M = 3.8$, $SD = 1.1$ and $M = 4.2$, $SD = 1.2$ for high- and low-educated mothers, respectively). Household composition was similar in both groups; 80% of high-educated and 65% of low-educated participants reported that they were living as nuclear families. The household of remaining mothers (20% in high-educated and 35% in low-educated groups) involved some relatives in addition to the spouse and children.

Recruitment Procedure

To recruit mothers, an invitation letter was sent to mothers that consisted of information regarding the aim of the study and the tasks that were required from the participants to accomplish. In this letter, participants were also informed about the procedure of the study and guaranteed confidentiality of the information they would provide.

The sample of the study partly evolved as a snowball sample. Snowball sampling involves recruitment of participants who are acquaintances of those already recruited. Since it was hard to find participants who satisfied all of the recruitment criteria, snowball sampling emerged as the best sampling method. However, the recruitment procedure also enabled the participation of mothers from different suburbs of Istanbul. Accordingly, high-educated mothers were recruited from four suburbs; whereas, low-educated mothers were recruited from five different suburbs of Istanbul.

MEASURES

Sociodemographic Questionnaire

A background information form was administered to mothers to gather information regarding the sociodemographic characteristics of the mother and the father (e.g., date of birth, birth place, education level, occupation, work hours, marital status, language, parents' education and occupation), the child/children (e.g., date of birth, sex, birth order) and the household composition (e.g., other adults living with the family).

Socialization Goals Interview

To measure parenting beliefs and long-term socialization goals of mothers, the Socialization Goals Interview (SGI) developed by Harwood (1992; Harwood et al., 1995) was used. SGI is an in-depth semi-structured interview which consists of four open-ended questions where mothers were asked to describe the attributes they would and would not like their children to have as adults and to describe a child they know possessing at least some aspects of the positive and negative qualities they mentioned (Harwood, 1992). Specifically, the interview consists of the following questions in the order they are given: a) "What are some of the qualities and/or behaviors that you would like to see your child to possess as adults?", b) "What are some of the qualities and/or behaviors that you would *not* like to see your child to possess as adults?", c) "Describe a child you know who possesses at least the beginnings of some of the positive qualities you mentioned" and d) "Describe a child you know who possesses at least the beginnings of some of the negative qualities you mentioned".

In the literature, it has been reported that these four questions provide a rich picture of mothers' indigenous beliefs and values regarding their long-term socialization goals and perceptions of desirable and undesirable child behaviors (Harwood, 1992; Harwood et al., 1995; Harwood et al., 1996; Harwood et al., 1999; Leyendecker et al., 2002).

Coding Schema for SGI Main Categories

The mothers' responses to the SGI questions were coded into culturally-relevant categories according to the procedure developed by Harwood (1992; Harwood et al., 1995: 1996; 1999; Leyendecker et al., 2002). Accordingly, participants' responses were analyzed at the

level of individual word and phase descriptors to examine the participants' long term socialization goals. Individual words pertain to the
words that characterize or describe the qualities of a person, such as
being "cheerful" or "kind". Phase descriptors, on the other hand, pertain to two or more word phrases that describe the characteristics of
a person, such as "being fond of parents" or "being able to stand on
his/her own two feet". For example, depending on the coding scheme,
"What I mean by justice is treating people equally and not discriminating against others." was considered as two phase descriptors
("treating people equally" and "not discriminating against others");
and "She is respectful and dignified and doing her job fastidiously,"
was considered as two word descriptors ("respectful" and "dignified") and one phase descriptor ("doing her job fastidiously"). Each
descriptor was coded into five mutually distinct main categories as
developed and used in previous studies (Harwood 1992; Harwood et
al., 1995; 1996; 1999; Leyendecker et al., 2002).

1. *Category of Self-maximization*: Endorsing the goal for Self-maximization refers to the concern that the child becomes a self-confident
and independent person and develops his/her abilities as an individual
(Harwood, 1992).

> Self confident...in every matter, in working life, in private life, in all
> aspects of life... I don't want him to lag behind. I want him to have
> the strength to struggle with the difficulties of life. That is, I think
> that a person who is not self-confident can never succeed in any-
> thing in life, cannot be happy. If he is self-confident, whenever he
> faces a problem, it will be easier for him to tackle it and overcome
> it. For everything, that is for life, I think that he has to be self-con-
> fident (Interview #54).

> I do not fear anything. I have faith in myself. I am self-confident in
> everything. If I had had enough education, I am sure that I would
> have accomplished some good job in life. That is, I would certain-
> ly have done. That is, I want my son to resemble me in this respect.

> I don't want him to be afraid of anything. In the last resort, we will face whatever we are supposed to live. Why should we have fear? That is, to be fearful means to set barriers for yourself. A person can create opportunities to the extent that he works. That is, in today's world, one has to struggle, to arrive at good ends. Before arriving at good ends, one needs to struggle to survive. I want my son not to fear but to fight for everything (Interview #89).

2) *Category of Self-control*: Endorsing the goal for Self-control refers to the concern that the child learns to control his/her negative impulses and behaviors toward greed, aggression and egocentrism, to put limits on himself/herself, or to accept limits (Harwood, 1992).

> There are some children...they react by hitting, pushing and kicking their friends even in a minor disagreement. Suppose that something happened, for example, a child took another's pencil, the kid then hits his friend saying "Why did you take my pencil?" For example, another child trips up his friend while they walking on the street. I don't want my child to display such negative behaviors, like hitting, kicking ... When he becomes a grown up in the future, in any minor argument, I don't know... not to control one self, hitting, pushing one another are quite undesirable things in my view. Human beings can come to an agreement by talking. If one cannot get along with another one, he can choose to be distant, not to see or communicate with that person, or you can leave the place you are in. I don't want my son to quarrel or fight in case of disagreement. Maybe because I don't have a quarrelsome nature.... ((Interview #62.)

> I don't like people who get nervous easily, who get angry and shout a lot when you make a mistake. I don't like these characteristics. I don't like those people who fight (Interview #61).

3) *Category of Lovingness*: Endorsing the goal for Lovingness refers to the concern that the child be a friendly and emotionally warm person and be able to maintain close affective relationships with others (Harwood, 1992).

...He is a very compassionate child; he shows his love too much. He hugs and kisses. He shows his love in a variety of ways since his infancy. He loves people without discerning. This is his most obvious characteristic as I have observed. He shows the same sympathy to the person whom he sees for the first time in his life and to the person whom he knows quite well. If he meets you now, he would come and kiss you. When we take a taxi, he tries to communicate with the taxi driver. I observe other kids of the same age; they draw themselves back, they don't want to talk, but my son is a kid whose communicative abilities are quite strong. He never discriminates against people. He shows the same warmth and concern to everyone. I would like him to show the same characteristics in the future... the same lovingness (Interview #54).

...There is a son of my friend... he is very kind, very talkative. He does every nice thing to make his mother do what he wants. He is very soft-spoken, not only towards me, but towards all. He is extroverted. He communicates with everyone. He makes every people love him. I can give him as an example. I would like my son to be like him (Interview #76).

4) *Category of Decency*: Endorsing the goal for Decency describes the mother's wish for her child to have the ability to meet basic social standards, such as being hardworking, responsible and honest, and not displaying illicit behavior (Harwood, 1992).

...I cannot tolerate people who are not effective in society, who harm society. Nowadays, we see theft everywhere. These are the things that I am afraid of most. They may happen as a result of false guidance, one cannot foresee what will happen. We don't know what will happen to us... I don't know if we will loose control in a city like Istanbul. In this city it is quite difficult to bring up a child. I am very afraid of that...We know that there is the problem of narcotic drugs in high school. I cannot tolerate that. Families, even if they are well-informed, cannot prevent it. Things like that are against society. They are harmful to oneself and to the society. These are intolerable for a child's family, I suppose. Theft, narcotic drugs are unacceptable. Besides that, I do not want him to be a person who does not respect human rights. These are the things which are important for me (Interview #69).

I don't want him to have negative habits. I mean drugs, gambling, rakı... these are negative habits. These are the things that I don't like most. I want him to choose good friends. Because all the ills come from bad friends. Bad friends have those kinds of habits. Kids leave home, God knows where they go. I don't want my child to have those kinds of friends (Interview #63).

5) *Category of Proper Demeanor*: Endorsing the goal for Proper Demeanor refers to the concern that the child be well mannered, well behaved, respectful, cooperative, obedient, and has good family relationships (Harwood, 1992).

...For example, my husband's sister has a daughter. She is in the fourth grade. Maybe she is young, but I like her personality. She is a very calm and compliant girl; she knows how to behave in a well-mannered way. She knows the right moment to interrupt when her parents talk to each other. Despite her age, she is very mature. She knows her parents so well that even at her young age she knows how to talk to them. And she is definitely very merciful. That is, if something bad happens to one of the kids here, she would immediately come and help that child (Interview #72).

...I want her to be a respectful child. That is, I want her to know how to behave toward people who are older and younger than her. I want her to behave appropriately. I want to bring her up like that. I hope that she will have those attributes. I don't want her to have bad habits like those kids on the street. Because, we bring up the child, but the child goes out and comes back home having learned quite different things from others. Then, she may start behaving quite differently. I don't want my child to be like that of course. I want my child to be a good natured person, a respectful person, a child who knows what she is doing (Interview #59).

Coding Schema for SGI Subcategories

Responses of mothers were further coded in terms of ten subcategories developed by Leyendecker et al. (2002). According to this categorization, the category of Self-maximization is divided into three subcategories;

a) *Emotional and physical well-being and integration,* or concern that the child be happy, positive, peaceful, highly motivated, and psychologically and physically healthy.

b) *Development of personal and economic potential,* or concern that the child will improve himself/herself both financially and psychologically. This includes being intelligent, getting a college degree, getting a good job, being ambitious and successful in life and not to give in easily.

c) *Psychological development,* or concern that the child be self-confident, self-reliant, assertive, decisive, and be one who insists on his/her rights.

The main category Decency was further divided into the two subcategories;

a) *Avoid illicit behavior,* which includes concerns regarding delinquency, sexual misconduct as well as the standard to find the right kind of friends.

b) *Personal integrity and moral values,* including socially desirable behaviors such as being honest, trustworthy, benevolent, and showing conformity to moral as well as religious values.

Mothers' goals regarding the Lovingness main category were evaluated under two subcategories;

a) *Interpersonal warmth in general,* or the concern that the child be sociable, compassionate, and communicate well with other people.

b) *Close and warm relationship with family,* or the concern that the child will appreciate his/her parents and also establish strong company with his/her friends.

Lastly, the Proper Demeanor category was divided into two

subcategories;

a) *Respectful and well brought up,* or the concern that the child behaves respectfully towards others who are older than him/her, behaves appropriately, is respectful and well mannered in his/her relationships.

b) *Role obligations within family,* or the concern that the child will be in contact with the family members throughout his/her life, be fond of his/her parents, and listen to the advice of his/her parents.

This elaborated SGI coding system enables the examination of goals of mothers in terms of different aspects of the main categories. In the present study, all the interviews were coded by two researchers who were blind to the educational status of the mothers. The inter-rater reliability (Cohen's kappa) in coding was .83.

Translation of Materials

All written materials were translated from German to Turkish by a professional translator and a team of Turkish psychologists. Original materials and their back-translations were compared and checked carefully by the researchers to ensure that every question had the same meaning in both the Turkish and German versions.

RESULTS

Preliminary analysis showed that mothers in the high-educated group ($M = 247.3$, $SD = 78.5$) provided more responses, in general, than mothers in the low-educated group ($M = 192.7$, $SD = 61.8$) to be coded under the SGI categories (F (1, 38) = 5.9, $p < .05$). Therefore, rather than frequencies, percentages were used in the multivariate analyses to examine the number of descriptors provided by the two groups of mothers for each category and subcategory. With this aim, percentage scores in all four SGI questions were pooled for each main category and subcategory. **Tables 4.2** and **4.3** give an overview of the percentages for the coding categories in the high-educated and low-educated groups.

TABLE 4.2

Mean Percentages of Main Categories in the Two
Groups Generated Across Four Questions (N = 40)

	Low-educated mothers		High-educated mothers		
	n = 20		n = 20		
Main Categories	M	SD	M	SD	p
Self-maximization	%29	9	%40.80	12.1	**
Self-control	%9.70	6.6	%8.80	4.9	
Decency	%15.20	8.5	%16.10	9	
Lovingness	%11	7.9	%13.20	5.7	
Proper Demeanor	%35	11	%21	7.5	**

"*p < .05; **p < .01."

TABLE 4.3

Mean Percentages of Subcategories in the Two
Groups Generated Across Four Questions (N = 40)

	Low-educated mothers		High-educated mothers		
	n = 20		n = 20		
Subcategories	M	SD	M	SD	p
Emotional and physical well-being and integration	%5.20	3.2	%9.60	5	**
Development of personal and economic potential	%17.30	8.1	%18.20	9.1	-
Psychological development	%6.50	5.3	%12.80	7	**
Self-control	%9.70	6.6	%8.80	4.9	-
Avoid illicit behavior	%6.30	5.4	%3.60	4.8	-
Personal integrity and moral values	%8.90	8	%12.40	5.9	
Interpersonal warmth	%6.40	5.2	%8.90	5.7	-
Close, loving family relations	%4.60	5.6	%4.30	3.4	
Respectful, well brought up	%19.40	9.8	%11.20	6.2	**
Role obligations within the family	%15.50	9.9	%9.80	6.3	*

" *p < .05; **p < .01."

Results for Five Main Categories

A descriptive analysis indicated that the distribution of scores around the mean percentages was quite similar across categories and in the two groups. Analysis of Variance (ANOVA) performed for the main SGI categories showed that the high-educated and low-educated mothers differed significantly in two of the five main categories. Mothers in the high-educated group were found to endorse self-maximization goals more highly. High-educated mothers (M = 40.7, SD = 12.5) were concerned with self-maximization of their children more than mothers in the low-educated group (M = 29, SD =9), (F (1, 38) = 12, p < .01). On the other hand, with regard to the category of Proper Demeanor, low-educated mothers (M = 34.9, SD = 11) were found to be concerned that their child be obedient, respectful and well mannered more than the high-educated mothers (M = 34.9, SD = 7.5), (F (1, 38) = 21.6, p < .001).

However, mothers did not significantly differ with regard to the category of Decency (e.g., being honest or a good person), Lovingness (ability to have close and warm relationships with others, to be kind and caring) and Self-control. **Table 4.2** shows the percentages for the main categories generated through the four questions.

Analysis of Subcategories of Self-maximization and Proper Demeanor

Subcategories of Self-maximization and Proper Demeanor were further analyzed in order to understand various aspects of these two main categories in which mothers in the high- and low-educated groups differed.

Analysis of Subcategories of Self-maximization

An ANOVA analysis performed on the subcategories of Self-maximization indicated that high– and low-educated mothers significantly differed from one another in the subcategory of emotional and physical well-being and integration (F (1,38) = 11, p <. 01).

Accordingly, high-educated mothers ($M = 9.6$, $SD = 5$) referred to goals related to emotional and physical well-being and integration more than low-educated mothers ($M = 5.2$, $SD = 3.2$). In addition, high-educated mothers ($M = 12.8$, $SD = 7$) provided more descriptive terms and phrases regarding psychological development of their children than low-educated mothers ($M = 6.5$, $SD = 5.3$), ($F (1, 38) = 10.2$, $p < .01$). However, high- and low-educated mothers did not significantly differ from one another in their reference to goals related to the development of personal and economic potential subcategory.

Analysis of Subcategories of Proper Demeanor

Analysis showed that high- and low-educated mothers significantly differed in both aspects of Proper Demeanor. Low-educated mothers ($M = 19.4$, $SD = 9.8$) generated more responses than high-educated mothers ($M = 11.2$, $SD = 6.2$) with regard to the subcategory of being respectful and well brought up ($F (1, 38) = 9.8$, $p <. 05$). Similarly, low-educated mothers ($M = 15.5$, $SD = 9.9$) referred to goals related to 'role obligations within the family' more than high-educated mothers ($M = 9.7$, $SD = 6.3$), ($F (1, 38) = 4.6$, $p <. 05$). **Table 4.3** shows the percentages for the subcategories generated across the four questions.

Differences in Mothers' Responses With Respect to the Sex of the Child

A comparison of mothers of boys and girls in both groups indicated that mothers of boys ($M = 6.6$, $SD = 5.4$) mentioned fears for delinquency and illicit behavior (falls under the main category of Decency) more often than mothers of girls ($M = 2.6$, $SD = 3.3$; $F (1, 38) = 7.5$, $p < .05$). **Tables 4.4** and **4.5** show the percentages for the main categories and subcategories, respectively, according to the sex of the child.

TABLE 4.4

Mean Percentages of Mothers' Responses in Main Categories
With Respect to Sex of the Child (N = 40)

Main Categories	Mothers of girls		Mothers of boys		
	n = 19		n = 21		
	M	SD	M	SD	p
Self-maximization	%38.20	12.4	%32.10	11.4	
Self-control	%10.10	5.5	%8.60	6.1	
Decency	%11.50	5.9	%18.50	8.2	*
Lovingness	%12.50	7.7	%11.20	6.1	
Proper Demeanor	%27.50	11.9	%29.30	10.9	

*$p < .05$.

TABLE 4.5

Mean Percentages of Mothers' Responses in Subcategories With Respect to
Sex of the Child (N = 40)

Main category	Subcategory	Mothers of girls		Mothers of boys	
		n = 19		n = 21	
		M	SD	M	SDp
Self-maximization					
Emotional and physical well-being		%8.30	4.3	%6.60	5.1
Personal and economic potential		%18.30	9.5	%17.50	7.8
Psychological development		%11.50	7.6	%7.80	6.1
Self-control		%10.10	5.5	%8.60	6.1
Decency Avoid illicit behavior		%2.60	3.3	%6.60	5.4 *
Personal integrity and moral values		%8.80	5.7	%11.80	8.1
Lovingness Interpersonal warmth		%8	6.2	%7.30	5.1
Close, loving family relations		%4.50	5.8	%3.90	2.5
Proper Demeanor					
Respectful, well brought up		%15.30	9.3	%15.70	9.1
Role obligations within family		%12.10	8.2	%13.60	9.2

*$p < .05$.

Within Group Ranking in the Categories

A descriptive analysis showed that high-educated mothers referred to goals that fall under the category of Self-maximization (M = 40.8; SD = 12.1) more than the other four main categories. Other goal categories mentioned most by high-educated mothers were Proper Demeanor (M = 21, SD = 7.5), Decency (M = 16.2, SD = 9) and Lovingness (M = 13.2, SD = 5.7). Goals related to Self-control (M = 8.9, SD = 4.9) were the least referred to among the five main categories. **Chart 4.1** shows the relative frequency of main categories

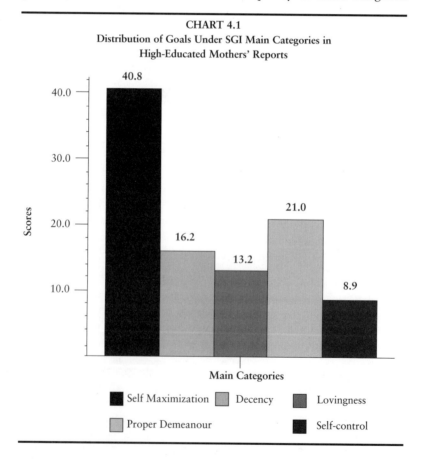

CHART 4.1
Distribution of Goals Under SGI Main Categories in
High-Educated Mothers' Reports

brought up by the high-educated mothers.

A descriptive analysis of low-educated mothers' reports showed that low-educated mothers mentioned goals that fall under the category of Proper Demeanor ($M = 34.9$, $SD = 11$) more than the other four main categories. The second, third and fourth main categories mentioned by low-educated mothers were Self-maximization ($M = 29.1$, $SD = 9$), Decency ($M = 15.3$, $SD = 8.5$) and Lovingness ($M = 11$, $SD = 7.9$), respectively. The category low-educated mothers referred to least was Self-control ($M = 9.7$, $SD = 6.6$). **Chart 4.2** shows the rela-

CHART 4.2
Distribution of Goals Under SGI Main Categories in
Low-Educated Mothers' Reports

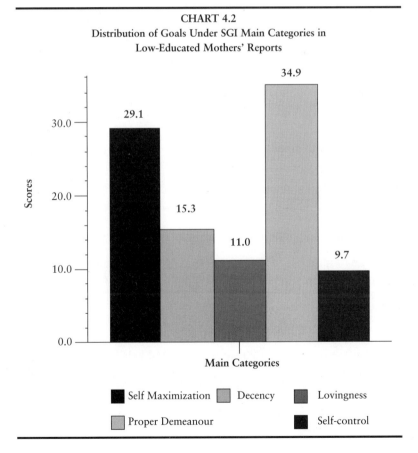

tive frequency of main categories mentioned by low-educated mothers. This analysis showed that, except for the categories of Self-maximization and Proper Demeanor, high and low-educated mothers gave importance to goals related to the categories of Decency, Lovingness and Self-control in the same order.

Reports of the high- and low-educated mothers were also analyzed in terms of goals that fall under subcategories. This analysis showed that high-educated mothers referred to goals related to the development of personal and economic potential (M = 18.3, SD = 9.1), psychological development (M = 12.8, SD = 7), which are subcategories of Self-maximization main category, and personal integrity (M = 12.5, SD = 5.9), which is a subcategory of Decency, respectively, more than the other subcategories. Low-educated mothers on the other hand, valued 'being respectful and well brought up' (M = 19.4, SD = 9.8), which is a subcategory of Proper Demeanor; development of personal and economic potential (M = 17.3, SD = 8.1), which is a subcategory of Self-maximization; and role obligations within the family (M = 15.5, SD = 9.9), which is a subcategory of Proper Demeanor, more than other subcategories. **Charts 4.3** and **4.4** show the distribution of subcategories for the high- and low-educated groups, respectively.

DISCUSSION

The primary purpose of the present study is to investigate the relationship between educational status of mothers and their long-term socialization goals in the Turkish context. Studying parental cognitions is important since they are closely related with child outcomes (Grusec et al., 1997; Harkness & Super, 1996). Literature has shown that parental characteristics, such as socialization goals and beliefs, affect their parenting styles and behaviors, which, in turn, are associated with child outcomes. For example, the qualities that mothers want their children to possess have been found to be in line with the child-rearing practices they display (Luster et al., 1989), and these practices predict psychoso-

CHART 4.3
Distribution of Goals Under SGI Subcategories in High-Educated Mothers' Reports

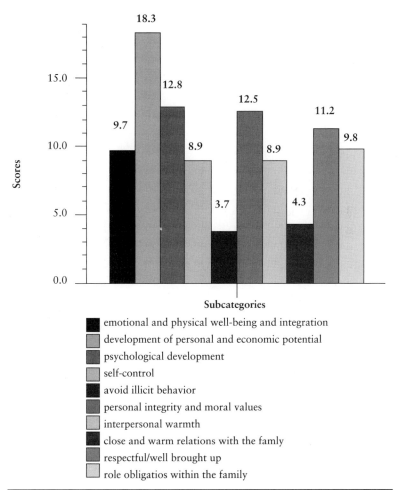

CHART 4.4
Distribution of Goals Under SGI Subcategories in Low-Educated Mothers' Reports

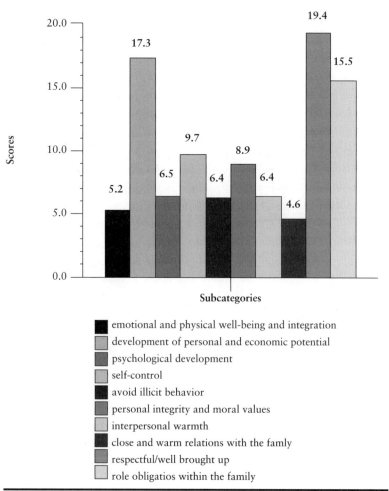

emotional and physical well-being and integration
development of personal and economic potential
psychological development
self-control
avoid illicit behavior
personal integrity and moral values
interpersonal warmth
close and warm relations with the famly
respectful/well brought up
role obligatios within the family

cial competence and academic achievement (Beckwith et al., 1992; Dornbusch et al., 1987; Grusec & Goodnow, 1994; Lamborn et al., 1991), vocabulary development (Huttenlocher et al., 1991), and language development of the child (Whitehurst et al., 1998).

Studying moderating variables, such as parental education, is another important target of investigation since education can shape the nature of the relationship between parenting and child outcomes. Goodnow (1988) emphasized parental education as a critical variable that has to be taken into account since differences in parenting cognitions and practices may diminish when parents' education level is controlled. However, "cultural models" regarding parenting may guide parental ideas and acts despite differences in social and educational background. In support of this claim, the literature has shown that mothers' long-term socialization goals related to self-enhancement/autonomy and compliance/relatedness to others highlight a robust difference across cultures (Harwood 1992; Harwood et al., 1999; Leyendecker et al., 2002; Miller & Harwood, 2001) regardless of socioeconomic status (Harwood et al., 1996). Cross-cultural differences in maternal socialization goals have been interpreted as indications of the normative cultural constructs that cannot be reduced to differences in socioeconomic status (Harwood et al., 1996). Nevertheless, Harwood et al. (1996) have also found that, in their reports regarding long-term socialization goals, Anglo mothers from a higher SES emphasized self-enhancement, and those from a low SES stressed the importance of being well mannered and compliant. This finding points to the fact that there are within-culture differences in mothers' socialization goals that is partly due to their socioeconomic background.

In this realm, comparing high- and low-educated mothers' long-term socialization goals, this study provided information regarding the relations between the education level of Turkish mothers and the attributes they want their children to attain in the long run. The present study showed findings similar to those reported by Harwood et al. (1996) regarding SES-related variation in Anglo-American mothers' socialization goals.

The present study indicated that socialization goals related with self-enhancement, development of individual potential and psychological development are emphasized more by high-educated mothers, whereas goals related with exhibiting being well brought up, respectful, compliant, and well-mannered are emphasized more by low-educated mothers in the Turkish context. In this study, high-educated mothers mentioned the importance of characteristics, such as being motivated, peaceful, psychologically healthy, diligent, and positive, and they also reported that they wish their children to have the necessary skills that will help them to accomplish their own ideals and actualize their potentials in life. Furthermore, they brought up features such as decisiveness, self-confidence, and intelligence as the qualities that they wish their children to possess as adults. High-educated mothers also emphasized the importance of being a person who knows what she/he wants and struggles for and what she/he believes to be true more than low-educated mothers. It should be noted that although all mothers mentioned these goals, such autonomy granting themes were more salient in the reports of high-educated mothers. Low-educated mothers' reports highlighted the importance of obligations and being related to others, especially to the family.

In regard to goals related to being well brought-up and well-mannered, low-educated mothers mostly mentioned respect for the elderly, being adaptive to the situation, being kind and considerate towards others and being compliant to societal norms as the desirable characteristics that they wished their children to possess as adults. They also highlighted the importance of close family ties and their expectation for their children to be obedient to values, opinions and decisions of the family more than the high-educated mothers did. Although these socialization goals were also endorsed by high-educated mothers, they were more often and strongly brought up by low-educated mothers.

Besides differences, there were also similarities between the long-term socialization goals of high- and low-educated Turkish mothers. Being successful in school and work life and being determined in the face of hardship were common goals shared by both high- and low-educated mothers. Mothers in both groups emphasized the importance of education and reported that they wished their children to be well-educated, meaning that they desired their children to have a college degree. Having an occupation that provides satisfactory and regular earning was also stressed by all the mothers.

Mothers of the two groups were also similar in their desire for their child to be a person who has good communication skills and the ability to share, and who is compassionate and sociable. Both low- and high-educated mothers underlined being on good terms with the family, as well as with other people, and establishing good friendships as the desirable qualities that they wish their children to possess as adults. All of the mothers emphasized honesty, sincerity, modesty, reliability and frankness as the qualities they wish their children to possess as adults, whereas they described hypocrisy, forgery, lying, and insincerity as the qualities that they do not want to see in their children. Similarly, anxiety regarding illicit behavior such as smoking, using drugs and gambling were mentioned by both groups of mothers. Mothers of girls in the low-educated group also emphasized the possibility of a premarital sexual relationship as an undesirable event that they want their daughter to refrain from.

Lastly, both low- and high-educated mothers showed similar concerns such that they all emphasized the importance of putting limits to one's temptations, knowing one's limits, and not harming and abusing others. Being aggressive, stubborn, violent, and arrogant were among the aspects all mothers loathed.

GENERAL DISCUSSION AND CONCLUSION

The present study contributes to the literature by showing that the educational level of mothers is related to their long-term socialization goals, and it is an important source of within-culture difference in the Turkish context. In this respect, findings of this study indicate that goals that emphasize self-enhancement and autonomy (self-maximization), and obligations, compliance, and relatedness (proper demeanor) are important cultural constructs, and examining these goals aids us to understand maternal socialization goals within the framework provided by the Family Change Model (Kağıtçıbaşı, 1996, 2007). The Family Change Model proposed by Kağıtçıbaşı (2007) provides an account of child-rearing beliefs and patterns adopted by families on the basis of the constitution of family structure within the context of socioeconomic development and urbanization.

As expected, the pattern found in the reports of low- and high-educated mothers justified the framework provided by the Family Change Model. Low-educated mothers, although recruited from Istanbul, were mostly born in rural areas of Turkey and migrated to Istanbul with their families before they married. Regardless of their birth place, all of the low-educated mothers were residing in poor suburbs of Istanbul in which traditional lifestyles, close kinship ties and intimate neighborhood relationships are valued and prevalent. As residents of these economically less-developed suburbs are first or second generation migrants, it is quite common to see such social relationships in these suburbs that are characteristic of rural areas. Since the participant low-educated mothers used to work in less prestigious jobs with inadequate earnings, financial concerns and matters regarding social security render the traditional family model still functional. Hence obedience, preserving intimate relationships with the family, giving importance to family ties, and, as most of the low-educated mothers overtly stated, expecting the child to look after his/her parents when they get older emerged as salient aspects in long-term socialization goals of low-educated mothers.

With regard to the high-educated mothers' goals, the findings also justify the theorization provided by the Family Change Model. Accordingly, high-educated mothers mentioned the high demands of today's world, especially demands of work life on the individual, and overtly emphasized their wishes regarding their children to be self-reliant and autonomous individuals. All of the high-educated mothers, especially the working mothers, saw characteristics of being self initiating, confident, and self reliant as necessary qualities to be successful and happy in both private and work lives.

Nevertheless, as the findings of the present study showed, high-educated mothers did not value total independence of the child. Instead, they shared similar concerns with low-educated mothers in terms of expecting their children to be close to them and be warm and loving children in their relationships with their family. As such, it might be argued that long-term socialization goals of high-educated mothers exemplify the child-rearing orientation of the family model of *psychological interdependence* (Kağıtçıbaşı, 1996, 2005). This model describes autonomy as well as the emotional connectedness of the child as desirable characteristics in the child-rearing orientations of the mothers. In this regard, it can be said that high-educated Turkish mothers value independence but not total separation from the family.

The Family Change Model has some implications regarding the types of selves to which the three family interaction patterns contribute. Accordingly, *the family model of interdependence* fosters the development of a relational self, which is high in relatedness and low in autonomy. *The family model of independence* engenders the separate self, which is high in autonomy and low in relatedness. *The family model of emotional interdependence* on the other hand, contributes to the development of an autonomous related-self, which is high in both autonomy and relatedness (Kağıtçıbaşı, 1996, 2007). Although the kinds of selves mothers try to foster in their children were not studied explicitly in the present study, mothers' reports on their parenting goals provide a description for the self that they encourage in their children. Accordingly, it might be claimed that the pattern reflected in the low-educated mothers' reports regarding desirable characteristics that they wish to see in their children fit the description of a related self model; whereas, the high-educated mothers' description is in congruence with the autonomous-related self model.

It has to be noted that the findings of the present study are consistent with previous research that assert the role of economic hardship in shaping the family structure and desirable child characteristics. Smith et al. (2006) stated that it is common that the child contributes to the family in material terms in socioeconomically less developed societies, particularly in rural agrarian contexts and in low-income groups in urban/semi-urban areas. In such societies where old-age asylum and social security benefits like insurance and retirement income are not well established, children have an old age security value. Kağıtçıbaşı (2007) and colleagues (Smith et al., 2006) argue that this pattern is typical in the family model of interdependence in which obedience-oriented child-rearing is valued; whereas, independence and autonomy are not promoted, since such attributes are considered as a threat to family solidarity.

In that respect, the present study confirms the theoretical framework provided by the Family Change Model and also consistent with previous findings (İmamoğlu, 1987; Kağıtçıbaşı, 1982a; Kağıtçıbaşı & Ataca, 2005) regarding the comparative desirability of a child's autonomy and obedience in varying socioeconomic backgrounds. Apparently, autonomy and relatedness themes emerge as proper socialization goals that have a function within the context of the socioeconomic niche of the family.

Limitations of the current study provide directions for future research. A larger sample size might have provided a more elaborate picture regarding other socialization goals of low- and high-educated mothers in Turkey. In this study, the definition of low- and high-educated groups was limited to at most five years and at least thirteen years of schooling, respectively, to examine the differences between the two ends of the educational spectrum. Examining parenting beliefs of secondary and high school graduates will highlight the relative closeness of mothers with varying educational attainments in respect with their socialization goals, and thereby might provide valuable information regarding which pattern of socialization goals is more 'typical' or out of the ordinary in the Turkish context.

Similar to most other studies (Harwood, 1992; Harwood et al., 1995; Harwood et al., 1996; Harwood et al., 1999; Leyendecker et al., 2002), the present study investigates the long-term socialization goals of *mothers* only. However, values of fathers can shape the home environment and affect mothers' goals and child-rearing practices. Future studies that examine paternal socialization goals may highlight another aspect of the topic that has basically remained unexplored until now and facilitate our understanding of 'socialization in the family'.

Lastly, the functional value and importance of mothers' long-term socialization goals can be shown by examining the link between these goals and child outcomes. The extant literature provides promising findings in this realm and suggests that parental beliefs and expectations (Okagaki & Sternberg, 1993; Luster et al., 1989), parental reasoning (Holden, 1997), parental cognitions (Grusec et al., 1997), and long-term and short-term goals (Boratav, 2003; Kuczynski, 1984; Hastings & Grusec, 1998) are related to cognitive and socioemotional abilities in children. Investigating the relations between parental cognitions and child outcomes in the Turkish context may carry the attempt started in this study and contribute further to our knowledge about socialization and children's development in Turkey.

REFERENCES

Abell, E., M. Clawson, W. N. Washington, K. K. Bost, and B. E. Vaughn, 1996, "Parenting Values, Attitudes, Behaviors, and the Goals of African-American Mothers from a Low-income Population in Relation to Social and Societal Contexts", *Journal of Family Issues*, 17(5): 593-613.

Abidin, R. R., 1992, "The Determinants of Parenting Behavior", *Journal of Clinical Child Psychology*, 21(4): 407-412.

Akşit, B., and B. Akşit, 1989, "Sociocultural Determinants of Infant and Child Morality in Turkey", *Social Science and Medicine*, 28(6): 571-576.

Ambert, A. M., 1994, "An International Perspective on Parenting: Social Change and Social Constructs", *Journal of Marriage and the Family*, 56(3): 529-543.

Baumrind, D., 1973, "The Development of Instrumental Competence through Socialization" in A. D. Pick (ed.), *The Minnesota Symposium on Child Psychology*, 7: 3-46, Minneapolis: University of Minnesota Press.

—, 1978, "Parental Disciplinary Patterns and Social Competence in Children", *Youth and Society*, 9(3): 239-275.

Beckwith, L., C. Rodning and S. Cohen, 1992, "Preterm Children at Early Adolescence and Continuity and Discontinuity in Maternal Responsiveness from Infancy", *Child Development*, 63: 1198-1208.

Bornstein, M. H. and R. H. Bradley, 2003, "Socioeconomic Status, Parenting, and Child Development: An Introduction" in M. H. Bornstein and R. H. Bradley (eds.), *Socioeconomic Status, Parenting, and Child Development*, Mahwah, NJ: Lawrence Erlbaum Associates, Publishers.

Boratav, A. B., 2003, "The Role of Child Temperament, Sociocognitive Abilities, Parenting and Social Context in the Development of Prosocial Behaviour", unpublished doctoral dissertation, University of Melbourne, Victoria, Australia.

Bornstein, M. H., C. Hahn, J. T. D. Suwalsky, and O. M. Haynes, 2003, "The Hollingshead Four-Factor Index of Social Status and the Socioeconomic Index of Occupations" in M. H. Bornstein and R. H. Bradley (eds.), *Socioeconomic Status, Parenting, and Child Development*, Mahwah, NJ: Lawrence Erlbaum Associates, Publishers.

Clausen, J. A., 1966, "Family Structure, Socialization, and Personality" in L. W. Hoffman and M. L. Hoffman (eds.), *Review of Child Development Research*, New York: Russell Sage Foundation.

Covell, K., J. E. Grusec, and G. King, 1995, "The Intergenerational Transmission of Maternal Discipline and Standards for Behavior", *Social Development*, 4(1): 32-43.

Cowan, P. A., D. Powell, and C. P. Cowan, 1998, "Parenting Interventions: A Family Systems Perspective" in W. Damon (ed.), *Handbook of Child Psychology*, 5(4): 3-72.

Darling, N. and L. Steinberg, 1993, "Parenting Style as Context: An Integrative Model", *Psychological Bulletin*, 113(3): 487-496.

Dix, T., D. N. Ruble, J. E. Grusec, and S. Nixon, 1986, "Social Cognition in Parents: Inferential and Affective Reactions to Children of Three Age Levels", *Child Development*, 57: 879-894.

Dornbusch, S. M., P. L. Ritter, P. H. Leiderman, O. F. Roberts, and M. J. Fraleigh, 1987, "The Relation of Parenting Style to Adolescent School Performance", *Child Development*, 58: 1244-1257.

Eisenberg, N., 1996, "The Conflict Talk of Mothers and Children: Patterns Related to Culture, SES, and Gender of Child", *Merrill-Palmer Quarterly*, 42(3): 438-452.

Ellis, G. J., G. R. Lee, and L. R. Petersen, 1978, "Supervision and Conformity: A Cross- cultural Analysis of Parental Socialization Values", *American Journal of Sociology*, 84(2): 386-403.

Ensminger, M. E., and K. Fothergill, 2003, "A Decade of Measuring SES: What It Tells Us and Where to Go from Here" in M. H. Bornstein and R. H. Bradley (eds.), *Socioeconomic Status, Parenting, and Child Development*, Mahwah, NJ: Lawrence Erlbaum Associates, Publishers.

Garcia Coll, C., A. Akerman, and D. Cicchetti, 2000, "Cultural Influences on Developmental Processes and Outcomes: Implications for the Study of Development and Psychopathology", *Development and Psychopathology*, 12: 333-356.

Georgas, J., S. Christakopoulou, Y. H. Poortinga, A. Angleitner, R. Goodwin, and N. Charalambous, 1997, "The Relationship of Family Bonds to Family Structure and Function across Cultures", *Journal of Cross-Cultural Psychology*, 28(3): 303-320.

Goodnow, J. J., 1988, "Parents' Ideas, Actions, and Feelings: Models and Methods from Developmental and Social Psychology", *Child Development*, 59: 286-320.

Göncü, A., U. Tuermer, J. Jain, and D. Johnson, 1999, "Children's Play as Cultural Activity" in A. Göncü (ed.), *Children's Engagement in the World*, Cambridge: Cambridge University Press.

Göregenli, M., 1997, "Individualist-collectivist Tendencies in a Turkish Sample", *Journal of Cross-Cultural Psychology*, 28(6): 787-794.

Greenfield, P. M., and L. K. Suzuki, 1998, "Culture and Human Development: Implications for Parenting, Education, Pediatrics, and Mental Health" in W. Damon (ed.), *Handbook of Child Psychology*, 5(4): 1059-1109.

Grusec, J. E., D. Rudy, and T. Martini, 1997, "Parenting Cognitions and Child Outcomes: An Overview and Implications for Children's Internalization of Values" in L. Kuczynski and J. E. Grusec (eds.), *Parenting and Children's Internalization of Values*, New York: John Wiley & Sons, Inc.

Harris, J. R., 1995, "Where is the Child's Environment? A Group Socialization Theory of Development", *Psychological Review*, 102(3): 458-489.

—, 2000, "Socialization, Personality Development, and the Child's Environments: Comment on Vandell", *Developmental Psychology*, 36(6): 711-723.

Harkness, S., and C. M. Super, 1996, "Introduction" in S. Harkness and C. M. Super (eds.), *Parents' Cultural Belief Systems: Their Origins, Expressions, and Consequences*, New York: The Guilford Press.

Harwood, R. L., 1992, "The Influence of Culturally Derived Values on Anglo and Puerto Rican Mothers' Perceptions of Attachment Behavior", *Child Development*, 63: 822-839.

Harwood, R. L., J. G. Miller, and L. N. Irizarry, 1995, *Culture and Attachment: Perceptions of the Child in Context*, New York: Guilford.

Harwood, R. L., A. Schoelmerich, P. A. Schulze, and Z. Gonzalez, 1999, "Cultural Differences in Maternal Beliefs and Behaviors: A Study of Middle-class Anglo and Puerto Rican Mother-infant Pairs in Four Everyday Situations", *Child Development*, 70: 1005-1016.

Harwood, R. L., A. Schoelmerich, E. Ventura-Cook, P. A. Schulze, and S. P. Wilson, 1996, "Culture and Class Influences on Anglo and Puerto Rican Mothers' Beliefs Regarding Long-term Socialization Goals and Child Behavior", *Child Development*, 67: 2446-2461.

Hastings, P. D. and J. E. Grusec, 1998, "Parenting Goals as Organizers of Responses to Parent-child Disagreement", *Developmental Psychology*, 34(3): 465-479.

Holden, G. W., 1997, *Parents and the Dynamics of Child Rearing*, Colorado: Westview Press.

Hortaçsu, N., L. Ertem, H. Kurtoğlu, and B. Uzer, 1990, "Family Background and Individual Measures as Predictors of Turkish Primary School Children's Academic Achievement", *The Journal of Psychology*, 124(5): 535-544.

Huttenlocher, J., W. Haight, A. Bryk, M. Seltzer, and T. Lyons, 1991, "Early Vocabulary Growth: Relation to Language Input and Gender", *Developmental Psychology*, 27: 236-248.

İmamoğlu, E. O., 1987, "An Interdependence Model of Human Development" in Ç. Kağıtçıbaşı (ed.), *Growth and Progress in Cross-cultural Psychology*, Lisse, The Netherlands: Swets & Zeitlinger.

Kağıtçıbaşı, Ç., 1970, "Social Norms and Authoritarianism: A Turkish-American Comparison", *Journal of Personality and Social Psychology*, 16(3): 444-451.

—, 1973, "Psychological Aspects of Modernization in Turkey", *Journal of Cross-Cultural Psychology*, 4(2): 157-174.

—, 1982a, "Old-age Security Value of Children", *Journal of Cross-Cultural Psychology*, 13(1): 29-42.

—, 1982b, "Sex Roles, Value of Children and Fertility in Turkey" in Ç. Kağıtçıbaşı (ed.), *Sex Roles, Family, and Community in Turkey*, Bloomington, Indiana: Indiana University Press.

—, 1984, "Socialization in Traditional Society: A Challenge to Psychology", *International Journal of Psychology*, 19: 145-157.

—, 1985, "Intra-family Interaction and a Model of Change" in T. Erder (ed.), *Family in Turkish Society*, Ankara: Turkish Social Science Association.

—, 1987, "Alienation of the Outsider: The Plight of Migrants", *International Migration*, 25: 195-210.

—, 1989, "Child Rearing in Turkey and an Intervention Research", *Psychology and Developing Societies*, 1(1): 37-52.

—, 1996, "The Autonomous-relational Self: A New Synthesis", *European Psychologist*, 1(3): 180-186.

—, 2005, "Autonomy and Relatedness in Cultural Context: Implications for Self and Family", *Journal of Cross-cultural Psychology*, 36(4): 403-422.

—, 2007, *Family, Self and Human Development across Cultures. Theory and Applications*, 2nd ed., Mahwah, NJ: Lawrence Erlbaum Associates.

Kağıtçıbaşı, Ç. and B. Ataca, 2005, "Value of Children and Family Change: A Three-decade Portrait of from Turkey", *Applied Psychology: An International Review*, 54(3): 317-137.

Kağıtçıbaşı, Ç., D. Sunar, and S. Bekman, 2001, "Long-term Effects of Early Intervention: Turkish Low-income Mothers and Children", *Applied Developmental Psychology*, 22: 333-361.

Kashima, Y., 1987, "Conceptions of Person. Implications in Individualism/Collectivism Research" in Ç. Kağıtçıbaşı (ed.), *Growth and Progress in Cross-cultural Psychology*, Berwyn, PA, US: Swets North America.

Kıray, M., 1976, "The New Role of Mothers: Changing Intra-familial Relationships in a Small Town in Turkey" in J. G. Peristiany (ed.), *Mediterranean Family Structures*, London: Cambridge University Press.

Kohn, M. L., 1963, "Social Class and Parent-Child Relationships: An Interpretation", *American Journal of Sociology*, 68: 471-480.

Kongar, E., 1976, "A Survey of Familial Change in Two Turkish Gecekondu Areas" in J. G. Peristiany (ed.), *Mediterranean Family Structures*, London: Cambridge University Press.

Korte, C., 1984, "The Helpfulness of Urban Villagers" in E. Staub, D. Bar-Tal, J. Karylowski and J. Reykowski (eds.), *Development and Maintenance of Prosocial Behavior*, New York: Plenum Press.

Kuczynski, L., 1984, "Socialization Goals and Mother-Child Interaction: Strategies for Long-term and Short-term Compliance", *Developmental Psychology*, 20(6): 1061-1073.

Lamborn, S. D., N. S. Mounts, L. Steinberg, and S. M Dornbusch, 1991, "Patterns of Competence and Adjustment among Adolescents from Authoritative, Authoritarian, Indulgent, and Neglectful Families", *Child Development*, 62: 1049-1065.

Leaper, C., K. J. Anderson, and P. Sanders, 1998, "Moderators of Gender Effects on Parents' Talk to Their Children: a Meta-analysis", *Developmental Psychology*, 34(1): 3-27.

Leyendecker, B., R. L. Harwood, M. E. Lamb, and A. Schoelmerich, 2002, "Mothers' Socialization Goals and Evaluations of Desirable and Undesirable Everyday Situations in Two Diverse Cultural Groups", *International Journal of Behavioral Development*, 26: 248-258.

Lloyd, A., and M. C. Fallers, 1976, "Sex Roles in Edremit" in J. G. Peristiany (ed.), *Mediterranean Family Structures*, London: Cambridge University Press.

Luster, T., K. Rhoades, and B. Haas, 1989, "The Relation between Parental Values and Parenting Behavior: A Test of the Kohn's Hypothesis", *Journal of Marriage and the Family*, 51: 139-147.

McLoyd, V. C., 1998, "Socioeconomic Disadvantage and Child Development", *American Psychologist*, 53(2): 185-204.

McNally, S., N. Eisenberg, and J. D. Harris, 1991, "Consistency and Change in Maternal Child-rearing Practices and Values: A Longitudinal Study", *Child Development*, 62: 190-198.

Miller, A. M. and R. L. Harwood, 2001, "Long-term Socialization Goals and the Construction of Infants' Social Networks among Middle Class Anglo and Puerto Rican Mothers", *International Journal of Behavioral Development*, 25: 450-457.

Miller, J., C. Schooler, M. L. Kohn, and K. A. Miller, 1979, "Women and Work: The Psychological Effects of Occupational Conditions", *American Journal of Sociology*, 85(1): 66-94.

Mueller, C. W. and T. L. Parcel, 1981, "Measures of Socioeconomic Status: Alternatives and Recommendations", *Child Development*, 52: 13-30.

Okagaki, L. and R. J. Sternberg, 1993, "Parental Beliefs and Children's School Performance", *Child Development*, 64: 36-56.

Oyserman, D., H. M. Coon, and M. Kemmelmeier, 2002, "Rethinking Individualism and Collectivism: Evaluation of Theoretical Assumptions and Meta-analyses", *Psychological Bulletin*, 128: 3-72.

Ross, G. F., 1984, "Styles of Discipline: Reported Responses to a Variety of Child Behaviors", *Australian Journal of Sex, Marriage and Family*, 5(4): 215-220.

Schneider, B., G. Attili, P. Vermigli, and A. Younger, 1997, "A Comparison of Middle-class English-Canadian and Italian Mothers' Beliefs about Children's Peer-directed Aggression and Social Withdrawal", *International Journal of Behavioral Development*, 21(1): 133-154.

State Institute of Statistics (SIS), 2003, *Census of population 2000; Social and Economic Characteristics of Population, Turkey*, Ankara: SIS Press.

—, 2003, *Census of Population 2000; Social and Economic Characteristics of Population, Istanbul*, Ankara: SIS Press.

Slaughter-Defoe, D. T., 1995, "Revisiting the concept of socialization. Caregiving and Teaching in the 90s-A Personal Perspective", *American Psychologist*, 50(4): 276-286.

Smith, P. B., M. H. Bond, and Ç. Kağıtçıbaşı, 2006, *Understanding Social Psychology across Cultures: Living and Working with Others in a Changing World*, London: Sage Publications.

Stevenson-Hinde, J., 1998, "Parenting in Different Cultures: Time to Focus", *Developmental Psychology*, 34(4): 698-700.

Szapocznik, J. and W. M. Kurtines, 1993, "Family Psychology and Cultural Diversity", *American Psychology*, 48(4): 400-407.

Taylor, R. D. and G. Oskay, 1995, "Identity Formation in Turkish and American Late Adolescents", *Journal of Cross-Cultural Psychology*, 26(1): 8-22.

Triandis, H. C., 1994, *Culture and Social Behavior*, New York: McGraw-Hill, Inc.

Tudge, J., D. Hogan, S. Lee, P. Tammeveski, M. Meltsas, N. Kulakova, I. Snezhkova, and S. Putnam, 1999, "Cultural Heterogeneity: Parental Values and Beliefs and Their Preschoolers' Activities in the United States, South Korea, Russia, and Estonia" in A. Göncü (ed.), *Children's Engagement in the World*, Cambridge: Cambridge University Press.

UNICEF, 1991, *The Situation Analysis of Mothers and Children in Turkey*, Ankara: UNICEF.

Vandell, D. L., 2000, "Parents, Peer Groups, and Other Socializing Influences", *Developmental Psychology*, 36(6): 699-710.

Volkan, V. D. and A. Çevik, 1989, "Turkish Fathers and Their Families" in S. H. Cath, A. Gurwitt and L. Gunsberg (eds.), *Fathers and Their Families*, Hillsdale, NJ: The Analytic Press.

Von der Lippe, A. L., 1999, "The Impact of Maternal Schooling and Occupation and Child-rearing Attitudes and Behaviours in Low-income Neighbourhoods in Cairo, Egypt", *International Journal of Behavioral Development*, 23(3): 703-729.

Whitehurst, G. J., F. L. Falco, C. J. Lonigan, J. E. Fischel, B. D. DeBaryshe, M. C. Valdez-Menchaca, and M. Caulfield, 1998, "Accelerating Language Development through Picture Book Reading", *Developmental Psychology*, 24: 552-559.

Appendices

INTERVIEWER: In this study, we are investigating mothers' wishes and expectations regarding their children's future; namely, what kind of personality characteristics and behaviors they want their children to possess in the future. To understand this, I will first ask you to tell me what you expect for your child in the future, and then to describe children that you know to possess at least the beginnings of the characteristics that you wish your child to possess. For each mother, there are some desirable and undesirable qualities that she would and would not like to see in her children. I want you to think of your child now and describe to me the personality characteristics and behaviors that you wish your children to possess in the future.

MOTHER: I would like him to be a respectful child in the first place. I wish him to have a good education. As his mother and father, we could not have a good education and had an occupation. I want my son to go to college; I will do everything in my power for this. Well...I don't know... in the future, I do not want my son to experience the bad things we have experienced. We neither lived our childhood nor are living a proper adult life. We do not have a career, an education. I want my child to be a well educated and respectable person. Just like all mothers, I want my child to be a respectful child in his environment and in the eyes of other people. But, my greatest wish is in fact to see him as an educated person.

INTERVIEWER: Some mothers say, for example, that they wish their child to be a cheerful child; they mention characteristics like that... do you have such expectations regarding your child's future characteristics?

MOTHER: Oh! This is not something that one can say right now. This may be related to the child's inborn characteristics...it must be something genetic. If the child is not cheerful, I can not do anything I suppose. I would like him to love people. We, as his mother and father, are very close to people. I notice that...it seems as if our child has inherited this characteristic; he is very close to other people, he is very friendly. For sure, I would like him to be like that when he is grown up. However, I mean... if he is sulky, I cannot do anything for that.

INTERVIEWER: Are there any other characteristics that come to your mind... that you would like to see in your son in the future?

MOTHER: Well...as a mother you want everything...but I cannot express them. You want everything when you have a child; you want him to wear the best clothes and eat the best food...well... I don't know, you want your child to live well. Now my son is eight months old, I want him to experience best of everything. That is, maybe because I could not live well, I wish all good things for him. I try to feed him with the best food and to dress him with the best cloths as far as I can do. That is, as I said, even if I know that I will starve to death, I will definitely provide him the opportunities for good education. I want him to have a good education and have an occupation. I dream of him in the future as a ...policeman...maybe one need not to spend years in the college to be a policeman...I want to see him as a policeman some day in the future. This idea impresses me even now when I dream of it. Maybe I will see the day my son comes home as a policeman, in his official dress.

INTERVIEWER: I see. You said you want your son to be a respectful person. Could you explain it to me? What is it like to be a respectful person?

MOTHER: A respectful person...For a person to be respectful, that person should be respectful to himself in the first place. Not to harm his/her social environment, not to have ill habits... I do not want him to have bad habits. If he does not have such habits, and his body is not addicted to something and his mind works a little bit, he would not be a disrespectful person. If you do not engage in illicit behaviors, you are not disrespectful towards others.

INTERVIEWER: What kind of bad habits and illicit behaviors?

MOTHER: Well...cigarette smoking, gambling, drinking alcohol...like that. But for today's world even alcohol and gambling are simple things, narcotic drugs are popular like alcohol or gambling...in the past it was not that much commonplace. Well...I don't know...there are strange things like homosexuality. I do not want to experience something like that as a mother.

INTERVIEWER: Could you give an example for respectful behavior? How would a respectful person behave?

MOTHER: A respectful person...I don't know...When he is grown up?

INTERVIEWER: In the future, at any age.

MOTHER: If he learns to be respectful, that is, if you teach the child to be respectful, you can see respectful behaviors from him in the future. Respect...well...is not to harm anybody, respect for yourself first and then respect for others, to respect people older than you and to love people younger than you, to be in service of one's business, to go to work and come back home regularly, to come home after work, to engage in social activities, to be with friends. Well... I mean... what is a disrespectful person like? Perhaps, because I do not see that kind of a person, I cannot describe it. A respectful person is a person who is busy with his/her own life, who gets along well with his/her neighbors, whose friendships are strong... If a person is disrespectful, nobody would like to be a friend of that person; he would not have any neighbors and a good job.

INTERVIEWER: Do you mean a person who is good at human relations?

MOTHER: Yes. I want him to be a person who gets along well with people.

INTERVIEWER: I understand. You said you wish your child to be well educated and have an occupation. Could you explicate it a little bit?

MOTHER: I don't know how to explicate it since I did not go to school after graduating from grade school.

INTERVIEWER: I mean what do you expect regarding education and occupation?

MOTHER: Well...as I said I really want my son to be a policeman. Maybe he does not need to go to school for too many years to be a policeman. But if a new law comes into force and requires people to have a college degree to be a policeman, I do not know, I will do everything in my power to make him go to college. I will try hard to accomplish this. I want him to have an occupation.

INTERVIEWER: I understand. Well, you said I do not want him to experience the bad things you have experienced. What kind of expectations do you have regarding this?

MOTHER: Oh! I did not live my childhood, frankly saying. That is, we did not experience things that today's children experience... I was brought up in a village. My spouse was brought up in Istanbul but he has not lived his childhood either. I mean...I could not express myself... ...I mean I want him to experience all good things that I have not seen in my life.

INTERVIEWER: What do you want him to do?

MOTHER: Well... everything...in my childhood was very simple but we did not have hamburgers for example. I ate a hamburger when I came to Istanbul. I want my child to know everything, to experience everything. Even now, as a child I want him to know everything and to start to grasp everything. I mean I want him to enjoy everything. We did not see an amusement park for example when we were children. Well...I don't know... we could not know what it means to go onto a swing. We have no such experiences. I want him to have nice toys.

INTERVIEWER: I see. You said you want him to be a respectable person? Could you explain this?

MOTHER: Respectable! In my understanding a respectable person is a well educated person. If you have an occupation you are already a respectable person. However, this does not mean that when you have a diploma and an occupation you will become a respectable person in any case; if you are a bad person you cannot be a respectable person. To be a respectable person you should be liked by people as well. Well...I want him to have a good career, not through our encouragement but with his own inclination. If you do not have an occupation, you cannot be a respectable person.

INTERVIEWER: I see. You also said "I want him to love people". What kind of expectations do you have regarding this characteristic?

MOTHER: Just before you came, I was watching a program on TV in which help is provided for people. Maybe to love people is to care for them, to be worried about them, to do something for them. I want to do everything for people. I want my child to be like that. I want to help people as much as I can. I wish I could have enough resources to help people. I want my child to be concerned with people. If he has financial resources, and if his neighbor needs financial help, I would like my child to be responsive to this need. I mean, I want him to be respectful to people older than him to care about these people. For example, I am very fond of my parents. This is related to love. I would like my son to be fond of his parents in a similar way. I mean, I want him a good observer. To love people, one needs to observe to care about people; he has to think whether his neighbors and friends have any problems...I want my son to be thoughtful about these matters.

INTERVIEWER: All right. Are there any other characteristics you would like to see in your son in the future?

MOTHER: My child is very smart. He is now eight months old... I mean his doctor –he has a private doctor...He is able to eat food that he should eat two months later according to the nourishment schedule determined by the doctor. If my child develops fast in all aspects, I want to see him having a good career.

INTERVIEWER: I see. I want you to think of your son again and tell me the characteristics that you do not want your child to possess in the future. Are there such characteristics or behaviors?

MOTHER: Of course there are. In the first place we, as his parents, are quite popular people in our surrounding. I want my child to be like that. I want him to refrain from ill habits and if possible I want him to refrain from such groups. I am afraid of his being a homosexual. It is very strange for me that homosexuality is ordinary nowadays. I don't know...it is strange, I suspect that there is homosexuality everywhere. Seeing on the television, one can easily be a homosexual. I am afraid of encountering such a thing in my child. I want him to be away from such things. I do not want to see him as a homosexual. However, if there is such an inclination in him, what can you do? You cannot do anything. As I said, I want him to be away from illicit habits.

INTERVIEWER: Alright...are there any other things that you want to say? What kind of personality characteristics of your son would make you unhappy?

MOTHER: If he becomes an unprincipled person that would make me unhappy. ... a person should have a characteristic...cheerfulness or sadness...but there must be something. I want my child to possess all human characteristics but not characterlessness. A person should have some qualities. I would like to see all qualities in my son except the bad ones. I want him to be a self-confident and a self-reliant child. I am like that. I want him to take these characteristics from me.

INTERVIEWER: Could you describe a person who is characterless?

MOTHER: A person who is characterless is capable of doing everything. This "everything" includes theft, dishonesty. Also...if you harm a characterless person, he would not care and would not react. The person who accepts everything is a characterless person. If a person has a character, he would not bear everything.

INTERVIEWER: I see. Can you think of an example for being characterless?

MOTHER: What do you mean?

INTERVIEWER: I mean...you said, for example, that a characterless person bears everything, accepts everything he would not bear if he has a character. Can you think of an example?

MOTHER: I mean I want him not to stand everything, he should show reaction if necessary, he should shout if the situation requires him to shout, if the situation requires him to sit, I want him to sit. I want him to behave properly. I don't know... there are things not all human beings can stand. These things are related to the personality characteristics. For example, I do not want my child to do something embarrassing. How can I say? I mean if somebody confronts him, I want him to stand against it, to overcome it.

INTERVIEWER: I see. Are there any other negative characteristics that you would not like your child to possess?

MOTHER: Well... let us put such things aside, none of the mothers would like her child to be an ill-mannered and a disrespectful child. No one would like to see her child like that. Which mother would like to see her child as a thief, as a vagabond? A child who cannot share anything with other people, neither takes anything good from others nor gives anything to them. If he has an occupation, he will have a chance to give and take something. My son is so pure that I would like to see him in a pure world. However, such a thing is impossible. I would not like to see my son as a vagabond.

INTERVIEWER: Are there any other things that you would like to add to what you have already said?

MOTHER: Well...Rather than negative things, one dreams of good things. I have been thinking of positive things for eight months. I think of good things that I will do in the future for him. For example, I think of which school to send him, which school is available for me financially. I think of sending him to a private school, I dream of good things. I have not allowed bad thoughts about my child to enter in my mind.

INTERVIEWER: Are there any other things that you would like to say?

MOTHER: No.

APPENDIX 4.2
A SAMPLE INTERVIEW WITH A DE-IDENTIFIED HIGH-EDUCATED MOTHER

INTERVIEWER: In this study, we are investigating mothers' wishes regarding their children's future; what kind of personality characteristics and behaviors they want their children to possess in the future. To understand this, I will first ask you to tell me what you expect for your child in the future, and then to describe children that you know possess at least the beginnings of the characteristics that you wish your child to possess. For each mother, there are some desirable and undesirable qualities that she would and would not like to see in their children. I want you to think of your child now and describe to me the personality characteristics and behaviors that you wish your children to possess in the future.

MOTHER: In the first place, I would like my daughter to be a child at peace with herself. I want her to be self-confident, self-contained, and a self-initiated person, a person who is capable of making her own decisions. In short, I want her to be a self-confident child.

INTERVIEWER: You said "a child at peace with herself". Could you describe a child who is at peace with herself/himself?

MOTHER: I mean...my child is a person who is already at peace with herself. She is now a friendly child; that is, she is a very positive child. For example, she knows her positive sides. Even if she is quite young, she is aware of things going around. That is, if she will be like that in the future, I think she will be a kind of person who knows how to be happy, be a kind of person who is self-confident. She is very happy and takes everything positively. She is quite a sociable person, she communicates quite well with people. She knows how to make people like her. Well, she is a quite friendly child.

INTERVIEWER: Alright; you also said you want your daughter to be a self-confident child. Could you elaborate on this a little bit?

MOTHER: We are already trying to give our child opportunities to learn and to try everything. That is, when she wants to do something, we do not say "No!". We want her to try and understand by herself if what she does is bad or good. That is, we let her try what she wants to do to distinguish the good and the bad. We do not try to protect her from everything. We let her try things, so that she can remember it better. We want her to learn the good and the bad not only from what we tell her about the good and the bad but also through trial and error. For example, instead of saying "It is hot, do not touch it!" I make her approach to the oven so that she can understand it herself, and does not touch it next time. Otherwise, if I say her "No!" she will want to try it in some way. I want her to do things, try things self-confidently and make her decisions in life.

INTERVIEWER: I see. You also said, "I want her to be a self-initiative person". Could you explain it?

MOTHER: Well... how can self-initiation be taught at that stage I do not know; but after I give her necessary training, I want her to distinguish good and bad things and make her own decisions by herself without asking me. That is, I do not want her to come and ask me everything, but to judge what is good and bad, and decide what to do by herself. Mothers provide their children opportunities like piano lessons and the like for example. I want to provide her such opportunities and give the chance to try, but then I want her to do what she wants to do. That is, I want her to tell me "Yes mom! I want to proceed with that". I do not want to compel her for anything; I want her to enjoy what she does. I want her to take the initiative in these matters. I do not want to manage her life.

INTERVIEWER: Do you think of other characteristics that you want your child to possess as an adult?

MOTHER: That I want in the future? I want her to be a mature person of course. In the last resort, nothing in life is in our control and in accord with our expectations. One has to react to everything with maturity. Honestly, I want my child to be logical and not too emotional. How can I teach that? I don't know but ... I do not want my child to be too emotional. She should be able to establish a balance between logic and emotion.

INTERVIEWER: Can you give an example?

MOTHER: ...for example, suppose that one day she wants to go abroad, and since she is my only child, as a mother I do not want her to go. She should not stay here just because her mother wants her to stay. If going abroad seems to her more reasonable to have an education and to live there, if that is what she wants to do, she should do it. She should learn to establish a balance between these things. She should be able to be logical in her relationships with humans and in decisions she makes. Therefore, she should develop skills that will help her to distinguish between what is reasonable and what is not. We should be helpful in such issues of course but I do not want to be obstructive in her life any way. I want my child to be able to make all kinds of decisions and be able to stand for the decisions she makes. I will guide her about the consequences of some decisions and of some actions of course, but I want her to decide what is good and what is bad by herself. I want to give her the necessary support; I want her to know that I am behind her whatever she does. The final decision is hers. She can do whatever she wants... also about choosing an occupation. Well, although I am an ambitious mother, I want her to become whatever she wants. If she wants to be a ballerina, let her be a ballerina. If she is doing what she likes, nothing is a problem for me. I will be in support of her.

INTERVIEWER: I see. Are there any other qualities that you want your child to possess?

MOTHER: I want my child to be analytical.

INTERVIEWER: Analytical? How?

MOTHER: I want her to be talented in mathematics. Of course, nobody has to be interested in mathematics, but I want her to know some basic math. I think that being logical is related to mathematics. I think my child should have some analytical abilities and practical intelligence. She should be able to approach issues both from a practical point of view and from an analytical perspective. That is, I want her to have thinking abilities and do not want her to be a child who memorizes what she learns. For example, in our educational system children learn to memorize things without questioning. That is, a child has a limited world in the end. I want my child to ask questions about what she wants to learn. I want her to be a person who questions things. My husband and I want to be supportive in the development of such a skill, and we want to give support to her in preschool as well as school years. That is, if she wonders about something, she can go and search for it. There is the internet, and today's children are already very talented; for example, our daughter can use a mouse even at that young age. For example, she can do some painting on the computer with the help of her father. I want her to have an interest in searching. I want her to search for whatever she is interested in and to have ability in some basic mathematics.

INTERVIEWER: You mean quantitative ability?

MOTHER: Yes, I mean quantitative ability.

INTERVIEWER: Do you think this ability will help her in areas other than mathematics?

MOTHER: Yes, I think so.

INTERVIEWER: Are there any other positive qualities that you would like to see in your child?

MOTHER: What else? Since she is now quite young I did not think about all these at length. As a result, after I became a mother I learned this: you plan something regarding your child, you say "I will do that", "I will never do this" kind of things... However, your child has her/his own nature, own abilities, and tastes from very early ages on. My daughter has already formed her tastes now. That is, she says what she likes and dislikes. She says "I like this food, but not this one" for example. The personality of the child has already started to form. Therefore, in spite of what I wish, she will be doing whatever she is interested in. My duty in this respect is to help her to be a more a curious person, a person who searches for things. Well...for example, I want her to be interested in classical music. As her parents, we are persons who read a lot. My daughter has her own books and she says "Let me bring my book and read it.". I want her to read and learn through reading. However, her personality will determine this in the future.

INTERVIEWER I see. I want you to think of your child again and tell me the characteristics that you do not want your child to possess in the future. Are there such characteristics or behaviors?

MOTHER: Yes. For example, I do not want her to be an aggressive person. In general, in our society, people communicate with each other by shouting. Even though I am a calm person, I sometimes find myself getting nervous. When I visited foreign countries, like America for example I saw that people do not shout at each other, they do not raise the volume of their voice. I do not want my daughter to be a person who is aggressive. I want her to solve her problems with other people by talking to them in a calm and self-possessed manner. She is too young now, since she is a child... at these ages children can get nervous easily, and express their anger in a higher voice. However, I do not want it to be that way in the future.

INTERVIEWER: What else?

MOTHER: I do not want her to be selfish.

INTERVIEWER: Could you elaborate a little on this?

MOTHER: For example, I try to guide her to share her toys with her playmates. Or, for example, she does not want to share her father with me. Such things can happen I suppose in childhood years. She has to know that we have different places in the eyes of her father. That is, she should not see me as a rival, and therefore she should learn to share. I try to teach her to share, but I do not know to what extent I am successful. I do not want her to be selfish. I do not want her to be aggressive at all. I want her to get along well with everyone. What else? I want her to be a smart and a logical girl. I do not want her to be an ignorant person.

INTERVIEWER: What do you mean by "ignorant person"?

MOTHER: Well... For example, I see many young people around, those high school students for example. It seems to me that their only concern is to adorn themselves. I do not want my child to be like that. Of course, she will adorn herself too; adorning herself is OK, if she is concerned with some cultural and intellectual activities also. I do not want her to be an ignorant girl. I want her to be intellectual.

INTERVIEWER: Are there any other negative characteristics that you would like to add?

MOTHER: What else? I do not want her to lie; never.

INTERVIEWER: Even the so-called "white lies"?

MOTHER: Well, she may tell some little lies, but I would like her to trust me. I would like to give her the feeling that she can trust me, that she needs not to tell lies to me. If she can talk to me about everything, she would not need to tell lies to me. When I was a child, there was an incident that I told a lie to my mother, but my mother realized this and thereafter I never told a lie to her throughout my life. I told everything to her. My mother was very nice, and she listened to me all the time. Since she knew my boyfriend and all my close friends, there was no need for me to tell a lie to her. She also taught me what is good and what is bad. I was knowledgeable about that. I want my daughter to be like that.

INTERVIEWER: Are there any other things that you would like to say?

MOTHER: Well? No.

INTERVIEWER: Alright!

MOTHER: And, I do not want her to smoke cigarettes and drink alcohol.

5

Analyzing the Aspects of International Migration in Turkey by Using 2000 Census Results

Yadigar Coşkun – A. Sinan Türkyilmaz

INTRODUCTION

Migration is as old as human history. Humans have been migrating since prehistoric times. Either as an individual, as a family or as a group; a multitude of people have migrated or are going to migrate from one place to another with different purposes and reasons. It is estimated that the number of international migrants is 185 million; that is, some three percent of the world's population (McKinley, 2004). Most of the world's developed countries have become diverse, multiethnic societies, and those that have not reached this state are moving in that direction (Massey et. al., 1993).

The extent of the emigration and the socio-economic and demographic characteristics of the migrants are very important and have direct influence on social and economic characteristics of both the country of origin and the country for destination. A full understanding of contemporary migratory mechanisms will not be achieved by depending on the tools of one discipline alone or by focusing on a single level of analysis.

Migration is more complex and multifaceted than any other demographic event. With the decline in fertility and mortality in many parts of the world, migration has taken on an increased significance, becoming an important component of population dynamics in many countries (Waki, 2004). As migration is seen as an important factor in the international economy, the studies on international migration have increased, especially in the last decade of the 20th century. Studying international migration seems to be a crucial issue for both the country of origin and the country of destination.

Turkey is one of the countries in the world with the greatest interest in international migration because of its geography, history and policy orientation. Throughout history, Anatolia and Thrace had become the homelands of different tribes, states and empires. In addition, because of their strategic locations, many migrants have preferred and still prefer these lands either to migrate within or to use as a transit region in their migration route.

Although the type of emigration changed after 80's and 90's, Turkey has been an important country of emigration; especially at the second half of the twentieth century. İçduygu (2005) mentions five main current types of emigration of Turkish citizens in the 2000's: family-related migration, asylum-seeking, irregular (undocumented or clandestine), labour emigration and international professional migration.

Under the heading of "family-related migration," long and short term family visits, family reunification, and marriage related migration are included. The international migration history of Turkey in the second half of the twentieth century reached its peak in the late 60's and 70's with labor migration mainly to Western European countries. Relying on the contracts between Turkey and European countries under German rule, hundreds of thousands of Turkish citizens migrated to Europe. Even after the oil crisis in the 70's, this type of migration first slowed and then finished totally. However, as a result of the network between relatives and friends in the homeland and the communities in the countries of destination, migration flows continued in terms of family-related migration, especially in Western countries.

Although the overall pace of migration has declined over the years, the proportion of marriage migration and family re-unification migration has become the main form of emigration.

At the end of the twentieth century, especially after the military intervention in 1980, thousands of asylum seekers migrated to western European countries from Turkey for political reasons. Especially in the 1990's, thousands of people, particularly from the east and southeast regions of Turkey, applied for asylum in various European countries because of the conflict between the armed forces and separatist rebels.

In addition, Turkey is one of the famous "highways" as a transit country for asylum-seekers to Europe, directly and indirectly (İçduygu, 2004; Mannaert, 2003). Turkey's strategic location, between East, West, South, and North, made Turkey an important transit country in terms of illegal migration and asylum-seekers. Data from the United Nations High Commissioner for Refugees (UNHCR) shows that the annual number of asylum-seekers from Turkey to industrialized countries was almost 26,600 in 1994. Although the number of asylum seekers fluctuated between 1994 and 2003, it did not fall under 20,000. The latest figures show that number of asylum applicants fell to 24,876 in 2003. In 2000, on the other hand, the number of applications was about 30,000 (UNHCR, 2006).

Undocumented, irregular migration includes: illegal entries, overstayers, and rejected asylum seekers. İçduygu and Ünalan (2002) in their study indicate that nearly one quarter of migrants stated that they either have tried to enter a country without the required papers, or attempted to overstay their visa or permit (İçduygu and Ünalan, 2002).

As mentioned above, Turkish labour migration gained speed in the 60's and 70's with contracted labor migration to western European countries, especially to Germany. In addition, after the 80's, temporary

labor migration to Arab countries gained importance. Family unification and temporary labor migration still continues to western
European countries but the direction of the latter changed to Eastern
European and Central Asian countries (İçduygu and Sirkeci, 1998;
recent statistics of Turkish Employment Office (TEO) in 2000).

Another type of migration, "brain migration", has also gained
speed recently. University graduates and highly qualified professionals
are migrating to European countries and the United States of America.

As can be clearly understood from above, Turkey has been one of
the main routes and sources of international migration. The information
about the number of transit migrants and/or the emigrants of Turkey
gain importance for both Turkey and other countries that are in the
migration process. The number of the migrants is very crucial for countries, not only for economic and security reasons, but also for the direct
or indirect effects on social and demographic situations. The relations
within the countries will be effected from the migration relations
between themselves. Any huge migration flow will affect both countries
economically, socially and politically. Every country aims to know the
number of emigrants and immigrants that pass through their borders.

Although the number of international migrants all over the
world has nearly reached 190 million, there is no clear definition of an
international migrant. In general there are five concepts which are
used to collect data and evaluate it: citizenship, residence, duration of
staying, purpose of staying, and place of birth (İçduygu and Toktaş,
2005). These concepts help the governors and social scientists to make
operational definitions. Every study on international migration should
be evaluated within these limitations.

This study aims to provide a picture on the international migration trends by using the 2000 census results. The question "How
many members of this household who are not in the house now are in
a) the country? or b) abroad?" is going to be the starting point of the
study. Emigration rates will be estimated for provinces and regional
divisions depending on the results of this question. The terms

"migrant" and "emigration" are directly related to the answer of this question. Any member of a household in Turkey who is abroad at the time of the census is considered an "emigrant", and the household who has such a member is considered an "emigrant household". These definitions do not include the duration or the purpose of the person abroad, but the results of this question will give us the geographic distribution of the international migrants for Turkey. Methodological discussions will be done in the methodology chapter of this study.

LITERATURE REVIEW AND POSSIBLE DATA SOURCES ON INTERNATIONAL MIGRATION

The literature on Turkish emigration is directly affected by different migration types and the period the migration occurred. At different periods, different migration topics are handled by the social scientists and researchers. The studies on international migration from and to Turkey are using various data sources. Like in many countries, there is little reliable data on migration in Turkey and that which does exist is far from providing a complete picture. Different institutions and organizations in Turkey and abroad collect different data that can be considered as emigration data. As mentioned above, the definition of international migration is very debatable and every attempt to understand the whole picture of international migration will help all social scientists and policy makers. Before the literature review, the current potential data sources will be discussed to understand the weak and strong aspects of the studies on international migration.

Data Sources on International Migration Data in Turkey[1]

There is no institution or organization that collects international migration data information. However, some organizations (State Statistics Organization, Ministry of Labor and Social Security, and

---

1   We would like to acknowledge to Neriman Can for her valuable efforts on the data sources for Turkey.

Ministry of the Interior) collect data that can be identified as international migration data for their own duties and purposes. The sources that can be used to supply the demand for international migration data directly and indirectly are: censuses, border statistics, administrative registers and sources, foreign country registers (for the citizens living abroad), and surveys.

Censuses: The censuses cover the information on both the natives and the foreigners at the time of census. A de facto type of census has been applied in Turkey. With the censuses, information on the birth place, nationality, and permanent residence is collected. At the time of the survey 5 years ago, the person who mentioned that he/she was abroad 5 years ago was accepted as an immigrant. As the information is taken directly from the person himself/herself, and only the persons residing in the country are counted, no direct information on the emigrants is taken.

In addition, permanent residence information can also be used for international migration data, by which the Turkish citizen who mentions his/her permanent residence as being abroad can be identified as an emigrant. Moreover, as mentioned above, census data contains information that can be used as an indirect source for international migration, and the information of the household members that are mentioned as being abroad at the time of census can be used as a secondary type of data for identifying the emigrants.

Border statistics: The General Directorate of Security for the Ministry of the Interior, has the current data for each border gate. Every person entering or going out from the border is registered in the system; therefore, each passenger's passport information is collected in detail. Indeed, 60 out of 103 border gates have computerized registration systems that are directly connected to the main system in the capital city, Ankara. The others record the information by hand and send it to the centre monthly.

Administrative Records: Administrative records on International migration can be considered in the following sub-groups:

Residence permissions: General Directorate of Security collects the information related with residence permissions. This can be considered as stock data for immigration. Residence permissions data are collected with the Certificate of Foreigner Residence. The applications done in each province are first evaluated in each province's directorate of security, then the ones accepted are sent to the centre and the final decision is made at the centre. Each household fills out one form for the application.

Work permissions: According to Law 5683, each foreigner who wants to work in Turkey has to obtain a residence permit within a month of arriving in Turkey and before starting work. In addition, the employer has to inform the security officers if he employs a foreigner within 15 days. Until 2003, the General Directorate of Security was the responsible unit for collecting the information; however, starting with Law 4817 (which passed September 6, 2003), the Ministry of Labor and Social Security is mentioned as the responsible organization.

Asylum seeker and refugee records: The General Directorate of Security and the UN Refugee Agency (UNHCR) keeps records of asylum seekers and refugees. The asylum seekers from countries other than Europe are forbidden to settle in Turkey. They are only able to apply to a third country from Turkey. Each asylum seeker has to fill a form that can be either from the UNHCR offices or from the province or sub-province Directorate of Security offices. The information, independent from the source where the form is filled, is sent to the General Directorate of Security and kept in computers.

Citizenship Information: The Ministry of the Interior, General Directorate of Population and Citizenship Affairs is the responsible unit that evaluates applications for citizenship. They keep all the forms (either acquiring or surrendering Turkish Citizenship) filled in Province Directorates of Population and Citizenship at the centre.

Visa Registers: The Ministry of Foreign Affairs keeps visa applications. These records carry potential immigration flow information. Visa applications to Turkey are done in Turkish Embassies or

Consulates. Each year they send the information about the visa applications to the Ministry of Foreign Affairs. Although the visa applications can be evaluated as a potential source of immigration, because they are not kept in computers, they can not be used. Moreover, for the citizens of some countries no visa is required as they can get their visa permission at the border gate. For these cases the information seems to be unclear about the visa applicants.

Migrant Information: Since 1934, the General Directorate of Village Services is the responsible unit for migrants. Coordination of the whole migration process is done with this directorate. Two types of migrants are defined in the Directorate: migrants coming through The Settlement Law, and free settling migrants. The three big migrant flows that came with different migration laws after 1934 are the Ahiska Turks, Afghans, and Bulgarian Turks. The laws for these groups are published for each migration flow separately and annulled after the migration flow ends.

Being a free migrant is a categorization that applies to only those coming from Turkic Republic Countries, like Azerbaijan, Turkmenistan and so-on. The application is done by a reference from a Turkish citizen living in Turkey in the name of the persons from the Turkic Republics. They apply to the Province Directorate of Village Services and the form goes to Province Directorate of Security. After investigating of the potential migrant, if there is no problem, all the documents are sent to General Directorate of Village Services. In coordination with the General Directorate of Security, Ministry of Foreign Affairs and Ministry of Interior, two forms are filled out by the migrant: the Emigrant Paper and (if the Turkish Citizenship application is done and accepted) the Form of Passing to the Family Ledger and Citizenship. These two forms are filled and recorded in the Province Directorate of Village Services.

Registers of the other countries: The Turkish citizens living abroad are used as an information source for emigration potential. In Turkey, the Ministry of Labor and Social Security keeps the numeric information of Turkish citizens living abroad. Of the 14 main immigration countries where Turkish citizens are living, the units related to the ministry records are kept. No matter if they have a job in these countries or not, each Turkish citizen is recorded. Each year the Ministry sends an "Annual Activity Report Form" to these attachés and Consulates and gets only the information they need in the report format about the Turkish citizens living abroad. Attachés and Consulates fill in the report with the records in the attachés' statistics offices of the countries they settled in, including local or regional media sources.

Surveys: TURKSTAT conducts a "Foreign Visitors Questionnaire" in terms of Tourism Statistics. Four times a year, the information of visitors to Turkey is collected from the commonly used border gates. The visitors are selected in a purposive sample. The results are published annually.

Hacettepe University Institute of Population Studies (HUIPS) conducted the Turkish International Migration Survey (TIMS) collaboration with Netherlands Interdisciplinary Demographic Institute (NIDI) in 1996 in twenty eight selected districts in eight provinces of Turkey. The survey was designed to provide information on the causes, mechanisms, dynamics, and consequences of migration flows from Turkey, with a retrospective time perspective set at ten years (1986-1996) (EUROSTAT, 2000). Survey results gave valuable information with respect to the characteristics of emigrants' in Turkey.

HUIPS conducts the Turkey Demographic and Health Surveys (TDHS) over a five year period. The latest TDHS was carried out in 2003 and included a special module in the household questionnaire named "Migration and Mobility," which can be helpful in providing valuable information on Turkish migration. For every member of the household, a question is asked regarding place of residence five years ago. The final report of the survey was published in 2004, and the data was made available for scientists outside the institute as of October 2006.

All these sources can be used to give direct or indirect estimations for the number of Turkish emigrants. However, they can not give the actual number of international migrants of Turkey. Although any attempt at estimating the number of emigrants will be imprecise the information gathered will nonetheless be valuable for this field of study where there is currently little information available. The potential data sources are commonly used by social scientists in their studies when referencing their limitations.

Studies on International Migration in Turkey
There are many studies on the direction and type of migration to and from Turkey. Former studies on international migration were focused on labor migration, as well as the economic, social and psychological effects on the migrants (Abadan, 1964; Tuna and Ekin, 1966; Gökdere, 1978; Gitmez, 1979, Tunalı, 1988). When the type of emigration started to change, the content and focus of the studies on emigration also changed.

The studies after the 1990's are mainly about the size and changing characteristics of the Turkish migrants in European countries (Martin, 1991; Çiçekli, 1998; Şen and Koray, 1993), problems in Turkey in relation to international migration, like transit migration and asylum seeking (Kirişci, 2003, 2004; Erder, 2004; Timur, 2004, Peker, 2004; İçduygu, 2000, Mannaert, 2003), and Turkey and European Union relations on the topic of migration (Erzan et. al. 2004; İçduygu, 2004; Toksöz, 2004). Recent studies commonly discuss the changing role of Turkey in the international migration agenda: from a sending country, to both receiving and transit country. However, with the lack of reliable information on the number of migrants these studies are considered limited.

The numbers of Turkish migrants in statistics are nothing more than a combination of the numbers from different sources. In Turkey, the number of international migrants is compiled mainly from the statistics collected by the Ministry of Labor and Social Security and from other official sources. On the other hand, in the countries of destination, the numbers are only about the Turkish migrants' legal status. However, as mentioned above these attempts are limited.

The State Institute of Statistics (SIS) of Turkey (with the Turkey Statistics law accepted in November 2005, the State Institute of Statistics is to be named as Turkey Statistical Institute-TURKSTAT[2]) is the responsible institution to conduct the censuses. The first census in the Turkish Republic was done in 1927, and after the second census in 1935, the SIS has held a census every five years. After 1990, SIS planned to make censuses in years ending with "0". The last two censuses were made in 1990 and 2000. Beginning with the 1975 census, SIS asked for the members of the households in Turkey who are not in Turkey at the time of Census. Although the numbers in 1975 and 1980 censuses are published only at the country level, since 1985 it has also published province totals (SIS, 1982, 1984, 1989, 1993). However, the 2000 census report does not include information about the individuals abroad or the households which have at least one member abroad at the time of census.

The only study published using this question from census was prepared by Ünalan and Türkyılmaz (2003). They presented their study at the Third Conference on Turkish Demography in 1997. In this study, they evaluated the results of the 1990 census and estimated emigration rates for Turkey in 14 regions and provinces. The emigration rates for the year 1990 given in this study are compared with the estimated rates of the 2000 census, to note the changes in the ten year period.

RESEARCH DESIGN

Hypothesis / Research Question
In Turkey, the aspects of international migration that attract attention of social scientists and policy makers have always been one of the issues marked by heavy debate. It is commonly accepted that the inter-

---

2   We would like to acknowledge TURKSTAT for their support in supplying the data of the study.

national migration statistics are conditioned by the scarcity and poor quality of the data. In Turkey, it is almost impossible to specify who emigrated, how and to which country. There is no trustworthy information on the chronology or route of migration flows into and out of Turkey (İçduygu, 2005).

The actual number of Turkish migrants living outside of Turkey is not known. There have been many studies on international migrational behavior of Turkish citizens, especially to Western European Countries. However, most of the studies on international migration are not based on census or demographic survey results, but on local or small scale studies usually carried out by academics or researchers. The studies conducted by national and international organizations are merely the gathering of information from different sources to give numerical estimates. These attempts do more than completing just a part of the whole picture.

The Ministry of Labor and Social Security is one of the major sources for estimations. Although it is estimated that around 3.6 million Turkish citizens (3.2 million in European Countries) are living abroad (Kirisçi, 2003), it is also known that illegal/undocumented migration will probably add to this number.

In this study, the 2000 census results are going to be discussed in terms of whether the information in the census can be used to estimate recent emigration trends in Turkey under certain limitations stemming from the nature of data sets.

Methodology

The definition of migrant/migration has always been debatable. The changing structure in migration led scientists to add different characteristics to the definition. The universal definition of migration includes special needs and approaches from special research topics. In many different statistics systems, international migrants are taken into consideration as directly related to the international laws and regulations that the Turkish government has accepted. Because of this, no universal definition of migration will be accepted and applied by going over the local laws. As migration is a multi-dimensional issue, limited definitions do not supply the demands of the researchers in different fields (İçduygu and Toktaş, 2005).

Even in countries which have a well-designed and well-working vital registration system, information on migration is more problematic then the information on births, deaths, or marriages; the system cannot give valid numbers of emigrants and immigrants. Turkey, like many other developing countries, has problems in vital registration systems. The availability and the question of if the system is up-to-date has always been suspicious for many social scientists studying migration. The whole registration system has many weaknesses and impeding points in itself. It is nearly impossible to get a total picture of international migration from the registration system. Therefore, the reported official numbers of international migrants are mostly legal workers and/or family reunification to other countries.

However, besides legal migration, the illegal migration of Turkish citizens is also important and the scope of this problem is still not clearly known. Local studies are not covering all of the country on international migration and can not answer the need for information countrywide. In addition to censuses, surveys giving estimations for Turkey on various demographic issues do not ask information about international migration because of the simple cost and benefit dilemma.

This study is aimed to estimate the aspects of international migration trends for Turkey; 2000 in total and the differences between the defined "classic" five regions and 14 sub-regions used in TDHS's and all three NUTS (The Nomenclature of Units for Territorial Statistics) levels. Studying the migration rates for the country as a whole and for different regional levels of definition make comparisons and conclusion more meaningful. Provinces are the most detailed levels in this study. The definitions and the backgrounds of regions used in this study are explained below.

The five regions, West, South, Central, North, and East, are the conventional five geographic regions. For the 1993 and 1998 TDHS, a 14 sub-region definition was used as a stratification criterion. The criteria for subdividing the five major regions into sub-regions were the infant mortality rates of each province, estimated from the 1990 Population Census using indirect techniques. Using the infant mortality estimates as well as geographic proximity, the provinces in each region were grouped into 14 sub-regions at the time of the 1993 TDHS. The sub-regional division developed during the 1993 TDHS was used in the 1998 survey (Türkyılmaz and Aliaga, 1999).

In addition, a new system of regional breakdown was adopted in late 2002. In accordance with the accession process of Turkey to the European Union, the State Planning Office and the State Institute of Statistics constructed three levels of NUTS regions, which have since become official (Law No. 2002/4720). "NUTS" stands for "The Nomenclature of Units for Territorial Statistics". NUTS is a statistical region classification that is used by member countries of European Union (EU). The 81 provinces were designated as the NUTS 3 level; these were further aggregated into 26 regions to form the NUTS-2 regions. The NUTS-1 regions were formed by aggregating NUTS-2 regions into 12 regions (Türkyılmaz, Hancıoğlu and Koç, 2004). The NUTS-1 levels were considered and used for the 2003 TDHS.

The definition of international migration in this study is limited to the answers given to the question: "How many members of this household who are not in the house now are in the: a) country? b) abroad?" The members mentioned as abroad at the time of census are considered as international migrants/emigrants. This definition does not contain the Turkish citizens who emigrated as a family/household (so that none of the household members were left in Turkey to answer this question); or the persons who are not mentioned as being abroad by any household head. Additionally, this migrant definition includes the members who are abroad temporarily for any reason: tourism, work, or other temporary reasons. Although the data has limitations in terms of the definition of international migration, the results should be important in identifying the regional and province based differences in terms of emigration. The information collected by this question does not contain the name of the country of destination. Without undervaluing the limitations of the data mentioned above, with this study international migration rates are estimated for the whole of Turkey, five regions and NUTS levels.

As mentioned above, censuses are one of the potential data sources for international migration. In addition to the evaluation of the answers to these questions, the question on the place of residence five years prior to the census will provide valuable insight for further research into other aspects of internal and international migration. The immigrant profile for Turkey will be evaluated with the results of this question. It seems that censuses can be accepted as one of the important data sources and with small modifications to the questions, which will improve both the quality and the content of the questions. Censuses can be easily used for giving estimations for international migration.

RESULTS

As mentioned above, the statistics of the Ministry of Labor and Social Security bring out important information about the Turkish migrants in other countries. According to the 2000-2001 statistics, there are 3.6 million Turkish citizens living abroad. Of these, 3.1 million are living in Western European Countries. Furthermore, as gathered from the labor statistics of the countries of destination, around 1.2 million of these are working in the countries where they have migrated. Around 1.0 million of Turkish citizens abroad are working in Western European countries (Ministry of Labor and Social Security, 2002). On the other hand, according to the 2000 census results, Turkey's population was 68,808,976. The household heads mentioned that 640,458 household members were out of the country at the day of census (9.4‰ of all the population). The detailed information from the district level is presented in Appendix 1. As compared to the former censuses with comparable data, the figure in 1975 was at 15.2%, in 1980 at 16.1‰, in 1985 at 13.9‰, and in 1990 at 11.1‰. The emigration rates seem to be decreasing, although in a ten year period, 13,425 more individuals are mentioned as migrants. The overall population growth rate is more than the growth rate of the migrant population. In other words, the proportion of emigrants has decreased in the last two decades. **Figure 5.1** shows the trend of the emigration rates estimated from census results.

FIGURE 5.1
Emigration Rates (‰) by Censuses

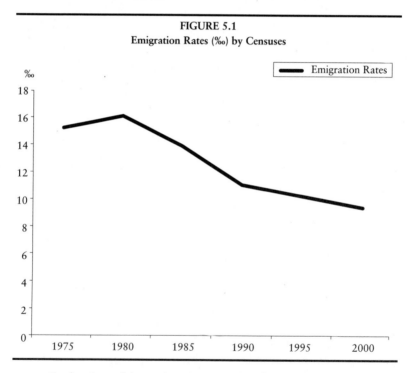

Evaluation of the emigration rates are from 2000 census will be presented both on individual level and on the household level.

Migration Rates on Individual Levels
In this study, emigration rates for NUTS-3 Level (81 provinces) for urban, rural, and total population are estimated and the results are shown in Appendix 2A. Moreover, province emigration rates are shown at Appendix 6, Map 1-3. It is clearly seen that none of the provinces from the western part of the country have high emigration rates.

For total emigration rates, three of the seven provinces that have high emigration rates are neighboring provinces from the eastern part of the country: Tunceli, Elazığ and Bingöl. Two of the seven are from central Anatolia and they are also neighboring provinces: Aksaray and Nevşehir. The other two provinces are Zonguldak in north Anatolia and Hatay in the South. On the other hand, **Table 5.1** indicates the emigration rates according to five regions (the provinces at the five region division are presented in Appendix 3) and type of residence. The highest emigration rates are in the northern region, both in urban and rural areas of the country.

In contrast, the lowest rates are in the eastern urban areas and the western rural areas. In the South, Central and North regions, the emigration rates are more than 10‰, whereas in the West and East it is below 9‰. In addition, **Table 5.1** indicates that except for the Western region, in all other regions, the rural emigration rate is high-

TABLE 5.1
Emigration Rates (‰) by Region and Place of Residence
(2000 Census Results, Turkey)

Region	Urban	Rural	Total
West	8.9	7.1	8.4
South	10.0	13.1	11.2
Central	10.0	12.3	10.9
North	10.2	13.5	12.0
East	6.4	8.0	7.1
Turkey	9.0	10.3	9.4

er than the urban rates. Although the rates are higher in rural areas of the regions, the West is seen as the only exception in which the emigration rate is higher in urban.

Migration rates are given in **Table 5.2** and Appendix 6 Map 4-6 according to 14 regions (14 region provinces are presented in Appendix 4 with place of residence. Fourteen region divisions are commonly used in the Turkish Demographic and Health Survey (TDHS) to give more detailed demographic estimates. The main criterion for dividing the country into 14 regions is geographic proximity and infant mortality estimates (Türkyılmaz and Aliaga, 1999). It is shown that the highest rates are seen in the "East 14" region for both Urban and Rural areas. Especially in the rural areas of "East 14", the emigration rate is nearly 25‰. On the other hand, the lowest rates are seen in "East 11". Both in rural and urban areas, the rates are below 4‰. There are 11.2‰ and 19.7‰ differences between "East 14" and "East 11" regions.

TABLE 5.2
Emigration Rates (‰) by 14 Regions and Place of Residence
(2000 Census Results, Turkey)

Region	Urban	Rural	Total
West 1	9.7	6.7	9.3
West 2	8.3	7.8	8.2
West 3	7.7	7.2	7.5
South 4	7.7	5.7	6.7
South 5	10.3	12.8	11.1
Central 6	9.7	10.2	10.0
Central 7	9.1	11.2	10.0
Central 8	10.3	13.2	11.2
North 9	11.2	12.5	11.9
North 10	9.3	14.4	12.1
East 11	3.9	3.5	3.7
East 12	6.5	8.1	7.4
East 13	7.1	13.5	10.0
East 14	15.1	23.2	19.0
Turkey	9.0	10.3	9.4

NUTS levels, as mentioned above, were constructed by State Planning Organization and State Institute of Statistics as part of efforts for statistical adaptations for the European Union. NUTS-3 Level classifies all provinces as 81 regions. NUTS-1 level has 12 region divisions and NUTS-2 has 26 region divisions. The provinces in NUTS-1 and NUTS-2 levels are mentioned in Appendix 5. **Table 5.3** and Appendix 6 Map 7-9 indicates the emigration rates for NUTS-1 level and place of residence.

The highest emigration rate in urban areas is seen in central Anatolia with 16‰. On the other hand, the highest emigration rate in rural areas is in northeast Anatolia with 19‰. In total, the highest rate is estimated to be in central Anatolia. However, the lowest rates are seen in southeast Anatolia in urban and rural areas (6‰ and 7‰ respectively). The overall picture indicates that 6 regions are over the national level: Istanbul, West Anatolia, the Mediterranean, Central Anatolia, West Black Sea, and East Black Sea; whereas, the other six regions are below the national average.

TABLE 5.3

Emigration Rates (‰) by NUTS-1 Level and Type of Place of Residence
(2000 Census Results, Turkey)

Region	Urban	Rural	Total
1) Istanbul	9,9	7,1	9,6
2) West Marmara	7,2	6,7	7,0
3) Aegean	8,2	8,5	8,3
4) East Marmara	8,4	8,3	8,4
5) West Anatolia	8,9	9,4	9,0
6) Mediterranean	10,0	13,1	11,2
7) Central Anatolia	13,9	18,5	16,0
8) West Black Sea	8,5	11,1	9,9
9) East Black Sea	10,9	12,6	11,9
10) Northeast Anatolia	5,9	8,1	7,1
11) Central East Anatolia	8,0	10,0	9,0
12) Southeast Anatolia	5,8	6,5	6,1
Turkey	9,0	10,3	9,4

NUTS-2 Level gives more detailed results about the distribution of the emigrant population. **Table 5.4** and Appendix 6 – Map10-12 shows the emigration rates according to the NUTS-2 level. The highest emigration rates in urban and rural areas are seen in NUTS-2 – 13 (15.1 ‰ and 25.1‰ respectively). The second highest rate in urban areas is seen in NUTS-2 – 14 with 15.1‰. Although the emigration

TABLE 5.4

Emigration Rates (‰) by NUTS-2 Level and Type of Place of Residence
(2000 Census Results, Turkey)

Region	Urban	Rural	Total
NUTS 2 – 1	9.9	7.1	9.6
NUTS 2 – 2	7.1	5.6	6.5
NUTS 2 – 3	7.2	7.4	7.3
NUTS 2 – 4	8.1	5.4	7.6
NUTS 2 – 5	8.2	9.3	8.8
NUTS 2 – 6	8.4	9.2	8.8
NUTS 2 – 7	7.7	4.9	7.1
NUTS 2 – 8	9.4	10.4	9.9
NUTS 2 – 9	8.6	7.6	8.5
NUTS 2 – 10	9.7	10.1	9.9
NUTS 2 – 11	7.8	5.9	7.0
NUTS 2 – 12	8.0	4.9	7.0
NUTS 2 – 13	15.2	25.1	20.0
NUTS 2 – 14	15.1	17.5	16.3
NUTS 2 – 15	13.1	19.3	15.8
NUTS 2 – 16	9.2	21.5	16.4
NUTS 2 – 17	5.8	7.5	6.8
NUTS 2 – 18	9.0	8.1	8.5
NUTS 2 – 19	10.9	12.6	11.9
NUTS 2 – 20	5.2	10.6	7.8
NUTS 2 – 21	6.9	5.9	6.3
NUTS 2 – 22	12.8	18.6	15.3
NUTS 2 – 23	2.7	3.5	3.1
NUTS 2 – 24	8.8	8.8	8.8
NUTS 2 – 25	3.3	5.5	4.3
NUTS 2 – 26	5.7	6.2	5.9
Turkey	9.0	10.3	9.4

rate in NUTS 2 – 16 is below 10‰ in urban areas, the rate is the second highest in rural areas with 21.5‰. On the other hand, the lowest rates are seen in NUTS-2 – 23 and NUTS 2 – 25, which are in total below 5‰.

Table 5.5 indicates the ten provinces with the highest emigration rates at the time of the 2000 census. The highest rate is seen in Tunceli with nearly 40‰ in province totals, which is followed by Aksaray and Hatay (30.9‰ and 26.3‰, respectively). These three provinces share the first three ranks in the urban and rural division. In the rural areas of Tunceli, the emigration rate reaches 46.5‰, which is the highest rate of all the country.

When the results are compared with the 1990 census results, it is seen that Tunceli and Aksaray again have the highest rates in total. However, Hatay was not among the highest emigration rated provinces listed in the 1990 census results in total and rural areas, and only ranked sixth in urban areas (Ünalan and Türkyılmaz, 2003).

Moreover, 14 different provinces found places on the list. Twelve of these are from the Eastern and Central regions (6 from each), 1 from Northern and 1 from Southern regions. It is noticeable that there is no province from the Western region in the first ten.

TABLE 5.5
10 Provinces Having Highest Emigration Rates (‰)
(2000 Census Results, Turkey)

Rank	Urban		Rural		Total	
1)	Aksaray	32.9	Tunceli	46.5	Tunceli	39.5
2)	Tunceli	31.9	Hatay	29.2	Aksaray	30.9
3)	Hatay	22.9	Aksaray	28.9	Hatay	26.3
4)	Iğdır	19.3	Elazığ	28.7	Elazığ	21.9
5)	Kırşehir	19.1	Nevşehir	26.6	Nevşehir	21.0
6)	Elazığ	17.8	K. Maraş	26.3	Zonguldak	20.3
7)	Bingöl	17.4	Zonguldak	25.3	Bingöl	19.7
8)	Uşak	17.0	Bingöl	21.6	Yozgat	19.3
9)	Yozgat	16.9	Yozgat	21.3	Kırşehir	19.2
10)	Bayburt	14.4	Kayseri	20.9	K. Maraş	18.6

The provinces having the lowest emigration rates are shown in **Table 5.6**. The first four ranks are shared by the East and Southeast region provinces. The exceptions are Karabük, Bilecik, Kırıkkale, Osmaniye and Manisa. Although there are nine different provinces from the Eastern region are seen in the table, only five provinces from other regions of the country found a place in the ranking. The lowest rates are estimated in Bitlis (Urban 1.1‰, Rural 0.7‰, Total 0.9‰) Van (Urban 2.2‰, Rural 1.4‰, Total 1.8‰) and Siirt (Urban 2.3‰, Rural 1.5‰, Total 1.9‰).

TABLE 5.6
10 Provinces Having Lowest Emigration Rates (‰) (2000 Census Results, Turkey)

Rank	Urban		Rural		Total	
1)	Bitlis	1.1	Bitlis	0.7	Bitlis	0.9
2)	Van	2.2	Siirt	1.4	Van	1.8
3)	Siirt	2.3	Van	1.5	Siirt	1.9
4)	Hakkari	2.4	Hakkari	1.9	Hakkari	2.2
5)	Şanlıurfa	3.3	Manisa	2.7	Diyarbakır	3.1
6)	Diyarbakır	3.4	Diyarbakır	2.7	Batman	3.6
7)	Batman	3.6	Kırıkkale	2.9	Karabük	3.6
8)	Erzurum	3.7	Osmaniye	3.2	Bilecik	3.7
9)	Bilecik	3.8	Kilis	3.2	Kilis	3.7
10)	Karabük	3.8	Karabük	3.3	Manisa	3.9

Migration Rates on Household Level
In addition to the results at an individual level, the study of emigration rates on household level are estimated for NUTS-3 level (Appendix 2B and Appendix 6 – Map 13-15). Similar to the results on an individual level, the highest emigration rates are seen in the same neighboring provinces. If any members of the household are out of Turkey, this household is mentioned as a migrant household. **Table 5.7** indicates the household emigration rates according to five regions and place of residence.

The highest household emigration rates are in the Southern

TABLE 5.7
Household Emigration Rates (‰) by Region and Place of Residence
(2000 Census Results, Turkey)

Region	Urban	Rural	Total
West	23.0	16.1	21.4
South	29.0	38.0	32.4
Central	24.7	30.2	26.5
North	24.2	30.2	27.1
East	23.6	31.7	26.7
Turkey	24.3	27.1	25.2

region (32.4‰), whereas the lowest emigration rates are in the Western region (21.4‰). As expected, it is clearly seen that when making an estimation on household emigration levels, the rates are higher than the rates made on the individual level. Excluding the Southern region, for all other four regions, the household emigration rates are above 20‰.

In addition, like the individual emigration rates, **Table 5.7** indicates that except for the Western region, in all other four regions, the rural household emigration rate is higher than the urban rates. Although the rates are higher in rural areas of the regions, the West is seen as the only exception in which the emigration rate is higher in terms of urban migration.

Household emigration rates are given in **Table 5.8** and Appendix 6 Map 16-18 according to the 14 regions and the type of residence. Like in individual rates, it is shown that the highest rates are seen in East 14 region for both urban and rural areas (43.5‰ and 66.7‰ respectively). Especially in the rural areas of the East 14, the household emigration rate is more than two times that of the country's average. In contrast, the lowest rates are seen in South 4 and East 11. There are 37.7‰ differences between the highest and lowest rates in total.

Table 5.9 and Appendix 6 – Map 19-21 indicate the household emigration rates for NUTS-1 level and places of residence. Like indi-

TABLE 5.8
Household Emigration Rates (‰) by 14 Regions and Place of Residence
(2000 Census Results, Turkey)

Region	Urban	Rural	Total
West 1	25.9	17.5	24.9
West 2	20.8	17.0	19.5
West 3	18.9	15.2	17.7
South 4	18.4	13.1	16.0
South 5	32.8	45.7	36.8
Central 6	25.5	29.6	27.4
Central 7	19.0	22.3	20.3
Central 8	25.8	32.3	27.5
North 9	28.1	30.8	29.4
North 10	20.9	29.0	24.8
East 11	17.7	16.3	17.2
East 12	22.7	32.2	27.4
East 13	21.8	41.0	29.7
East 14	43.5	66.7	53.7
Turkey	24.3	27.1	25.2

TABLE 5.9
Household Emigration Rates (‰) by NUTS-1 Level and Place of Residence
(2000 Census Results, Turkey)

Region	Urban	Rural	Total
Istanbul	26.6	20.3	26.1
West Marmara	16.9	13.0	15.2
Aegean	19.3	17.2	18.6
Eeast Marmara	21.2	19.3	20.6
West Anatolia	23.5	24.1	23.6
Mediterranean	29.0	38.0	32.4
Central Anatolia	34.1	48.1	39.7
West Black Sea	20.8	25.1	22.8
East Black Sea	27.7	31.4	29.6
Northeast Anatolia	18.3	27.9	23.0
Central East Anatolia	28.3	39.4	32.9
Southeast Anatolia	22.9	28.4	24.7
Turkey	24.3	27.1	25.2

vidual results, the highest household emigration rate in urban areas is seen in Central Anatolia (34.1‰ in urban, 48.1‰ in rural and 39.7‰ in total). In contrast, the lowest rates are seen in west Marmara. The overall picture indicates that only five regions are over the national level (Istanbul, the Mediterranean, central Anatolia, the east Black Sea and central east Anatolia); whereas seven of the regions are below the country average.

As mentioned above, NUTS-2 Level gives more detailed results about the distribution of the migrant households. **Table 5.10** and Appendix 6 – Map 22-24 shows the household emigration rates according to the NUTS-2 level. Similar to the individual emigration rates, the highest household emigration rates in urban and rural areas are seen in NUTS 2 – 13 (46.7‰ and 82.2‰ respectively). Second highest rate is seen in NUTS 2 – 22 with 46.8‰ which is 15.8‰ lower than NUTS 2 – 13. On the other hand, the lowest rates are seen in NUTS 2 – 23 and NUTS 2 – 03 which are in total below 15‰.

Table 5.11 indicates the ten provinces having the highest household emigration rates at the time of 2000 census. The highest rate is seen in Tunceli in total and rural areas (95.4‰ and 118.7‰ in that order). On the other hand, Aksaray has the highest household emigration rates for urban rates in province totals, which is followed by Hatay (30.9‰ and 26.3‰ respectively). These three provinces share the first three ranks in urban and rural division. In the rural areas of Tunceli, the household emigration rate reaches 118.7‰, which is the highest rate of all the country. In rural areas of Tunceli and Hatay, more than one of each ten households had at least one of their members outside Turkey on the day the census was taken.

The provinces having the lowest emigration rates are shown in **Table 5.12**. The first rank is filled by Bitlis (Urban 5.2‰, Rural 3.7‰, Total 4.6‰) followed by Karabük and Van. It is interesting that there is a 90.8‰ difference between the highest and lowest household emigration rates.

TABLE 5.10

Household Emigration Rates (‰) by NUTS-2 Level and Place of Residence
(2000 Census Results, Turkey)

Region	Urban	Rural	Total
NUTS 2 – 1	26.6	20.3	26.1
NUTS 2 – 2	17.9	12.3	15.7
NUTS 2 – 3	15.9	13.5	14.7
NUTS 2 – 4	20.3	12.8	19.0
NUTS 2 – 5	18.7	18.2	18.4
NUTS 2 – 6	18.0	18.4	18.1
NUTS 2 – 7	19.6	12.0	18.0
NUTS 2 – 8	23.8	24.2	24.0
NUTS 2 – 9	22.8	19.2	22.4
NUTS 2 – 10	25.5	26.8	26.0
NUTS 2 – 11	18.9	13.9	16.9
NUTS 2 – 12	25.6	15.6	22.6
NUTS 2 – 13	46.7	82.2	62.6
NUTS 2 – 14	36.3	43.9	39.6
NUTS 2 – 15	32.7	51.5	39.8
NUTS 2 – 16	19.1	36.9	28.3
NUTS 2 – 17	14.4	17.2	15.9
NUTS 2 – 18	23.0	22.4	22.7
NUTS 2 – 19	27.7	31.4	29.6
NUTS 2 – 20	15.9	33.3	23.5
NUTS 2 – 21	22.5	22.1	22.3
NUTS 2 – 22	38.4	61.1	46.8
NUTS 2 – 23	12.0	17.0	14.4
NUTS 2 – 24	28.9	34.9	30.4
NUTS 2 – 25	14.7	25.1	18.7
NUTS 2 – 26	25.9	27.3	26.4
Turkey	24.3	27.1	25.2

CONCLUSION

As is clearly evident from the results, emigration rates are higher in the eastern and central parts of the country, and hardly any provinces from the western region, which is developed both economically and socially. Except this region, in rural areas the rates are higher than in

TABLE 5.11
10 Provinces Having Highest Emigration Rates (‰)
(2000 Census Results, Turkey)

Rank	Urban		Rural		Total	
1)	Aksaray	78.3	Tunceli	118.7	Tunceli	95.4
2)	Tunceli	73.9	Hatay	110.3	Hatay	91.9
3)	Hatay	73.3	Elazığ	93.5	Aksaray	79.7
4)	Bingöl	66.7	Bingöl	91.5	Bingöl	78.9
5)	Elazığ	54.2	Aksaray	81.4	Elazığ	66.8
6)	Iğdır	48.7	Yozgat	62.4	Yozgat	53.4
7)	Kırşehir	47.9	K. Maraş	61.3	Bayburt	50.9
8)	Yozgat	44.2	Bayburt	59.0	Kırşehir	46.9
9)	Şırnak	39.9	Nevşehir	55.2	K. Maraş	43.0
10)	Bayburt	39.1	Kayseri	48.1	Nevşehir	42.9

TABLE 5.12
10 Provinces Having Lowest Emigration Rates (‰)
(2000 Census Results, Turkey)

Rank	Urban		Rural		Total	
1)	Bitlis	5.2	Bitlis	3.7	Bitlis	4.6
2)	Karabük	9.4	Bilecik	7.1	Karabük	9.1
3)	Van	10.4	Manisa	7.4	Van	9.3
4)	Bilecik	10.7	Van	8.0	Bilecik	9.3
5)	Kastamonu	10.8	Karabük	8.2	Çanakkale	9.8
6)	Çanakkale	11.5	Çanakkale	8.4	Kastamonu	10.0
7)	Siirt	11.8	Siirt	8.8	Manisa	10.2
8)	Manisa	12.2	Kastamonu	9.4	Siirt	10.6
9)	Hakkari	13.0	Kırıkkale	9.5	Hakkari	12.0
10)	Erzurum	13.0	Eskişehir	9.8	Muğla	13.3

urban areas. Although the overall emigration rates seem to be decreasing in some provinces, the overall national emigration rates are increasing. The trends in emigration in a 50 year period will be seen easily. It is known that the first migrants settled in the destination countries, and although the labor migration is more or less finished to western European countries, short term migrants and asylum seekers are still increasing the number of Turkish citizens outside Turkey. This

is especially true for the provinces where relatives are from the frontiers of the labor migration that happened in the 60's and 70's and
where there is conflict between the separatist Kurds and the armed
forces. The picture in which the central and eastern regions have the
highest emigration rates should be explained by these two reasons.
Hatay on the other hand, has a different structure, as an important
part of the population has relatives in Syria. Therefore, the high rates
will be explained by the continuation of close relations between the
families inside and outside the Turkish border.

Individual level rates seem more reliable when they are compared to household level rates, since the latter can be affected by any
members' movement and name any household as an "emigrant" one.
In addition, the way of wording the question and the content of the
information gives more accurate estimates on the individual level.

As mentioned above, there is no reliable information about the
emigration rates and the number of Turkish citizens living outside
Turkey. If the actual number of emigrants is considered as a big picture,
each attempt to give the number of emigrants and each statistic about
emigrants is a part of this picture. Therefore, census results must be
taken into consideration as a part of this big picture which gives important results especially on temporary migrants and asylum seekers.

Moreover, evaluating the results by regions and NUTS levels
will help not only the social scientists but the policy makers as well. In
order to understand the social and economic reasons for emigration in
the provinces/regions, comprehensive studies should be done. The
direction of emigration can roughly be collected by changing the structure of the questions in the census and by adding the "country of destination".

Additionally, the censuses include questions that can be used to
estimate both the emigrants and immigrants. However, the questions
should be reformulated with some modifications to the content of the
question that will be suitable to make estimations on international
migration. The next census in Turkey should have the same questions

with modifications that will close the gap of information on international migration. The studies on the problems of data of international migration in Turkey must be taken into consideration, and the group that is responsible for designing the census questionnaire must also include an expert on international migration.

REFERENCES

Abadan, N., 1964, *Batı Almanya'daki Türk İşçileri ve Sorunları*, Ankara: Devlet Planlama Teşkilatı.

Çalışma ve Sosyal Güvenlik Bakanlığı, 2002, "Yurtdışındaki Vatandaşlarımıza İlişkin Gelişme ve Sayısal Bilgiler", Yayın No.110, Ankara.

Çiçekli, B., 1998, *The Legal Position of Turkish Immigrants in the European Union*, Ankara: Karmap Publishing Inc. Co.

Erder, S., 2004, "Irregular Migration and Turkey", Population Challenges, International Migration and Reproductive Health in Turkey and the European Union: Issues and Policy Implications, Turkish Family Health and Planning Foundation.

Erzan, R., U. Kuzubaş, and N. Yıldız, 2004, "Growth and Immigration Scenarios: Turkey-EU", Population Challenges, International Migration and Reproductive Health in Turkey and the European Union: Issues and Policy Implications, Turkish Family Health and Planning Foundation.

European Commission, Statistical Office of the European Communities (EURO-STAT), 2000, *Push and Pull Factors of International Migration*, Country Report, Population and Social Conditions, 3/2000/E/No.8.

Gitmez, A. S., 1979, *Dışgöç Öyküsü*, Ankara: Maya Matbaası.

Gökdere, A. Y., 1978, *Yabancı Ülkelere İşgücü Akımı ve Türkiye Ekonomisi Üzerine Etkileri*, Türkiye İş Bankası Kültür Yayınları, General Publication No.196, Economy Series: 14.

—, 1994, "An Evaluation of Turkey's Recent Migration Flows and Stocks", *Turkish Journal of Population Studies*, 16: 29-56.

İçduygu, A. and İ. Sirkeci, 1998, "Changing Dynamics of the Migratory Regime between Turkey and Arab Countries", *Turkish Journal of Population Studies*, 20: 3-16.

İçduygu, A. and T. Ünalan, 2002, "Tides between Mediterranean Shores: Undocumented Migration in the South of Europe", *Papers in Demography*, No.7, Hacettepe University Institute of Population Studies.

İçduygu, A. and Ş. Toktaş, 2005, "Yurtdışından Gelenlerin Nicelik ve

Niteliklerinin Tespitinde Sorunlar", TUBA Reports No.12, Türkiye Bilimler Akademisi, Ankara.

İçduygu, A., 2000, "The Politics of International Migratory Regimes: Transit Migration Flows in Turkey", *International Social Science Journal*, 165: 357-369.

—, 2004, "Migration from Turkey to Europe: A Debate of the Past, Peresent, and Future within the Context of Turkey's EU Membership", Population Challenges, International Migration and Reproductive Health in Turkey and the European Union: Issues and Policy Implications, Turkish Family Health and Planning Foundation (TAPF), Istanbul.

—, 2005, Turkey and International Migration, SOPEMI Report for Turkey 2004, for the Continuous Reporting System on Migration (SOPEMI) of the Organization for Economic Cooperation and Development (OECD), Istanbul.

IOM, 1995, *Transit Migration in Turkey*, Migration Information Programme, Budapest.

Kirişci, K., 2003, "Turkey: A Transformation from Emigration to Immigration", *Migration Information Source*, available at (http://www.migrationinformation.org).

—, 2004, "Turkey's Pre-Accession and Immigration Issues", Population Challenges, International Migration and Reproductive Health in Turkey and the European Union: Issues and Policy Implications, Turkish Family Health and Planning Foundation (TAPF), Istanbul.

Mannaert, C., 2003, "Irregular Migration and Asylum in Turkey", New Issues in Refugee Research, Working Paper No.89, The UN Refugee Agency (UNHCR), Geneva, Switzerland.

Martin, P. L., 1991, "The Unfinished Story: Turkish Labour Migration to Western Europe", with special reference to the Federal Republic of Germany, International Labour Office, Geneva, Switzerland.

Massey, D. S., J. Arango, G. Hugo, A. Kouaouci, A. Pellegrino and J. E. Taylor, 1993, "Theories of International Migration: A Review and Appraisal", *Population and Development Review*, 19(3): 431-466.

McKinley, B., 2004, *Migration Management Today*, Population Challenges, International Migration and Reproductive Health in Turkey and the European Union: Issues and Policy Implications, Turkish Family Health and Planning Foundation (TAPF), Istanbul.

Peker, M., 2004, "The Changing Structure of the Turkish External Emigration", Population Challenges, International Migration and Reproductive Health in Turkey and the European Union: Issues and Policy Implications, Turkish Family Health and Planning Foundation (TAPF), Istanbul.

State Institute of Statistics, 1982, "Census of Population, 1975, Social and Economic Characteristics of Population", Publication No.988, Ankara, Turkey.

—, 1984, "Census of Population, 1980, Social and Economic Characteristics of Population", Publication No.1072, Ankara, Turkey.

—, 1989, "Census of Population, 1985, Social and Economic Characteristics of Population", Publication No.1369, Ankara, Turkey.

—, 1993, "Census of Population, 1990, Social and Economic Characteristics of Population", Publication No.1616, Ankara, Turkey.

Şen, F. and S. Koray, 1993, "Türkiye'den Avrupa Topluluğu'na Göç Hareketleri", Türkiye Araştırmalar Merkezi, Cologne.

Toksöz, G., 2004, "Demand for Highly Skilled Workforce in the European Union and New Migration Arrangements: The German Example", Population Challenges, International Migration and Reproductive Health in Turkey and the European Union: Issues and Policy Implications, Turkish Family Health and Planning Foundation (TAPF), Istanbul.

Timur, S., 2004, "International Migration and Turkey: Changing Trends", Population Challenges, International Migration and Reproductive Health in Turkey and the European Union: Issues and Policy Implications, Turkish Family Health and Planning Foundation (TAPF), Istanbul.

Tuna, O. and N. Ekin, 1966, "Türkiye'den F. Almanya'ya İşgücü Akımı ve Meseleleri 1. Rapor", Istanbul University, Department of Economics, Institute of Economic and Social Sciences, Publication No.1196, Istanbul.

Tunalı, İ., 1988, "Migration and Remigration in Turkey: Micro-Econometric Evidence from 1963-1973", Working Paper No.409, Cornell University, Department of Economics, College of Arts and Sciences, New York.

Türkyılmaz, A. S. and A. Aliağa, 1999, "Appendix B. Survey Design" Turkish Demographic and Health Survey, 1998, Hacettepe University Institute of Population Studies (HUIPS) and Macro International Inc, Ankara.

Türkyılmaz, A. S., A. Hancıoğlu and İ. Koç, 2004, "Appendix B. Survey Design" Turkish Demographic and Health Survey, 2003, Hacettepe University Institute of Population Studies (HUIPS), Ankara.

UNHCR, 2006, "2003 UNHCR Statistical Yearbook", available at ⟨http://www.unhcr.org/cgibin/texis/vtx/statistics/opendoc.pdf?tbl=STATISTICS&id=41d2c1a40&page=statistics⟩.

Ünalan, T. and A. S. Türkyılmaz, 2003, "1990 Genel Nüfus Sayımı Bilgileri Kullanılarak Uluslararası Göç Bilgilerinin Analizi", 3rd Conference on Turkish Demography, Ankara 1997, Hacettepe University Institute of Population Studies (HUIPS), Ankara.

Waki, K., 2004, "Opening Remarks", Population Challenges, International Migration and Reproductive Health in Turkey and the European Union: Issues and Policy Implications, Turkish Family Health and Planning Foundation (TAPF), Istanbul.

Appendices

TOTAL POPULATION AND THE NUMBER OF MIGRANTS
BY PROVINCES AND DISTRICTS

		Urban		Rural		Total	
		Population	Migrants	Population	Migrants	Population	Migrants
01.	**Adana**	**1,414,040**	**11,220**	**466,358**	**2,415**	**1,880,398**	**13,635**
	01. Seyhan	820,000	7,190	40,964	333	860,964	7,523
	02. Yüreğir	323,890	2,677	125,451	625	449,341	3,302
	03. Aladağ	6,969	10	18,974	10	25,943	20
	04. Ceyhan	111,010	588	70,579	490	181,589	1,078
	05. Feke	4,863	6	18,396	60	23,259	66
	06. İmamoğlu	30,339	68	14,063	30	44,402	98
	07. Karaisalı	6,175	16	28,911	41	35,086	57
	08. Karataş	9,256	167	23,404	137	32,660	304
	09. Kozan	77,182	325	61,015	196	138,197	521
	10. Pozantı	8,704	23	13,057	41	21,761	64
	11. Saimbeyli	4,944	26	14,486	71	19,430	97
	12. Tufanbeyli	5,915	87	18,733	271	24,648	358
	13. Yumurtalık	4,793	37	18,325	110	23,118	147
02.	**Adıyaman**	**340,472**	**2,421**	**313,706**	**2,452**	**654,178**	**4,873**
	00. Merkez	182,366	720	79,079	468	261,445	1,188
	01. Besni	33,846	300	71,902	831	105,748	1,131
	02. Çelikhan	9,608	41	9,410	16	19,018	57
	03. Gerger	4,028	4	27,801	42	31,829	46
	04. Gölbaşı	28,631	1,127	26,140	848	54,771	1,975
	05. Kahta	62,741	157	64,015	168	126,756	325
	06. Samsat	6,848	2	6,888	11	13,736	13
	07. Sincik	5,248	1	19,330	21	24,578	22
	08. Tut	7,156	69	9,141	47	16,297	116
03.	**Afyon**	**359,851**	**4,398**	**459,563**	**6,309**	**819,414**	**10,707**
	00. Merkez	123,239	536	73,536	137	196,775	673
	01. Başmakçı	7,770	37	7,569	21	15,339	58
	02. Bayat	5,168	93	4,486	46	9,654	139
	03. Bolvadin	47,414	530	28,234	328	75,648	858
	04. Çay	17,954	125	27,987	175	45,941	300
	05. Çobanlar	8,422	11	4,198	3	12,620	14
	06. Dazkırı	5,420	23	9,523	22	14,943	45
	07. Dinar	34,800	367	54,111	597	88,911	964
	08. Emirdağ	19,666	1,181	30,727	2,282	50,393	3,463

		Urban		Rural		Total	
		Population	Migrants	Population	Migrants	Population	Migrants
09.	Evciler	5,439	170	4,491	33	9,930	203
10.	Hocalar	2,884	56	11,509	350	14,393	406
11.	İhsaniye	4,339	3	29,731	104	34,070	107
12.	İscehisar	10,628	19	11,982	89	22,610	108
13.	Kızılören	2,865	144	2,089	49	4,954	193
14.	Sandıklı	38,036	945	41,741	1,429	79,777	2,374
15.	Sincanlı	5,903	35	53,815	397	59,718	432
16.	Sultandağı	6,834	82	16,710	96	23,544	178
17.	Şuhut	13,070	41	47,124	151	60,194	192
04.	**Ağrı**	**238,911**	**929**	**299,361**	**1,342**	**538,272**	**2,271**
00.	Merkez	76,020	268	43,456	120	119,476	388
01.	Diyadin	13,550	33	31,025	28	44,575	61
02.	Doğubeyazıt	54,055	264	51,947	65	106,002	329
03.	Eleşkirt	11,995	220	36,160	853	48,155	1,073
04.	Hamur	3,658	7	20,042	50	23,700	57
05.	Patnos	68,938	106	67,434	88	136,372	194
06.	Taşlıçay	5,017	5	18,264	29	23,281	34
07.	Tutak	5,678	26	31,033	109	36,711	135
05.	**Amasya**	**187,713**	**1,253**	**179,565**	**1,193**	**367,278**	**2,446**
00.	Merkez	66,597	298	61,234	218	127,831	516
01.	Göynücek	2,565	6	16,137	41	18,702	47
02.	Gümüşhacıköy	14,522	122	17,281	96	31,803	218
03.	Hamamözü	1,590	11	5,105	16	6,695	27
04.	Merzifon	43,750	306	23,018	322	66,768	628
05.	Suluova	44,191	362	11,771	42	55,962	404
06.	Taşova	14,498	148	45,019	458	59,517	606
06.	**Ankara**	**3,426,921**	**29,564**	**460,923**	**3,505**	**3,887,844**	**33,069**
01.	Altındağ	381,930	1,846	7,026	26	388,956	1,872
02.	Çankaya	710,232	9,966	5,747	46	715,979	10,012
03.	Etimesgut	149,655	824	1,030	3	150,685	827
04.	Gölbaşı	32,422	247	26,315	224	58,737	471
05.	Keçiören	626,535	5,105	46,439	203	672,974	5,308
06.	Mamak	405,806	2,158	17,573	45	423,379	2,203
07.	Sincak	270,070	1,110	20,295	62	290,365	1,172
08.	Yenimahalle	525,495	4,632	17,776	118	543,271	4,750
09.	Akyurt	7,489	12	10,539	22	18,028	34
10.	Ayaş	7,102	8	13,289	17	20,391	25
11.	Bala	6,348	18	33,933	226	40,281	244
12.	Beypazarı	34,351	129	17,615	49	51,966	178
13.	Çamlıdere	5,283	15	9,198	30	14,481	45
14.	Çubuk	45,166	101	27,550	38	72,716	139
15.	Elmadağ	22,928	100	19,768	95	42,696	195
16.	Evren	4,294	150	2,329	110	6,623	260
17.	Güdül	5,272	61	14,271	96	19,543	157

		Urban		Rural		Total	
		Population	Migrants	Population	Migrants	Population	Migrants
18.	Haymana	10,098	177	46,036	1,066	56,134	1,243
19.	Kalecik	11,227	17	13,879	56	25,106	73
20.	Kazan	14,825	31	12,354	32	27,179	63
21.	Kızılcahamam	14,988	59	17,612	39	32,600	98
22.	Nallıhan	15,620	49	24,614	98	40,234	147
23.	Polatlı	78,432	936	36,900	171	115,332	1,107
24.	Ş. Koçhisar	41,353	1,813	18,835	633	60,188	2,446
07.	**Antalya**	**864,642**	**7,027**	**659,500**	**2,495**	**1,524,142**	**9,522**
00.	Büyükşehir	585,497	5,515	109,131	455	694,628	5,970
01.	Akseki	8,648	23	32,117	45	40,765	68
02.	Alanya	66,785	606	121,969	611	188,754	1,217
03.	Elmalı	13,922	34	25,844	47	39,766	81
04.	Finike	9,399	38	32,064	89	41,463	127
05.	Gazipaşa	16,056	79	29,562	75	45,618	154
06.	Gündoğmuş	2,402	6	17,476	45	19,878	51
07.	İbradi	7,009	5	3,908	15	10,917	20
08.	Kale	13,948	25	8,452	13	22,400	38
09.	Kaş	4,786	89	42,754	131	47,540	220
10.	Kemer	7,434	134	16,033	208	23,467	342
11.	Korkuteli	16,169	50	35,785	107	51,954	157
12.	Kumluca	25,142	58	35,927	64	61,069	122
13.	Manavgat	56,024	278	88,727	403	144,751	681
14.	Serik	31,421	87	59,751	187	91,172	274
08.	**Artvin**	**80,887**	**446**	**129,145**	**843**	**210,032**	**1,289**
00.	Merkez	21,248	70	12,576	78	33,824	148
01.	Ardanuç	5,288	23	10,866	37	16,154	60
02.	Arhavi	14,551	156	6,374	68	20,925	224
03.	Borçka	8,006	31	21,454	85	29,460	116
04.	Hopa	15,128	95	18,802	128	33,930	223
05.	Murgul	3,898	12	4,997	14	8,895	26
06.	Şavşat	7,028	33	25,735	188	32,763	221
07.	Yusufeli	5,740	26	28,341	245	34,081	271
09.	**Aydın**	**486,968**	**4,136**	**437,921**	**2,321**	**924,889**	**6,457**
00.	Merkez	143,265	950	64,433	291	207,698	1,241
01.	Bozdoğan	8,413	27	28,921	146	37,334	173
02.	Buharkent	7,197	105	6,006	49	13,203	154
03.	Çine	17,918	32	35,946	64	53,864	96
04.	Didim	24,962	435	11,959	112	36,921	547
05.	Germencik	11,953	89	32,755	89	44,708	178
06.	İncirliova	17,937	149	23,616	105	41,553	254
07.	Karacasu	6,145	37	17,158	62	23,303	99
08.	Karpuzlu	2,279	3	11,651	15	13,930	18
09.	Koçarlı	8,664	19	24,749	50	33,413	69
10.	Köşk	8,446	47	17,289	12	25,735	59

		Urban		Rural		Total	
		Population	Migrants	Population	Migrants	Population	Migrants
11.	Kuşadası	41,447	630	18,592	359	60,039	989
12.	Kuyucak	7,505	57	24,663	449	32,168	506
13.	Nazilli	105,881	997	40,890	179	146,771	1,176
14.	Söke	61,862	489	54,483	245	116,345	734
15.	Sultanhisar	6,233	53	16,689	82	22,922	135
16.	Yenipazar	6,861	17	8,121	12	14,982	29
10.	**Balıkesir**	**569,586**	**4,632**	**520,666**	**4,829**	**1,090,252**	**9,461**
00.	Merkez	208,213	1,736	75,049	439	283,262	2,175
01.	Ayvalık	32,089	353	26,734	295	58,823	648
02.	Balya	1,870	20	18,031	122	19,901	142
03.	Bandırma	98,883	675	23,031	113	121,914	788
04.	Bigadiç	14,971	149	39,001	1,442	53,972	1,591
05.	Burhaniye	30,845	432	12,216	79	43,061	511
06.	Dursunbey	14,864	55	35,496	125	50,360	180
07.	Edremit	37,912	251	55,771	1,022	93,683	1,273
08.	Erdek	18,151	228	14,048	113	32,199	341
09.	Gömeç	4,094	43	6,936	55	11,030	98
10.	Gönen	36,373	215	37,002	140	73,375	355
11.	Havran	9,505	30	17,232	19	26,737	49
12.	İvrindi	5,831	22	34,112	129	39,943	151
13.	Kepsut	5,794	85	24,633	145	30,427	230
14.	Manyas	5,537	31	20,514	124	26,051	155
15.	Marmara	2,153	9	6,815	83	8,968	92
16.	Savaştepe	9,808	42	13,314	86	23,122	128
17.	Sındırgı	10,262	79	39,204	164	49,466	243
18.	Susurluk	22,431	177	21,527	134	43,958	311
11.	**Bilecik**	**113,684**	**427**	**71,809**	**251**	**185,493**	**678**
00.	Merkez	27,194	91	18,921	46	46,115	137
01.	Bozüyük	45,999	193	13,757	75	59,756	268
02.	Gölpazarı	7,120	44	6,841	15	13,961	59
03.	İnhisar	2,233	9	4,319	25	6,552	34
04.	Osmaneli	12,719	19	8,375	3	21,094	22
05.	Pazaryeri	6,514	14	7,286	25	13,800	39
06.	Söğüt	10,630	55	8,765	47	19,395	102
07.	Yenipazar	1,275	2	3,545	15	4,820	17
12.	**Bingöl**	**116,987**	**2,038**	**140,171**	**3,025**	**257,158**	**5,063**
00.	Merkez	68,814	1,434	50,932	1,635	119,746	3,069
01.	Adaklı	3,175	49	9,212	161	12,387	210
02.	Genç	16,721	97	27,279	65	44,000	162
03.	Karlıova	7,524	41	25,510	440	33,034	481
04.	Kiğı	3,139	81	3,175	238	6,314	319
05.	Solhan	13,635	184	20,648	221	34,283	405
06.	Yayladere	2,497	90	1,582	213	4,079	303
07.	Yedisu	1,482	62	1,833	52	3,315	114

		Urban		Rural		Total	
		Population	Migrants	Population	Migrants	Population	Migrants
13.	**Bitlis**	**205,703**	**232**	**176,264**	**126**	**381,967**	**358**
00.	Merkez	43,764	65	20,607	6	64,371	71
01.	Adilcevaz	32,857	31	21,822	35	54,679	66
02.	Ahlat	32,826	31	19,078	14	51,904	45
03.	Güroymak	22,168	41	26,288	10	48,456	51
04.	Hizan	10,359	12	34,188	24	44,547	36
05.	Mutki	3,247	0	36,027	21	39,274	21
06.	Tatvan	60,482	52	18,254	16	78,736	68
14.	**Bolu 125,344**	**1,053**	**140,531**	**1,296**	**265,875**	**2,349**	
00.	Merkez	73,336	661	53,650	505	126,986	1,166
04.	Dörtdivan	2,744	27	8,101	191	10,845	218
06.	Gerede	21,910	235	17,602	250	39,512	485
08.	Göynük	4,641	16	14,229	35	18,870	51
10.	Kıbrıscık	2,180	2	3,331	1	5,511	3
11.	Mengen	4,986	28	12,752	119	17,738	147
12.	Mudurnu	5,289	21	21,187	81	26,476	102
13.	Seben	4,094	27	5,427	58	9,521	85
14.	Yeniçağa	6,164	36	4,252	56	10,416	92
15.	**Burdur**	**134,935**	**1,065**	**123,692**	**1,188**	**258,627**	**2,253**
00.	Merkez	58,116	356	27,263	135	85,379	491
01.	Ağlasun	5,006	16	6,830	34	11,836	50
02.	Altınyayla	4,273	28	3,056	99	7,329	127
03.	Bucak	28,094	93	29,681	65	57,775	158
04.	Çavdır	4,765	62	11,824	77	16,589	139
05.	Çeltikçi	2,423	8	4,491	11	6,914	19
06.	Gölhisar	12,881	228	10,140	245	23,021	473
07.	Karamanlı	5,315	58	3,169	10	8,484	68
08.	Kemer	2,284	48	2,581	15	4,865	63
09.	Tefenni	5,451	57	6,999	43	12,450	100
10.	Yeşilova	6,327	111	17,658	454	23,985	565
16.	**Bursa**	**1,635,274**	**13,770**	**495,470**	**2,607**	**2,130,744**	**16,377**
01.	Nilüfer	127,961	1,089	38,561	281	166,522	1,370
02.	Osmangazi	578,365	4,429	62,983	332	641,348	4,761
03.	Yıldırım	489,176	4,512	994	12	490,170	4,524
04.	Büyükorhan	3,635	18	13,709	32	17,344	50
05.	Gemlik	63,779	572	25,582	311	89,361	883
06.	Gürsu	21,756	199	6,212	44	27,968	243
07.	Harmancık	3,538	10	7,935	65	11,473	75
08.	İnegöl	106,093	1,039	81,028	462	187,121	1,501
09.	İznik	20,421	91	25,155	68	45,576	159
10.	Karacabey	41,291	209	35,913	99	77,204	308
11.	Keles	3,453	12	16,507	59	19,960	71
12.	Kestel	28,604	543	15,913	54	44,517	597
13.	Mudanya	20,715	162	33,314	391	54,029	553

		Urban		Rural		Total	
		Population	Migrants	Population	Migrants	Population	Migrants
14.	M. Kemalpaşa	47,769	235	56,642	195	104,411	430
15.	Orhaneli	7,940	9	22,743	39	30,683	48
16.	Orhangazi	45,479	566	24,339	126	69,818	692
17.	Yenişehir	25,299	75	27,940	37	53,239	112
17.	**Çanakkale**	**199,159**	**939**	**250,102**	**910**	**449,261**	**1,849**
00.	Merkez	68,698	417	27,914	161	96,612	578
01.	Ayvacık	6,447	17	24,671	83	31,118	100
02.	Bayramiç	12,006	35	21,032	36	33,038	71
03.	Biga	27,592	127	51,058	142	78,650	269
04.	Bozcaada	2,088	20	0	0	2,088	20
05.	Çan	26,226	82	25,438	52	51,664	134
06.	Eeceabat	4,373	13	4,982	17	9,355	30
07.	Ezine	11,828	31	21,712	77	33,540	108
08.	Gelibolu	21,497	107	18,303	91	39,800	198
09.	Gökçeada	4,459	47	1,980	114	6,439	161
10.	Lapseki	8,581	36	17,885	77	26,466	113
11.	Yenice	5,364	7	35,127	60	40,491	67
18.	**Çankırı**	**125,929**	**532**	**137,458**	**826**	**263,387**	**1,358**
00.	Merkez	60,442	348	17,977	45	78,419	393
01.	Atkaracalar	4,394	10	4,507	7	8,901	17
02.	Bayramören	2,006	9	4,350	9	6,356	18
03.	Çerkeş	10,852	37	14,111	35	24,963	72
04.	Eldivan	5,674	8	3,981	2	9,655	10
05.	Ilgaz	9,524	12	17,642	53	27,166	65
06.	Kızılırmak	2,541	14	9,039	70	11,580	84
07.	Korgun	5,638	13	3,360	7	8,998	20
08.	Kurşunlu	10,116	15	14,533	8	24,649	23
09.	Orta	5,469	52	21,772	86	27,241	138
10.	Şabanözü	4,644	13	8,593	120	13,237	133
11.	Yapraklı	4,629	1	17,593	384	22,222	385
19.	**Çorum**	**316,115**	**3,650**	**315,878**	**2,497**	**631,993**	**6,147**
00.	Merkez	164,523	2,131	63,514	879	228,037	3,010
01.	Alaca	25,930	535	31,350	556	57,280	1,091
02.	Bayat	7,528	17	26,585	34	34,113	51
03.	Boğazkale	2,276	107	7,115	49	9,391	156
04.	Dodurga	3,634	80	7,678	160	11,312	240
05.	İskilip	19,939	118	30,642	72	50,581	190
06.	Kargı	5,805	30	16,241	20	22,046	50
07.	Laçin	2,094	12	7,981	57	10,075	69
08.	Mecitözü	5,951	29	22,062	144	28,013	173
09.	Oğuzlar	5,057	66	4,995	9	10,052	75
10.	Ortaköy	3,578	36	9,957	105	13,535	141
11.	Osmancık	25,658	202	28,805	166	54,463	368
12.	Sungurlu	36,266	250	49,726	230	85,992	480
13.	Uğurludağ	7,876	37	9,227	16	17,103	53

		Urban		Rural		Total	
		Population	Migrants	Population	Migrants	Population	Migrants
20.	**Denizli**	**411,250**	**3,568**	**447,426**	**7,660**	**858,676**	**11,228**
00.	Merkez	276,564	2,343	119,503	1,352	396,067	3,695
01.	Acıpayam	9,798	139	59,120	1,157	68,918	1,296
02.	Akköy	2,450	15	3,170	28	5,620	43
03.	Babadağ	4,894	25	3,470	10	8,364	35
04.	Baklan	3,004	31	6,259	91	9,263	122
05.	Bekilli	4,158	103	8,000	598	12,158	701
06.	Beyağaç	2,781	10	5,072	22	7,853	32
07.	Bozkurt	4,287	81	8,583	277	12,870	358
08.	Buldan	13,624	81	13,137	79	26,761	160
09.	Çal	4,538	35	29,180	637	33,718	672
10.	Çameli	2,295	5	18,883	31	21,178	36
11.	Çardak	4,363	60	6,195	144	10,558	204
12.	Çivril	13,642	247	51,809	1,375	65,451	1,622
13.	Güney	6,435	24	7,617	86	14,052	110
14.	Honaz	7,505	46	16,265	122	23,770	168
15.	Kale	6,807	9	15,559	52	22,366	61
16.	Sarayköy	16,297	129	16,656	246	32,953	375
17.	Serinhisar	15,926	90	6,566	55	22,492	145
18.	Tavas	11,882	95	52,382	1,298	64,264	1,393
21.	**Diyarbakır**	**813,582**	**2,795**	**572,812**	**1,558**	**1,386,394**	**4,353**
00.	Büyükşehir	546,005	1,907	179,438	398	725,443	2,305
01.	Bismil	62,866	206	68,727	207	131,593	413
02.	Çermik	15,611	256	35,307	527	50,918	783
03.	Çınar	12,857	53	47,502	80	60,359	133
04.	Çüngüş	4,255	9	12,279	39	16,534	48
05.	Dicle	8,770	10	32,271	18	41,041	28
06.	Eğil	4,853	10	17,708	17	22,561	27
07.	Ergani	50,082	166	45,516	87	95,598	253
08.	Hani	10,635	29	21,587	21	32,222	50
09.	Hazro	5,812	18	13,476	16	19,288	34
10.	Kocaköy	5,507	6	7,718	1	13,225	7
11.	Kulp	14,842	19	25,683	31	40,525	50
12.	Lice	8,281	16	14,012	40	22,293	56
13.	Silvan	63,206	90	51,588	76	114,794	166
22.	**Edirne**	**213,542**	**1,533**	**171,408**	**997**	**384,950**	**2,530**
00.	Merkez	110,069	838	18,891	137	128,960	975
01.	Enez	3,823	12	8,167	27	11,990	39
02.	Havsa	8,150	95	16,523	119	24,673	214
03.	İpsala	7,478	29	25,936	91	33,414	120
04.	Keşan	42,209	256	31,386	159	73,595	415
05.	Lalapaşa	1,383	10	8,050	34	9,433	44
06.	Meriç	3,270	16	16,573	40	19,843	56
07.	Süleoğlu	2,610	6	5,888	64	8,498	70
08.	Uzunköprü	34,550	271	39,994	326	74,544	597

		Urban		Rural		Total	
		Population	**Migrants**	**Population**	**Migrants**	**Population**	**Migrants**
23.	**Elazığ**	**365,155**	**6,492**	**221,200**	**6,354**	**586,355**	**12,846**
00.	Merkez	275,051	4,247	81,546	1,497	356,597	5,744
01.	Ağın	3,623	7	2,138	10	5,761	17
02.	Alacakaya	3,531	1	6,228	17	9,759	18
03.	Arıcak	3,566	8	16,113	10	19,679	18
04.	Baskil	10,457	17	17,716	53	28,173	70
05.	Karakoçan	19,570	1,028	25,218	2,770	44,788	3,798
06.	Keban	5,832	24	3,851	2	9,683	26
07.	Kovancılar	21,980	1,042	26,655	1,728	48,635	2,770
08.	Maden	6,842	30	15,107	56	21,949	86
09.	Palu	9,812	69	16,338	176	26,150	245
10.	Sivrice	4,891	19	10,290	35	15,181	54
24.	**Erzincan**	**148,174**	**1,177**	**159,551**	**2,711**	**307,725**	**3,888**
00.	Merkez	89,622	881	67,523	1,437	157,145	2,318
01.	Çayırlı	6,538	78	11,714	263	18,252	341
02.	İliç	2,232	4	6,632	22	8,864	26
03.	Kemah	2,438	25	8,431	220	10,869	245
04.	Kemaliye	1,908	18	6,299	23	8,207	41
05.	Otlukbeli	3,526	49	1,330	16	4,856	65
06.	Rrefahiye	3,586	21	13,774	94	17,360	115
07.	Tercan	8,736	15	23,384	268	32,120	283
08.	Üzümlü	29,588	86	20,464	368	50,052	454
25.	**Erzurum**	**522,128**	**1,924**	**412,138**	**2,941**	**934,266**	**4,865**
00.	Büyükşehir	343,370	1,186	27,497	64	370,867	1,250
01.	Aşkale	13,046	32	19,877	57	32,923	89
02.	Çat	5,466	6	20,487	59	25,953	65
03.	Hınıs	25,501	106	25,595	521	51,096	627
04.	Horasan	16,562	160	32,741	188	49,303	348
05.	Ilıca	10,698	30	18,532	46	29,230	76
06.	İspir	7,508	62	21,120	173	28,628	235
07.	Karaçoban	12,840	51	18,629	129	31,469	180
08.	Karayazı	5,864	12	32,145	356	38,009	368
09.	Köprüköy	3,638	6	18,795	92	22,433	98
10.	Narman	7,583	10	19,528	23	27,111	33
11.	Oltu	22,466	102	19,283	178	41,749	280
12.	Olur	2,746	15	9,891	56	12,637	71
13.	Pasinler	19,835	56	22,432	34	42,267	90
14.	Pazaryolu	4,527	16	5,683	94	10,210	110
15.	Şenkaya	3,997	8	27,278	48	31,275	56
16.	Tekman	3,885	36	31,803	653	35,688	689
17.	Tortum	7,827	24	32,365	77	40,192	101
18.	Uzundere	4,769	6	8,457	93	13,226	99

		Urban		Rural		Total	
		Population	**Migrants**	**Population**	**Migrants**	**Population**	**Migrants**
26.	**Eskişehir**	**546,042**	**3,571**	**150,173**	**673**	**696,215**	**4,244**
00.	Büyükşehir	479,397	3,181	36,075	207	515,472	3,388
01.	Alpu	5,719	15	11,234	44	16,953	59
02.	Beylikova	4,644	8	5,144	16	9,788	24
03.	Çifteler	12,106	203	6,914	77	19,020	280
04.	Günyüzü	3,891	1	11,347	6	15,238	7
05.	Han	2,293	11	2,054	9	4,347	20
06.	İnönü	4,741	36	4,212	41	8,953	77
07.	Mahmudiye	5,077	34	5,102	32	10,179	66
08.	Mihalgazi	4,031	5	5,923	3	9,954	8
09.	Mihalıççık	4,205	17	14,236	26	18,441	43
10.	Sarıcakaya	7,515	19	6,805	9	14,320	28
11.	Seyitgazi	3,315	11	18,985	46	22,300	57
12.	Sivrihisar	9,108	30	22,142	157	31,250	187
27.	**Gaziantep**	**1,015,857**	**9,826**	**282,949**	**3,008**	**1,298,806**	**12,834**
01.	Şahinbey	506,715	5,022	40,727	187	547,442	5,209
02.	Şehitkamil	355,229	3,699	56,098	232	411,327	3,931
03.	Araban	10,584	98	23,905	725	34,489	823
04.	İslahiye	38,392	236	42,760	310	81,152	546
05.	Kargamış	4,213	11	9,926	31	14,139	42
06.	Nizip	73,958	644	45,941	423	119,899	1,067
07.	Nurdağı	10,340	35	23,985	746	34,325	781
08.	Oğuzeli	10,095	55	22,404	128	32,499	183
09.	Yavuzeli	6,331	26	17,203	226	23,534	252
28.	**Giresun**	**279,773**	**3,712**	**271,377**	**3,763**	**551,150**	**7,475**
00.	Merkez	83,458	1,372	31,707	436	115,165	1,808
01.	Alucra	12,077	17	12,603	49	24,680	66
02.	Bulancak	33,628	410	31,788	350	65,416	760
03.	Çamoluk	4,123	11	11,740	47	15,863	58
04.	Çanakçı	7,059	99	9,817	166	16,876	265
05.	Dereli	8,052	215	23,016	219	31,068	434
06.	Doğankent	4,199	20	4,128	16	8,327	36
07.	Espiye	13,546	289	19,076	202	32,622	491
08.	Eynesil	11,117	178	11,933	180	23,050	358
09.	Görele	25,989	151	27,678	188	53,667	339
10.	Güce	3,773	52	5,849	59	9,622	111
11.	Keşap	9,004	185	15,233	639	24,237	824
12.	Piraziz	8,782	131	8,969	44	17,751	175
13.	Ş. Karahisar	34,038	130	16,016	49	50,054	179
14.	Tirebolu	16,588	179	24,885	423	41,473	602
15.	Yağlıdere	4,340	273	16,939	696	21,279	969

		Urban		Rural		Total	
		Population	Migrants	Population	Migrants	Population	Migrants
29.	**Gümüşhane**	**67,781**	**374**	**122,799**	**1,814**	**190,580**	**2,188**
00.	Merkez	27,399	146	18,489	148	45,888	294
01.	Kelkit	17,102	105	47,399	887	64,501	992
02.	Köse	7,535	13	12,017	121	19,552	134
03.	Kürtün	3,312	4	14,034	86	17,346	90
04.	Şiran	8,042	80	17,743	374	25,785	454
05.	Torul	4,391	26	13,117	198	17,508	224
30.	**Hakkari**	**120,102**	**294**	**96,684**	**188**	**216,786**	**482**
00.	Merkez	53,492	98	19,510	18	73,002	116
01.	Çukurca	3,597	0	3,721	0	7,318	0
02.	Şemdinli	9,120	36	31,172	69	40,292	105
03.	Yüksekova	53,893	160	42,281	101	96,174	261
31.	**Hatay**	**599,620**	**13,731**	**694,215**	**20,254**	**1,293,835**	**33,985**
00.	Merkez	150,639	3,912	206,132	8,648	356,771	12,560
01.	Altınözü	5,809	547	57,198	1,962	63,007	2,509
02.	Belen	19,570	232	10,067	102	29,637	334
03.	Dörtyol	56,050	239	73,125	286	129,175	525
04.	Erzin	26,488	135	8,448	28	34,936	163
05.	Hassa	9,230	36	42,253	136	51,483	172
06.	İskenderun	163,505	3,598	127,889	3,335	291,394	6,933
07.	Kırıkhan	64,926	748	36,014	276	100,940	1,024
08.	Kumlu	6,499	103	9,488	259	15,987	362
09.	Reyhanlı	52,454	1,457	23,868	597	76,322	2,054
10.	Samandağı	38,617	2,706	79,382	4,430	117,999	7,136
11.	Yayladağı	5,833	18	20,351	195	26,184	213
32.	**Isparta**	**266,822**	**1,842**	**216,680**	**2,248**	**483,502**	**4,090**
00.	Merkez	136,870	962	22,645	62	159,515	1,024
01.	Aksu	3,011	14	6,203	12	9,214	26
02.	Atabey	6,862	4	2,082	0	8,944	4
03.	Eğirdir	12,864	59	24,588	93	37,452	152
04.	Gelendost	7,038	64	15,882	396	22,920	460
05.	Gönen	6,684	32	5,143	23	11,827	55
06.	Keçiborlu	9,289	45	13,090	119	22,379	164
07.	Senirkent	13,095	53	11,103	150	24,198	203
08.	Sütçüler	3,106	22	17,081	20	20,187	42
09.	Şarkikaraağaç	23,624	177	29,146	517	52,770	694
10.	Uluborlu	7,746	92	1,552	19	9,298	111
11.	Yalvaç	31,492	305	67,648	836	99,140	1,141
12.	Yenişarbademli	5,141	13	517	1	5,658	14

		Urban		Rural		Total	
		Population	Migrants	Population	Migrants	Population	Migrants
33.	**İçel**	**1,011,054**	**8,294**	**647,079**	**2,988**	**1,658,133**	**11,282**
00.	Büyükşehir	553,042	5,525	194,604	1,452	747,646	6,977
01.	Anamur	48,695	211	35,365	114	84,060	325
02.	Aydıncık	7,839	32	3,854	2	11,693	34
03.	Bozyazı	24,203	60	17,376	55	41,579	115
04.	Çamlıyayla	8,557	29	10,078	24	18,635	53
05.	Erdemli	40,459	220	95,941	338	136,400	558
06.	Gülnar	10,041	24	29,057	41	39,098	65
07.	Mut	33,579	194	39,282	196	72,861	390
08.	Silifke	64,609	257	91,853	278	156,462	535
09.	Tarsus	220,030	1,742	129,669	488	349,699	2,230
34.	**Istanbul**	**8,923,552**	**87,938**	**898,658**	**6,349**	**9,822,210**	**94,287**
01.	Adalar	14,600	372	0	0	14,600	372
02.	Avcılar	233,971	3,228	0	0	233,971	3,228
03.	Bağcılar	556,109	3,540	0	0	556,109	3,540
04.	Bahçelievler	477,764	4,804	0	0	477,764	4,804
05.	Bakırköy	192,677	3,958	0	0	192,677	3,958
06.	Bayrampaşa	238,430	2,053	0	0	238,430	2,053
07.	Beşiktaş	180,721	4,629	0	0	180,721	4,629
08.	Beykoz	170,426	1,576	36,628	307	207,054	1,883
09.	Beyoğlu	221,196	1,860	0	0	221,196	1,860
10.	Eminönü	30,596	200	0	0	30,596	200
11.	Esenler	374,539	1,815	0	0	374,539	1,815
12.	Eyüp	233,526	1,520	18,851	144	252,377	1,664
13.	Fatih	389,127	3,319	0	0	389,127	3,319
14.	G.O. Paşa	658,594	3,878	92,597	291	751,191	4,169
15.	Güngören	273,129	2,494	0	0	273,129	2,494
16.	Kadıköy	658,453	11,560	0	0	658,453	11,560
17.	Kağıthane	342,237	2,108	0	0	342,237	2,108
18.	Kartal	338,360	3,924	67,557	272	405,917	4,196
19.	K. Çekmece	591,704	4,076	952	2	592,656	4,078
20.	Maltepe	347,537	4,074	0	0	347,537	4,074
21.	Pendik	384,558	3,228	4,479	47	389,037	3,275
22.	Sarıyer	212,990	2,787	20,811	312	233,801	3,099
23.	Şişli	254,756	2,858	0	0	254,756	2,858
24.	Tuzla	101,466	834	13,422	51	114,888	885
25.	Ümraniye	440,937	3,692	161,122	930	602,059	4,622
26.	Üsküdar	484,437	5,563	0	0	484,437	5,563
27.	Zeytinburnu	242,667	2,055	0	0	242,667	2,055
28.	B. Çekmece	34,624	513	339,328	2,852	373,952	3,365
29.	Çatalca	15,495	108	59,763	355	75,258	463
30.	Silivri	44,056	445	62,086	648	106,142	1,093
31.	Sultanbeyli	175,477	766	0	0	175,477	766
32.	Şile	8,393	101	21,062	138	29,455	239

		Urban		Rural		Total	
		Population	Migrants	Population	Migrants	Population	Migrants
35.	**İzmir**	**2,688,700**	**21,731**	**615,679**	**3,314**	**3,304,379**	**25,045**
01.	Balçova	65,688	916	0	0	65,688	916
02.	Bornova	381,078	2,742	5,286	24	386,364	2,766
03.	Buca	308,356	2,410	5,996	19	314,352	2,429
04.	Çiğli	108,749	921	3,956	10	112,705	931
05.	Gaziemir	62,446	381	17,929	185	80,375	566
06.	Güzelbahçe	12,420	198	3,220	15	15,640	213
07.	Karşıyaka	446,825	4,417	334	1	447,159	4,418
08.	Konak	775,853	5,742	951	1	776,804	5,743
09.	Narlıdere	46,237	697	0	0	46,237	697
10.	Aliağa	35,995	250	18,294	128	54,289	378
11.	Bayındır	15,897	25	31,469	74	47,366	99
12.	Bergama	51,302	211	53,873	104	105,175	315
13.	Beydağ	5,385	36	8,464	25	13,849	61
14.	Çeşme	19,817	387	11,290	121	31,107	508
15.	Dikili	12,819	120	18,588	189	31,407	309
16.	Foça	9,230	151	15,361	141	24,591	292
17.	Karaburun	2,606	26	10,121	148	12,727	174
18.	Kemalpaşa	25,831	116	46,806	255	72,637	371
19.	Kınık	12,155	32	19,225	31	31,380	63
20.	Kiraz	9,726	35	36,260	40	45,986	75
21.	Menderes	16,879	102	54,145	629	71,024	731
22.	Menemen	45,680	280	64,531	271	110,211	551
23.	Ödemiş	62,069	193	66,173	116	128,242	309
24.	Seferihisar	15,775	147	16,237	285	32,012	432
25.	Selçuk	23,964	202	8,292	82	32,256	284
26.	Tire	43,756	178	34,701	93	78,457	271
27.	Torbalı	38,403	325	51,958	164	90,361	489
28.	Urla	33,759	491	12,219	163	45,978	654
36.	**Kars**	**124,628**	**584**	**208,426**	**1,193**	**333,054**	**1,777**
00.	Merkez	72,855	435	39,043	309	111,898	744
01.	Akyaka	2,952	12	11,444	62	14,396	74
02.	Arpaçay	3,564	29	24,670	137	28,234	166
03.	Digor	2,427	9	25,675	85	28,102	94
04.	Kağızman	17,846	48	31,918	264	49,764	312
05.	Sarıkamış	18,128	30	38,441	140	56,569	170
06.	Selim	4,159	13	23,993	136	28,152	149
07.	Susuz	2,697	8	13,242	60	15,939	68
37.	**Kastamonu**	**167,435**	**721**	**230,818**	**847**	**398,253**	**1,568**
00.	Merkez	61,846	199	38,636	44	100,482	243
01.	Abana	3,721	51	904	6	4,625	57
02.	Ağlı	2,898	7	1,466	1	4,364	8
03.	Araç	5,315	21	21,486	29	26,801	50
04.	Azdavay	3,223	24	7,256	9	10,479	33

		Urban		Rural		Total	
		Population	Migrants	Population	Migrants	Population	Migrants
05.	Bozkurt	5,203	9	5,190	21	10,393	30
06.	Cide	5,749	87	20,432	145	26,181	232
07.	Çatalzeytin	2,867	28	7,683	169	10,550	197
08.	Daday	4,640	7	7,885	10	12,525	17
09.	Devrekani	6,213	34	11,249	71	17,462	105
10.	Doğanyurt	1,431	13	9,996	70	11,427	83
11.	Hanönü	2,339	19	3,705	9	6,044	28
12.	İhsangazi	2,937	6	4,796	2	7,733	8
13.	İnebolu	8,642	47	19,808	87	28,450	134
14.	Küre	3,412	4	7,948	26	11,360	30
15.	Pınarbaşı	1,904	2	5,192	29	7,096	31
16.	Seydiler	3,015	7	2,444	9	5,459	16
17.	Şenpazar	2,715	23	4,895	20	7,610	43
18	Taşköprü	16,296	52	30,278	47	46,574	99
19.	Tosya	23,069	81	19,569	43	42,638	124
38.	**Kayseri**	**738,132**	**9,560**	**357,561**	**7,490**	**1,095,693**	**17,050**
01.	Kocasinan	277,888	4,051	50,546	1,115	328,434	5,166
02.	Melikgazi	260,446	2,561	48,130	446	308,576	3,007
03.	Akkışla	3,446	180	7,375	193	10,821	373
04.	Bünyan	12,993	102	29,214	682	42,207	784
05.	Develi	36,965	456	39,214	550	76,179	1,006
06.	Felahiye	5,808	147	11,618	677	17,426	824
07.	Hacılar	18,534	99	1,178	1	19,712	100
08.	İncesu	8,616	53	15,091	131	23,707	184
09.	Özvatan	7,670	663	3,973	418	11,643	1,081
10.	Pınarbaşı	12,503	254	28,674	325	41,177	579
11.	Sarıoğlan	5,247	153	24,995	1,035	30,242	1,188
12.	Sarız	5,056	150	14,422	866	19,478	1,016
13.	Talas	35,798	338	21,008	302	56,806	640
14.	Tomarza	11,276	146	28,026	517	39,302	663
15.	Yahyalı	22,656	134	22,754	173	45,410	307
16.	Yeşilhisar	13,230	73	11,343	59	24,573	132
39.	**Kırklareli**	**174,793**	**1,174**	**140,418**	**769**	**315,211**	**1,943**
00.	Merkez	47,933	291	27,564	94	75,497	385
01.	Babaeski	23,232	203	28,907	267	52,139	470
02.	Demirköy	4,468	8	6,030	20	10,498	28
03.	Kofçaz	797	4	2,924	23	3,721	27
04.	Lüleburgaz	75,917	533	37,935	195	113,852	728
05.	Pehlivanköy	3,246	36	3,112	21	6,358	57
06.	Pınarhisar	9,494	48	11,869	75	21,363	123
07.	Vize	9,706	51	22,077	74	31,783	125

		Urban		Rural		Total	
		Population	Migrants	Population	Migrants	Population	Migrants
40.	**Kırşehir**	**152,751**	**2,918**	**114,146**	**2,197**	**266,897**	**5,115**
00.	Merkez	91,118	1,999	29,176	1,075	120,294	3,074
01.	Akçakent	1,312	4	7,432	72	8,744	76
02.	Akpınar	3,820	39	10,779	115	14,599	154
03.	Boztepe	5,282	78	5,403	65	10,685	143
04.	Çiçekdağı	7,011	101	15,917	177	22,928	278
05.	Kaman	29,330	487	34,750	589	64,080	1,076
06.	Mucur	14,878	210	10,689	104	25,567	314
41.	**Kocaeli**	**709,314**	**5,854**	**471,772**	**3,241**	**1,181,086**	**9,095**
00.	Büyükşehir	192,279	1,235	170,037	1,177	362,316	2,412
01.	Gebze	253,853	2,015	165,407	1,081	419,260	3,096
02.	Gölcük	46,469	464	50,731	619	97,200	1,083
03.	Kandıra	11,054	60	40,602	186	51,656	246
04.	Karamürsel	29,465	302	18,829	81	48,294	383
05.	Körfez	81,154	830	22,851	94	104,005	924
06.	Derince	95,040	948	3,315	3	98,355	951
42.	**Konya**	**1,289,238**	**12,042**	**919,325**	**9,215**	**2,208,563**	**21,257**
01.	Karatay	181,631	1,447	30,773	70	212,404	1,517
02.	Meram	226,816	1,884	36,679	130	263,495	2,014
03.	Selçuklu	325,780	2,924	20,787	42	346,567	2,966
04.	Ahırlı	5,619	33	8,804	25	14,423	58
05.	Akören	10,642	68	6,755	154	17,397	222
06.	Akşehir	62,726	770	55,908	317	118,634	1,087
07.	Altınekin	8,817	1	13,882	9	22,699	10
08.	Beyşehir	40,246	470	77,001	395	117,247	865
09.	Bozkır	10,699	73	48,377	627	59,076	700
10.	Cihanbeyli	18,374	480	60,787	2,229	79,161	2,709
11.	Çeltik	5,084	248	10,137	90	15,221	338
12.	Çumra	40,613	462	62,078	286	102,691	748
13.	Derbent	7,340	1	7,099	1	14,439	2
14.	Derebucak	5,125	58	14,204	92	19,329	150
15.	Doğanhisar	9,500	39	27,672	63	37,172	102
16.	Emirgazi	8,552	21	6,616	9	15,168	30
17.	Ereğli	87,096	731	45,009	190	132,105	921
18.	Güneysınır	9,787	134	14,462	184	24,249	318
19.	Hadım	14,487	58	42,967	76	57,454	134
20.	Halkapınar	1,857	7	4,815	10	6,672	17
21.	Hüyük	7,986	17	43,017	96	51,003	113
22.	Ilgın	27,400	84	50,881	93	78,281	177
23.	Kadınhanı	14,951	28	28,206	103	43,157	131
24.	Karapınar	36,624	78	21,064	107	57,688	185
25.	Kulu	29,003	1,351	47,099	2,393	76,102	3,744
26.	Sarayönü	10,267	17	26,531	193	36,798	210
27.	Seydişehir	48,837	226	38,685	287	87,522	513

		Urban		Rural		Total	
		Population	**Migrants**	**Population**	**Migrants**	**Population**	**Migrants**
28.	Taşkent	9,524	13	33,494	37	43,018	50
29.	Tuzlukçu	5,986	18	4,304	14	10,290	32
30.	Yalıhüyük	4,929	151	228	0	5,157	151
31.	Yunak	12,940	150	31,004	893	43,944	1,043
43.	**Kütahya**	**309,773**	**2,153**	**350,983**	**3,140**	**660,756**	**5,293**
00.	Merkez	160,094	1,070	41,608	324	201,702	1,394
01.	Altıntaş	6,228	105	20,231	333	26,459	438
02.	Aslanapa	2,261	18	11,624	139	13,885	157
03.	Çavadarhisar	4,589	24	9,623	163	14,212	187
04.	Domaniç	4,576	63	16,330	252	20,906	315
05.	Dumlupınar	3,281	75	2,467	98	5,748	173
06.	Emet	18,719	63	27,581	322	46,300	385
07.	Gediz	18,907	191	58,224	602	77,131	793
08.	Hisarcık	6,159	33	15,237	144	21,396	177
09.	Pazarlar	5,396	17	7,323	18	12,719	35
10.	Simav	26,519	185	78,285	327	104,804	512
11.	Şaphane	4,804	45	7,487	30	12,291	75
12.	Tavşanlı	48,240	264	54,963	388	103,203	652
44.	**Malatya**	**501,890**	**3,161**	**382,228**	**3,053**	**884,118**	**6,214**
00.	Merkez	386,317	2,483	77,713	188	464,030	2,671
01.	Akçadağ	12,755	65	39,852	1,149	52,607	1,214
02.	Arapkir	9,819	23	8,598	45	18,417	68
03.	Arguvan	2,688	107	10,401	89	13,089	196
04.	Battalgazi	14,486	35	13,072	43	27,558	78
05.	Darende	13,770	37	43,703	139	57,473	176
06.	Doğanşehir	13,985	151	48,904	430	62,889	581
07.	Doğanyol	5,458	0	6,062	16	11,520	16
08.	Hekimhan	12,989	157	34,443	485	47,432	642
09.	Kale	3,546	24	7,174	20	10,720	44
10.	Kuluncak	5,934	15	16,338	133	22,272	148
11.	Pötürge	4,782	25	28,669	34	33,451	59
12.	Yazıhan	4,162	16	16,260	145	20,422	161
13.	Yeşilyurt	11,199	23	31,039	137	42,238	160
45.	**Manisa**	**703,683**	**3,398**	**542,361**	**1,469**	**1,246,044**	**4,867**
00.	Merkez	208,214	974	58,648	133	266,862	1,107
01.	Ahmetli	10,006	40	7,760	8	17,766	48
02.	Akhisar	83,036	401	69,691	155	152,727	556
03.	Alaşehir	39,419	180	55,252	176	94,671	356
04.	Demirci	20,214	143	40,627	75	60,841	218
05.	Gölmarmara	11,408	9	6,767	2	18,175	11
06.	Gördes	11,009	19	28,260	76	39,269	95
07.	Kırkağaç	18,220	70	23,541	47	41,761	117
08.	Köprübaşı	5,220	14	6,189	14	11,409	28
09.	Kula	22,116	53	29,956	63	52,072	116

		Urban		Rural		Total	
		Population	**Migrants**	**Population**	**Migrants**	**Population**	**Migrants**
10.	Salihli	85,057	507	63,782	203	148,839	710
11.	Sarıgöl	12,257	56	23,826	76	36,083	132
12.	Saruhanlı	12,990	74	52,478	171	65,468	245
13.	Selendi	7,657	19	20,895	46	28,552	65
14.	Soma	62,034	391	27,427	143	89,461	534
15.	Turgutlu	94,826	448	27,262	81	122,088	529
46.	**K. Maraş**	**530,025**	**6,031**	**505,064**	**13,273**	**1,035,089**	**19,304**
00.	Merkez	316,917	1,687	144,293	1,490	461,210	3,177
01.	Afşin	36,792	295	60,062	1,115	96,854	1,410
02.	Andırın	8,074	30	38,664	97	46,738	127
03.	Çağlayancerit	12,373	34	18,509	822	30,882	856
04.	Ekinözü	6,928	36	11,140	435	18,068	471
05.	Elbistan	73,822	1,346	62,303	1,952	136,125	3,298
06.	Göksun	27,503	159	50,003	579	77,506	738
07.	Nurhak	8,648	367	9,870	397	18,518	764
08.	Pazarcık	26,703	1,986	56,989	5,835	83,692	7,821
09.	Türkoğlu	12,265	91	53,231	551	65,496	642
47.	**Mardin**	**386,249**	**3,098**	**327,625**	**2,736**	**713,874**	**5,834**
00.	Merkez	61,895	298	44,227	341	106,122	639
01.	Dargeçit	16,847	102	11,876	50	28,723	152
02.	Derik	20,472	34	38,245	228	58,717	262
03.	Kızıltepe	113,223	498	72,359	313	185,582	811
04.	Mazıdağı	10,814	27	17,655	24	28,469	51
05.	Midyat	53,567	789	73,508	671	127,075	1,460
06.	Nusaybin	75,529	962	31,413	436	106,942	1,398
07.	Ömerli	7,274	92	7,356	33	14,630	125
08.	Savur	7,295	32	28,592	595	35,887	627
09.	Yeşilli	19,333	264	2,394	45	21,727	309
48.	**Muğla**	**247,766**	**1,715**	**416,462**	**2,096**	**664,228**	**3,811**
00.	Merkez	41,582	160	39,199	92	80,781	252
01.	Bodrum	23,470	364	57,251	615	80,721	979
02.	Dalaman	16,644	124	11,131	12	27,775	136
03.	Datça	7,907	130	5,911	61	13,818	191
04.	Fethiye	50,512	321	99,380	283	149,892	604
05.	Kavaklıdere	3,106	8	9,417	47	12,523	55
06.	Köyceğiz	7,567	76	22,102	75	29,669	151
07.	Marmaris	21,000	289	35,187	432	56,187	721
08.	Milas	37,925	121	72,724	175	110,649	296
09.	Ortaca	17,055	64	16,255	101	33,310	165
10.	Ula	5,194	17	17,071	104	22,265	121
11.	Yatağan	15,804	41	30,834	99	46,638	140

	Urban		Rural		Total	
	Population	**Migrants**	**Population**	**Migrants**	**Population**	**Migrants**
49. Muş	**151,368**	**951**	**306,888**	**2,646**	**458,256**	**3,597**
00. Merkez	64,800	285	104,081	487	168,881	772
01. Bulanık	24,100	110	78,905	254	103,005	364
02. Hasköy	20,262	50	18,835	42	39,097	92
03. Korkut	5,250	7	27,298	47	32,548	54
04. Malazgirt	21,723	48	48,803	71	70,526	119
05. Varto	15,233	451	28,966	1,745	44,199	2,196
50. Nevşehir	**132,767**	**1,791**	**177,472**	**4,727**	**310,239**	**6,518**
00. Merkez	69,083	613	34,850	537	103,933	1,150
01. Acıgöl	6,925	44	20,039	197	26,964	241
02. Avanos	10,750	144	32,888	1,364	43,638	1,508
03. Derinkuyu	9,892	53	13,400	147	23,292	200
04. Gülşehir	8,332	234	24,226	1,049	32,558	1,283
05. Hacıbektaş	6,019	140	13,159	506	19,178	646
06. Kozaklı	7,757	299	17,018	342	24,775	641
07. Ürgüp	14,009	264	21,892	585	35,901	849
51. Niğde	**124,295**	**679**	**231,890**	**1,371**	**356,185**	**2,050**
00. Merkez	76,339	431	101,264	342	177,603	773
01. Altunhisar	4,255	46	20,438	166	24,693	212
02. Bor	29,208	133	34,728	134	63,936	267
03. Çamardı	3,756	7	17,275	72	21,031	79
04. Çiftlik	4,405	20	29,769	318	34,174	338
05. Ulukışla	6,332	42	28,416	339	34,748	381
52. Ordu	**407,112**	**4,973**	**515,110**	**4,685**	**922,222**	**9,658**
00. Merkez	114,787	1,543	44,379	962	159,166	2,505
01. Akkuş	5,273	54	43,181	103	48,454	157
02. Aybastı	15,850	605	19,393	568	35,243	1,173
03. Çamaş	11,437	85	4,336	13	15,773	98
04. Çatalpınar	8,837	41	14,798	42	23,635	83
05. Çaybaşı	5,171	81	12,054	22	17,225	103
06. Fatsa	59,663	704	59,865	631	119,528	1,335
07. Gölköy	23,404	22	44,805	77	68,209	99
08. Gülyalı	5,342	18	5,665	78	11,007	96
09. Gürgentepe	18,197	50	18,905	23	37,102	73
10. İkizce	8,197	94	20,225	53	28,422	147
11. Kabadüz	3,694	40	8,226	133	11,920	173
12. Kabataş	9,401	83	12,888	48	22,289	131
13. Korgan	15,508	349	27,153	168	42,661	517
14. Kumru	14,481	81	29,168	186	43,649	267
15. Mesudiye	4,280	9	25,415	275	29,695	284
16. Perşembe	10,611	143	31,540	555	42,151	698
17. Ulubey	8,617	154	24,718	394	33,335	548
18. Ünye	64,362	817	68,396	354	132,758	1,171

		Urban		Rural		Total	
		Population	Migrants	Population	Migrants	Population	Migrants
53.	**Rize 198,725**	**1,540**	**190,632**	**2,181**	**389,357**	**3,721**	
00.	Merkez	79,673	499	54,090	484	133,763	983
01.	Ardeşen	38,577	450	16,165	285	54,742	735
02.	Çamlıhemşin	1,871	39	8,219	155	10,090	194
03.	Çayeli	22,471	142	34,410	325	56,881	467
04.	Derepazarı	6,396	47	4,931	84	11,327	131
05.	Fındıklı	10,428	107	6,618	72	17,046	179
06.	Güneysu	3,752	20	13,240	171	16,992	191
07.	Hemşin	3,306	23	1,753	55	5,059	78
08.	İkizdere	2,392	27	10,723	106	13,115	133
09.	İyidere	6,088	64	5,113	29	11,201	93
10.	Kalkandere	9,390	40	12,402	104	21,792	144
11.	Pazar	14,381	82	22,968	311	37,349	393
54.	**Sakarya**	**450,845**	**4,552**	**305,135**	**4,398**	**755,980**	**8,950**
00.	Merkez	276,569	2,559	57,912	829	334,481	3,388
01.	Akyazı	11,902	227	12,403	180	24,305	407
02.	Ferizli	7,832	80	6,712	89	14,544	169
03.	Geyve	23,389	440	55,513	1,064	78,902	1,504
04.	Hendek	16,313	43	28,261	110	44,574	153
05.	Karapürçek	28,213	362	36,521	500	64,734	862
06.	Karasu	4,158	28	6,988	53	11,146	81
07.	Kaynarca	25,033	387	32,088	958	57,121	1,345
08.	Kocaali	4,818	14	20,364	237	25,182	251
09.	Pamukova	14,138	113	17,522	161	31,660	274
10.	Sapanca	13,021	105	11,023	38	24,044	143
11.	Söğütlü	21,686	171	14,320	164	36,006	335
12.	Taraklı	3,773	23	5,508	15	9,281	38
55.	**Samsun**	**650,302**	**6,825**	**628,762**	**6,798**	**1,279,064**	**13,623**
00.	Büyükşehir	369,242	3,418	74,778	715	444,020	4,133
01.	Alaçam	12,609	90	27,835	128	40,444	218
02.	Asarcık	1,857	27	18,529	118	20,386	145
03.	Ayvacık	6,420	94	21,933	103	28,353	197
04.	Bafra	86,205	894	79,175	885	165,380	1,779
05.	Çarşamba	51,273	586	89,356	1,822	140,629	2,408
06.	Havza	20,263	370	38,475	340	58,738	710
07.	Kavak	7,513	26	22,610	88	30,123	114
08.	Ladik	8,863	101	14,613	189	23,476	290
09.	19 Mayıs	9,708	547	18,799	561	28,507	1,108
10.	Salıpazar	6,464	56	21,558	127	28,022	183
11.	Tekkeköy	15,259	139	37,886	692	53,145	831
12.	Terme	26,370	329	62,386	661	88,756	990
13.	Vezirköprü	23,262	90	94,041	342	117,303	432
14.	Yakakent	4,994	58	6,788	27	11,782	85

		Urban		Rural		Total	
		Population	Migrants	Population	Migrants	Population	Migrants
56.	**Siirt**	**148,434**	**342**	**112,360**	**155**	**260,794**	**497**
	00. Merkez	95,784	222	9,682	18	105,466	240
	01. Aydınlar	2,421	7	2,193	17	4,614	24
	02. Baykan	7,412	23	23,804	24	31,216	47
	03. Eruh	6,692	8	7,212	7	13,904	15
	04. Kurtalan	25,772	75	29,963	38	55,735	113
	05. Pervari	5,334	4	22,306	36	27,640	40
	06. Şirvan	5,019	3	17,200	15	22,219	18
57.	**Sinop**	**97,776**	**1,026**	**143,399**	**2,148**	**241,175**	**3,174**
	00. Merkez	29,403	192	19,520	117	48,923	309
	01. Ayancık	11,178	279	19,200	686	30,378	965
	02. Boyabat	22,956	90	23,744	26	46,700	116
	03. Dikmen	1,155	14	9,510	33	10,665	47
	04. Durağan	9,249	64	22,708	34	31,957	98
	05. Erfelek	3,672	38	11,035	63	14,707	101
	06. Gerze	10,387	95	15,163	65	25,550	160
	07. Saraydüzü	3,345	0	5,265	3	8,610	3
	08. Türkeli	6,431	254	17,254	1,121	23,685	1,375
58.	**Sivas**	**404,599**	**4,275**	**374,455**	**5,863**	**779,054**	**10,138**
	00. Merkez	249,179	2,545	52,555	452	301,734	2,997
	01. Akıncılar	4,271	6	3,993	11	8,264	17
	02. Altınyayla	4,941	85	12,057	251	16,998	336
	03. Divriği	14,164	52	10,710	95	24,874	147
	04. Doğanşar	3,959	17	3,112	6	7,071	23
	05. Gemerek	11,003	75	44,313	924	55,316	999
	06. Gölova	3,731	10	3,129	9	6,860	19
	07. Gürün	10,728	108	18,859	224	29,587	332
	08. Hafik	3,307	17	15,801	94	19,108	111
	09. İmranlı	5,164	37	9,035	225	14,199	262
	10. Kangal	11,836	62	28,903	296	40,739	358
	11. Koyulhisar	5,163	17	20,506	62	25,669	79
	12. Suşehri	21,508	91	22,238	65	43,746	156
	13. Şarkışla	21,507	851	31,674	907	53,181	1,758
	14. Ulaş	2,800	32	13,437	155	16,237	187
	15. Yıldızeli	14,520	162	64,990	1,802	79,510	1,964
	16. Zara	16,818	108	19,143	285	35,961	393
59.	**Tekirdağ**	**381,551**	**2,742**	**223,138**	**1,255**	**604,689**	**3,997**
	00. Merkez	105,884	723	32,316	164	138,200	887
	01. Çerkezköy	37,791	128	40,388	147	78,179	275
	02. Çorlu	138,288	1,167	32,192	195	170,480	1,362
	03. Hayrabolu	17,311	73	22,374	110	39,685	183
	04. Malkara	23,142	190	35,632	300	58,774	490
	05. Marmaraereğli	7,796	83	11,250	167	19,046	250
	06. Muratlı	18,161	93	8,334	34	26,495	127

		Urban		Rural		Total	
		Population	Migrants	Population	Migrants	Population	Migrants
07.	Saray	16,422	97	23,412	66	39,834	163
08.	Şarköy	16,756	188	17,240	72	33,996	260
60.	**Tokat**	**399,457**	**2,300**	**452,675**	**2,224**	**852,132**	**4,524**
00.	Merkez	111,066	583	64,439	215	175,505	798
01.	Almus	5,820	12	39,988	180	45,808	192
02.	Artova	4,964	13	11,655	26	16,619	39
03.	Başçiftlik	5,662	2	7,296	18	12,958	20
04.	Erbaa	48,257	285	59,959	168	108,216	453
05.	Niksar	44,770	342	49,906	196	94,676	538
06.	Pazar	5,199	17	15,609	56	20,808	73
07.	Reşadiye	14,831	30	86,865	664	101,696	694
08.	Sulusaray	4,319	28	8,100	291	12,419	319
09.	Turhal	95,617	581	37,118	168	132,735	749
10.	Yeşilyurt	6,609	151	9,069	73	15,678	224
11.	Zile	52,343	256	62,671	169	115,014	425
61.	**Trabzon**	**469,586**	**5,422**	**539,455**	**9,075**	**1,009,041**	**14,497**
00.	Merkez	213,895	2,836	70,474	989	284,369	3,825
01.	Akçaabat	40,064	468	84,304	1,902	124,368	2,370
02.	Araklı	21,973	264	45,739	1,080	67,712	1,344
03.	Arsin	12,535	26	25,315	414	37,850	440
04.	Beşikdüzü	28,253	164	19,719	197	47,972	361
05.	Çarşıbaşı	7,445	70	10,646	131	18,091	201
06.	Çaykara	5,769	9	32,045	477	37,814	486
07.	Dernekpazarı	5,272	147	3,799	106	9,071	253
08.	Düzköy	6,970	117	19,377	521	26,347	638
09.	Hayrat	7,120	34	15,980	209	23,100	243
10.	Köprübaşı	5,253	109	7,197	189	12,450	298
11.	Maçka	6,753	50	33,900	605	40,653	655
12.	Of	25,162	277	58,472	536	83,634	813
13.	Sürmene	16,488	164	25,516	253	42,004	417
14.	Şalpazarı	7,686	60	18,620	334	26,306	394
15.	Tonya	14,494	264	17,115	239	31,609	503
16.	Vakfıkebir	31,096	242	22,592	495	53,688	737
17.	Yomra	13,358	121	28,645	398	42,003	519
62.	**Tunceli**	**45,453**	**1,452**	**48,962**	**2,279**	**94,415**	**3,731**
00.	Merkez	22,711	1,084	7,177	634	29,888	1,718
01.	Çemişgezek	3,205	14	7,087	35	10,292	49
02.	Hozat	4,367	74	3,939	181	8,306	255
03.	Mazgirt	2,717	64	11,270	395	13,987	459
04.	Nazımiye	1,866	52	3,750	306	5,616	358
05.	Ovacık	3,320	35	3,649	69	6,969	104
06.	Pertek	5,366	75	9,470	375	14,836	450
07.	Pülümür	1,901	54	2,620	284	4,521	338

		Urban		Rural		Total	
		Population	**Migrants**	**Population**	**Migrants**	**Population**	**Migrants**
63.	**Şanlıurfa**	**836,012**	**2,722**	**619,247**	**5,034**	**1,455,259**	**7,756**
00.	Merkez	384,643	1,252	149,024	234	533,667	1,486
01.	Akçakale	30,162	26	45,246	95	75,408	121
02.	Birecik	39,786	382	36,838	691	76,624	1,073
03.	Bozova	19,431	44	51,000	978	70,431	1,022
04.	Ceylanpınar	43,854	89	23,414	55	67,268	144
05.	Halfeti	2,807	77	37,025	2,245	39,832	2,322
06.	Harran	7,949	4	47,090	41	55,039	45
07.	Hilvan	16,182	31	23,372	44	39,554	75
08.	Siverek	124,508	236	99,762	185	224,270	421
09	Suruç	45,590	152	38,101	94	83,691	246
10.	Viranşehir	121,100	429	68,375	372	189,475	801
64.	**Uşak**	**186,698**	**3,175**	**148,578**	**2,886**	**335,276**	**6,061**
00.	Merkez	139,887	1,894	43,664	679	183,551	2,573
01.	Banaz	17,101	527	29,357	849	46,458	1,376
02.	Eşme	11,885	249	28,816	403	40,701	652
03.	Karahallı	5,295	23	10,294	198	15,589	221
04.	Sivaslı	7,174	336	20,612	351	27,786	687
05.	Ulubey	5,356	146	15,835	406	21,191	552
65.	**Van**	**430,899**	**941**	**461,173**	**681**	**892,072**	**1,622**
00.	Merkez	283,733	721	75,663	136	359,396	857
01.	Bahçesaray	3,111	1	14,014	40	17,125	41
02.	Başkale	11,153	18	42,457	62	53,610	80
03.	Çaldıran	11,076	12	47,680	56	58,756	68
04.	Çatak	5,213	5	19,267	29	24,480	34
05.	Edremit	6,220	3	12,441	14	18,661	17
06.	Erciş	65,801	120	82,826	120	148,627	240
07.	Gevaş	10,748	19	20,023	15	30,771	34
08.	Gürpınar	4,684	18	33,738	63	38,422	81
09.	Muradiye	18,598	14	37,359	52	55,957	66
10.	Özalp	6,236	8	57,921	79	64,157	87
11.	Saray	4,326	2	17,784	15	22,110	17
66.	**Yozgat**	**316,079**	**5,330**	**394,517**	**8,386**	**710,596**	**13,716**
00.	Merkez	71,326	566	41,844	275	113,170	841
01.	Akdağmadeni	19,897	657	44,623	1,668	64,520	2,325
02.	Aydıncık	6,469	31	20,211	72	26,680	103
03.	Boğazlıyan	29,636	646	39,697	922	69,333	1,568
04.	Çandır	13,414	124	5,603	79	19,017	203
05.	Çayıralan	14,307	364	20,697	1,340	35,004	1,704
06.	Çekerek	12,028	165	30,712	133	42,740	298
07.	Kadışehri	5,049	27	19,734	209	24,783	236
08.	Saraykent	9,516	260	18,222	650	27,738	910
09.	Sarıkaya	22,425	432	40,002	1,211	62,427	1,643
10.	Sorgun	56,187	1,240	71,158	1,167	127,345	2,407

		Urban		Rural		Total	
		Population	Migrants	Population	Migrants	Population	Migrants
11.	Şefaatli	13,912	269	17,413	429	31,325	698
12.	Yenifakılı	8,414	63	7,674	139	16,088	202
13.	Yerköy	33,499	486	16,927	92	50,426	578
67.	**Zonguldak**	**250,522**	**3,002**	**411,652**	**10,414**	**662,174**	**13,416**
00.	Merkez	106,353	742	122,787	1,516	229,140	2,258
01.	Alaplı	18,098	197	29,838	531	47,936	728
02.	Çaycuma	19,110	318	92,686	2,939	111,796	3,257
03.	Devrek	20,478	573	57,869	3,140	78,347	3,713
04.	Ereğli	78,711	870	88,021	1,807	166,732	2,677
05.	Gökçebey	7,772	302	20,451	481	28,223	783
68.	**Aksaray**	**207,657**	**6,826**	**205,784**	**5,951**	**413,441**	**12,777**
00.	Merkez	135,777	5,009	109,576	2,979	245,353	7,988
01.	Ağaçören	5,205	178	12,809	735	18,014	913
02.	Eskil	22,113	25	6,813	19	28,926	44
03.	Gülağaç	5,120	163	23,779	763	28,899	926
04.	Güzelyurt	3,835	42	14,271	388	18,106	430
05.	Ortaköy	27,768	1,288	33,709	846	61,477	2,134
06.	Sarıyahşi	7,839	121	4,827	221	12,666	342
69.	**Bayburt**	**38,672**	**558**	**62,009**	**1,096**	**100,681**	**1,654**
00.	Merkez	29,820	445	42,938	828	72,758	1,273
01.	Aydıntepe	7,031	96	6,415	125	13,446	221
02.	Demirözü	1,821	17	12,656	143	14,477	160
70.	**Karaman**	**139,443**	**1,851**	**111,617**	**1,243**	**251,060**	**3,094**
00.	Merkez	105,738	1,542	50,278	979	156,016	2,521
01.	Ayrancı	3,026	18	11,179	30	14,205	48
02.	Başyayla	5,508	17	3,065	43	8,573	60
03.	Ermenek	14,280	106	29,295	106	43,575	212
04.	Kazımkarabekir	3,843	141	1,863	17	5,706	158
05.	Sarıveliler	7,048	27	15,937	68	22,985	95
71.	**Kırıkkale**	**282,067**	**1,382**	**101,815**	**298**	**383,882**	**1,680**
00.	Merkez	209,403	1,233	19,742	68	229,145	1,301
01.	Bahşılı	5,513	15	2,858	4	8,371	19
02.	Balışeyh	2,671	18	10,433	28	13,104	46
03.	Çelebi	2,992	2	4,192	13	7,184	15
04.	Delice	8,803	25	21,353	73	30,156	98
05.	Karakeçili	7,669	18	469	0	8,138	18
06.	Keskin	32,718	37	24,882	20	57,600	57
07.	Sulakyurt	5,731	28	12,034	80	17,765	108
08.	Yahşihan	6,567	6	5,852	12	12,419	18

	Urban		Rural		Total	
	Population	**Migrants**	**Population**	**Migrants**	**Population**	**Migrants**
72. Batman	**308,278**	**1,110**	**159,521**	**556**	**467,799**	**1,666**
00. Merkez	252,006	953	26,945	69	278,951	1,022
01. Beşiri	8,402	73	26,880	311	35,282	384
02. Gercüş	8,094	18	25,662	105	33,756	123
03. Hasankeyf	3,609	22	4,017	7	7,626	29
04. Kozluk	26,407	31	48,770	33	75,177	64
05. Sason	9,760	13	27,247	31	37,007	44
73. Şırnak	**195,585**	**1,399**	**133,248**	**1,095**	**328,833**	**2,494**
00. Merkez	44,653	101	16,260	20	60,913	121
01. Beytüşşebap	5,424	4	13,190	2	18,614	6
02. Cizre	68,951	578	12,468	143	81,419	721
03. Güçlükonak	3,130	3	5,301	1	8,431	4
04. İdil	19,194	336	43,687	761	62,881	1,097
05. Silopi	46,829	350	21,094	127	67,923	477
06. Uludere	7,404	27	21,248	41	28,652	68
74. Bartın	**48,240**	**585**	**154,662**	**3,168**	**202,902**	**3,753**
00. Merkez	36,569	456	105,597	2,394	142,166	2,850
01. Amasra	6,273	66	11,396	220	17,669	286
02. Kurucaşile	1,743	21	7,384	80	9,127	101
03. Ulus	3,655	42	30,285	474	33,940	516
75. Ardahan	**31,286**	**219**	**110,049**	**760**	**141,335**	**979**
00. Merkez	14,120	117	32,046	196	46,166	313
01. Çıldır	1,606	9	13,800	21	15,406	30
02. Damal	1,767	26	7,433	15	9,200	41
03. Göle	7,860	27	32,155	172	40,015	199
04. Hanak	3,968	6	12,737	58	16,705	64
05. Posof	1,965	34	11,878	298	13,843	332
76. Iğdır	**80,511**	**1,556**	**93,043**	**864**	**173,554**	**2,420**
00. Merkez	61,187	1,237	45,575	478	106,762	1,715
01. Aralık	6,806	73	14,066	41	20,872	114
02. Karakoyunlu	3,306	152	14,180	295	17,486	447
03. Tuzluca	9,212	94	19,222	50	28,434	144
77. Yalova	**98,563**	**1,277**	**63,669**	**646**	**162,232**	**1,923**
00. Merkez	70,565	801	15,479	152	86,044	953
01. Altınova	3,015	36	15,025	159	18,040	195
02. Armutlu	3,905	46	3,629	13	7,534	59
03. Çınarcık	8,976	162	11,781	138	20,757	300
04. Çiftlikköy	9,965	223	14,857	163	24,822	386
05. Termal	2,137	9	2,898	21	5,035	30

		Urban		Rural		Total	
		Population	Migrants	Population	Migrants	Population	Migrants
78.	**Karabük**	**157,832**	**597**	**76,291**	**255**	**234,123**	**852**
00.	Merkez	101,118	309	17,056	38	118,174	347
01.	Eflani	2,714	8	10,708	21	13,422	29
02.	Eskipazar	7,941	28	9,018	26	16,959	54
03.	Ovacık	1,397	0	5,430	5	6,827	5
04.	Safranbolu	32,990	141	15,886	40	48,876	181
05.	Yenice	11,672	111	18,193	125	29,865	236
79.	**Kilis**	**73,163**	**295**	**41,672**	**135**	**114,835**	**430**
00.	Merkez	69,359	284	16,368	49	85,727	333
01.	Elbeyli	1,921	8	5,874	58	7,795	66
02.	Musabeyli	1,259	2	14,196	11	15,455	13
03.	Polateli	624	1	5,234	17	5,858	18
80.	**Osmaniye**	**312,541**	**2,148**	**155,909**	**493**	**468,450**	**2,641**
00.	Merkez	180,507	1,391	35,940	161	216,447	1,552
01.	Bahçe	10,370	65	8,578	19	18,948	84
02.	Düziçi	37,589	125	47,234	81	84,823	206
03.	Hasanbeyli	4,615	6	2,517	7	7,132	13
04.	Kadirli	69,415	543	39,876	130	109,291	673
05.	Sumbas	2,167	3	15,554	72	17,721	75
06.	Toprakkal	7,878	15	6,210	23	14,088	38
81.	**Düzce**	**112,023**	**1,395**	**187,814**	**2,542**	**299,837**	**3,937**
00.	Merkez	53,740	677	97,346	1,038	151,086	1,715
01.	Akçakoca	20,415	191	19,711	271	40,126	462
02.	Cumayeri	6,474	204	6,589	102	13,063	306
03.	Çilimli	5,676	19	11,114	123	16,790	142
04.	Gölyaka	4,938	57	13,613	319	18,551	376
05.	Gümüşova	8,998	64	7,022	135	16,020	199
06.	Kaynaşlı	8,100	112	12,723	240	20,823	352
07.	Yığılca	3,682	71	19,696	314	23,378	385
Türkiye Toplamı		**43,140,273**	**386,181**	**24,668,703**	**254,277**	**67,808,976**	**640,458**

APPENDIX 5.2
PROVINCIAL LEVEL (NUTS – 3) EMIGRATION RATES (‰),
2000 CENSUS RESULTS, TURKEY

Apendix 5.2A
Individual Level Rates

Province	Urban	Rural	Total
Adana	7,9	5,2	7,3
Adıyaman	7,1	7,8	7,4
Afyon	12,2	13,7	13,1
Ağrı	3,9	4,5	4,2
Amasya	6,7	6,6	6,7
Ankara	8,6	7,6	8,5
Antalya	8,1	3,8	6,2
Artvin	5,5	6,5	6,1
Aydın	8,5	5,3	7,0
Balıkesir	8,1	9,3	8,7
Bilecik	3,8	3,5	3,7
Bingöl	17,4	21,6	19,7
Bitlis	1,1	0,7	0,9
Bolu	8,4	9,2	8,8
Burdur	7,9	9,6	8,7
Bursa	8,4	5,3	7,7
Çanakkale	4,7	3,6	4,1
Çankırı	4,2	6,0	5,2
Çorum	11,5	7,9	9,7
Denizli	8,7	17,1	13,1
Diyarbakır	3,4	2,7	3,1
Edirne	7,2	5,8	6,6
Elazığ	17,8	28,7	21,9
Erzincan	7,9	17,0	12,6
Erzurum	3,7	7,1	5,2
Eskişehir	6,5	4,5	6,1
Gaziantep	9,7	10,6	9,9
Giresun	13,3	13,9	13,6
Gümüşhane	5,5	14,8	11,5
Hakkari	2,4	1,9	2,2
Hatay	22,9	29,2	26,3

Province	Urban	Rural	Total
Isparta	6,9	10,4	8,5
İçel	8,2	4,6	6,8
Istanbul	9,9	7,1	9,6
İzmir	8,1	5,4	7,6
Kars	4,7	5,7	5,3
Kastamonu	4,3	3,7	3,9
Kayseri	13,0	20,9	15,6
Kırklareli	6,7	5,5	6,2
Kırşehir	19,1	19,2	19,2
Kocaeli	8,3	6,9	7,7
Konya	9,3	10,0	9,6
Kütahya	7,0	8,9	8,0
Province	Urban	Rural	Total
Malatya	6,3	8,0	7,0
Manisa	4,8	2,7	3,9
K. Maraş	11,4	26,3	18,6
Mardin	8,0	8,4	8,2
Muğla	6,9	5,0	5,7
Muş	6,3	8,6	7,8
Nevşehir	13,5	26,6	21,0
Niğde	5,5	5,9	5,8
Ordu	12,2	9,1	10,5
Rize	7,7	11,4	9,6
Sakarya	10,1	14,4	11,8
Samsun	10,5	10,8	10,7
Siirt	2,3	1,4	1,9
Sinop	10,5	15,0	13,2
Tekirdağ	7,2	5,6	6,6
Sivas	10,6	15,7	13,0
Tokat	5,8	4,9	5,3
Trabzon	11,5	16,8	14,4
Tunceli	31,9	46,5	39,5
Şanlıurfa	3,3	8,1	5,3
Uşak	17,0	19,4	18,1
Van	2,2	1,5	1,8
Yozgat	16,9	21,3	19,3
Zonguldak	12,0	25,3	20,3
Aksaray	32,9	28,9	30,9
Bayburt	14,4	17,7	16,4

Province	Urban	Rural	Total
Karaman	13,3	11,1	12,3
Kırıkkale	4,9	2,9	4,4
Batman	3,6	3,5	3,6
Şırnak	7,2	8,2	7,6
Bartın	12,1	20,5	18,5
Ardahan	7,0	6,9	6,9
Iğdır	19,3	9,3	13,9
Yalova	13,0	10,1	11,9
Karabük	3,8	3,3	3,6
Kilis	4,0	3,2	3,7
Osmaniye	6,9	3,2	5,6
Düzce	12,5	13,5	13,1

Appendıx 5.2B
Household Level Rates

Province	Urban	Rural	Total
Adana	25,4	17,4	23,7
Adıyaman	26,0	35,3	30,0
Afyon	24,3	29,0	26,6
Ağrı	17,6	19,7	18,7
Amasya	16,4	15,7	16,1
Ankara	22,8	19,2	22,4
Antalya	20,8	11,2	17,0
Artvin	16,6	18,0	17,4
Aydın	19,8	11,6	16,1
Balıkesir	17,5	16,2	16,9
Bilecik	10,7	7,1	9,3
Bingöl	66,7	91,5	78,9
Bitlis	5,2	3,7	4,6
Bolu	20,0	18,0	19,0
Burdur	14,9	17,7	16,2
Bursa	21,9	13,4	20,1
Çanakkale	11,5	8,4	9,8
Çankırı	13,4	19,2	16,1
Çorum	29,5	22,0	26,3
Denizli	19,2	32,0	25,5
Diyarbakır	15,7	14,0	15,1
Edirne	17,5	12,5	15,4
Elazığ	54,2	93,5	66,8
Erzincan	19,5	41,3	30,2
Erzurum	13,0	25,4	17,9
Eskişehir	15,1	9,8	14,1
Gaziantep	30,9	37,4	32,1
Giresun	30,6	31,0	30,8
Gümüşhane	15,6	40,4	31,6
Hakkari	13,0	10,6	12,0
Hatay	73,3	110,3	91,9
Isparta	14,8	20,3	17,0
İçel	25,8	14,4	21,4
Istanbul	26,6	20,3	26,1
İzmir	20,3	12,8	19,0

Province	Urban	Rural	Total
Kars	15,3	23,0	19,6
Kastamonu	10,8	9,4	10,0
Kayseri	31,1	48,1	36,0
Kırklareli	16,7	12,3	14,9
Kırşehir	47,9	45,3	46,9
Kocaeli	22,2	19,3	21,1
Konya	24,5	26,6	25,3
Kütahya	15,9	17,5	16,7
Malatya	18,0	22,6	19,7
Manisa	12,2	7,4	10,2
K. Maraş	28,7	61,3	43,0
Mardin	32,3	36,4	34,0
Province	Urban	Rural	Total
Muğla	15,8	11,8	13,3
Muş	25,6	40,8	35,0
Nevşehir	29,6	55,2	42,9
Niğde	14,6	17,7	16,4
Ordu	30,3	23,2	26,6
Rize	21,8	31,6	26,4
Sakarya	24,9	32,6	27,7
Samsun	24,9	28,8	26,5
Siirt	11,8	8,8	10,6
Sinop	21,8	28,2	25,4
Tekirdağ	18,7	12,2	16,4
Sivas	27,3	44,1	34,4
Tokat	16,6	16,2	16,4
Trabzon	29,6	41,4	35,3
Tunceli	73,9	118,7	95,4
Şanlıurfa	13,7	35,0	22,2
Uşak	32,7	38,4	35,0
Van	10,4	8,0	9,3
Yozgat	44,2	62,4	53,4
Zonguldak	24,4	42,1	34,2
Aksaray	78,3	81,4	79,7
Bayburt	39,1	59,0	50,9
Karaman	34,2	28,3	31,7
Kırıkkale	14,8	9,5	13,6
Batman	17,0	16,3	16,8
Şırnak	39,9	34,2	37,7

Province	Urban	Rural	Total
Bartın	22,3	39,7	34,4
Ardahan	16,4	19,2	18,5
Iğdır	48,7	30,5	39,9
Yalova	30,8	23,8	28,1
Karabük	9,4	8,2	9,1
Kilis	13,2	15,2	13,8
Osmaniye	22,0	11,9	18,9
Düzce	27,7	29,5	28,8

APPENDIX 5.3
FIVE REGION PROVINCES

5 Region and Provinces

1) West	Aydın, Balıkesir, Bursa, Çanakkale, Denizli, Edirne, Istanbul, İzmir, Kırklareli, Kocaeli, Manisa, Sakarya, Tekirdağ, Yalova
2) South	Adana, Antalya, Burdur, Gaziantep, Hatay, Isparta, İçel, Muğla, Kilis, Osmaniye
3) Central	Afyon, Amasya, Ankara, Bilecik, Bolu, Çankırı, Çorum, Eskişehir, Kayseri, Kırşehir, Konya, Kütahya, Nevşehir, Niğde, Tokat, Uşak, Yozgat, Aksaray, Karaman, Kırıkkale, Düzce
4) North	Artvin, Giresun, Kastamonu, Ordu, Rize, Samsun, Sinop, Trabzon, Zonguldak, Bartın, Karabük
5) East	Adıyaman, Ağrı, Bingöl, Bitlis, Diyarbakır, Elazığ, Erzincan, Erzurum, Gümüşhane, Hakkari, Kars, Malatya, K. Maraş, Mardin, Muş, Siirt, Sivas, Tunceli, Şanlıurfa, Van, Bayburt, Batman, Şırnak, Ardahan, Iğdır

APPENDIX 5.4
14 REGION PROVINCES

14 Region and Provinces

West 1	Edirne, Istanbul, Kırklareli, Tekirdağ, Yalova
West 2	Balıkesir, Bursa, Çanakkale, Kocaeli, Sakarya
West 3	Aydın, Denizli, İzmir, Manisa
South 4	Antalya, Burdur, Isparta, Muğla
South 5	Adana, Gaziantep, Hatay, İçel, Kilis, Osmaniye
Central 6	Amasya, Çankırı, Çorum, Tokat, Yozgat
Central 7	Afyon, Bilecik, Eskişehir, Kütahya, Uşak
Central 8	Ankara, Bolu, Kayseri, Kırşehir, Konya, Nevşehir, Niğde, Aksaray, Karaman, Kırıkkale, Düzce
North 9	Artvin, Giresun, Ordu, Rize, Trabzon
North 10	Kastamonu, Samsun, Sinop, Zonguldak, Bartın, Karabük
East 11	Bitlis, Diyarbakır, Hakkari, Mardin, Siirt, Van, Batman, Şırnak
East 12	Ağrı, Bingöl, Erzurum, Kars, Muş, Ardahan, Iğdır
East 13	Adıyaman, Malatya, K. Maraş, Sivas, Şanlıurfa
East 14	Elazığ, Erzincan, Gümüşhane, Tunceli, Bayburt

Appendix 5.5
NUTS 1 (12 Regions) and NUTS 2 (26 Regions)

NUTS 1 – 12 Region

1) Istanbul	Istanbul
2) West Marmara	Balıkesir, Çanakkale, Edirne, Kırklareli, Tekirdağ
3) Aegean	Afyon, Aydın, Denizli, İzmir, Kütahya, Manisa, Muğla, Uşak
4) East Marmara	Bilecik, Bolu, Bursa, Eskişehir, Kocaeli, Sakarya, Yalova, Düzce
5) West Anatolia	Ankara, Konya, Karaman
6) Mediterranean	Adana, Antalya, Burdur, Hatay, Isparta, İçel, K.Maraş, Osmaniye
7) Central Anatolia	Kayseri, Kırşehir, Nevşehir, Niğde, Sivas, Yozgat, Aksaray, Kırıkkale
8) West Black Sea	Amasya, Çankırı, Çorum, Kastamonu, Samsun, Sinop, Tokat, Zonguldak, Bartın, Karabük
9) East Black Sea	Artvin, Giresun, Gümüşhane, Ordu, Rize, Trabzon
10) Northeast Anatolia	Ağrı, Erzincan, Erzurum, Kars, Bayburt, Ardahan, Iğdır
11) Central East Anatolia	Bingöl, Bitlis, Elazığ, Hakkari, Malatya, Muş, Tunceli, Van
12) Southeast Anatolia	Adıyaman, Diyarbakır, Gaziantep, Mardin, Siirt, Şanlıurfa, Batman, Şırnak, Kilis

Nuts 2 – 26 Region

1) Istanbul
2) Edirne, Kırklareli, Tekirdağ
3) Balıkesir, Çanakkale
4) İzmir
5) Aydın, Denizli, Muğla
6) Afyon, Kütahya, Manisa, Uşak
7) Bilecik, Bursa, Eskişehir
8) Bolu, Kocaeli, Sakarya, Yalova, Düzce
9) Ankara
10) Konya, Karaman
11) Antalya, Burdur, Isparta
12) Adana, İçel
13) Hatay, K. Maraş, Osmaniye
14) Kırşehir, Nevşehir, Niğde, Aksaray, Kırıkkale

15) Kayseri, Sivas, Yozgat
16) Zonguldak, Bartın, Karabük
17) Çankırı, Kastamonu, Sinop
18) Amasya, Çorum, Samsun, Tokat
19) Artvin, Giresun, Gümüşhane, Ordu, Rize, Trabzon
20) Erzincan, Erzurum, Bayburt
21) Ağrı, Kars, Ardahan, Iğdır
22) Bingöl, Elazığ, Malatya, Tunceli
23) Bitlis, Hakkari, Muş, Van
24) Adıyaman, Gaziantep, Kilis
25) Diyarbakır, Şanlıurfa
26) Mardin, Siirt, Batman, Şırnak

APPENDIX 5.6
MAPS

MAP 5.1
Emigration Rates (‰), 2000 Census Results, Turkey, Total

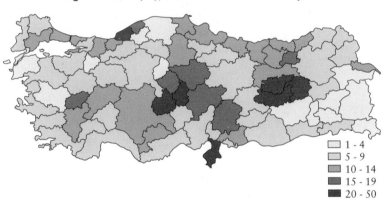

1 - 4
5 - 9
10 - 14
15 - 19
20 - 50

MAP 5.2
Emigration Rates (‰), 2000 Census Results, Turkey, Urban

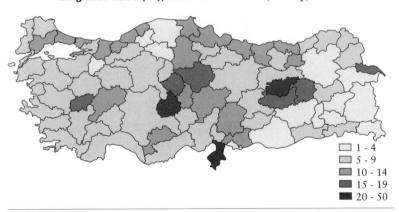

1 - 4
5 - 9
10 - 14
15 - 19
20 - 50

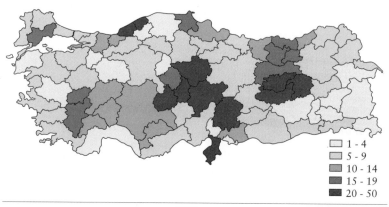

MAP 5.3
Emigration Rates (‰), 2000 Census Results, Turkey, Rural

□ 1 - 4
▨ 5 - 9
▨ 10 - 14
▨ 15 - 19
■ 20 - 50

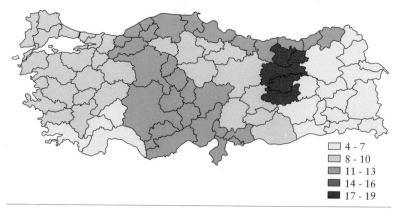

MAP 5.4
Emigration Rates (‰), 2000 Census Results, Turkey, 14 Region, Total

□ 4 - 7
▨ 8 - 10
▨ 11 - 13
■ 14 - 16
■ 17 - 19

MAP 5.5
Emigration Rates (‰), 2000 Census Results, Turkey, 14 Region, Urban

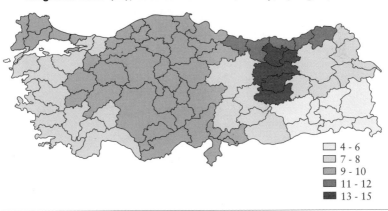

- 4 - 6
- 7 - 8
- 9 - 10
- 11 - 12
- 13 - 15

MAP 5.6
Emigration Rates (‰), 2000 Census Results, Turkey, 14 Region, Rural

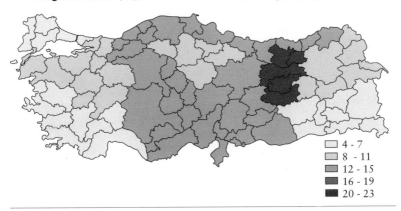

- 4 - 7
- 8 - 11
- 12 - 15
- 16 - 19
- 20 - 23

MAP 5.7
Emigration Rates (‰), 2000 Census Results,
Turkey, NUTS-1 Level (12 Region), Total

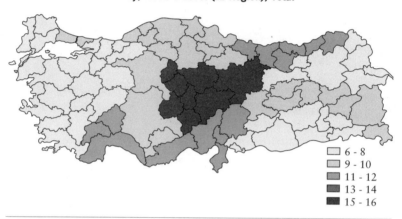

- ☐ 6 - 8
- ☐ 9 - 10
- ◼ 11 - 12
- ◼ 13 - 14
- ◼ 15 - 16

MAP 5.8
Emigration Rates (‰), 2000 Census Results,
Turkey, NUTS-1 Level (12 Region), Urban

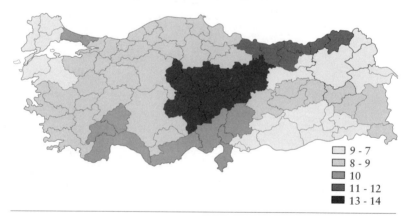

- ☐ 9 - 7
- ☐ 8 - 9
- ◼ 10
- ◼ 11 - 12
- ◼ 13 - 14

MAP 5.9
Emigration Rates (‰), 2000 Census Results,
Turkey, NUTS-1 Level (12 Region), Rural

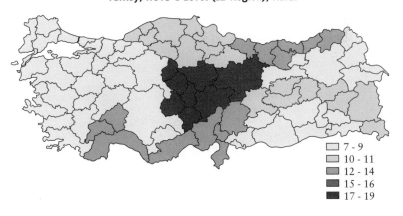

7 - 9
10 - 11
12 - 14
15 - 16
17 - 19

MAP 5.10
Emigration Rates (‰), 2000 Census Results,
Turkey, NUTS-2 Level (26 Region), Total

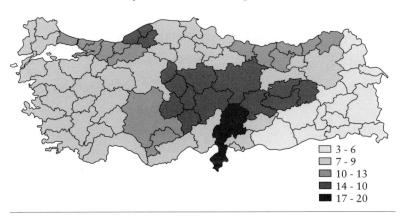

3 - 6
7 - 9
10 - 13
14 - 10
17 - 20

MAP 5.11
Emigration Rates (‰), 2000 Census Results,
Turkey, NUTS-2 Level (26 Region), Urban

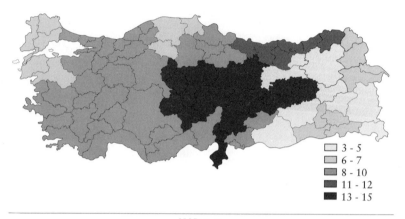

3 - 5
6 - 7
8 - 10
11 - 12
13 - 15

MAP 5.12
Emigration Rates (‰), 2000 Census Results,
Turkey, NUTS-2 Level (26 Region), Rural

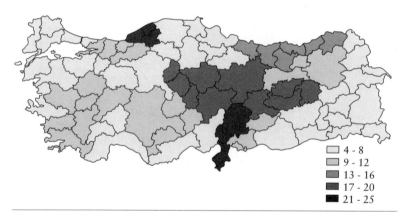

4 - 8
9 - 12
13 - 16
17 - 20
21 - 25

MAP 5.13
Household Emigration Rates (‰), 2000 Census Results, Turkey, Total

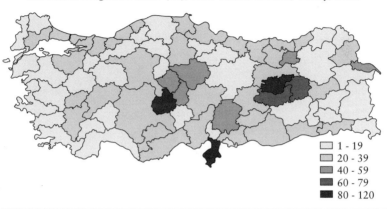

□	1 - 19
▨	20 - 39
▨	40 - 59
▨	60 - 79
■	80 - 120

MAP 5.14
Household Emigration Rates (‰), 2000 Census Results, Turkey, Urban

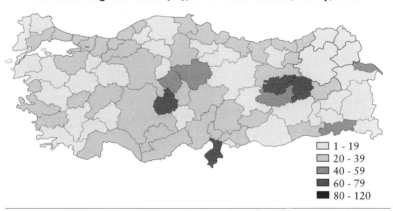

□	1 - 19
▨	20 - 39
▨	40 - 59
▨	60 - 79
■	80 - 120

MAP 5.15
Household Emigration Rates (‰), 2000 Census Results, Turkey, Rural

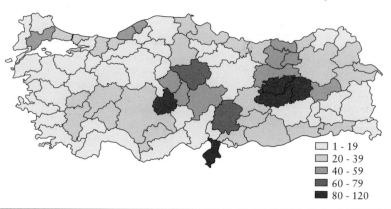

1 - 19
20 - 39
40 - 59
60 - 79
80 - 120

MAP 5.16
Household Emigration Rates (‰), 2000 Census Results, Turkey, 14 Region, Total

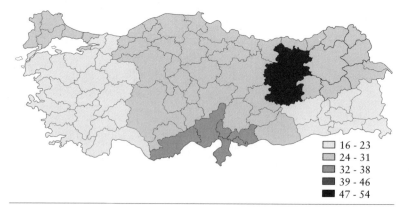

16 - 23
24 - 31
32 - 38
39 - 46
47 - 54

MAP 5.17
Household Emigration Rates (‰), 2000 Census Results, Turkey, 14 Region,
Urban

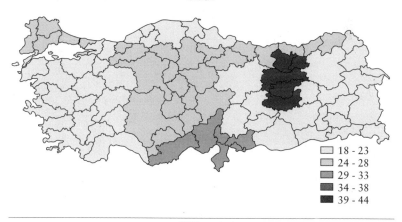

- 18 - 23
- 24 - 28
- 29 - 33
- 34 - 38
- 39 - 44

MAP 5.18
Household Emigration Rates (‰), 2000 Census Results, Turkey, 14 Region,
Rural

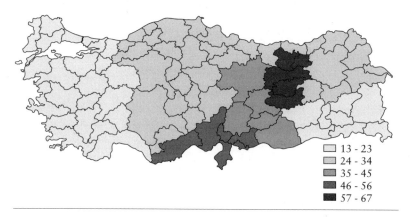

- 13 - 23
- 24 - 34
- 35 - 45
- 46 - 56
- 57 - 67

MAP 5.19
Household Emigration Rates (‰), 2000 Census Results,
Turkey, NUTS-1 Level (12 Region), Total

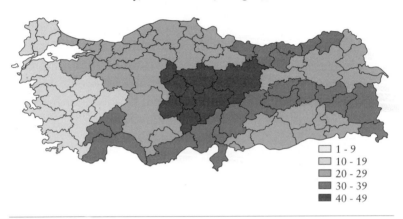

☐ 1 - 9
☐ 10 - 19
▨ 20 - 29
▨ 30 - 39
■ 40 - 49

MAP 5.20
Household Emigration Rates (‰), 2000 Census Results,
Turkey, NUTS-1 Level (12 Region), Urban

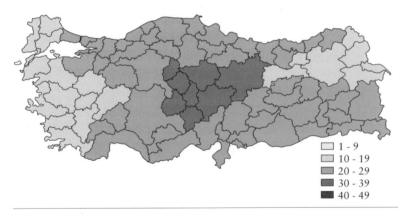

☐ 1 - 9
☐ 10 - 19
▨ 20 - 29
▨ 30 - 39
■ 40 - 49

MAP 5.21
Household Emigration Rates (‰), 2000 Census Results, Turkey, NUTS-1 Level (12 Region), Rural

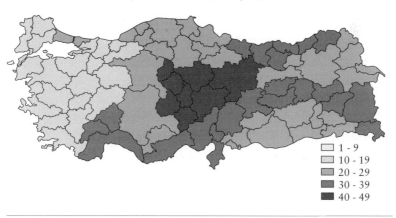

- ☐ 1 - 9
- ☐ 10 - 19
- ☐ 20 - 29
- ☐ 30 - 39
- ■ 40 - 49

MAP 5.22
Household Emigration Rates (‰), 2000 Census Results, Turkey, NUTS-2 Level (26 Region), Total

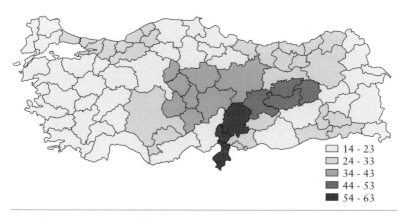

- ☐ 14 - 23
- ☐ 24 - 33
- ☐ 34 - 43
- ■ 44 - 53
- ■ 54 - 63

MAP 5.23
Household Emigration Rates (‰), 2000 Census Results,
Turkey, NUTS-2 Level (26 Region), Urban

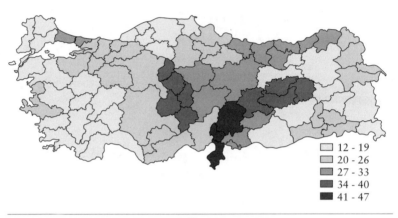

□ 12 - 19
▨ 20 - 26
▨ 27 - 33
▨ 34 - 40
■ 41 - 47

MAP 5.24
Household Emigration Rates (‰), 2000 Census Results,
Turkey, NUTS-2 Level (26 Region), Rural

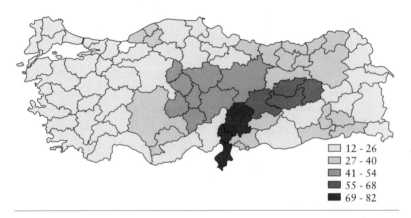

□ 12 - 26
▨ 27 - 40
▨ 41 - 54
▨ 55 - 68
■ 69 - 82

PART TWO

Immigration to Turkey

6

"Integration in Limbo": Iraqi, Afghan, Maghrebi and Iranian Migrants in Istanbul

A. Didem Danış, Cherie Taraghi
Jean-François Pérouse

INTRODUCTION[1]

Research Question

Turkey's position in migration systems has radically transformed due to the changes in the volume and modes of migration waves to and via the country. The last twenty-five years have witnessed the emergence of new regions of origin and new flows fuelled by the country's geographical position at the crossroads of Asia, the Middle East, and Europe (İçduygu, 2003). Migrants from politically turbulent and economically unstable non-European countries account for a very sizeable component of overall arrivals in Turkey. Most of these migrants have been kept out of the legal structure, due to the lack of any regularization of undocumented migrants and Turkey's geographical limitation in the Geneva Convention (Kirişci, 1996b). Despite this legal hindrance, the increasingly restrictive immigration policies of EU

---

1   A. Didem Danış. Lecturer, Sociology Department, Galatasaray University and Ph.D. candidate, Ecoles des Hautes Etudes en Sciences Sociales. Galatasaray University, Sociology Dept., Ciragan Cad. No.36, Ortakoy, 34357 Istanbul, Turkey. ddanis@gsu.edu.tr

countries result in the gathering of larger numbers of undocumented migrants in Turkey. However, there is a vacuum in terms of reception policies concerning migrants due to the limited financial and institutional capacities in Turkey. This lack of official reception mechanisms obliges migrants to seek their own ways of survival and incorporation, and they thus realize *a 'de facto* integration'.

The aim of our project is to investigate 'unofficial integration' models of four specific migrant groups in Istanbul, namely Iraqi, Afghan, Iranian and Maghrebi migrants (the latter includes Moroccan, Algerian, Tunisian and Libyan). We have chosen these four migrant groups because they are the most significant[2] nationalities among non-European migrants who do not have the right to settle in Turkey as a refugee due to the geographical limitation on Geneva Convention. We focus on how these four groups survive in an environment of extreme precariousness and on their mechanisms of incorporation into employment and housing markets. We analyze their patterns of networking and their struggle for economic and social inclusion in Istanbul.

In the following chapters, we depict group profiles and present the socio-economic characteristics of Iraqi, Afghan, Iranian and Maghrebi migrants in Istanbul, without disregarding fluidity and elusiveness among the categories related to migrants' status. The vagueness between the boundaries of these categories complicates the job of the researcher. One of our solutions for overcoming this difficulty was to focus on each group's migration history. In this manner, we tried to discern characteristics of 'flow diversities' as well as the impact of a migratory past and status on migrants' integration patterns. Additionally, we scrutinize social networks that the migrants benefit from to find employment and accommodation, since they constitute the main resource for these migrants. We thus aim to reveal the patterns of unofficial integration of Iraqi, Afghan, Iranian and Maghrebi

---

2   The only source to evaluate their demographic significance is the statistics provided by General Directorate of Security Forces (see Table 1.1).

migrants in Istanbul and to contribute to the international literature by bringing to light the example of these overlooked groups and their conditions of sojourn.

TABLE 6.1

Irregular Migrants Apprehended by Turkish Security Forces During 1995-2001

Country of Origin	1995	1996	1997	1998	1999	2000	2001	Total
Iraq	2,128	3,319	5,689	14,237	11,546	17,280	23,444	77,643
Iran	252	362	364	1,116	5,281	6,825	8,504	22,704
Afghanistan	24	68	81	921	3,046	8,476	9,542	22,158
Maghreb (total)	58	126	243	366	547	2,086	2,631	9,126
Algeria	27	25	69	207	102	430	429	1,289
Morocco	28	53	93	295	369	1,401	1,905	7,033
Tunisia	3	48	81	44	76	255	297	804
Libya	NA	NA	NA	NA	NA	NA	NA	NA

Source: Ahmet İçduygu (2003). *Irregular Migration in Turkey*, IOM Migration research series, p.25 (based on data provided by General Directorate of Security Forces, Bureau for Foreigners, Borders and Asylum).

Among undocumented migrants in Turkey, the Iraqis have been the most populous group for the last decade. The Iraqi migration to Turkey started during the Iran–Iraq War with individual cases, and later continued with massive refugee flows during the 1991 Gulf War. The three main Iraqi groups in Turkey are Kurds, Turkmens and Assyro-Chaldean Christians. Kurds and Christians are mostly irregular transit migrants whose stay in Turkey ranges from a few months to a decade. Unlike them, Turkmens are more permanent due to their 'Turkish origin'; they could obtain residence permits relatively easily until recent years, and thus there emerged a small but established Turkmen community in the country.

Afghan migration to Turkey commenced during the early 1980s after the Russian invasion of Afghanistan and the downfall of the monarchic regime. A limited number of Afghan migrants were officially invited to live in Turkey by the Turkish government in the early 1980s. These were Afghans of Uzbek and Turkmen ethnicity, who already spoke the Turkish language and shared a common Turkish heritage. These individuals were officially settled in various regions of the country, however many selected an internal migratory route and chose to live in the city of Istanbul. Aside from these official migrants, there is a group of Afghans, mainly composed of younger, single men or single female-headed families, who apply to the United Nations High Commissioner for Refugees (UNHCR) and focus effort upon third country resettlement. There is also a group of Afghans, mainly men, who have either not applied to the UNHCR, and therefore lack status in the country, or who have applied and been rejected status thus slipping into an unofficial status, lacking necessary documents for a legal stay in the country.

Maghrebis (here we are speaking about a 'Great Maghreb', ranging from Libya to Morocco) have a triple presence in Istanbul. First of all, there has been an increase in the number of Maghrebi who use Turkey as a temporary home on their way to Europe, which can be observed in the statistics showing apprehended, clandestine migrants (see **Table 6.1**). Second, there is the Maghrebi 'suitcase trade'. The Maghrebi are among the pioneers of shuttle traders who started the business of trading in spare parts back in the 1970s and 1980s in Istanbul's Yenikapı district. Finally, there are professional niches filled by the Maghrebi who serve as an interface between suit-case traders and Turkish economic actors. Concurrently, there is a Moroccan nanny network, particularly within the French or French-speaking families of Istanbul.

Iranian migration started after the fall of the monarchic regime and large numbers of Iranians transited to Europe via Turkey. Currently there are two predominant groups of Iranians in Istanbul: a small established community that acquired Turkish citizenship or permanent residence permits on the one hand, and the Iranian asylum seekers, mostly of religious and ethnic minorities on the other. There are also Iranian cyclical migrants who take part in the suitcase trade.

Terminology

We first need to clarify some terminological points since there are diverse expressions utilized to describe 'undocumented migrants'. Academics and Non Governmental Organizations (NGO) prefer to use terms such as 'irregular', 'illegalized' or 'illegally resident/working immigrant', whereas state authorities draw more on the term 'illegal'. In this discussion, we utilize the term 'undocumented' or 'irregular', even though these migrants have very often been depicted by the press and security forces as clandestine or illegal migrants. During our fieldwork, the irregularity of the migrants that we encountered was generally related to the absence of work and residence permits. Actually, very few migrants are involved in real criminal activities. For this reason, we refrain from using the term 'illegal' in order to wipe out a connection with criminality.

> In the words of Nobel Peace Prize winner, Elie Wiesel, *"There is no such thing as an illegal human being"*, human beings can be tall, short, rich or poor, but not illegal. The term of illegal immigrant also subconsciously suggests a close linkage to criminality, which stokes fears among local populations. (Italic in the original, Hofbauer, 2005: 16)

For this reason, in our research we utilize 'undocumented migrant' or 'irregular migrant' as interchangeable terms to represent foreign nationals who stay and work in Turkey without having the necessary official permits for residence and work.

Design and Methodology

Undocumented migration in Turkey is a new field that has rarely been sociologically analyzed.. Except for a few important studies which usually approach the subject with a macro perspective (İçduygu, 1996, 2003, 2004; Kirişci, 1996, 2000; Erder, 2000; Erder and Kaşka, 2003), there is a serious lack of ethnographic studies on foreign migrant groups. Our field research on the *de facto* integration mechanisms of non-European undocumented migrants intends to contribute to the literature and fill this analytic gap. Despite the earnestness of this intention, we should openly state that it is not an easy task to fulfill. One of the major difficulties is related to methodological problems. First of all, little is known about the social and demographic characteristics or economic behaviors of undocumented foreign migrants, especially those from non-European countries, although they represent a significant proportion of foreigners in the country. Even the most rudimentary demographic information on these groups is either lacking or inconsistent. The only statistical source we do have about the size of these groups is provided by the Bureau for Foreigners, Borders, and Asylum of the General Security Directorate of the Ministry of Interior. Unsurprisingly, the collection and distribution of these statistics are shaped according to various concerns (see the section below for the discussion on the accuracy and reliability of the statistical information about irregular migration in Turkey).

The absence of precise information about the immense source from which we are supposed to choose our sample leads us to use snowball sampling. This method is especially suitable for explorative studies and in situations where there is a scarcity of knowledge about the field. It is useful in cases where it is not possible to determine an exemplary quota to choose the sample. Last but not least, the snowball sampling method is particularly convenient and meaningful when working out the problem of confidence that emerges due to the tenuous status of the interviewees.

Undocumented migrants are vulnerable groups that are trying to survive in precariousness. In some cases, they are suffering stigmatization and are often perceived as 'illegal' persons. The fact that they do not have the required papers to stay and work in the country creates a constant fear of 'foreigners'. The snowball sampling method helps the researcher to overcome the anxiety of the interviewees and facilitates entry into groups. Our first step in using this method was to find out 'entry points' or 'hooks' to be able to penetrate into our specific migrant groups. In some cases, these entry points have been migrant neighborhoods such as Zeytinburnu (for the Afghans), whereas in others we started at the places of economic activity, such as Laleli-Aksaray or Osmanbey (in particular for the Maghrebi and Iraqi Turkmens). We also used some associations (for the Iraqi and Afghan Turkmen and Iraqi Kurd) and churches (for the Iraqi Assyro-Chaldeans) to make the first step into their groups. In most cases, an introduction by a community cohort helped to alleviate migrants' fears and resulted in a relatively smooth internal acceptance. In short, snowball sampling has been our main instrument to overcome the greatest research challenge: that of gaining acceptance by the migrant groups.[3]

After we made contact with migrants, we conducted semi-structured face-to-face interviews using open-ended questions. We did more than one hundred forty in-depth interviews. Given the variation in the sizes of the four migrant groups, we conducted around seventy interviews with Iraqis, forty with Afghans, twenty with Maghrebis, and ten with Iranians. The interviews were conducted in neighborhoods that are mostly inhabited by foreign migrants, such as Aksaray-Laleli, Zeytinburnu, Tarlabasi-Dolapdere, and Osmanbey in Istanbul. These localities appeal to irregular migrants due to the predominance of informal economy and an abundance of low-skilled jobs in textile and leather shops. They also provide the possibility of a more permanent shelter to a wide variety of migrants. In addition to these interviews, we conducted a number of case studies in order to deepen our knowledge on the details of everyday life and personal stories. We also benefited from the ethnographic method of observing human interactions in their social settings and activities. We believe that the open-ended questions of in-depth interviews allowed us to discover the nature of these migrant populations in Turkey and their ways of socio-economic incorporation.

---

3   It is worth mentioning that while this method has functioned quite well in some groups, such as Iraqi Turkmen and Christians or Afghans, it did not suffice for creating an atmosphere of confidence in more precarious groups, such as Iraqi Kurds or some Maghrebi groups.

During the interviews, each researcher benefited from his/her specific resources in order to get in contact with the migrants. An important obstacle shared by each researcher was the difficulty to wipe out the fog of suspicion that prevails among undocumented migrants. Most of them were afraid of talking to 'researchers', whose work was unclear and dubious to them. We had to explain our objectives repeatedly in order to convince them that we were not working for security forces. At that point, we tried to bring our various 'capital assets' into play to access the migrant world, as migrants do to facilitate their incorporation into the receiving society. Cherie Taraghi had the advantage of speaking Farsi and Dari as well as having Iranian origins to help create an environment of confidence. Being a 'foreigner' and speaking their same languages, (even though she mostly spoke Turkish), she could easily build a bridge of trust. Thus she made her first contacts while wandering the streets of Zeytinburnu, and subsequently visited the houses of these persons. To enter into the field was relatively easier for Jean-François Pérouse, since he had previously undertaken a research project on Mahgrebi suitcase traders a few years ago. He held new interviews thanks to his old contacts in Laleli and Aksaray, yet some national groups were more difficult to build a connection with. Despite the facilitating factor of the French language shared by the researcher and the interviewees, some Maghrebi migrants, in particular those who intend to cross into Greece clandestinely, were aloof and unapproachable. Unlike Taraghi and Pérouse, A. Didem Danış did not share linguistic contact with her respondents. In addition, her Turkish citizenship has been a disadvantage in building confidence, except for amongst Turkmens. For each Iraqi subgroup she looked for specific entry points: the Turkmen Association, Kurdish persons of Turkish nationality, and the head of the Turkish Chaldean Church (for the last one, she had established contacts in late 2003). After building these links, she was able to conduct interviews at the houses or workplaces of Iraqi migrants, in various localities of Istanbul, including Tarlabaşı, Dolapdere, Elmadağ and Kurtuluş for

Iraqi Christians, Aksaray, Laleli and Osmanbey for Turkmens, and Tarlabaşı and Aksaray for Kurds.

Another difficulty shared by all researchers was misunderstandings about our research. Even after we had built confidence, some migrants remained convinced that we were working for the UNHCR or some other migrant associations that came to the field 'for choosing the ones to be granted acceptance'. In some cases, their desperate search for any sign of hope had also affected us psychologically. In such cases, we sometimes refrained from asking our standard questions so as to make them believe that we were not working for a migrant organization.

During the field research, we tried to reach a saturation level in order to assure that our groups were adequately representative. Thus we conducted interviews until we began to garner similar responses to our questions. In each interview, we tried to ask questions about the characteristics of the migrant's group, so as to increase our knowledge about each migrant group. In each following chapter, we present data on the migratory patterns and the approximate size of migration flows of each migrant population. Nevertheless, we do not go into a detailed statistical study; rather, we use statistics provided by the General Security Directorate and Turkish researchers. By combining quantitative information based on secondary sources with our in-depth analysis rooted in qualitative survey and ethnographic methodologies, we try to portray profiles of each migrant group.

The interviews with these four groups are composed of three main sections:

1. Migrant profile: The objective of this first section is to identify the group profile of each migrant community in order to observe the impact of migratory experience on socio-economic incorporation. We thus explored the socio-economic, ethnic, and religious characteristics of migrant groups in order to examine the social borders; the markers of exclusion and inclusion in these four populations. Whenever possible, we also asked questions on basic demographic characteristics.

2. Migration history and further migration plans: For this section, we gathered information about the migratory journey by asking questions such as why and how migrants left their homeland, why they chose Turkey, the ways they used to arrive in Istanbul (visas, passports, transportation modes, etc), individuals who accompanied them during the journey, and so on. The objective is to present itineraries, patterns, and modes of migration. We also inquired about their intentions concerning the continuation of their migration journey. Which countries do they prefer to settle in and why, which methods do they plan to use (official applications for refugee status and family migration or irregular methods, such as smuggling), and whether they have relatives in these countries, are among the questions asked. Here, we try to see the impact of social networks on the further migration plans.

3. Living status / integration possibility in Istanbul: In this section we attempt to understand how the migrant and his/her household members experience the migration process and temporary or permanent stay in Istanbul. Questions about previous and current accommodation and employment conditions (where they work, how they find jobs, employer-employee relations, and whether work conditions affect their familial setting) are raised in order to investigate migrants' survival strategies in situations of extreme precariousness. The findings of this section are used to evaluate various capitals (social, economic or human) migrants have and the social networks they build.

In addition to these semi-structured interviews, we interviewed some officials, such as the representatives of the UNHCR in Istanbul, representatives of the Foreigners' Department of the Ministry of Interior Affairs and various NGOs working specifically on transit migrant groups including the Helsinki Citizens' Assembly-Refugee Bureau, IIMP, Caritas, and the ICMC. These officials allowed us to see structural factors, such as legal and political attitudes that affect the performance of migrant networks and integration. In addition, we benefited from the news archives at the French Anatolian Studies Institute (IFEA).

Theoretical Significance

Incorporation of Migrants in Developing Countries

The integration of migrants in developing countries is a neglected area of study. Integration literature is almost exclusively concerned with the cases of migrants in Western final settlement areas (Van Hear, 1998, Faist, 2000). The few studies thus far on undocumented migrants' incorporation into developing countries have been conducted on the African continent (Sommers, 2000; Dick, 2002; Lindstrom, 2003). Given the high ratio of refugee and migrant populations in various developing countries, the case of undocumented or 'transit'[4] migrants necessitates a thorough analysis of the subject.

The existence of abundant research conducted on migrant integration in final destinations provides a starting point for our theoretical framework. According to Maja Korac (2001) there are two main theoretical approaches to conceptualize integration: race relations and minorities' literature on the one hand, and refugee studies on the other. These two approaches are distinguished on the basis of cultural integration contrasting with structural and institutional integration models. The former describes integration as "the process of change that occurs when two groups of different cultures are in some way forced to co-exist in one society" (Korac, 2001: 31). This cultural perspective focuses on issues such as acculturation, identity and belonging (Berry, 1997), whereas the latter's emphasis is on the practical or functional aspects of refugee settlement (Brink, 1997). The focus of the structural integration model is on social protections provided to refugees. Maja Korac specifies assistance in housing, language training, education and re-training, and access to the labor market as main areas of social protection offered by state agencies.

In our project we conceive integration by focusing on its practi-

---

4   As we observe in many cases, most of the irregular migrants claim to be in transit in Istanbul, even though this 'temporary' transit period lasts sometimes over five years or consists of cyclical journeys.

cal and structural aspects, rather than cultural elements. In other words, we concentrate on the access to employment and housing markets as indicators of social participation in the wider society. Non-European migrants in Turkey face serious difficulties during their stay in Turkey, including multi-faceted vulnerability. Social and economic problems, as well as legal exclusion (being status-less), worsen their conditions.

Irregular migrants in developing countries are unlikely to receive official assistance provided to refugees and migrants in the West. Similarly, Turkey does not provide any kind of formal assistance to migrants, except for some very basic aid provided to recognized refugees. The lack of a government-based integration policy and the limits of available help by the UNHCR leave very few options for migrants in Turkey. Thus migrants must rely upon their own resources – be this the material resources which they brought with them, their physical body as a means to work, their educational background, or the housing and employment networks established by fellow religious, ethnic or national cohorts.

In the absence of official assistance for integration, there occurs a '*de facto integration*', a term that we borrow from Karen Jacobsen (2001). Non-European migrants construct and benefit from social networks to overcome their socio-economic difficulties and to supply their basic needs. Migrants mobilize various social capitals (ethnic, religious, and so on) to activate *de facto integration*. Despite the positive connotations of the term, it should also be reminded that *de facto integration* often construes a partial and incomplete incorporation. Social networks that foster such incorporation are bounded by social and legal limitations and are reliant upon external factors, such as police keeping a closed eye to the workshops where irregular workers are employed, sectarian peace permitting the functioning of informal schooling at religiously oriented associations.

The *de facto integration* of non-European migrants in Istanbul depends on the capacity of their social capital. Migrants' social capital used for entering into the core society can be distinguished as bridging or bonding, as expressed by Putnam (2000). Bridging social capital includes networks that link migrants with the wider society and bonding social capital enhances the communication and solidarity of migrants with each other. Bridging social capital is of considerable importance in the job search, and illustrates the crippling strength of weak ties in securing employment (Granovetter, 1974).

Micheal Piore's pioneer book *Birds of Passage: Migrant Labor and Industrial Societies* (1980) provides an analytical framework for the fractional integration of migrants.[5] His dual 'labor market assumption' places migrants within the secondary labor market, whereas skilled unionized native workers fill the primary market. His theory is instructive when trying to grasp the diversification in the labor markets; however his clear-cut separation between primary and secondary markets, as well as native and migrant laborers is too narrow to conceptualize the diversity in current employment markets. In order to develop the dual labor market theory, we suggest a model based on *fractional integration*. Migrants who mobilize distinct social capital are inserted into specific social niches in the receiving society. The concept of 'segmented assimilation' by Portes & Zhou (1993), which we choose to read as '*segmented incorporation*', provides a useful analytical tool to understand different patterns of foreigners' insertion into Turkish society. As Portes & Zhou claim, migrant incorporation is not a 'straight-line progression', but it is a process that often leads to multiple endpoints. Non-European migrants in Istanbul exhibit a 'segmented incorporation' in terms of their occupational as well as residential incorporation. Thus we observe uneven clustering of the migrants both in the economic and spatial distribution of the city. This is certainly an unequal and hierarchical incorporation because of the differences in the content and impact of the 'bridges' (i.e. mediating agents) which influence the success of the migrants' incorporation process.

---

5   I am grateful to Nermin Abadan Unat who brought Piore's dual labor market approach to my attention.

Social Networks

Social ties are an important factor that migrants benefit from in difficult times. Social networks of migrants form channels facilitating the migration process and relieving the burdens of it, and is one of the topics being studied in full measure by international migration scholars (Kearney, 1986; Brettel, 2000).

The earliest studies about migrants' networks focus on the role of social networks in sustaining the continuation of migration after it started out, and increasing the likelihood of mobility of non-migrants (Massey et.al., 1993). Aside from this, Massey and his colleagues assert the advantages of having some kind of familial or amicable affiliation which brings a significant social capital owing to the familial and friendship values that compel the migrant to provide support to newcomers (Massey et.al., 1993: 448). Various researches conducted in this field also attest to the facilitating and encouraging role of the migrant networks (Gurak & Caces, 1992; Böcker, 1995; Pessar, 1999; Boyd, 1989). Nevertheless, what is lacking in the overall social networks approach is a focus on the role of networks built and used by migrants during their stay in transit countries.

Vertovec (2002: 3-4) notes that social networks benefited by migrants vary according to local history, national circumstances and common socio-cultural features of the groups. In our case, two main components that play a significant role in the migrants' networks are the existing social diversity in Istanbul and various social capital that migrants do have. The social and economic heterogeneity in Istanbul, which came about due to the influence of internal and international migrations, provides the necessary milieu to nourish various social networks. Thus new foreign migrants find a prolifically heterogeneous environment to build special niches for themselves or to link with already built niches. What facilitates their access to these niches is the various social capital they have or they construct.

There are various sources of social capital used to build social networks in the host society: familial, social, religious or ethnic ties are mobilized to create networks in/with the host society. First and foremost, there are familial networks even though some family members become impoverished in the course of migration. Still, for many migrants familial ties furnish the primary support for the exigencies of survival and incorporation in Istanbul. Family is the principal source of assistance and relief for almost all migrants, regardless of the national, ethnic, religious or economic status. In cases where migrants lose contact with their family members, either because of ongoing violence in their home country or lack of communication facilities, material and psychological endurance becomes harder.

An important capital for some migrants is related to the ethnic affiliations. For instance, having a 'Turkish origin' turns to a precious capital thanks to the 1934 Law of Settlement which states that only persons of 'Turkish descent and culture' have the right to immigrate and find refuge in Turkey. It is clear that being Turcophone becomes important capital in Turkey thanks to this law. Nevertheless, ethnic capital is not a fixed resource: the category of migrants 'having Turkish descent' is very vague and migrants of Turkish origin are treated differently in distinct periods, as will be seen in the chapter on the Iraqi Turkmen.

Ethnic affiliation is not always a constructive social capital, as is clear in the case of Kurds from Iraq or Iran. Unreceptive policies of Turkish authorities towards Kurdish undocumented migrants seem to affect the effectiveness of their networking mechanisms. Another factor that influences the weakness of Kurdish ethnic networks is the disadvantaged status of local Kurds in Istanbul. Internal Kurds, who came to Istanbul with the involuntary migration waves of the 1980s and 1990s, are dwelling in inner city slums, such as Tarlabaşı, where poverty and deprivation prevail. Impoverishment during this traumatic migration together with their lack of educational credentials and professional competence in an urban setting seem to dissolve all kinds of possibilities for building a basis of solidarity with Iraqi or Iranian Kurds.

Another basis of network formation is related to the linguistic capital. Knowledge of local language creates a sense of cultural familiarity with the receiving society and helps to emphasize the 'ethnic closeness'. Typical examples are the Iraqi Turkmen, Iranian Azeri or Afghan Turkmen who, thanks to their linguistic skills, i.e. Turkish comprehension, become incorporated relatively easily. The advantages that linguistic capital brings are not limited to Turkish language. Knowledge of the Arabic language becomes a linguistic competence for migrants. This is true in particular for the persons working in the re-flourishing shuttle trade, which is increasingly attracting clients from Arab countries, mainly from Maghreb, and recently from Iraq. The case of Mardinli and Iraqi Turkmen, two Arabic speaking migrant groups with different migration pasts, is interesting in this sense, as they are the two biggest competitors in Laleli and Osmanbey in attracting Arabic speaking clientele.

Last but not least we need to discuss religious ties that benefit undocumented migrants. In terms of religious networks, non-Muslim, and in particular Christian, networks seem to be function better than other religious ties. Contact to various local Christian communities and organizations provides a basis of networking for some groups, such as Iraqi Assyro-Chaldeans and Iranian Christians. However, it is worth mentioning that these church organizations are often constrained in their effort to assist migrants because of the tacit concerns of the national political bodies.

The American literature on migrant incorporation provides us with some fruitful theoretical tools. Being an ancient country of immigration, there have been several studies on migrant integration in the United States since the 1920s. The early concepts, such as assimilation, that were introduced by Robert Park and Milton Gordon, were later criticized, and there then occurred four major shifts in the American immigrant incorporation theory in the last decades, which we think is illuminating for our research, too:

1) A shift from focusing on immigrants and their efforts to adapt to their new environment, toward focusing on the interaction between immigrants and the structure of American society. 2) A shift from an undifferentiated and amorphous conceptualization of the latter to one that takes into account existing economic (in particular labor market) ethnic and class structures and inequalities. 3) A shift from focusing primarily on cultural variables to emphasizing structural/economic variables, that is, the conditions of labor markets and the skills of immigrants. 4) A shift from a single model identifying various steps and stages in the process of incorporation (i.e. assimilation) to the coexistence of several models, projecting a variety of conditions and possible outcomes (Schmitter and Heisler, 2000: 79).

The theoretical tools developed by the American incorporation scholars draw attention to the importance of studying the interaction between migrants and the receiving society and emphasize the role of structural factors to understand migrant incorporation. They also warn us about the incorrectness of attributing a homogenous, monolithic character to migrant groups or to the host society. In order to better grasp the interaction between the migrants and receiving society, we need to discern changes of the migration waves, reception policies and attitudes towards migrants. Below we first focus on changing migratory patterns and how the recent migrants are perceived and received in Turkey. Then we present the socio-spatial and economic setting that migrants face in their arrival and during their incorporation in Turkey.

Changing Patterns of Migration Waves To Turkey

'Muhacirs': Welcomed Migrants of the Nation-State Formation Era

Turkey has a long history of immigration, even though it is known in the West as an emigration country. During the retreat of the Ottoman Empire from the territories in the Balkans, Caucuses and the Middle East, there have been many Turkish-speaking or Muslim people who migrated to Istanbul and Anatolia (McCarthy, 1983 and

2001). Emigrations from former Ottoman territories into the new Turkish state continued significantly in the early Republican period (Danış & Pérouse, 2005). According to the government statistics provided by Kemal Kirişci (1996) more than 1.6 million persons immigrated to Turkey from 1923 to 1997. Most of these immigrants were from Greece, Bulgaria, Yugoslavia and Romania; in other words, from territories that were once part of the Ottoman Empire, as seen in the Table 6.2. Kirişci (2000) argues that the migration policies of the young Turkish state intended to create a homogeneous population out of an ethnically and culturally heterogeneous Ottoman population. To realize this objective new administrators gave priority to immigrants having a Muslim and/or Turkish background. During this formal reception period groups who were most welcomed were the ones which were supposed to easily melt into a Turkish identity. Thus, Albanians, Bosnians, Circassians, Pomaks, and Tatars from the Balkans were embraced whereas ethnic and religious groups such as the Gagauz Turks (Turkish speaking Christians in Moldova) were not encouraged to immigrate to Turkey (Kirişci, 2000).

TABLE 6.2
Immigration from the Balkans Between 1923 and 1960

Country of origin	Approximate number
Greece	480,000
Bulgaria	374,000
Yugoslavia	269,000
Romania	121,000
Total	1,244,000

Source: Akgündüz 1998: 112.

Sema Erder (2000) reminds us of the significance of the term *'muhacir'* to demonstrate the differences between the government-supported migrations which continued until the 1970s, and the recent irregular migrations into Turkey. Whether *iskânlı* or *iskânsız*, the muhacirs of those years were warmly welcomed and relatively easily incorporated into Turkish society. The incorporation of *muhacirs* was facilitated by various arrangements. First of all, on the legal level, newcomers were easily granted Turkish citizenship. On the economic level, resettlement of *iskânlı* was assisted by the authorities and they were assigned farmland and houses. This mostly prevailed for the ones who arrived as a result of the Greek-Turkish population exchange of 1922-1924. The *İskânsız* did not benefit from government-assistance for their resettlement, yet they could bring into play familial and social networks, mostly interwoven around having common homeland origins. Another factor that contributed to the smooth incorporation was the social and demographic diversity that predominated during the years of *muhacirs* arrivals. Zürcher (2003) indicates that "at the time the Republic of Turkey was founded in 1923, over twenty percent of its population had a *muhacir* background". Compared to newcomers in recent years, the migrants of those early Republican years could incorporate relatively smoothly into the highly heterogeneous society.

Non-European Undocumented Migrants in Istanbul

There has occurred a striking shift in the immigration history of Turkey in the early 1980s when new migrant and refugee groups poured into Turkey in unexpected volumes. Unlike the migrants of early Republican years, most of the post-1980 migrants were 'uninvited' and unwelcome. One of the reasons for this unreceptive attitude was related to the fact that Turkish authorities were not willing to receive any more migrants, even Turkish and/or Muslim ones, since they believed that population growth in Turkey has reached its optimum and there was not anymore land to distribute to newcomers (Apap et al., 2005: 33). However, these new population movements were triggered by factors over which the authorities did not have great control: Dissolution of the Cold War brought about a global political and social turnover. The destabilization of political equilibriums in the Balkans and the Middle East resulted in the massive and continuous emigration from these regions. Refugee and migratory waves related to political disorder affected Turkey as well. Beginning with the 1979 Iranian Islamic Revolution, followed by the 1980 Soviet invasion of Afghanistan, the 1980-88 Iran-Iraq War, the 1988 Halabja massacre, the 1989 Bulgarian mistreatment of its Turkish-speaking citizens, the 1991 Gulf War, wars in Bosnia (1992), in Kosovo (1999 and 2001) and lastly the American invasion of Iraq in 2003, the last two and half decades have been characterized by constant political and social instability for Eastern, as well as Western neighbors of Turkey (Corliss, 2003). The result was massive and sudden forced migration. In most cases, population movements that begun as abrupt, forced migration flows, helped to build new migrant networks that facilitated emigration of potential migrants in the homeland. The asylum movements continued later on as irregular transit migration.

The irregular migration transiting via Turkey towards Europe has been a hot issue of discussion between Turkish and EU authorities. Especially in the late 1990s and 2000s, Turkey appeared as a major route of irregular migration towards Europe. The agenda on migration and asylum issues in EU have concentrated on curbing irregular migration towards EU member states. One of the main methods employed by the EU to fight against these movements has been pressuring neighboring countries to strengthen their border controls against undocumented crossings. Among many, the European Council Presidency meeting in Seville during 21-22 June 2002 witnessed bitter discussions on the subject; in this instance Turkey was severely criticized for not effectively controlling its borders (Danış, 2004). The massive pressure of EU countries to prevent irregular transit migration via Turkey has included demands such as improvement of border controls, construction of reception centers, and the signing of readmission agreements with countries of origin as well as with the EU (Gresh, 2005).

In spite of the hot debate on how to control and manage irregular migration, we still do not have precise information on the amount of irregular migration in Turkey. All the numbers given are only estimates. For instance, Kemal Kirişci argues that the number of irregular migrants in Turkey varies between 150,000 and 1 million, whereas Nilüfer Narlı estimates a population of 4.5 million irregular foreigners in 2003 (cited by Gresh, 2005: 13). Ahmet İçduygu (2003) highlights the difficulty of calculating the volume of irregular migration flows due to its complexity and overlapping categories. The difficulty of this calculation is also related to statistical manipulations of different interest groups, as mentioned by Michael Jandl:

> Despite these strong arguments for the production of more reliable estimations, in most European countries policy-making in the area of illegal migration is based on guesswork and rumors rather than sophisticated methods of estimation. Moreover, all actors in the field of illegal migration have their own interests in producing certain numbers on illegal migration. Some may deliberately overstate the size of their estimates; others may want to understate it. In the best case, this will render policies on illegal migration merely irrelevant. In the worst case, the lack of reliable information will lead to misguided policies that will aggravate the problem (Jandl, cited by Gresh, 2005: 11).

The only exact figures that we have about undocumented migration in Turkey are the statistics provided by the Turkish Security Directorate regarding foreigners apprehended for being irregularly present in the country. According to the figures presented on the website of the General Security Directorate, half a million foreigners have been arrested by police between 1995 and 2004 (see **Table 6.3**).

The numbers of irregular migrants apprehended by the authorities steadily increased until their numbers peaked in 2000 with almost 95,000. Since then the there has been a downward trend with the number of apprehended migrants falling to 56,219 in 2003. In addition to the decrease in the trend of irregular migration via Turkey there is also a transformation in the country of origin of undocumented migrants since 2001. While the number of undocumented migrants from the Middle Eastern countries has decreased, the share of citizens from former Soviet republics has increased (see **Table 6.4**).

TABLE 6.3
Irregular Migrants Arrested by Turkish Authorities

1995	11,362
1996	18,804
1997	28,439
1998	29,426
1999	47,529
2000	94,514
2001	92,364
2002	82,325
2003	56,219
2004 (until 22.9.2004)	31,686

Source: General Security Directorate, Foreigners' Bureau. http://www.egm.gov.tr/yabancilar/default.htm

TABLE 6.4
Beakdown of Irregular Migrants Arrested by Turkish Security Forces Between 1995 and June 2004 by Their Nationalities

Countries	The Number of People
Afghanistan	28,911
Bangladesh	13,418
Pakistan	28,442
Iran	22,199
Iraq	99,402
Syria	50,18
Sub-total	197,390
North Africa	9,397
Former Soviet Republics*	100,018
Central Asian Countries**	6,473
Albania	3,988
Bulgaria	9,111
Romania	19,067
Turkey	24,419
Others	107,986
Total	477,849

(*)   Former Soviet Republics: Russia, Ukraine, Moldova, Georgia, Azerbaijan, Armenia, Belarus, Lithuania, Latvia, Estonia.

(**)   Central Asia Countries: Kyrgyzstan, Kazakhstan, Turkmenistan, Uzbekistan, Tajikistan

Source: J. Apap, S. Carrera and K. Kirişci (2005: 34) Data obtained from the Foreigners Department of MOI.

Based on the sizes of irregular migration flows, Ahmet İçduygu (2005) distinguishes four periods of the irregular migration trends in Turkey. According to him, the first period takes place between 1979 and 1987 and is called a 'fertilization period'. Secondly, in 1988-1993 there is a 'maturation period', followed by a 'saturation period' in 1994-2000/2001. And lastly, since 2001 there occurs a 'degeneration period' due to the decrease in the number of irregular migrants entering Turkey. Despite the significance of such a categorization based on the quantity of irregular migrants, we believe that it is necessary to nourish this periodization with the social, political, and legal background of these flows. For instance, as will be seen in the following chapters, from the undocumented migrants' perspective, the recent years seem to be more of a maturation period rather than degeneration in the sense that migrants have improved their contacts with the host society.

Debates about the number of irregular migrants highlight the importance of constructing analytical categories pertaining to undocumented migrants. Until now, there have been very few attempts to categorize migrant groups in Turkey. One of the first accounts on the subject is provided by Sema Erder in an article where she argues that Turkey is more of a 'waiting room' rather than a genuine 'receiving country' (2000). According to her, international migrants who come to Turkey can be categorized under three main groups, based on their motivations in migration. These are 'political refugees' who arrive in the country in massive waves and seek asylum in a third country; 'transit migrants' who come to Turkey in small groups or with their family members with the aim of moving to a developed country with better economic opportunities and higher life standards; and lastly 'suitcase traders' and 'temporary clandestine workers' who come to the country in cyclical patterns to engage in commerce.

Erder's classification provides the first full-fledged categorization on foreign migrants in Turkey; however her clear-cut separations do not seem to fit with what we have observed during our fieldwork. In the first place the term 'political refugee' is misleading because few of the 'refugees' in Turkey can obtain an official refugee status. There are many persons who are running away from the generalized violence in their country of origin but do not apply for asylum in Turkey, or if they do so, are rejected by the UNHCR officers. This is why it is difficult to distinguish clearly between 'refugees' and 'transit migrants'. As argued by Aslan and Pérouse (2003), the legal, social or economic status of migrants may easily change during their period of stay in Istanbul. There are many examples for the fluidity and elusiveness of migrants' status. For instance, many recognized asylum seekers or transit migrants began to work without having necessary work permits, out of mere obligation to survival. Or correspondingly, there are irregular transit migrants who are waiting to cross to Greece or any EU country to apply for refugee status. Last but not the least, suitcase trade and other economic activities of foreign migrants are not as strictly detached as expressed by Sema Erder. For instance, Iraqi Turkmens (who have already become Turkish citizens or received long-term residence permits) run export/cargo companies in Laleli and Osmanbey or work as salespersons and translators in shops serving foreign clientele from Arabic-speaking countries. In addition, there are many undocumented foreign migrants ('transit migrants', as called by Erder) who are working as unskilled workers in textile factories or other related domains, such as belt or button producing sweatshops.

These migrants who produce the goods that are sold in Laleli or Osmanbey shops to foreign suitcase traders are thus serving to supply the huge foreign trade sector of Istanbul. Transit migrants provide the most suitable reserve labor pool for temporary, unskilled, low-wage jobs in the manufacturing sector, which fluctuates according the tides of the global neo-liberal economy. They thus make it possible to change the level of production quite flexibly in proportion to the number of suitcase traders in Istanbul. Yet, any flight of clients to new and cheaper global markets, to China for instance, results in joblessness of foreign undocumented migrants. In short, whether transit migrant or asylum-seeker, as defined by Erder, or whether documented or not, most of the migrants do contribute to the growing economic domain related to the foreign trade and informal economy.

In his more recent article, Kuvvet Lordoglu (2005: 109-110) categorizes migration motives of 'clandestine foreign workers' in Turkey under three groups: The first group he mentions are transit foreigners who mostly come from the Eastern neighbors of Turkey, such as Iraq, Iran, Afghanistan and who prefer to engage in small business and to be self-employed. Secondly he writes about clandestine workers from ex-Soviet countries entering into the country with a tourist visa and who work temporarily during their visa period. They perform cyclical movements and go back and forth between their home country and Turkey, in order to comply with visa requirements. And lastly, there are migrants of Turkish descent from countries such as Bulgaria, Greece, Azerbaijan and Iran who get into the country with tourist visas and then stay in Turkey and acquire residence and work permits through to the opportunities provided to them.[6]

Our findings collected from the field indicate some deficiencies in Lordoğlu's conceptualization regarding foreigners' employment in Turkey. It seems that country-based categorizations are not effective and eloquent due to the subgroups of migrants from the same origin countries. For example, Turkmen, Christian, and Kurdish migrants from Iraq incorporate in very distinct ways into the labor market. Besides, there are many overlapping cases because of the fluidity and vagueness among the categories. For instance, among the cyclical workers there are many who continue to stay in Istanbul despite the expiration of their visa periods. In the research report on "Clandestine Migration in Turkey", Ahmet İçduygu (2004: 48) provides examples of cyclical workers who overstay their visa period and thus refutes Lordoğlu's categorization. In short, evaluation of Sema Erder's and

---

6   Lordoglu claims that migrants of Turkish descent began to fall into irregularity after 1997, since before that year they could easily acquire residence and work permits based on the Law no. 2527, signed in 25.9.1981. ("Türk soylu yabancıların Türkiye'de meslek ve sanatlarını serbestçe yapabilmelerine, kamu, özel kuruluş veya işyerlerinde çalıştırılabilmelerine ilişkin kanun").

Kuvvet Lordoglu's (2005) categorizations indicates the significance of the fluidity and elusiveness between categories.

An attempt to conceptualize migrant types and their employment prospects in Istanbul has to take into account the general social, economic and legal background that migrants join in. Below, we provide the economic setting that migrants deal with during their stay in Istanbul.

The Socio-Spatial and Economic Setting for Migrants' Incorporation

Urban Scenery: Istanbul – Home for Migrants

The heterogeneity and dynamism of urban areas where there is a wide range of ethno-linguistic, national and economic varieties offer many advantages to irregular migrants. The abundance of interactions in cities raises the possibility of new identities and novel forms of social organization, whereas the anonymous crowd provides the best conditions to evade the control of authorities.

Istanbul is one of the major cities in the region that provides a favorable environment for all kinds of exchanges due to the anonymity and availability of encounters (Pérouse, 2004). Aslan and Pérouse (2003) designate this Eurasian metropolis as a hub of opportunities and networks that offers both material and non-material resources to enhance initiation of mobility and circulation. The supply of legal services (such as travel agencies, translation offices, consulates, airline companies) is infinitely diverse. Istanbul is also well-known for its illegal services such as fake passports, smugglers, and so on)\. This 'burgeoning gigantism' allows migrants to find the means of contacting people who furnish the necessary resources to cross the borders. In short, Istanbul is the principal *loci* of international migration systems in the region and it functions like a *relay* and a *switch* where the migrants not only accumulate economic, but also social, linguistic and professional capital in order to create the necessary conditions for the next step of their mobility (Aslan and Pérouse, 2003).

Despite this vivid diversity, many migrants are excluded or prefer staying away from the public spaces of the city. Undocumented migrants seek invisibility due to their fear of facing police; very few of them feel free to stroll in the streets or visit other districts than their own. Even the Afghans, a large number of whom acquired Turkish citizenship, live in a quite limited space in Zeytinburnu. The police raids in public spaces prevent foreign migrants from meeting in open places. The exceptions are hotel lobbies, shops, workshops, coffeehouses or churches, for example Algerian coffeehouse in Laleli, and churches for Iraqi and Iranian Christians in Beyoglu and Aksaray. Neighborhoods where most migrants feel more secure are Aksaray and Laleli as they offer a segregated spot in the city, reserved mainly for various foreigners. Thus it is relatively easy for the migrants to get lost in the crowds of these places. Except for marginal cases of street sellers (işportacı), there are very few migrant small businesses, like. shop owners, in the city. Concealed places for work such as sweatshops located in basements create a more intimate employer-employee relationship, and decrease the risk of facing police at the cost of increasing migrants' vulnerability. For female migrants, child or elderly care work in private households provides this kind of discretion and isolation from the rest of society.

Undocumented migrants also seek 'invisibility' in their residential choices. What we observe for many undocumented migrants is a kind of integration into the host society from the periphery (Sommers, 2000). This peripheral aspect of undocumented migrants' stay in Istanbul is further underlined by locations of residency (Tarlabaşı, Kurtuluş, Dolapdere, Zeytinburnu, Kumkapı). Even though these districts are geographically at the center of the city, unlike the *gecekondu* of internal migrants built in the urban outskirts, they are in the underprivileged and impoverished areas of central districts. In this sense we prefer to call these locations 'the periphery of the center'.

Landau (2004) notes the co-existence of marginalized internal migrants and undocumented foreign migrants in particular neighbor-

hoods. This is congruent with what we observe in shabby neighborhoods such as Kumkapı or Tarlabaşı. These run-down districts are
inhabited by Kurds who migrated from Southeast Anatolia in the last
decades due to the armed clashes between Kurdish fighters and the
Turkish army (Bayraktar, 2006).[7] The national and foreign residents
of these districts often share a similar destitution and poverty. Actually
this fact helps to refute Piore's argument, presented above, about dual
labor market theory. The work conditions of the locals are often as
poor as the foreigners in these neighborhoods. Nevertheless, despite
the socio-economic similarities between internally displaced Kurds
and undocumented foreign migrants, the latter face worse conditions
due to their lack of residence permits. The precariousness of legal status of foreign migrants contributes to their exclusion from public education and health systems.

Undoubtedly, one area that does not require citizenship for participation is the informal employment market. The intensity of unregistered economic activities in Turkey provides employment opportunities for foreign migrants, as will be seen in the next section.

A Vibrant Informal Economy: A Pole of Attraction
For All Migrants

The extent of informal economic activities and the flexibility of
regulations in the country are the two factors that pull many migrants
to Turkey. The absence of strict regulations, supervision, and law
enforcement contributes to the spread of informal economic activities.
In Northern European countries, which present a sharp contrast to
Turkey, the control against unregistered economic activities is much
stricter, and thus there is less room for migrants' informal integration

---

7   During the rural-to-urban migration of the 1960s and 1970s, the self-built *gecekondu* houses
    had compensated the absence of state assistance to housing problem. The populist and clien-
    telist politics of the pre-1980 era had encouraged the spread of informal housing (Keyder 2005).
    Yet since the 1990s, the *gecekondu* cycle slowed down and many involuntary migrants of
    Kurdish origin lost the opportunity of getting socially incorporated through constructing a
    gecekondu on peripheral public land.

into labor markets (Boissevain and Grotenbreg, 1987). In the Turkish case, the weakness of state control on labor markets provides a relatively flexible environment for migrants in Istanbul, compared to the strict regulations in the Northern European countries. Thus the deficiency of state provisions, such as the nonexistence of rights to housing and education, or of work for migrants is in some way compensated for by the flexibility of labor and housing markets where they can participate due to the widespread informality in these sectors.

The vividness of unregistered economic activities provides employment opportunities as well as other possibilities for the relatively smooth incorporation of migrants into the host society. Rural-to-urban migration in Turkey in the 1960s had created a similar environment of informal incorporation into labor and housing sectors. In those years, the modernization paradigm suggested that the spread of informal labor among internal migrants was a temporary short-term phenomenon that would vanish and become formalized in due time (Keyder, 2005: 125). However, as we observe in the year 2000, the informal labor market did not fade away; on the contrary, it became more and more entrenched throughout the globalisation era.

In 2000, the Istanbul Chamber of Commerce (İTO) claimed that there were around 10.5 million workers who did not pay taxes and were not registered in any social security system. According to this report called "Artificial Employment and Employment Policies in Turkey", the informal economy is spreading into all economic sectors and is accompanied by problems of low income, poverty and unemployment.[8] According to the Turkish Statistical Institution (TURK-STAT), 55.4% of those employed in Turkey are working in the informal sector, comprising the unregistered economy.[9] In the third quarter of 2004, 22.2% of the salaried workers, 91.5% of the daily workers

---

8   *Radikal*, 30.10.2000 "10.5 milyon işçi kaçak".

9   One should clearly distinguish informal economy from illicite economy. In this text, we utilize the term 'informal' for economic activities that are not registered formally by public authorities. It does not include illicite or illegal economic activities.

(*yevmiyeli*), 25% of the employees, and 91.5% of the unpaid family workers were informally employed. In 2004, 48.2% of the16,511,000 male workers, and 74.4% of the 6,323,000 female workers were employed in the informal sector.[10] The magnitude of the informal economy in Turkey has been a concern for politicians as well as international economic organizations, including the IMF.[11]

Within the environment of the severe economic crisis in 2000, the informal employment of foreign migrants had been presented as the scapegoat of economic problems by the media and politicians; foreign migrants, especially the ones from former Soviet countries, were accused of causing unemployment problems.[12] Unemployment has been an acute problem in Turkey and this has made competition in the labor market much tougher. According to *Turkey's Statistical Yearbook 2004* published by TURKSTAT, unemployment rates increased from 6.5% in 2000 to 10.3% in 2001, 10.3% in 2002, 10.5% in 2003 and 10.3% in 2004.[13]

For the year 2005, it is estimated to be around 10%.[14]

The unemployment rate in urban areas is much worse than rural areas. In the same yearbook, the urban unemployment rate has been presented as 8.8% in 2000, 11.6% in 2001, 14.2% in 2002, 13.8% in 2003 and 13.6% in 2004. These statistics have also been confirmed by the records of the Turkish Labor Institute (İş-Kur). The three major cities which host the highest portions of the unemployed population in Turkey are Istanbul, with 13,7% of the Turkish average), Zonguldak at 7.8%, and Ankara representing 7.01% in 2000.[15]

---

10 *Zaman*, 10.12.2004, "Büyüme, işsizliğe çare olamıyor". The number given for women working in the informal sector seems to be very low compared what we observe in the field and in the academic texts. As argued by many researchers, informalization goes hand in hand with feminization of the labor force in the globalisation era (Standing 1989; Standing 1999).

11 *Zaman*, 22.6.2005, "IMF: Kayıt dışı, vergi indirimiyle önlenemez."

12 *Evrensel*, 30.12.2000 "İşsizliğin nedeni yabancı işçiymiş."

13 http://www.die.gov.tr/yillik/10_Calisma.pdf (accessed on January 2006).

14 *Hürriyet*, 27.12.2005, "Paranı istemiyoruz dersek IMF bozulur". Unemployement rate was 11.5% in February 2005, whereas it decreased to 9.4% in August in the same year.

15 *Radikal*, 23.10.2000, "Kentler işsiz dolu".

Photo 6.1. Afghan migrants waiting for work in Aksaray (JFP).

The promotion of a new law against the foreign undocumented workers has occurred in this environment of high unemployment and a large informal economic sector. In the late 1990s and early 2000s, the Ministry of Labor had claimed that there were one million foreign 'illegal' migrants, the majority of whom are from countries such as Moldova, Russia, Iran and the Far East. The Ministry's statements were backed by media coverage against undocumented foreigners. The result has been the creation of a new law to penalize companies that employ undocumented workers. The objective of the law was to diminish informal employment of foreigners by charging 2,500 Yeni Turk Lirası (YTL) from the company owners who employ informal foreign workers. The law had been put on the agenda by the former minister of labor, Yaşar Okuyan, in the year 2000,[16] however, it took three years for its implementation.[17] "The law about the work permits of foreigners" (Law no. 4817 published on March 6, 2003 in the official gazette) is designed to prevent the employment of foreign undocumented migrants and to harmonize Turkish labor laws with EU acquis.

Given the difficulty of calculating the size of the undocumented labor force, there are only estimations about the numbers of foreigners who are informally employed. What complicates the picture more is the search for jobs by foreigners who enter the country with a tourist visa (see **Table 6.5**). For instance, the Istanbul Chamber of Commerce, (İTO), sets the number of undocumented laborers at 450.000,[18] while trade union projections shoot it up to 2 million.[19] This huge disparity in the estimations is clearly due to the conflicting interests of entrepreneurs and labor unions. At the same time for instance, the Turkish Confederation of Employer Associations (TİSK) admits that the employment of foreign undocumented migrants creates an advantage for the company owners.

The strongest opposition to foreign undocumented migrants is asserted by textile unions. The Textile Workers' Trade Union (TEKSİF) argued in 2000 that every three in twenty workers employed in textile factories in Thrace are undocumented migrants from Romania.[20] In fact, informal employment in the textile sector is an acute problem: the Social Security Institute (SSK) estimated that 85% of textile workers are unregistered and thus devoid of any social security. They also argue that most of the foreign undocumented migrants in Turkey are employed in textile production.[21] In a report published

---

16 *Sabah*, 30.1.2001, "Kaçak işçi çalıştıran yandı".
17 *Dünya*, 2.9.2003, "Yabancı kaçak işçi çalıştırma cezaları 6 Eylül'de yürürlüğe giriyor".
18 *Türkiye*, 9.10.2000, "450 bin kaçak işçimiz var".
19 *Radikal*, 30.10.2000, "10,5 milyon işçi kaçak".
20 *Radikal*, 30.10.2000, "10,5 milyon işçi kaçak".
21 *Radikal*, 23.10.2000, "İşçiler de işyerleri de kaçak".

TABLE 6.5
Entries of Persons from the Balkan and Middle Eastern Neighboring States Between 1964 and 2003

	1964	1970	1980	1990	1996	2000	2003
Middle Eastern Countries							
Iran	12,796	14,247	42,082	219,958	379,003	380,819	484,269
Iraq	3,919	6,518	14,046	13,372	14,137	20,776	29,940
Syria	9,996	13,184	26,384	113,959	92,033	122,417	154,108
Gulf States*	–	–	–	43,088	40,029	19,537	43,503
Pakistan	1,961	7,383	4,800	7,347	12,410	7,908	12,336
Subtotal	28,672	41,332	87,312	397,724	537,612	551,457	724,156
Balkan States							
Albania	–	–	–	1,924	20,971	29,748	32,682
Bosnia	–	–	–		12,115	28,631	35,119
Bulgaria	693	18,214	26,523		139,648	381,545	1,007,535
Greece	3,042	11,313	19,477	203,720	147,553	218,092	368,425
Macedonia	–	–	–	–	41,269	108,928	117,819
Romania	–	–	–	352,034	191,203	265,128	184,182
Serbia Montenegro	–	–	–	–	44,600	128,383	186,423**
Yugoslavia	5,661	28,352	13,817	296,843	–	–	–
Sub Total	9396	57,879	59,817	854,521	597,359	1,160,455	1,932,185
Total	38,068	99,211	147,129	1,252,245	1,134,971	1,711,912	2,656,341
General Total	229 347	724,754	1,057,364	2,301,250	8,538,864	10,428,153	13,461,420

(*) Gulf States: Bahrain, Kuwait, Oman, Qatar, Saudi Arabia, United Arab Emirates.
(**) In the statistics used for preparing this table Serbia Montenegro is sometimes referred to as Federal Republic of Yugoslavia.
Source: (Apap, et al., 2005: 58) Compiled from data obtained from the Foreigners Department of MOI and State Statistical Institute Annual Reports.

by Teksif in 1999, only a quarter of the two million persons who are employed in the textile sector are registered. An exceptionally high incidence is observed in Merter, where only 4.000 among the 60.000 textile workers are registered.[22]

---

22 *Radikal*, 30.10.2000, "10,5 milyon işçi kaçak".

Photo 6.2. Afghan migrants waiting for daily work in the field of construction. (JFP)

Suitcase Trade

The majority of the employment opportunities for migrants in the informal sector are related to the extensive presence of export centers in Istanbul. Most migrants work either directly or indirectly in the suitcase related fields; many migrants work at the production level, (for example in textile sweatshops). while others work as salespersons, porters, or simple workers. Production and market centres for textile, leather and other products in Laleli, Osmanbey, Merter and other places attract cyclical migrants or shuttle traders, especially from the former Soviet Union, but also from Middle Eastern and North African countries.

Istanbul is an outstanding regional economic center: In 2003, it has realized over 60% of declared foreign trade of Turkey. More than 65% of import and export companies in the country are located in this city. Above all, Istanbul serves as the nodal point of a vast

Photo 6.3. Shops serving for suitcase trade in Laleli. (JFP)

hinterland from Central Asia to the Middle East. Part of the presence of temporary foreigners in Turkey is associated with the commercial appeal of Istanbul. This is mainly valid for the citizens of ex-Soviet and Eastern European countries, in addition to North Africans (mainly Libyans), as their access to European markets becomes tougher (Péraldi, 2001).

'Suitcase tourism' or the 'shuttle trade' started in the early 1990s, after the collapse of the Soviet Union. The hunger for consumption in those countries that had been repressed for so long under communist regimes has been fulfilled by suitcase traders who shuttle between their countries and Turkey. 'Suitcase trade' is exercised mainly by 'çelnok', which means 'shuttle traders' in Russian (Yükseker, 2003). Typical suitcase traders travel regularly, such as once every two months, and stay for a short period in Istanbul to buy relatively cheap and higher quality textile and leather products, automobile spare parts, or other goods produced in Turkey. Due to the repetitiveness and frequency of their movement, they are often called 'cyclical migrants' (Erder, 2000; Aslan and Pérouse, 2003).

It is not easy to distinguish 'classic tourists' from 'suitcase tourists' statistically, since the latter enter the country with the same type of documents (see **Table 6.6**).

It is also difficult to grasp the volume of this foreign trade since it is a non-declared economic activity. Nevertheless, it is certain that 'the golden age' of 'commercial tourism' that took place between 1992 and 1996 finished after the big economic crises in Turkey and the governmental efforts to document these exchanges. Similarly, on January 1, 2004, the Russian government changed the law that allowed Russian passengers to bring goods weighing 200 kg without paying tax. Since then, passengers to Russia can take only 50 kg and a maximum of $1,000 United States Dollars (USD).[23] In 2004, the Consul General of Russia in Istanbul, Sergei Velichkin, claimed firmly that they want to completely terminate the suitcase trade between Turkey and Russia, the volume of which had already decreased from 20 billion USD in 1990s, to 3.5 billion USD in 2004 (see **Table 6.7**).[24] Even though the Russian representative's estimate about the trade volume is very high, the decrease he is pointing at reveals the reality.

---

23 *Zaman*, 17.10.2004 "Laleli esnafı, bavul ticaretinde Başbakan'dan yardım istedi".
24 *Zaman*, 6.10.2004 "Rusya, bavul ticaretini tamamen durduracak".

TABLE 6.6
Foreign Tourist Entry in Turkey, Based on Country of Origin (1981-2003)

Country	1981	2002	2003
Germany	181,773	3,480,844	3,327,800
Great Britain	67,273	1,040,228	1,091,200
Russian Federation	12,134 (USSR)	945,678	–
Netherlands	19,759	871,560	938,700
Bulgaria	15,901	833,848	1,006,000
France	134,945	524,170	470,200
Iran	11,286	432,224	494,800
Austria	36,664	376,995	379,700
Belgium	–	313,436	308,100
Greece	18,335	280,307	393,400
Israel	–	271,024	321,100
United States	101,966	247,837	222,600
Italia	74,971	211,069	236,800
Sweden	11,451	203,830	188,600
Ukraine	–	191,202	–
Other countries	&	3,023,985	–
Total	1,158,125*	13,246,875	13,958,000

(*): among them, 450-519 are single day transit passengers.
The above table presents a selection of nationalities. The total number includes all nationalities.
Source: Ministry of Tourism 2004, cited by Perouse 2004.

TABLE 6.7
The Volume of Suitcase Trade With Russia (USD)

1997	5,800,000,000
1998	3,700,000,000
1999	2,300,000,000
2000	2,900,000,000
2001	3,100,000,000
2002	4,100,000,000
2003	4,500,000,000
2004	2,000,000,000*

(*) Approximate.
Source: Zaman, 07.03.2005 "Bavul ticareti bitti firmalar Laleli'yi Rusya'ya taşıyor".

The withdrawal of Russian clients has been a recurring theme during our fieldwork in Osmanbey and Laleli, too. Many shop owners told about the negative role of China and the overvaluation of Turkish lira in the export-oriented trade of Istanbul. The changing parity of TL v USD has increased the costs of production for Turkish companies and made it more difficult for them to compete with Chinese producers. It has been stated that the volume of trade in Laleli has decreased 60-70%, and may lead to the bankruptcy of big companies since they have less flexibility to adjust to the shrinking volume of trade. Actually, all of these unfavorable conditions seem to result in a replacement of Russian clients by Arabs, namely Algerian, Iraqi and Libyan. Another consequence has been an increasing specialization between different locations such as Osmanbey, Laleli, Merter in terms of quality and price of the goods.

Laleli is like a Tower of Babel, where one can encounter all kinds of migrants in its streets and shops. Bosnian and Bulgarian *muhacir*, Arabs from Mardin, and Turkmens from Iraq are the most easily detected amongst shop owners. Among the clients there is greater variety: members of ex-Soviet countries (the withdrawal of Russians and Ukrainians have been substituted by Azerbaijani, Georgian and even Armenian migrants), and Arabs mainly from Northern Africa and Iraq, as well as from the Arab peninsula. Most of the undocumented migrants that we are studying have contacts with this lively blend, either as shop owners, clients, or workers in the sweatshops that produce goods for the shops of Laleli or Osmanbey. In one sense, there is kind of a *cocoon* interwoven around export-oriented economic activities. In the following chapters, we analyze different ways that migrants connect with this sector and how this affects their socio-economic incorporation.

In the subsequent sections, we investigate three main points for the cases of Iraqi, Afghan, Maghrebi and Iranian migrants. First of all, we portray migrant profiles for each group by presenting their migration histories and modes. The questions that we try to answer in this section are when and how the pioneers have arrived in Turkey; what are the turning points that affect the size and the content of these migration flows; and what are the migrants' socio-economic backgrounds. Secondly, we focus on the migrants' employment patterns. We investigate their ways of incorporation into the Turkish labor market, the channels and networks they mobilize to find employment in the highly competitive and fragile Turkish labor market. Thirdly, we investigate their incorporation into housing markets. We analyze their ways of finding accommodation, as well as characteristics of the neighborhoods they settle in. Finally, we concentrate on other fields of social incorporation such as education and health services. When it is valid, we investigate means of schooling for children and ways of solving health problems.

The transformation of formerly emigrating countries into immigration centres brings about new challenges, such as incorporating migrant groups into the housing and employment markets. We hope that our research on Iraqi, Afghan, Iranian and Maghrebi migrants' unofficial ways of integration in Turkey will contribute to the academic field by its special focus on migrant incorporation in a developing country. Sound knowledge on the non-European migrants, some of whom have a propensity to become permanent residents may also contribute to the enhancement of migration policies in Turkey.

IRAQIS IN ISTANBUL: SEGMENTED INCORPORATION[25]

Iraqis: A Large but Invisible Migrant Group

The Iraqis have been one of the largest foreign migrant groups in Turkey. Particularly in the late 1990s and early 2000s we frequently encountered their names in the daily newspapers, either as 'clandestine

---

25 A. Didem Danış. Lecturer, Sociology Department, Galatasaray University and Ph.D. candidate, Ecoles des Hautes Etudes en Sciences Sociales. Galatasaray University, Sociology Dept., Ciragan Cad. No.36, Ortakoy, 34357 Istanbul, Turkey. ddanis@gsu.edu.tr

migrants' arrested around the borders, or as 'refugees' in shipwrecks on the Aegean coasts. This news, despite the significance in terms of pointing at the reality of Iraqi migration via Turkey, obscures the intricacies of the Iraqi presence in Turkey by using only one label to describe a more complex process. As observed during the fieldwork, Iraqis in Turkey represent a wide array of differences, in terms not only of legal status but also ethnic and religious backgrounds corresponding to the diversities of Iraqi society. They display different chronologies and patterns of migration to Turkey. These differences, which are presented below, are partly due to their distinct migratory capitals, as well as to the differing treatment by Turkish authorities.

The objective of this section is to analyze modes of incorporation of the Iraqis and to question the factors that play a role in this process. The variations in the patterns of Iraqi incorporation into Turkish society in general are contingent on two factors. At first, various social capital, either based on economic, cultural or political ties, provide the main characteristics of distinct incorporations for each group. For instance, the Christianity of Iraqi Assyro-Chaldeans which instigated their emigration from Iraq, becomes the most significant resource with which to build social networks during their temporary stay in Istanbul. In the case of Iraqi Kurds, the political ties between Kurds from Iraq and Turkey congregated around various oppositional political organizations begat construction of a Kurdish social space in certain localities of Istanbul. Lastly, in the Turkmen case, their ethnic similarity with the mainstream Turkish society contributes to their integration into Turkish society. Yet as seen below in the section on Turkmens, this 'privileged' status of Turkishness brings about various ups and downs owing to the political meaning and importance of this ethnic identity for the Turkish state.

The second fundamental factor for migrants' incorporation is related to political reception. Government policies toward different migrant groups, such as granting refugee status, regularizing the status of undocumented migrants, or creating social programs targeting migrants, all affect the success of migrant incorporation (Portes, 1995: 24). To argue that Iraqi migrants' incorporation in Istanbul takes place in a social space devoid of state would be a mistake. The Turkish state, which looks inexistent in some periods of these migratory processes, certainly plays a special role, even though under different appearances. First of all, legal instruments and their various utilizations by the state imply significant consequences for migrants. The political authorities sometimes become a criminalizing agent, as in its treatment of Kurds, or negatively affect migrants' socio-economic conditions by changing policies regarding residence permits, as in the case of recently immigrated Turkmens.

One should also highlight differences in the manifestations of the authorities: as in the latter example, suspension of granting residence permits on a more institutional level may go together with a growing understanding on the individual level, as seen in the tolerance of the police toward undocumented Turkmens in their daily face-to-face interactions. Even in the example of Assyro-Chaldeans, where the Turkish state gives the impression of being totally invisible, we can argue that it is a *'deliberate indifference'*, since authorities seem to ignore the mostly undocumented existence of Iraqi Christians.

If we substitute the term assimilation with incorporation, the concept of 'segmented assimilation' postulated by Portes and Zhou (1993) can be helpful to understand different patterns of the Iraqi insertion into Turkish society. As Portes and Zhou claim, migrant incorporation is not a 'straight-line progression' but it is a process that often leads to multiple endpoints. They observe three possible patterns of adaptation that may occur among migrants and their offspring. What we observe in the case of Iraqis in Istanbul is certainly a 'segmented incorporation'. It can be discerned in the specific socio-cultural and occupational niches they occupy, as well as their spatial distribution in the city. For instance, while Iraqi Christians are inserted into the non-Muslim communities, or to be more precise Catholic and Syriac milieus in Istanbul, the Iraqi Kurds, in particular the politically active ones, develop a social network around the Kurdish political institutions in Turkey. Lastly, the Turkmens are incorporated via the Turkmen Association and interconnect to job markets with the help of Turkmen businessmen in Laleli and Osmanbey. The main incorporating agents are the Assyro-Chaldean Church, the Kurdish political structures, and the Turkmen Association, as will be elaborated below, in each section.

The spatial scattering of Iraqis in Istanbul reveals the impact of these networks for each group. Despite the temporary character of many Iraqis' stay in Turkey, they already have a settlement presence in certain quarters of the city. Assyro-Chaldeans dwell almost exclusively in the overpopulated valley connecting Tarlabaşı, Dolapdere, Kurtuluş and Elmadağ. These neighborhoods, in particular the streets that meet downhill, were known in the late 19th century by the working class non-Muslim populace that inhabited there, which can still be noted by the prevalence of churches (Bayraktar, 2006; Danış & Kayaalp, 2004). The same districts are also lodging a number of Iraqi Kurds together with the involuntary Kurdish migrants coming from southeast Anatolia in the late 1980s and 1990s. Yet it is certain that Iraqi Kurds congregate predominantly in the derelict Kumkapı-Yenikapı axis, next to both internally displaced Kurds of Turkey and various undocumented foreign migrants such as Africans or Iranians. Kumkapı, which is located just a few hundred meters down from the Laleli area, had also a non-Muslim, mainly Armenian character in the past, and was highly degraded during the 1980s when first migrants began to arrive.

The traditional settlement areas for Turkmens are Aksaray, Fatih, Çapa and Fındıkzade, which are always associated with the predominance of Muslim population. These neighborhoods were also preferred by the pioneer Turkmen youth who came to Istanbul for educational reasons. The medical schools of Istanbul University in Cerrahpaşa and Çapa, as well as a few other private dentistry and pharmacology schools in the vicinity have been important pull factors for these residential choices. Today, the young single men dwell mostly in Kurtuluş and Feriköy and thus decrease the time and money they spend to commute between home and work, since the latter is located in Osmanbey. Besides, the location of the Iraqi Turks Culture and Solidarity Association in Aksaray creates an attraction and influences the residential preferences of the Turkmen families. Today, there is a wider spatial dispersal for the Turkmen community in the city, owing to their high level of integration. Even though some of the newly arrived families still prefer to live in the Aksaray-Fatih axis, many of the established families are already scattered to distant places as far as Mecidiyeköy, Kadıköy and Maltepe.

In Between Legal Categories

There are various patterns for the general Iraqi presence in Turkey. Large numbers of Iraqi have irregular status, that is to say that they either enter into the country without having the valid documents, or they slip to irregularity after entering legally due to expiration of their visas (İçduygu, 2003). However, this is not the only status for Iraqis in Turkey. There are some who apply for asylum; these are mostly the Christian transit migrants who want to regularize their status during the long waiting period for family unification in Australia and Canada. A smaller group among the asylum seekers consists of the Kurds.[26] There are also some who had once been migrants but eventually acquired Turkish citizenship. It is difficult to grasp the size of this group through statistics, due to the absence of detailed official data on the nationalization of foreigners. Yet it is certain that this group consists almost exclusively of Turkmens who could acquire Turkish nationality under the 1934 Law of Settlement. Besides, although in smaller numbers compared to the other cyclical migrants,

---

26 The un-receptive attitude of the Western governments towards Kurdish refugees has been intensified after the 2003 American intervention to Iraq; after that date the asylum requests of many Kurds arriving from the North of Iraq has been rejected in reference to the 'newly-built security' in the Kurdish populated areas of the country.

there are also Iraqis who commute back and forth between Iraq and Turkey, mainly for commerce. Now, let us analyze each category.

Iraqis have been the largest group among the irregular migrants arrested by Turkish security forces in Turkey for the last ten years. Almost 100,000 persons from Iraq have been apprehended, constituting half of all the apprehended cases from the Middle East and Asia, and one-fifth of all the apprehended cases in Turkey between 1995 and 2004 (Apap, et al., 2005: 34).

TABLE 6.8

Top Ten Countries of Origin for Irregular Migrants Arrested by Turkish Authorities Between 1995 and 2003

Country of Origin	1995	1997	1999	2001	2003
Moldavia	19	17	3,098	7,980	7,728
Pakistan	708	307	2,650	5,618	6,258
Iraq	2,128	5,689	11,546	23,444	3,757
Roumania	68	107	3,395	4,533	2,785
Russia	5	52	1,695	4,694	2,130
Afghanistan	24	81	3,046	9,542	2,178
Ukraine	9	52	1,695	4,694	1,947

Source: Compiled from the data provided on the website of Foreigners Department of MOI.

As seen in the table above, the volume of Iraqi irregular migration has been in a serious decline in the last years. 2001 has been the peak and since then there has been a continuing decrease. It is certain that the statistics provided by security forces should be treated cautiously, since they reveal only the figures of apprehended cases of foreigners, and not the number of all irregular foreigners in the country. As we observed during the fieldwork, there are many undocumented migrants who are not 'touched' by authorities. Nevertheless, we can agree to the decrease in the figures provided by authorities, due to the slowing down of overall emigration from Iraq after 2003, when American occupation persuaded many Iraqi Kurds to stay in the country. If we remember that a large section of Iraqi irregular migrants in

Turkey were comprised of Kurds running away from serious attacks by the regime, then the decline in the Iraqi emigration after the overthrow of Saddam Hussein becomes understandable. Nevertheless, it is obvious that Iraqi irregular migration still continues even though in much smaller numbers.[27]

A large majority of irregular migrants in Turkey consists of persons who enter the country with valid documents which eventually expire. Thus to better grasp the size of this group, we should also take a look at the official entry statistics of the Iraqis.

TABLE 6.9
Number of Iraqis Arriving (With Official Papers) in Turkey Between 1984 and 2004

1984	8,162
1985	8,674
1986	7,154
1987	8,558
1988	8,216
1989	12,508
1990	15,473
1991	3,859
1992	12,664
1993	12,085
1994	15,045
1995	14,381
1996	13,558
1997	17,574
1998	18,277
1999	17,591
2000	20,759
2001	16,378
2002	15,765
2003	24,727
2004	111,475

Source: Compiled from data provided on the website of Ministry of Culture, www.kultur.gov.tr (accessed on January 2006).

---

27 For instance, in October 2005 it was reported that some 180 Iraqi irregular migrants were arrested during the previous few months. Siverek and Viranşehir are two towns in the South

The tables on legal entries of Iraqi nationals into the country demonstrate the ups and downs of the officially registered border crossings from Iraq to Turkey. The year 1991 is remarkable with the sudden decrease in the official entries of Iraqis. The insecurity during and after the Gulf War and the massive flight of almost half a million Iraqis in the same year elucidate this abrupt fall. Even though legal entries of Iraqis increased almost twice from 1996 to 2003 and reached 24,727, it was still low in comparison with the total entries from Middle Eastern countries (see **Table 6.10**). This inconsistency is probably related to very restricted passport delivery policies of the Saddam Hussein regime (Chatelard, 2005). In particular after the 1991 Gulf War, when escapes from Iraq soared due to worsening economic conditions, the Ba'ath [MSOffice1}[RTF annotation: }Changed to mean the Baas hit "replace all"]leaders looked for new policies to impede out-migration from the country. One of the methods, for instance, was to oblige professionals, mainly doctors and engineers, to deposit $1,000 USD for tourist visas as a guarantee to ensure their return (Hiro, 2003: 15). Given the economic instability in the country and overvaluation of the USD over the Iraqi Dinar, it was not possible to cover this warranty without selling valuable properties. In this sense, the immense increase in 2004, almost ten times of the 2002 figures, represents the fall of Saddam Hussein and easy access to passports in Iraq. The liberalization of the passport regime and its implications on economic transactions between Turkey and Iraq is discussed below in the section on Iraqi Turkmens' ethnic niche in Laleli and Osmanbey.

East Anatolia that most of these arrests took place (*Zaman* 2.10.2005, "Sàhte pasaportla yakalandılar"). Likewise in Mardin, twelve Iraqi minors from Mosul, aging between 13 and 17 were caught by gendarmerie. Despite their request not to be deported to Iraq where they are believed to have been killed, soon after they were driven out of Turkey. *Zaman* 5.10.2005, "Irak'tan kaçan 12 mülteci yakalandı"; *Milliyet*, 25.07.2004, "Son durakları karakol..."

It is not necessary to go into the details of extreme instability and insecurity in Iraq, yet just to give a simple example, it is worth mentioning that in September 2005, 702 Iraqis were murdered in a single month. (*Zaman*, 02.10.2005, "Irak'ta geçen ay 702 Iraklı öldürüldü").

TABLE 6.10
Entries of Persons from the Balkan and Middle Eastern
Neighboring States Between 1964 and 2003

	1964	1970	1980	1990	1996	2000	2003
Iraq	3,919	6,518	14,046	13,372	14,137	20,776	29,940
Subtotal for Middle Eastern Countries	28.672	41.332	87.312	397.724	537.612	551.457	724.156
General Total	229 347	724,754	1,057,364	2,301,250	8,538,864	10,428,153	13,461,420

Source: Deduced from the table provided by Apap, Carrera & Kirişci (2005: 58) who compiled it from data obtained from the Foreigners Department of MOI and State Statistical Institute Annual Reports).

Another legal status significant for some of the Iraqis has been related to asylum requests. Iraqis together with Iranians constitute the two largest asylum seeker groups in Turkey; the maximum Iraqi asylum case load has been 4,895 in 1998 (İçduygu, 2003: 23). Subsequently it followed a decreasing trend and reached the minimum in 2003, when there were only 363 asylum applications submitted by Iraqis in Turkey. Since then there has been a steady increase again.

Despite the intensity of assaults against ethnic and religious minorities in Iraq and ongoing departures in the 1990s, the number of Iraqi asylum applicants was of a limited nature in Turkey. Given the size of total out-migration from Iraq, this is certainly a low figure. One of the factors that contribute to these limited statistics is the geographical limitation that Turkey maintains in the 1951 Geneva Convention (Kirişci, 2000). Aware of the fact that they will not be able to obtain refugee status in Turkey, many non-European potential asylum seekers merely transit the country without showing up before officials. A similar movement happens in Jordan, too; between 1991 and 2003, over 1.5 million Iraqis are estimated to have arrived in Jordan. Most of these Iraqis "have merely transited the country, which is not a party to the 1951 Geneva Convention relating to the Status of Refugees, and which has offered them neither asylum nor

TABLE 6.11
Asylum Applications in Turkey Between 1995 and 2005

	Iran	Iraq	Other	Total
1994	1,803	2,475	179	4,457
1995	935	2,890	152	3,977
1996	1,552	2,691	192	4,435
1997	1,484	3,028	129	4,641
1998	2,206	4,895	229	7,330
1999	4,221	2,635	435	7,309
2000	4,185	2,160	664	7,019
2001	3,708	1,933	1,034	6,675
2002	2,815	1,128	388	4,331
2003	3,310	366	604	4,280
2004	2,064	954	916	3,934
2005	1,047	1,717	1,150	3,914
Total	29,330	26,872	6,072	62,302

Source: Collected from UNHCR official website. http://www.unhcr.org.tr/ MEP/FTPRoot/Dosyalar/turkiyedebmmyk/sayilarlailtica/Basvuru%20Dagilimi%20199 4-2005.xls

economic integration" (Chatelard, 2004). Chatelard claims that there are some 300,000 Iraqis in Jordan and only 30,000 of these have legal status.

Another factor that restrains the figure of Iraqi asylum seekers is the suspension of Iraqis' cases in UNHCR offices. Since the 2003 American invasion, many Western countries have postponed the processing of Iraqi cases until a political resolution emerges in the country. According to the UNHCR website, in early 2006 some 2,200 Iraqi refugees and asylum-seekers were present in Turkey. Their cases are at a halt; in other words, they are stuck between the continuing instability and insecurity in Iraq and their expectations of confronting final resettlement countries that have stopped the processing of applications by Iraqi refugees.[28]

---

[28] http://www.unhcr.org/cgi-bin/texis/vtx/home/opendoc.pdf?tbl=PUBL&id=4371d1a90&page= home (accessed on January 2006).

TABLE 6.12
Statistics Concerning Applications Under the
1994 Asylum Regulation from 1995 to Sept. 2003

Country	Applications	Accepted Cases	Rejected Cases	Pending Cases	Cases not assessed
Iraq	12,196	4,459	3,491	3,227	453
Iran	19,982	11,850	1,291	5,891	230
Afghanistan	655	201	148	249	56

Source: Kirişci 2003 (Data obtained from the Foreigners Department of MOI).

Given the complexity of the picture concerning Iraqi migrants' legal status, we propose to begin with elucidating major turning points in the history of Iraqi migration to Turkey. Subsequently we analyze the migration patterns and incorporation modalities of each group separately.

A Short Chronology of Iraqi Migration

We can distinguish four main periods in the Iraqi emigration to Turkey. The first arrivals from Iraq occurred in the early decades of the new republic. As elaborated below in the section on Turkmens these first arrivals were mainly seeking educational opportunities and were exclusively the Turkmen. Since then Turkmen immigration has continued in small but constant flows. Especially in the 1980s there were increases in its volume particularly in periods of maltreatment by the Iraqi regime. There were also marginal cases of Iraqi asylum seekers in Turkey or choosing Turkey for transit to Europe during the Iran-Iraq War between 1980 and 1988. In those years, it consisted of young men deserting the army and escaping from the long and exhausting military service.

The second period consists of massive refugee arrivals between 1989 and 1992. The Anfal campaign and the death of five thousand people at Halabja in March 1988 initiated these abrupt population movements. Halabja and other similar attacks on the Kurds, who were blamed for collaborating with the Iranian authorities, triggered the escape of tens of thousands of Iraqi Kurds to Southeast Anatolia in 1988 (Ciğerli, 1998). Later in 1992, one of the biggest refugee flows in world history occurred. After the Iraqi army's violent suppression of uprisings in the North, some half a million Iraqis, consisting mostly of Kurds but also other minorities, fled to Turkey, while another one million escaped to Iran (Kaynak, 1992; Mannaert, 2003; Van Hear, 1995).

The third period consists of irregular migration movements of the 1990s that were instigated after the massive refugee arrivals. The continuing oppression of the regime against dissidents and decreasing life standards as a result of political instability and economic embargoes in the aftermath of the Gulf War presented the main motivations of this out-migration. Eventually, a combination of political and economic reasons chased many northern Iraqis across Turkey in order to reach Europe throughout 1990s. In these huddles of irregular migration there were Kurds as well as Turkmens and Assyro-Chaldean Christians, even though they all used their own means and networks to accomplish the perilous journey towards the west.

The fall of Saddam Hussein in 2003 opened the last era of Iraqi migration. Iraqi Kurdish emigration came to a halt, with the hopes of building a new life in newly acquired lands that are both economically and politically promising under the supervision of American occupation forces. In the case of Kurds, we can even talk of a reverse migration: some of the Iraqi Kurds who were stuck in Istanbul choose to return to their homelands with the emergence of a new political structure in the north of the country. After 2003, there have also been some Turkish nationals, mostly of Kurdish origin, who sail to Iraq with the hope of having a well-paid job in the blooming economy of the country. However, while the group making up the largest portion of the emigration demographic throughout the 1990s decided to stay in their homeland at the present, other minorities, or "minorities of minorities" such as Turkmens and Assyro-Chaldeans, continue evacuating Iraq due to their ongoing fear of maltreatment.

Iraqi Kurds: Changing Patterns in a Long-Standing Migration Wave

A great majority of the Iraqi migrants until the early 2000s was from northern Iraq, and consisted mostly of Kurds. Even though Iraqi Kurdish migration begins much earlier with smaller border crossing activities after the emergence of nation-states in the region, it was boosted with massive Kurdish refugee flows in the 1988 and 1991.

Massive Refugee Arrivals Between 1988 and 1991

First arrivals of Iraqi Kurds date back to the 1980s when young Kurdish men escaping military service crossed into Turkey in order to transit to Europe during the Iran-Iraq War years. Unfortunately we have no systematic information on these early marginal cases. The earth-shaking period in the Iraqi emigration to Turkey came about between 1988 and 1991. Mainly Kurds, but also other groups took refuge in the southeast of Turkey when the oppressions of the Iraqi regime reached an unbearable level. Iraqi asylum seekers have arrived in three waves into Turkey between 1988 and 1991 (Kaynak, 1992). The first wave was related to the "Anfal" Campaign of 1988. Anfal is the name of a series of military operations conducted by the Iraqi rule against Kurds, who were accused of collaborating with Iran during the Iran-Iraq War. According to Middle East Watch, the Anfal Campaign that took place between February and September 1988 and led to the murder of about 50,000 to 100,000 persons, the majority of whom were women and children (Bruinessen, 2000; Cigerli, 1998: 35). The campaign was also known for the utilization of chemical gases, and the most tragic event of all happened when the Iraqi air forces bombed the town called Halabja in March 17, 1988 and caused the immediate death of 5,000 persons.

The chemical bombs together with other military assaults during the Anfal Campaign compelled the Iraqi Kurds to take shelter in the north. Thus some 100,000 Kurds[29] escaping the persecutions of

---

29 Even though there are different estimations about the size of refugee population, according to Turkish officials 117,000 Iraqis arrived in 1988, of which 51,000 were eventually settled in the camps (Cigerli 1998; Kaynak 1992).

Saddam Hussein's regime crossed the mountains and then the Iraqi-Turkish border in late August 1988 (Ciğerli, 1998: 59-60). Turkish authorities were not very welcoming toward the Iraqi Kurdish asylum seekers because of the ongoing armed struggle with the Kurds of Turkey in the southeast of the country. The state was afraid of the potential involvement of Iraqi Kurdish refugees in the Kurdish guerilla movement. Nevertheless, owing to humanitarian concerns in the country and pressure from the international community they eventually decided to officially accept the asylum seekers. There were two main points that the Turkish state insisted on in order to curb any potential 'threat to national security'. First of all, Turkish authorities have never granted refugee status to Iraqi Kurds; instead they persistently called them 'temporary guests for humanitarian reasons'. Secondly, authorities gave them shelter in special camps that were deliberately constructed in zones far from the Kurdish settlement areas.[30] Both of these arrangements aimed to make Iraqi Kurds' stay temporary and short in nature as well as to limit their interactions with the local Kurdish villagers. The camps continued to exist up until 1992 even though the majority of the refugees returned home in a shorter span of time.[31]

The subsequent and most significant refugee movement happened in April 1991, after the suppression of the Kurdish uprising by the army loyal to Saddam Hussein. After the victory of the governmental authority over Shiites in the south and on Kurds in the north, and fearful of recurrent massacres, some 460,000 Iraqis fled to Turkey, and a million to Iran (Mannaert, 2003; Van Hear, 1995). This

---

30 They were initially staying on five temporary camps in Yüksekova (Uzunsırt and Suüstü), Silopi, Dicle and Mardin (Kızıltepe). Three months later, they were transfered to three permanent camps in Mardin, Diyarbakır and Muş (Ciğerli 1998: 71).

31 Whether this was really a voluntary return or a refoulement depends on from which side you listen the story. There are two main books about the Iraqi refugee flows between 1988 and 1992. Sabri Ciğerli's book (1998) is written from Kurdish perspective, while Muhteşem Kaynak's book (1992) provides the point of view of the Turkish state about these population movements.

last influx of asylum-seekers to Turkey consisted mostly of Kurds, but also included significant numbers of Turkmens, Assyro-Chaldeans, and Arabs from northern Iraq. As in 1988, Iraqis who took refuge to Turkey in 1992 were recognized as *'temporary guests for humanitarian reasons'* and could not obtain the refugee status due to Turkey's geographical limitation in the Geneva Convention. Almost all of the persons escaping from Iraq in 1991 left Turkey in the nick of time. According to the survey conducted under the supervision of Muhteşem Kaynak, there remained only 25,000 asylum-seekers in temporary settlements six months after their arrival (Kaynak, 1992: 147). The UNHCR, who did not take an active part in 1988, was in action during the massive influx of 1991 and intervened for the resettlement of Iraqi refugees in third countries. Some of these Iraqis, who attained camps in southeast Turkey in 1991, subsequently continued their journey forward and opted for crossing the European borders 'by their own means'.

1990s and Early 2000s: 'Explosion' of Iraqi-Kurdish Irregular Migration

In recent years, the biggest group among the irregular migrants apprehended by Turkish authorities were the Iraqis (İçduygu, 2003). According to the Foreigners' Bureau of the General Security Directorate, during the first ten months of the 2000, 3,174 of the 12,921 irregular migrants who were arrested in Istanbul were from Iran and Iraq.[32] These two were the largest among the apprehended irregular migrants in 2000, and it is estimated that Kurds are the largest group within the apprehended cases of irregular migrants of Iraqi and Iranian nationality.

While the statistics provided in **Table 6.8** in this section only show the apprehended cases, they display the variations in the volume of the Iraqi irregular migration, whose majority is believed to be

---

32 *Radikal*, 28.12.2000.

Kurdish.[33] The number of Iraqis apprehended by the security forces rose from 2,128 in 1995 to 11,546 in 1999 (almost a five times increase in four years).[34] This was then followed by an 'explosion' in 2001 and reached 23,444 detainees. As a matter of fact, during 1999 and 2002 there has been plenty of news about Kurdish 'boat people'.[35] The doubling up of the irregular population between 1999 and 2001 was then followed by a sudden decrease in 2003, when only 3,757 Iraqis were apprehended by Turkish security forces. Thus, in 2003, for the first time, Iraqis lost their top ranking in the number of irregular migrants, and fell to third position behind the Moldavian and the Pakistani populations in Turkey.

A very large majority of the Iraqi Kurdish migrants consists of young single men. They run away from poverty, deteriorating living standards, as well as the ongoing civil war in northern Iraq.[36] The increase in the volume of Iraqi Kurdish emigration throughout the 1990s is also associated with the clashes between PDK (Party Democratic of Kurdistan) and PUK (Patriotic Union of Kurdistan) that started in 1994 and continued sporadically until the signing of the Washington Agreements in September 1998. It later on continued with the skirmishes between Barzani forces and PKK (Workers Party of Kurdistan) in 2001. In fact, Kurdish history in the 1990s until 2003 was characterized by a number of armed struggles between various Kurdish groups, which created a sense of political and economic

---

33 This presumption about the Kurdishness of Iraqi migrants is based on the personal interviews with various Iraqi migrants and the data gathered from newspapers. The official sources do not differentiate ethnic, religious or hometown origins of the Iraqi citizens.

34 It is clear there have been many more who crossed Turkey without being caught by security forces. According to the UN sources, 22,000 Iraqi Kurds asked asylum in European countries in 1996. *Yeni Gündem*, 19.9.2000, "Sessiz ama büyük göç".

35 *Özgür Bakış*, 14.3.2000, "Kürt göçü durmuyor"; *Yeni Gündem*, 21.7.2000, "Kürt mülteciler İtalya sahilinde"; *Yeni Gündem*, 13.8.2000, "İtalya'da 250 mülteci daha". In those years, hundreds of persons were apprehended every day, particularly in Italian coasts.

36 *Yeni Gündem*, 12.07.2002, "Güney Kürdistan'da iç kanama: Göç". The reporter writes meticulously about the social problems, such as gender imbalances, increasing divorce cases, familial shattering caused by the emigration of young Kurdish male.

despair, as well as an environment of insecurity.

These motivations that instigated Iraqi Kurdish emigration have been brought to fruition as a result of various factors. The familial ties of Kurds scattered on different sides of the Iraqi-Turkish border provide the first migratory asset to Iraqi Kurds who want to cross to Turkey. The only study about smuggling networks in Turkey (İçduygu and Toktaş, 2002) points at the role of family and kin-based relationships in the functioning of smuggling networks in the east of Turkey. For the Iraqi Kurdish migrants, extended familial ties that include both kinship and tribal relations, provide the first basis of networking to cross the border.

Another resource, which is probably much more important than the familial ties, has been derived from the irregular migration expertise of the Kurds of Turkey. When Iraqi Kurds poured into Turkey in the 1990s, the Kurds of Turkey had already gained experience in crossing European borders to seek asylum (Pérouse, 1999c; Sirkeci, 2003). During the late 1980s and early 1990s Turkey had been in the top three ranking in the list of origin country of refugees in Europe (Danış, 2004). For instance, in 1985-1994 Turkey was in the third position on the list of asylum seekers into EU countries, with a population of 264,000 persons (Böcker and Havinga, 1997: 34). Many of these Turkish asylum seekers in the EU were using clandestine ways to pass the national borders: for instance, between 1997 and 2000, 17,000 Turkish citizens irregularly entered into England with the result being that they ranked third, behind Indians and Pakistanis, on the 'list of illegal entries'.[37]

Among the accommodating factors of Kurdish emigration in 1990s, one should also add the positive attitude of European politicians and society towards the Kurdish asylum seekers. Until the early 2000s, some human rights associations and media agencies emphasized the oppression endured by the Kurds and tried to raise public

---

[37] *Cumhuriyet*, 21.5.2002.

sensitivity in Europe towards the 'Kurdish tragedy'.[38] Accordingly, many European governments were less reluctant to deport Kurdish irregular migrants. On one occasion in 2001, a boat full of 600 migrants of Sri Lankan, Iranian and Kurdish origins was apprehended while boarding to Italy. Despite the fact that Italian authorities immediately expelled Sri Lankan and Iranian migrants, they stayed silent about the Kurds –whose nationality was not specified, but referred to simply as 'Kurds' in this news.[39] This sympathetic approach of Europeans has changed in recent years in line with their anti-immigration attitude.[40] Many countries began to refuse asylum requests of the Kurds. Diaspora Kurds organized hunger strikes against EU countries that stopped positively discriminating their cases in the deportation operations.[41]

This changing attitude by the European nations was partly justified by the prevalence of Kurds in human smuggling networks. There is not wholly reliable information on the ethnic character of the smuggling networks. Turkish authorities, as well as Turkish newspapers, talk about the role of Kurdish human smuggling groups and the enhancement of political networks interwoven around the PKK (the Kurdistan Workers' Party). A report published in 2002 by the Foreigners Bureau indicated that the PKK has been smuggling Kurds into Europe and has subsequently earned a huge sum of money.[42] On the other hand, Kurdish media emphasizes the role of Turks, and also of the Turkish state and administration, in the human smuggling networks to Europe (Çiçek, 2005). In fact, the pervasiveness of Turks in

---

38 The spokesperson of the French Human Rights Association expressed her concerns about the Kurdish migrants' tragedy and indicated that only in 2000, 271 Iraqis were drowned in Indonesia, Australia and the Aegean sea. She also invited France to call a UN Security Council to discuss Kurdish emigration and to improve their life standards in their homelands. (*Yeni Gündem*, 24.02.2001 "Kürt mültecilere ilgi devam ediyor").

39 *Radikal*, 24.04.2001, "Kürt göçmene 'kalış bileti'".

40 *Özgür Politika*, 27.12.2002, "Avrupa mültecileri istemiyor".

41 *Özgür Politika*, 27.12.2002, "Mülteciler açlık grevinde".

42 The report is called 'Illegal Migration in the World and in Turkey' (*Radikal*, 11.06.2002).

the 'business' has been confirmed by the statistics provided by Turkish police authorities, as well as some Turkish newspapers.[43] As indicated by the table below, a great majority of smugglers are of Turkish nationality. However, Turkish authorities accentuate the prevalence of Kurds among the human smugglers of Turkish nationality.

TABLE 6.13
Nationalities of Human Smugglers Apprehended by Security Forces

Nationality	1998	1999	2000	2001	2002	Total
Turkey	75	139	701	1021	102	2038
Afghanistan			14			14
Azerbaijan			7			7
Banghladesh		6	11	1		18
Unkown				13		13
Bulgaria	2		2	1	1	6
Morocco			9			9
Georgia			3	4		7
India		2	2			4
Iraq	14	13	48	47	3	125
Iran	1	12	19	35	4	71
Lebanon	1			4		5
Malezia			2			2
Egypt	1					1
Moldova			1			1
Nigeria			2			2
Pakistan	3	9	8	10		30
Poland			1	1		2
Romania			2			2
Russia	1		2	2		5
Syria		6	5	10		21
Crotia						0
Ukraine			1	2		3
Greece			10	4		14
Total	98	187	850	1155	110	2400

Source: EGM website.

---

43 *Vatan*, 01.01.2005, "İnsan tacirlerine en büyük darbe"; *Radikal*, 20.10.2000, "'İnsan ticaretini Türk mafyası düzenliyor'".

As presented in the above table, Iraqis are the second largest group in the list of human smugglers' nationalities. Owing to the informal data collected during the interviews, it would not be entirely wrong to assume that many of these Iraqi nationals are of Kurdish origin and have contacts with other smugglers. The Kurdish dispersal to Europe has certainly contributed to the expansion of all kinds of Kurdish networks in the Schengen territories (Wahlbeck, 1998). Additionally, some Iraqi Kurds, who once had passed through Europe to seek asylum, later became actors in the human smuggling business.[44] The evaluation of the weight of Kurdish organizations in the smuggling networks is out of the scope of this research. Still, based on media news we can argue that these smuggling networks often have a transnational character: Operations conducted against human smuggling networks by the British police, in cooperation with Italian, French, Greek, and Turkish authorities in December 2005, pinpoint the transnational connections among these organizations.[45]

The general discourse toward irregular migrants in Turkey is shaped by a tone of criminalization. In newspapers Iraqis as well as other Asian migrants are presented only under the heading of irregular migration. In January 2004, the head of the International

---

[44] Nevzat Aydın who wrote an article on Kurdish refugees, illustrates two northern Iraqi Kurds involved in the smuggling business in Istanbul. *Yeni Gündem*, 19.9.2000, "Zaxo-Roma Hattında Mülteciler".

[45] The head of the network arrested by British police, which is accused of smuggling over 5,000 people from Middle East to Europe, was an Iraqi; there have been 22 additional members of the gang in France, 18 in Italy, 7 in England, 3 in Greece and 3 in Turkey (*Cumhuriyet*, 17.12.2005). According to British authorities, the Turkish gang was charging $7,000 USD per person, which allowed them to earn around $1.4 billion USD out of this lucrative job. Just two months before this operation, British police had arrested 18 Turkish smugglers in England and thus crushed a big Turkish smuggling network, which was supposed to be involved in the irregular crossing of 200,000 people into England. However, there is no data on their ethnic origins (*Vatan*, 12.10.2005). Iraqis are also involved in small smuggling networks installed in Istanbul. In 2004, a bunch of Somalian clandestine migrants complained of being cheated by an Iraqi smuggler who promised them passage across the Greek border. They realized that they had been deceived, after waiting two months in an apartment in Kurtuluş without any sign from the smugglers whom they paid $4,500 USD (*Vatan*, 27.02.2004).

Transportation Association, (UND), Çetin Nuhoğlu complained bit-terly about human smuggling networks that utilize Turkey as a transit route. After monitoring the activities of smugglers, the association detected several points that served as a passageway to Europe and sent an elaborate report to various ministries in order to make them "inter-vene in these illegal networks which negatively affect the activities of transportation companies".[46]

Iraqi Kurds in Istanbul: Fractional Incorporation

Iraqi Kurds, who poured to Turkey in the 1990s and early 2000s, incorporated very weakly, partly because of the Turkish State's resentful attitude towards Kurds in general. As we have discussed above in the section on Iraqi- Kurdish massive asylum movements between 1988 and 1992, Turkish authorities were afraid of their potential participation in the Kurdish uprisings in Turkey. The hostile stance of the state and its attempts to curb potential contacts between Turkish and Iraqi Kurds further weakened Iraqi Kurds' resources of incorporation.

Another factor that hinders the socio-economic incorporation of Iraqi Kurds is related to the social and economic incapacity of their co-ethnics in Turkey and their precarious conditions in Istanbul. Kurds in Turkey have been migrating mostly involuntarily to metropolitan areas, particularly to Istanbul in the last decades (Bayraktar, 2006). Many were forced to migrate due to the environment of insecurity in the regions they originally inhabited. Çağlar Keyder explains this involuntary population movement with a focus on the macro dynam-ics of the country:

> It is the last two decades' devastation of what had already been the poorest regions of the country which has pushed people toward the big cities. This devastation is primarily due to the ethnic/separatist

---

46 *Sabah*, 16.01.2004, According to Nuhoğlu, these key points include Çeşme harbor, Erenköy Custom Zone, Haydarpaşa harbor and Ambarlı harbor.

war, itself in part related, in various ways, to globalisation and the
collapse of national developmentalism (Keyder, 2005: 131).

This sudden and unprepared displacement of the Kurds of
Turkey brought about a malfunctioning settlement in Istanbul, where
they were unable to build new social networks. The absence of
prospects for return because of the devastation of the villages, the cut-
ting of ties with the homelands, as well as the dearth of capital available to them gave rise to "a danger that these new immigrants have
now calcified into a permanent underclass, moving back and forth
between unemployment, self-employment and casual, informal work,
always in need of outside assistance for survival" (Keyder, 2005: 132).
Hence, Kurdish internal migrants face a somber social, as well as political exclusion because of the lack of economic and social resources,
and cannot provide an opportunity for socio-economic integration to
Iraqi Kurds.

Within this restricted setting, we can distinguish two patterns of
Iraqi Kurdish incorporation: One the one hand, there are large numbers of undocumented Iraqi Kurdish migrants composed largely of
young single men. In the second group, there are Kurds who are characterized by a high level of political activity. They are much more
resourceful during their stay in Istanbul and in their further migration
thanks to their ties with Kurdish political organizations in Turkey.

The first group is poorer in terms of their social ties with Turkish
society in general. Their stay is undocumented in every sense;[47] they
enter the country without proper documents, and they look for smugglers to take them across to Greece. They try to make their transit stop
in Istanbul as short as possible and reach Europe before long. Their
work and housing conditions are awful. They are mingling in the non-
European, undocumented migrant crowds in Aksaray waiting to find
employment. They work in daily jobs, whenever they can find one, par-

---

47 We are unable to use first hand quotations since none of the Iraqi Kurdish interviewees accepted to use a tape recorder.

ticularly in the construction sector. They are mostly dwelling in the Kumkapı-Yenikapı axis and frequent coffeehouses in this area. They live in 'inns' or share a room with other undocumented migrants in the inner city slums. They rarely go to other districts of the city because of fear of being arrested by the police. In consequence, their world is limited both in spatial and social senses.

The second group is more significant in terms of their social capital based on political ties with the Kurdish political circles of Turkey. This includes Iraqi Kurds who already had political affiliation in northern Iraq, and thus benefits from the common ground of working for the 'Kurdish cause' with the Kurds of Turkey. Their migration process as well as their stay has been assisted by Kurdish organizations, in particular the political parties in Turkey.

> There have been large numbers of people arriving into Turkey in the 1990s, especially in 1998, after the attacks had started. I remember that the network for their arrival into Istanbul was carried on through Hadep. They first came to cities like Nusaybin, Cizre where they already had kinship relations. Then most of them were directly coming to Istanbul, after being organized via Hadep (Interview with Osman, 4.1.2006).[48]

Ethnic and political ties intermingle in the formation of social networks that are utilized by the politicized Iraqi Kurdish migrants. The Kurdish 'structure' in Turkey through its political parties, cultural centers, and newspapers provide an important niche for the organization of Iraqi Kurdish migration, as well as the temporary incorporation of Kurds in Istanbul.

> They were using whatever skills they had in order to solve their accommodation and employment problems. For instance, I know

---

48 Osman is a 24 year-old university student in Istanbul, once active in Kurdish organizations. In this section, he is the only one whose testimonies are used because the others did not accept being tape recorded. Interview on 4.1.2006.

one who was a graphic designer there [in Iraq], he started to work for a newspaper after he came here. There were also many musicians; they constructed the infrastructure of music and folk dance activities here in the cultural center (Osman, 4.1.2006).

Spatial loci of Kurdish irregular migrants in Istanbul until the early 2000s corresponds with this political networking. Yenikapı and Tarlabaşı were certainly the two main locations for both the internally displaced and the Iraqi Kurds. The relationships between Turkish and Iraqi Kurds were not one-sided; in line with the Kurdish solidarity ethos, "they were contributing to each other with whatever they had to offer" *(Osman, 4.1.2006)*. Iraqi Kurds' most important contribution was certainly political participation in Kurdish organizations.

Even though they were in a very precarious position, they were politically participating. There were many who tutored language courses in the cultural center. Knowledge of the language was very low among the Kurds of Turkey; they knew Kurdish so they were teaching them. If the police arrested them they would be immediately deported, but they were not afraid of this (Osman, 4.1.2006).

It is not only the Iraqi Kurds who benefit from this ethno-political solidarity. Kurds from Syria may also integrate into the political networks. Social and spatial concentrations of Kurds in some inner city neighborhoods help the newcomers to make contact with the local Kurdish inhabitants.

Last year, after the events erupted in Kamışlı [in the north of Syria], lots of Kurds came here. They were not very open to interaction. For instance I remember the women. We went to visit them because we were collecting some money for them. They had to return, but they did not have money to pay the bus. They had come to stay temporarily, only to be away during the clashes. So they came to us too, to collect the necessary money. The women were all in black veils and were not talking at all. It was only the men who were talking. But still, they had found their way somehow, they had come to Tarlabaşı and me[e]t Kurds there. In Tarlabaşı, all the shops belong to Kurds, the language spoken in the streets is Kurdish. I think they somehow made the first contact with them and then told about their problems. So, the Kurds in Tarlabaşı collected money for them and sent them back (Osman, 4.1.2006).

Kurds in Iraq and Turkey, as well as the ones in Syria or Iran, possess limited human capital due to the absence of educational and professional opportunities. Unlike the Iraqi Turkmens in Istanbul who first came in the 1960s. Earlier on in the work says that they have been coming since the founding of the Republic –a few pages later it says since the 1950's and enhanced their qualifications through educational attainment, Kurds have not been able to improve their credentials. Their being stigmatized as 'dangerous minorities' is one of the factors that compel them to 'illegal' spheres, even to the world of crime in some instances.

> Various kinds of criminal underground organizations in Tarlabaşı ares in the hands of Kurds from Diyarbakır. They know who arrives, who leaves. They take care of them [Iraqi Kurds]; they even help them when necessary. They are also politically active. These people who do organize car robberies or the simplest purse-snatching have a political affiliation because of their history or their ethnic background. And it still goes on. (...) The Kurdish migrants, Turkish citizen or foreigner, in Tarlabaşı have very few skills or qualifications. This is why they are unable to create solidarity ties (Osman, 4.1.2006).

Owing to the lack of social networks, except 'illegal' ones, it is very difficult for the Iraqi Kurds to build a new life in Istanbul. The sole option to earn a livelihood for many is to work daily burdensome jobs until the day of departure comes.

The Fading Out of Kurdish Emigration from Iraq After 2003
The Kurdish emigration which had continued mostly of an irregular nature during the last decade came to a halt in the last several years.

Currently most of the Iraqi Kurds are going back to their homeland, while still very few attempt to go forward, to Europe. However it is certainly clear that the volume of Kurdish emigration is not as high as it was once. The number of Iraqi nationals who were apprehended by Turkish security forces dropped from 23,444 in 2001 to 3,757 in 2003. Even though we do not have the statistics for the last two years, it would not be wrong to estimate that it decreased further.

The American occupation in Iraq as well as the establishment of a new regime after the overthrow of Saddam Hussein changed the conditions in the north that once pushed many out of the country. The reconciliation between Barzani and Talabani, as well as rapid development of a new political and economic system in the Iraqi Kurdish areas resulted in a slowing down, even an ending, of the Kurdish departure. Furthermore, since 2003, European countries have changed their policies towards Iraqi Kurds and insisted on the 'voluntary return' of Kurdish asylum seekers whose claims are rejected. All of these changes signified a weakening both in push and pull factors for Kurdish emigration.

Apart from the newly emerged circumstances in the departure and destination countries, there have also been changes in Turkey. The year 1999 has been a critical turning point for the Kurdish political setting in Turkey. The apprehension of Abdullah Öcalan on February 16, 1999 resulted in a hot debate among Kurdish groups in Turkey, and in the end, led to the weakening of Kurdish organizations in the country. This remarkable event had also consequences for the politically active Iraqi Kurdish irregular migrants in the country.

> The apprehension of Öcalan and the change of the paradigm in the Kurdish movement, the discourse of 'let's leave the guns', completely changed the situation. As a result, I met very few Kurds from Iraq or Iran in this structure after 2000. (...) Even if they [Iraqi Kurds] come, there are not anymore people to get in contact with here. Many Kurds from Turkey went to Europe. I can say that 80% of whom I know went; most of these people were very tal-

ented, very qualified persons. Because of the dismantling process of the structure here, the newcomers prefer to stay out and to develop their own means of emigration in Yenikapı or other places. Most of them left eventually. The people [Iraqi Kurds] whom I met this summer for instance were staying here and did not join any political or social activity. In the end, they left (Osman, 4.1.2006).

After 2003, a reverse movement, of Kurdish migration in the region started. Many Iraqi Kurds who were stuck for a long time in Turkey opted for returning to their native soils. Furthermore, increasing numbers of Kurds from Turkey are going to Northern Iraq to benefit from education and work opportunities. One aspect of the post-2003 population movements between the two countries is the work-related circulation of Turkish nationals, mainly of truck drivers. Unfortunately the price of this desperate search for work in Iraq is very high for many. Between 2003, and 2005 110 Turkish truck drivers died and 87 were injured in Iraq.[49] Seventy-four of the hundred-ten were killed as a consequence of armed assaults. Most of the truck drivers originated from southeastern Anatolian cities such as Diyarbakır, Mardin, Urfa, Mardin, and Adana. Even though the truck drivers are the most mentioned in the media, they are not alone in their journey; artisans, technicians, cooks, and construction workers are amongst the many searching for new prospects in Iraq. Poverty and unemployment are the two main reasons that force them to undertake such perilous and risky jobs.[50] Besides, among the migrants to Iraq there are also university candidates who could not receive the necessary score on the national examination for university entrance. These young persons from the southeast of Turkey, especially Hakkari, Şemdinli, and Şırnak, go to Erbil or Suleymaniye in northern Iraq where they can study in Kurdish.

To summarize, even though it lost its previous pace, the Iraqi

---

49 *Zaman*, 26.9.2005, "2003 yılından bu yana Irak'ta 110 Türk şoför hayatını kaybetti".

50 *Zaman*, 30.9.2005, "Istanbul'daki işinden daha fazlasını kazanmak için Irak'a giden mobilyacının cenazesi geldi"; *Radikal*, 01.12.2004, "Irak'ta işgal üstü kebap"; *Milliyet*, 18.10.2004, "Sadece yaşamak için".

Kurdish emigration via Turkey is continuing. Most of the Kurds from Iraq are joining the ranks of undocumented transit migrants in Istanbul and constitute one of the most disadvantaged groups in terms of their capacity to build social networks. Most of them adhere to the cheap, unqualified labor reserve of undocumented foreigners and dwell in shabby neighborhoods inhabited by their Turkish co-ethnics, who themselves arrived in Istanbul involuntarily in the 1980s and 1990s in response to the insecure environment in their homeland. Social exclusion that the Kurds of Turkey experience limits the resources to be shared with Iraqi Kurds. The only resource that seems to be helpful is the dense network interwoven around various Kurdish organizations. Thus Iraqi Kurds who already had political contacts in their homeland affiliate with the politically active Kurdish environment in Istanbul. Undoubtedly, this presents a restricted social space for the steady incorporation of Iraqi Kurds due to the continuing control and pressure of Turkish authorities on Kurdish institutions, which are seen as a potential threat to the security and integrity of the state.

Iraqi Turkmens: Ethnic Brotherhood, Easier Incorporation?

A Mystery: The size of the Iraqi Turkmen Population

The population of Iraqi Turkmens in Turkey has been a controversial subject, in particular since January 2005, when the Iraqi parliamentary election took place. In line with the weakness of statistical information on any ethnic, migrant, or naturalized group, there is no official data about the size of the Iraqi Turkmen population in Turkey. The only hints we could gather are mostly of an informal nature, based on the newspapers and our own interviews with Turkmen representatives. During the 2005 parliamentary election in Iraq, more than 280,000 expatriates were registered for out-of-country voting in 14 countries,[51] as seen in the table below.

---

51 "Iraqis worldwide celebrate landmark vote" http://www.cnn.com/2005/WORLD/meast/01/28/
iraq.expat.voting/index.html (accessed on 29.01.2005).

TABLE 6.14
Iraqi Expatriate Voters

Australia: 11,806
Canada: 10,957
Denmark: 12,983
France: 1,041
Germany: 26,416
Iran: 60,908
Jordan: 20,166
Netherlands: 14,725
Sweden: 31,045
Syria: 16,581
Turkey: 4,187
UAE: 12,581
UK: 30,961
US: 25,946

Source: BBC, 28.01.2005.

The tiny number of Iraqis registered in Turkey had been hotly discussed in Turkish newspapers, which argued that the size of the Turkmen community in Turkey is around 40,000.[52] However, there were only 4,178 persons who had registered for out-of-country voting in the January elections, and the Iraqi Turkmen Front (ITC) had gained 3,500 of those votes. Turkmens in Turkey were severely criticized and blamed for not being organized as well as the Turks of Bulgaria, who made an impressive showing in the parliamentary elections.[53] Turkmen respondents explained this low registration by referring to the reactions against the American-led election. Many did not want to participate in elections thinking that such participation would mean justifying the American occupation in the country. Besides, all over the world, the Iraqi diaspora's participation in the election was limited; only a quarter of expatriate Iraqis were registered to vote.[54]

---

52 www.ntvmsnbc.com, 26.01.2005 "Yurtdışındaki Iraklılardan seçime destek yetersiz".

53 *Zaman*, 19.01.2005, "Türkiye'deki Iraklılar seçime ilgi göstermiyor"; *Zaman*, 23.01.2005, "Türkiye'deki Türkmenler, Kerkük'ün geleceğini etkileyecek sürece ilgisiz".

54 "Expatriate Iraqis head to polls" http://news.bbc.co.uk/2/hi/middle_east/4215393.stm (accessed on 28.01.2005).

The head of the Iraqi Turks Culture and Solidarity Association (*Irak Türkleri Kültür ve Yardımlaşma Derneği*, for a brief time, the Turkmen Association hereafter) repudiates the 40,000 estimation of the Turkmen population in Turkey, and claims that none of them have established such a figure. According to him, probably *the* expert on the Turkmen migrants, the 40,000 guesstimate is just an invention of the media, and the correct number is between 7,000 and 10,000 in Turkey, and 5,000 to 7,000 in Istanbul.[55]

Yet the Turkish Minister of Foreign Affairs, Abdullah Gül, does not seem to share this opinion. The minister stated that there are almost 40,000 Iraqi citizens in the country and 30,000 of these are Turkmen, who should certainly go to the ballot if they want to contribute to the restructuring of their homeland.[56]

Despite the low participation in Turkey in the January 2005 out-of-country voting, there were more people in voting cabins in the December 2005 election. Twenty-thousand persons participated in the elections and 21,000 voted for the Turkmen parties.[57] On the other hand, this unexpected and sudden explosion of votes in Turkey annoyed Iraqi Kurdish groups who claimed that it was a deception organized by extreme nationalists. The Turkish representative of the Patriotic Union of Kurdistan (PUK) had declared that they would dispute the results. In return, Turkish electoral representatives explained the increase in the votes in terms of the facilities provided by the authorities, such as permission for clandestine Iraqis to participate in voting without the intervention of police officers.[58]

Whatever its real size, two groups can be distinguished within the Turkmen community in Istanbul: the old and the new. Kemal

---

55 Turkmens are also settled in Ankara, Antalya, İzmir and Konya in addition to Istanbul, which is the favorite destination for the Iraqi Turkmen, like for other foreign nationalities..
56 *Milliyet*, 15.12.2005, "Gül'den Türkmenlere, 'Oy ver' çağrısı".
57 *Milliyet*, 17.12.2005, "Kürtler Istanbul'a itiraz edecek".
58 *Milliyet*, 17.12.2005, "Kürtler Istanbul'a itiraz edecek". Turkish columnists rationalize this sudden increase of votes by referring to the unjust demographic manipulations of Iraqi Kurdish parties in Kirkuk. See, *Milliyet*, 17.12.2005, "Kerkük'ün dört kapısı", Fikret Bila.

Beyatlı, the head of the Turkmen Association, indicates that the migration from Iraq to Turkey has to be distinguished as pre-1991 and post-1991. He claims that 60%-70% of the actual Turkmen population in Turkey has arrived after 1991. Nevertheless, it is certain that there is a continuing emigration ongoing since the 1950s, mostly motivated by educational aspirations.

From the Loss of Mosul to the Gulf War: Educational Migration of the Turkmen

Turkey has long been paying attention to the Turkmen of Iraq, although with changes in the degree and content of its interest. The loss of Mosul in 1926, after long diplomatic negotiations with Britain and the League of Nations, created a large Turkish speaking community within Iraqi territories. To protect, and if possible to improve, the rights of the Iraqi Turkmen has been a continuing concern for Turkish authorities (Şimşir, 2004: 47-68). We will not go into the details of the relations between Turkey and Iraqi Turkmen, since it is out of the scope of this research. Still we should state that arguments about the figures of the Turkmen have been a significant political instrument for Turkish authorities to raise anxiety about the oppression over the Turkmen minority in northern Iraq.[59] As a matter of fact, this instrument has sometimes turned to the disadvantage of the Turkmen who were forced to leave Iraq as a result of worsening social and political circumstances in the 1990s. The Turkish state, which then realized the importance of having a sizeable Turkmen community in Iraq in order to have a say in the future restructuring of the country, slowed down delivery of permanent resident permits, let alone citizenship, to the Turkmen who sought refuge in Turkey.

---

59 Population statistics in Iraq have always been a boiling battlefield since the 1920s, however its intensity has particularly increased in the last years. Turkmens have been trying to demonstrate that their population in Iraq is around 2,000,000 despite the 'Arabization' and 'Kurdification' policies in the country. (See Al-Hirmizi 2003: 91-104 for a detailed account of various documents and researchers on the subject).

The attitudes of the Turkish state towards Turkmen minorities in Iraq were affirmative in the first half of the 20th century. The first shock that was experienced after the loss of Mosul had been mitigated by policies aiming to improve the historical and social ties between Iraqi Turkmens and Turkey. There are two important agreements between Turkey and Iraq that have considerable implications for the Turkmen migration to Turkey. The first one is *the Turkish-Iraqi Residence Contract* signed on January 9, 1932 (*Türkiye-Irak İkamet Mukavelenamesi*), and the other is *the Educational and Cultural Cooperation Protocol (Eğitim, Öğretim ve Kültür İşbirliği Protokolü,)* signed under article No.3 of *The Friendship and Good Neighborhood Agreement (Dostluk ve İyi Komşuluk Antlaşması)*, in March 29, 1946.

The Residence Contract of 1932 granted the citizens of Iraq and Turkey the right to live, to work, and to have properties in the reciprocal country.[60] Evidently, it has been the Turkmen who have benefited the most from this agreement. Consequently, back-and-forth movements increased and the Iraqi Turkmen obtained the right to settle, to work, and to study in Turkey without losing their Iraqi nationality. This law also made possible the restoration of the social ties of the Turkmen kindred who are spread to the two sides of the Iraqi-Turkish border (Şimşir, 2004: 89-90).

The Educational and Cultural Cooperation Protocol had considerable implications for the Iraqi Turkmen migration in Turkey (Şimşir 2004: 115-121). In consequence of this protocol, Iraq and Turkey agreed reciprocally to recognize the equivalence of all diplomas obtained in the other country. In addition, Turkey accepted Iraqi students into public boarding schools and covered all of their expenses in the country. Consequently, in the 1950s and 1960s many Turkmen students benefited from the right to study in Turkey. The 1946 Protocol together with the 1932 Residence Contract facilitated the settlement of the Turkmen who came to Turkey to study.

---

60 The law (Law No.2003) has been ratified in 4.6.1932 by the Turkish National Assembly and been implemented in 6.7.1933 (Şimşir 2004: 89).

These two agreements have been official doors opened for the entry of Turkmen into the country. In particular after the Kirkuk Massacre in 1959 (Al-Hirmizi, 2005), there have been many Turkmen youth who benefited from this protocol of education. The importance of having academic credentials has always been acknowledged and education is highly encouraged by Turkmens.[61] Nevertheless, the emigration of the Turkmen owing to educational purposes in the 1950s and 1960s is not related to the supposedly better quality of education in Turkey. As far as the interviews conducted reveal, most of the Turkmen students decided to study in Turkey because of their lower grades in the Iraqi national *baccalauréat* exam (a secondary school examination giving university entrance qualification). The alternative for the Turkmen who could not achieve the score required to get into a 'decent' faculty was Turkey.

> In our university entrance system, there is an examination at the end of high school, like here. However, we do suppose a young person as 'educated', if he is a graduate of medical school, dentistry, engineering or pharmacology. If he cannot enter into these faculties, he thinks about going abroad. For us, the closest country is Turkey (Interview with Hasan, 24.11.2005).[62]

One of the important features of the study-in-Turkey program was certainly related to the ethnic/linguistic 'closeness' between Turkey and Iraqi Turkmen, as elaborated above. In addition to this linguistic competence, the strength of the Iraqi economy in the 1960s had facilitated the realization of studying abroad for many Turkmen.

> Iraqi families could easily support the children they sent to study to Turkey because of the strength of the Iraqi economy at that peri-

---

61 A recent research study conducted in Iraq about the migration patterns of the Iraqi Turkmen points at their high-level of education: accordingly a quarter of the women and one third of the men have attended university and only one in ten had no education (Sirkeci 2005: 14).

62 Hasan is a dentist born in 1951, in Mosul. He has lived in Turkey since 1969, the year when he came to study. The interview was conducted in his private clinic in Taksim, on 24.11.2005.

od. One Iraqi Dinar was equal to 3.30 USD. Even middle income families could easily send their kids. Avoiding military service was also a reason to come to Turkey for some young people who finished high school but could not get into university. And of course, parents who are doctors want their children to study certainly in medical school; if he cannot enter into medicine in Iraq, they send him to Turkey or to other countries. In those years, every country was known with the high quality of education in some specialties; for example the Eastern Bloc, especially Romania and Czechoslovakia, were favorite destinations to study orthopedics (Interview with Kemal Beyatlı, 22.4.2005).[63]

The importance paid to education is certainly a significant element of Iraqi Turkmen culture. Most of the interviewees expressed the high level of education among the Turkmen community in Iraq. This emphasis on education was valid for people of urban backgrounds as well as rural. Besides, networks based on extended family ties encouraged the dissemination of information about possibilities in Turkey, as well as providing initial contacts for young students, who were mostly male:

> My father was a farmer. One of my brothers came to Turkey to study after me. The other one got a degree inf political sciences in Baghdad and then a Masters degree in Cairo and completed his doctorate in Turkey. He is now an associate professor in a Turkish university.... The son of my aunt studied here, in the department of mechanical engineering at the Technical University, also the son of my uncle studied medicine in Istanbul (Interview with Hasan, 2005).

While many of the Iraqi Turkmen students went back home after they finished their education, there were a considerable number of people who could not return because of the political turbulence in their country. The relations of these early comers with the homeland

---

63 Kemal Beyatlı is the head of the Turkmen Association (Irak Türkleri Kültür ve Yardımlaşma Derneği). He himself immigrated to Turkey in 1991, after the Gulf War, together with his wife and two children. The interview has been realized at the headquarters of the Association in Aksaray, on 22.4.2005.

are shaped by the political and military unrest. The 'never-ending wars' in Iraq give rise for many to the impossibility of returning home, and to limited interactions with family members and friends. Once again, the distinction between volunteer and forced migration is hard to delineate, as is seen in the words of İhsan:

> All my relatives went back after they graduated. At those times, the situation in Iraq was very good. Me too, I would return. I got my degree but I wanted to stay for a doctorate. Then, the year I got my doctoral degree, the war began [Iran-Iraq War]. In that case what could I do? I decided to stay and open a private clinic so as not to hang around jobless. In those years, the economic conditions in Iraq were good, and ours was better. The short term opening of the clinic became eternal, I could not go back again and I stayed here. When the war with Iran ended, the Gulf War started, the situation in Iraq became terrible, and I could not go home, again. I did not have even a tiny idea of opening a clinic here. Before my arrival here, I had a plan in mind that I would return to Iraq in 1973. It is now 2005, how many years have passed away from my homeland (in gurbet)? My parents and my siblings are there; homesickness is hard. But the conditions in Iraq are so bad that nothing can be done (Interview with İhsan, 2005).

We can categorize these educational migrants under three categories:

1. Persons who stay in Turkey. Even though most of them did not have such an intention upon their arrival, problems related to political chaos and military service under the Ba'ath Regime caused many to prefer to stay in Turkey and build a new life. Their education credentials and their well-to-do families' financial support have been two important means of their adjustment. Above all, the easy access to Turkish citizenship has facilitated their incorporation. Never ending political problems in Iraq made them stay permanently in Turkey.

Today, the general profile of the old Iraqi Turkmen community in Istanbul is characterized by high levels of education, professional middle class positions, and reasonable incorporation into Turkish society. During the interviews, many of the early comers put an emphasis on the fact that they are not migrants.

2. Persons who return to Iraq. This category went back to Iraq at the end of their education in Turkey, before the beginning of Iran-Iraq War. Some people with sizeable wealth back home could not give it up for the sake of escaping military service. Among these students some have become circular migrants and continued back-and-forth movements between Iraq and Turkey, mostly for business activities.

3. Persons who go to third countries. This further migration is motivated by work prospects. These migrants' diplomas and linguistic skills (speaking Arabic and Turkish) have been their main competencies. Most of them have been working in Turkish companies based in Arab countries, such as the United Arab Emirates or Libya. The ethnic and linguistic capitals seem to play a pivotal role in these networks. There are also others who are settled in northern European countries, after finishing their education in Turkey.

Post-1991: Mass Departure

Even though Turkmen emigration continued throughout the 1970s and 1980s, its most critical year, like for other Iraqi minority groups, was 1991. According to İbrahim Sirkeci (2005: 40) 80% of Iraqi Turkmen migrants have emigrated after 1990. In the same way, the head of the Turkmen Association claimed that the majority of the current Turkmen population in Turkey (60-70%, in his words) arrived after 1991. According to Sirkeci, "17,000 Turkmen have entered into Turkey in 1991, 12,000 of those have returned home." The 'Altunköprü Massacre' in March 1991 was one of the remarkable moments worsening the conditions of the Iraqi Turkmens (Saatçi, 2004). As expressed by many, the conditions during and after the Gulf War were worsened to an intolerable degree, and many had to seek refuge in Turkey, together with large numbers of Kurds and Assyro-Chaldeans.

Because of our social structure we do not easily migrate, but then the conditions became unbearable.... I write literature, poetry. But in those years, it was not possible to publish what we wrote. Obviously, if you write rose-flower-love things there was no problem but the regime did not allow the publication of what we wanted to write. There were all kinds of coercions by the regime towards the Turkmen; there were executions, obstacles to employment, rejections from universities and forbiddances to buy and sell properties. Finally, together with a group in 1991, we crossed to Turkey by walking on the mountains. We stayed in the Silopi camp. Then the government reached a decision and said that persons [Turkmens], who have money in the bank or have relatives here, can pass through (Interview with Mustafa, 23.4.2005).

The Turkmens who arrived in 1991 were advantaged in terms of the reception policies of the Turkish authorities. Many Turkmen who arrived that year experienced a hospitable atmosphere. Many could easily acquire residence permits just after their arrival. A special decree that passed in late April 1991 has regulated the right to residence of the 1991 refugees. According to this regulation, "persons who have a first or second degree relative in Turkey, as well as persons who have sufficient economic resources to guarantee their livelihood" could obtain residence permits.[64] This decree privileged mainly the Turkmen who could easily mobilize their close as well as distant relatives to acquire the right to residence. As asserted by some of the interviewees who came in 1991, in addition to this state assistance which soothed the legal status of the Turkmen, many also benefited from informal state assistance in finding jobs in the public or private sectors.

Some of the asylum seekers in 1991 were well educated professionals, even though there were also several who had lesser credentials. While a great majority of them went back home soon after a brief stay in the southeast of Turkey, there were significant numbers of people (5,000 according to Kemal Beyatlı) who did not. Actually, for

---

64 "Hangi mültecilere oturma izni var", *Sabah*, 30.4.1991.

the latter, the alternatives were not limited to staying in Turkey. There were some who continued their migration and tried to reach their relatives abroad, particularly those in Europe. Among these, there were very few who obtained refugee status by the UNHCR. According to the representatives of the association, the last five years in particular have been a total frustration for Iraqi Turkmen who applied to UNHCR for asylum.[65] Among the post-1991 Turkmen, although in small numbers, there were also some who crossed to Europe through clandestine ways.

After the massive and sudden flight in 1991, the emigration has not come to an end. It has continued until today, even though in a decreased quantity. According to Sirkeci's research (2005: 24), Turkmen households have a high level of migration with at least one member migrating abroad (35% of the overall Turkmen households). Ahmet Sirkeci argues that this migration appears to be forced due to their good socio-economic conditions (2005: 32). During our own fieldwork in Istanbul, we observed that in the post-1991 era, political and economic motivations for migrating go hand-in-hand. War, political turbulences and poverty are the most mentioned topics, as well as political and physical oppression towards the Turkmen minority. Saime, who is a 30 year-old Turkmen woman from Kirkuk, arrived with her husband in Istanbul via Jordan in 1994.

> We came from Iraq in 1994 and we settled here. We could not bear the cruelty of Saddam, we ran away and we came here. There were constant assaults on our houses. For instance, we are sitting here, and then we see that soldiers are jumping over the garden walls and enter into the house.... They were searching for guns, but they were messing everything up, cupboards, wardrobes... We spent two days to rearrange the house after they left (Interview with Saime, 14.12.2005).[66]

---

65 It seems that the UNHCR in Turkey single out the Turkmen files by considering their cases 'less urgent' owing to the relatively warm reception by the Turkish authorities.

66 Interview with Saime conducted in 14.12.2005.

Besides, for the Turkmen migrants of 1991, an important motivation of departure was to escape the military service that became intolerable after years spent in the army.

> Living conditions in Iraq are very hard. There is poverty, famine and war. After the Gulf War, the situation became insecure and restless. Moreover, we had difficulty of livelihood there. In fact, we were starving. And I was afraid of being called again for the military service. I decided to go to Europe to have a better life with my family. Before going to Europe, we decided to go to Istanbul, because our relatives too had migrated similarly (Interview with Ahmet,16.12.2006).[67]

The principal sources of networking that facilitate the integration of Iraqi Turkmen in Turkey are familial solidarity, knowledge of the Turkish language, and finally the networks provided by associations. Familial ties are the first source of solidarity and help to overcome the difficulties faced during irregular stays in Istanbul.

> We did not face great difficulty when we came here. The fact that our relatives had arrived here earlier helped us a lot for our adaptation. We did not have a place to stay when we first came here; we stayed at their houses. And above all, we benefited a lot from the support of our relatives to find a job. Probably if we did not have relatives here, we would suffer a lot (Interview with İhsan).

> My brother-in-law had arrived here earlier. Three of my brother-in-laws went to Canada with United Nations permission, and one of them stayed here and became a Turkish citizen. In fact, we first came to his house. He helped us; we stayed at his place for a while. (...) Our family is very attached to each other, in every subject. It was the same there, as also here. If anybody needs something, everybody make a contribution. For instance, when we bought this

---

67 Ahmet is a 35 year-old man with a university degree from Kirkuk. He had arrived in Istanbul with his wife and children 9 months before the interview. At that time he had recently stopped working at the construction sites and started to work in a small textile factory. The interview was conducted in 16.12.2005.

house, my brother-in-law paid more than half of its cost, without expecting any return. We bought most of our furniture with the money sent by my brother-in-laws in Canada (Interview with Saime).

Turkmen are certainly advantaged thanks to their familiarity with the Turkish language, even though many who studied in Iraq did not know how to write in Turkish. Unlike the earlier migrants, the post-1991 arrivees are characterized by a relatively lower level of education. The general specialty of Turkmens had been their education; however, the atrocities committed against them and war-related destruction in the country seems to diminish the educational credentials of the newcomers.[68]

The Association and its Identity Cards: Certificate of Turkishness

The Iraqi Turks Culture and Solidarity Association (*Irak Türkleri Kültür ve Yardımlaşma Derneği*) is the hub of Turkmen presence in the city. Even though there are a few more Turkmen associations in Istanbul,[69] the Turkmen Association in Aksaray is a social, cultural and geographical attraction center for the Iraqi Turkmen migrants since its foundation in 1959. The Association has two types of members. In the first group there are the persons who have already acquired Turkish citizenship or residence and have held work permits

---

68 Turkmens account for this decrease in the education level with Saddam Hussein's ultra-nationalist policies and his attempts 'to wipe out Turkmens'. They claim that the ex-Iraqi president did not appreciate education when he said that, "I do not need educated men, but I need soldiers to die for me."

69 There are also other Turkmen organizations in Istanbul: Kerkük Vakfı (Kirkuk Foundation) headed by İzzettin Kerkük in Beyoğlu, Türkmeneli İnsan Hakları Derneği (Turkmen Human Rights Association) headed by Nefi Demirci in Fatih and Irak Türkmenleri Kardeşlik ve Kültür Derneği (Iraqi Turkmen Brotherhood and Culture Association) headed by Yaşar Kevser in Osmanbey. However, none of them have a constituency as large as the Turkmen Association in Aksaray. The first two are specialized in publishing activities to raise awareness about oppressions towards Turkmens in Iraq, whereas the last one serves more as a professional association for the Turkmen businessmen in Osmanbey.

for more than two years. This group consists of around 350 persons. In the second group, there are the Turkmen who have a short-term, if any, residence permit. The Turkmen Association processes their registration and gives them an identity card for the association. This group is much larger and comprises 2,000 people.

The disinterest of the old migrants towards the Turkmen Association is mostly due to the fact that all of them have citizenship and established lives in Istanbul for many years. Until the 1990s it was very easy to get Turkish citizenship for the Iraqi Turkmen, as asserted by many of the respondents who arrived in the pre-1991 era. They acquired Turkish nationality within six months after their simple application. They thus feel less dependent on an official mediator for their daily problems.

The membership figures provided by the head of the Association correspond to what is observed during the interviews with the old comers. Affiliation with the Association creates a differentiation among the old Turkmen migrants. The group who stays in touch with the newcomers through the channel constructed by the Association is more concerned about the political developments in Iraq and are, generally speaking much more nationalistic, whereas others who stay away from the association are less involved in homeland issues. The latter seems to be much more assimilated into Turkish society, in socio-economic as well as political terms, to such a degree that their ties to their country of origin are gradually becoming a mere folkloric issue. The comment of an interviewee who came to Turkey in the 1960s, clarifies the distance that many old Turkmen migrants feel towards the Association:

> The Association has a political aspect. I have never been involved in politics; this is why I am not interested in [the Association]. I know those people, but I do not have a relation. In fact, the Association is useful for the newcomers (Interview with Hasan).

Despite this aloofness of the old migrants, the Association means a lot for the newcomers and serves as an important hub for them. It mainly assists with the legal and economic problems of its members. One of its important roles is to help them to find employment:

> We act as a go-between for the well-behaved and polite newcomers from Iraq or for the ones who recently quit their work; we try to find them a job in Osmanbey and Laleli. Thankfully, persons who have business there notify us when they need new personnel. We mediate to get them together, and then we leave them alone (Interview with an employee of the Association, 22.04.2005).

The undocumented Turkmens in Istanbul are also benefiting from the legal assistance of the Turkmen Association. The formalities of applying for residence permits are often administered by the staff of the Association. However, what is most significant among its activities is the delivery of a special identity card, which facilitates the interaction of the undocumented Turkmen with the police. On one side of this card there is basic information about the cardholder, including name, surname, and birth date. Below on the same side, it says "this cardholder is of Turkish origin". On the other side, there is a map of Kirkuk and its surroundings in a bright red color, and above it is written "Kirkuk is Turk and will always be so" (Kerkük Türktür, Türk kalacak). This identity card which stirs the nationalist feelings of Turkish policemen serves as the unofficial residence permit for many Iraqi Turkmen who have recently arrived.

The Association does not have an official service to find accommodation; nonetheless they help newcomers to find a residence thanks to information disseminated by word-of-mouth. They have a better organization for health services; the representatives of the Association made an agreement with a hospital in Beyazıt for a 50-60% discount to Turkmen patients. Similarly, members benefit from the solidarity networks of Turkmen doctors, often from the previous generation of

Turkmen migration, providing medical treatment for undocumented Turkmen migrants who are unable to use public health services. Last but not least, they organize social events like picnics or special nights at restaurants. All these events together with the activities carried out in the Association's headquarters help to build a social space that the Turkmen link up with.

Ethnic Business in Osmanbey and Laleli

Commerce is an important economic activity for the Turkmens' socio-economic incorporation. Thanks to their linguistic capital, knowledge of Turkish as well as Arabic, they are one of the biggest groups who sell textiles and other products to Gulf and North African countries in shops located in Laleli and Osmanbey. Turkmen seem to date back to the 1980s in Laleli when the first migrants after the students of the 1960s began to arrive to Istanbul. While few benefited from the economic capital they could bring from Iraq, most of them started 'from the bottom' by working in the shops as salespersons or interpreters for the Arab clientele.

> In the past there were plenty of Arabs; this was our chance. We worked as interpreters for them; we acted as brokers (komisyoncu) and we got hold of a position in the market. We started our own businesses. Similar to the Russians who made the Bosnians rich, Arabs made us rich(Interview with Nefi).[70]

There are basically two groups who work with the Arab clientele: the Mardinli and Iraqi Turkmen. According to the accounts of the Turkmen shop owners, the Mardinli have recently appeared in this business community in the last ten years. As a matter of fact, there is competition between these two, and the Iraqi whom we interviewed expressed their feelings of dislike quite openly:

---

70 Nefi was at this time director of an export company in Laleli. He immigrated in 1986, at age 21 and since then "worked in all kind of jobs in Laleli", such as sale person, interpreter-guide. Interview on 7.7.2005, in Laleli.

> The people from the East steal from the merchandise; if they write
> size forty on a cloth, they produce it two sizes smaller, just to prof-
> it from the material. In particular, the Mardinli do this a lot: they
> are swindlers, freeloaders. They think they are smart but they harm
> both the customer and Turkey. Certainly, sooner or later customers
> run away. (...) The only thing they know is money, money, money.
> Don't misunderstand, maybe it is not only the Mardinli, but these
> men do not have a work ethic. They say they will deliver the goods
> \on that day, but then you wait weeks and weeks to receive it. For
> us, work ethic is the most important thing. If we give our word, we
> accomplish it whatever happens (Interview with Nefi).

The unfriendliness between the Mardinli and the Turkmen is
also related to different careers they pursue. While Mardinli are often
shop owners in Laleli (Deli, 2002), most of the Turkmen specialize in
the export companies. These are cargo firms that mediate between
wholesalers and Arab customers for the transportation as well as
arrangement of the merchandise bought. Their earnings are based on
a TVA (Katma Değer Vergisi) they collect from the state out of the
amount processed; thus they need to receive official invoices in order
to get their share.

> People from the East and Southeast want to become rich through
> shortcut. They do not like official business; actually they don't even
> know it. In the past, they were smuggling at the borders, they still
> think the same way here. Asking for an invoice appears strange to
> them. That discipline of smuggling doesn't work out here. When
> you ask for an invoice, they say 'don't botherwith the invoice'; they
> suppose they can do business this way (Interview with Ömer).[71]

Iraq is the dazzling new target-customer for export-oriented
shops and cargo companies in Laleli and Osmanbey. Many Turkmen

---

71 Ömer came from Kirkuk in 1994 and worked in various companies as a % 50 shareholder until
    1998 when he started his own export company in Laleli. They convey textile and construction
    merchandise mostly to Iraq, but also to other Middle Eastern countries, including Syria and
    Lebanon. Interview on 7.7.2005, in Laleli.

companies who were once targeting Arabs from the Gulf countries and Maghreb now have a closer relationship with Iraqi customers. One of the Turkmen firms that we visited during the fieldwork has been the biggest foreign trade company that transports goods for Arab countries, including Iraq. According to their accounts, commerce with Iraq started in 1996-1997, however in a very limited capacity because of the embargo. At that time it was only possible to send food, and to a lesser extent some textiles "if the companies could arrange custom guards who would close their eyes". Since 2003, there has been a significant boom in commerce with Iraq, in particular with the easy access to passports and the freedom of export and import in the country. Even though it is not possible to verify, Turkmen businessmen in Laleli argue that the volume of commerce with Iraq is four to five million USD yearly.

> There were Iraqi customers in the past too. However, after the fall of Saddam when it became possible to get a passport and to carry out American dollars, an explosion happened. Before the fall of Saddam, Kurds were collecting very high duties on the custom. They were charging half a dollar for each trouser or shirt; if you calculate it for each large truck it made three to four thousand dollars. After his [Saddam's] fall, they did not intervene for a while, now they establish a customs system with lower duties than before: they charge 100-200 dollars for each truck (Interview with Tarık).[72]

Even though commerce in Laleli seems to be part of the informal economy, states have a significant role in shaping the volume and direction of these flows. The embargoes, custom duties, granting of visa permits, and TVA payments are all instruments used by the

---

72 Tarık is a Turkmen in his mid-30s working in Company T since 1991 when he arrived. All the Turkmen shop owners directed me towards this company which they designated as the biggest Turkmen firm in Laleli. I was quite surprised when I entered the firm, which was, in sharp contrast to other Turkmen shops in Laleli, in a complete Islamic decoration: no men without beard, "selamünaleyküm" as the only greeting and pictures of Hajj and other sacred places on the walls. Interview on 8.7.2005, in Laleli.

authorities to control how and who benefits from this business. Correspondingly, the Turkish state subtly privileges Turkmens in the growing commerce with Iraq. The Iraqi customers unsurprisingly are relatives of the Turkmen merchants in Istanbul who buy mostly textile products and construction equipment.

> Commerce with Iraq started before the fall of Saddam, yet it now goes on with a growing speed. We send goods to our relatives in Iraq and they sell them little by little. Life isn't stopped there, it continues; and they want to dress up nicely too. (...) Turkey impedes visa procedures of non-Turkmens from Iraq, so that they want to punish the Kurds for what they do to us" (Interview with Ömer).

Ethnic businesses targeting Arab customers provided an important employment niche for the Iraqi Turkmen who migrated in the 1980s and 1990s. Unlike the ones who came for educational reasons in the 1960s, Turkmens who arrived in the later decades took advantage of the flourishing, informal sector, in particular of the commercial centers in Laleli and Osmanbey. Nevertheless, prosperous years of suitcase trade did not last long and the golden years of 1996-97 ended with a stagnation period that still somehow reigns in Laleli and Osmanbey markets (Pérouse, 2002).

Competition with China, overvaluation of the Turkish currency, and regularization attempts by the Turkish authorities, including putting high taxes on the unregistered export activities, play a part in the shrinking of the market. The recently arrived Turkmens, who thus lose one of the important sources of employment, face difficulties acquiring what other undocumented migrants in the country experience. Ahmet, who arrived nine months ago from Kirkuk, articulates these problems very clearly:

> At the beginning I worked in construction, and then painted houses. Now I am working in a textile workshop. Our work hours are very long and exhausting. I was working in difficult conditions in Iraq too, but I don't remember that I had ever been so tired. I work

> very hard but I earn very little. I can't receive what I deserve.
> Changing jobs is not a solution. When you are a migrant they
> always treat you the same way. At the end, I am working without
> security and for a little salary. We can't say a word because we are
> migrants (Interview with Ahmet).

The recent arrivals to the Iraqi Turkmen community in Istanbul, are in a precarious position. A 15 year-old boy working as a salesperson in a shoe shop in Gedikpaşa owned by a Turkmen and Bulgarian Turk said that he had been working in various jobs since age 13. He emigrated with his family from Kirkuk five years ago and he had to work together with his older sister to secure their living. He could not attend school due to economic hardship as well the absence of residence permits which are required for enrollment in primary schools in Turkey.

Nevertheless, despite the legal obstacles that hinder newcomers in acquiring official documents, face-to-face interactions with the state, such as encounters with the police, are relatively easier for the Turkmen:

> I don't have a residence [permit], I am clandestine, but the police
> close their eyes. They would rather catch the Arabs or the Kurds.
> It is now very difficult to obtain residency, but the police do not
> touch the Turkmen, they sympathize with us and they tolerate
> (Interview with Muhammed, 12.8.2005).[73]

An important obstacle for the newcomers' incorporation has been the difficulty of obtaining Turkish nationality. Many Turkmens, who easily acquired citizenship up until the last five years, highlight the difficulty for the recently arrived in getting citizenship or even a

---

73 Muhammed came from Iraq in 1998, in age 18, to escape the military service after seeing his older brother's destiny who spent many years in the Iraqi army and five more in the Iranian prisons. Since his arrival he has been working in various shops in Osmanbey thanks to his relatives' assistance. As a single man, he lives in Kurtuluş, like many of his colleagues working in Osmanbey (Interview on 12.8.2005, in Osmanbey).

residence permit. Actually, very few of the Turkmens who arrived after 2000 could obtain citizenship. This is probably related to the population politics of the Turkish state that prefers the Turkmen to stay in Iraq rather than immigrate. To sum up, even though it can be argued that the incorporation of the Iraqi Turkmen has been facilitated by their ethnic origin, i.e. their 'Turkishness', as seen above there have been periods during which this ethnic affiliation has turned out to be a disadvantage due to the changes in the foreign policy of the Turkish state towards Iraq.

Iraqi Assyro-Chaldeans: Religious Networks and 'Deliberate Indifference'

A small but steady part of the Iraqi migrants in Turkey consists of the Christians. Being one of the smallest minorities in their homeland they have been massively evacuating Iraq since the 1991 Gulf War.

A Community En Route: Iraqi Assyro-Chaldeans[74]

The recent Iraqi Christian emigration has begun as a consequence of worsening conditions during the 1991 Gulf War, and has been ongoing since then in a small but constant way.[75] Aiming to get out of Iraq as soon as possible, Assyro-Chaldeans first head off to Turkey, Jordan or Syria in order to initiate their applications to affluent third countries, and thus perform a step migration since they cannot reach their preferred destinations directly. The religious identities that restrict their political participation and access to economic resources in Iraq and eventually engender their exile, turns into a crucial instrument for easing the difficulties they face in the migration process.

---

74 The information on this section is substantiated by my previous research on Iraqi Christian transit migration (Danış, 2005).

75 Catholic Chaldeans, Assyrians, Syrian Orthodox and Armenians are the main Christian minority groups in Iraq, of which the Chaldeans constitute the largest (Yakan, 2002: 18). In this paper, I interchangeably use Christians and Chaldeans since almost all of the Iraqi Christian migrants in Istanbul belong to this sect. Statements made on Chaldeans apply for other Christians as well.

The Iraqi Christians, who have been *en route* to developed countries via Istanbul, provide an intriguing example among the other migrant groups reckoning Turkey as a 'waiting room'. With an educated guess, we can suggest that in 2006 there was a population of three to four thousand persons, with constant entrants and exits. In total, some hundred thousand Iraqi Christians have used this route to reach their final destinations which include such countries as Australia and Canada in the course of twenty years of incessant migration. The Christians in Iraq, a minority estimated at around half a million currently, constituted 3% of the Iraqi society and had twice this population three decades ago (Heyberger, 2003). This means that in the last two decades some half a million Iraqi Christians have run away to the west via transit countries surrounding Iraq.

The Assyro-Chaldeans are considered among the ancient Christian communities living in the Middle East (Joseph, 1961; Valognes, 1994).[76] Christian minorities in Iraq have been in a vulnerable position, similar to other communities in the country, due to the environment of instability that has been going on for the last 25 years in Iraq. First, the Iran-Iraq War, then the incidents of the Gulf War in 1991 worsened living conditions. The increasing level of oppression against dissidents in the aftermath of the Gulf War and the decreasing living standards as a result of political instability and economic embargoes induced a massive emigration of Iraqis (Mannaert, 2003; Van Hear, 1995). And finally, after the fall of Saddam Hussein, sharing the difficulties of the prevalent chaos with other Iraqi citizens, Christians are further threatened due to accusations of collaborating with the United States. They thus face incidents of persecution, such as assaults on churches, intimidation of Christian youth, kidnappings, and religious discrimination in schools and other public spaces.

---

76 Chaldeans split from Assyrians in 1553 and united to the Catholic Church. Despite this separation, Assyrians and Chaldeans have very similar rituals and traditions.

> We came in July 2003 from Mosul. I was working as taxi driver
> before the war [in 2003] but my taxi was put on fire during the war,
> I could not ask who did it. After the war the situation became hard-
> er for Christians. Shiites discriminate against Christians and Muslims.
> My son was the only Assyrian in his school, all the other kids blamed
> him, saying that 'you are Christian, you called the Americans'. Every
> afternoon, we were waiting anxiously for his return from the school.
> After a while we could not bear this anymore and we left (Interview
> with Varda, 35 year-old man, married with two children).

The migratory movement of the Iraqi Chaldean community in
the last twenty years operates as both a chain migration and a refugee
movement owing to the collapse of the political and social order in
Iraq. The blurring of the dichotomy between political and economic
migrants complicates to differentiate labor migration and refugee
movements (Hein, 1993; Chatelard, 2002). The same is valid for Iraqi
Christians too; the increasing discrimination against their Christian
identities in their daily lives on the one hand, and day-by-day worsening living standards due to embargoes and economic constraints on
the other, reinforces their determination to emigrate. Whatever the primary reason is, their religious identity is one of the pertinent factors in
their departure from Iraq. In his study on emigration of the Kurds of
Turkey, Ibrahim Sirkeci (2005) remarks that the environment of ethnic conflict in Turkey for the last twenty years acts as a push factor as
well as an opportunity framework for those potential migrants who
do not have the necessary means to realize this aspiration. Parallel
conditions exist in the case of Christian Iraqis; while discrimination
against their religious identity forces them to leave the country, the
maltreatment they have endured as members of a minority group qualifies them for refugee status or for humanitarian protection. In short,
being deprived of the most basic means of sustenance, including protection for their lives, renders the classical distinction of forced/volun-
tary or economic/political migration insignificant.[77]

---

77 Nevertheless, for the ease of expression I use the term migrant in this section.

Social Networks of the Assyro-Chaldeans

Two factors seem to be crucial for the organization of Iraqi Christian migration: these are kin and religion-based social networks. The facilitating and encouraging roles of the migrant networks have been observed in various migratory contexts (Boyd, 1989; Gurak and Caces, 1992; Pessar, 1999). Social networks of migrants are often conceived as an independent factor sustaining the continuation of migration after it starts out (Massey et.al., 1998; Brettel, 2000). They have an influential role in designating migration routes and in getting over the difficulties that have been encountered during the transit migration period as well. The pioneers of the Iraqi Christian emigration, those who had departed in the early 1990s and now reside mostly in Australia and Canada, establish an important basis of support for today's migrants; they provide invaluable assistance at several steps such as departure from Iraq, arrival to Istanbul, and further on.[78] Transit migrants in Istanbul benefit from their 'successful' relatives' help in order to overcome the economic straits they have gone through during the tense waiting period which amounts to two to five years (with exceptional cases lasting more than seven years). Fadiya, a 65 year-old widowed woman, illustrates the role of the family network in the migration process:

> Life was very difficult in Iraq. My son in Australia told us to come first to Istanbul and then to Australia. We could not yet receive an answer to our application. My son left Iraq six years ago; he stayed for a while in Greece and two years ago he went to Australia. He thinks of us all the time, he calls once or twice every month. He sends us money too, otherwise we would not be able to pay the rent (Fadiya arrived in Istanbul in early 2003 together with her two sons and a daughter ranging in age between 24 and 35).

---

78 By the estimates of the Australian Department of Immigration, Iraq-born immigrants constitute one of the fastest growing groups, and Assyro-Chaldeans come first within Iraqi population in Australia. According to the figures of 2001 census, the largest group among the people of Iraqi origin, a population of 24,760, is the community of Assyro-Chaldean descent with 40% (9,710 people). It has been reported that over 40,000 Iraqi of Assyro-Chaldean descent resideed in Australia by the end of 2003 (http://www.immi.gov.au).

On their arrival to Istanbul, newcomers stay for a while near the relatives who came before; 'veterans' open up their houses to the newly arrived and reveal the intricacies of living and being a migrant in Istanbul. The people without relatives relate that they have gone through miseries upon their arrival, having to stay at hotels for a while, especially unnerved by being unable to speak Turkish and the lack of relatives to guide them through. Bes, a 39 year old man who arrived in 2002 with his wife, five children and his 69 year old mother recalls:

> When we came to Istanbul, my sister was here, they received us. She came in 1999 and spent almost four years here before they went to Australia. They helped us in every sense. After a while we rented a place of our own. All my relatives are in Australia, there is nobody left back in Iraq, I was the last one. Me too, I want to go to Australia. We came here after we sold all our belongings. There is not even a cigarette behind.

Religious ties constitute a more pertinent means for survival than familial networks during Iraqi Christians' temporary stay in Istanbul. Religion, which is the most fundamental element in the Iraqi Christian social organization and self-identification, enables them to get hold of a wider social network and helps them sustain their lives in the period of dire straits during the transit migration period.

The role of religion in the process of international migration has been evaluated from different angles. The classical perspective conceives religion as a source of social, economic, and psychological assistance for migrants' adaptation and integration into the host society. Hirschman (2003), for instance, points at the church organizations' role as information sharing communities, enhancing survival strategies and the socioeconomic opportunities of migrants, in his account of migrants in the United States. In the same way, Orlando Mella emphasizes psycho-social benefits of religion for exile communities. She emphasizes the role of religion in enhancing mental integrity in the life of Chilean refugees in Sweden (Mella, 1994). Reaffirmation of traditional beliefs through religion provides cognitive means to begin a new life in an unfamiliar setting where migrants feel themselves alien. Religion also provides a sense of belonging in cases of forced migration; refugee communities embrace religion to reclaim and rebuild their history and culture. References to religious identities and symbols foster the reconstitution of the community (Stelaku, 2003).

Agreeing with Vasquez (2003), I believe that one should consider micro, meso, and macro contexts simultaneously in order to better understand the embeddedness of religious practices and institutions. Below, three remarkable functions that religion plays in the process of Iraqi Christian transit migration are analyzed. Firstly, from a religious organizational context, I scrutinize the role of religion in creating a social network that Catholic Chaldeans benefit from. Then, I portray the distinguished position of priests in these religious networks. Finally, I focus on the impact of the Turkish state in shaping the boundaries and the content of this network.

Religious Networks: Church as the Center of Community

The secularization paradigm, which assumed a gradual secularization of migrants and the public decline of religion as a result of social change related to the migration process, has been challenged by many scholars recently. More and more researchers recognize the significance of religion and indicate the role of religious participation in the adaptation and integration of migrants (Levitt, 2001; Ebaugh and Chafetz, 2002). Religiosity is a frequently observed phenomenon among new immigrants (Hirschman, 2003). Particularly, soon after arrival, migrants seek to participate in religious ceremonies which provide a spiritual calm to endure the difficulties of adjusting to a new life. As Handlin puts it, religion becomes a bridge that connects the old world with the new (Handlin, 1973, cited by Hirschmann, 2003: 7). Father George, a renowned figure in the community, summarizes the significance of religion for the Chaldeans in Istanbul:

> We are foreigner here, we have to be together all the time. This is
> why we all live in the same neighborhoods. This is why the Sunday
> mass is so important for us (see box no.1).

High religiosity of new migrants is also observed in churches in
Istanbul. Local churches that have gradually lost their original members are now filled up by foreigners. On Sundays, a heterogeneous
crowd including Philippinos, Africans, Iraqis, Iranians, Poles, and others get together in the churchyard and form a formidable Tower of
Babel while waiting for their denominational service.

Religion certainly has a more important meaning to a community with a religious minority status, both in the departure and arrival
countries. Accordingly, a major source of support for Iraqi Christians
during their migration is the social networks interwoven around
church and affiliated institutions. They create a religious milieu that
both replenishes feelings of belonging and identity, and provides
socioeconomic opportunities during the transit period in Turkey. In
addition to moral support, churches provide material services such as
opportunities for social interaction, information sharing on housing or
job opportunities, education facilities for children, provision of food,
clothing or medical assistance, and so on. Churches and other religious institutions thus serve as a fundamental source of support for the
practical problems.

The central spatial element for the Iraqi Christian community in
Istanbul is the church of Catholic Italians in Beyoğlu which has been
used by the Chaldeans since their abrupt arrival. Chaldeans are
dwelling in run-down city center districts like Tarlabaşi, Dolapdere,
Elmadağ, and Kurtuluş, in the vicinity of the church and Caritas.[79] It is
my understanding that Caritaas no longer exists as a result of a dispute
that emerged between the two groups that made up the oundation.
This residential concentration is also remarkable since the area was

---

[79] Caritas is a Catholic charity organization offering basic social services such as legal consultation, education, provision of food and clothing to Iraqi Christians.

once populated by a native Christian population who gradually left the country by the mid-20th century. Sunday rituals held at the church provide a unique occasion to gather the community together. A minimum of 200-300 Iraqi Chaldeans participate in the Mass, which plays a notable social role in reinforcing the relations among community members, hence serving as a channel of solidarity. The chats after the prayer in the yard of the Catholic Church constitute a lively social field where job opportunities for youngsters are discussed, anxieties are exchanged, or possibilities of further migration are considered. Having lunch together after the church service and performing house visits within the community ensure that Sundays become a remarkable socialization day for Chaldean transit migrants in Istanbul.

Apart from offering religious services to Chaldean Catholic Iraqi migrants, church officials of the Chaldean Church in Istanbul arrange semi-official meetings with institutions like the governorship and the Foreigners' Bureau in the General Security Department. These church officials follow up on the cases of Chaldean Iraqis who got into trouble with police or cannot get permission to leave the country as a result of failing to complete the papers in spite of gaining admission from a third country. In brief, they 'keep an eye on them'; a situation resembling the *millet* system of the Ottoman period, a model of governance where non–Muslim communities were both overseen and represented officially by their religious leaders (Mardin, 1990: 39). Given that most of the Chaldeans are undocumented during their stay in Turkey due to entering Turkey without passports or overstaying their visas in due course, such interventions before the police officials are of utmost importance.

The eminence of religion for Chaldean Iraqi migrants does not come to an end there. Most of the Chaldeans in Istanbul either work near a non-Muslim, Istanbulite family, or rent houses owned by local non-Muslims. In this sense, the limits of the network that Chaldeans in Istanbul inhabit are marked by Christianity. 'Intermediaries' or 'brokers' between Chaldean Iraqi migrants and natives of Istanbul, who assist new arrivals to find housing and employment connections, are the church watchmen, who are recognized by almost all recently-arrived Chaldean families in Istanbul. Connecting the Chaldean migrants to non-Muslim Istanbulite employers and landlords, these church employees act as a bridge connecting two social networks, in the sense employed by Granovetter (1973), hence conducing the incorporation of Chaldean Iraqis with strong internal ties to a wider social milieu through the link of Oriental Christianity. As such, Christian Iraqi families rent the houses owned by non-Muslim Istanbulites, and Chaldean girls are employed in their households as babysitters and cleaning-ladies. Sara's story of how she found her first job is typical in this sense:

> When we first came here, we went to the Assyrian Catholic Church on our first Sunday in Istanbul. We said that we had just arrived; we explained our situation to the priest. He advised my mom that there is such a job for girls; he enthusiastically told that it is a good job and he convinced my mom. The next day, my sister and I got prepared and went [to the church] to meet the people; they told us to start one week later. So on the fifteenth day of our arrival, we began to work.

Sara and her older sister began to work at ages 13 and 14 due to the meagre amount of monetary resources they could bring from their homeland. In other families whose economic conditions are better, daughters work at a later age. All Iraqi Christian girls looking for 'a job at a house' receive their information from the churches. Churches and church personnel are the glue in Iraqi Christians' social networks that serve as 'sources for the acquisition of scarce means, such as capital and information' (Portes, 1995: 8). The 'intermediaries' between Chaldean Iraqi migrants and natives of Istanbul, who make connections on the housing and employment fronts, are priests or church staff. The networking mechanism works like this: Newly arrived Iraqi Christians inform the church staff of their need for a job during the Sunday service. Then the staff distributes the news to local non-Muslim women who are looking for household workers. The two steps of the recruitment happen by word-of-mouth and take place in the church, through the mediation of the church personnel, known by all the recently-arrived Iraqi families. Connecting the Iraqi migrants to non-Muslim Istanbulite employers, church personnel act as a bridge linking two social networks, in the sense employed by Granovetter (1973). They thus help the incorporation of Iraqi Chaldeans marked by strong internal ties into a wider social milieu through the link of Christianity and assist them in building an Iraqi Christian ethnic niche in the domestic work sector.

In accordance with the employment pattern of Iraqi Christian domestic service workers, unmarried girls work in live-in arrangements, whereas married women take daily house cleaning jobs. In both cases, the employers are members of the local Assyrian community. Nine-teen year-old Jaklin answers explicitly the question on why they do not work in Turkish, (i.e. Muslim), households:

> Because we do not have a circle of relations. Because we do not know any other circle. If you know people, they will tell you when there will be a job, but because you do not have acquaintances, you can't do it. Here, Assyrians are better known, besides they know each other, they inform each other and then tell us. We then go.

Membership in a social network is generally based on ascriptive criteria, such as ethnicity, gender, and religion, and social capital refers to the 'individual's *ability* to mobilize them on demand' (Portes, 1995: 12-13). For Iraqi Christians, religious affiliations serve as the main social capital and offer them a potential resource, which is apparently embedded in the overall network of social interactions (Schmitter-Heisler, 2000: 83).

Despite all its positive aspects, the Iraqi Christian religious social network has oppressive and exclusionary characteristics as well. One should not imagine this social milieu as a setting organized merely on principles of solidarity and consensus (Pessar, 1999). It also includes hierarchies of power and community control mechanisms, and creates an order of discipline and punishment in the transit period. It is mostly younger members of the community who suffer most, since they are better incorporated into mainstream society owing to their work experiences. In brief, religion which serves as an important means of survival, easily develops into an apparatus of social control to enhance safeguarding of communal norms and attitudes, and creates generational conflicts as well.

Caritas: Social Services for the Assyro-Chaldeans

Another branch of Iraqi Christians' religious social network is the Catholic charity organization, Caritas, which offers basic social services.[80] Being a Catholic organization of humanitarian aid, development, and social services, Caritas gives support to Chaldean Catholic Iraqis, especially on legal matters; it looks over the paperwork for those who have applied to the UNHCR to attain refugee status and makes connections with the representatives of countries admitting immigrants based on sponsorship systems, like Australia and Canada. In the year 2000 alone, Caritas-Turkey followed up on the forms of 745 Iraqis, as stated in the leaflet of the organization. In 2004, they opened 328 new files, (which makes approximately 1312 people in 2004). According to Caritas, the decrease in the number of Iraqis arriving in Turkey compared to the period before war is because of the closure of the borders between Iraq and Turkey just after the war.

They also provide counseling services whose "main targets are to provide information, give advice and guidance the migrants, asylum seekers or refugees regarding their needs. This service also provides a reliable source of information and opportunity to discuss the various

---

80 Caritas-Turkey is a member of the *Caritas Internationalis* confederation, based in Rome and represented in 198 countries. The Caritas office in Turkey was founded in 1950 by Domenico Caloveras, then director of the Greek Catholic community, and moved to its current location in Harbiye in 1985 (Danis & Kayaalp, 2004).

legal options that may exist for the client." In addition to these services, they deliver food, clothing and urgent medical aid to needy migrants. Another important service is the provision of education to the children of Christian Iraqi families who cannot attend to public schools for lack of official residence permits to stay in Turkey. Basically, they teach English to migrants leaving for Australia and Canada in language courses, in addition to rudimentary subjects at a modest level. Caritas and the Church also step forward in favor of Chaldean men and women to find employment in the wide informal sector of the country.[81]

Priests at the Center of the Religious Network

In the Iraqi Christian case, as with other migrant communities, the nodal point of religious life is religious leaders, who have a special responsibility to maintain communal bonds and to transmit long-established values and attitudes. In the Chaldean tradition, priests were eminent figures in the past, as much as they have been today, having a say in the affairs of community life. The priests emerged at the forefront mainly in the 19th century, which was a turning point for Chaldeans and Assyrians. The 19th century, setting the stage for great political and social turmoil in the Ottoman territory, witnessed the destabilization of the existing order that had prevailed for centuries. The two main stimulating factors behind this breakdown were the western-inspired Ottoman centralization reforms that extended to the eastern provinces and the proliferation of American and British missionary activities in the region (Bruinessen, 2003: 268-301). Abrogation of the Kurdish emirates neighboring Chaldeans and Assyrians by the Ottoman authorities, and the missionary activities oriented to the Christian minority dwelling in the region, bred sentiments of fear and suspicion among Kurds, which later on led to massacres targeting these Christian groups in the second half of the 19th

---

81 http://www.caritas-tr.org/eng/multeci.htm (accessed on 11.11.2005).

century (Yonan, 1999). This period, occupying a noteworthy place in the collective memory of Assyrians and Chaldeans, occasioned the emergence of religious leaders who assumed political roles as Christians, as well as Kurds (Bruinessen, 2003: 277). The head of the Hakkari-based Patriarchate of Assyrians, Patriarch Mar Shimun, acted as both religious authority and political representative negotiating with neighboring Kurdish tribes and Ottoman tax-collectors (Foggo, 2002: 21). The patriarch was also the leading person in the emigration of Assyrians from Hakkari to Urmiyah and eventually to Iraq, which was under British rule in 1918 (Joseph, 1961: 163).

In these years of turbulence, religion-based social organization and religious leaders became even more crucial for Assyrians and Chaldeans. In the course of the shift from the multi-ethnic Ottoman Empire to various nation-states, religion became the major agent of the definition of group identity and the foundation of social structure for stateless minorities like Assyrians and Chaldeans. Religious leaders undertook a unifying role during times of exile and resettlement, and thus bolstered their social and political power over the community. Correspondingly, the Chaldean migration from the northern Iraqi countryside to urban areas such as Baghdad and Mosul in the 1960s and 1970s was influenced by the relocation of the Chaldean Patriarchate to Baghdad in 1950.

Religious leaders also played significant roles in the mass migration of the Assyrian and Chaldean community from Iraq between 1988 and 1992. The 1992 influx of asylum-seekers, making up one of the major refugee movements of the 20th century, consisted mostly of Kurds, as well as Assyro-Chaldeans, Turkmens, and Arabs of Northern Iraq. The pioneers of Christian emigration have been mentioned in the reports of those days. For instance, it has been recorded that three thousand people comprising more than half of the Silopi temporary refugee camp were Christians, that is to say, Chaldean, Assyrian, and Syrian Orthodox (Kaynak, 1992: 147). Even during such a sudden displacement, religion was a significant aspect of the

Christian asylum seekers; in Silopi one of the three main sections of the camp was allocated to Christians who had immediately established a tent-church.[82] An article published in *Le Monde* at the time, reports that 500 Chaldeans lodged in the temporary settlement in Silopi communicated their request to be accepted as refugees by European countries through their priests (cited in Kaynak, 1992).

Priests stand out as the main actors of the current migration, too; they are the most notable personalities of the Chaldean community in Istanbul. Priests of the local Chaldean church in Istanbul and the ones affiliated to Caritas perform the role of go-between among Turkish authorities and the migrant community, whereas Iraqi or European priests who wander in different cities of the Middle East contribute to build a transnational social space organized around religion. These persons can appropriately be called '*transnational professionals*', possessing a high prestige and social recognition in the eyes of the migrant community (Cook, 2002). Iraqi Chaldean priests have attended to the application procedures of the community members in addition to their religious duties. In short, these priests have a prominent role in constructing an extensive religious space.

Father George[83] is an intriguing example of the eminence of religious figures in Iraqi Chaldean migration. He is one of the most well-known figures of the Iraqi Christian community in Istanbul. He stayed in Turkey for approximately two years and left for Canada at the end of 2003, with the aim of working as a religious personnel for the recently migrated Chaldean community; he thus departed for Canada with his work permit, a fact that increased his reputation among his compatriots. The responsibility of Father George in Canada is not only religious leadership; he also acts as 'the boss' of the community in the small Canadian town. He is in charge of the communitarian sponsorship system and selects families 'to be invited' under the community quota, some 20-25 families every year. While he was still in Istanbul, he had

---

82 Interview with UNHCR field assistant, 23.12.2004.
83 Interviews with Iraqi Chaldean priest in Istanbul, in October 24 and October 31, 2003.

undertaken detailed research on the families with a lower possibility of admission. He then earned considerable social capital and admiration in the eyes of Chaldean migrants for his diligence with the details of application and admission procedures, like file numbers and form sheets. As a *transnational professional*, Father George had contacts with migrant and refugee-related institutions as well, such as the ICMC (International Catholic Migration Committee), the IOM (International Organization for Migration), and of course Caritas. He was also in touch with Australian and Canadian consulates when he was in Istanbul.

The Limits of Socio-Economic Incorporation Through Religious Ties

State policies and institutional arrangements have serious implications for the Assyro-Chaldean migrants' socio-economic integration in Turkey. The 'institutional capacity' of Chaldean or Catholic religious structures in Turkey is not very strong, compared to American and European cases. In the United States, the absence of state religion, a religiously pluralist setting, and a highly religious society all provide a favorable environment for religious congregations working in favor of migrant communities, in addition to encouraging migrants' religious participation (Hirschman, 2003). The highly secular European system, on the contrary, does not encourage migrants' religious activities, (the last headscarf debate in France, for instance). However, it still recognizes religious groups' rights of institutionalization. In Turkey, a nation-state based on a predominantly Sunni-Turkish population, two factors seem to be most significant in setting the context: The adoption of laicism as a founding ideology of the new Republic, and the Lausanne Treaty of 1923, which have resulted in the official recognition of only three religious communities (Greeks, Armenians, and Jews), as minorities. These two principles hinder the development of community services to be offered to Iraqi Assyro-Chaldean Christians. The weakness of institutional representation of local religious minorities in Turkey, (unlike the 'millet' system of Ottoman

Empire which allowed a legitimate representation of religious communities), thus has a negative impact on the construction of a transnational religious field.

Notwithstanding the engaging work of Catholic networks worldwide and their attention to refugees and migrants, it needs to be stated that the Chaldean Church in Istanbul is a member of neither the Middle East Council of Churches (MECC) nor the Catholic Near Eastern Welfare Association (CNEWA). The reasons for this detachment are distrustful and precautionary state policies towards non-Muslim minorities and 'the fear of missionary activities' that may occur due to the potential development of such inter and transnational connections. The absence of reliable reception and admission policies towards asylum-seekers and migrants, as well as a skeptical attitude towards Christian minorities influence the range of social space that Iraqi Christian migrants may benefit from. While social networks established at religiously plural contexts contribute substantially to the sustenance of migrants (Hagan, 2002), such networks seem to be relatively sluggish in Turkish transit country context. In short, the extent of the transnational religious space of Christian migrants in Turkey seems to be delimited through state regulations.

AFGHANIS IN ZEYTINBURNU: A CROSS BETWEEN 'PERMANENCY' AND 'TRANSITION'[84]

Turkey lacks a common border with Afghanistan, however specifically the last quarter century has been witness to a considerable movement of Afghanis to Turkey. The recent history of Afghani movement to Turkey dates back to 1982 when then Turkish President Kenan Evren officially invited some 4,000 Afghans of Turkish origin to move to Turkey as residents. The following year, this same request was extended another 1,200. These individuals were invited to Turkey based upon the 2641 Numbered Special Law and were provided with permanent

---

84 Cherie Taraghi. Cultural orientation trainer, ICMC-Turkey. Poyracık Sok. No.35, Nişantaşı, Şişli, Istanbul. taraghi@icmc.net

residency, which included the right to employment, education, and the attainment of Turkish citizenship. These individuals were initially kept in quarantine in the city of Adana for some months and then dispersed to various regions within the country. These regions were mainly in the center, south, and southeast of Turkey, as **Table 6.15** indicates. This was the only official regularized act of migration between the two countries. An offspring of the migration of 6,200 Afghan Turks into Turkey has been a steady stream of 'family reunification' or 'migration through marriage'. Aside from this 'official' migration, Afghans of all ethnic backgrounds, not just Turkic, have entered Turkey legally with documents, or have been smuggled into the country in order to seek asylum or a safer, calmer life. Also, every year the Turkish government offers a number of scholarships to Afghan students so that they may enter and study at Turkish universities.

TABLE 6.15
1982 Migrant Afghan Families: Settled Location and Family Size

| | | Type of Residence | | | |
| | | Rural | | Urban | |
Region	District	Family	Population Number	Family	Population Number
Tokat	Artova-YeşilYurt	113	505	82	353
Hatay	Reyhanlı-Horlak	171	716	–	–
Gaziantep	Merkez	–	–	68	349
Şanlıurfa	C.Pınar	210	840	–	–
Van	Erci-Altındere	298	1.130	–	–
Kayseri	Merkes	–	–	64	270
	Total	792	3.191	214	972
		1,006 Families			
		4,163 Population			
	Grand totals				

Source: General Directorate of Rural Services. Information for 1983 is not available

Interviewed participants were asked to provide a date for their arrival in Turkey. The dates, the related narratives, and the statistics maintained by organizations such as the ICMC and the UNHCR indicate the following chronological pattern.

Throughout the 1980s, there was a small but regular flow of Afghans, particularly single young men, into Turkey, most of who were subsequently resettled in other countries through the UNHCR and refugee programs. This was followed by a lag in the flow of Afghans into Turkey in the 1990s, which is confirmed by statistics maintained by the Resettlement Program at the ICMC. These indicate that no Afghan cases were presented by the UNHCR for resettlement between 1992 and 1998. The rate of the movement of Afghans into Turkey picked up once more in 2001. This can be seen in the substantial number of individuals interviewed who have come to Turkey since that date.

An interesting contradiction can be noted between the comments made by Afghan Turkmen participants who arrived in the 1980s and individuals who have arrived since 2001. Most of the Afghan Turkmen insisted that the rate of Afghan migration to Turkey has dwindled to zero and there are almost no 'asylum seekers' any more.

> Almost everyone living here is Afghan Turkmen. Of course there are a lot of other Afghans here too. We are all Afghans and there is no difference between us. But still most of us are Turkmen. In the past, before 2001 there used to be more. Afghans of other backgrounds – Uzbeks, Tajiks, Pashtuns. Most of them would arrive illegally and they would apply for asylum, then they would leave Turkey for Europe. We don't have asylum seekers anymore. Now almost everyone here is legal (Abdul Majid, male, mid-30s, arrived in 1987).

Interviews conducted with numerous asylum seekers who have arrived since 2001, and mainly since 2003, indicate a different reality from the perception offered by the more established Afghan Turkmen. More recently arrived Afghans indicate that a large number of asylum seekers fled to Iran and Pakistan following the American led attack in 2001, and many came to Turkey due to growing difficulties for asylum seekers or refugees, including the establishment of a UNHCR run repatriation program in Iran. Although they are vague on numbers and rather uncomfortable when probed about possibilities for further migration other than applying for refugee status and possible third Country Resettlement by the UNHCR, all recently arrived Afghans indicate that there are many more individuals like themselves.

Due to the fluid state of the legal and irregular migration of Afghans into Turkey, it is difficult to offer any statistics about the population of Afghans living in Turkey. No known records have been kept of the progress of the 6,200 Afghan Turkmen who were invited in 1982-1983, although there are occasional newspaper articles referring to the 'surprising' fact that there are 1000s of Afghans living amidst the Turks, or the fact that Afghans have been very successful in establishing themselves as leaders in the leather market in their regions of residence, in particular in Antakya, (for example, an article in *Hurriyet* Newspaper dated 10.09.2002). Similarly, it is possible to find reference to their 'successes' as carpet dealers, silversmiths, dealers of silver trinkets and ornaments, and artifact salesmen, with 25 stores specifically in the Istanbul Grand Bazaar, (for example, a *Zaman* Newspaper article dated 13.12.2001, a *Milliyet* Newspaper article dated 26.10.2001 or a *Radikal* Newspaper atricle dated 01.10.2001).

These articles generally avoid statistics about the population of Afghans in Turkey. Only the article in *Hurriyet* newspaper admits that it is difficult to provide statistics due to the 'irregular' status of many of the Afghans, particularly those living in Istanbul. It is of course no coincidence that the largest spate of articles published about Afghans in Turkey were produced at a time when the world's eyes were focused upon Afghanistan, as the US prepared a military attack there following the establishment of links between the terrorist group Al Qaeda and its leader Osama Bin Laden's presence in Afghanistan and the tragic events of 11th of September 2001 orchestrated by Al Qaeda.

Afghans in Zeytinburnu: A Brief History
As **Table 6.15** above shows, Istanbul was not a government-designated region for the Afghan Turkmen who settled in Turkey in 1982-83. The decision to reside in Zeytinburnu appears to have been spontaneous. Two reasons can be offered. The preponderance of Afghans who arrived in 1982-1983 were skilled leather workers and the district of Zeytinburnu, among several other neighborhoods in Istanbul, is famous for its many leather workshops and ateliers. Also, research conducted in Turkey to date indicates that much of the settlement in rural areas of the country did not meet with success. Due to difficult environmental condition or the negative reaction of the local population, many could not withstand the pressure to move to larger cities, where they densely inhabited peripheral districts. In Istanbul, they inhabited Zeytinburnu, and in Ankara, they inhabited Telsizler, Altındağ, Ayaş and Kayaş. Some also chose to move to Bursa, Eskişehir, and several districts of Izmir (Özbay–Balpınarı).

> Initially we spent several months in quarantine in Adana. Those were strange days. Then we moved to a rural area in Hatay. It was difficult there because we were isolated from the people living in Hatay. There were kilometers and kilometers of empty land between us and the closest settlement... One day my father told us that he had heard some of the other Afghans we had traveled to Turkey with had settled in Zeytinburnu. He had heard there was a lot of work in Zeytinburnu and it was not hard to get employed. He had decided we would move to Zeytinburnu (Zahra, female, mid-30s, arrived in 1982).

> Zeytinburnu was not a nice place in the 1980s. It was a kind of shantytown. It was uncomfortable, very low quality with damp housing and no heating. Now that I think about it, these problems continue for many today. Many of the old houses are occupied by poor Afghans now, especially newcomers. But we appreciated the fact that we could work on our own trade. We were attracted to Zeytinburnu because of the leather ateliers. We were able to start working in the ateliers without a lot of trouble. At least I had little

trouble. I just settled into one of the ateliers and the rest of my family settled in with me. We were happy enough, when you think
Afghanistan was under occupation... (Ahmed, male, mid 60s,
arrived in 1983).

Zeytinburnu is a large and sprawling district of Istanbul.
According to the Zeytinburnu municipality website, it is the city's 8th
densest district with a population of 284,814, 13 quarters, 58 avenues
and 970 streets (www.zeytinburnu.bel.tr). The Afghans settled in two
of the thirteen quarters: Yeşiltepe or Nuripaşa. Interviewees repeatedly point out that they choose to live in these quarters because of the
other Afghans living there who serve to reinforce their sense of identity.

I like living in Yeşiltepe because there are so many other Afghans
here. I like hearing my language mixed with Turkish and people in
local dress as well as modern clothes. I've lived in Turkey almost
all my life. I don't remember anything about Afghanistan; only
some pictures and film footage on news or films. So it is nice to
have the feeling that although I live in Turkey, I can have my own
culture with me too. I can imagine what 'my' culture actually is. It
is comforting to be able to do that (Kadir, male, 21, arrived in
Turkey 1985).

Almost all of the Afghans live here (in Zeytinburnu). Of course
there are some who have moved to other neighborhoods – some
live in Adapazari or Sultanbeyli on the Asian side- but movement
is rare. Afghans like to be close to one another. We are like mer-
cury. We can split apart but in the end we roll into one ball all
together again. We can't do with being apart. Personally, I could
not imagine living far from my community. My mother is here. My
husband's family is here. It can be difficult because everyone knows
everything about you. Everyone can maintain control over what
you do and everyone tells everyone everything. You understand,
everyone is too close. But I would not move to another area in
Istanbul. Not even for comfort or if I won the lottery. I like the feeling of being an Afghan (Soraya, female, 32, arrived 1998).

Interviewees repeatedly pointed out their lack of desire for moving on from or out of Zeytinburnu. Regardless of legal status, the time period spent in Turkey or the conditions of their lives, including conditions of considerable social and economic upward mobility by some of the Afghan Turkmen, interviewees claimed that they were firmly rooted in the neighborhood which they and those who are interested in Afghans, identify with their Afghan identity. Zeytinburnu is not only an embodiment of Afghan identity. It also represents the network of local advice, support and economic or material help other individuals from the same national background offer.

> There were some complications during my wife's pregnancy. I had to place her in hospital. In the end the hospital bill was more than 600 YTL. I had no idea how to pay this. Some friends suggested I try ICMC, but they couldn't help me. So I knocked on the door of all the people I could think of in Zeytinburnu – all the people who might have that much money and in the end I raised the amount. No one else could have helped me (Interview with Kaawa: male, early 40s, arrived 2003).

Legal Status

The legal status of the Afghans plays a major role in their flexibility and ability to maneuver, change, or improve their conditions of life in the country. Legal status places marked distinctions between the Afghan populations living in Istanbul. The Afghan Turkmen who arrived in 1982-1983 were invited to the country and were therefore received with residence permits and the right to work.[85] These individuals have obtained Turkish passports and been naturalized as Turkish citizens. This is the only group which has been living in Turkey fully documented and legally since arrival.

---

[85] The receipt of a residence permit in Turkey does not imply the right to work. Work permits need to be applied for and are provided on the digression of Turkish authorities. Until 2003 the Foreigner's Police branch was responsible for provision of work permits. Since September 2003, work permits are provided by the Ministry of Labor.

Most of the Afghans who have traveled to Turkey during the last quarter century have been asylum seekers. Although Turkey is a party to the 1951 United Nations Convention on the Rights of Refugees, it retains a geographic limitation to its ratification of the Convention, which means that only those fleeing as a consequence of events occurring in Europe can settle in Turkey on a permanent basis. Afghan migrants have faced a limited range of possibility for settlement. One option has been to remain in the country regardless of legal status. A second option has been to apply for refugee status through the UNHCR. In order to circumvent the 'geographical limitation' clause, local authorities have since the 1990's, been pressing for recognition of Asylum seekers and pushing for the issuance of short-term resident permits until eventual resettlement in a third country has been granted. This option, of course, contains the risk of not obtaining refugee status and therefore facing the choice of deportation or remaining in the country with no legal status.

Afghans who apply for refugee status generally wait for one, two, and in some occasions more years before a decision is made on their case. The number of years of spent waiting lengthens if an initial rejection by the UNHCR is appealed. An asylum seeker, much like a 'statusless' individual, does not have the right to work in Turkey until refugee status is granted. Asylum seekers and irregular migrants debate the merit and risk of placing their children in school due to the need to provide status information and an address as a part of school registration. Government health benefits and free or subsidized hospital usage are not provided to individuals without legal status.

As stated above, throughout the 1980s there was a steady stream of Afghan 'refugees' who were resettled in Turkey. This flow stopped in the 1990s and recommenced in 1998. It has been relatively constant since. However, it is difficult to judge the balance between the numbers of individuals who applied and were granted refugee status, and those who have remained obscure and unregistered. Understandably, information is not forthcoming when this issue is raised. Most of the Afghans interviewed were reluctant to discuss the issue of legal status. More succinctly, individuals who had obtained Turkish citizenship or had refugee status did not express any qualms about mentioning this fact. This singled out individuals who were reluctant or unwilling to discuss the subject, leaving one with a tacit understanding that the subject was off bounds and too sensitive or perhaps self-incriminatory to be pursued.[86] Only three of the individuals interviewed openly admitted that they had been denied refugee status by the UNHCR and were now weighing options for the future.

Overall, regardless of legal status, the individuals interviewed were extremely careful to not discuss 'irregular' or 'statusless' Afghans living among them in Zeytinburnu, indicating a strong sense of allegiance and protection between members of the Afghan community. Nonetheless, it is important to point out that many of the interviewees made general reference to the difficulties faced by the 'statusless' or to their own difficulties living in Turkey prior to their receiving status.

The state of Afghans in Istanbul can be simplified to three categories:

1) Afghan Turkmen who were invited in 1982-83 and were received with residence permits and the right to work and become openly incorporated into Turkish society. They came to Turkey with the intention of remaining in Turkey.

2) Afghans who apply for and receive refugee status by the UNHCR and Turkish authorities. Permanent leave to remain in Turkey is impossible for these individuals, if they should so desire, due to Turkey's adherence to the 'geographical limitation' clause in the 1951 Refugee Convention.

3) Afghans who enter Turkey with documents and a visa and overstay their visa or who are smuggled into the country. They do not

---

86 Individuals interviewed were not openly aware of one another, unless recruitment had occurred in a group situation where several were asked if they were willing to speak to me at the same time. Therefore, to my knowledge, the individuals were not aware of one another or the fact that some willingly indicated their 'legal' status while others tacitly refrained.

register with authorities, and they lead undocumented lives in Turkey. Another group can be added to this category: Individuals who fail to receive refugee status and therefore slip into an irregular status.

Integrating in Istanbul

The various conditions of 'reception' or lack of reception upon arrival in Turkey results in different lives for the Afghans interviewed.

The Afghan Turkmen

Istanbul was not a designated city or region of settlement for the Afghan Turkmen. Those who arrived in 1982-83 and chose to live in Zeytinburnu at some stage in their sojourn in Turkey did so of their own accord. It is important to note that other Afghan Turkmen have come to Turkey subsequent to the initial group. However, for the sake of clarity and simplicity, discussion of Afghan Turkmen will imply individuals from those 2 groups unless clearly stated otherwise. Zeytinburnu became associated with Afghans due to the internal migration of individuals from these initial groups to that district.

> My family must have been one of the first Afghans to come to Zeytinburnu. I really don't recall meeting Afghans when we first arrived. We came to Zeytinburnu in 1984. But I remember how exciting it was to notice more and more people coming. It was like reuniting with old friends. We already knew many people and many came in groups together. They seem to have made the decision to come together and they came. If you are wondering, I don't believe it mattered that we left the space the Turkish government allocated us when we came here. We had migrated legally and no one ever got angry with us. So as long as we had money to pay rent no one cared. And anyway, Zeytinburnu was not a popular place in the early 1980s. It was the slums. Poor. Unwanted. I don't think the locals cared that we came here. They probably thought we were stupid actually. (Interview with Malikzay: Male, 43, Arrived 1983)

From all indications, the process of finding work in Zeytinburnu in the 1980s was not that difficult for the Afghans. Almost every individual interviewed recalls a rather simple process. Interestingly, few of the interviewees offered concrete personal experiences. Many of the individuals interviewed arrived in Turkey or Zeytinburnu in the early to mid-1980s. Only one of the individuals explained experiences in Zeytinburnu outside the frame of the collective. Others all referred to the 'royal we'.

> Yes, it was easy for us to find work here. We were experienced leather workers. All we needed to do was ask around and the doors were opened to us. We were lucky that we were experienced. We could prove our skill rather quickly. (Nasrat, male, early 50s, arrived 1983)

These individuals repeatedly refer to the same themes and ideas. One such theme is the fact that they were skilled leather workers and therefore deserved to receive jobs without any difficulty soon after arrival. A second theme is the fact that Zeytinburnu was very much a poor, peripheral neighborhood in Istanbul, lacking in many senses, including decent housing, roads, or public amenities. Therefore there was no reason for the local population to be concerned or disturbed with their presence in the 2 quarters they chose to inhabit. A couple of the interviewees believe their growing presence was hardly noticed by the local population considering the extent of internal migration going on in Zeytinburnu at the time.

> Really, I don't think people specifically noticed us settle in Zeytinburnu. Zeytinburnu was hardly developed enough for people to notice and it was the start of internal migration then, wasn't it? Yes, people started moving from central and southern Turkey at the same time as us. When we arrived, Zeytinburnu was still a slum neighborhood. There were hardly any proper streets and roads. People were constructing buildings without licenses (gecekondu) overnight. No one noticed anything then (Karim, Male, Early 50s, 1982).

Yet another theme which comes through clearly from reminiscences of the early days in Zeytinburnu is the language factor. As Turkmen, this first group of Afghans spoke a Turkish dialect. They understood and could make themselves understood by the local population. Looking back, all of the Afghan Turkmen acknowledge the advantage they had with their language skills. Being able to communicate reduced the barrier between the Afghans and the local population. It must have been a relief for tanneries and leather workshop owners to have a group of skilled and grateful workers who could speak the language and understand when directions were given, or when they were told how things needed to be done in the work environment. The Afghan Turkmen certainly speak of the advantage that their language ability provided compared to other ethnic Afghan groups who could not speak Turkish and therefore lacked the independence and communication skills needed to establish oneself in Istanbul.

> We [the Turkmen] all speak Turkish. We could speak with the people as soon as we arrived. Our children had few problems in school because they understood the teachers. We had few problems at work because we could explain what we needed and the boss could tell us what he wanted. Our wives could go shopping and ask for what they needed. This was very fortunate. I only realized what an advantage this was when the Uzbek and Tajik or Pashtun Afghans started to arrive. They don't speak Turkish. They speak the main Afghan languages, Dari and Pashtu. They couldn't do anything by themselves. We all became translators for them. We had to help them with every situation... (Ahmed, male, mid 60s, arrived in 1983).

Not all of the Afghan Turkmen who settled in Zeytinburnu were leather workers and tanners. Several were university graduates, including an English teacher and an economist, who were active in the Afghan government prior to the Russian invasion. Some had been carpet weavers, shopkeepers and tradesmen in Afghanistan, who proceeded to find employment as salesmen or traders in the Grand Bazaar in Istanbul. Several of these have proceeded to open their own stores. Although such individuals are in the minority, their stories are proudly mentioned and repeated by others in the community as examples to emulate. The Afghan Turkmen point out that the chance to educate their children or to attain an education in Turkey was a major positive factor during their initial days in the country. Almost all of the interviewees enthusiastically acknowledge the fact that education was a stabilizing factor in their settlement in Zeytinburnu.

> Once the children started going to school we really felt we belonged here. It is interesting because it created a sense of routine –it gave my wife a reason to want to rise in the morning, prepare breakfast, prepare the children, arrange for them to go to school. The children had responsibilities, homework. They had to work on their Turkish accent and the difference in words we used in Afghanistan and the Istanbul Turkish. For some reason these things made us feel at more at home here (Ahmed, male, mid-60s, arrived 1983).

A young interviewee who went to school in Zeytinburnu refers to a similar occurrence in her household.

> There was nothing like going to school to help me feel at home here in Zeytinburnu. Like I said we first arrived in Adana and then we were in rural Hatay. My parents were reluctant to send me to school in Hatay. I was small then and the school was several kilometers away. It was a long and tiring walk and my mother was convinced I would come to some harm. When we moved to Zeytinburnu one of the first things my father did was get me and my brother enrolled in school. The school was just a few minutes walk away. I got a lovely uniform and books and in class, I sat next to a girl who quickly became my best friend. We spent hours out of school together. So like I said, there was nothing like school to help me feel at home. I felt like I belonged (Zahra, female, mid-30s, arrived in 1982).

Zahra also points out that her teacher played an important role in her feeling welcomed and comfortable, thus highlighting the vital role teachers or mentors can play in the process of integration.

> My teacher was young and I thought she was really beautiful. She had a big smile and she was very enthusiastic about my being in the class. She really played an important role in my feeling welcome and comfortable in the school and I guess that also helped me feel like I belonged in Zeytinburnu. My teacher would get angry when the other children made fun of my accent or when they laughed at my mistakes. She asked my father to come to school and offered a lot of ideas on how my parents could help me adapt in the school. It's strange actually now that I think about it. I wonder why she cared. But it is great that she did. She really helped me feel good and fit in (Zahra).

Other Afghan Turkmen joined the first group on an individual basis throughout the 1980s due to the relative ease with which they could obtain Turkish residency and Turkish citizenship at that time. Most of these individuals did not come directly from Afghanistan. Quite the contrary, they had already fled their own country due to the Russian occupation and ensuing war in Afghanistan, and were living and working in Iran. Family and social networks, along with word-of-mouth, were very influential in the decision making process for many of these individuals. As one of the interviewees point out:

> I got word from my uncle and cousins in Istanbul that I should try and come here. I was in Iran at the time. My uncle assured me that there was shelter for me in Istanbul and the possibility to get work. He also let me know that I should not worry. I would be able to get Turkish residency and if I had a difficult time with that it would be arranged for me to get married in Istanbul and then I would get residency for sure. You know arranged marriage is quite common among us Afghans and that's how I ended up getting residency in Turkey (Nasseer, male, mid 30s, arrived in 1987).

Along a similar tone, one of the interviewees related the story of a cousin who arranged for his wife to be brought from Iran using family and social networks:

> When my cousin decided to get married he thought it would be nice to help a girl come to Turkey from Iran or Afghanistan. Our conditions were already quite good here so he was considered a good catch! He let some of the family in Iran know that he was looking for a wife and you know how news travels quickly. Within days he was alerted of several choices. One included a picture. Can you imagine that? My cousin was struck by the romance of falling in love through a picture and then meeting the girl on his wedding day. It was arranged and she arrived soon after (Zahra).

It is interesting to note that while the Afghan population in Zeytinburnu is open to friendship with the local Turkish population living in Zeytinburnu or beyond, close to none of the interviewees acknowledged the possibility of establishing romantic links with Turks or getting married to a Turk. The insularity of an Afghan identity and the desire to maintain Afghan blood is considered imperative:

> When I get married, of course it will be with an Afghan. Don't misunderstand – I have nothing against the Turks. At university, there were a lot of pretty Turkish girls and some liked me. But I could not consider a serious relationship with a Turkish woman. I would choose an arranged marriage to marriage with a Turkish girl. I can't explain why. I just like to stay with the Afghans. Perhaps it's because there are few of us here and we are far from home. It would feel like a betrayal. Does this make sense? (Abdul Majid, male, mid-30s, arrived in 1987)

Today a number of the Afghan Turkmen are by all means economically established and have experienced economic upward mobility. Many own leather workshops and tanneries. It is estimated that Afghans own more than 500 confection and leather workshops in Zeytinburnu today, along with up to 40 leather goods, carpet and silversmith/ silver trinket shops in the Istanbul Grand Bazaar, and another 25 carpet and silver trinket stores on Terlikçiler Street, an extension of the Grand Bazaar.[87] Conversation with shop owners in the Bazaar revealed an intricate extended network of trade and business between Turkey, Pakistan, and Afghanistan. Several of the shop owners indicated that they or family members-partners travel to Pakistan and on occasion to Afghanistan in order to locate and buy new and interesting material to sell on the market in Istanbul. Some pointed out that they have established contacts and links with Afghan refugees in Pakistan who produce the various amulets and trinkets on sale in Istanbul, or act as local agents, helping to locate and buy goods at reasonable prices. One of the interviewees also mentioned his excitement about the growing possibilities for official trade and business relations between Turkey and Afghanistan. He mentioned looking into the possibility of setting up agency representation for various Turkish food and household items in Afghanistan:

> I have been looking into the possibility of gaining the agency representation for Turkish companies in Afghanistan. A lot of food items such as Ülker and Eti chocolates and biscuits are sold in Kabul and North Afghanistan. I wonder how it is done legally. I have started to research how it is done and talking to people about possibilities. I would like to be involved in this (Ahmed, male, mid 60s, arrived in 1983).

This interest is not confined to the Afghans living in Zeytinburnu. The Turkish government has been actively involved in the reconstruction and development of Afghanistan since 2002. An August 2005 report by the Foreign Economic Relations Board (Dış Ekonomik İlişkiler Kurullu or DEIK) in Turkey is devoted to Turkish-Afghan economic relations and refers to a $115 million investment in the Afghan economy, and distinctly refers to the fact that there are

---

87 Reference to numbers of shops is made in *Milliyet* Newspaper, 26/10/2001 and *Hurriyet*, 10/09/2002.

'increasingly higher numbers of Turkish firms opening representative or liaison offices in Afghanistan' (DEIK Report: 2).[88] According to the report, the trade volume between Turkey and Afghanistan rose from $38.7 million in 2003 to $76.1 million in 2004 (DEIK Report: 4). The governments of Turkey and Afghanistan signed an Agreement on Trade and Economic Cooperation in Kabul in June 2004. The Turkish-Afghan Joint Economic Commission met in April 2005 to set higher targets for annual trade volume between the two countries over the next five years. Between the 4th and 7th of January 2006 the President of Afghanistan, Hamid Karzai paid an official visit to Turkey, accompanied by several Ministers, including the Minister of Foreign Affairs, Finance, Health, Education and Women's Affairs. This was the first visit of an Afghan head of state to Turkey since the visit by King Muhammed Zahir Shah, between the 26th of August and the 8th of September 1957. President Karzai's visit culminated in the signing of a Cooperation Accord to facilitate further construction and development aid between the two countries, and in a Press Conference President Karzai urged for 'greater investments from Turkish firms'.[89]

Another example of growing interest and relations between the two countries can be seen in the fact that Aryana Afghan Airlines conducts two direct flights a week between Istanbul and Kabul, and one flight a week between Kabul and Ankara. Also the Turkish Aviation News portal, Gökyüzü Haberci, announced the commencement of Turkish Airlines direct flights to Dushanbe, Tajikistan, in January 2006 as part of a plan to establish 24 new flight destinations in Central Asia and the Middle East due to an increase in trade relations.[90]

Back in Zeytinburnu, besides the confection and leather workshops, Afghan Turkmen also own odds–and-ends shops where any-

---

[88] The Report can be found at the DEIK website, www.deik.org.tr/bultenler/200582511515 TurkeysRoleinreconstructionofAfghanistanaugust2005. pdf

[89] Radio Free Europe Radio Liberty, 5/01/2006 www.rferl.org/featuresarticle/2006/1/6B4F5781-0E02-4577-990D-C9608AB030BD.html

[90] Gökyüzü Haberci, www.gokyuzuhaberci.com, 27/01/06.

thing from plastic piping and iron nails to Basmati rice and green tea is sold; news about home in Afghanistan is exchanged and droppers by are invited to drink tea and chat. During fieldwork in Zeytinburnu, individuals interviewed mentioned the existence of an Afghan bakery but I was not able to locate it. However, I did locate the music and film store which, although it is not owned by an Afghan, certainly caters to their interests and presence in the neighborhood. The store was filled with Indian, Pakistani, Iranian, and Afghan music tapes, and films, along with an occasional Turkish artist or film.

There also used to be an Afghan restaurant in the area, but it reportedly closed down in 2002. The Afghans' established and integrated existence in Zeytinburnu or Turkey at large is easily evidenced by the words and means the interviewees choose to explain their feelings and aspirations about work and employment. The younger interviewees offered a familiar range of comments and complaints concerning employment, salaries, making ends meet and the need for skills one frequently hears from local Turkish youth. Many of the statements indicated distance and an oblivious lack of awareness to the sensitive issue of the poverty of possibilities commented upon by Afghans with an irregular status.

> I came to Turkey 7 years ago. I came here to join my husband. I started working as a hairdresser soon after I arrived. First I started as an apprentice but after a few months I became a proper hairdresser. My husband works in one of the little corner shops (bakal) a few streets away. We don't get paid very much and he has to work very long hours but we manage. Fortunately my mother-in-law lives very close to us and she takes care of our child during the day... (Soraya, female, 32, arrived in 1998).

> I am working in my father's carpet shop at the moment. It is not bad but it is not what I really want to be doing. I have 3 older brothers and they also work in the shop. They can run the shop for my dad when he wants to retire. I would like to work in a bank or in finance. A few years ago you didn't need a degree to work in a

bank but now they ask for a degree, there is a lot of competition and you have to know somebody who can get you an interview. I don't know of an Afghan working in a bank or the finance sector that could help so I will have to be a trendsetter by myself (Kadir, male, 21, arrived in Turkey 1985).

Some older Afghan Turkmen express a more astute awareness of their advantageous situation, particularly with reference to their legal status in Turkey today:

I have been employed in different places in Zeytinburnu, all in the leather industry for many years. I have no problem. But during the past couple of years – maybe three- new employment laws were passed for foreigner workers. The employers have become a lot stricter with checking legal papers since these laws were passed. A number of friends lost jobs (Ali Osman, male, early 40s, arrived in Turkey 1985).

The Afghan Turkmen Social and Solidarity Foundation

The establishment of the Afghan Turkmen Social and Solidarity Foundation in 1999 can be seen as a symbol of Afghan Turkmen social and economic integration in Zeytinburnu. The Foundation has a double mission. On the one hand it aims to help Afghans in Turkey by organizing economic and material help where possible, arranging dinners and gatherings during religious festivals and the Afghan new year (March 21); arranging weddings, funerals and other social activities; organizing Farsi and Dari classes and Afghan cultural events specifically for Afghan children.

The Foundation has also been known to advocate in the local municipality or Education Ministry on behalf of Afghans with irregular legal status. Several members and participants refer to the efforts of the Foundation General Secretary Hekim Erturk in 2001-2 to convince the Education Ministry to allow local schools in Zeytinburnu to enroll Afghan children regardless of legal status in the country. However, overall members of the Foundation, including the President

Ali Çağrı, are reluctant to refer to the 'irregular' Afghans living in Zeytinburnu. Instead, all focus and interest is on the campaigns run by the Foundation to raise money for development and construction in Afghanistan. So far the Foundation has raised enough money to open 2 schools in north Afghanistan and has turned its attention to a campaign to raise money for a hospital. It is with reference to these efforts that the Foundation's President suggests:

> The Foundation and our campaigns represent our success in Turkey. We have succeeded in moving beyond our own needs and existence here. We are now able and in a position to turn our attention to our countrymen, to our motherland. I think this is a very exciting development for the Afghans living in Turkey (Ali Çağrı, mid 30s, arrived in 1982).

Afghan Refugees and Afghans with an 'Irregular' Status

As pointed out earlier, it is often difficult to distinguish between Afghan 'asylum seekers' or 'refugees' and those with an 'irregular' legal status. Most individuals are not willing to admit that they are living in Turkey with no official documentation; an act of self-preservation which is more than understandable. The boundary between the two statuses can be easily blurred. Until 2004 all asylum seekers and refugees in Turkey had to register with the UNHCR and the local Turkish police at the border where they entered the country within 10 days. For many this 10 day limitation literally meant the difference between being documented and residing in Turkey 'legally' or not.

Many enter Turkey irregularly from a border in the southeast of the country and make their way up to Istanbul – a journey which may take several days depending on conditions of travel. If the individual does not register with the local police authorities at the point of entry before traveling on to Istanbul, then the person has to re-trace steps, return to the point of entry, and approach local border police. In many cases 10 days was just not sufficient time and the possibility of slipping into a state of 'statuslessness' was very simple.

Some of the individuals enter Turkey with the hope of earning enough money to continue their journey to a 'more lucrative' destination but discover conditions for saving money more difficult than they had imagined. Some enter with no plan to apply for refugee status and are convinced by fellow country people that this is the best or the only course of action available. Others enter with a conscious plan to apply, but it cannot be assumed that they are aware of the rules and regulations involved.

The situation is further complicated by the fact that regardless of their good intentions, organizations working with refugees in Istanbul are few and generally lack the resources and time to be able to be as open and transparent in relating information to the refugees as they would like. The environment in which the migrants live is another factor which must be taken into consideration because it is conducive to rumors and misinformation. Once the individual has applied for refugee status it can take many months and at times years to be recognized or denied. The UNHCR has been working upon improving the bureaucracy and paperwork which impedes the speed with which they can offer refugee status determinations (RSD). Thus far legal officers and researchers in the field have pointed out that a system of response to 'vulnerable'[91] cases has been established but a faster, more efficient system for all applicants is still being worked on.[92]

Until a person is granted refugee status, that individual is not eligible for financial or medical support, and even after attaining refugee status, due to limited resources, few among the refugees qual-

---

[91] It is difficult to define 'vulnerable' in this context. There is no single clear cut definition. Vulnerable may be a minor refugee living in the country alone or a single woman with children for whom daily survival under precarious conditions would be more difficult in Turkey than for families. Vulnerable maybe defined as a family with a member who is seriously ill and in need of medical help or cases where the individual or family continues to be under threat from forces persecuting them in Turkey, etc. In such cases RSD provision is expedited.

[92] Kagan, Michael (*Refugee Rights Clinic, Tel Aviv University, Faculty of Law*) defined the changes in UNHCR's RSD procedure at the Helsinki Citizen's Assembly 'Refugee Support Program Workshop, 1/10/2005.

ifies for help. In almost all cases refugees and asylum seekers are responsible for their own housing, cost of school attendance, and other forms of education, including learning the Turkish language. Since September 2003, refugees officially have the right to apply for a work permit with the Department of Labor, however very few do and most potential employers are reluctant or unwilling to undertake the effort of applying and following through with the procedures to get a refugee a work permit. As an Afghan refugee points out:

> You know how it is. I found a job and told the employer I want to work legally. When I travel to another country I want to be able to say I worked in such and such a shop working as a salesman and prove it with documents. But the employer was not willing to apply for my work permit. He was suspicious at first, said I have no right to work so why was I making a mockery of him. When I explained to him that I was eligible for a work permit, that he and his company had to endorse and file for me, he made a call and tried to find out what the procedure was. I was very excited but then he told me he was unwilling. He said it wasn't worth all the effort, that it sounded complicated and I wasn't going to stay in Turkey long enough to merit the effort. I could work for him anyway if I wanted to but now he said I could work in the back loading and carrying boxes so I wouldn't be seen. It is funny, no? I got demoted for trying to be legal and I get paid less than others doing the same work because I cannot complain but I need the money to live here and pay rent. So I work (Noorahmed, male, 22, arrived 2003).

One could argue that there is very little difference in terms of official support and aid provided to individuals with refugee status and those without. The greatest difference appears to be psychological, for those with refugee status are aware of their 'legal' presence in the country. They do not fear the presence of police or authorities as avidly as undocumented individuals.

> Sure, I feel safer now that I have a card from the UN saying I am a refugee. I feel a big difference, like a mountain has been removed

from my shoulders. You have to understand, there are a lot of Afghanis who never applied or who apply and don't get accepted by the UN. What to do then? Questions start all over again – the risk of being caught by the police, detention, being deported. You need money. Every time you leave the house it is a risk. These are such difficult questions I don't have to face (Mahboobullah, male, 32, arrived 2004).

Due to the adherence to the geographic limitation clause (discussed above) most Afghan refugees living in Turkey remain for a limited period of time. Generally once they are recognized as refugees by the UNHCR, their files are passed on for possible resettlement to a third country, such as the United States, Canada, Sweden, Norway, and so-on.[93] Timewise, the whole process from the RSD application to leaving the country cannot be pre-determined. In some cases it may take a year, and in some it may take up to 5 or more years. Details and reasons are clearly outside the scope of this paper and shall not be discussed here. However, relevant here is the effect this period of waiting has upon the process of 'integration' in Turkey. This can be considered the biggest difference between individuals with documentation and those who are undocumented.

Persons who lack documentation have to face either the option of remaining in the country with the permanent risk of being caught by the police and local authorities, or trying to be smuggled to European countries. There is also a third option: returning to Afghanistan. 'Undocumented' Afghans and refugees interviewed underline a similar terrain of difficulties and sense impermanence in their lives in Istanbul. The highlight of their position in Istanbul is the network established by their fellow citizens in Zeytinburnu. This network denotes the possibilities for shelter, employment, financial help, translation services, etc. But finite material and personal possibilities

---

[93] Some countries such as Canada and Australia accept a limited number of refugees based upon sponsorship programs, in which case the refugee does not require recognition by UNHCR. However, these are few and most of the refugees in Turkey traverse the UNHCR based path.

in Istanbul outshine the positive aspects that the network provides.

The well established Afghan community in Zeytinburnu offers shelter to the documented and undocumented Afghanis who arrive in Istanbul. The realization that a whole community exists, a network of fellow country people with local Turkish language skills, an understanding of how local life functions, the possibility of a roof over one's head and some food to start off with plays a factor in the decision to come to Turkey.

> There are so many Afghans living everywhere. It is not that hard to inquire where to go and how things work in different places. We get fairly accurate information from friends, family, and people who have lived in one place or another. Many Afghans in Iran know there is a neighborhood in Istanbul with Afghans. They might not know the name exactly but they know it exists. That's how I came. It was arranged that I be brought to Zeytinburnu. It was explained that I would be able to live among Afghans and they would help me (Mansoor, male, 20, arrived 2003).

> It was a long journey from Zahedan to Mashhad and then Tehran and on to the border with Turkey and then across the border... the travel in Iran was okay. It was normal. I traveled alone but still, it's a strange experience. The imagination wanders and one feels nervous even though you are doing nothing wrong ... we traveled as a group. Sometimes by truck and sometimes by foot... the mountain passes were steep and difficult. We crossed at night and there were maybe 20 people in the group. We kept stopping and doing a head count but then we were told not to make noise. Some were slower, some were faster. I get nervous when I remember the experience. In the end we crossed without incident and once we were in Turkey the group divided. Some went to the city of Van, I don't know wherelse. There were four of us Afghanis and the smuggler brought us all the way to Zeytinburnu. That's how it works. We paid to be brought to Zeytinburnu... (Asim, male, 19, arrived 2004).

Several of the Afghans who have been living in Zeytinburnu for many years pointed out that there used to be an Afghan restaurant in

Zeytinburnu where Afghans of all ethnic backgrounds, status, and positions could meet and talk. This restaurant was identified as a network 'center' where needs such as housing, translation services, etc., could be organized and arranged. This restaurant closed down in 2002.

> Oh yes, there was a restaurant in Zeytinburnu. It was a meeting point where all the Afghans could ask or offer help. I helped as a translator several times. I wrote letters in Turkish and took people to the health clinic (sağlık ocak). People could mention if they needed a job or if their work place had an opening. The restaurant was important when there were a lot of refugees. A lot of things could be arranged for them from there but it was no longer necessary after 2002. The refugees don't come anymore (Nasseer, male, mid 30s, arrived in 1987).

Nasseer's belief that there are few or no Afghan refugees living in Zeytinburnu today is typical of the view put forth by many of the Afghan Turkmen who came to Turkey in the 1980s. This is not a surprise. Statistics of 'undocumented' Afghans arrested by Turkish police offered by the Directorate of National Security for Afghans indicate a distinct drop after an all-time high in 2001.

TABLE 6.16
Afghans Arrested by the Turkish Police

Year	Number
1995	24
1996	68
1997	81
1998	921
1999	2,476
2000	8,746
2001	9,701
2002	1,927
2003	2,178
2004	1,112

Source: General Security Directorate.

The distinct drop in the number of arrests verifies the view that there are fewer refugees in Zeytinburnu today. It is likely that the Afghan Turkmen simply do not notice the refugees due to the reduction in numbers. It is likely that with settlement and personal engagements and activities, they have lost touch with daily goings-on in the district. Perhaps many of the Afghan Turkmen no longer have the time or the inclination to keep up with the arrival and departure of refugees. Another reason may simply and understandably be that the Afghan Turkmen do not wish to draw attention to the continuing movement of 'documented' and 'undocumented' Afghans living in their midst. With their own social and economic climb, they may well be unwilling to taint the whole community with questions of 'legality'.

During fieldwork it was difficult to establish exactly how the Afghan network is contacted the first time by a newly arrived Afghan or activated to help. With the closing of the Afghan restaurant clearly the visible and contactable 'center' has been removed. What we have to rely upon is the words of the interviewees. The interviewees intersperse their conversation with mentions of friends of whom were brought by smugglers to Zeytinburnu, the fact that they asked for financial help when they were in need, that they could have an injection at the local health clinic for free because they were Afghan, or that they could find a job or a place to sleep because of the community living in Zeytinburnu. The existence of the community and network appears to be such an established fact that with the exception of one Consi der finding another word: maybe 'uninformed' Afghan lady living in the neighborhood of Aksaray, all the other Afghans met or interviewed simply referred to its existence. Direct questions such as how they heard of the community, how they found the community in the first place and how they could find a house, were received with looks of surprise and comments such as 'we just know'. Or 'everyone knows'. One of the interviewees reversed the question by asking how I knew to come to Zeytinburnu to look for the Afghans!

Many of the recently arrived Afghans refer to difficult housing conditions in Zeytinburnu. There is a constant reference to high cost in rent, the low quality of available housing, and crowdedness. Housing conditions appear to change from individual to individual but some clear trends are visible. One of the principle factors taken into consideration is cost. Single young men tend to rent one room in an apartment or house and live together. On some occasions 3-4 or more young men choose to live in one room together. Families are often the same. A whole family may choose to live in one room together, although more often families prefer to rent an apartment of their own, thus maintaining privacy. Single mothers with children on the other hand often live in a room and prefer to find/ are offered a room in the apartment or house of another Afghan family. Typically, this provides the lady and her children a form of male protection and security. Single women, if any, are taken in by families, regardless of kin or family relations. The housing is of low quality. Some of the interviewees draw links between the housing conditions and their feeling of isolation or sense of not being welcome in Turkey. The comments are rarely made in a comparative sense. The interviewees do not choose to compare their past lives in Afghanistan or Iran or Pakistan with their present life in Turkey. On the contrary, many refer to conditions in Turkey with reference to their hopes for a 'better' life in Europe, Canada or America:

> My house is awful here. It is cold – no heating other than an electric heater and it is winter now. My children and my wife are cold all the time. They complain but my wife keeps reading to us letters written by her mother in Canada and her brothers in England. There they have warm comfortable houses. This momentarily helps us forget the cold, the damp, the cold water the cramped lack of space, the thin walls.. Things will be better when we go to my wife's family in England (Suleyman, male, early-40s, arrived 2002).

Language skills are one of the areas Afghans have difficulty with in Istanbul. While the Turkmen speak a dialect of Turkish and

can make themselves understood, the Dari speakers experience alien-
ating distance by their inability to communicate or easily do things for
themselves. This problem is accentuated for women:

> It is difficult to not be able to speak Turkish. Everyone here just
> expects you to be able to. I have learnt some but it very difficult for
> my sister. I am able to leave the house and do things for myself. She
> is a girl, so it is more difficult for her. She has to be in the house.
> So she has learnt almost no Turkish. If something happened to me,
> I don't know how she would manage. I can do a lot of things by
> myself here now but for her it is like she never left Afghanistan. My
> biggest difficulty is I can't do any of the official work by myself.
> Every time I have to call the UN I need to make sure someone who
> speaks Turkish is close by. Every time I have an interview, the same
> (Munir, male, 18, arrived 2004).

> I am in the house the whole time taking care of the children. I
> couldn't wander around even if I didn't have the children. It is not
> that easy for an Afghan woman with no man. I go shopping of
> course but I prefer it when my downstairs neighbor offers to go
> shopping or I send my son. So I haven't been able to learn the lan-
> guage. I do not feel a part of life here and anyway, why should I? I
> won't be here for long. My children have learned. They go down-
> stairs and watch TV with our neighbors and they go to classes with
> their children (Samira, female, mid- 30s, arrived 2004).

Some children are better integrated and have established a life
for themselves in Zeytinburnu. Children of many of the interviewees
play football or hang around in small groups talking in the street or
offer to go to a friend's house to do homework or watch TV while I
talk to their parents or siblings. Many of the female interviewees who
have children admit that they rely upon their children for many chores
and activities. Children typically shop for their mothers, pay bills,
make phone calls, write letters, etc.

Employment is a critical difficulty for the Afghans. While most
mention some form of employment or other, many complain about
how difficult it is to gain and maintain employment. Typical employ-

ment remains working in the leather workshops. It is important to note that the interviewees work for both Turks and Afghans, although finding initial employment with an Afghan is considered much easier.

> A lot of us work in the workshops. I work for a Turk now, but in the beginning – that is when I first arrived, I worked for an Afghan. I asked for work directly, explaining that I had experience. My boss then just smiled and asked me to come the next morning. He gave me work clothes and that was that (Abbas, male, mid-20s, arrived 2001).

A number of the interviewees mention working as casual salesmen or day laborers along the pedestrian walkway at the harbor in Eminönü. These salesmen generally sell leather vests, coats, pouches, wallets and other little and inexpensive items. Some of the interviewees also mention the possibility of joining other Turkish and Iranian casual work seekers early in the morning in Aksaray.

> You have to go early in the morning. There is always a crowd of men waiting to see if there is any work for the day. A lot of the work is for construction workers. It is hard long hours and not a lot of pay. You are not lucky everyday but when available, it is work (Munir, male, 18, arrived 2004).

Overall a theme which seeps through by the comments made by interviewees is a sense of growing desperation and exasperation at the inability to find steady work. Comments by several of the interviewees indicate an increase in the enforcement of employment restrictions through police control or fear of police control instilled upon the employer. As one of the interviewees states:

> You start working in a place – horrible place, small and tight, with chemical fumes everywhere – probably unlawful health conditions but the boss comes after a couple of weeks and asks if you have papers or not and all of us who have no legal employment papers are excused (Yusef, male, mid-30s, arrived 2002).

Others make many similar comments:

> It is so hard to find work these days. I have to feed my wife and children but work is not available. This year has been hardest since we came here. I no longer know what to do (Suleyman, male, early 40s, arrived 2002).

These comments are not isolated. They are backed up by statements made by several of the Afghan Turkmen who now have their own work places but feel that conditions for employment provision have tightened during the last two to three years – in fact it seems to date from the enactment of the Law on Work Permit for Foreigners by the Turkish government on the 27th of February 2003:

> I used to employ Afghans readily in the past because I know how hard it is when one is new in the country and in need of help. But I have to admit, I have started to think twice about it these days. I still want to employ Afghans and most of my employees are Afghans but I had a visit from the police about a year and a half ago. They demanded to see the record of our accounts and the health insurance records for my employees. I was very worried but they left with only a warning. They asked me not hire anybody without proper documentation (Malikzay, male, 43, arrived 1983).

There is no doubt that the unofficial employment of workers in the informal economy in Istanbul, dominated by artisan work and trade, has been a source of possibility and in an odd sense protection to international migrants. It has offered the Afghans the chance to establish a comfortable niche in the leather workshops and the leather trade in general. However, if the trends mentioned by the interviewees persist and the local police manage to curb employment in the leather workshops, then economic survival for the 'undocumented' Afghan migrants in Zeytinburnu will become extremely constricted.

Another area of concern is education. Several of the refugees point out that they consider their time spent in Turkey a waste for their children. While they insist that they are grateful for the protection offered and the general safety of their environment, when prodded three types of responses emerge. One group points out that their children are going to school in Turkey and have learnt some Turkish, which is seen as a positive effect of their stay in Zeytinburnu.

> My children are happy here. All three of them go to school. They like their friends. I think it is very good that they are learning Turkish. At least they will be able to take this experience and learning with them wherever we go next. I am told it will give them confidence and strength. I am illiterate and my biggest fear is that my children will not get an education but so far we have managed. I am lucky because my uncle and 2 of my brothers are in Canada. They help me so my son does not have to work (Samira, mid-30s, arrived 2004).

A second group has decided not to enroll their children in school here in Turkey due to the expectation that they will be resettled in a third country soon. So why force their children to learn the language, get used to a school system, make friends and establish life just to tear them away from it all in short while?

This is in fact one of the greatest weaknesses of the present situation for refugees and asylum seekers in Turkey. The lack of perspective on the period of time the individual or family will spend in Turkey results in a resolve to avoid integration or habituation to life in the country.

> I don't see why my children should go to school here. We won't be here long so I see no reason why they should learn Turkish. If we knew the country we will really settle in then my children could learn the language of that country. For now I have decided they should just learn some English. That will be useful everywhere. But for Turkish I see no use (Fariba, female, mid-30s, arrived 2003).

This sentiment of course can backfire when the period of stay in Turkey turns out to be longer than initially anticipated, as another interviewee is discovering:

I saw no point to my children going to school here in Turkey. Why should they? It was a hassle and it is not cheap to buy uniforms and books and pens. I could not afford such costs. But now we have been here three years and still we do not know what is going to happen. My children are tired of the house. They are tired of having nothing to do. They fight a lot and they fight with my wife and even with me... (Ghasem, male, mid-40s, arrived 2002).

The third view is formed by the lack of 'status' in Turkey:

I am afraid of sending my children to school. I made inquiries and was told we have to give our address when we register the children and we cannot risk doing that. That's like inviting the police to your house. Anyway, even if we register the children, I have no regular employment at the moment. I cannot afford to send my children to school (Suleyman, male, early 40s, arrived 2002).

The lack of security and certainty places a great strain upon the option of 'integration' for the 'undocumented' migrants and refugees in Istanbul. The interviewees repeatedly mention their desire for a calm and settled life. When probed further it is often difficult for the individuals to further qualify 'calm and settled'. It appears self-evident and obvious for them:

A calm and settled life- you know- peaceful. Without worry (Fariba, female, mid-30s, arrived 2003).

But some are able to define their feelings very distinctly:

I would like to live a quiet comfortable life. You know exactly what I mean by that. I would like a stable job and to be able to afford education for my children. I would like for my wife to stop dreaming up schemes about how we shall go to Europe and live a life of luxury. I do not want luxury. I just want to feel like my life and my skills are being used to produce the chance for a future for my children and if Turkey cannot offer this, then we just may have to consider going back to Afghanistan (Suleyman, male, early-40s, arrived 2002).

Sadly, the undocumented migrants and refugees leave one with the impression that the process of integration leaves a lot to be desired. The interviewees repeatedly emphasize the 'insecurity' and lack of permanence inherent in their conditions. The conditions described and referred to indicate a bare struggle for survival and a vision of a desire for life in the EU or North America. Many of the interviewees point out that they would in fact be willing to live in Istanbul and settle on a permanent basis. Those who have been granted 'refugee status' are aware that there is no such option and consider a move to the EU, America or Canada a definite move up the ladder. Almost all of the undocumented feel that conditions are not suitable. Life in Istanbul is looked upon as 'transient' due to the lack of possibilities. This leaves two options: saving money and being smuggled to Europe, (typically Greece and on from there), or returning to Afghanistan. As can be imagined, the first option is by far the more popular, but interviewees indicate that if Europe becomes an impossibility, then they will consider the option of return.

> We have nothing in Afghanistan. My family is scattered everywhere. My father was killed. I have property to return to. No security. But if I cannot find security here and I cannot find a safe way to get my children to my brother in England, I will consider going back to Afghanistan. My brother advises it. I still cannot consider it. But if there is no choice, then there is no choice. Things will work out, God willing (Samira, female, mid-30s, arrived 2004).

At this stage, there is no possibility for integration for refugees or asylum seekers in Turkey. The lack of governmental or formal support and the lack of possibilities to permanently remain in Turkey have produced social networks which help with the basic survival of the recently arrived Afghans in Istanbul, addressing conditions such as housing, short term employment, translation, advice on going to the UNHCR, and so on. Long term possibilities are not available at this time.

In April 2005 the Turkish government introduced what is known as the 'National Action Plan', which defines the country's short and long term policy towards refugees and asylum seekers. The National Action Plan foresees the removal of the geographical limitation denying the chance for Asian, African, or Middle Eastern refugees settling in Turkey on a permanent basis in 2012. Genuine planning and preparation is needed to ensure a successful integration program by that time. By all means a deeper, more detailed examination of the division between 'permanently' settled, socially and economically rising Afghans living in Zeytinburnu and the 'transitory' refugees and asylum seekers could be a helpful way for the Turkish government to establish what areas need to be focused upon.

TRANSIT MAGHREBIS IN ISTANBUL: TRAJECTORIES, PROFILES AND STRATEGIES[94]

An early morning at the "Foreigners' Bureau" of Istanbul (November 2005)

I am in a queue hard to imagine its size and its mixture, waiting to be able to obtain the right to wait, i.e. to make me give a queue number, in order to still be able to wait at the successive counters. Certain people arrived at five o'clock in the morning in front of the Security Directorate (where the "Foreigners' Bureau" is located), close to Aksaray, famous pole of all the migrants. The Bulgarians and the citizens of the Russian Federation, who are the most populous, appear with the Iraqis; their knowledge of the Turkish language makes it easy to identify them, because it consists of Iraqi Turkmens in general. Scuffles, disputes, signs of aggravation, but also gestures of mutual aid, accomplice smiles, patience, resignation... Two young people with shaved heads introduce themselves at the "information office" for which the person in charge, who is generally absent, seems to be pleased to send them to the end of the queue. They are two Algerians; one of them speaks Turkish

---

[94] Jean-François Pérouse. Institut Français d'Etudes Anatoliennes (IFEA), Observatoire Urbain d'Istanbul. IFEA, Fransız Sarayı, Nuru Ziya Sok. 22, PK. 54, 34333, Beyoğlu, Istanbul.

well; he looks like an intermediary, even an organizer (I would come across him one month later at the Atatürk airport, engaged with the "Algerian suitcase tourists" in the departure hall). The other one has recently arrived. They show to the civil servant the passport of the man who does not speak Turkish and ask how to regularize his situation. Apparently, he exceeded the expiration date of his visa which was granted to him at the border. The police officer starts to be irritated. He resentfully repeats his favorite refrain: "To stay here, it is necessary to speak Turkish and to have real work". The Turkish-speaking Algerian insists, however, so that a solution is found... An Iraqi intervenes and proposes in Arabic to mediate. After several minutes of sharp discussions, with the volume increased, the Algerians realize that no compromise is possible and give up. And the civil servant pushes them to leave as fast as possible.

The terrible history of five young Moroccans, arrested by the Turkish coastguards in December 2001, draws attention on the fact that the Maghrebis also took part in the "great transit" towards Europe, via Turkey. Arriving in Turkey in 2000 as tourists, these five young people quickly slipped into clandestine life, after having tried to find work in Istanbul (as waiters or maintenance workers). Disappointed by their experience in Istanbul, they finally made the decision to reach Europe by way of Greece. In conjunction with their compatriots already installed in Greece, they tried to depart in boats by themselves from Çeşme, (close to Izmir), towards the Sakız Island. The adventure turned into a tragedy.[95] Likewise, five years later, the same image emerged again in the vicinity of Izmir, where this time two Tunisians drowned.[96]

Istanbul, located on the western periphery of Turkey – which has become an interface country on a regional and international scale, a corridor or a platform between rich and poor countries – after several years seems to have taken a central position in the international

---

[95] Because one of the five youngsters drowned.
[96] At the end of June 2005; see *Cumhuriyet*, 27/06/2005, p.4.

irregular migrations system. The function of this huge metropolitan area as an active pole of transit passages and various opportunities for the migration candidates has already been demonstrated (İçduygu, 2003). The Turkish press very frequently echoes the almost daily arrests, providing one of the most convincing signs of this vitality.[97]

Within the framework of this chapter, our aim is to examine these general patterns through the case of the Maghrebis[98] whose analysis was already undertaken a few years ago from the perspective of the movements of suitcase traders (Péraldi, 1998 and 2001; Délos, 2004). The geographical extension selected here – that we will not discuss – represents the "Larger Maghreb" spreading from Libya to Morocco, together with Mauritania.[99] Nevertheless, the criterion of nationality is not a restrictive criterion in the definition of our population of study. In other words, the fieldwork and the interviews led us to integrate the European citizens of Maghrebi origin in Istanbul into our sample as well.

Consequently, whatever the quantitatively modest character of their presence, one can wonder whether the Maghrebis in transit in Istanbul, beyond the different projects and trajectories which animate them, constitute a "society" (Tarrius, 2001), or a "community", however transitory. What are their modes of socialization in situations of passage and their strategies of incorporation into the metropolis of Istanbul, given that the duration of their transit sojourn in the city is always uncertain?

---

97 Elsewhere we have described the modes of foreigners' presense in Istanbul and outlined the modalities of the transit territory. In particular, we described the "counter", the "hub", the "hopper", and the "dead end". (Aslan and Pérouse, 2003; Pérouse, 2002 and 2004).

98 Which represents only 10,000 of the 478,000 irregulars apprehended in Turkey between early 1995 et June 2004, which is around 2%; see Apap, Carrera & Kirişci, 2004 (cited par Gresh 2005: 14).

99 It could appear strange to include Mauritania, but we can not forget the fact that this country, which emerged as an independent country very late (in November 1960), is historically strongly linked with Morocco; see *Aksiyon,* Sayı 516, 25/10/2004.

A Distinct Presence with Varying Chronologies for Each 'National Group'

Even if the attacks on Madrid (March 2004) and then on London (July 2005) which drew the attention of certain media to the Maghrebi presence in Istanbul[100] succeeded to present them as suspect and to criminalize them, their presence still remains isolated. Within the scope of the Turkish Republic's history, (we will not go up till the Ottoman period here), informal trade relations between Istanbul and the Maghreb, in the form of suitcase trade, have existed since the end of the 1970s. During the 1980s the Maghrebis were already identified as customers around Kapalı Çarşı (the Grand Bazaar), Mahmutpaşa, and Yenikapı (for automobile spare parts). Many tradesmen that we interviewed at Laleli have admitted to having relations with the Maghreb for more than twenty years. This lapse of time thus made it possible to weave now old relations, with replays in different forms and with various objectives. However, the transit movements seem to be more recent. They are related to the relative closure of the access to Europe by the "natural" ways, namely via Spain, Italy or France; this closing has to do with the emergence of the Schengen space (Délos, 2004). The interviews confirmed the idea of a Maghrebi presence which intensifies at the beginning of the 1990s. Thus, an Algerian of Laleli, a tradesman described by his compatriots as "the oldest Algerian of Laleli", has been in Turkey since 1991. The Libyans ultimately fit well in this chronology, whose presence in Istanbul is mainly of a commercial nature which dates back to the late 1970s, with the relative normalization of the relations of Libya with the external world, and Turkey in particular (the first commercial protocol signed between the two countries goes back to 1975). For the Mauritanians,

---

100 Two Canadians of Tunisian origin, were suspected to have bonds with El-Kaida (Al-Qaeda), and were intensely investigated. In October 2000, already, the police had arrested in Fatih three Moroccan nationals and an English national suspected to have bonds with terrorist organizations. After the attack of Madrid (2004), it appeared that these Moroccans, expelled in 2000, had played a part in the preparation of the assault.

with whom we did not conduct interviews, and for which we do not have any specific data, their presence is affirmed, (by the police apprehension reports), as late as the beginning of the 2000s.

Even if they offer us only a relative or indicative interest, the official figures of the entries of Maghrebi tourists are not spectacular, unlike those of Bulgarians, Russians, Iranians, or Ukrainians. Nevertheless, they are not negligible and record an appreciable increase since the early 2000s. This increase does not necessarily mean an increase in the flow of transit migrants, of which some enter illegally into Turkey, and are thus not taken into account by these tourist statistics. According to Tunisian consular authorities in 2004 more than 60,000 Tunisian nationals came to Turkey, which constitutes a strong increase compared to the early years starting in 2000 (see **Table 6.17**).

TABLE 6.17
Official Entry Statistics of the North Africans (1990-2005)

	1990	2000	2001	2002	2003	2004	2005 (the first six months)
Libya	22,500	24,000	31,473	29,970	28,185	27,846	12,440
Tunisia	16,330	39,692	44,961	51,271	46,718	52,470	30,389
Algeria	9,737	33,421	39,904	41,473	42,140	44,124	20,941
Morocco	5,695	11,635	11,798	12,643	13,794	15,987	11,008

Source: www.kultur.gov.org

Itineraries and Methods of Entry into Turkey

According to the data provided by the Turkish Ministry for Culture and Tourism, in 2004 a large majority of the Maghrebis legally entering Turkey used airways. However, it is noted that about a quarter of the Tunisians entered by a territorial border post. There is thus a Tunisian singularity which remains to be explained. Are they Tunisians of Europe who come by bus or car? Are they Tunisians on the way to Mecca transiting by Turkey? On the basis of 2004 statistics comprised of the entries at the various border posts, one realizes in fact that it consists of the Syrian land route. Indeed, in 2004 the main portion, (more than 9/10), of the Tunisian territorial entries were realized at the Turco-Syrian border at Hatay, Cilvegözü. Even if the share of the territorial entries is less important for the others – it is almost negligible for the Libyans – more than three quarters of the Moroccan and Algerian territorial entries are also done via Syria, the rest done via Greece (**Table 6.18**). Besides, the Algerians seem to be characterized by an exceptionality, which is due to their share of the arrivals by sea, relatively more important than the rest of the other national groups. Moreover, in 2004, almost all of these arrivals by sea landed in Thrace, in the region of Tekirdağ (**Table 6.18**). With regard to territorial passage, one puts aside other obviously'illegal' territorial ways, via Iraq or Bulgaria, to which we were incidentally referred, but on which we do not have a precise data.

TABLE 6.18
Modes and Points of Entry of Maghrebis Into Turkey in 2004

Country of origin	By airplane to Istanbul	By land via the Syrian border in Hatay	By land (road, train) in Edirne	By sea from Tekirdağ	Antaya
Libya	27,185	161	11	4	41
Algeria	39,481	1,005	251	1,617	640
Tunisia	39,278	10,691	377	–	785
Morocco	9,484	2,031	169	–	1,820
Mauritania	–	–		–	–

Source: www.kultur.gov.org

Two principal entry roads thus seem to emerge: the air route, mainly with arrival in Istanbul, on the one hand, and the land route, with entry via Syria, on the other hand. With regard to the more easily observable air route, the multiplication of the flights is one of the most obvious indications of the intensification of flows between Turkey and the Maghreb. In 2005, for example, there were ten scheduled flights per week between Tunisia and Turkey, five ensured by the

Turkish Airways and the other five by the Tunisian National Company. There are seven regular weekly flights between Libya and Turkey, ensured by the two respective national companies and a private company. And between Algeria and Turkey, there are three weekly flights assured by the two national companies. Lastly, following the inauguration of a new line by Turkish Airlines between Istanbul and Casablanca as of March 27, 2005, the airway relations between Turkey and Morocco also intensified.

For the moment, under the principle of reciprocity in the treatment of the nationals, the Maghrebis do not need visas to enter Turkey, except for the Libyans, who however may very easily obtain a one month visa. The Maghrebis with passports can thus enter Turkish territory without difficulty for three months duration. But the methods of entering and the intensity of the visits are likely to be modified with the setting-up of visas for the Tunisians and the Moroccans[101] as announced for the beginning of 2006. This new visa measure is imposed within the framework of the harmonization of Turkey into the European Union acquis. After this date, only the Algerians will be able to enter Turkey without visas. One sees in this case how the legal frameworks and opportunities established on the state level conditions the dynamics and the morphology of flows.

Profiles of 'Transitors' And Forms of Transit
It should be immediately underlined that these profiles are rather facets or roles (more than of the statuses), which can coexist, transfer or follow one another in the same person.

The Tourist
Tourism is the initial facet for all those who legally enter Turkey. Whether it consists of "banal" tourism, of *shopping* tourism, or religious tourism, (Istanbul is an important international place for all the

---

[101] According to a declaration of the Turkish Ministry of Foreign Affairs in February 2005, *Radikal*, 11/02/2005, p.5.

Sunnites in this sense), a number of the Maghrebis interviewed specifically or incidentally presented themselves as "tourists". If commercial tourism has been often mixed with visitor tourism, the articulation of both is to be taken into account. Still, we cannot deny *a priori* the Maghrebis the possibility of endorsing the role of a "normal" tourist, under the terms of a tourist hierarchy, based on the purchasing power, as often described by our Turkish interlocutors. Thus it is not necessary to doubt the sincerity of this fifty year-old Tunisian man who was very concerned to distinguish himself from his compatriots described as "profiteers". This Tunisian traveller insistently assured us that his first motive was tourism and not commerce, declaring that it was "out of the question to leave Istanbul without visiting Topkapı Palace."

The Shuttle Trader and the Merchant

The shuttle trader is one who operates with regular return tickets between his country of origin and Istanbul during a one year period. He sometimes stays only a few days, on average a week, in order to buy a reduced quantity of products, (which he carries back with him), with the intention of selling them in the black market or in a shop in his country. The frequency of these back and forth movements is changing; it goes from one to three in a year for "amateur" shuttlers, for whom the suitcase trade is a complementary activity,[102] and is easy to assimilate into a form of commercial tourism (this appears to also be the case for a number of Tunisian women met during the fieldwork). These trips go up to ten per year for certain Tunisians,[103] Algerians, and Libyans,[104] increasingly inclined to establish more for-

---

[102] For instance, a Tunisian civil servant comes during his holidays and thus performs suitcase trade only once per year to improve his income.

[103] Such as this 33 year old man we met in a hotel at Laleli, which told us that he comes every month at the rate of twice per month since 1991.

[104] However, the prohibition of the cargo airplanes enacted by the Libyan government in July 2005 caused a brake in the exchanges between Istanbul and Libya. Since then, the trade has to be made by the normal lines of "travelers" and this causes some prejudicial obstructions. See, *Radikal*, 23/08/2005, p.3.

malized import/export trade relations. It was even revealed to us in Osmanbey that there are Libyans[105] who come "two to three times every month". The typical shuttle trade, however, has a seasonal character, subject to the national, religious, and commercial calendars. The shuttle trade activity is apparently gainful, with a large profit margin, since a product bought in Turkey can be resold four times more expensively in Tunisia, for example.

The presence of the shuttle traders is generally articulated around a local contact, a Turkish merchant, with whom ties of relative confidence were woven as a result of a series of back and forth movements. This Arabic-speaking merchant often originates from the southeast of the country, and primarily from the city of Mardin (Deli, 2002). He becomes the principal contact for the shuttle traders, providing services that go well beyond simple commercial exchanges. Based on two series of observations and interviews, one in a shop at Osmanbey and the other in a shop at Laleli, we can specify the part played by the Turkish tradesman. He is involved with the facilities of travel, accommodation and all kinds of advice. Actually he provides all manner of services, greatly exceeding trade relations. One of these tradesmen showed us the integrality of his address book, including addresses of cargo companies, restaurants, hotels, translators, change offices, wholesalers, and workshops at the same time (Photo 6.4).

In a similar context, here we can refer to the case of another migrant. V is owner of a small shop in Laleli in one of the multiple commercial complexes of this emblematic place of the suitcase trade (incidently, the owner of the next-door shop is married to a Tunisian). He was born in 1971, and is married with two children. He was born in Mardin ("in the city itself", he insists), in an Arabic-speaking family; he has nine brothers and sisters. He also speaks Kurdish and understands some French. His father was a porter in Mardin, then in Istanbul. V came to Istanbul when he was 12, and he worked in par-

---

105 Interview, 25/04/2005.

Photo 6.4. A page from the address book of a merchant in Osmanbey (JFP).

ticular as a guide for the Tunisians or the Libyans "on the right, on the left" until 1988. In 1988, he started doing trade with the Maghreb, particularly those from Tunisia. He goes to Tunisia to sell textiles in small quantities and to build a network of customers. He thus acquires personal experience in the Maghreb. According to his words, he was devoted to this gainful employment between 1988 and 1994. He went bankrupt in 1999 because, he says, of his Tunisian partner, who had betrayed his confidence, (he did not make any claim at the court, since their relations were not officially formalized). Since then, he has a feeling of resentment towards Tunisians in general.

Between the end of 1999 and 2004, he was obliged to work as a salesman in somebody else's store in Osmanbey; this was the time necessary to again accumulate the money needed for the reset of his independence. At the end of 2004, he managed to restart his own business as a result of great sacrifices. He has his shop again. He goes to Tunisia at least once every three months to maintain his contacts, to widen his address book, as well as to engage in tourism. His customers are primarily Tunisians, "80% to 85% of which are women". He pays a rent of $500 dollars per month for his shop and manufactures his products in Merter and Kagithane. V has quite stereotypical ideas about Maghrebis; he distinguishes betweem national types, which he considers very different from each other. According to him, the Tunisians, unlike the Libyans, are not reliable in businesses...

One notes a relation between the country of origin and the gender of the traders. Indeed, all of the observations and interviews lead us to differentiate, for both the Libyans and the Algerians a suitcase trade conducted in great majority by young men; and for the Tunisians and the Moroccans a suitcase trade practiced predominantly by women. We were unable to find a satisfactory explanation to attribute to gender and national differences. This characteristic, in any case, makes national differences even more visible, and facilitates the procedures of identification at sight and from distance, inevitable in any initiation of a commercial relation.[106]

Socially speaking, it appears that those who are performing this trade belong to the middle class, are relatively educated, and have the essential capital for the frequent mobility required by this activity. Moreover, it is in this "category" that one finds most of the European

---

[106] Anthropological investigations, that we were not able to carry out, in the countries of origin would be necessary for a better grasp of this aspect.

citizens of Maghrebi origin, whether they are of Swiss nationality, Italian,[107] or French, to quote those who were introduced to us and those which we could meet. Suitcase trade conducted amongst these Maghrebi coming from Europe often take a convivial, family and/or tourist form and usually take place less frequently. Very often they occur during holidays celebrated in Europe. Lastly, some districts appear to polarize the presence of these Maghrebian shuttle traders; they have a mental image of Istanbul with the invariably convened poles of Osmanbey, Merter, Zeytinburnu, and Laleli. Sometimes, the suitcase merchants know only these places in Istanbul which represent circumscribed small islands at the centre of the metropolis, which in effect limit their experience of the city.

However, the number of those that can be catagorized as "Maghrebi suitcase trader" seems to be declining since the beginning of the 1990s, in parallel with the general constriction in the estimated incomes of this trade (**Table 6.19**). In any case, all of the Turkish tradesmen with whom we spoke made it clear that the Maghrebi countries do not represent very interesting markets for them, and that they constitute kinds of markets *par défaut*, except perhaps for the Libyan market, which is described as the 'entry door to the entire African market'. Libya indeed is regarded as a kind of 'soft belly' of the African customs by which enter more and more products intended not only for the Libyan market, but also for all of Africa. In the same way, as we were told on several occasions, certain Tunisians pass through Libya when importing goods because of the considerably lower rate of customs tax when compared to Tunisia. It was reported that these traders would then pass irregularly to Tunisia, (in the south of Tunisia there are multiple ways for trans-border smuggling).

In addition to distinctions made by the Turkish tradesmen between the 'good Maghrebis' (Libyan and Algerian) and the others, the emergence of Arabic-speaking customers with stronger purchasing

---

107 Like the young Italo-Tunisian met in Laleli one evening.

TABLE 6.19
The Decline of Suitcase Commerce Revenues in Laleli

Year	Estimated Revenue (in billions of dollars)
1997	5,8
1998	3,7
1999	2,3
2000	2,9
2001	3
2002	4,1
2003	4,5
2004	2

power, including Iraqis, Egyptians, nationals of Gulf countries and Saudis, caused a certain marginalization of the Maghrebi customers, in the hierarchy of the tradesmen. In the same way, the passage to more organized forms of trade, (import/export by cargo), plays a part in the degeneration of the image of the Maghrebi suitcase trader, described now with some contempt as "*torbacı*" (carrier of bag), a term with clearly pejorative connotations. Thus, more and more Turkish tradesmen make a distinction between these *torbacı*, considered with some derision, and the wholesalers, (*toptancı*), who are the favorites. There are still *torbacı*, but in the margins of the more noble activity which is represented by the trade carried out by the cargo companies (*kargocu*). Suitcase trade appears to be increasingly regarded only as a precondition, in the case of a first contact or a complementary activity at the periphery of the wholesale activity. Thus opposition between *torbacı* and *kargocu* is ultimately not as clear as one might think; many *kargocu* declare at the customs only some of their goods, and thus carry out the rest of their trade in an informal model.

The Candidate for Exile Toward Europe

At the beginning, let us highlight the fact that the Maghrebis constitute only a limited part of the overall irregular transit migration

Photo 6.5. Libyans checking in at the Atatürk airport (JFP, 2003) and packages for destination to Algeria in the same airport (JFP, 2005).

flows, if we stick to the statistics of apprehension provided by the security forces. During the first seven months of the year 2002, for example, of the 536 irregular migrants apprehended, there were only six Maghrebis, four Moroccans and two Algerians (along with 265 Iraqis, 127 Turkish citizens, 59 Afghans, 47 Palestinians, and 21 Iranians).[108] Table 6.20 offers another example of the proportions of each "national group" generally met.

TABLE 6.20

An Example of Apprehensions, late June 2002 at the Border Province of Edirne

Nationality	Number of nationals arrested
Iraqis	52
Afghans	52
Pakistanis	42
Bangladeshis	19
Palestinians	18
Sierra-Leonese	10
Algerians	8
Moroccans	4
Tunisians	2
Somalis	2
Nigerians	1

Source: *Radikal*, 21/06/2002, p.5.

From a chronological perspective, this pattern of a Maghrebi presence in Istanbul is not old. It emerges after the early 1990s, with the opening of the land routes in the Balkans, subsequent to the lifting of the Iron Curtain. In 2003, one observes a decrease in the statistics of apprehension collected at the territorial borders, (which concerns especially Moroccans and Algerians), if one trusts the data of the Security Directorate circulated by the press. This drop, which involves not only the Maghrebis but all the national groups, can be interpreted in different ways. It can be regarded as a sign of the fact that surveillance and

---

[108] *Cumhuriyet*, 12/08/2002.

supervision systems begin to bear fruit, or as an indication of changes in the transit strategies of migrants, their adaptation to the policies developed by the United States, and of a rearrangement of migration routes.

It is a question neither of a pure type of Maghrebi migratory movement that excludes others, nor of a type characterized by final objectives; it can be combined with a number of types and "statuses" all of which being extremely unstable. Arriving by multiple irregular or regular ways, they aim to go to Greece by land, or Italy by sea. Putting aside some not easily verifiable meetings and allusions, only arrests that regularly occur can give us indices concerning this profile. In almost all of the cases, we note that the irregular migrants apprehended on the Aegean coasts or near the territorial borders with Greece or Bulgaria stayed for a while in Istanbul, which appears as a true pole of redistribution from which the networks of clandestine migration are reframed and redeployed.[109] It does not seem that the Maghrebis have their own network for clandestine passage of the borders. According to the interviews and to the list of nationalities comprising the groups that have been arrested, it seems that the Maghrebis are inserted into the networks which offer services to citizens of varied countries, such as Pakistan, Afghanistan, Egypt, and Palestine (**Table 6.20**). On the other hand, many have their own 'national' relays in Greece.

Even if it was difficult for us to meet individuals identifying themselves as candidates for exile in Europe, we can say that they consist of a great majority of men, and often young men. Thus the Tunisian that we met one evening in the lobby of a hotel in Laleli confessed towards the end that he was waiting for a good 'plan' to pass by boat to Greece (for 800 Euros). Another young Tunisian thus told us that he went to Izmir, where he had met a compatriot who had settled there, and later learned about the conditions of passage to a Greek island (for 1,500 Euros). Not having the required sum, he explained

---

109 Thus the irregular migrants, whose majority were Afghans, apprehended lastly at Gebze (oriental periphery of Istanbul urban zone) while they were preparing to go to the Aegean coast; *Radikal*, 14.09.2005, p.3.

to us that his intention was to go back to Tunisia to find the necessary amount, then to return and attempt the adventure with friends whom he would make come with him. Occasionally, one also finds individuals with very high educational levels, motivated by the idea of making the most of this cultural capital in a European country where salaries are eminently more appealing. In many cases, Turkey is clearly recognized – during interviews – as 'the easiest way' to reach the EU irregularly. We note the example of an Algerian of forty years met at Beyazıt[110] who told us that he had transited via Turkey seven times since 1991, after being expelled six times from European countries which he had accessed from Turkey, (crossing the Turco-Greek border by foot each time, after a passage in Istanbul). Fifteen years after his first attempt, he is thus ready to repeat his endevour with the ultimate objective of reaching the Netherlands.

What stands out in this typology is the extreme uncertainty to which the candidates are condemned in the irregular crossing to Greece. In any case, those who do not have the proper means to do this, put the highest price on it. Rumors, gossip, inaccuracies, improvisations, hesitations, and chances typify this form of transit. Lastly, this picture of the "transitor" does not exist without its correlate, namely the human smuggler and merchant of forged identity papers; they can be of various nationalities. One evening, we encountered one of these in the streets of Laleli. He was a Tunisian, living for more than four years in Istanbul, and he was wandering near the hotels where prospective customers could be. On another occasion, we were told that one of the persons whom we had just met, having dual nationality, (Turkish and Italian), was in fact a supplier of forged documents.

The Nanny

Like the example of the Moldavians, who operate in another segment of the market, (not in competition therefore), there exists in

---

110 Interviews in Beyazıt/Laleli on 7.06.2005.

the domestic service market of Istanbul a genuine niche for the Maghrebi nannies, mostly occupied by Moroccan women to our knowledge. This Maghrebi network concerns single young women, unlike what one observes in the case of Moldavian, Armenian, or Georgian women in the same sector. This network is structured around a special milieu characterized by French-speaking professionals living in Istanbul, and seems to have made its first emergence ten years ago in the surroundings of the French diplomats. Since then, this employment has developed by word-of-mouth and has expanded with the arrival of new female candidates, and their circulation by recommendation from one family to another. These young nannies that are often without educational credentials are in a process of accumulation and emancipation from their family of origin.

The Employee and the Worker

We will not speak here about the Maghrebis engaged in formal business relationships under the title of Turco-Maghrebi trade which is significantly on the rise[111] (Photo 6.6). There are indeed some import/export companies and counseling firms where Maghrebis work.

In Laleli, we were able to conduct a long interview in an import/export company specializing in Maghrebi countries. Among the employees there were a Lebanese, a French, (converted to Islam and married to a Tunisian), and a Moroccan, all living in Turkey for a long time. Meanwhile, these companies, in Laleli or elsewhere, can also informally play the role of a social space full of resources, thanks to the possibility of newcomers meeting the experienced. We have witnessed several times the first contact between old and new migrants in this company. In the margin of the legal structures there are non-declared persons, with a blurred status according to the Turkish and Maghrebi laws.

---

111 On this subject, see studies conducted by the Chamber of Commerce on commercial relations with each countries of the Maghreb or the studies conducted by KOSGEB (Küçük ve Orta Ölçekli Sanayi Geliştirme ve Destekleme İdaresi Başkanlığı, *Cezayir*).

Photo 6.6. Import-export Company "Casablanca" in Laleli (disappeared in 2005) (JFP).

But in the shops of Osmanbey, Merter, and Zeytinburnu one finds Maghrebis employed for their linguistic skills in a more or less stable way (Photo 6.7). They are usually young women, who have generally "settled down" for a certain time in Istanbul – the time for the acquisition of a Turkish language level sufficient for the business-

Photo 6.7. "Available job for a female Arabic speaking salesperson" (Osmanbey, 2004)

es. These young women, following the example of the Bulgarians or Russians recruited to serve for the Russian speaking clientele, are used as the interface with all of the Arabic-speaking customers, whether they are Maghrebi or not. It was very difficult to carry out interviews with these employees due to their employers' protective manners, making us understand clearly that they did not like such questions. However, we observed that the Maghrebis tend to be increasingly replaced by Iraqis who are considered to be less expensive for ensuring this type of linguistic interface in the trade. In Laleli, one nevertheless finds at certain periods of the year, one Tunisian woman per shop at the shopping centers, and a Tunisian human advertiser at the entry of the *han*. To our knowledge, as opposed to what we observed for the Afghans or the Iraqis, (and even Romanians up until a certain period), the Maghrebis do not seem to engage in all types of informal labor in Istanbul. Construction and textile production are in the forefront of the informal sectors, together with, and in a more discrete manner, restaurants and manufacturing (Lordoğlu, 2005). Moreover, if the methods used in the fight against informal work are reinforced through a series of laws (in particular law number 4817 which came into effect on September 6, 2003[112]) and recently adopted measures[113] one could presume that the number of informal workers will certainly decline in number.[114]

The Student and the Apprentice

The number of Maghrebi students identified by their consular authorities, or among the scholarship holders of the Turkish State or a Maghrebi State, is very low. For Tunisia during the year 2004-2005, the number was put at nine according to the vice-consul whom we interviewed:[115] five in the department of Ottoman history and civilization, two in medicine, one in law school, and one in aviation. In addition to this type of student there is the mobility of former students and of students who are not registered by their consular authorities. Thus, some employees met in import/export companies and counseling firms were thus registered, often in language or literature programs. For the Libyans too, the official presence of students is limited; according to the president of the Association of the Turkish-Libyan

---

112 Law titled "Law on the authorization of foreigners' work", see *Dünya*, 02.09.2003, p.4.

113 A telephone number aiming to inform against this kind of practices is already put on line. See *Radikal*, 12.02.2005 and *Cumhuriyet*, 7.12.2005, p.13.

114 About the apprehension of eleven foreign undocumented workers in Laleli in October 2005, see *Vatan 34*, 19.10.2005, p.2.

115 Interview.

Parliamentary Friendship Group,[116] a total of 180 Libyan students would have been educated in Turkey since the two countries established steady relations. Among the former students, one also finds Algerians who studied in the USSR or in the Federation of Russia, and never returned to their country. It consists of relatively well settled people, 'references' respected for their social and cultural capital. One of our privileged respondents in 2001 to 2002 was an Algerian graduate of Arab literature at the University of Damascus and fluent in English (because he was married to an Anglophone for a time) and Turkish. He enjoyed this kind of esteem by his compatriots, until he decided to return to Syria because of the impossibility of obtaining an appropriate residence permit. In addition, there are Maghrebi apprentices in at least two spheres of activity, namely in the goldsmith and tourism sectors. Unfortunately, our knowledge about this category is currently incomplete.

The Prostitute

Prostitution is a category that became inevitable and recurring in the representations and conversations about foreigners' presence in Istanbul.[117] It corresponds to a status for the Maghrebis as well, even though we never noticed Maghrebis in the prostitution-related deportation statistics published by the Security Directorate. Nevertheless, at the beginning of January 2005, a police operation revealed the existence of 'massage saloons' where Tunisian women worked (they had become Turkish citizens by marriage).[118] Except for some various facts published in the press, we are using here only reported discourses. However, when a discourse is reported so repetitively, one is tempted to grant some credit to it. It consists primarily of the talk of tradesmen in Osmanbey or Laleli, who differentiate among different nationalities

---

116 Interview published by the newspaper *Sabah*, 05.12.2004.
117 Newspapers excel to nourish the fusion between prostitution and foreign presence; for a recent example of tendentious information see the magazine *Haftalık*, n°×140, 2005, pp.22-24.
118 See *Cumhuriyet*, 20.01.2005, p.3, "Şişli'de fuhuş operasyonu".

and tend to stigmatize especially the Moroccan women and more incidentally the Tunisians. They accuse them of performing acts of prostitution in the hotels of Taksim or Lâleli. Prostitution can be practiced very temporarily to secure an additional income or to prolong the stay in Istanbul, as it was admitted to us one night at Laleli by a Tunisian young woman whom we had encountered in a small shop in search of alluring clothing. The practice of prostitution with the tradesmen also makes it possible for certain Maghrebi women to pay in kind for the products they choose.

The Person in Escape

Lastly, Turkey acts as a haven of peace for people having problems with the law of their country. Although we do not know the details, these problems with the law were reported to include bankruptcy, bad checks, family difficulties, military service, and political opposition. In this case, it is not a question of 'transiting' but rather searching for a refuge. For example, we met a Tunisian in his thirties who lived in Germany for three years, then in Switzerland, where he married a Swiss citizen of Slovenian origin, then stayed one year in Ankara before going to Istanbul where he has lived for four years. This man told us that he has some problems, and for the moment is unable to return to Tunisia or to Switzerland. It was thus out of constraint and obligation that he was in Istanbul, where he carried on the activity of advertiser for Maghrebi customers at the entry of one of the most well known *han*s in Laleli. We later learned that he also carried on another activity, related to finding 'girls' for men in search.

The Articulation Between the Categories or the Risks of Classification

The categories that are presented, as we have already stated, are not exclusive from one another. None of the types correspond to an autonomous field of activity; they each have relations with the others. They consist of states or roles sometimes successively endorsed, consistent with the opportunities and the constraints, as with the passing of time. A tourist may quickly become a transit migrant; a merchant may turn into a prostitute; an employee to a married citizen. In the same way, there can also be co-presence of different categories in time and space. Thus, it was asserted to us during an interview that the suitcase trader would benefit from his back and forth movements and experience in Turkey to eventually build a business to deal with young compatriots and to connect them in Istanbul with clandestine migration networks towards Europe. This articulation between suitcase trade and clandestine emigration thus associates distinct categories at first sight, but which, on the basis of familial, emotional or economic relation, can converge in one moment.

In the same way, certain candidates for exile in Europe can become asylum applicants, like a Tunisian arrested in 1993 at the territorial border post of Dereköy who tried to pass clandestinely into Bulgaria.[119] Known for his opposition to the Tunisian regime, he wanted to go to France to solicit political asylum. Yet, he was presented by the Tunisian authorities contacted after his arrest as a criminal, and his expatriation had been considered, in accordance with the bilateral agreement of 1982 between Turkey and Tunisia.

Strategies Implemented

The Inscription in a Network More or Less Pre-Constructed and Stable

Each migrant fits *de facto* in a system of informal reception which serves him as the first framework of 'integration' (the term being employed here in a minimal sense). This system, which is always open to re-definitions and new complexities, can be perhaps regarded as a more or less dense, stable and integrated unit, with material or non-material (social) resources, that can be mobilized at the arrival and even before the arrival (thanks to the telephone). The access to this

---

119 See *Evrensel*, 10.04.1993, p.3.

network is always dealt with in one way or another, directly by differing money payments (the means of contraction of debt from the
beginning) or not, by work, or indirectly by formation of a moral debt
(requiring a payment which takes multiple forms, on very variable
temporalities). The access to an effective network is paid; and the construction of a network of integration or survival is always delicate and
precarious. In every case, networks are thus set in motion, involving
and mobilizing those which are 'installed' for long periods of time on
the one hand, and those whose relative situation is better. These networks are nationally segmented, in spite of the intervention of Turkish
people who ensure bridges or links. In other words, it is initially by
applying for the segment of the Algerians of Istanbul that a recently
arrived Algerian, whatever his profile, undertakes to invest in Istanbul.
For the Moroccan nannies network for example, it has been possible
for us to trace the entire chain, beginning with a true pioneer, originating in Casablanca and married to a Moroccan doing a declared
activity in the historical peninsula. She urged her close relatives from
Morocco to come, and she took care of their lodging and work in the
first phase, until they became relatively self-sufficient. This role of pioneer can be redistributed in time, as far as the material and legal situations evolve. Thus, an old newcomer can become an autonomous
nanny at the end of a few years, being able to play in its turn the part
of protective 'pioneer'. Also, in each "national group", as in the image
of the young Algerian encountered at the Foreigners' Bureau and at
the Atatürk airport, more adept small leaders emerge. They sometimes
become genuine "social contractors", who can assert themselves near
their compatriots – his 'natural' clientele – like a useful contact, and
can convert their knowledge of the terrain and their social capital
accumulated in the big city into cash.

Furthermore, the implication of associations in the reception
and integration mechanisms remains extremely limited, even non-existent, except in cases of some extreme events, and this is for the
moment a norm in Turkey, aside from some positions, declarations

and specific services.[120] Ultimately, only the Turkish office of Amnesty International develops policy on the subject, regularly drawing the attention of the authorities to the files of the candidates in transit.[121] Likewise, we did not remark upon exploitation by the Maghrebi of the Turkish religious networks as a component of the integration strategies, even though religious networks in Turkey are known to nourish all the society, businesses milieus and political circles. In other words, beyond the sometimes heard assertions about a common membership in a 'community of believers', the practice of religion seems to remain a private and a 'national' issue at the same time. If there is an inscription of the private practices in the collective calendar of Sunnite Islam, the intersections between these practices and the practices of the host country remain very limited, except for the frequenting of a "Turkish" mosque on some occasions. In the same way, we did not hear them speak about the Maghrebis going to charity associations with marked religious references, like Deniz Feneri or the IHH (*İnsani Yardım Vakfi*: http://www.ihh.org.tr(cgibin/index.pl.).

Lastly, what can be named as the visible *community's infrastructure*, which would be made up of associations and well known meeting places. is much reduced for the Maghrebis. Except for high class Tunisian or Moroccan restaurants, there exists only, to our knowledge, the "Algeria" Restaurant in Beyazıt, on the first floor of a rather sordid building (see Photo 6.8) on a street toward the Marmara Sea. It is the only hang-out place known by Algerians addressing the newcomers. It appears to also be known by the Moroccans and certain Tunisians. However, it was very difficult for us to conduct inter-

---

120 Like the Association of Affectionate Hearts (*Şevkatli Kalpler Derneği*), Human Rights Association (İHD) or Mazlumder.

121 See for instance the daily newspaper *Zaman*, 4.06.2005, p.16 ("Türkiye'deki mülteci hukuku yeni bir yol ayrımında" by Taner Kılıç"). Also *Zaman*, 9.08.2005, p.1, about the modification of the regulation on the granting refugee status (since March 2005, Turkey is actually in the obligation of taking into consideration refugee status requests from the nationals of Asian, African and Middle Eastern countries). This change will certainly have implications on the migratory strategies.

Photo 6.8: "Algéria" café-restaurant at Beyazıt in 2001 (The sign disappeared in 2006).

views there, since the then owner, (the management changes at an intensive pace), showed an extreme reticence at each of our appearances/intrusions.

Components of the Network

Invaluable Family

Understood in a broad sense, family is one of the principal resources, providing essential services in the initial times of arrival and even a long time after, due to the compulsory refunding of the contracted debts (money makes relatives). They also become an important resource in the case of a serious problem such as an accident or disease.

Let us take the example of A, a Moroccan female originating from the poor peripheries of Casablanca. She arrived in 2000 in Turkey to live with her elder sister. The latter is married to a captain in the Turkish merchant navy, whom she met in Valencia, Spain, under conditions which we are unaware of. She was thus regularized very quickly in terms of status, and invited her sister to join her. For three years, A lived at her sister's place, who introduced her to L, working in the nanny network and married to a Moroccan who had been settled for a long time in Turkey. L, a friend of A's sister, quickly ensured the integration of A in the network of Moroccan nannies serving the French-speaking clientele. An important percentage of the money earned was being sent to Morocco. The sister of A was also involved in the fake marriage of her younger sister, who, since 2003, started to gain her autonomy, in particular by moving to a place to live by herself. Having refunded her debts to her sister, A in her turn invited friends from Casablanca, some of whom lived for a while at her place. Since spring 2005, A became a Turkish citizen, married to a Turk, who is the cousin of the mother of a child whom she took care of for a time.

Thus when the family does not exist, it is 'manufactured', by the recourse to marriage which appears especially for women as a major element in their integration strategies. Friends, too, sometimes provide a replica of family networks.

The Boss/Protector

The participation in the informal labor market is one of the most sensitive stages in the process of local incorporation. It performs informal relays including the possession of minimal information on the available opportunities. We have presented above the branches of economic activities where there are the most Maghrebis, particularly the female Maghrebis. A central figure, the boss/protector is the provider of employment, and because of this has considerable power over them. Two types exist: in the case of informal employment, as is mostly the case at least in the initial periods, the dependence is strong; in the case of formal employment, the relations are clearer and less subjected to the arbitrary attitudes of the boss. The boss is sometimes a Turkish citizen, sometimes a Maghrebi settled for a certain time, having a status that confers on him a relative visibility in the eyes of his co-nationals. No philanthropy exists in the relations between boss and 'subject'. The boss is often also the landlord of the migrant, and this factor reinforces the relation of dependence. In this case, accommodation is found on the upper floor of the shop or the workshop, often under very miserable conditions.

Housing

Except for those who are welcomed by a friend, a friend of a friend, a relative, or the employee of a hotel – which is increasingly frequent for the tradesmen – housing remains the principal enigma and the first problem to be solved. For the migrants who do not have a pre-existent family network, it was done mainly, until recently, in the small pensions and other 'furnished' rooms held by slumlords in the historical peninsula (districts of Fatih and Eminönü), but also in certain districts of Beyoğlu. For the Maghrebis in transit, during the interviews we pinpointed some hotels, located in the bottom of Laleli and around

Kadırga, Nişanca or Cankurtaran. These neighborhoods are places to get in contact with providers of employment, as well as with the smuggling networks to Greece. They also constitute one of the privileged spaces of contact between Maghrebi and Turkish citizens, some of the latter who are themselves immigrants too in their own country, sharing the same living and working conditions. There is a hierarchy of hotels in terms of the quality and services offered. It is highly probable that the function of certain hotels is not only lodging. If we can speak about a hotel supply segmented by nationality, the hotels are nevertheless places of articulation between various categories specified above.

However, it should be noted that currently there is a movement of reorganization of the 'hiding places', in particular for the most precarious migrants, as the degraded districts of the inner city[122] cease being the principal poles of lodging. This redeployment is due at the same time to a change of clandestine lodging strategies that seek a greater invisibility,and to the politics of 'cleaning' the historical peninsula by the local authorities. The district of Küçükpazar[123] in the historical peninsula, (in the Eminönü district), is thus the object of such a re-conquest, as a result of the shutting down of pensions and other lodging, (called 'rooms for single people'), where the foreign as well as internal migrants dwell. This re-conquest is accompanied by a stigmatization campaign in the media, in particular in the daily newspapers with large audiences, towards foreign migrants who are presented to be at the origin of the insecurity in the districts concerned.[124] Thus in April 2005, special teams of the Eminönü municipality, supported by the rapid deployment force (*çevik kuvvetler*) of the Ministry for the Interior, proceeded with evacuation by force[125] and sealed tens of pen-

---

122 In one example in Fatih where, 38 irregular migrants were caught in late May 2005 in a house abandoned by the smuggling networks (to whom they paid 2,000 to 3,000 dollars each, to reach Europe) were kicked out by the police; see *Vatan-34*, 29.05.2005.

123 Where, for instance, after an accusation, 30 Pakistanis had been arrested at the beginning of the July 2002.

124 See *Sabah*, 31.05.2005.

125 See *Zaman*, 16.04.2005, p.19.

sions considered to be suspect for medical hygiene as well fiscal rea- sons. They thus initiated a genuine 'cleaning' of the sectors in the city centre where irregular migrants, whether they are Turkish citizens or foreigners, dwell. Besides, the apprehension of 37 irregular migrants in Güngören, on November 19, 2005 and the arrest of 81 clandestine Pakistani and Mauritanians on November 29, 2005 in a low quality district of the Asian periphery – in Aydınevler, a neighborhood of Maltepe – confirm this assumption, in addition to the references made during the interviews (concerning for example the peripheral districts of Küçükçekmece or Gaziosmanpaşa). The solution adopted in this case is to rent an apartment in one of the innumerable buildings under- occupied in the urban periphery of Istanbul.

School, Health and the Question of 'Relationships With Turks'

We have little information about these topics in the daily life of the Maghrebi. With regard to education, based on two interviews con- ducted with Maghrebis installed in Istanbul, we notice that the pref- erence seems to go to private schools, and for the girls, to Koranic courses which constitute the only form of education provided. In the two cases, Turkey is perceived to be more tolerant than the countries of origin in terms of religious education.

The discourse on 'the Turks' oscillates according to our respon- dents between a discourse of rejection and that of closeness. It is thus impossible to generalize, since the judgments are conditioned by the individual experience of each person and by the more or less adapted and spread discourses. So from one side, as can be signified by mixed marriages, Turks are seen as similar people, particularly in terms of religion and a common history. From another side, they are presented as radically different people, rather Asian than Mediterranean in ori- gin. But the participation in a Turco-Moroccan wedding showed us that cleavages, even in this case, could remain rather strong, (not only for linguistic reasons). That night the two 'camps' involved socialized very little with each other, and a crystallization even appeared at some moments about the respective differences.

Strategies to Exit

The Regular Exit from the Country and Intra-Urban Mobility

For the Maghrebis who only have tourist visas, the solution is to leave the Turkish territory every three months – and this is the same solution for the other foreigners, including the Europeans – so as to, to some extent, rebuild their statutory virginity vis-à-vis the Turkish authorities. It comes out from our observations that one of the most privileged destinations to undertake these steps is northern Cyprus. Many of our respondents thus go regularly to Cyprus, generally by plane but also by boat, in order to carry out these formalities. Generally, they only make a return trip, and the Turkish and Cypriot customs officers close their eyes to these repeated exits/re-entries in return of some money taken under the table. For the most deprived Moroccan and Algerians, Syria[126] also constitutes a solution for this type of action.

The Exit Ways of the Transit

In addition to the pure and simple return, which is not always possible, we note two main exit routes of the transit: marriage on the one hand and formal work on the other. These two methods, which mostly concern the women, are also very frequently linked one to another. In the network of the nannies, observed since late 1999, we had already attended several weddings; the same woman being able to marry twice, the first time in the "fake" way with a Turk and with the complicity of a civil servant, the second time in a more serious mode with a Turk or not. Until early 2003, the first marriage made possible the acquisition of Turkish nationality at the end of one year. From then

---

126 Interview on 12.04.2005 with V.

on, three years became necessary. In a Turco-Moroccan counseling and import/export company we met a woman married to a Turk for five years, who worked in his brother's company. A graduate from the University of Marrakech in geology, she wanted, at the moment of the interview, to continue her studies at the University of Istanbul. To survive, she was tutoring French and Arabic courses.

The Reign of Contingency and Subversion of the Codes

Even if the Maghrebis do not constitute the most representative 'populations' of the transit migrants in Istanbul, their case, which presents sensitive differences according to their countries of origin, once more makes it possible to evaluate the appeal of Istanbul, the gigantic pole and switch in the system of circulations and international mobility. In all of the cases, the term 'transit' to qualify certain forms of foreigners' presence should be used with great prudence, since the trajectories are dubious, and since the scales of time and space of this transit are variable. We will thus be careful not to draw very general conclusions. The experience of transit in Istanbul is an experience personal and a collective at the same time, struck by precariousness, full of risks and difficulties to communicate, except for perhaps that of the suitcase traders. The continuously contingent character of the transit experience in the complex of multiple opportunities provided by the Istanbul metropolitan environment prevails. For those who want to pass clandestinely towards the European Union, the transit is everybody's personal concern, and the solidarities mobilized limit themselves to the closest companions of adventure, in a universe where information circulates poorly,[127] is segmented, and always suspect.

In the same way, legal changes which profile the Moroccans and the Tunisians are thus likely to modify these persons' conditions of stay in Turkey, and result in the change of direction of the strate-

---

[127] For instance, the accident that took place in late July 2005 in the Aegean sea, which caused the death of two Tunisians, did not seem to be known by the Maghrebis interviewed at the same period.

gies, toward other territories of transit – similar to the example of suitcase traders shifting borders of entry based on favorable tax treatment of goods. The likely result of the bilateral negotiations in progress between Turkey and each Maghrebi country about the readmission procedures can also have consequences for the migration practices (Kirişci, 2004: 19-20). What is striking is the reproduction, even reinforcement, of the national differences in transit situation; differences which, one could believe in the beginning, do not constitute a determining factor. However, nationality seems, if not to determine then at least largely to condition, the modes of presence of the Maghrebis in Istanbul (which do not constitute anything like a 'community' structured by common interests and practices of solidarity). In other words, far from erasing and transcending them, international circulations even seem to exacerbate the criteria of nationality. Besides, the transit stay and circulation in a foreign metropolis can redistribute gender roles, by upsetting the dominant division of labor, responsibilities and initiatives, while proceeding in fact to an emancipation of women. And finally, to try to answer the question asked at the beginning, the mental construction of 'transit societies' remains very limited, and in any case due to a function of the time and the conditions of transit, the candidates of exile appearing to be the last concerned about the forms of 'other integration' still to be explored (Tarrius, 2001: 47).

CHRONOLOGY

24.03.2000: Moroccans and Iraqis are arrested in a double-decker bus in Kadıköy.

01.05.2000: A Libyan sailor survives with difficulty one year in Turkey in writing signs in arabic at Beyazit and Taksim.

18.20.2006: Moroccans are arrested at the land border between Turkey and Greece

21.07.2000: Moroccans (together with Afghans, Iranians, Egyptians, Palestinians...) are arrested in Edirne province, trying to reach Greece by the terrestrial border.

23.08.2000: Moroccans are arrested at Kadiköy with Afghanis: they expected to leave Turkey for Europe.

05.05.2001: 40 Moroccans among a total of 449 people, including Iraqis, are arrested at Pendik in a boat leaving for Europe.

13.12.2001: 5 Moroccans are arrested on a pneumatic boat off Cesme; they lived one year in Istanbul, working as waiters, cleaners,...

22.05.2002: 12 Moroccans are arrested at Silifke on a boat, among 233 escapees.

02/09.06.2002: 9 Algerians, 4 Moroccans and 2 Tunisians are arrested in Edirne.

07.01.2002: 1 Moroccan is arrested in Edirne when trying to go across the terrestrial boundary with Greece.

12.08.2002: Moroccans are arrested at Marmaris, on a boat, among 222 escapees, including Afghanis, Iraqis, Egyptians and Palestinians.

28.08.2002: Algerians are arrested trying to go across the Turkish-Greek terrestrial border.

Beginning of 2002: 4 Moroccans and 2 Algerians are arrested.

01.01.2003: 2 Algerians are arrested at Edirne, in the road-station. They were with 5 Somalis and each of them had given $400 to get to Greece where they wished to go, from Istanbul. They were without passports.

11.02.2004: 4 Moroccans and 1 Mauritanian are arrested in the province of Edirne (with Iranians, Somalians...), when trying to cross the Turkish-Greek boundary; See: *Evrensel*, 12/02/2004, p.3.

04.10.2004: 130 alien irregulars, including Moroccans, are founded crushed together in a building at Ayazaga/Sisli. They paid $2500 to get to Europe.

28.03.2004: Mauritanians are arrested near the Greece-Turkey border in Ipsala and Meriç districts; see *Özgür Gündem*, 30/03/2004, p.3.

19.01.2005: A Turkish woman of foreign origin is arrested in a suspected massage center. Some irregular Tunisian girls were working with her.

18.02.2005: Robbery in the house of a partner of the company "Tarablus Dis Ticaret Limited Sirketi".

29.05.2005: 4 Mauritanians died between Ayvacik (Çanakkale) and the Greek island of Midilli, after the shipwreck of their boat; see: *Zaman*, 30/05/2005, p.3.

26.06.2005: 2 Tunisians died in a boat accident between Dikili (Izmir) and the Greek island of Midilli. See: *Cumhuriyet*, 27/06/2005, p.4.

02.11.2005: Many Algerians and Mauritanians died in the Aegean Sea, trying to pass to Greece in a little boat; see: *Radikal*, 3/11/2005, p.7.

IRANIANS IN ISTANBUL: CHANGING MIGRATORY PATTERNS AND MODES OF INCORPORATION[128]

The models and chronologies of Iranian migration have significant implications for their patterns of socio-economic incorporation in Turkey. Iranians have a lot of similarity with the Iraqis in Turkey, as they both include documented as well as undocumented migrants. Their migration started as a result of political turnover in the country that led to the flow of large numbers of Iranians in the 80s who perceived Turkey merely as a transit country. It later changed shape and continued mostly as irregular migration, even though it has always consisted of asylum seekers as well.

More Than a Million Transit Migrants!

The Iranians' initial massive movement to Turkey was instigated by the fall of the monarchic regime and continued throughout the 1980s. According to some estimates, the overall number of Iranian migrants who transited through Turkey is around 1.5 million (Kirişci, 2000). However it is probably an exaggerated estimation if we project that the overall number of Iranian immigrants in the United States, the most favorite destination, is around 1 million (Roy, 2003; cited by Koser-Akcapar, 2004: 6). If Turkey was the only transit country for Iranian emigration in the 1980s, the 1,5 million estimation could be reasonable, yet Cyprus and Dubai were also used as transit stops in that period. Ahmet İçduygu (2003) seems to provide a more reasonable estimation and argues that between half a million and one million Iranians have transited through Turkey.

Thus, in the 1980s, Istanbul served as a stepping stone to the West for many Iranians. Among them, there was a large group of

128 A. Didem Danış. Lecturer, Sociology Department, Galatasaray University and Ph.D. candidate, Ecoles des Hautes Etudes en Sciences Sociales. Galatasaray University, Sociology Dept., Ciragan Cad. No.36, Ortakoy, 34357 Istanbul, Turkey. ddanis@gsu.edu.tr. Cherie Taraghi. Cultural orientation trainer, ICMC-Turkey. Poyracık Sok. No.35, Nişantaşı, Şişli, Istanbul. taraghi@icmc. net

Iranian professional middle classes who used official channels to attain their preferred countries, mostly in Europe and North America. Yet there were also some who benefited from the newly flourishing human smuggling networks located mostly in Aksaray.

Even though many of these early migrants were merely in transit in Turkey, there remained a small legally established community as a residue of this massive flow. İçduygu (2003) estimates that some 10,000 Iranian persons have remained in Turkey. Among the remnants of the pioneer group in Turkey, most have acquired Turkish nationality or long term residence and work permits and settled in Istanbul. Many of those are of the educated, professional, middle class. Iranian Azeris, (Turcophone Iranians), acquired Turkish nationality relatively easily thanks to the Settlement Law of 1934.

Some of these naturalized Iranians, as well as the members of a small Iranian expatriate community, have contacts with some key Iranian institutions in Istanbul, such as the primary school in Sultanahmet next to the Iranian Consulate, and the Iranian National Bank in Şişli. Life in Istanbul is quite comfortable for them and they do not face serious problems in their socio-economic incorporation thanks to their legal status in the country as well as their middle class positions. Another significant institution is called the Iranians' Charity Association (İranlılar Hayır Derneği), a long-standing Iranian association established in the mid 1940s. The association does not seem to be active except in organizing events during special dates such as Nevruz (the Iranian spring festival), and contributing in kind and money to the needy. According to the executive of the association '99% of their members consist of Iranians with Turkish citizenship'.[129]

Among these early transit migrants of the 1980s, there were also some persons who used clandestine ways to cross into Europe. In those years, irregular border crossings were relatively easier and cheaper. The cost and risks of such an alternative was much less com-

---

[129] Interview on January 2006.

pared with today, thanks to the relatively flexible border controls in Europe and Turkey.

Since the 1990s: Ethnic and Religious Minorities on Route

In the 1990s, obtaining refugee status or realizing irregular migration became tougher for Iranians, like other Middle Eastern and African migrants. The emphasis put on 'the control against illegal migration' in the EU agenda and increasing European pressure on Turkish authorities to improve border controls against irregular entries made things harder for new migrants.

Since the 1990s, Iranian emigration has continued in small but consistent numbers. Iranians are the largest group among the asylum applicants in Turkey, even though they cannot acquire refugee status in Turkey due to the geographical limitation in the 1951 United Nations Convention on the Rights of Refugees. Between 1997 and 2001 14,615 Iranians applied for asylum in Turkey. Among the Iranian asylum applicants, there are particular ethnic and religious minorities, such as Kurds, Bahais, Christians and some others.

TABLE 6.21
Asylum Applications of Iranians in Turkey

Year	Applications
1997	1.392
1998	1.979
1999	3.843
2000	3.926
2001	3.475
Total	14.615

Source: Icduygu (2003: 23). *Irregular Migration in Turkey*, IOM Migration Research Series.

Iranian Kurds are in the most difficult conditions among the Iranian minorities seeking asylum. Turkish authorities are cautious about accepting Iranian Kurds, as in the case of the Iraqi Kurds, due to the ongoing Kurdish problem in the country. Concerned about their possible collaboration with Kurdish dissidents in the country, Turkish authorities kept recognized Iranian Kurdish asylum seekers in satellite cities where they can be watched closely. From time to time, Iranian Kurds organize angry protests at being stuck in the east of Turkey or in satellite cities, and they criticize what they call the 'politics of cruelty and discouragement'. The hunger strikes organized in the summer of 2005 by a group of Iranian Kurds is very revealing in this sense. These Iranian Kurdish refugees had passed from Iran to Iraq and then into Turkey in 2001, running away from internal war among Iraqi Kurdish parties. They had applied for refugee status on their arrival in Van, the famous entry point for many Iranians, and were granted the right of asylum. However, until now they have not yet been sent to a third country, which made them engage in a hunger strike in front of the UNHCR Van office.[130]

Van is one of the most significant localities for Asian and Middle Eastern migrants in Turkey. It is the first entry point for many foreigners, particularly Iranian. The majority of the population consists of Kurds, both Turkish nationals and foreign. Van is seriously impoverished due to the massive flow of Kurds in the 1980s from the rural areas surrounding to the city, and thus has very little to offer to Iranian asylum seekers and migrants. The conditions are tough, particularly for undocumented Iranian Kurdish migrants.[131]

Bahais are another minority group from Iran. Bahais are typical transit migrants, or to put it more correctly, transit refugees. They submit their asylum application as soon as they enter into Turkey and almost all of them eventually leave the country with refugee status. The Bahai applicants receive a positive answer and acquire refugee status in particular from the USA. Thanks to the success of this procedure

---

130 http://www.kurdisinfo.com/modules.php?name=News&file=article&sid=2725 (accessed on January 2006)

131 A documentary prepared by Serkan Şavk, Barış Şahin ve Şevket Onur Cihan from Ankara University Short Film and Documentary Center provides striking scenes about the difficulties Iranians are enduring in Van ("Arka Bahçenin İnsanları" – people of the backyard).

administered by the UNHCR and the ICMC (International Catholic Migration Commission)[132] most of the Bahais go to satellite cities as recognized refugees and they wait there until their paperwork is completed.

Christians are yet another group among Iranian religious minorities in Turkey. Most converted just before departing their homeland, or in Turkey. The antagonistic attitudes against Christian converts in the Islamic Republic of Iran became a strategy for some Iranians who seek acceptance by Western countries. The persons who are baptized in Iran have more chances than the ones who are converted in Turkey. The latter are often treated with suspicion by UNHCR officers and migration departments of embassies. Iranian Christians in Istanbul benefit from services provided by Christian charity organizations, in particular by the Istanbul Interparish Migrants Program (IIMP). IIMP organizes courses to teach English and Turkish to migrant children and serves food twice a week in the garden of an ancient church in Beyoğlu.

The IIMP, like the Caritas, is not officially recognized by Turkish authorities. The restrictions to acquire a formal NGO status create problems for these organizations. The unwelcome attitude by the authorities is mostly related to their anxiety toward possible missionary activity, as well as the intention of limiting the activities of these organizations which are believed contribute to the "pull factor" for Middle Eastern Christians by relieving the difficulties of survival in Istanbul. The attacks against Christian organizations have also been supported by the media, who accused missionaries of 'seducing Turkish Muslims in dire economic conditions'.[133] Finally in 2005,

---

[132] ICMC Turkey also administers a "fast-track" program in Istanbul for Iranian Bahais. http://www.icmc.net/docs/en/null/turkeyback#4

[133] See especially articles by Ali Bulaç "Misyonerlik ve azınlıklar", *Zaman*, 05.02.2005; "Misyonerlik" *Zaman*, 26.01.2005; "'Yeni Hıristiyan azınlık' oluşturmak!" *Zaman*, 26.01.2005 and Hulki Cevizoğlu (2005) *Misyonerlik ve Siyasal Hıristiyanlık*, Ceviz Kabuğu Yayınları: Istanbul, for a compilation of accusations against Christian missionaries broadcasted in the television program called "Ceviz Kabuğu".

Turkish authorities insisted that the IIMP serve only non-Muslims and not receive any Muslim foreigners at their locale in Beyoğlu.

These non-Muslim religious organizations are very significant, particularly in an environment where there is limited, if any, support provided to foreigners by mainstream organizations. Nevertheless, mechanisms such as religious networks that help migrant incorporation or survival are always delicate and precarious, as is recently observed in the unexpected closing down of the IIMP, after the murder of a Catholic priest in Trabzon in January 2005.

In Search of a Better Life
Aside from Iranian Kurds and non-Muslims recognized as refugees, there is an ongoing migration from Iran by persons who are "seeking a better life". Once more it is very difficult to differentiate between economic and political migrants (see the section on Iraqi Christians for a critique of political vs. economic migrant distinction). The repressive political and social conditions in Iran push many Iranians out of their country, and Turkey attracts many of them thanks to the geographical and cultural proximity, in addition to the 'extent of freedoms' it has to offer.

Iranian students provide a remarkable example within this category. Even though Turkey is not the most favored destination for affluent families who want their child to study abroad, it still serves as an attractive option for those having limited money but still wanting to 'taste the freedom for a while'.

A larger group 'in search of a better life' is the Iranian transit migrants who are trying to reach "Western paradise" (Koser-Akcapar, 2004). They are often benefiting from human smuggling networks, since border crossings have become more difficult as a result of the rapprochement between Turkey and the EU. Under the pressure of the EU member states, Turkey increased its border controls in the Eastern provinces, in particular around Van. Unlike the middle and upper class Iranians who smoothly transited through Turkey in the 1980s, the migrants of the 1990s are less affluent and use different travel networks and arrangements. The key location in Istanbul for many of those Iranians, together with others from the Middle East and North Africa is Aksaray.

Aksaray is a very famous spot for most Iranians. Whether they are tourists or migrants, they know about it much before their arrival to Istanbul. A variety of services offered in Aksaray is the main reason of its appeal to Iranian, as well as other foreigners in the city. Travel agencies, restaurants, hotels, leather and garment shops, and nightclubs all are welcoming the strangers in the city, including the Iranians. Aksaray also serves to accommodate some undocumented migrants of Iranian, African, Afghan, or Iraqi origin. The relatively cheap rents for dilapidated and miserable lodging attract mostly single destitute men, but also families, though in smaller numbers.

Despite the increasing significance of undocumented transit Iranian migrants in Turkey, the total number of Iranians that are arrested by security forces is relatively low. The total number between 1995 and 2001 was 22,704. It was only 252 in 1995, 362 in 1996, 364 in 1997, and 1,116 in 1998 (İçduygu, 2003, see also **Table 6.1** in the introduction for a comparison). After 1999 there occurred a sharp increase and it reached 5,281 in 1999, 6,825 in 2000 and 8,502 in 2001. According to the statistics provided by Koser-Akcapar (2004: 9) these figures are much lower for 2001 (3,514) and 2002 (2,508). In any case, compared to the Iraqis (77,643) who are apprehended in the same period between 1995 and 2001, and Afghans (22,158), it is certainly a small number, particularly if we remember that Iranians have always been on the top of the asylum seekers list in Turkey. One of the explanations for the low number of Iranians that are being apprehended by Turkish security forces is related to the liberal visa regulations for Iranian nationals.

Visa-Free Regulation between Turkey and Iran
An important factor that facilitates Iranians' entry into Turkey has been the visa-free travel agreement that was signed between Turkey

and Iran in 1964 (Apap, et al., 2005: 47). Many Iranians who transited through Turkey in their immigration have benefited from this regulation, which allowed them to enter and stay in Turkey for three months without visa obligations. Thus, despite the low number of Iranian undocumented migrants apprehended by Turkish authorities, there have been hundreds of thousands of Iranians who entered officially into the country. As seen in the table below, official entries of Iranians in 2003 were almost half a million in 2003.

The visa-free arrangement with Iran has contributed to the commercial relations between Iran and Turkey. Iranian merchants, in particular Iranian Azeri, have been one of the pioneers in the suitcase trade. They have been shuttling between Turkey and Iran conducting suitcase trade or for border trade around Van. Some of these Iranian cyclical migrants have later on overstayed their visa-free time and slipped into a clandestine state. Some of these undocumented Iranians are the persons who do not want to return to Iran, which they describe as a "prison life". Today, Iranians are among the foreign undocumented workers in Istanbul. In addition to construction, they have been working in textiles, in the same conditions with other undocumented migrants.

TABLE 6.22
Entries of Persons from the Balkan and Middle Eastern Neighboring States
Between 1964 and 2003

Middle Eastern Countries	1964	1970	1980	1990	1996	2000	2003
IRAN	12,796	14,247	42,082	219,958	379,003	380,819	484,269
IRAQ	3,919	6,518	14,046	13,372	14,137	20,776	29,940
SYRIA	9,996	13,184	26,384	113,959	92,033	122,417	154,108

Source: Apap, Carrera & Kirişci (2005: 58). See Table 1.5 in the introduction for the complete version of this table.

The liberal visa regime has also increased the tourist appeal of Turkey, especially its Mediterranean shores, for the Iranian middle classes who cannot travel easily to European countries because of visa restrictions. The increase in the number of Iranian tourists has been observed by the media as well.[134] It is estimated that there were around half a million Iranian tourists in 2004. The favorite destinations of the Iranian middle and upper classes are mostly the five star hotels or holiday villages in Bodrum, Antalya, and Alanya. The increasing attractiveness of Turkey can also be observed by the increase in the airline companies that carry passengers between Iran and Turkey. While in 1999 there was only one company, (the Iranian, Mahan Air), it was later joined by Turkish Airlines, Iranian Airlines, and Kish Air. In 2003, there was a boom in airline transportation between Iran and Turkey, and the number of companies rose to ten.

The flexible visa policy with Iran does not seem destined to last very long due to new regulations to be implemented for Turkey's harmonization with the EU acquis. Within the framework of the harmonization process, Turkey decided to abolish its visa-free travel for six countries including Iran in 2005 (the others are Bosnia-Herzegovina, Kyrgyzstan, Macedonia, Morocco, and Tunisia). Aware of its possible negative consequences for tourism and trade, the Minister of Foreign Affairs declared that they will implement some special facilities for the citizens of these countries through bilateral agreements.[135]

Networks for Survival, Networks for Incorporation

Şebnem Köşer Akçapar (2004), an expert on Iranian migration, argues that there is no form of integration for Iranian transit migrants in Turkey, because they perceive Turkey as a "waiting room". According to her, Iranian undocumented migrants are enduring a multi-faceted exclusion due to their political, legal, social, and economic vulnerability. Based on our observations in the field, we agree with her argument. Nevertheless, we believe that there are still some social networks that Iranians utilize either as a survival or as an incorporation strategy.

---

134 "İranlılar Türkiye'de tatilde", *Hürriyet*, 25.07.2004.
135 "Türkiye vizede AB'ye uyacak", *Radikal*, 11.2.2005.

The networks that Iranians mobilize in Istanbul are mostly familial and ethnic-religious ones. Familial ties provide a crucial resource for Iranians, as for other migrant groups. They utilize and mobilize contacts with family members who are in Istanbul or relatives abroad and at home. Relatives furnish social, mental, as well as economic assistance that relieve to some extent migrants' vulnerability and thus facilitate their survival in Istanbul.

Religious networks in Istanbul seem to offer more institutionalized services than other types of social networks. Both Bahai circles and Christian charity organizations such as the IIMP provide an environment of security and solidarity for Iranian migrants. The IIMP office for instance provides material assistance, including the serving of food on special days, financial support for medical care, in addition to educational services such as language courses in their domicile in Beyoğlu. Nevertheless, as mentioned above, they have been accused of missionary activities and are forbidden to provide services to Muslim foreigners. Such non-Muslim religious organizations work in precarious conditions, as observed very recently in the closing down of the IIMP office for security reasons after the murder of a Catholic priest in Trabzon.

These networks help more with the survival of newly arrived Iranian migrants rather than their integration. It is particularly more difficult to talk about incorporation in the case of undocumented transit migrants. Because their main objective is to reach Europe, even though it becomes harder day by day, they perceive their stay in Istanbul as temporary. Besides, the prevalence of a deep lack of trust among Iranians prevents the construction of a wider social space that Iranians, regardless of their ethnic, religious, or legal background, can participate in.

Despite the significance of the networks that serve different Iranian groups, there is no appearance of a diaspora community. Instead, what is observed is a segmented community, where each segment is numerically very small, and there is an established suspicion among each communal segment. Iranians do not trust one another, and rumors within the community worsen the in-community suspicion. Thus, long-established Iranians who acquired a regular status owing to their Turkish citizenship or long-term residence permits seem to avoid lending a hand to the newcomers. This communal fragmentation is also related to the authoritarian rule in Iran which promotes an environment of suspicion and untrustworthiness among the nationals. In short, what is observed in the case of the social networking of Iranian migrants is a pragmatic relationship constructed and maintained out of necessity.

CONCLUSION

Since the beginning of our research a significant question that has concerned us has been the validity of the concept that we utilize in our project title: 'integration in limbo.'[136] Could we really talk about integration, or socio-economic incorporation more precisely, in the case of undocumented migrants in Turkey whose conditions are extremely precarious because of the legal as well as social deficiencies they face? Above and beyond, these migrants are supposed to be 'transient' both in their own eyes and in those of the authorities. The Iraqi, Afghan, Maghrebi, and Iranian migrants that we focus on constitute 'unstable' groups, whose membership changes continuously. Nevertheless, as we realized during the fieldwork, even though some of these migrants are merely transiting, these communities are slowly settling in Istanbul, or have already done so, as in the cases of the Iraqi or Afghan Turkmen. In consequence, we have been convinced to use the title 'Integration in Limbo' which connotes here an unofficial incorporation where migrants are integrated by mobilizing their own resources in the absence of state assistance.

As fieldwork proceeded it was discovered that our initial plan to study whole populations of Iraqis, Afghans, Maghrebi, and Iranians

---

136 In this study we used integration as a short-hand for the migrants' socio-economic incorporation and 'limbo' to signify the vagueness and fluidity of the status of migrants whom we concentrated on.

was too ambitious, given the heterogeneity of each migrant population in terms of their legal status and the effect that this has on their ability to integrate. There are overlapping characteristics between the migrant populations from each different country and it must be pointed out that their migratory and legal profile determines the features they share with other groups more than with their co-nationals holding different legal status and migratory plans. In other words, the categorization according to nationalities is not an exhaustive index to understand Iraqi, Afghan, Maghrebi and Iranian migrants' modes of incorporation in Istanbul. As we have presented in the above chapters, each nationality has inner differentiations regarding their ethnic, religious, and other characteristics. For instance Kurds from Iran and Iraq have more resemblance to each other than they have to their Turkish-speaking or Christian co-nationals. Above all ethnic or religious affiliations, *the* distinguishing characteristic for many migrants is their official status: whether one is legal or not, (thanks to acquiring refugee status, residence permit or citizenship; or owing to have a non-expired tourist visa), mean a lot for socio-economic, as well as mental relief.

Another question was to what extent we may talk of a successful integration for the migrants concerned. We should make it clear that our findings on Iraqi, Afghan, Maghrebi, and Iranian migrants do not illustrate a fully accomplished socio-economic integration for all of them. As a matter of fact, it is out of the question to accomplish a full incorporation for the migrants who do have limited material or non-material resources, insecure legal status, and no state assistance. As we observed, migrants' incorporation necessitates some sort of bond between the migrants and the receiving society, or more correctly, with a fragment of the society. In this sense, what we observe is a 'segmented incorporation', whenever we may talk of integration. For instance, Iraqi Christians' incorporation through the link of Syriac community in Istanbul or the Iraqi and Iranian Kurds' insertion via their contacts with Kurdish political milieus indicates a 'segmented incorporation'. The segmented incorporation points also at an 'integration from the periphery' in terms of participation in labor and housing markets. Large proportions of these migrants work in informal sectors and dwell in residential locations that can easily be called either the 'periphery of the center' or the 'center of the periphery'.[137]

The strength and success of the migrants' incorporation depends on the capacity of each social segment they incorporate. For instance, the remnants of the Syriac community in Istanbul can offer employment opportunities to their Iraqi co-religious thanks to their relatively well-off economic standing, even though the population and the societal infrastructure of Christian minorities in Turkey have substantially diminished in the last century. On the other hand, the Kurds of Turkey, another segment of the Turkish receiving society, are socio-economically and politically incapacitated, particularly because of the involuntary migration that they had to endure in the last decades. Thus, the integration of Kurds from Iran and Iraq is feeble, since they are inserted into the deprived and disadvantaged setting of their co-ethnics in Istanbul. Their conditions have further been worsened due to their ethnic identity which is perceived as a threat against the integrity of the Turkish state and society.

Social Networks Facilitating 'Segmented Incorporation'

Given the weakness of state assistance or authorized non-governmental organizations providing services for regular or irregular migrants, social networks of migrants become of primary importance for migrant survival and incorporation in Turkey. Since the first moments of their arrival, every migrant gets into contact with an informal reception mechanism. The components of these networks carry certain similarities and differences for different migrant groups.

In the absence of formal organizations, family – in its extended and imaginary form – is the foremost resource to ease the migration,

---

137 It is no coincidence that the neighborhoods that these migrants are clustered in (e.g. Tarlabaşı, Kurtuluş, Dolapdere, Zeytinburnu, Kumkapı) have been characterized by internal migration waves much before the arrival of the foreign migrants.

incorporation, and survival of undocumented migrants. Various members of the family play an active role in the migration process. First of all, they make possible the dissemination of information, even though it sometimes consists of incorrect information, about opportunities in different countries and cities. Thus, for instance Iraqi Christian transient migrants learn about whether Turkey, Syria, or Jordan is better to head off to in order to submit their subsequent application for Australia and Canada. For all migrant groups, family members, whenever they exist, provide shelter and help their relatives to find employment. They thus incorporate newcomers into an already constructed employment network, such as the Afghan tannery network, Maghrebi nanny network, or the Iraqi Turkmen trade niche in Laleli.

If the migrants do not have relatives in Istanbul as the primary basis of networking, they look for other resources of sociability and mobilize their social capital to build social networks to get in contact with the segments of the receiving society. Types of social capital benefited from are various, depending on the resources and needs of migrants. As in the case of Iraqi Assyro-Chaldeans it can be a religious network enhanced by contact with the local Syriac in Istanbul, or as in the case of Iraqi Kurds, it can be an ethno-political network built around the Kurdish political and solidarity ethos. What seems interesting in terms of networks is that they are always built as a result of the special ties that migrants may mobilize to construct a relationship with a segment of the receiving society.

Linguistic, religious and ethnic capitals are the most significant resources that migrants mobilize for their survival and incorporation. Linguistic capital, which also signifies an ethnic affiliation in the case of Iraqi and Afghan Turkmen or Iranian Azeri, creates a sense of cultural closeness with the receiving society. The benefits of linguistic capital for migrants' incorporation are not limited to the knowledge of the Turkish language. Knowledge of Arabic, for instance, becomes a remarkable skill for Iraqi and Maghrebi migrants who look for a job in the economic sphere that flourished around the suitcase trade in

Laleli and Osmanbey, and which attracts cyclical migrants from Arab countries.

Another form of social capital that is mobilized is religious affiliation. In this sense, non-Muslim milieus seem to offer more than their Islamic counterpart, as observed in the Assyro-Chaldean networks of the Iraqis, or the Bahai, Christian affiliations of Iranians. This is also related to the non-Muslim character of a few charity organizations and to the stronger solidarity among Christian communities in Istanbul, probably due to their minority identity. Surprisingly, the fact that Maghrebis in Istanbul are mostly Sunni Muslim does not help them to get in contact with Sunni Turkish society, quite possibly because they cannot find a particular niche to fit in.

Lastly we may talk of ethnic networks, as in the case of Kurds. However, we have observed that Kurdish ethnic ties are not as fruitful as other networks, unless in combination with some sort of political affiliation. Thus in the case of Iraqi or Iranian Kurds one needs to talk about an ethno-political network rather than a purely ethnic network. One explanation for the failure of the Kurdish ethnic networks is probably related to the unfriendly attitudes of Turkish authorities and the weakness of the Kurdish communal infrastructure in Istanbul.

Incorporation into Housing and Labor Sectors
One of the significant contributions of these networks for the newly arrived migrants is to find accommodation, and they mostly resort to their co-nationals to solve this problem. This is why there is a particular spatial clustering for certain migrant groups in Istanbul. For instance, while Maghrebis as well as Iraqi Kurds (in addition to other foreigners such as sub-Saharan Africans) inhabit Kumkapı-Yenikapı, Afghans dwell in Zeytinburnu and Iraqi Christians prefer the surroundings of Tarlabaşı-Dolapdere-Elmadağ. One should note that despite this concentration in certain neighborhoods, many of the migrants are trying to keep a low profile, owing to the precariousness of their legal status. This is also observed in the weak communal infra-

structure of certain groups, in particular of Maghrebis, who have a very small community and very limited resources to initiate particular associations and meeting places. Unlike them, Iraqi or Afghan Turkmen have been able to build a social space, with some representative spots such as the Iraqi Turkmen association in Aksaray or Afghan coffeehouses in Zeytinburnu.

Networks certainly play a significant role for the participation of newly arrived migrants in the employment market. This is realized sometimes by a simple word-of-mouth process, and sometimes a more organized, (via migrant associations), dissemination of information regarding employment opportunities. This distribution of employment news via social networks results in the clustering of certain groups in certain jobs and the creation of ethnic niches. Accordingly there appears a domestic labor niche for Maghrebi nannies working for the Francophone ex-patriates, or Iraqi Christian women working at the houses of local Syriac families. Niche formation is much weaker for the men. The newly arrived undocumented migrants, whatever their ethnic or religious background, have the most precarious conditions. They work mostly in low status, low paid jobs in construction or textile industries. Iraqi or Afghan Turkmen represent a more settled migrant class; after all of the years since their initial migration, they have been able to build special employment sectors, in part, due to their various competencies or capital brought from their homeland. Thus many Afghans are employed in tanneries, and Iraqis conduct their own businesses in the export centers of Laleli and Osmanbey. The few Iraqi Turkmens who arrived seeking educational opportunities and eventually acquired Turkish nationality have surely been fully integrated both economically and socially, and are now working in high-status professions, such as doctors, engineers, academicians, or pharmacists.

One significant cornerstone of the migrants' networks are the 'pioneers', or those who are already settled in Istanbul. They construct a social milieu that provides necessary contacts for the newcomers, particularly in the problematic areas of employment and accommodation. These pioneers are of course benefiting from their intermediary or bridging role between newcomers and the reception society. These bridges are often Turkish citizens, sometimes with a migrant background, like in the case of the Turkmen who have acquired Turkish citizenship before the 1990s. Sometimes these persons may be members of an ethnic or religious minority group, like the Kurds or Syriacs of Turkey. In the case of suitcase traders, they become 'social entrepreneurs', as observed in the Maghrebis.[138]

School, Health and Other Social Services

The requirement for enrollment into public schools in Turkey was to have an official residence permit; this was changed in late 2004. Thus the children of undocumented migrants may attend public educational institutions, however registering for school requires the provision of an address and most of the irregular migrants do not wish to risk such an exposure of their whereabouts. For that reason, the parents try to find alternative solutions wherever possible. During our fieldwork we observed that the most effective alternative is religious or religious-affiliated educational institutions. For instance, some Moroccan families opt for Koranic schools, and Iraqi Christians attend the unofficial school in Caritas along with Iranian Christian children who attended courses that were offered by the Istanbul Interparish Migrant Program (IIMP). This latter educational provision was closed down by IIMP administration, because of the murder of a priest in Trabzon in January 2006.

Access to health services is better than access to schools, owing to the abundance of private clinics offering health services to anybody who has sufficient money to pay the bill. However, as a matter of fact

---

[138] Among these intermediaries there are also persons who are mediating not for integration but for the continuation of the migration; they are the dealers between smuggling networks and the potential clients, i.e. candidates to exile. These 'unlawful'" bridges can be Turkish as well as foreigner, like the early-arrived undocumented migrants who work for smuggling networks.

many undocumented migrants do not have enough economic resources to pay the high cost of medical services. In this case, either familial or communal solidarity, sometimes through the money transfers sent by relatives abroad, or in rare cases charity organizations intervene to pay the costs.

In Turkey there was almost no possibility for undocumented migrants to benefit from basic social services such as health and education unless they acquired official status. During recent discussions on the social security reform in Turkey it has been mentioned that asylum seekers will be able to benefit from public health services, although this new law seems to exclude undocumented migrants and rejected asylum seekers. It is likely that this approach in Turkey will change during the EU harmonization process.

Implications of State Policies for 'Integration in Limbo'
The policies adopted and implemented by states certainly have an important say in the migration and incorporation strategies of new migrants. First of all, they affect the volume and morphology of migration flows. For example, the visa-free entry right of Iranians and Maghrebis until recently, has pulled many of them into Turkey; yet similarly new visa laws in line with EU regulations will certainly decrease the intensity of these flows. Moreover, the intensification of Turkish authorities' 'struggle against illegal migration' leads to a re-arrangement of irregular migratory routes, and diminishes the volume of undocumented migrants in the country. Yet it should be remembered that the improvement of border controls results also in the besieging of more and more undocumented migrants in Istanbul.

The policies also have an effect on modes of socio-economic incorporation of new migrants. The attempts of the Turkish authorities to regularize the so-called 'suitcase trade' in Laleli and Osmanbey diminishes the volume of this trade and thus restrains the employment opportunities for some migrants. Besides campaigns against informal foreign workers, supported both by new laws and media coverage, regulation pushes foreign undocumented workers into invisibility and worsens their work conditions due to their increased precariousness.

State policies and institutional arrangements bound the limits of migrants' social networks. The segmented incorporation of migrants via social networks in an environment of limited financial and institutional capacities and the weakness, if not absence, of reception policies in Turkey, is very precarious. Furthermore, migrants' incorporation is contingent on policies as well as on the official treatment of foreigners in the country. Thus such incorporation, even though it is highly important for the survival of undocumented migrants, is condemned to stay 'in limbo', unless an improvement in the migrants' status occurs. Mechanisms that help migrant incorporation or survival are always delicate and precarious, as was recently observed in the unexpected closing down of the IIMP, one of the most significant non-official Christian charity organizations providing services for African and Iranian Christians.

In summary, in concert with the instability of transient or undocumented migrants' stays in Istanbul, their social networks are likewise unsteady. Migrant networks are vulnerable and potentially jeopardized by legal or political changes.

REFERENCES

Akgündüz, A., 1998, "Migration to and from Turkey, 1783-1960: Types, Numbers and Ethno-religious Dimensions", *Journal of Ethnic and Migration Studies*, 24(1): 97-120.

Al-Hirmizi, E., 2003, *The Turkmen and Iraqi Homeland*, Istanbul: Kerkük Vakfı.

—, 2005, *The Turkmen Reality in Iraq*, Istanbul: Kerkük Vakfı.

Apap, J., S. Carrera and K. Kirişci, 2005, "EU-Turkey Relations in the Pre-Accession Period: Implementing the Schengen Regime and Enhancing Border Control", CERP report.

Aslan, M. and J. F. Perouse, 2003, "Istanbul: le Comptoir, le Hub, le Sas et L'impasse", *Revue Europeenne des Migrations Internationales*, 19(3): 173-204.

Baily, S., 2004, "Is Legal Status Enough? Legal Status and Livelihood Obstacles for

Urban Refugee", (http://fletcher.tufts.edu/research/2004/Bailey-Sarah.pdf.
html)

Bauman, Z., 2001, *Community Seeking Safety in an Insecure World*, Cambridge: Cambridge Polity Press.

Boissevain, J. and H. Grotenberg, 1987, "Survival in spite of the Law: Surinamese Entrepreneurs in Amsterdam", *Revue Européenne des Migrations Internationales*, 3(1&2): 199-222.

Boyd, M., 1989, "Family and Personal Networks in International Migration: Recent Developments and New Agendas", *International Migration Review*, 23(3): 638-70.

Bocker, A., 1995, "Migration Networks: Turkish Migration to Western Europe", Causes of International Migration, proceedings of a workshop, Luxembourg, Eurostat.

Bocker, A. and T. Havinga, 1997, *Asylum Migration to the European Union: Patterns of Origin and Destination*, Luxembourg: Office for Official Publications of the European Communities.

Brettel, C. B., 2000, "Theorizing Migration in Anthropology: the Social Construction of Networks, Identities, Communities and Globalscapes" in C. B. Brettel and J. H. Hollifield (eds.), *Migration Theory: Talking Across Disciplines*, London: Routledge.

Brink, M., 1997, "The Labor Market Integration of Refugees in the Netherlands" in P. Muus (ed.), *Exclusion and Inclusion of Refugees in Contemporary Europe*, Utrecht: Utrecht University, ERCOMER.

Bruinessen, M., 2003, *Ağa, Şeyh, Devlet*, Istanbul: İletişim.

Chatelard, G., 2002, "Jordan as a Transit Country: Semi-protectionist Immigration Policies and Their Effects on Iraqi Forced Migrants", Working Paper No.61, Robert Schuman Centre for Advanced Studies European University Institute.

—, 2004, "Jordan: A Refugee Haven", Migration Information Source, consulted January 2006, (.html).

Ciğerli, S., 1998, *Les Réfugiés Kurdes d'Irak en Turquie: Gaz, Exode, Camp*, Paris: Harmattan.

Cook, D. A., 2002, "Forty Years of Religion across Borders: Twilight of a Transnational Field?" in H. R. Ebaugh and J. S. Chafetz (eds.), *Religion across Borders: Transnational Immigrant Networks*, Walnut Creek: Altamira Press.

Corliss, S., 2003, "Asylum in Turkey Today and Future Prospects" in E. Zeybekoglu and B. Johansson (eds.), *Migration and Labor in Europe: Views from Turkey and Sweden*, Istanbul: MURCIR & NIWL joint publication.

Çiçek, E., 2005, *Ararat Yolcuları: İnsan Tacirleri, Göç ve Mültecilik*, Istanbul: Peri Yayınları.

Danis, D., 2004, "Yeni Göç Hareketleri ve AB yolunda Türkiye", *Birikim*, 184: 216-224.

—, 2005, "Waiting on the Purgatory: Religious Networks of Iraqi Christian Transit
Migrants in Istanbul", paper presented at the Sixth Mediterranean Social and Political Research Meeting of the Mediterranean Programme of the Robert Schuman Centre for Advanced Studies at the European University Institute, held in Montecatini Terme, March16-19.

Danis, D. and E. Kayaalp, 2004, Elmadağ: a Neighborhood Influx, *Les dossiers de l'IFEA*, 18, Istanbul: IFEA.

Danis, D. and J. F. Perouse, 2005, "La Politique Migratoire Turque: Vers Une Normalisation?", *Migrations Société*, 17(98).

Deli, F., 2002, "La MaîÓtrise du Commerce International du Textile par les Patrons Arabes de Mardin à Laleli" in M. Peraldi (ed.), *La Fin des Norias? Réseaux Migrants Dans les É...conomies Marchandes en Méditeranéé*, Paris: Maisonneuve et Larose.

Délos, H., 2004, "Entre Maghreb et Turquie: Mobilités et Recompositions Territoriales", *Revue Européenne des Migrations Internationales*, 19(2): 47-67.

Dış Ekonomik İlişkiler Kurulu (DEİK), 2005, "Turkey's Role in the Reconstruction of Afghanistan", available at (http://www.deik.org.tr/bultenler/200582511515 TurkeysRoleinReconstructionofAfghanistan-august2005.pdf.html).

Dick, S., 2002, "Liberians in Ghana: Living without Humanitarian Assistance", New Issues in Refugee Research, Working Paper No.57.

Doboson, J. and J. Stillwell, 2000, "Changing Home, Changing Schools: Towards a Research Agenda on Child Migration", *AREA*, 32(4): 395-401.

Ebaugh, H. R. and J. S. Chafetz (eds.), 2002, *Religion across Borders: Transnational Immigrant Networks*, Walnut Creek: Altamira Press.

Erder, S., 2000, "Uluslararası Göçte Yeni Eğilimler: Türkiye "Göç Alan" Ülke mi?" in F. Atacan, Türkay and Kurtuluş (eds.), *Mübeccel Kıray için Yazılar*, Istanbul: Bağlam.

Erder, S. and S. Kaska, 2003, "Irregular Migration and Trafficking in Women: The Case of Turkey", IOM, 86.

Faist, T., 2000, *The Volume and Dynamics of International Migration and Transnational Social Spaces*, Oxford: Oxford University Press.

Foggo, H. Y., 2002, *Kırmızı Püskül: 1843-1846 Nesturi Katliamı*, Istanbul: Çiviyazıları.

Granovetter, M., 1974, "The Strength of Weak Ties", *American Journal of Sociology*, 78(6): 1360-1380.

Gresh, G., 2005, "Acquiescing to the Acquis: Combating Irregular Migration in Turkey", *Insight Turkey*, 7(2): 8-27.

Gurak, D. T. and F. Caces, 1992, "Migration Networks and the Shaping of Migration Systems" in M. M. Kritz, L. L. Lim and H. Zlotnik (eds.), *International Migration Systems: A Global Approach*, Oxford: Clarendon Press.

Hagan, J. M., 2002, "Religion and the Process of Migration: A Case Study of a Maya Transnational Community" in H. R. Ebaugh and J. S. Chafetz (eds.), *Religion across Borders: Transnational Immigrant Networks*, Walnut Creek: Altamira Press.

Hein, J., 1993, "Refugees, Immigrants and the State", *Annual Review of Sociology*, 19: 43-59.

Heyberger, B. (ed.), 2003, *Chrétiens du Monde Arabe: Un Archipel en Terre d'Islam*, Paris: Autrement.

Hiro, D., 2002, *Iraq: A Report from the Inside*, London: Grante Books.

Hirschman, C., 2003, "The Role of Religion in the Origins and Adaptation of Immigrant Groups", paper presented at the conference on 'Conceptual and Methodological Developments in the Study of International Migration' at Princeton University, May 23-25.

Hofbauer, S. (coor.), 2005, "Illegal Immigration in Austria, a Survey of Recent Austrian Migration Research", Austrian Contribution to the European Research Study Project II: "Illegally Resident Third Country Nationals in the EU Member States: State Approaches Towards Them and Their Profile and Social Situation", available at () (accessed in January 2006).

İçduygu, A., 1996, "Transit Migrants and Turkey", *Bogazici Journal Review of Social, Economic and Administrative Studies*, 10(1-2): 127-142.

—, 2003, "Irregular Migration in Turkey", IOM Migration Research Series, Geneva.

—, 2004, *Türkiye'de Kaçak Göç*, Istanbul: Istanbul Ticaret Odası Yayınları.

—, 2005, "Transit Migration in Turkey: Trends, Patterns and Issues", CARIM Research Report, European University Institute, Robert Schuman Center for Advanced Studies, San Domenico di Fiesole.

İçduygu, A. and Ş. Toktaş, 2002, "How do Smuggling and Trafficking Operate via Irregular Border Crossings in the Middle East: Evidence from fieldwork in Turkey", *International Migration*, 40(6): 25-50.

International Organization for Migration (IOM), 1995, *Transit Migration in Turkey*, Budapest: IOM Migration Information Programme.

Jacobsen, K., 2001, "The Forgotten Solution: Local Integration for Refugees in Developing Countries", New Issues in Refugee Research, Working Paper No.45.

Joseph, J., 1961, *The Nestorians and their Muslim Neighbors: A Study of Western Influence on Their Relations*, Princeton: Princeton University Press.

Kaynak, M., 1992, *The Iraqi Asylum Seekers and Türkiye 1988-1991*, Ankara: Tanmak Yayınları.

Kearney, M., 1986, "From Invisible Hand to Visible Feet: Anthropological Studies of Migration and Development", *Annual Review of Anthropology*, 15: 331-61.

Keyder, Ç., 2005, "Globalisation and Social Exclusion in Istanbul", *International Journal of Urban and Regional Research*, 291: 124–34.

Kibreab, G., 2001, "Displaced Communities and the Reconstruction of Livelihoods in Eritrea", available at ().

Kirişci, K. 1996, "Coerced Immigrants: Refugees of Turkish Origins since 1945", *International Migration*, 34(3): 385-412.

—, 2000, "Disaggregating Turkish Citizenship and Immigration Practices", *Middle Eastern Studies*, 36(3): 1-22.

—, 2003, "Harmonizing Turkish Asylum and Immigration Policy with the EU: Civic and Human Rights Approach vs. Security Approach", paper presented at the conference on Turkey and the EU, From Association to Accession?, 6-7 November 2003, Amsterdam.

—, 2004, "Reconciling Refugee Protection With Combating Irregular Migration: Turkey and the EU", *Perceptions*, 9(2): 5-20.

Koff, H., 2002, "Let's Talk Across Disciplines on Immigration and Integration Issues", Working Paper No.60, Centre for Comparative Immigration Studies, UCSD.

Korac, M., 2001, "Dilemmas of Integration: Two Policy Contexts and Refugee Strategies for Integration", final report of a comparative study of the integration experiences of refugees from former Yugoslavia in Rome and Amsterdam.

Koser, Akçapar, S., 2004, "Iranian Transit Migrants in Turkey: 'Waiting Room' before Entering the 'Paradise'", paper presented at the Fifth Mediterranean Social and Political Research Meeting of the Mediterranean Programme of the Robert Schuman Centre for Advanced Studies at the European University Institute, Montecatini Terme, 24-28 March 2004.

Landau, L. B., 2004, "Urban Refugees: Networks, Livelihood, Trade and the Informal Economy", FMO Research Guide, available at (html..html).

Levitt, P., 2001, "Between God, Ethnicity and Country: An Approach to the Study of Transnational Religion", paper presented at the conference on Transnational Migration: Comparative Perspectives at Princeton University, 30 June-1 July.

Lindstrom, C., 2003, "Urban Refugees in Mauritania", *Forced Migration Review*, 17: 46-47.

Lorduglu, K., 2005, "Türkiye'de Yabancıların Kaçak Çalışması ve Bu Çalışmaya İlişkin bir Araştırma", *Toplum ve Bilim*, 102: 103-127.

Mannaert, C., 2003, "Irregular Migration and Asylum in Turkey", Working Paper No.89, New Issues in Refugee Research, UNHCR Evaluation and Policy Analysis Unit.

Mardin, Ş., 1990, *Türkiye'de Toplum ve Siyaset*, Istanbul: İletişim.

Massey, D., J. Arango, H. Graeme, A. Kouaoucci, A. Pellegrino, and E. Taylor, 1998, *Worlds in Motion: Understanding International Migration at the End of the Millennium*, Oxford: Oxford University Press.

Massey, D. et al., 1993, "Theories of International Migration: A Review and an Appraisal," *Population and Development Review*, 19(3): 431-466.

McCarthy, J., 1983, *Muslims and Minorities. The Population of Ottoman Anatolia and the End of Empire*, New York: New York University Press.

—, 2001, *The Ottoman Peoples and the End of Empire*, Oxford: Hodder Arnold Publication.

Mella, O., 1994, *Religion in the Life of Refugees and Immigrants*, CEIFO: Stockholm.

Peraldi, M., 1998, "Le Cycle Algérien Dans Lâleli Morose", *Lettre d'Information de l'OUI*, 14: 19-22.

—, 2001, "L'esprit du Bazar. Mobilités Transnationales Maghrébines et Sociétés Métropolitaines. Les Routes d'Istanbul" in M. Peraldi (ed.), *Cabas et Containers. Activités Marchandes Informelles et Réseaux Migrants Transfrontaliers*, Paris: Maisonneuve et Larose.

Pérouse, J. F., 1999a, "Istanbul, Capitale du Nouveau Monde Turc?", *Revue de Géoéconomie*, 9: 45-53.

—, 1999b, "Irruption et É...clipse des Navetteurs 'Russes' à Istanbul (1988-1999). Remous et Rumeurs Dans la Mégapole", *Slavica Occitania*, 8: 273-312.

—, 1999c, "La Diasporization Kurde en Méditerranée ou la GenèÉse Contemporaine d'une Diaspora" in C. Vallat (ed.), *Les Méditerranées Dans le Monde*, Amiens: Presses de l'université d'Artois.

—, 2002a, "Laleli, Giga-bazar d'Istanbul? Appréhender les Caractéristiques et les Mutations d'une Place Commerciale Internationale" in M. Peraldi (ed.), *La Fin des Norias? Réseaux Migrants Dans les É...conomies Marchandes en Méditerranée*, Paris: Maisonneuve et Larose.

—, 2002b, "Istanbul Est-elle Une Métropole Méditerranéenne? Critique d'un Lieu Commun Tenace" in R. Escallier (ed.), *Cahiers de la Méditerranée, Actes du Colloque* (Les enjeux de la nouvelle métropolisation dans le monde arabe et méditerranéen, Grasse 22-24 Novembre 2000), Nice, CMMC, 64: 167-198.

—, 2002c, "Migrations, Circulation et Mobilités Internationales à Istanbul", Migrations et Mobilités Internationales: la Plate-forme Turque, (Coor. P. Dumont, JF.Pérouse, S.de Tapia, S. Akgönül), IFEA, Istanbul.

—, 2004a, "La Complexité de la Migration de Transit à Istanbul", paper presented in the regional conference Migrants in Transit Countries: Sharing responsibility for management and protection organized by Council of Europe, Istanbul, 30 September – 1 October 2004.

—, 2004b, "Nouvelles Configurations Migratoires et ProblèËmes des Immigrants en Turquie" (en collaboration avec M. Aslan) in A. A. Manco (ed.), *Turquie: vers de nouveaux horizons migratoires?*, Paris: l'Harmattan, Coll.

Pérouse, J. F. and S. Gangloff, 2001, "La Présence Roumaine à Istanbul. Une Chronique de l'É...phémère et de l'Invisible", *Les Dossiers de l'IFEA*, 8: 47.

Pessar, P. R., 1999, "The Role of Gender, Households and Social Networks in the Migration Process: A Review and Appraisal" in C. Hirschman, P. Kasinitz, and J. DeWind (eds.), *The Handbook of International Migration: The American Experience*, New York: Russell Sage Foundation.

Portes, A., 1995, "The Economic Sociology and the Sociology of Immigration: A Conceptual Overview" in A. Portes (ed.), *The Economic Sociology of Immigration: Essays on Networks, Ethnicity and Entrepreneurship*, New York: Russel Sage Foundation.

Portes, A. and R. Rumbaut, 2001, *Legacies: the Story of the Immigrant Second Generation*, California: University of California Press.

Portes, A. and M. Zhou, 1993, "The New Second Generation: Segmented Assimilation and Its Variants among post-1965 Immigrant Youth", *Annals of the American Academy of Political and Social Science*, 530: 74-96.

Saatçi, S., 2004, *Altunköprü*, Istanbul: Irak Türkleri Kültür ve Yardımlaşma Derneği Yayınları.

Schmitter, H. B., 2000, "The Sociology of Immigration: from Assimilation to Segmented Integration, from the American Experience to the Global Arena" in C. B. Brettel and J. H.

Hollifield (eds.), *Migration Theory*, New York: Routledge.

Sirkeci, İ., 2003, "Migration from Turkey to Germany: An Ethnic Approach", *New Perpsectives on Turkey*, 28: 189-207.

—, 2005, *Irak'tan Türkmen Göçleri ve Göç Eğilimleri*, Ankara: Global Strateji Enstitüsü Yayınları.

Sommers, M., 2000, "On the Margins, in the Mainstream: Urban Refugees in Africa" in S. C. Lubkemann, L. Minear and T. G. Weiss (eds.), *Humanitarian Action: Social Science Connections*, Rhode Island: Brown University publications.

Sperl, S., 2001, "Evaluation of UNHCR's Policy on Refugees in Urban Areas, A Case Study Review of Cairo", available at ().

Standing, G., 1989, "Global Feminization through Flexible Labor", *World Development*, 17(7): 1077-1095.

—, 1999, "Global Feminization through Flexible Labor: A Theme Revisited", *World Development*, 27(3): 583-602.

Stelaku, V., 2003, "Space, Place and Identity: Memory and Religion in Two Cappadocian Greek Settlements" in R. Hirschon (ed.), *Crossing the Aegean: An Appraisal of the 1923 Compulsory Population Exchange between Greece and Turkey*, New York and Oxford: Beghan Books.

Şimşir, B., 2004, *Türk-Irak İlişkilerinde Türkmenler*, Ankara: Bilgi Yayınevi.

Tarrius, A., 2001, "Au-delà des Etats-nations: des Sociétés de Migrants", *Revue Européenne des Migrations Internationales*, 17(2): 37-61.

Valognes, J. P., 1994, *Vie et Mort des Chrétiens d'Orient: Des Origines a Nos Jours*, Paris: Fayard.

Van Hear, N., 1995, "Displaced People after the Gulf Crisis" in R. Cohen (ed.), *The Cambridge Survey of World Migration*, Cambridge: Cambridge University Press.

—, 1998, *New Diasporas: the Mass Exodus, Dispersal and Regrouping of Migrant Communities*, London: UCL Press.

Vasquez, M., 2003, "Religion and Transnational Migration: What Religion Brings and Gains in the Conversation" in SSRC text on "Transnational Religion, Migration and Diversity", project background and conceptual framework paper.

Vertovec, S., 2002, "Transnational Networks and Skiled Labour Migration", WPTC-02-02, (), (working papers, Transnational Communities Programme).

—, 2004, "Trends and Impacts of Transnational Immigration", Centre on Migration, Policy and Society, Working Paper No.3, University of Oxford.

Wahlbeck, O., 1998, *Kurdish Diasporas: A Comparative Study of Kurdish Refugee Communities*, Centre for Research in Ethnic Relations, Warwick: University of Warwick.

Yakan, F., 2002, "Doğu Kilisesi Tarihçesi Üzerine Toplu Bir Bakış, Türkiye'de Keldaniler", *Hıristiyanlık: Dünü, Bugünü ve Geleceği*, Ankara: Dinler Tarihi Derneği.

Yenal, D., 1999, "Enformel Ekonominin Uluslararasılaşması: Bavul Ticareti ve Laleli Örneği", *Defter*, Kış 1999: 48-72.

Yılmaz, B. B., 2006, "Migration, Exclusion et Taudification Dans le Centre-Ville Istanbuliote: Etude de cas de Tarlabaşı", unpublished Ph.D. Dissertation, Saint-Denis: Université de Paris VIII.

Yonan, G., 1999, *Asur Soykırımı: Unutulan Bir Holocaust*, Istanbul: Pencere.

Yükseker, H. D., 2003, *Laleli-Moskova Mekiği: Kayıtdışı Ticaret ve Cinsiyet İlişkileri*, Istanbul: İletişim Yayınları.

Zurcher, E. J., 2003, "Greek and Turkish Refugees and Deportees 1912-1924", available at (http://www.let.leidenuniv.nl/tulp/Research/efz18.htm) (accessed on 16.01.2006)

7

A Survey on African Migrants and Asylum Seekers in Istanbul

KELLY T. BREWER - DENİZ YÜKSEKER

INTRODUCTION

In the past decade, an increasing number of Africans have arrived in Turkey as transit migrants or asylum seekers. Although they enter Turkey from various points, the majority of them live in Istanbul. The objective of this report is to describe the demographic characteristics of African migrants, their reasons for and patterns of migration, as well as their living conditions and problems in Istanbul.[1] As there are no previous studies on Africans in Turkey, one of the aims of this report is to open up a field for studying African migration rather than reaching conclusions.

The report is based on the findings of the research we conducted from February 2005 to 2006 in Istanbul, which included a survey of 133 Africans. In-depth interviews were conducted with a number of these Africans, as well as interviews with elite informants in non-governmental organizations (NGOs), the Turkish police in Istanbul and

---

1   Our research focused on migrants from Sub-Saharan African countries plus Mauritania, but we also present some data about North African migrants in Turkey.

the United Nations High Commissioner for Refugees (UNHCR) office in Ankara.[2]

The major findings of our research in synopsis are the following: (*i*) The increase in the numbers of Africans who arrive in Turkey for transit and asylum seeking and the mode of their stay here should be assessed within the framework of Turkey's bid for accession to the European Union (EU); (*ii*) Africans in Istanbul should not be considered as a homogeneous group; (*iii*) there are migrants from West, East and Central Africa in Istanbul and their motivations for migration are diverse; (*iv*) there are both men, women and families with children; (*v*) irregular migration[3] and asylum seeking are intertwined processes whose goal is often to reach Western Europe; (*vi*) the difficulty, however, of getting into Europe prolongs Africans' stay in Turkey, leading them to engage in a variety of survival strategies; (*vii*) asylum seekers especially have poor living conditions; (*viii*) poor living conditions are related to the paucity of income earning opportunities, social aid and services targeting them, as well as the weakness of asylum seekers' social networks.

An important conclusion we draw is that "transit" migration is not so transitory for many of the people going through it. Although the majority of the migrants have the goal of reaching Europe, their "transit" puts them in an indeterminate state in terms of their livelihoods. Consequently, African migrants and asylum applicants seek to make a living through informal income earning opportunities alongside Turkish citizens who also operate in the city's large, informal economy. As Turkey prepares to harmonize its migration regime with that of the EU, humanitarian and social needs of migrants and asylum

2 We would like to thank MiReKoc (Migration Research Program at Koc University) for a grant in 2005 which funded this research. We are also grateful to Harun Ercan for data entry and the construction of tables; Gaspard Bizimana, Adem Siyaad Omar and Ishmael Gasle for help with conducting the survey, and the latter two also for interpreting from Somali; and Şefika Kumral for assistance with library research and transcription of some interviews.
3 Irregular migration refers to the movements of people who, owing to illegal entry or the expiry of their visas, lack legal status in a transit or host country (IOM, 2005).

seekers need to be addressed. However, given Turkey's limited resources, methods of burden sharing between Turkey and the EU should be devised.

LITERATURE REVIEW

International Migration in a Globalizing World

The increasing volume and changing patterns of international migration have marked the last several decades and are likely to be one of the major social phenomena shaping the world in the twenty-first century. Since the 1970s, transformations in the world economy, such as economic crisis and declining industrial employment in the core, and the impact of the debt crisis and changing economic structures in many peripheral countries, have brought about major changes in migration trends. Emerging patterns and types of international migration were also bolstered by political turmoil and ethnic, as well as internal, wars in the Middle East, Africa, Central Asia, and Eastern Europe. Regular labor migration to Western Europe declined. However, illegal migration and flows of asylum seekers and refugees gained pace from Sub-Saharan and North Africa, from Southwest Asia (Middle East) and Central Asia, and from Eastern Europe towards the European Union (IOM, 2005).

As asylum seekers and illegal economic migrants flocked to the doors of the European Union during the 1980s and 1990s, Southern Europe (Spain, Portugal, Greece and Italy) became transit routes for migrants from Asia and Africa. Human smugglers organized illegal migration as the profits from clandestine passages through dangerous land and sea routes rose in tandem with the risks of such operations (Wallace and Stola, 2001). Alarmed by this wave and being in the process of stronger regional integration, countries of the European Union sought to tighten their asylum regulations and border controls (Castles and Miller, 1998). In 1991, the Maastricht Treaty established European citizenship, and in 1995, the notion of Schengen Citizenship was introduced. The objective of the emerging "Fortress Europe" was to keep out non-Europeans while making it easier for Europeans to move freely within the EU.

Against the background of the changes just mentioned, the emerging patterns of people's cross-border movements since the 1970s have been marked by the (*i*) globalisation, (*ii*) differentiation, (*iii*) feminization, and (*iv*) politicization of migration (Castles and Miller, 1998).

(*i*) First of all, intra-regional migration has been on the rise compared to south-to-north migration. Cases in point are: flows of people within cultural regions in Africa (previously divided by colonial rule), from the Horn of Africa to the Middle East, from the Mediterranean Basin to Western Europe and from North Africa and South Asia to the Gulf region (IOM, 2000).

(*ii*) Secondly, illegal and transit migration, refugee flows, waves of asylum seekers and temporary contract labor migration are on the rise compared to legal labor migration and legal immigration, which used to be more characteristic of the postwar period. This is a result of Western Europe's and North America's tightening immigration and asylum rules, the nature of demand for migrant labor in the Gulf Arab region, as well as push factors such as economic collapse and internal wars in sub-Saharan Africa and Eastern Europe. Transit migration refers to the movement of third country nationals who target Western Europe. Transit migrants spend an indefinite time in transit countries until they gain illegal entry into the West. Such flows are often intertwined with asylum seeking and are organized by criminal rings (Stola, 2001: 80). As such, the differentiation of types and direction of migratory flows since the 1980s has fuelled the creation of a "migration industry," with illicit aspects such as human smuggling[4] and trafficking.[5]

---

4   Human smuggling is defined as "the procurement, in order to obtain, directly or indirectly, a financial or material benefit, of the illegal entry of a person into a State Party of which the person is not a national or a permanent resident" (UN, 2000a).

5   Trafficking in persons refers to the "recruitment, transportation, transfer, harboring or receipt of persons, by means of the threat or use of force or other forms of coercion, of abduction, of fraud, of deception, of the abuse of power or of a position of vulnerability or of the giving or

(*iii*) Until the 1980s, men constituted the majority of migrants. Since then, about half of international migrants have become women as a result of the growing demand for domestic labor and other low-end service sector jobs in core countries and in the middle classes of middle income countries. Migrant women's jobs are often characterized by strict labor contracts, few worker rights, but relatively higher wages, making their remittances to their home countries an important source of foreign currency earnings (Parrenas, 2000).

(*iv*) Domestic and international political upheavals and power plays form a backdrop to many of these new patterns of population movements. For instance, the Iran-Iraq War and the First Gulf War led to the termination of the labor contracts of migrants from some Arab countries, whereas these wars, as well as the Iranian Revolution and repression by the Saddam Regime in Iraq, precipitated significant refugee flows originating from the region (Castles and Miller, 1998). Anti-immigration political currents in Western Europe and the USA have also shaped and reshaped the kinds and directions of flows of people; for instance, illegal migration, human smuggling and asylum seeking are reactions to restrictions to entry into the EU.

In this regard, the creation of literal buffer zones on the eastern borders of the EU is a telling example. It has been argued that a "buffer zone" was "politically and socially constructed" between western and eastern Europe during the 1990s, running through Hungary, Ukraine and Belarus (Wallace, 2001). "Buffer zone" countries entered into readmission[6] agreements with each other under political pressure from the EU and invested in policing their borders more effectively in order to stem transit and illegal migration (Stola, 2001: 83). This would thus curb illegal entries into "Fortress Europe" not only by limiting the number of people who are able to enter into

---

receiving of payments or benefits to achieve the consent of a person having control over another person, for the purpose of exploitation" (UN, 2000b).

6   Readmission agreement refers to an agreement which addresses procedures for one state to return aliens in an irregular situation to their home state or a state through which they passed en route to the state which seeks to return them (IOM, 2005).

the buffer zone, but more importantly, by also enforcing that a buffer country would readmit an illegal migrant if she/he escapes into and then is caught by a bordering EU nation.

Buffer countries respected the 1951 Geneva Convention on Refugees and became "safe third countries" for asylum seekers while their applications for refugee status were considered by the UNHCR. It is thought that during the Yugoslavian refugee crisis in the early 1990s, most refugees ended up in Hungary and other buffer countries rather than in the EU. Thus, Central European countries acted as a "safe sieve" that distinguished between bona fide and false claims for asylum (Stola, 2001: 85). It may be argued that the buffer zone has been expanded farther east after the accession of countries such as Hungary and Poland into the European Union. A case in point is Albania, which has recently accepted the Geneva Convention in full, thus agreeing to accept refugees (Peshkopia, 2005).

Refugee Flows and Asylum Seeking

In the twentieth century, there have been several major flows of refugees. The first two took place in the context of World Wars I and II, and were limited mostly to Europe. The signing of the Geneva Convention on Refugees in 1951 followed the displacements of World War II. The third wave started with the Partition in the Indian subcontinent in the 1940s with millions of refugees in both Pakistan and India. Since then, there have been massive refugee movements everywhere in the non-Western world, the most notable being: Palestinians in the Middle East, Ethiopians and Eritreans in the Horn of Africa, Afghans in Central Asia, Salvadorans in Central America, and Rwandans and Burundians in Central Africa (Castles and Miller, 1998). The global refugee population increased from 2.4 million in 1975 to 10.5 million in 1985 and nearly 15 million in 1990. Since 1995, the number of refugees has decreased while the number of internally displaced persons (IDPs) has sharply risen (Castles, 2003). While in 1982, 1.2 million IDPs were counted in 11 countries; today, an estimated 25 million IDPs live uprooted in 49 countries (IDMC, 2005). The fall in the number of "convention refugees" (see below) since the 1990s and the rise in the number of IDPs is attributed to the "non-arrival regime" established by western countries, whose objective is to contain refugees in or near their areas of origin. A result of this is that increasing numbers of people fall prey to human smugglers as the only way to reach countries where they can make asylum applications (Castles, 2003).

It has been argued that these flows arise out of two main historical processes: the formation of new states, and confrontation over the social order in a given state. Key drivers behind refugee movements are wars of national liberation, nation-building processes, inequalities in access to power and resources among different groups in a multi-ethnic society, and revolutionary processes leading to generalized violence (Zolberg, 1989; Keely, 1996). The overwhelming majority of refugee flows has originated in postcolonial countries in the twentieth century, and the overwhelming majority of refugees have stayed within the developing world, often within their own regions (Wood, 1994). Put differently, the Western world has shared only a small portion of the burden of refugee flows, although the after effects of European colonization and political and military interventions by Western states, as well as the former Soviet Union, have often triggered the events that led to refugee movements in the first place.

The 1951 "Convention Relating to the Status of Refugees" defined a refugee as anyone who:

> as a result of events which occurred prior to January 1, 1951, and owing to a well-founded fear of being persecuted for reasons of race, religion, nationality, membership of a particular social group or political opinion, is outside the country of his nationality and is unable or, owing to such fear, is unwilling to avail himself of the protection of that country; or who, not having a nationality and being outside the country of his former habitual residence as a result of such events, is unable or, owing to such fear, is unwilling to return to it.

In 1967, the "Protocol Relating to the Status of Refugees" expanded the scope of the meaning of refugee enshrined in the 1951 document both spatially and temporally to include anyone in the world and not just Europeans (Hyndman, 2000). It has been argued that the status of "convention refugees" is granted on politically outdated and Eurocentric criteria enshrined in the 1951 Geneva Convention and the 1967 Protocol. To be more specific, refugee status is granted to those persons whose civil and political liberties are abrogated. Yet, this definition does not include a broader understanding of the violation of socio-economic human rights. It also does not comprise of threats based on generalized violence rather than specific threats towards individuals (Hyndman, 2000). In this sense, the 1969 Organization for African Unity (OAU) "Convention Governing the Specific Aspects of Refugee Problems in Africa" broadened the scope of the definition of refugees to include not only those fleeing individual persecution, but also people who escape situations of generalized violence, such as internal wars (*ibid.*: 13).

Since the 1990s, at the behest of UNHCR's principle donors, many of which are also the traditional resettlement countries that now wish to lessen their responsibilities, refugee protection in safe countries is systematically eroding, while *refoulement*[7] has reemerged through the back door, and repatriation into unstable "home" countries has become an option (Barnett, 2001; Goodwin-Gill, 2001; Koser, 2001). In this context, some argue that UNHCR's original mandate is being transformed from an agency providing protection to refugees in safe countries to one providing humanitarian assistance to displaced groups *in situ* (Hyndman, 2000; Loescher, 2001). Meanwhile, the "camp" model of provision of humanitarian services by the UNHCR to refugees in Africa has also come under

---

7   *Refoulement* is the return by a state or an individual to the territory of another state in which his or her life or liberty would be threatened, or s/he may be persecuted for reasons of race, religion, nationality, membership of a particular social group or political opinion; or would run the risk of torture (IOM, 2005).

criticism by social scientists (e.g. Harrell-Bond, 1986; see also Hyndman, 2000).

Although humanitarian policies are increasingly important in a world where refugee flows and internal displacement are constant problems, these practices also carry a number of problems in their applications. Anthropologists working on forced migration emphasize that international agencies create new forms of knowledge and new categories in the course of handling the problems of asylum seekers (Harrell-Bond, 2002). For instance, international agencies operate on well-defined categories based on which they dispense with humanitarian aid and decide on resettlement in safe countries (Sorensen, forthcoming). Such subject categories also objectify target populations by assuming that their characteristics, needs and wants are homogeneous, regardless of nationality, ethnicity and reasons for migration (Malkki, 1995). Of particular concern for us in this paper is the definition of vulnerability, which restricts access to assistance, and of the "refugee," which restricts eligibility for international protection. For this reason, hundreds of thousands of people in Africa escaping ethnic violence or economic ravages brought about by war are not eligible to become "convention refugees." And so, the UNHCR and international humanitarian agencies serve them in camps in surrounding countries where they are *de facto* refugees – so-called "mandate refugees,"[8] and have little right to participate in the life of the society to which they have escaped.

From 2002 onwards, the number of refugees around the world decreased steadily down to 9.2 million by the end of 2005, the lowest figure of refugees in 25 years (UNHCR, 2005) (see **Table 7.1**). Yet, this figure climbed up to 9.9 million by the end of 2006, the highest number in 5 years (UNHCR, 2007a). The ten largest origins of refugee populations in 2004 were: Afghanistan, Sudan, Burundi, Democratic

---

[8] A mandate refugee is a person who qualifies for UNHCR protection regardless of whether the country he or she is a party to the 1951 Convention or the 1967 protocol and regardless of whether that country recognizes him or her as a refugee (IOM, 2005).

TABLE 7.1
Estimated Number of Refugees

Year	Refugees	Year	Refugees
1980	8,446,000	1993	16,306,000
1981	9,706,000	1994	15,754,000
1982	10,310,000	1995	14,896,000
1983	10,610,000	1996	13,357,000
1984	10,717,000	1997	12,015,000
1985	11,851,000	1998	11,481,000
1986	12,620,000	1999	11,687,000
1987	13,114,000	2000	12,130,000
1988	14,331,000	2001	12,117,000
1989	14,716,000	2002	10,594,000
1990	17,378,000	2003	9,680,000
1991	16,837,000	2004	9,237,000
1992	17,818,000		

Source: UNHCR, 2005.

Republic of Congo (DRC), Somalia, Palestine, Vietnam, Liberia, Iraq and Azerbaijan (see **Table 7.2**). In 2004, the ten countries that generated the largest flows of refugees were: Sudan, DRC, Somalia, Iraq, Ivory Coast, Burundi, Liberia, Central African Republic, Rwanda and the Russian Federation (see **Table 7.3**). In addition, there were about 839,000 asylum seekers (those people who apply for "asylum" – the right to be recognized as bona fide refugees and receive legal protection when they seek sanctuary in another country). Reportedly, the number of new asylum seekers in the Western world dropped to its lowest level in 16 years as of 2004 (UNHCR, 2005). As is clear from **Table 7.4**, 34 percent (3,120,223) of all refugees in the world (9,236,521) were from African countries as of the end of 2004. **Tables 7.2** and **7.3** also show that most African refugees are clustered in the countries surrounding their county of origin.

TABLE 7.2
Origin of Major Refugee Populations in 2004

Country of Origin	Main Countries of Asylum	Total
Afghanistan	Pakistan / Iran / Germany / Netherlands / United Kingdom	2,084,900
Sudan	Chad / Uganda / Ethiopia / Kenya / D.R. Congo / Central African Rep.	730,600
Burundi	Tanzania / D.R. Congo / Rwanda / South Africa / Canada	485,800
Democratic Rep. Congo	Tanzania / Zambia / Congo / Burundi / Rwanda	462,200
Somalia	Kenya / Yemen / United Kingdom / USA / Djibouti	389,300
Palestinians	Saudi Arabia / Egypt / Iraq / Libya / Algeria	350,600
Vietnam	China / Germany / USA / France / Switzerland	349,800
Liberia	Guinea / Côte d'Ivoire / Sierra Leone / Ghana / USA	335,500
Iraq	Iran / Germany / Netherlands / United Kingdom / Sweden	311,800
Azerbaijan	Armenia / Germany / USA / Netherlands	250,500

Source: UNHCR, 2005.

TABLE 7.3
Major Refugee Arrivals in 2004

Origin	Main Countries of Asylum	Total
Sudan	Chad / Uganda / Kenya	146,900
D.R. Congo	Burundi / Rwanda / Zambia / Uganda	38,100
Somalia	Yemen / Kenya	19,100
Iraq	Syria	12,000
Côte d'Ivoire	Liberia / Mali	5,900
Burundi	Rwanda / Tanzania	4,200
Liberia	Sierra Leone / Côte d'Ivoire / Guinea	3,700
Central African Rep.	Chad	500
Rwanda	Malawi / D.R. Congo	500
Russian Federation	Azerbaijan	500

Source: UNHCR, 2005.

TABLE 7.4
African Refugees (End of 2004)

Country	Total population	Country	Total population
Algeria	10,691	Libya	1,720
Belize	9	Mali	483
Benin	309	Mauritania	31,131
Botswana	6	Morocco	1,319
Burundi	485,764	Mozambique	104
Cameroon	7,629	Niger	689
Central African Rep.	31,069	Nigeria	23,888
Chad	52,663	Rwanda	63,808
Congo	28,152	Senegal	8,332
D.R. Congo	462,203	Sierra Leone	41,801
Djibouti	495	Somalia	389,272
Egypt	5,376	South Africa	272
Eritrea	131,119	Sudan	730,612
Ethiopia	63,105	Swaziland	14
Gambia	684	Togo	10,819
Ghana	14,767	Tunisia	2,518
Guinea	4,782	Zimbabwe	9,568
Kenya	3,847	Western Sahara	165,729
Lesotho	7	Total	3,120,223
Liberia	335,467	Grand Total	9,236,521

Source: UNHCR, 2005.

Transit and Irregular Migration Through Turkey

The prevalent patterns of migration to and from Turkey fit into the changing types and patterns of migratory movements explained in the "International Migration in a Globalizing World" section above. Turkey has constituted a major component of the labor migration system in Europe since the 1960s, especially through the guest worker system. Although Western European countries stopped labor recruitment during the 1970s, Turkish migration to Germany, France, Austria, Sweden, Switzerland and the Netherlands has continued through family unification (e.g. Faist, 2000). Types of Turkish migration to Europe diversified after 1980. In the wake of the military coup in 1980, a strong wave of asylum seekers knocked at the doors of Western Europe, and continued during the 1990s in the course of the Kurdish conflict.

Simultaneously, illegal migration to European Union countries gained pace, often organized by human smugglers. It has been argued that economic migration and the asylum movement were intertwined during the 1990s, as some asylum seekers were not bona fide refugees but illegal economic migrants (Sirkeci, 2003). Directions of population movements were also altered. From a major sending country during the postwar decades, Turkey has been transformed into both a sending and a receiving country for the past two and a half decades. This has been a result of manifold factors, including political changes: the Iranian revolution, the Gulf War, the collapse of the Soviet Union and political oppression of the Turkish minority in Bulgaria. It has also been a result of economic distress (the collapse of socialist economies) in the surrounding regions, as well as political and economic turmoil in far reaching areas. Situated in a geographical area that provides both land and sea routes from the Middle East and North Africa toward Western Europe, Turkey has especially been home to waves of transit migration and illegal labor migration as well as movements of asylum seekers (İçduygu, 2000 and 2003). Such illegal flows are often organized by human smugglers (İçduygu and Toktaş, 2002).

Illegal labor migration mostly concerns people from former Soviet republics and Romania. Among them, the majority are proba-bly women, who find informal employment in domestic services or as sex workers (Keogh, 2004; Ünal, 2004). There is also trafficking of Eastern European women as sex workers that takes place through Turkey (Erder and Kaşka, 2003). Migrants transiting through Turkey with a view to reaching the European Union are more diverse as to their origins, encompassing people from Africa as well as South Asia. Likewise, asylum seekers arriving in Turkey are also diverse in terms of their origins, although the greatest numbers have come from two countries, Iran and Iraq. The Revolution in Iran and the Iran-Iraq war triggered large waves of refugees through Turkish borders during the 1980s (İçduygu, 2000). Iraq's repression of Kurds and the First Gulf War precipitated two large influxes of refugees in 1988 and 1991 (Kirişci and Winrow, 1997). In 1990, about 300,000 thousand ethnic Turks arrived from Bulgaria during a campaign against the Turkish minority by the communist regime; although, since then some of them have returned, the majority settled in Turkey, and were subsequently granted citizenship (Vasileva, 1992). A group of Afghan refugees arrived during the 1980s, and during the 1990s, there were relatively small refugee inflows from Bosnia, Kosovo and Chechnya.

Since the mid-1990s, the number of Africans arriving in Turkey as irregular migrants or asylum seekers has been on the rise. However, there are no scholarly studies on current African migration to Turkey. The only information collected comes from studies on transit migration (IOM, 1995; İçduygu 2000 and 2003) and refugee flows (Frantz, 2003). There are also several descriptive or journalistic accounts of the experiences of African migrants in Istanbul (Yaghmaian, 2003; Çalkıvık, 2003; Öcal, 2005; Ekberzade, 2006).

Turkey is a signatory to the 1951 Geneva Convention and the 1967 Protocol, but it has maintained a "geographical reservation" to the 1967 Protocol. Thus, it has only accepted Europeans as "convention refugees"; namely, people from the Soviet Union and other Soviet bloc countries in Eastern Europe (Kirişci, 1996). The resettlement of Turks from Bulgaria as citizens was made possible under Turkey's citizenship and resettlement laws dating from the 1930s. These laws limit immigration into Turkey to persons of Turkish ethnicity and Muslims who were culturally part of the Ottoman heritage (Çağaptay, 2002). However, since the early 1990s, Turkey gives temporary asylum to non-western persons who have pending asylum applications at UNHCR's office in Turkey (Kirişci, 2002). Temporary asylum is implemented through a government regulation dated 1994, which was revised twice in 1999 and 2006 (*Resmi Gazete*, 1994, 1999 and

2006). It may be argued that the catalyst for this change was the influx of Iraqi Kurds to Turkey during the first Gulf War.[9] The humanitarian aspect of that incident led Turkey to take steps to ensure non-*refoulement* for non-Western people who sought refuge within Turkish borders.

In addition to that development, Turkey has been under the impact of the changes in asylum and migration policy to its west, namely in the European Union. The EU accepted Turkey's candidacy for accession at the Helsinki Summit in 1999, and then Turkey accepted a National Programme for Adoption of the EU *Acquis Communautaire* in 2001. The National Programme includes measures to be taken; such as, more effective patrolling of borders to stem illegal entries, altering its visa policy in order to discourage transit and irregular migrants, creating reception centers for asylum seekers, and eventually lifting the geographical limitation to the Geneva treaties (İçduygu, 2003). Turkey has also entered into readmission agreements with a number of origin and destination countries including Syria and Greece since 2000. Although the lifting of the geographical reservation will probably be postponed until later in the accession negotiations between Turkey and the EU, it will eventually open the way for more non-European refugees to stay in Turkey (*ibid.*).

African International Migration
Nearly half of Sub-Saharan Africa's[10] overall population (more than 300 million people) lives below the poverty line (UNDP, 2003), constituting the most significant push factor for the mobility of people in search of livelihoods. Sub-Saharan Africa is considered to contain the

---

9 When the Iraqi army advanced on the Kurdish region in March 1991, over a million people fled their homes towards the Iranian and Turkish borders. Although Turkey decided to keep its borders shut, partly in an effort to prevent a renewal of the refugee crisis in 1988 after the chemical bombing of Halabja, it could not resist the waves of displaced Kurds who were gathering in the mountains. Later, US troops entered Northern Iraq and created a "safe haven" into which the Kurdish refugees were repatriated (Kirişci and Winrow, 1997).

10 Sub-Saharan Africa excludes Egypt, Algeria, Morocco, Tunisia, Libya and Mauritania.

most mobile population in the world. In 2000, there were an estimated 16.3 million migrants in Sub-Saharan Africa, making up 9 percent of the global stock of migrants (IOM, 2005).

Migration flows originating in Sub-Saharan Africa display the following patterns (see also Appendix 7.1): internal and cross-border migration, movements towards regions of relative prosperity, transit migration through North Africa towards Europe, clandestine and irregular migration towards Europe, (sometimes involving trafficking in persons), and increased feminization of migration (IOM, 2005). Among these, irregular migration flows to and through the Maghreb (North Africa) merits some attention due to its relevance to transit migration of Africans to and through Turkey. Although Sub-Saharan populations' movement towards the Maghreb is a long-standing historical phenomenon since the 1980s, this migratory flow has been on the rise. In the recent years, about 65,000 to 80,000 Sub-Saharan Africans are estimated to arrive annually to the region (IOM, 2005). The reasons for this intensifying flow are numerous: the Maghreb stands out as a more prosperous region where informal work can be found in some of the countries in comparison to West and Central Africa where conflict, political instability, desertification and economic hardship render life difficult. Also, as Western European countries combat irregular migration and discourage flows of asylum seekers, Sub-Saharan transit and irregular migration to Europe through the Maghreb has increased. Especially This is especially true for Libya, which adopted a Pan-African policy that turned it into a destination country over the past five years, as well as Tunisia and Morocco which are all significant receivers of irregular and transit migration from Sub-Saharan Africa (IOM, 2005).

Today, international migration from Africa is motivated by various reasons, two of which are of paramount concern: (*i*) firstly, economic collapse and poverty in many countries triggers population movements in search of survival and economic betterment (Adepoju, 2000); and (*ii*) secondly, ethnic conflict and state failure lead to internal displacement and refugee flows (Jamal, 2003) (see Appendix 7.2). In both contexts, human smuggling and trafficking are great concerns (Adepoju, 2005). Migrants are sometimes deceived into paying large sums of money for clandestine passage to South European countries often to be dumped somewhere along the Turkish or North African coasts. Even when migrants first apply for asylum or refugee status in the countries where they arrive, they face an uphill battle. The European Union, in line with policies that sustain the so-called "Fortress Europe," de-emphasizes granting protection, refugee status and resettlement to asylum seekers, while it actively pursues the non-arrival of potential asylum seekers into European soil. As part and parcel of these policies, it promotes protection and humanitarian aid for asylum seekers and refugees in other African countries without seeking political solutions to conflicts that created the refugee flows in the first place. Hence, Africa today is faced with "protracted refugee situations" (Jamal, 2003) and camps full of refugees living in uncertain conditions (Hughes, 2003). More frequently nowadays, refugee repatriation is suggested as a possible solution, without paying enough attention to the voluntary degree of such return (Kindiki, 2005). Somalis, as one of the largest groups of refugees originating from Africa in the past decade, are at the center of these debates and have the most precarious situation. As is known, there is no operational state in Somalia, and different parts of the land are ruled by competing clans (see Appendix 2). Hundreds of thousands of Somalis have fled the country and been placed in refugee camps primarily in neighboring Kenya (Hyndman, 2000) and Yemen (Hughes, 2003). For this reason, it is not surprising that Somalis constitute the majority of African asylum seekers in Turkey.

RESEARCH DESIGN

Research Questions
There are no studies that focus particularly on the flow of Africans into Turkey. We undertook this research in order to shed light on this understudied phenomenon. Although Africans are not as numerous as some

other groups who illegally enter and/or stay in Turkey, their presence is indicative of certain pressing issues in international and forced migration. First, Africans constitute one of the most significant refugee populations in the world today, and secondly, they constitute a significant group of irregular migrants in Europe. Given Turkey's geographical location at the crossroads of land and sea routes between the Middle East, North Africa and Europe, the relative ease of legal or illegal entry into the country, as well as the weakness of regulations against undocumented migrants, the number of Africans arriving in Turkey as migrants and asylum seekers increased considerably by the turn of this decade.

As we wanted to lay the groundwork for further research on this phenomenon, the questions that motivated our research were the following: (1) What are the similarities and differences between the flows of African asylum seekers and irregular migrants? In this respect, we wanted to learn who the African migrants in Turkey are, why they have left their countries, what their final destinations are, what methods they have used to enter Turkey, how long they have been staying in Turkey, how much longer they plan to do so, and, if they are asylum seekers, what their reasons for seeking refuge were.

(2) Another set of questions pertains to the living conditions of Africans in Istanbul. How do Africans survive while staying in Istanbul? To what extent are irregular economic migrants' and asylum seekers' living conditions differentiated? To answer these questions, we collected information on such issues as their survival strategies and income earning activities in Istanbul, the available forms of social assistance, as well as Africans' perceptions of how they are treated by Turkish law enforcement officers and Turkish citizens.

(3) We also want to describe the legal parameters of Africans' presence in Istanbul. How has the Turkish asylum regime been changing in the past few years? Are African and other illegal migrants tolerated or not? We sought to answer these questions within the framework of Turkey's changing perspective on asylum and irregular migration during the EU integration process.

Methodology

Research Methods

The research for this report was based on a review of secondary sources as well as fieldwork. We examined relevant reports by the International Organization of Migration (IOM), the UNHCR, scholarly literature on African migration and refugees and on transit migration and asylum seeking through Turkey.

The fieldwork consisted of a survey with 133 Africans in Istanbul, in-depth interviews with 21 African migrants (seven women and three men from Somalia; one Sierra Leonean, two Senegalese, three Ghanaians, three Nigerians, one Rwandan and one Sudanese, all of whom were men), interviews with the representatives and workers of several NGOs and church organizations in Istanbul that cater to asylum seekers and migrants, representatives of the UNHCR Office in Ankara, and officers at the Foreigners, as well as Borders and Asylum Department of the General Directorate of Security (hereafter, Foreigners' Police) in Istanbul.

The sample for the survey is not a probabilistic one, as this was impossible to do among an undocumented, floating population. However, we sought to reach members of different nationalities, both men and women, and both asylum seekers and illegal migrants. The representation of persons from each country of origin in the sample is unfortunately not representative of our estimations of the actual size of each group because there were difficulties in reaching West Africans, who were more reluctant to speak about their situation. This may be expected since many of them are irregular migrants and mistrustful of researchers, whereas asylum seekers from East Africa are often legally registered in Turkey and are somewhat more used to being "interviewed." Two Somalis and one Rwandan helped us to fill out the survey questionnaire. All three men had some experience interpreting for and working with NGOs that cater to African migrants and asylum seekers in Istanbul.

The Somalis – both registered asylum applicants – also assisted in interpreting from Somali into English during the interviews, and their presence facilitated a degree of trust between the researchers and the informants. The interviews with Africans were conducted mostly in English and some in Somali, and were based on open-ended questions. Most of the interviews with Africans and non-participant observation of their social activities were carried out by Kelly T. Brewer. The data on the questionnaires were entered into MS Excel and SPSS by a work-study student at Koc University, who also helped with constructing the tables.

We should note that both the interviews and the survey had some drawbacks in terms of the quality of information, owing to the fact that some of our questions pertained to the illegal aspects of Africans' presence here, and some to their reasons for asylum seeking. As we will argue in this report, asylum seeking and irregular migration are intertwining processes, and personal testimonies may not always be truthful. Conducting a number of interviews helped us gain at least some degree of insight into the overall situation so as to assess the truthfulness of the information. Nevertheless, vague areas remain.

Kelly T. Brewer attended various church services, football games, and charity activities where Africans gathered. He also visited several establishments (cafes) operated by Africans. Non-participant observation in these venues enriched our knowledge of Africans' lives in Istanbul. Kelly T. Brewer and Deniz Yükseker conducted the interviews with these institutions in English, with the exception that Yükseker interviewed the police in Turkish.

Plan of the Report

In the "African Migrants in Istanbul: A Demographic Profile" section of this report, we examine the findings of our fieldwork on African migrants and asylum seekers in Istanbul. The section of "Framework of Africans' Presence: Asylum, Illegality and Charity" draws on interviews with representatives of institutions, as well as secondary literature, to define the parameters of Africans' presence in Turkey in terms of: procedures for asylum seeking, access to social and humanitarian aid, law enforcement, and Turkey's migration and asylum regimes, which will soon be transformed due to the impact of EU accession negotiations.

In "The Survey" section, 4.2, Africans' demographic characteristics and social problems are examined based on information gained from the survey. The survey outlines their reasons and methods for traveling to Turkey, their length of stay, reasons for asylum seeking, plans for further migration, income earning activities while in Turkey, sources of income, major problems in Istanbul and access to social and humanitarian aid.

A description of the lives of African migrants and would-be refugees is offered in the section "A view of African Migrants' Lives in Istanbul" based on non-participant observation and interviews. Here, we focus on the transient nature of Africans' lives and on the difficulty of passage into Europe that prolongs a transient state. Faith-based community building, informal entrepreneurship, playing football, and marriages within the group or with Turkish citizens are various aspects of the efforts of many African migrants in Istanbul to build their lives.

In the conclusion, we discuss ways of improving the living conditions, especially of African asylum seekers and the prospects for illegal African migration, in light of the legal responsibilities Turkey will undertake as part of adopting the *Acquis Communautaire*.

AFRICAN MIGRANTS IN ISTANBUL: A DEMOGRAPHIC PROFILE

Framework of Africans' Presence: Asylum, Illegality and Charity

The legal framework of Africans' presence in Turkey is governed by the law on passports, the law on legal residence, the law on the movements of foreigners, government regulations on asylum, as well as Turkey's rights and obligations under international law. First, we briefly overview the regulations on asylum and then, based on interviews with the police and UNHCR, we discuss the particular situation of African asylum seekers, as well as irregular African migrants. Finally, we describe the types of social services and aid available to them in Istanbul.

African migrants in Istanbul may be asylum applicants/ refugees, short term visitors with valid visas, irregular migrants who have illegally entered Turkey, or who have legally entered but overstayed their visas or legal aliens married to Turkish citizens. There are also many African university students in Turkey, especially in Ankara, staying on student visas. Our fieldwork did not concern them. Our survey included 45 people who legally entered Turkey (most of whom later overstayed their visas), 86 people who entered illegally and two who did not specify their legal status. Sixty-three respondents had made asylum applications. Among the interviewees, there were asylum seekers as well as irregular/transit migrants. In addition, a couple of male interviewees had legal residence in Turkey based on marriages to Turkish citizens.

The Asylum Process

In 1994, the Turkish government adopted a regulation on asylum applications by individuals and groups. This regulation stipulated that asylum seekers who have legally or illegally entered Turkey can file an asylum application in a governorship within five days of their arrival (*Resmi Gazete*, 1994). After the initial interview with the asylum seeker, until his or her application is accepted by the authorities, he or she would be kept under detention. Once the application is accepted, the applicant would be issued a residence permit which allows him or her to freely reside in Turkey. The regulation states that the Ministry of Interior (MOI), in cooperation with UNHCR and the IOM, would decide whether to accept or reject an individual's application to become a refugee. If a person's refugee application is rejected, then he or she would be deported. An amendment to the regulation in 1999 extended the period of application to 10 days. It also allowed individuals to petition a rejection of their application to obtain refugee status within 15 days (*Resmi Gazete*, 1999). A new amendment in January 2006 further modified this regulation in favor of the asylum applicants. Now, there is no time limit as to when a foreigner who has entered Turkey can apply for asylum. The regulation says that a person who applies for asylum would be hosted in a reception center or may freely reside in a place to be determined by the MOI. Then, a person whose asylum application is accepted may stay in a reception center or may freely reside in a place to be determined by the MOI while his application for refugee status is considered. A person whose application for refugee status is rejected twice would be notified that he or she needs to leave Turkey (*Resmi Gazete*, 2006).

Significant in the last modification of the regulation is the mention of "reception centers". As part of the National Programme, Turkey promised to set up reception centers for incoming asylum seekers. However, officials say that it may take at least several years for this project to materialize. Currently, there is only one reception center in Turkey, in the Central Anatolian province of Yozgat, which is reserved for asylum applicants who are sick or infirm. We do not know of Africans currently staying there. Another significant change in the amended regulation is the requirement for asylum applicants to have "free residence" (i.e., not in a reception center) in places to be determined by the MOI. Authorities have introduced this requirement so that people whose applications for asylum have been accepted would reside in designated provincial centers[11] and register with the police there, instead of in Istanbul. This regulation was new when we conducted the fieldwork, and therefore, among the asylum applicants who answered our survey, only five reported having registered in Eskişehir and Kayseri. Some of the interviewed asylum seekers expressed that they would prefer to stay in Istanbul. They said that it would be difficult to survive in these provincial places because of the

---

11 These provinces are Afyon, Aksaray, Amasya, Bilecik, Burdur, Çankırı, Çorum, Eskişehir, Isparta, Karaman, Kastamonu, Kayseri, Kırıkkale, Kırşehir, Konya, Kütahya, Nevşehir, Niğde, Sivas, Tokat and Yozgat.

lack of income earning opportunities, separation from their national communities, and also because the locals would not be welcoming towards them. A police officer acknowledged that there is at least one province where the local population complained about the presence of asylum seekers, but he did not specify the province or the nationality targeted. However, since we completed the fieldwork, more people have registered in provincial centers. For instance, two Somalis, who were granted refugee status since our fieldwork ended, have moved to Konya and Burdur. In order to receive the monthly allowance for refugees and to take advantage of social services, they need to remain and be registered in those cities.

Once a person's application for asylum is rejected twice, the Foreigners' Police notify this person that his or her residence permit has expired and that he or she needs to leave the country in 15 days. However, police officials say that this is only a notification; deportation of rejected asylum seekers is not pursued. It is difficult to determine the whereabouts of such persons, and such a pursuit would be costly in terms of labor and time. In their words, such individuals become "tolerated foreigners". Rejected asylum applicants could only be deported if they were caught during a routine check of papers (ID, passport, visa), a procedure that is occasionally carried out in places known to host irregular migrants, such as bars, cafes and clubs in certain districts. Such identity checks do not specifically target Africans; in fact, they are more likely to target irregular migrants from Romania and other former Soviet republics, who constitute a much larger group of undocumented migrants in Istanbul. Nevertheless, Africans' physical distinctiveness makes them more prone to impromptu identity checks compared to other groups.

Among African asylum applicants, the majority of whom are Somalis, the main form of entry into Turkey is illegal (see "The Survey" section below). It is plausible to argue that, for some African asylum applicants, asylum seeking and irregular migration are intertwined, not only on the way to Turkey, but also, in the event that their refugee applications are rejected. Data provided by the Foreigners' Police supports this argument. For instance, the number of apprehensions of persons from Somalia is much higher than the number of Somalis who have applied for asylum in Turkey (**Tables 7.5 and 7.6**).[12] This may mean that only a fraction of the Somalis who illegally enter Turkey end up applying for asylum, which suggests the enmeshing of irregular migration and refugee flows.[13] Our survey also indicates that African asylum seekers remain in Turkey long after their cases get a final rejection from the UNHCR (see "The Survey Section"). In addition, our interviews suggest that, once an asylum seeker's application is rejected, he or she may attempt to illegally cross into Greece, and if his or her effort is unsuccessful, he or she may continue to stay illegally in Turkey.

How does the asylum process work in Turkey? The International Catholic Migration Commission (ICMC), an international NGO, the UNHCR's Office in Ankara, and the Turkish police cooperate in processing asylum applications. Once a person applies to Turkish authorities, he or she is interviewed by the police and then the UNHCR (or the ICMC in Istanbul) is notified about this person. In Istanbul, the ICMC makes the pre-interview preparations. Funded by the UNHCR, the ICMC acts as a liaison between applicants and the UNHCR. The UNHCR then registers this person as an asylum applicant and the Turkish police gives him or her a "residence permit for asylum applicants." The UNHCR then invites this person for an interview in Ankara and reaches a decision on each application sometime after the interview. If the decision is negative, the applicant can ask for reconsideration of his or her case and may subsequently be inter-

---

12 The total of new applications, pending cases and closed cases of Somali asylum seekers was 839 by the end of 2005 according to UNHCR figures (Table 4.1); whereas 8,512 Somalis were apprehended for illegal entry/exit/stay between 1995 and 2005 according to figures provided by the Foreigners' Police (Table 4.3).

13 However, the number of Somalis apprehended for illegal entry/exit and visa violations may not be accurate since authorities say that some Africans falsely declare themselves as Somalis, and some Somalis may have been apprehended more than once.

viewed again. If he or she is rejected for a second time, then the residence permit is rescinded within 15 days.

The active caseload of the UNHCR office in Ankara consists of Iranians, Iraqis, Africans and small numbers from other nationalities. The Iraqis' applications were stalled in 2003 in the wake of the American occupation of Iraq and the regime change in that country. But more recently in December 2006, the UNHCR declared that Iraqis fleeing from the central and southern regions, where it described the situation as one of generalized violence and grave violation of human rights, need international protection. It recommended the Turkish government non-*refoulement* of Iraqis in irregular status in Turkey (UNHCR, 2007b). Most of the Iranian asylum seekers in Turkey belong to the Bahai community. In contrast, until the American invasion of Iraq most of the Iraqi asylum seekers in Turkey were Chaldean Christians. As **Table 7.5** shows, Somalis are the largest African group with asylum applications. According to information we obtained from UNHCR officials, 42 percent of the active caseload of Somali asylum seekers in Turkey in 2005 were women. **Table 7.6** indicates the number of recognized refugees in Turkey as of the end of 2005; it should be noted that these are "mandate refugees," not "convention refugees."[14] According to figures we obtained from UNHCR officials, in 2002, 73 percent of Iraqi asylum seekers, 38 percent of Iranians and 35 percent of "others" (including Africans) were recognized. In 2003, 79 percent of Iranian applicants and 45 percent of "others" were recognized. In 2004, 75 percent of Iranians and 31 percent of "others" were recognized.[15] UNHCR officials say that the recognition rate for Somalis (included in "others") is lower than for Iranians because there is a high rate of applications that are not cred-

---

14 Clearly, in Turkey, all refugees except those coming from European countries would be mandate refugees rather than convention refugees because of Turkey's geographical reservation to the 1967 Protocol.

15 No figures for Iraqis are available for 2003 and 2004 because of the freeze on their applications following the American occupation of and the regime change in Iraq.

TABLE 7.5

Individual Asylum Applications and Refugee Status Determination in Turkey (2005)

	Pending Begin Year	Applied During Year	Decisions During the Year-Rejected	Decisions During the Year-Rejected	Otherwise Closed	Pending End Year
Congo	0	1	0	0	0	1
Burundi	3	5	3	0	1	4
D.R. Congo	14	12	2	1	7	16
Eritrea	17	18	6	1	12	16
Ethiopia	23	32	2	3	19	31
Ivory Coast	0	1	0	0	0	1
Liberia	5	2	5	0	2	5
Mauritania	0	14	0	0	1	13
Nigeria	7	8	0	2	8	5
Sierra Leone	0	0	0	0	0	0
Somalia	214	473	82	16	152	437
Sudan	39	76	6	4	35	70
Rwanda	0	1	0	0	1	0
Total, African C.	322	643	106	27	238	599
Grand Total*	3,929	3,914	1,368	377	2,874	4,969

Source: UNHCR Office, Ankara.

(*) Grand total includes Iran, Iraq and other countries.

ible. Often, Somalis do not have identification. Besides, some non-Somali persons also apply for asylum claiming to be Somalis. All of these factors make it difficult to get credible statements and information on an applicant's identity. It is also for these reasons that it may take longer for a Somali (or another African nationality) application to be processed than for someone from another nationality. In general, an African asylum seeker's application process lasts a couple of years.

UNHCR officials say that they look into both "subjective" and "objective" conditions in determining African applicants' status. That is, not only threats of individual persecution (subjective factors) – the ground for refugee status determination based on the Geneva

TABLE 7.6

Refugee Population in Turkey by Legal Status and type of Recognition (End of 2005)

	Legal Status		Type of Recognition	
Country of Origin	UNHCR Mandate	Total	Indiv. Recogn.	Total
Burundi	3	3	3	3
D.R. Congo	2	2	2	2
Eritrea	4	4	4	4
Ethiopia	3	3	3	3
Mauritania	7	7	7	7
Rwanda	1	1	1	1
Sierra Leone	1	1	1	1
Somalia	66	66	66	66
Sudan	7	7	7	7
Tunisia	1	1	1	1
Total	95			
Grand Total*	2,342	2,399	2,342	2,399

Source: UNHCR Office, Ankara.

(*) Grand total includes Iran, Iraq and other countries.

Convention – but also objective factors, such as generalized violence in the region where the person comes from, are taken into account.

Once a person is recognized as a refugee, then he or she is referred for resettlement. UNHCR has separate departments handling status recognition and resettlement. Recognized refugees in Turkey may be resettled in the USA, Canada or Australia, and in some cases, in European countries. ICMC's office in Istanbul processes the resettlement of refugees in the USA. This office is an "Oversees Processing Entity" for the US government's Refugee Resettlement Program and covers Turkey, Lebanon, Yemen, Pakistan and Kuwait. ICMC officers say that most of the refugees resettled through their office in the last few years were Iranian Bahais. They also say that the resettlement of Iranian refugees takes place much faster compared to Somalis.

According to UNHCR officials, the slowness of the pace of Africans' resettlement stems from the fact that resettlement is an entirely different process than recognition; and in this case, traditional resettlement countries' criteria for accepting refugees into their land are important, not the refugee recognition criteria. Therefore, for instance, after the attacks in the USA on September 11, 2001, resettlement has slowed down. This is conceded by both the ICMC staff and UNHCR officials. Resettlement countries' admission criteria regarding security is now stricter, with the result that the process is much slower, especially for refugees who do not have identification (i.e., Somalis) and more generally for Muslim men.

While status recognition is decided only based on convention criteria, resettlement decisions take into account the pre-existence of refugee communities from a given country of origin in a receiving country as well as vulnerability. In general, unaccompanied women and children are considered vulnerable and their resettlement process can be prioritized and expedited on that basis.

However, the interviews for status determination may also be expedited for unaccompanied women and children. This sometimes gives rise to an interesting situation, according to the UNHCR officials we interviewed. They explained that sometimes the husband of a woman who initially declared herself as unaccompanied would subsequently appear after her interview. Meaning, while the woman would get an individual recognition interview, sometime later, her husband would get a "derivative status" interview. UNHCR officials were of the opinion that human smugglers may be advising women to declare themselves as "unaccompanied" so that they are eligible to be considered vulnerable. However, our survey indicates that many Somali and Ethiopian women indeed traveled alone to Turkey.

Therefore, it may be argued that somewhat of a gender and generation bias may exist in refugee resettlement, and perhaps also in status determination to some extent, although UNHCR officials denied that. While women and children are seen by international agencies as the paradigmatic refugees because of their vulnerability (Malkki, 1995), adult African men may be viewed with suspicion on the grounds that they may have been combatants, drug smugglers, or worse yet, Islamic terrorists. This, alongside other reasons, might partially explain why fewer African asylum seekers in Turkey are referred for resettlement compared to non-Muslim Iranians and Iraqis.

There has been for some time a UNHCR training program for Turkish police, and currently, it is run by the ICMC with UNHCR funding. The training, which targets the Foreigners' Police, involves methods of identifying asylum seekers, interviewing them and recognizing vulnerabilities. UNHCR officials point out that training should also be provided to police officers at reception centers in the regions where potential asylum seekers enter the country; as well as places from where they attempt to leave Turkey en route to Europe.[16] UNHCR officials say that the Turkish Foreigners' Police's approach towards asylum seekers has improved over the years. The police are supposed to register asylum seekers regardless of country of origin and availability of identity documents. One problematic practice used to be that Turkish police were unwilling to register a person's asylum application if he or she had been staying in Turkey for a long time without documents, arguing that these were "abusive" claims by irregular migrants.[17] The January 2006 government regulation in effect solved this problem by removing the 10-day limit for filing an asylum application after arriving in the country (*Resmi Gazete*, 2006).

Irregular Migrants

In this section, we turn our attention to irregular African migrants in Istanbul, who arrive here in the hope of going further west, but often have to live in the city for several years. NGO repre-

---

16 This is quite important considering the fact that in recent months, local Turkish police in some border areas deported a number of Iranians of Bahai conviction and dozens of Iraqi irregular migrants back to their countries in violation of the non-refoulement principle. Many of these people would have applied for asylum, had they been given the chance (UNHCR, 2007b; HCA and AI, 2007).

17 Turkish Foreigners' Police's opinions about the "abusive" claims must be based on the large discrepancy between the number of apprehended illegal migrants from a particular country, and the number who actually apply for asylum.

sentatives and officials we interviewed estimate the number of irregular African migrants in Istanbul to be between 4,000 and 6,000. NGO workers say that this number increases in winter and drops during the summer months, when Africans travel to the Aegean coast to search for clandestine passage to Greece by boat. Since it is difficult to get into Western Europe illegally, and because many people are unable to return to their countries (because of economic reasons or for lack of safety), irregular migrants and rejected asylum seekers often spend several years in Turkey. Thus, the duration of their "transit" becomes prolonged. However, the reverse is also possible. Since the living conditions of many migrants in Istanbul are dismal, some people continue making dangerous attempts to cross into Europe.[18]

Turkey has a relatively liberal visa system for travelers. Citizens of former Soviet republics and Eastern European countries can obtain tourist visas upon entry to Turkey, and some Turkic republics have visa exemptions for 90-day stays. Irregular migrants from those countries overstay their visas or legal duration of stay and find informal or illegal employment in Turkey. If they are caught or when they want to leave Turkey, they have to pay a fine in proportion to the length of their unauthorized stay; however, they are allowed to re-enter Turkey once during the year in which they have overstayed their visa.

In the case of Africans, visa regulations were quite liberal until recently. According to police officers, citizens of many Sub-Saharan countries used to be able to receive 15-day visas for a business meeting, for inquiring about employment by a football club, as well as regular tourist visas upon applying to a Turkish consulate in their country or to one that is authorized in their country. In their opinion, the majority of irregular African migrants (not the asylum seekers) currently residing in Istanbul are such persons who arrived legally and then overstayed the duration of their visas. Our survey also indicates

---

18 As an NGO worker explained to us, if a migrant cannot find housing in the cold months of the winter, he or she might risk harsh weather conditions and pay a human smuggler to be taken to Greece or Italy.

that among non-asylum seeking migrants, most of whom are from West African countries, the main form of entry is legal (see "The Survey Section" 4.2 below).

Compared to Eastern European irregular migrants, African migrants' movements to and from Turkey appear less circular; that is, most of them do not exit and re-enter Turkey over the course of a year. However, there may be an exception to this in the case of traders from West Africa, particularly some Nigerians, Senegalese and Ghanaians, who enter and exit Turkey to carry on their informal suitcase trade. The difference between the patterns of Eastern European irregular migrants' and Africans' movements may stem from several reasons: Africans' objectives are to secure transit on to Western Europe, not employment in Turkey; in addition, Turkey has tightened its visa regime in an effort to curb irregular migration as part of its obligations towards the EU. At the beginning of 2005, the Turkish visa regime for 48 Sub-Saharan African countries was changed. Since then, the applications of persons from those countries need to be approved by the MOI before a Turkish consulate can issue visas (*Zaman*, 2005). Moreover, Turkey cancelled tourist visa exemptions for Kenya and South Africa in 2003 (*Resmi Gazete*, 2003a). Police officers said that since the visa regime change, the number of irregular African migrants who arrive with valid visas and then overstay the duration of their visas has declined.

Overall, the number of irregular African migrants in Turkey is only a fraction of irregular migration from other countries, most notably former Soviet republics and Romania. The number of people apprehended by Turkish police for "illegal entry and exit, illegal stay, and visa and residence permit violations" between 1995 and 2005 gives us an indication, however imperfect, of this. Only about 6 percent (35,101) of the total number of people detained for the mentioned reasons (580,139) were from African countries, including North Africa (**Table 7.7**). When the annual figures of the people detained for illegal migration are examined, one can see that appre-

TABLE 7.7
Breakdown by Country of Origin of Apprehensions for
Illegal Migration (1995-2005)*

	Algeria	2,857	Ghana	401	Rwanda	480
	Belize	6	Guinea	123	Senegal	548
	Benin	6	Kenya	224	Sierra Leone	940
	Botswana	2	Lesotho	1	Somalia	8,512
	Burundi	149	Liberia	211	South Africa	952
African	Cameroon	124	Libya	574	Sudan	735
Countries	C. African					
	Republic	39	Mali	42	Swaziland	18
	Chad	56	Mauritania	6,598	Togo	8
	Djibouti	1	Morocco	4,625	Tunisia	1,789
	Egypt	1,602	Mozambique	3	Zaire	10
	Eritrea	145	Niger	345	Zimbabwe	21
	Ethiopia	477	Nigeria	2,049	West Sahara	4
	Gambia	159	Congo	265		
Total, African Countries						35,101
	Afghanistan	64,922	India	4,044	Poland	929
	Albania	4,424	Iraq	107,712	Romania	21,519
	Azerbaijan	10,618	Iran	24,248	Russia	16,892
					Serbia and	
Selected	Bangladesh	17,389	Kazakhstan	2,445	Montenegro	3,666
Countries	Belarus	1,161	Kyrgyzstan	1,698	Syria	6,906
	Bulgaria	9,846	Latvia	149	Tajikistan	285
	China	3,513	Lithuania	290	Ukraine	17,224
					Unknown	
					Country of	
	Armenia	3,723	Macedonia	1,853	Origin	13,801
	Georgia	16,445	Moldova	51,434		
Total						407,136
Grand Total						580,139

(*) Data provided by the Foreigners' Police. "Grand Total" includes all apprehensions from all countries, including "Selected Countries" and "African Countries."

hensions of some countries' nationals (e.g. Nigeria and South Africa) increased significantly until 2002-2003, but then dropped in the last two years. This may have resulted from the impact of the change in visa regulations for Sub-Saharan countries. But at the same time, detentions of Somalis and Mauritanians increased in the past several years, suggesting an increase in the inflows of people from these countries, which must be related to ongoing political turmoil in those regions.

It is difficult for foreigners to obtain work permits in Turkey, although this procedure was somewhat liberalized in 2003. According to the Law on Work Permits for Foreigners (No. 4817), foreigners can apply for a work permit to the Ministry of Labor and Social Security (MLSS) if they have a job offer from a Turkish employer. After four years of legally working and residing in Turkey, they can apply for an extension of the work permit without having a certain employer hiring them, and after eight years, the work permit can be indefinitely extended (*Resmi Gazete*, 2003b). The law obviously is concerned with legal employment and would in theory apply to those persons who enter Turkey on valid visas and then seek employment. However, given that labor migrants in Turkey can often only find jobs in low-skill and low-wage sectors where informal employment is already prevalent, the law has so far not benefited irregular migrants from African countries, or for that matter, those from Eastern Europe . In any case, African irregular migrants often do not work in the same sectors as, say, Moldovans and people from other former Soviet republics (with the possible exception of Ethiopian women working in domestic labor). As we discuss in the following sections, the kinds of income earning activities to which Africans resort to or have access to are quite different than those for Eastern Europeans and may be quite erratic and not enough to live on.

Another issue is the criminalization of irregular migration. In this regard, interesting issues emerge from data provided by Istanbul Foreigners' Police Bureau pertaining to criminal charges against

Africans in Istanbul. Although this data should be interpreted with caution given that we do not have comparable data for migrants from other countries and we cannot assess the reliability of this information (**Table 7.8**).[19] First, the data confirms that Somalis mostly enter illegally.[20] Secondly, people from North and West African countries are involved in illegal entry/exit and visa violations. Third, arrests under the heading of forgery are high among North Africans (Tunisians, Moroccans, Algerians), Nigerians and Congolese. Forgery, together with fraud, may refer to apprehensions for carrying falsified travel documents, but could also suggest arrests for supplying transit migrants with forged visas and passports. This would mean that some African nationals are involved in the "illegal migration industry" in Turkey. On the other hand, only four African persons (one Sudanese, Egyptian, Somali, and Tunisian) had been arrested for "human smuggling" since 2001. Our Somali interviewees reported having paid several hundred up to a thousand dollars at each stage of clandestine passage from Africa into Turkey. But in general, interviewees did not provide information about the particulars of their illegal entry into Turkey. Also, respondents to the survey did not answer the questions on whether and how much they paid human smugglers for getting passage into Turkey.

What does the data on criminal offenses by Africans suggest? Irregular migration inevitably leads people into legal gray zones, precisely because their entry into the territory of another country is criminalized by definition and the legal scope of their activities within that territory are severely restricted.[21] Therefore, African migrants' very presence in Turkey, as well as various strategies they employ to acquire cash to live on or in order to travel to Europe, may lead to their involvement with criminal activities.

---

19 Although our report is concentrated on Sub-Saharan Africa, the police data also includes information on North Africans.

20 However, this data might be misleading because officials we interviewed said that sometimes Africans from other countries falsely claim to be Somalis hoping to apply for asylum later on.

21 For a parallel argument regarding human trafficking, see Munck (2005).

TABLE 7.8
Africans Apprehended for Selected Criminal Offenses*

Country of Origin	Visa Violations	Illegal Entry/exit	Forgery	Smuggling	Froud
Africa	0	22	1	0	0
Burundi	0	4	1	0	0
Algeria	35	43	54	0	1
Eritrea	0	4	7	0	0
Ethiopia	1	47	2	0	0
Morocco	49	66	93	0	6
Gambia	10	6	1	0	0
Ghana	15	51	10	0	0
So. Africa	1	6	14	0	0
Cameroon	2	1	6	0	2
Kenya	9	4	15	0	0
Congo	6	10	28	0	0
Liberia	0	5	1	0	4
Libya	1	1	8	0	0
Egypt	12	187	18	1	0
Mauritania	0	180	6	0	0
Nigeria	89	84	53	0	24
Rwanda	0	16	0	0	0
Senegal	22	50	11	0	5
Sierra Leone	0	37	10	0	0
Somalia	1	637	15	1	7
Sudan	6	27	3	1	0
Tanzania	6	27	8	0	0
Tunisia	31	21	100	1	2
Total	301	1543	473	4	53

(*) Data provided by the Foreigners' Police.

If an irregular migrant is apprehended for crimes, he or she would be deported; however, if he or she is in legal status, the person would be deported after imprisonment (if he or she is convicted and sentenced for a particular crime). However, as we discussed in the previous section, deportation is not effectively implemented. Until recently, a person would be taken to a border and expected to leave the country. In the past couple of years, Turkey has started to pay for the travel expenses of foreigners who are deported because of undocumented status. In an incident on July 7, 2001, between 250 and 300 people, citizens of 11 African countries, were picked up by police in several neighborhoods of Istanbul, detained for several days and dumped at the border with Greece in İpsala, Edirne. For several days, the group, which included two people with UNHCR protection, was tossed between Greek authorities who refused entry, and Turkish authorities who did not allow them to return. Eventually, they were allowed to come back to Istanbul, but in the meantime, three people reportedly died, one woman had a miscarriage and several women claimed to have been raped (HRA, 2001; UNHCR, 2001). During this incident, which took place a few months before the Readmission Protocol between Turkey and Greece was signed in November 2001, both sides claimed that the persons had first passed through the other's territory. This incident also highlighted the particular vulnerability of Africans to police harassment. Their physical distinctiveness and visibility in Istanbul allowed the police to round them up indiscriminately. Turkey reportedly continues to deport irregular Africans, but UNHCR officials said an en-masse deportation effort on the scale of the 2001 incident has not recurred.

Based on the discussion in this section, it may be argued that irregular African migrants' presence in Istanbul is relatively "tolerated" by the Foreigners' Police, but they may be at greater risk of police harassment or deportation compared to other groups because of their physical distinctiveness. Two incidents that occurred relatively recently highlighted Africans' particular vulnerability and raised concerns about deliberate police ill-treatment toward them. In an incident in Istanbul in December 2006, several African asylum seekers who were in detention were forced by police officers to work in the removal of roadblocks used for security during Pope Benedict's visit earlier that day. The asylum seekers complained of police mistreatment to the Refugee Support Program of the Helsinki Citizens' Assembly (HCA)

– Turkey (Akşam, 2006). In another incident in August 2007, a Nigerian man was detained by police in Istanbul's Beyoğlu police station and was killed there by a gunshot. The police claimed that the man was taken inside the station on suspicion of drug possession and that he was accidentally killed when he tried to resist a police officer. According to news reports, the man had previously been in police custody for six months and had been released a month before he was killed, upon declaring his intension to apply for asylum (*Radikal*, 2007a).[22] The Beyoğlu police station had been in the news in 2007 for several incidents in which police officers who work there were accused of mistreatment and physical abuse of innocent passersby including a transvestite street vendor, a taxi driver and a lawyer (*ibid.*). The evidence from the two incidents involving police and African migrants is not enough to conclude that the police systematically target Africans for ill-treatment since human rights violations in the hands of police is a broader problem in Turkey. However, migrants also claim that police harassment of Africans is regular in Beyoğlu (a district where many Africans live), and that the killing of a Nigerian was just the tip of the iceberg that urged them to hold a public protest against the police on August 31 (*Radikal*, 2007b). What these two cases show is that physical distinctiveness and lack of legal status in Turkey make African migrants and (potential and actual) asylum seekers more vulnerable to human rights abuses. In this light, UNHCR officers' emphasis on the urgency for training not only the Foreigners' Police, but also other units within the General Directorate of Security on the rights of asylum seekers (and more generally on human rights) is quite important.

Humanitarian and Social Aid

NGOs, police and the UNHCR are unanimous in saying that in terms of social and humanitarian aid, African asylum seekers are

---

22 The UNHCR Office in Ankara asked the Ministry of Foreign Affairs for an explanation regarding the killing of this Nigerian man (CNN Türk.com, 2007).

worse off than other groups. This is related to the fact that they lack strong social networks in Turkey, they are denied access to Turkish institutions and aid provided by NGOs or others is meager.

The conditions of asylum seekers' stay in Turkey is defined in the relevant government regulations (particularly, *Resmi Gazete*, 1994). Asylum seekers and refugees do not have work permits. Groups who enter Turkish borders and seek refuge en masse are supposed to undergo periodic health checks and receive medical care in state hospitals. However, the government regulations do not address the health care needs of individual asylum applicants. There is a vague mention of refugee children's eligibility for primary education in one of the government regulations (*Resmi Gazete*, 1994), but this is not implemented in practice. In general, asylum seekers and refugees do not have access to education for their children in Turkish schools. In Istanbul, Caritas, a Catholic aid organization, runs a school program for Iraqi Christian asylum seekers' children. ICMC also has had a small program for the education of non-European migrants and asylum seeker children in recent years, but attendance by African migrants' children appears to be low based on the information ICMC provides on its web site (ICMC, not dated).

Recognized refugees are eligible to receive health care paid for by the UNHCR. Registered asylum seekers can receive medical care only in case of emergencies in a couple of designated hospitals in Istanbul to be paid for by the UNHCR. In Istanbul, ICMC is the contact point for arranging these services for asylum applicants. Tuberculosis patients can receive free medication at government-run TB clinics (*Veremle Savaş Dispanserleri*), but at least in one prior case in which a Congolese man had a treatment-resistant variant of TB, his need for expensive medication was rejected by government-run hospitals. ICMC also provides psychological counseling to asylum seekers when they first apply for registration.

When a person files for asylum for the first time, UNHCR provides a one-time cash assistance. Recognized refugees receive a small monthly payment from UNHCR (about 100 USD per person). Other than this, cash assistance to asylum seekers and refugees is virtually non-existent.

The Istanbul Interparish Migrants' Programme (IIMP) provides emergency healthcare, food, clothing, blankets and small travel allowances for both economic migrants and asylum seekers, and it has recently started a voluntary repatriation program. IIMP workers say that their major clients are Africans. However, since their budget, which several churches in Istanbul contributed to, is very small, they can only help vulnerable groups. Therefore, they prioritize women and children. Other than the IIMP, individual churches also have small programs. For instance, a Greek Orthodox Church provides free lunch on Saturdays to economic migrants and asylum seekers. The Dutch Union Church runs a weekly program for mothers and children. At the time we conducted our fieldwork, an NGO, the Refugee Legal Aid Program (RLAP), assisted asylum seekers with writing their applications and appeal letters to UNHCR. Since then, RLAP has been turned into the Refugee Support Program of the Helsinki Citizens' Assembly (HCA) – Turkey.[23]

There is almost no Turkish social aid or charity for which asylum seekers are eligible. Our survey and interviews show that they take advantage of the free dinners provided by the Istanbul Metropolitan Municipality during the month of Ramadan, and those who have residence permits for asylum seekers are eligible to receive food donations given by district municipalities during Ramadan. In interviews, some people also reported receiving food and clothing donations by Turkish citizens, but there is no organized manner in which this is done. However, it should be mentioned that, under the amended regulation (*Resmi Gazete*, 2006), persons who have been granted refugee status are entitled to some social aid and services through government agencies.

---

23 However, we will use the abbreviation RLAP, since it used that name when we conducted the fieldwork.

By NGOs' own admission, social aid and services available to Africans are extremely limited and far from meeting the demand. Because of the limited amount of resources and donations, the IIMP, for instance, prioritizes "vulnerable" groups as the target of food aid, cash assistance and medical aid. In line with international humanitarian practice, women with children and men and women in need of emergency medical assistance are defined as "vulnerable." As we argued in the section "Refugee Flows and Asylum Seeking" above, defining vulnerability for purposes of humanitarian policy automatically excludes some people at the same time that it includes others (Sorensen, forthcoming). Indeed, as some aid workers acknowledged, while there is no doubt about the vulnerability of a Somali woman with many children, a single male asylum seeker could be equally vulnerable under certain circumstances. In fact, "aid for migrants" excludes the majority of migrants for two reasons: the majority of asylum seekers and migrants are males, and furthermore, the majority of all "migrants" are irregular migrants, not asylum seekers. Hence, the practice of prioritizing vulnerable groups for assistance has a built-in bias against males and non-asylum seekers.

Overall, we may argue that social aid and services for African migrants and asylum seekers in Istanbul operate as a charity flowing mostly from Europeans to people from poor countries, whereas Turkish civil society and Turkish government agencies are not sufficiently involved.

Social Networks

African asylum seekers also lack resourceful social networks that could provide them with any kind of help. This contrasts with the situation of Iranian and Iraqi asylum seekers and refugees in Turkey. Especially Iranians (Muslims and Bahais alike), because of their history of asylum seeking since the early 1980s, have communities in Turkey and in Europe. Iraqi Chaldeans are also reportedly a more resourceful group in term of their social networks as well as in terms of the availability of faith-based humanitarian and social aid through Caritas's office in Istanbul. In addition, NGO workers point out that Iranians and Iraqis are financially much better off here compared to Somalis, Sudanese and Ethiopians. It should further be mentioned that Somalis often do not have any ties to home – another point of contrast with Iraqis and Iranians.

The lack of social and humanitarian aid and the dearth of social networks may make African asylum seekers especially vulnerable to hunger and disease, and also to abuse. A recently published journalistic account of the experiences of two Somali and Ethiopian asylum seekers in Istanbul tells about how an evangelical proselytizing church in Kadıköy provided help to these (and apparently other) refugee women in return for conversion and church attendance (Ekberzade, 2006). The relationship between proselytizing churches and foreign migrants would constitute a fruitful area to expand on in future studies of migration and asylum seeking in Turkey.

The situation of African irregular economic migrants is somewhat different than the asylum seekers. West Africans, such as Ghanaians and Nigerians, appear to have stronger social networks in Istanbul, as well as networks spanning Istanbul and their countries. One nexus of such social networks is church. Some of the Ghanaians and Nigerians we interviewed said they regularly attended church here. Two of the churches we visited were evangelical churches headquartered in North America, whose branches in Istanbul served foreigners and Turkish nationals. Africans attended the English-language service; therefore most of the attendees were other West Africans. Another nexus of social networks is football. Nigerians have been at the forefront of organizing an "African Cup" in Istanbul; an event that brings together the nationals of various African countries. We have observed that there is an overlap between people who attend church services and who go to football games, suggesting that there is not much differentiation in the social networks of West Africans.

The West Africans we interviewed and those who responded to the survey have active ties to their families back at home. Some reported that their families send them money. Furthermore, some Nigerians and Ghanaians also have business ties to home in the form of informal importation of goods and exportation of Turkish apparel products. Sixty-four percent of the respondents who answered our survey, mostly West Africans, reported having contact with their families in their countries through telephone and e-mail. This contrasts with asylum seekers from East and Central Africa and Mauritania who mostly reported having no or little contact with relatives. In response to the question about why they did not have contact, especially Somalis said that they had no family left behind.

It must be conceded that we might have been able to observe only the positive aspects of Africans' social networks during our research, although participation in a certain social group can also have negative consequences for a person. Particularly women may become vulnerable to personal harm through exposure to individuals or groups engaged in criminal behavior. We were told by several NGO workers that there have been incidents in which African women were sexually exploited by human smugglers or other migrants. In a similar vein, Ekberzade's book (2006) tells about the vulnerability of a Somali asylum seeker woman in the face of money offers in exchange for sexual favors by irregular migrants from another African country. An NGO volunteer worker told us the particulars of one Ethiopian and one Eritrean female asylum seeker's experiences in Istanbul. Both of these women were obliged to offer sexual favors to their housemates from two West African countries, and they were both impregnated by these men. What needs to be emphasized here is that it is extremely difficult for an asylum seeker or irregular migrant to file complaints against such abusers. NGOs that provide aid for asylum seekers and migrants are the only places where they can complain about such incidents and ask for help.

The Survey

The respondents to the survey[24] were from 11 different nationalities, Somalis (53) and Nigerians (21) being the largest groups.[25] The other respondents were from Ghana, Democratic Republic of Congo, Mauritania, Eritrea, Ethiopia, Kenya, Burundi, Sudan, and Djibouti.[26] Seventy-eight were men and 55 were women. Somalis contained the largest group of women (30) (**Table 7.9**). The breakdown of age groups among the respondents were as follows: 41 people were between 25 and 30, 36 were between 19 and 24, and 33 were between 31 and 40. There were 10 people below the age of 19, and 11 people above 40. The majority of the respondents were single (48 men and 27 women). Half of the female respondents (27) were married, divorced or widowed (**Table 7.10**). The educational level of the men was much higher than the women. About 42 percent of the women were illiterate and about 9 percent were merely literate. In contrast, about 29 percent of men had high school degrees, and about 13 percent had higher education. Among women, the majority of whom were Somalis, there were many widows and the level of education was low (**Table 7.11**).

We asked the survey respondents how they/their families made a living in their country. We found that 31.6 percent said their parents were small business owners, 21.8 percent said they were workers, 18.8 percent said they were government employees, 13.5 percent said they were farmers, 6 percent said they were merchants and 2.3 percent reported having no income. Among the 6 percent who marked "other," several indicated that their parents were killed. Although we did not ask about rural/urban backgrounds, the answers to this ques-

---

24 The variations in the number of "total" answers to each question in the tables in this sub-section stem from the fact that some questions were left unanswered by some of the respondents.

25 We also asked respondents to ethnically identify themselves. Among the Somalis, persons belonging to the Ashraaf, Reer-Hamaar and Jareer clans were predominant. Among the Nigerians, Ibos and Yorubas constituted the majority. Among Ethiopians, Oromos and Tigres were significant. Mauritanians and Sudanese in our sample were mostly "blacks."

26 The responses by six Sudanese and two Djiboutian respondents are shown under the title of "other" under "country of origin."

TABLE 7.9
Gender Breakdown of Respondents According to Country of Origin

	Somalia	Nigeria	Ghana	D.R. Congo	Mauri-tania	Eritrea	Ethiopia	Kenya	Bu-rundi	Otler	Total
Male	24	16	6	5	6	2	3	3	6	7	78
Female	30	5	0	5	1	5	6	2	0	1	55
Total	54	21	6	10	7	7	9	5	6	8	133

TABLE 7.10
Marital Status of Respondents According to Gender

	Single	Married	Divorced	Widowed	Total
Male	48	25	1	1	75
Female	27	10	3	14	54
Total	75	35	4	15	129

TABLE 7.11
Gender Breakdown of Education

	Illiterate	Able to read and write	Elementary school	Middle school	High school	University	Total
Male	10	3	12	19	22	10	76
	13.2%	3.9%	15.8%	25.0%	28.9%	13.2%	100%
Female	23	5	12	5	6	4	55
	41.8%	9.1%	21.8%	9.1%	10.9%	7.3%	100%
Total	33	8	24	24	28	14	131
	25.2%	6.1%	18.3%	18.3%	21.4%	10.7%	100%

tion may suggest that the majority of the migrants must have come from cities. We also asked what the respondent's own occupation prior to migration was. Of them, 24.8 percent said they were students, 18.8 percent said they had small businesses, 14.3 percent said they were athletes or football players, 10.5 percent said they were workers, 9 percent said they were farmers and 6 percent reported themselves as merchants. The high ratio of those who marked "other" (15.8 percent) stemmed from women's answers as having no job. Nevertheless, there were also women who reported being traders.

Migration Process

West African respondents mostly cited economic difficulties as the reason why they left their countries, whereas Somalis predominantly cited threats against their security[27] (**Table 7.12**). A full 64.3 percent and 77.8 percent of Nigerians and Ghanaians respectively cited economic difficulties as their reason for migrating, while 66.7 percent of Somalis said an attack against their family prompted their decision to leave. A further 30 percent cited other threats and increasing violence. Another 27.3 percent of D.R. Congolese marked increasing economic difficulties as the cause of their decision to leave the country, and 63.7 percent of them cited violence and security threats. Except 14.3 percent of Mauritanians who said they left the country because of economic difficulties, the rest of them cited threats and attacks against their family. Ethiopians cited both economic reasons (57.1 percent) and security threats (42.9 percent) as the causes of their migration, whereas Eritreans only marked security related options to this question. Sudanese and Djiboutians ("other" in the nationalities) also mostly marked economic difficulties. The mixed responses to this question by members of many nationalities can be interpreted as supporting our argument in this report that asylum seeking and economically motivated irregular migration are intertwined. However, it should be kept in mind that, most often, generalized violence and economic collapse are also correlated. As we discussed in the section "Refugees Flows and Asylum Seeking", the current legal definition of refugees and asylum seekers does not match the extant conditions in refugee-sending areas where armed conflict, poverty and human rights violations are entangled (Hyndman, 2000).

Among the respondents, 34 percent entered Turkey on valid visas and passports and 66 percent entered illegally. Almost all Nigerians, D.R. Congolese and Kenyans had entered legally, whereas almost all Somalis, Mauritanians, Eritreans, Ethiopians entered illegally (**Table 7.13**). Of Somali respondents, 44 said they traveled to

---

27 More than one option could be marked in response to this question.

TABLE 7.12
"Why Did You Decide to Leave Your Country?"

	Threat Against My/My Family's Security	An Attack Against Me/My Family	Increasing Violence Where I Lived	Persecution/ Threat of Persecution Against Me/My Family	Increasing economic Difficulties	Other
Somalia	13.3%	66.7%	10.0%	6.7%	3.3%	
Nigeria		3.6%	7.1%	7.1%	64.3%	17.9%
Ghana			22.2%		77.8%	
D.R. Congo		9.1%	36.4%	18.2%	27.3%	9.1%
Mauritania	57.1%	28.6%			14.3%	
Eritrea	33.3%	33.3%		33.3%		
Ethiopia	28.6%	14.3%			57.1%	
Kenya			25.0%		75.0%	
Burundi	50.0%	50.0%				
Other				25.0%	75.0%	
Total	12.8%	26.6%	11.0%	7.3%	36.7%	5.5%

Turkey by boat, three on foot and five reported having come on foot and by boat. Only one Somali flew into Turkey. All 21 Nigerians arrived in Turkey by airplane, as did all nine D.R. Congolese and five Kenyans. Mauritanians mostly came by boat, and Ethiopians traveled on foot through the land border (**Table 7.14**).

Nearly half of the Somalis could not remember through what border they entered Turkey; but those who reported a place cited Istanbul, İzmir, Hatay, Van, the land border with Greece (Edirne), and the Iraqi border as their points of entry. All Nigerians, D.R. Congolese, Kenyans and Burundians entered the country through Istanbul's airport. Most of the Eritreans and Ethiopians entered through Syria into the Hatay province (**Table 7.15**).

The reasons why the respondents chose to come to Turkey demonstrates a stark fact: many human smugglers promised illegal migrants that they would take them to a European Union country, and

TABLE 7.13
Legal Status in Turkey by Country of Origin

Country of origin	Legal entry	Illegal entry	Total
Somalia	1	52	53
	2%	98%	1
Nigeria	20	1	21
	95%	5%	1
Ghana	4	2	6
	67%	33%	1
D.R. Congo	9	0	9
	100%	0%	1
Mauritania	0	7	7
	0%	100%	1
Eritrea	1	6	7
	14%	86%	1
Ethiopia	1	8	9
	11%	89%	1
Kenya	5	0	5
	100%	0%	1
Burundi	2	4	6
	33%	67%	1
Other	2	6	8
	25%	75%	1
Total	45	86	131
	34%	66%	1

then abandon them off the coasts of Turkey. In response to the question "Why did you come to Turkey and not some other country?"[28] 40.8 percent of the respondents marked, "I was deceived that I would be taken to Greece but was left in Turkey" (**Table 7.16**).[29] Of Somali

---

28 Respondents could mark more than one option in answering this question.

29 We were told by officials at both the Foreigners' Police Bureau in Istanbul and the UNHCR office that on several occasions African asylum seekers testified that the Greek coast guard steered their boats away from the Greek coast into Turkish territorial waters. Although these officials said that it is not possible to verify such claims, news and video footage showing Greek authorities leaving illegal migrants in Turkish territorial waters in the Aegean have recently appeared in the Turkish media (e.g. *Radikal*, 2006a and 2006b).

TABLE 7.14
Method of Entry Into Turkey by Country of Origin

	Somalia	Nigeria	Ghana	D.R. Congo	Mauritania	Eritrea	Ethiopia	Kenya	Burundi	Other	Total
Airplane	1	21	4	9	0	1	1	5	2	2	46
	2.17%	45.65%	8.70%	19.57%	0 %	2.17%	2.17%	10.87%	4.35%	4.35%	100%
By boat	44	0	0	0	6	3	2	0	1	2	58
	75.86%	0 %	0 %	0 %	10.34%	5.17%	3.45%	0 %	1.72%	3.45%	100%
On foot	3	0	2	0	1	1	6	0	0	3	16
	18.75%	0 %	12.50%	0 %	6.25%	6.25%	37.50%	0 %	0 %	18.75%	100%
On foot and by boat	5	0	0	0	0	2	0	0	3	0	10
	50.00%	0 %	0 %	0 %	0 %	20.00%	0 %	0 %	30.00%	0 %	100%
Total	53	21	6	9	7	7	9	5	6	7	130
Total Percentage	40.77%	16.15%	4.62%	6.92%	5.38%	5.38%	6.92%	3.85%	4.62%	5.38%	100%

TABLE 7.15
Province or Border of Entry Into Turkey

Country of Origin	Istanbul	İzmir	Hatay/ Syria	Don't Remember	Greece	Van & Iraq	Total
Somalia	9	2	2	20	7	2	42
Nigeria	16	0	0	0	0	0	16
Ghana	4	0	2	0	0	0	6
D.R. Congo	5	0	0	0	0	0	5
Mauritania	3	2	0	1	0	0	6
Eritrea	1	0	3	0	0	1	5
Ethiopia	1	0	6	1	0	0	8
Kenya	3	0	0	0	0	0	3
Burundi	3	0	0	1	0	0	4
Other	2	1	3	0	0	0	6
Total	47	5	16	23	7	3	101

respondents, 79.6 percent marked this answer, as well as 77.8 percent of Mauritanians and 57.1 percent of Eritreans. Another 31.3 percent of the respondents said they came to Turkey because they had friends here. Half or more of the Nigerians, Ghanaians, D.R. Congolese, Ethiopians, Kenyans and Burundians marked this option. A total of 11.6 percent of the respondents expressed the opinion that it was easy to enter Turkey legally or illegally, and easy to move on to Europe via Turkey. A couple of Nigerians said they came to Turkey to find jobs as football players.[30] Although no Ghanaians marked this option in the survey, our interview with one Ghanaian man indicates that finding employment in a Turkish football team was what motivated him to travel to Turkey. Another 8.8 percent said they came to Turkey for

---

30 Several Burundians marked "to play football professionally" in their answers. This unlikely answer may be due to their misunderstanding of the question. After they arrived in Turkey and applied for asylum, they may have thought that playing football was a possibility, rather than having based their migration decision on this. Indeed, our interview with a young Sierra Leonean man gives a similar impression. Having entered Turkey illegally and then having applied for asylum, this 20 year-old man said the only thing he could do for a living was to play football.

TABLE 7.16
"Why Did You Come to Turkey and Not Some Other Country?"

Country of origin	I had friends who had come to Turkey	I had relatives who had come to Turkey	Turkey's borders are easy to enter	It is easy to get a visa to Turkey	I heard I could appl to the UNHCR in Turkey	It is easy to enter Europe via Turkey	It is easy/ cheap to get an illegal visa/ passaport in Turkey	To play football profes- sionally	I was decived that I would be taken to Greece but left in Turkey	Other
Somalia	3.7%	1.9%				3.7%			79.6%	11.1%
Nigeria	53.6%	3.6%	3.6%	7.1%		10.7%		3.6%	3.6%	14.3%
Ghana	62.5%			12.5%		25.0%				
D.R. Congo	53.8%	23.1%		7.7%		7.7%				7.7%
Mauritania				11.1%	11.1%				77.8%	
Eritrea	28.6%	14.3%							57.1%	
Ethiopia	77.8%					11.1%	11.1%			
Kenya	50.0%	16.7%							16.7%	16.7%
Burundi	50.0%				16.7%			16.7%		16.7%
Other	28.6%					14.3%			57.1%	
Total	31.3%	4.8%	0.7%	3.4%	1.4%	6.8%	0.7%	1.4%	40.8%	8.8%

"other" reasons and their explanations included various economic factors as well as hopes to pursue higher education in Turkey.

The duration of stay in Turkey exhibited some variation across different nationalities. Twenty-eight people had arrived in Istanbul during the preceding three months before they answered the questionnaire. Fifty-five had been here for three months up to one year, 29 had been staying in Turkey for one year to three years and 17 had been here for more than three years. Nearly 80 percent of the Somalis have been here for up to one year, whereas the majority of Nigerians and Ghanaians have lived in Istanbul for more than a year (**Table 7.17**). This pattern is in line with our observation that West African migrants have been here for some time as irregular economic migrants, whereas the inflow of Somali asylum seekers is ongoing.

An indicator of irregular migration was the duration of expiry of visas. We asked those respondents who entered Turkey legally but who were now in irregular condition when their visas expired (**Table 7.18**). Of those who answered this question, 35.5 percent said it has been 1 to 3 years since their Turkish visa expired. Another 25.8 percent said it has been 3 months to one year, while 22.6 percent of the respondents' visas had expired more than 3 years ago. Almost half of those who overstayed their visas were Nigerians. Next were Ghanaians and D.R. Congolese.

Respondents did not have a clear idea about how much longer they would stay in Turkey. A full 64.7 percent said they had no plan about when to leave, 19.3 percent said they would stay until they attained their goals, 9.2 percent said they would remain here until they found a chance for clandestine passage to Europe and 6.7 percent said they were waiting for UNHCR's decision on their application. In response to the question "What would you do if you fail to cross the border into Europe?" 35.2 percent of the respondents said they would somehow continue to stay in Turkey, 22.5 percent expressed the intention to go back to their countries and 24 percent had no idea.

TABLE 7.17
Duration of Stay in Turkey

Country of origin	0-10 Days	11 days 90 days	3 months- 12 months	1 year- 3 years	More than 3 years	Total
Somalia	7	7	27	11	1	53
Nigeria	0	4	4	7	6	21
Ghana	0	0	1	3	2	6
D.R. Congo	0	1	2	4	2	9
Mauritania	0	1	6	0	0	7
Eritrea	0	1	4	2	0	7
Ethiopia	0	1	3	1	4	9
Kenya	0	0	4	0	0	4
Burundi	0	5	1	0	0	6
Other	0	1	3	1	2	7
Total	7	21	55	29	17	129

TABLE 7.18
"When Did Your Visa Expire?"

Country of origin	0-90 days ago	3-12 months ago	1-3 years ago	More than 3 years ago	Total
Nigeria	3	3	6	3	15
Ghana	0	0	1	3	4
D.R. Congo	0	3	2	0	5
Mauritania	1	0	0	0	1
Eritrea	0	1	0	0	1
Ethiopia	0	1	1	0	2
Kenya	1	0	0	0	1
Burundi	0	0	1	1	2
Other	5	8	11	7	31
Total Percentage	16.1%	25.8%	35.5%	22.6%	100%

Those who entered Turkey legally said they would leave Turkey by air travel, whereas those who entered illegally said they would seek to find passage through Turkey's land borders (68.2 percent) or wait for UNHCR resettlement (18.8 percent) and 11.8 percent said they would not leave Turkey (**Table 7.19**).

TABLE 7.19
"How do You Plan to Leave Turkey?"

Form of entry into Turkey	Air travel	Through the land border	Refugee resettlement by UNHCR	Won't leave Turkey	Total
Legal	45	0	0	0	45
Illegal	1	58	16	10	85
Total	46	58	16	10	130

The responses to the question "What country do you want to go to from Turkey?" demonstrates that many African migrants hope to reach Western Europe through Turkey, but that some of them have other plans such as going back or staying in Turkey. Twenty-three people specified Greece and 22 specified Western Europe (45.9 percent of all responses) to this open-ended question. While 21.4 percent (21 persons) said they wanted to stay in Turkey, 11.2 percent (11 persons) expressed a wish to go back to their country (**Table 7.20**). The breakdown of the responses according to nationalities shows some interesting patterns. A total of 70.5 percent of Nigerians said they wanted to go to Western Europe or Greece and 23.5 percent said they planned to go back home. Likewise, 80 percent of Ghanaians expressed a wish to go to Western Europe or Greece, and 20 percent wanted to return home. Somalis were most confused about this question: around 30 percent said they did not know, and about 38 percent said they would not leave Turkey, almost 19 percent answered Western Europe or Greece, 5.4 percent said they would wait for UNHCR's decision on their application, and another 5.4 percent wanted to return home.

Of the respondents, 63 said they had made asylum applications and 64 had not. 43 Somalis had made applications, whereas nine had not, which might be due to the fact that they had just arrived in the country. Less than half of all of the D.R. Congolese, Mauritanians, Eritreans and Ethiopians had asylum applications, as opposed to all Burundians (**Table 7.21**). This may be an indication that irregular

TABLE 7.20
"To What Country do You Want to Go?"

Country of origin	Don't know	I won't leave	Greece	Western Europe	Other	I'll wait for UNHCR Decision	Back to my Country	Total
Somalia	11	14	6	1	1	2	2	37
Nigeria	0	0	3	9	1	0	4	17
Ghana	0	0	2	2	0	0	1	5
D.R. Congo	2	1	2	3	0	0	1	9
Mauritania	1	3	0	2	0	0	0	6
Eritrea	1	2	2	0	0	0	0	5
Ethiopia	0	0	4	1	1	0	1	7
Kenya	0	0	0	2	0	0	1	3
Burundi	1	0	0	2	0	0	0	3
Other	0	1	4	0	0	0	1	6
Total	16	21	23	22	3	2	11	98

TABLE 7.21
Asylum Applications by Country of Origin

Country of origin	Asylum Application		Total
	No	Yes	
Somalia	9	43	52
Nigeria	19	0	19
Ghana	6	0	6
D.R. Congo	6	2	8
Mauritania	4	3	7
Eritrea	4	3	7
Ethiopia	6	3	9
Kenya	4	1	5
Burundi	0	6	6
Other	6	2	8
Total	64	63	127

migration and asylum seeking are intertwined for those countries' nationals, but it also may reflect the fact that not all regions or ethnic/religious groups in a country are affected by civil war or persecution (e.g. Eritrea, Ethiopia and Mauritania).

There was a link between the reasons for migrating or leaving one's country and whether one has made an asylum application. Of those who applied for asylum in Turkey, 35 people said they left their country because of a security threat, a persecution threat, an attack against them or because of violence, whereas 15 people who cited similar reasons for migrating did not. 35 people who cited economic difficulties or other reasons for why they decided to migrate had not made asylum applications (**Table 7.22**).

Life in Istanbul: Social Interactions

In this section, we examine African migrants' life experiences in Istanbul in terms of their interactions with each other and with Turkish citizens and authorities.

The majority of the respondents to the survey lived in the derelict neighborhoods of the Beyoğlu District (Tarlabaşı and Dolapdere) (38.2 percent) and in the neighborhoods of Kumkapı and Aksaray (48.1 percent), which are attraction points for irregular migrants from various regions. There were others who lived in the Şişli district and other neighborhoods. African migrants mostly live with their compatriots in Istanbul. Of the respondents, 42.4 percent said they shared apartments or rental rooms with others from their country, 16.2 percent lived with their co-ethnics and 19.2 percent lived with their co-religionists (some respondents gave multiple answers, therefore these percentages overlap). A reported 12.2 percent lived with their family members. Only 5.2 percent lived with Africans from other countries and 2.2 percent lived with non-African migrants (**Table 7.23**).

Another indicator of in-group social interactions is church-going. In our sample, 73 people described themselves as Muslims and 55 persons as Christians. Among the Christians, 61.5 percent said they went to church in Istanbul, and among Muslims, 40.3 percent said they went to mosque. Among the church-goers, 46.9 percent said their church was frequented by other Africans, 18.8 percent said the regu-

TABLE 7.22

Reason of Migration and its Relation to Asylum Applications

	Asylum Application		
Reasons of Migration	No	Yes	Total
A Threat against Me/My Family's Security	5	8	13
An Attack against Me/My Family	6	19	25
Increasing Violence Where I Lived	2	4	6
Persecution/Threat of Persecution against My Family/Me	2	4	6
Increasing Economic Difficulties	33	0	33
Other Reasons	2	0	2
Total	50	35	85

TABLE 7.23

Your Relationship to the People You Live With

Relationship	Percent
None	0.9
My family members	12.2
People from the same country	42.4
People from the same ethnic group	16.2
People from the same religious group	19.2
Africans from another country	5.2
Non-African migrants	2.2
Turkish citizens	0.4
Other	1.3
Total	100.0

lar attendees consisted of non-African foreigners and 25 percent said the regular attendees consisted of Turkish citizens (**Table 7.24**). Indeed, two evangelical churches that we attended had a mixed West African following. These churches had Turkish language mass at a different time on Sundays, suggesting that some Africans might attend the services where Turks are present. Among the mosque-going Muslim migrants, all said that the worshippers were Turks. Attending Christian worship services fosters a West African community, whereas attending mosque may possibly foster greater interaction between

TABLE 7.24
"Who are the Other Worshippers in the Church/Mosque Where
You Attend Worshipping Services?"

	Religion			
	Muslim	Christian	Other	Total
People from my country			100.0%	2.0%
Other Africans		46.9%		29.4%
Foreigners who are not Africans		18.8%		11.8%
Turkish citizens	100.0%	25.0%		51.0%
All of them		9.4%		5.9%

Muslim migrants and Turkish citizens. However, we cannot make a generalization since not all Muslims (mostly Somalis in our sample) and only men pray in the mosque.

Although social interactions among Africans across different nationalities is not very high, respondents' opinions about their relations with other Africans was overall positive. Whereas 36.5 percent said they had no problems with other Africans and 38.8 percent said they had good relations, only 1.2 percent said their relations were bad. While 5.9 percent had no opinion yet because of recent arrival, 15.3 said they had no relations with other Africans (**Table 7.25**).

In parallel fashion, respondents' opinions of their relationship with Turkish citizens were not negative overall. Of them, 35.6 percent said they had no problem with Turks, 28.8 percent said they had good relations, whereas only 4.8 percent said their relationship to Turks was bad. Another 26 percent reported having no relationship with Turkish citizens, which may be partly because of having very recently arrived in Istanbul (**Table 7.26**).

A related question in the survey was on the greatest problems that African migrants face in Istanbul. "Discrimination" was cited as a problem in only 4.7 percent of the responses and "ill treatment by neighbors" was cited by only 0.4 percent (see **Table 7.32**). However, the low report of "discrimination" might be misleading because of the

TABLE 7.25
"How are Your Relations With Africans in Istanbul?"

	No. of persons	Percent
No Relation	13	15.3
Not Bad / No Problem	31	36.5
Very Good	33	38.8
Bad	1	1.2
Don't Know Yet	5	5.9
Total	85	100

TABLE 7.26
"How are Your Relations With Turkish Citizens?"

	No. of persons	Percent
No Relation	27	26.0
Not Bad / No Problem	37	35.6
Very Good	30	28.8
Bad	5	4.8
Don't Know Yet	5	4.8
Total	104	100.0

abstract conceptual wording of this option in the question. During the interviews, people's perceptions about others' treatment toward them became apparent in their accounts of personal experiences and anecdotes, rather than through abstract concepts such as "discrimination." Perhaps confirming this observation, 29.5 of the respondents mentioned "ill treatment by strangers" as a problem, although they did not mention discrimination (see **Table 7.32** below).

One of the reasons why respondents did not have much interaction with Africans from other nationalities, let alone Turkish citizens, may have to do with language barriers. Only 26.5 percent spoke English, 13 percent spoke Arabic and 11.4 percent spoke French. We found that 47 percent spoke various native languages.[31] Regarding the

---

31 More than one option could be ticked for this answer. Our survey was conducted with the help of two assistants speaking English, Arabic and Somali and another one who spoke French and English.

weakness of their interactions with Turkish citizens, African migrants' weak Turkish language skills might be a hindrance. Only 13 people rated their knowledge of Turkish to be "quite well," 18 said they knew some Turkish, 41 knew very little Turkish and 55 did not speak Turkish at all. The great majority of those who said they spoke some Turkish or knew Turkish well (20 out of 31) had been staying in Turkey for more than a year.

Encounters with the police constitute perhaps the most important aspect of irregular African migrants' and asylum seekers' interactions with Turkish society. We asked the survey respondents if and how many times they were stopped by the police and asked for their identity documents, and if they were ever detained by the police. We also asked their opinions about police treatment of African migrants.

Eighty-one people said they were never stopped by the police. Among the 43 who answered "yes," 33 said they were stopped more than three times (**Table 7.27**). Among the people who answered the question on detentions, 87 people said they were never detained by the police, whereas 40 said they were detained once (**Table 7.28**). However, there may have been some inaccuracy in the responses to this question for two reasons. First, the question did not specify whether the detention was at the point of illegal entry into Turkey or during one's stay in Istanbul. We know that many Somalis are initially detained and then they apply for asylum. Secondly, some people might have given a false negative answer to this question.

Seventy-two people who responded to the question "Do you think Turkish police treat Africans differently than other migrants?" answered in the negative while 20 said "yes," and 33 said they did not have an opinion.[32] The largest group who thought police treatment towards them was poor were Nigerians (6 people), but more Nigerians thought that police treatment towards them was no different (12 people) (**Table 7.29**). Regarding the question on the greatest problems of

---

32 Although the wording of the question did not specify in what way police treatment was different, in face-to-face surveying, we explained that it meant negative treatment.

TABLE 7.27
Encounters With Police

"Were you ever stopped by Police?"	No. of persons	Percent
No	81	65.3
Yes	43	34.7
Total	124	100.0

"How many times were you stopped?"	No. of persons	Percent
Once	2	4.7
Twice	7	16.3
Three Times	1	2.3
Four Times	3	7.0
Five Times	1	2.3
Several Times	14	32.6
Many Times	15	34.9
Total	43	100.0

TABLE 7.28
"Were You Ever Detained by Police?"

Country of origin	No	Yes, once	Total
Somalia	40	11	51
Nigeria	15	6	21
Ghana	3	3	6
D.R. Congo	6	3	9
Mauritania	5	2	7
Eritrea	3	3	6
Ethiopia	3	5	8
Kenya	4	1	5
Burundi	4	2	6
Other	4	4	8
Total	87	40	127

African migrants in Istanbul, only 1.7 percent of the respondents cited "ill treatment by police" (See **Table 7.32**).

We also asked those respondents who have been in Turkey for more than one year their assessment of the changes in the police's treatment of Africans. Of the respondents, 82.4 percent said police

TABLE 7.29
"Do You Think Turkish Police Treats Africans Differently Than Other Migrants?"

Country of origin	No	Yes	Don't know	Total
Somalia	25	4	19	48
Nigeria	12	6	3	21
Ghana	4	2	0	6
D.R. Congo	6	1	2	9
Mauritania	3	0	4	7
Eritrea	5	0	2	7
Ethiopia	3	3	3	9
Kenya	5	0	0	5
Burundi	2	3	0	5
Other	7	1	0	8
Total	72	20	33	125

treatment has improved considerably, 5.9 percent said it has not changed and 5.9 percent said it has worsened. Those respondents (5.9 percent) who marked "other" cited discrimination and mistreatment against them.

How should we interpret the findings of the questions pertaining to police treatment in the light of the cases of mistreatment we reported the section "Irregular Migrants". People may be unwilling to give candid answers to survey questions that they perceive to be related to their personal security. Indeed, in interviews, we heard more complaints about the police. However, we are unable to conclude, based on the evidence we collected, that there is systematic discrimination and/or targeted human rights violations against Africans by Turkish authorities. Further in-depth studies that take into account the general state of respect for human rights by the police need to be conducted in order clarify this issue. For instance, one point to keep in mind in future studies is the impact of the amendment of the law on police duties in June 2007 in a way that broadened the scope of unchecked police authority in law enforcement. It has been argued that reports of police brutality in detention have increased since then, although there have been improvements in the human rights record of the Turkish police in the past several years thanks to EU reforms. This may also be the reason why complaints about abuse of authority by the police were not palpable in our survey, which we conducted more than a year before the amendment of the police duties law.

Life in Istanbul: Problems

In this section, we discuss the problems that Africans face in Istanbul in terms of income earning, social aid, housing and health.

We asked the respondents how they provided for themselves financially (**Table 7.30**).[33] The largest number of responses was "I do odd jobs" (31.3 percent). Sixteen percent of the respondents said they had no source of income, 13 percent said they "worked for wages in a factory/workshop/firm," 10.7 percent said they sold goods and 6.9 percent said they received money from charities. Some said they borrowed money from friends (6.1 percent), and some said their families sent money to them (5.3 percent). Among the 6.1 percent of the respondents who marked "other" in answering this question, some mentioned that they were living on money which they brought with them to Turkey, and a couple mentioned working for NGOs.[34] Among Somalis, the largest group said they had no source of income; among Nigerians and Ghanaians, doing odd jobs was more common. Nigerians and Ghanaians also reported selling goods, which may mean peddling goods on the street or trading in goods. Mauritanians likewise most commonly reported doing odd jobs and selling goods. Ethiopians reported working for wages more than any other group, which stems from the fact that some women worked in domestic service. Several people (Somalis, a Sudanese, and a Djiboutian) said they begged for money. Begging for money was also reported by a couple of newcomer asylum seekers we interviewed. However, we should

---

33 More than one option could be selected in answering this question.

34 We know that a few people work as interpreters and volunteers at RLAP and IIMP. Also, several people may have marked "other" in order to conceal illicit forms of income earning.

TABLE 7.30
"How do You Provide for Yourself Financially?"

Country of origin	I work for wages	I do odd jobs	I sell goods	My family sends money	I receive money from UNHCR	I receive money from charity	I borrow money from frends	I beg for money	I have no source of income	Other
Somalia	7.7%	23.1%		7.7%	3.8%	7.7%	13.5%	1.9%	32.7%	1.9%
Nigeria	9.5%	33.3%	38.1%	4.8%		4.8%			4.8%	4.8%
Ghana	33.3%	50.0%	16.7%							
D.R. Congo		30.0%	10.0%		20.0%				10.0%	30.0%
Mauritania		57.1%	42.9%							
Eritrea	14.3%	42.9%				14.3%				28.6%
Ethiopia	66.7%	11.1%		11.1%					11.1%	
Kenya	20.0%	20.0%	20.0%	20.0%						20.0%
Burundi		33.3%				33.3%	16.7%		16.7%	
Other	12.5%	62.5%				12.5%		12.5%		
Total	13.0%	31.3%	10.7%	5.3%	3.1%	6.9%	6.1%	1.5%	16.0%	6.1%

note that based on our interviews Africans mostly beg for money from other Africans.

There are only a handful of places where asylum seekers and migrants can ask for social aid. We asked the survey respondents if they had applied for and received any aid (**Table 7.31**).[35] Reportedly 22.2 percent said they never applied for any aid. 18.8 percent of Somalis never applied for aid, a finding that seems surprising at first, since Somali asylum seekers most often get into contact with NGOs soon after they arrive in Turkey. The fact that there were newcomers among the respondents may explain this finding. Nigerians and Ghanaians were the least likely to have sought financial assistance, with 48.3 percent and 36.4 percent, respectively. The largest group among all respondents, 34.5 percent, said they had applied for aid to IIMP, which provides emergency medical care, blankets, food, etc., to both migrants and asylum seekers. Seventeen percent had applied to the Refugee Legal Aid Program (RLAP), while 14.9 percent said they asked for financial assistance from UNHCR and 6.2 percent from ICMC. Although respondents reported the last two (UNHCR and ICMC) separately, in fact, ICMC dispenses UNHCR financial assistance to asylum seekers and refugees.[36] Only 3.6 percent of the respondents received aid from independent churches (not part of the IIMP) and several asked Turkish charities for help.

The greatest problem faced by the respondents was finances. In answer to the question, "What are your greatest problems in Istanbul?" about 42 percent of the respondents pointed out "lack of income"[37] (**Table 7.32**). As mentioned in the previous section, the second most cited problem was "ill treatment by strangers" (29.5 percent) and the third most mentioned problem was housing (9.8 per-

---

35 Respondents were allowed to select more than one option in answering this question.

36 We report the answers to this question, although there is some inconsistency in the responses. Some Nigerians and Ghanaians marked UNHCR and ICMC as institutions to which they applied for aid, although UNHCR and ICMC obviously do not provide any aid to economic migrants; and no Nigerians and Ghanaians in our sample reported having applied for asylum.

37 Respondents could choose more than one option in answering this question.

TABLE 7.31
Financial Aid Applications

Country of origin	Never applied	ICMC	RLAP	IIMP	UNHCR	A church	Turkish charity	Other
Somalia	18.8%	8.8%	18.8%	31.3%	21.3%			1.3%
Nigeria	48.3%	6.9%	3.4%	24.1%	6.9%	10.3%		
Ghana	36.4%			36.4%	9.1%	18.2%		
D.R. Congo	22.2%	11.1%	11.1%	55.6%				
Mauritania		7.1%	42.9%	42.9%	7.1%			
Eritrea	30.0%		20.0%	30.0%	20.0%			
Ethiopia	13.3%		13.3%	46.7%	26.7%			
Kenya	12.5%			50.0%	12.5%	12.5%	12.5%	
Burundi		12.5%	50.0%	25.0%		12.5%		
Other	20.0%		20.0%	40.0%	10.0%			10.0%
Total	22.2%	6.2%	17.0%	34.5%	14.9%	3.6%	0.5%	1.0%

TABLE 7.32
"What Are Your Greatest Problems in Istanbul?"

Country of origin	Lack of income	Disc- rimi- nation	Ill treat- ment by police	Ill treat- ment by neigh- bours	Ill treat- ment by Stran- gers	Housing	Hunger	Other
Somalia	45.3%	7.4%	1.1%		27.4%	8.4%	3.2%	7.4%
Nigeria	38.9%	11.1%			22.2%	16.7%	5.6%	5.6%
Ghana	45.5%				36.4%	9.1%		9.1%
D.R. Congo	40.0%				26.7%	6.7%	6.7%	20.0%
Mauritania	35.7%				50.0%	14.3%		
Eritrea	41.7%				33.3%	8.3%		16.7%
Ethiopia	35.3%		5.9%	5.9%	29.4%		11.8%	11.8%
Kenya	30.0%				40.0%	10.0%	10.0%	10.0%
Burundi	36.4%		9.1%		45.5%	9.1%		
Other	53.8%		7.7%		15.4%	15.4%		7.7%
Total %	41.9%	4.7%	1.7%	0.4%	29.5%	9.8%	3.8%	8.1%

cent). Discrimination came fourth with 4.7 percent and "hunger" was cited in 3.8 percent of the responses. Those people who marked "other" in response to this question cited their health problems, psychological problems and feelings of hopelessness. An interesting finding is that the ratio of people who highlighted lack of income as their greatest problem did not show much variance across different nationalities. This appears to be in contrast to our observation that West Africans are somewhat better off than asylum seeking East Africans. We may explain this finding by saying that there is a generalized perception of lowness of incomes among Africans, although there is variation between different national groups in terms of living standards.

We inquired about the health problems of the respondents. Among 118 who answered the question about whether they had serious health problems, 101 answered in the negative. Five people reported having tuberculosis, two people had diabetes, two had heart disease and two had epilepsy. Six people who marked "other" reported psychological depression and various infections. We also asked if they ever got sick in Istanbul and if they received medical attention. Forty-six people reported that they received medical care for their illnesses. Of these, 21 said the IIMP provided/paid for the medical care, 13 people said they paid for it themselves, seven said the UNHCR or ICMC covered their hospital bill, three people borrowed money from their friends and two received medical care at Turkish tuberculosis clinics (*Verem Savaş Dispanseri*).

Although not many people reported having chronic diseases, we should draw attention to the frequency of tuberculosis among migrants and asylum seekers. Given that many migrants, especially asylum seekers, live in crowded apartments, there is a danger that the roommates of persons infected with TB can contract the disease. This danger may be especially serious because many asylum seekers do not have proper nutrition due to poverty and may have no other recourse than to live in damp places without proper heating during the winter months. Although screening for TB is available at Turkish tuberculosis clinics, there has been at least one case in the past when a certain hospital refused treatment of a multi-drug resistant TB patient because of the high cost of the medication. An NGO worker told us the details of this Congolese man's case, who was repatriated in 2004 when he received a "contagion-free" document. His illness was not diagnosed on time and he initially received a wrong medical treatment while living in very poor conditions with several other men from his country.

A significant problem for irregular migrants and asylum seekers who have children is access to education. People who do not have legal residency in Turkey are unable to send their school-age children to primary school, although there is a vague mention of education for asylum seekers' and refugees' children in the relevant government regulations. Among the respondents to the survey, 14 people said they had children in Istanbul. Five of them were able to send their kids to a school program run by a church, while eight said their children received no schooling here. One person's child was too young to go to school.

In concluding this section, we may describe the respondents' opinions of their living conditions in Istanbul. Among the 82 persons who answered the question on this, 44 said their living conditions in Istanbul were "better in terms of personal security," 20 said their living conditions here were about the same as in their country. Seven people said they were better off in Istanbul economically, but eight said they were economically worse off. And three said their conditions in Istanbul were worse than in their country in terms of personal security. We asked the respondents if they would like to go back to their countries. Only 18 answered this question positively, and they were from West Africa. Among them, 10 said they would like to do so because their life was much harder in Turkey than before. One said it was impossible to cross into Europe. Two said they were not able to make enough money here to send back home. And two stated the economic conditions back in their country were improving. Among "other" reasons for wanting to go back, some expressed a desire to return home if plans for crossing into Europe did not materialize. Although few people wanted to go back, those who did were apparently disappointed with what they found in Turkey or hopeless about prospects for getting into Europe.

A View of African Migrants' Lives in Istanbul

Social Interactions Among Africans and Their Living Conditions

As we were conducting the fieldwork in August 2005, the annual "African Football Cup" took place in a football field in the neighborhood of Kurtuluş.[38] The Nigerian team won the final game against Guinea to the loud cheers of their fans. Although most of the spectators were Africans, the turnout of Turkish citizens was high. The teams had been preparing for this tournament in the fields of Kurtuluş, Dolapdere, Tarlabaşı, and Hacıhüsrev for some time. Many West Africans play football in Istanbul regularly, as some of them have come to Turkey in the hope of getting into a second or third division Turkish team. This was one of the few social events in which Africans from diverse countries (and not just West Africans) come together in Istanbul. Football is also a medium through which Turkish citizens and Africans can interact with each other, as Turks and Africans often play against each other. Apart from that, the only social venues where young Turkish citizens and African migrants socialize with each other are a couple of reggae clubs in Beyoğlu.

It may be argued that Africans from the east and the west of the continent do not intermingle and form strong social bonds with each other in Istanbul. This may have various reasons which would be applicable to irregular migrants and asylum seekers from other regions of the world. There are cultural and ethnic differences and even animosities, and there is often a language barrier. For instance, people from D.R. Congo are said to be an insular group because they

---

38 The African Football Cup is becoming an institution as the fourth was held in Summer 2007.

are Francophone. In general, English language skills of persons are weak if they do not come from countries where English is an official language.

Among the asylum seekers, persons from the same country often share apartments, interact with each other and help each other to the extent that this is possible. For instance, several Somalis and a Sierra Leonean man we interviewed mentioned that when they first arrived in Istanbul they were taken in by their fellow countrymen and not charged money for rent for several months. However, since nobody is resourceful enough, the offer of a free place ends after a few months.

Asylum seekers from Somalia, Ethiopia and Eritrea mostly live in the Galata neighborhood of the Beyoğlu district and in the Kumkapı and Aksaray neighborhoods. Some asylum seekers live in the Aşağı Laleli neighborhood of Eminönü district, not far from Aksaray. Buildings are older and more derelict in Galata, but not much better in Aksaray and Laleli. Often, more than ten people share an apartment and several people share a room. In interviews we were told that persons who share a room or apartment might have to take turns to sleep due to the lack of space. These apartments usually lack heating and people use electric space heaters and small electric ranges or small LPG (liquefied petroleum gas) tubes for cooking. Several persons said that their apartments were damp and infested with insects. West Africans are more likely to live in the Tarlabaşı neighborhood of Beyoğlu, and many Somalis also live there. The apartments and rental rooms in Tarlabaşı are also derelict. Certain parts of Tarlabaşı are distinct because many West Africans live there and there are some stores that cater to them. For instance, international telephone call centers are a gathering place for West Africans.

Some of the interviewees complained about the prejudicial attitudes of Turkish citizens towards them. For instance, a complaint expressed by those who have lived here for several years was that landlords were hesitant to rent them apartments. However, a Nigerian and a Sudanese said that once their current landlords got to know them those prejudices were removed. In addition, some complained that the word "African migrant" was associated with "illegal migration." During the African football cup in summer 2005, Nigerians expressed the hope that this event would give a positive picture of Africans to the Turkish society, but the event was hardly covered in the Turkish press. In general, it may be argued that Istanbul's citizens know very little about African migrants and the conditions and reasons that brought them here.

Survival Strategies and Income Earning

The interviewees, like the survey respondents, complained of the dearth of income earning opportunities. West Africans were aware of the difficulty – and hence did not have much expectation – of finding employment, given that the Turkish citizens in the areas where they lived were also jobless and poor. There appears to be a difference between West African irregular migrants and East African asylum seekers in terms of how they survive in Istanbul. Although this difference is not a sharp line, it may be argued that economically motivated irregular/transit migrants engage in some kind of income generating activity and are better off, whereas asylum seekers lead a barren existence in Istanbul based on marginal survival activities.[39]

West Africans are more likely to be engaged in some kind of "trade" compared to East Africans in Istanbul. Some ethnic groups in Nigeria, Ghana, and Senegal have traditionally been long distance traders (Diouf, 2000; Coquery-Vidrovitch, 1997). In the face of economic collapse and civil strife, people from Central African countries such as Congo and the Democratic Republic of Congo have started to engage in informal trade between their countries and Western Europe

---

39 Here, the term "survival strategy" refers to activities targeting income maximization (working, begging, peddling, etc.) as well as those targeting the minimization of expenditures (sharing crowded apartments, staying hungry, etc.) (for instance see, Gonzalez Arriagada, 2000 and Gonzalez De La Rocha, 1994).

in the past two decades (MacGaffey and Bazenguissa-Ganga, 2000). In Istanbul, too, it is possible to see various commercial activities by West Africans, as well as by people from Congo and D.R. Congo. We interviewed two young Senegalese men who peddled goods in street markets. Their wares were not African "souvenirs" but small trinkets that Turkish peddlers also sold. A Ghanaian man we interviewed said he went back and forth between his country and Turkey in order to buy and sell goods.

Indeed, such "suitcase trade," that is, informal exports from Turkey to various African countries, is a significant form of commercial activity. Three men, a Ghanaian, a Nigerian and a Senegalese, told us that they assisted their compatriots who came to Istanbul for "suitcase trade." Sometimes they would send a batch of clothes from Istanbul to someone who made an order back at home. Apparently, some Congolese irregular migrants also engage in such small-scale "suitcase trade" (Öcal, 2005). In fact, suitcase traders from various African countries regularly come to Turkey to buy clothing and their business is centered in the Beyazıt and Laleli neighborhoods, which have long been the center of informal exports to former Soviet republics, Eastern Europe and North Africa. Our interviews indicate that the suitcase trade to Africa is sometimes intertwined with irregular migration, since some of the traders overstay their visas in Istanbul.[40]

There are several small shops operated by Africans in Istanbul. In Tarlabaşı, we visited a restaurant, Lady V's, operated by a Nigerian woman, situated in an apartment on the second floor of an old building. The restaurant offered Nigerian food and some imported items for personal care. In Tarlabaşı, several Nigerian men sell/rent African movie videos, music tapes and CDs, which are brought to Turkey by Nigerian traders. In Laleli, a small store operated as an "African café"

---

40 This observation is in line with the findings of earlier research on the informal "shuttle trade" between Turkey and former Soviet republics: in that case, poorer shuttle traders switched back and forth between working illegally as Russian speaking salespersons in Laleli and shuttling goods to their countries (Yükseker, 2004).

where some imported food items were on sale. All of these establishments appeared to be informal.

There are a few formal establishments operated by Africans as well. The easiest way to have a legal business for a foreigner is to be married to a Turkish citizen and to have obtained a residence and a work permit in this way. Some people can earn a residence and a work permit in Turkey after graduating from a Turkish university and finding employment.[41] A Sudanese man we interviewed operated a music club in Beyoğlu frequented by Africans, Turkish citizens and European expatriates alike. Two Nigerians we interviewed who were married to Turkish citizens also said that they had small trading businesses in Istanbul. Based on the accounts of the interviewees, other African-operated cafes existed a few years ago, indicating a high turnover in such entrepreneurial activities.

Some African migrants and asylum seekers find informal work in Istanbul, but for sub-minimum wages. In Tarlabaşı, Aksaray, Kumkapı, Galata and Laleli, Africans' neighbors are poor Turkish citizens, often the Roma or internally displaced Kurds, or sometimes both. These neighborhoods, although centrally located, in general lack opportunities for regular income earning. In these areas, most jobs are in street vending, construction work and irregular wage work in informal workshops. Therefore, the income earning activities that Africans engage in are not unique to them, but exist in a continuum of coping strategies in which the poor inhabitants of those areas are involved. Below, we describe some cash generating activities that were reported by asylum seekers and East Africans.

Several Eritrean and Ethiopian women who answered our survey reported working as domestic laborers in private homes. These women entered Turkey illegally through the Syrian border and had

---

41 Student visas for foreigners do not permit them to work in Turkey, and graduation from a Turkish university does not automatically entitle foreigners to work permits either; however, if they find legal employment, several years later the residence and work permits can become indefinite.

previously been working in Lebanon as domestic laborers.[42] There is also evidence that members of evangelical churches who help African asylum seekers may employ them as domestic help (Ekberzade, 2006).

Some East and West Africans work informally in workshops especially in lighting fittings and garment production in the back streets of the Beyoğlu district. Their reported monthly wages are lower than the legal minimum. We also heard complaints that employers sometimes simply do not pay, knowing that an undocumented migrant cannot report such an incident to Turkish authorities. In Kumkapı, some Africans said they worked at the wholesale fish market for the equivalent of a few dollars a day.

Odd jobs such as cleaning or carrying boxes for storeowners are called *çabuk çabuk* by African migrants in Istanbul. Meaning "do it quickly" or "hurry up" in Turkish, this term refers to doing some work for food or for a little cash. From the perspective of the "employer," this is something that needs to be done quickly. But from the Africans' perspective, *çabuk çabuk* has a double connotation. On the one hand, it means that some Turks order them around. On the other hand, *çabuk çabuk* is literally a fleeting experience that fails to provide for their daily needs.

Some of the survey respondents reported a few survival strategies that are unique in highlighting the extreme precariousness of their living conditions in Istanbul. Some newly-arrived young male asylum seekers mentioned begging for cash to buy food from other Africans. Some said they "worked for food" or worked for an employer who provided shelter but no wages. Indeed, some newcomer asylum seekers report hunger ("Sometimes I do not eat for 2-3 days") and lack of shelter ("I have been sleeping on the street") as their greatest problems in Istanbul. Under these conditions, the life of African asylum seekers

---

42 Many Ethiopian and Eritrean women, alongside many more Sri Lankan and Filipina women, work as domestic servants in middle class homes in Lebanon, where they have limited rights vis-à-vis their employers and labor recruiters. When some of them seek to escape from abusive work environments and/or indebtedness to their recruiters, undocumented entry into Turkey is one option, if not a very frequent one.

in Istanbul becomes stripped down to a bare existence, where even food and shelter are precarious "amenities."

Finally, it appears that some Africans in Istanbul may be involved in the forged visa/passport business, although our survey and interviews did not give us any information about this. Nevertheless, the observations of some NGO volunteers as well as the Foreigners' Police crime statistics mentioned in the section "Framework of Africans' Presence: Asylum, Illegality and Charity" suggest that some Africans are involved in the document forging/human smuggling business.[43]

Discussion

Turkish filmmaker Berke Baş's documentary "Transit" [In Transit] (2004) portrays the lives of three migrant families in Istanbul in the first half of this decade: one Iraqi Christian, one Iraqi Kurdish family who sought asylum in Turkey and a young Nigerian couple. The Nigerian man and woman had arrived in Turkey as transit migrants separately, but after a few attempts, they were both unable to achieve clandestine passage into Western Europe. As the director followed the lives of the Nigerian couple over a year, Rosaline and Jonathan accepted that their stay in Turkey was not as "temporary" as they had hoped it to be. They got married in an evangelical church in Istanbul and were trying to improve the poor conditions of their life in Istanbul's Tarlabaşı neighborhood. Watching the film leaves one with the thought that, not only for the Nigerian couple, but also for the Iraqi Christian family who were resettled in Canada after several years' wait, "transit migration" was not so much about "transiting" Istanbul as it was about seeking to create a meaningful life in this city.

Our objective in this report was to provide a broad overview of the various ways in which African migrants and asylum seekers create a life in Istanbul. More than being merely statistics on irregular migration and refugee flows, Africans in Istanbul actively struggle to make a living,

---

43 According to the Turkish Criminal Code, making false visas and passports would be offenses under the titles of fraud and forgery, the categories listed in **Table 4.4**.

build communities, provide for their basic needs and shape the patterns of their journeys, but in this process they come across many hurdles.

The findings of our research raise questions for further research on irregular migration through Turkey in general, Africans' lives in Istanbul in particular, rather than provide definitive answers. Future research on the following issues would supplement the findings of this study and provide a better picture of the flows of people from Africa to and through Turkey: the organization of irregular migration by human smugglers and other migration entrepreneurs, the patterns of trade between West Africa and Turkey and the relation between informal trade and irregular migration, community building by Africans in Istanbul, especially the role of evangelical churches and the patterns of social interaction between Turkish citizens and African migrants.

CONCLUSION

As we argue above, irregular migration and asylum seekers who flow from Africa through Istanbul are not a temporary or "transitory" phenomena. These processes affect migrants' lives in profound ways. As such, irregular migration also affects Turkish society. NGO representatives, police officers and the migrants themselves point out that the Africans in Istanbul have important problems. From a humanitarian perspective, the most urgent problems are access to healthcare for all asylum seekers, access to education and decent housing. From a socioeconomic perspective, all asylum seekers and irregular migrants complain that they cannot work legally.

As Turkey gradually harmonizes its asylum and migration regime with that of the EU, it fears that the number of irregular migrants and asylum seekers would increase. For the reasons that we explained in the section of "International Migration in a Globalizing World" the EU's anti-immigration and anti-asylum policies have already increased the flows of irregular migrants and refugees in surrounding regions such as Eastern Europe, Turkey and North Africa. In this sense, this fear is not unfounded. Recalling the experience of

Central and Eastern European countries on their way to integration with the EU, one may claim that Turkey could become a "ditch" for irregular migrants and asylum seekers as they struggle to enter "Fortress Europe." Indeed, recent news about Greece's reported misuse of (or failure to implement) the readmission protocol raises concern in this regard.[44] Therefore, as Turkey harmonizes its immigration and asylum regime with the EU, the increasing humanitarian and financial burden should be shared rather than turning Turkey into a buffer for unwanted illegal migrants.

However, when we examine the numbers of apprehended irregular migrants, which must constitute only a small portion of the total number irregular migrants in Turkey, and asylum seekers in Turkey in the last decade, three observations emerge: irregular African migrants constitute a very small group compared to irregular migrants from former Soviet republics, the number of asylum seekers (African and other) makes up only a small proportion of all irregular migrants and African asylum seekers constitute a minority of all asylum applications. With these facts in mind, it may be argued that adopting policies that would address the humanitarian needs and human rights of asylum seekers and irregular migrants are unlikely to significantly increase the flow of migrants from Africa to Turkey.

Therefore, Turkey should take steps to provide access to healthcare, housing and education for the African asylum seeking population. It should also consider policies for granting work permits to asylum applicants and refugees as well as simplify the application for work permits by migrants.

Turkey plans to create reception centers for asylum seekers and refugees as part of its National Programme. On the one hand, the establishment of reception centers should be hastened. On the other

---

44 According to the Turkish coast guard command, Greek coast guard boats steered illegal migrants' boats into Turkish waters in two incidents in July 2004 and May 2006 in violation of both humanitarian principles and the readmission protocol (*Radikal*, 2006a). More recently in September 2006, six illegal migrants were drowned in an incident in which the surviving illegal migrants accused Greek authorities' for having dumped them in the sea off İzmir (*Radikal*, 2006b).

hand, allowing asylum seekers and refugees to work and letting them reside freely in an integrated manner with the society may yield more humane results, which may be more efficient and cost-effective in comparison to "camp style" solutions.

Furthermore, Turkish civil society should also assume a role in providing humanitarian and social assistance to migrants and asylum seekers. Although under-funded, we observed that the existing NGOs catering to asylum seekers (mainly Africans) played a vital role in helping these people adjust to the new realities of their lives in Turkey. Given that the number of asylum seekers is not overwhelming, if domestic NGOs become more involved, social and humanitarian assistance would become more widely available.

REFERENCES

Adepoju, A., 2005, "Review of Research and Data on Human Trafficking in Sub-Saharan Africa", *International Migration*, 43(1/2): 75-98.

—, 2000, "Issues and Trends in International Migration in Sub-Saharan Africa", *International Social Science Journal*, 52(3): 383-394.

Akşam, 2006, "Polisin Yalanladığı 'Köle' Skandalını Akşam Kanıtladı", 11 December.

Barnett, M., 2001, "UNHCR and the Ethics of Repatriation", *Forced Migration Review*, 19: 31-34.

Castles, S., 2003, "Towards a Sociology of Forced Migration and Social Transformation", *Sociology*, 37(1): 13-34.

Castles, S. and J. Mark, 1998, *The Age of Migration: International Population Movements in the Modern World*, London: Macmillan.

Çağaptay, S., 2002, "Kemalist Dönemde Göç ve İskan Politikaları: Türk Kimliği Üzerine bir Çalışma", *Toplum ve Bilim*, 93: 218-241.

Çalkıvık, A. F., 2003, "Yaşam ve Ölüm Alanları arasında Afrikalı Göçmenler", *Birikim*, November-December: 149-152.

Coquery-Vidrovitch, C., 1997, *African Women, A Modern History*, Boulder, CO: Westview Press.

CNN Türk.com., 2007, "BM Ölen Nijeryalı için Bilgi İstedi", 3 September, available at (http://www.cnnturk.com).

Diouf, M., 2000, "The Senegalese Murid Trade Diaspora and the Making of a Vernacular Cosmopolitanism", *Public Culture*, 12(3): 679-702.

Ekberzade, B., 2006, *Yasadışı*, Istanbul: Plan B.

Erder, S. and S. Kaşka, 2003, "Irregular Migration and Trafficking in Women: The Case of Turkey", International Organization for Migration (IOM), Geneva.

Faist, T., 2000, *International Migration and Transnational Social Spaces*, Oxford: Oxford University Press.

Frantz, E., 2003, *Report on the Situation of Refugees in Turkey: Findings of a Five-Week Exploratory Study, December 2002-January 2003*, available at (http://www.aucegypt.edu/academic/fmrs/Reports/TurkeyReport.pdf).

Gonzalez Arriagada, A., 2000, *Surviving in the City – The Urban Poor of Santiago de Chile 1930-1970*, Acta Universitatis Upsaliensis, Uppsala Studies in Economic History, 51.

Gonzalez De La Rocha, M., 1994, *The Resources of Poverty – Women and Survival in a Mexican City*, Oxford: Blackwell.

Goodwin-Gill, G., 2001, "After the Cold War: Asylum and the Refugee Concept Move On", *Forced Migration Review*, 10: 14-16.

Harrell-Bond, B., 1986, *Imposing Aid: Emergency Assistance to Refugees*, Oxford: Oxford University Press.

—, 2002, "Can Humanitarian Work with Refugees Be Humane?", *Human Rights Quarterly*, 24: 51-85.

HCA and AI, 2007, Helsinki Citizens' Assembly and Amnesty International Joint Statement, August, available at (http://www.hyd.org.tr).

Hughes, N., 2003, "Yemen and Refugees: Progressive Attitudes – Policy Void", *Forced Migration Review*, 16: 36-38.

Human Rights Association (HRA), 2001, "Preliminary Report on African Immigrants and Refugees in Turkey", Istanbul, July 27, available at (http://www.ihd.org.tr/repspec/african/prelim.html).

Hyndman, J., 2000, *Managing Displacement: Refugees and the Politics of Humanitarianism*, Minneapolis: University of Minnesota Press.

International Catholic Migration Commission (ICMC), "Turkey", available at (http://www.icmc.net/docs/en/programs/turkeyback#10).

International Organization for Migration (IOM), 1995, "Transit Migration in Turkey", IOM Migration Information Programme, Budapest.

—, 2000, "World Migration Report: 2000", International Organization for Migration (IOM), Geneva.

—, 2005, *World Migration, Costs and Benefits of International Migration*, Geneva: IOM.

İçduygu, A., 2000, "The Politics of International Migratory Regimes: Transit Migration Flows in Turkey", *International Social Science Journal*, 52(165): 357-367.

—, 2003, *Irregular Migration in Turkey*, IOM, available at (http://www.iom.int).

İçduygu, A., and Ş. Toktaş, 2002, "How do Smuggling and Trafficking Operate via Irregular Border Crossings in the Middle East? Evidence from Fieldwork in Turkey", *International Migration*, 40(6): 25-52.

Jamal, A., 2003, "Camps and Freedoms: Long-Term Refugee Situations in Africa", *Forced Migration Review*, 16: 4-6.

Keely, C. and B. Winter, 1996, "How Nation States Create and Respond to Refugee Flows", *International Migration Review*, 30(4): 1046-1066.

Keough, L., 2004, "Driven Women. Reconceptualizing the Traffic in Women in the Margins of Europe through the Case of Gagauz Mobile Domestics in Istanbul", *Focaal, European Journal of Anthropology*, 43: 14-26.

Kindiki, K., 2005, "Europe and the Rebuilding of Somalia", *Forced Migration Review*, 23: 37-38.

Kirişci, K., 1996, "Is Turkey Lifting the 'Geographical Limitation'? The November 1994 Regulation on Asylum in Turkey", *International Journal of Refugee Law*, 8(3): 293-318.

—, 2002, "UNHCR and Turkey: Cooperating for Improved Implementation of the 1951 Convention relating to the Status of Refugees", *International Law of Refugee Law*, 13(1-2): 71-97.

—, Kirişci, K. and G. Winrow, 1997, *The Kurdish Question and Turkey: An Example of a Trans-State Ethnic Conflict*, London: Frank Cass.

Koser, K., 2001, "New Approaches to Asylum?", *International Migration*, 39(6): 85-101.

Loescher, G., 2001, "UNHCR and the Erosion of Refugee Protection", *Forced MigrationReview*, 10: 28-30.

MacGaffey, J. and R. Bazenguissa-Ganga, 2000, *Congo-Paris, Transnational Traders on the Margins of the Law*, Bloomington: Indiana University Press.

Malkki, L., 1995, "Refugees and Exile: From 'Refugee Studies' to the National Order of Things", *Annual Review of Anthropology*, 24: 495-523.

Munck, R., 2005, "Irregular Migration and the Informal Labour Market: The Underside of Globalisation or the New Norm?", unpublished keynote address at the "International Workshop on Irregular Migration, Informal Labour and Community in Europe" organized by IMILCO, December 1-2, Istanbul.

Öcal, A., 2005, "Türkiye'deki Afrikalı Göçmenler. Bir Yiğit Gurbete Gitse...", *Express*, 52: 41-44.

Parrenas, R. S., 2000, "Migrant Filipina Domestic Workers and the International Division of Labor", *Gender and Society*, 14(4): 560-580.

Peshkopia, R., 2005, "Albania – Europe's Reluctant Gatekeeper", Forced Migration Review, 23: 35-36.Radikal, 2006a, "'Kaçak' Bırakan Yunan Botuna Suçüstü", September 20, available at ⟨http://www.radikal.com.tr/haber.php?haberno=199178⟩.

—, 2006b, "Yunanistan Hiç Acımıyor", September 27, available at (http://www. radikal.com.tr/haber.php?haberno=199857).

—, 2007a, "Ölüm Yeri: Beyoğlu Emniyeti", August 30, available at (http://www. radikal.com.tr).

—, 2007b, "Karakolda Ölüme 'Siyah' Tepki", September 1, available at (http:// www.radikal.com.tr).

Resmi Gazete, 1994, "Türkiye'ye İltica Eden veya Başka Bir Ülkeye İltica Etmek Üzere Türkiye'den İkamet İzni Talep Eden Münferit Yabancılar ile Topluca Sığınma Amacıyla Sınırlarımıza Gelen Yabancılara ve Olabilecek Nüfus Hareketlerine Uygulanacak Usul ve Esaslar Hakkında Yönetmelik", (22127), November 30.

—, 1999, "Türkiye'ye İltica Eden veya Başka Bir Ülkeye İltica Etmek Üzere Türkiye'den İkamet İzni Talep Eden Münferit Yabancılar ile Topluca Sığınma Amacıyla Sınırlarımıza Gelen Yabancılara ve Olabilecek Nüfus Hareketlerine Uygulanacak Usul ve Esaslar Hakkında Yönetmelikte Değişiklik Yapılmasına Dair Yönetmelik", (23582), January 13.

—, 2003a, "Yabancı Ülkelerden Bazılarının Vatandaşlarına Tanınmış Olan Vize Muafiyetlerinin Kaldırılmasına İlişkin Karar", (25067), April 2, available at (http://rega.basbakanlik.gov.tr/Eskiler/2003/04/20030402.htm#2).

—, 2003b, Yabancıların Çalışma İzinleri Hakkında Kanun No.4817, RG No.25040, March 6, available at (http://rega.basbakanlik.gov.tr/Eskiler/2003/03/20030306.htm#5).

—, 2006, "Türkiye'ye İltica Eden veya Başka Bir Ülkeye İltica Etmek Üzere Türkiye'den İkamet İzni Talep Eden Münferit Yabancılar ile Topluca Sığınma Amacıyla Sınırlarımıza Gelen Yabancılara ve Olabilecek Nüfus Hareketlerine Uygulanacak Usul ve Esaslar Hakkında Yönetmelikte Değişiklik Yapılmasına Dair Yönetmelik", (26062), January 27, available at (http://rega.basbakan-lik.gov.tr/Eskiler/2006/01/20060127.htm).Sirkeci, İ., 2003, "Migration from Turkey to Germany: an Ethnic Approach", New Perspectives on Turkey, 28-29: 189-208.

Sorensen, B. R., (forthcoming), "Anthropological Contributions to Forced Migration Studies: Critical Analysis and Ethnography", Acta Geographica.

Stola, D., 2001, "Two Kinds of Quasi-Migration in the Middle Zone: Central Europe as a Space for Transit Migration and Mobility for Profit" in C.Wallace and D. Stola (eds.), Patterns of Migration in Central Europe, London: Palgrave Macmillan.

United Nations Development Programme (UNDP), 2003, Human Development Report 2003- Millenium Goals: A Compact among Nations to End Human Poverty, New York: Oxford University Press.

United Nations High Commissioner for Refugees (UNHCR), 2001,

"Turkey/Greece: confusion on dumped Africans", UNHCR Briefing Notes, available at (http://www.unhcr.ch/cgi-bin/texis/vtx/home/+kwwBmenGVO).

—, 2005, 2004 Global Refugee Trends: Overview of Refugee Population, New Arrivals, Durable Solutions, Asylum-Seekers, Stateless and other Persons of Concern to UNHCR, available at (http://www.unhcr.org/statistics).

—, 2007a, 2006 Global Trends, Refugees, Asylum-seekers, Returnees, Internally Displaced and Stateless Persons, available at (http://www.unhcr.org.statistics).

—, 2007b, "UNHCR Türkiye'nin 135 Iraklı'yı Sınır Dışı Edişinden Esef Eder", press release, available at (http://www.unhcr.org.tr).

United Nations (UN), 2000a, Protocol against the Smuggling of Migrants by Land, Sea and Air, Supplementing the United Nations Convention against Transnational Organized Crime, available at (http://www.unodc.org/pdf/crime/a_res_55/res5525e.pdf).

—, 2000b, Protocol to Prevent, Suppress and Punish trafficking in Persons, Especially Women and Children, Supplementing the UN Convention Against Organized Crime.

Ünal, B., 2004, "Sermaye Olarak Yaş ve Eğitim. Türkiye'de Ev İçi Hizmet Sektöründe Çalışan Kadınlar Üzerine Karşılaştırmalı Bulgular", Sosyoloji Araştırmaları Dergisi, 7(2): 137-161.

Wallace, C., and D. Stola, 2001, "Introduction: Patterns of Migration in Central Europe" in C. Wallace and D. Stola (eds.), Patterns of Migration in Central Europe, London: Palgrave Macmillan.

Wallace, C., 2001, "The New Migration Space as a Buffer Zone?" in C. Wallace and D. Stola (eds.), Patterns of Migration in Central Europe, London: Palgrave Macmillan.

Wood, W. B., 1994, "Forced Migration: Local Conflicts and International Dilemmas", Annals of the Asociation of American Geographers, 84(4): 607-634.

Yaghmaian, B., 2003, "Afrika Diyasporası: Türkiye'deki Afrikalı Göçmenlerin Dramı", Birikim, November-December: 140-148.

Vasileva, D., 1992, "Bulgarian Turkish Emigration and Return", International Migration Review, 26(2): 342-352.

Yükseker, D., 2004, "Trust and Gender in a Transnational Marketplace: Laleli, Istanbul", Public Culture, 16(2): 47-65.

Zaman, 2005, "Ankara'nın Onaylamadığı Afrikalılar'a Vize Verilmeyecek", February 17, available at (http://www.zaman.com.tr/?bl=butun&trh=20050217&hn=143918).

Zolberg, A. R., 1989, "The Next Waves: Migration Theory for a Changing World", International Migration Review, 23(3): 403-430.

Appendices

APPENDIX 7.1
REFUGEE FLOWS AND INTERNAL DISPLACEMENT IN AFRICA*

East Africa and the Horn of Africa: Environmental disasters and ethnic, border and guerilla wars in the Horn of Africa (Somalia, Eritrea, Ethiopia and southern Sudan) led to massive flows of refugees and IDPs during the 1980s and 1990s.

Central Africa: Refugee flows and internal displacement reached a climax during the mid-1990s in the wake of the genocide in Rwanda and the civil war in Burundi. Turmoil in the Republic of Congo and the civil war in the Democratic Republic of Congo (previously Zaire) starting in 1997 further fuelled refugee and IDP flows. Although civil strife and warfare in the region abated after that, recently tensions have been rising between the DRC and Rwanda.

West Africa: Since 1989, the region covering Guinea Bissau, Sierra Leone, Liberia and Ivory Coast has experienced rebellions, civil wars and military uprisings, uprooting millions of people.

Southern Africa: Wars of independence and liberation struggles in Angola, Mozambique, Zimbabwe and South Africa (against Apartheid) have led to refugee flows in the past several decades.

(*) Adopted from IOM, 2005.

Appendix 7.2
Political Conditions that Create Refugee Flows
in Selected African Countries*

SOMALIA: The ethnic composition of the country: Somali 85 percent, Bantu and other non-Somali 15 percent (including 30,000 Arabs). Majority are Sunni Muslims with a Christian minority.

Mohamed Siad Barre's regime was overthrown in January 1991 which led to civil war, turmoil, and anarchy. Because of the ongoing fighting, UN initiated a peacekeeping operation (United Nations Operation in Somalia – UNOSOM II) in 1993. A Transitional Federal Assembly was formed in 2004 and now, a transitional federal government is in force. There are an estimated 400,000 IDPs due to civil war since 1988, clan-based competition for resources; 5,000 IDPs due to the December 2004 tsunami; and 389,272 refugees.

MAURITANIA: The ethnic composition of the country: mixed Maur/black 40 percent, Moor 30 percent, black 30 percent. Population is Muslim.

President Taya was ousted by a bloodless coup in August 2005. Colonel Ely Ould Mohamed Vall, leader of the coup, is the chief of state. Mauritania is an autocratic state, and ethnic tensions between the black population and different Moor (Arab-Berber) communities continue, resulting in the displacement of blacks.

SUDAN: Ethnic composition: black 52 percent, Arab 39 percent, Beja 6 percent, foreigners 2 percent, other 1 percent. Religious composition: Sunni Muslim 70 percent (in north), indigenous beliefs 25 percent, Christian 5 percent (mostly in south and Khartoum).

Military regimes favoring Islamic-oriented governments representing the Arab population have dominated national politics vis-à-vis blacks with indigenous beliefs and the Christian blacks. There have been two civil wars in its history, the second one beginning in 1983. This and famine resulted in more than 4 million IDPs, and approximately 2 million people died in two decades. In January 2005, the Naivasha Peace Treaty granted the southern rebels autonomy for six years. In another conflict in the western region of Darfur in 2003 more than 200,000 people were killed and nearly 2 million displaced; and since late 2005, peacekeeping troops struggle for stabilization. Field Marshal Umar Hassan Ahmad al-Bashir has been the president since October 1993.

(*) Compiled from CIA-The World Factbook (http://www.cia.gov/cia/publications/factbook/) and IDMC – Country Reports (http://www.internal-displacement.org/).

There are 110,927 refugees in Eritrea; 5,023 in Chad; 7,983 in Uganda); 14,812 in Ethiopia. Besides, there are between 5,300,000 to 6,200,000 IDPs due to the internal conflict since the 1980s and ongoing genocide. Refugees and displaced people are principally non-Arab populations, those residing in the South and West (Darfur).

DEMOCRATIC REPUBLIC OF CONGO: There are more than 200 African ethnic groups in DR Congo whose majority are Bantu (the four largest tribes – Mongo, Luba, Kongo (Bantu), and the Mangbetu-Azande (Hamitic) constitute nearly half of the population. Religious composition is: Roman Catholic 50 percent, Protestant 20 percent, Kimbanguist 10 percent, Muslim 10 percent, other syncretic sects and indigenous beliefs 10 percent.

In 1997, the Mobutu regime in Zaire was overthrown by a rebellion led by Laurent Kabila, after a period of ethnic conflict and civil war. The new regime, named Democratic Republic of Congo was challenged by a rebellion backed by Rwanda and Uganda. In October 2002, the new president Joseph Kabila was successful in negotiating the withdrawal of Rwandan forces occupying eastern DRC. A transitional government was set up in July 2003.

There are 5,277 refugees in Republic of Congo; 11,816 in Rwanda; 18,953 in Uganda; 19,400 in Burundi; 45,226 in Sudan; and 98,383 in Angola. There were an estimated 1,664,000 displaced people since the end of 2005; and 1,680,100 were reported to have returned home from the end of 2004 to the end of 2005. Main reason of displacement was fighting between government forces and rebels since the mid-1990s (The number of the displaced reached 3.4 million in 2003 as its peak, most of them in the east.)

ETHIOPIA: Ethnic composition is: Oromo 40 percent, Amhara and Tigre 32 percent, Sidamo 9 percent, Shankella 6 percent, Somali 6 percent, Afar 4 percent, Gurage 2 percent, other 1 percent

Religious composition is: Muslim 45 percent-50 percent, Ethiopian Orthodox 35 percent-40 percent, animist 12 percent, other 3 percent-8 percent.

The socialist regime which was destroyed by coups, insurrections, drought, and massive refugee problems, was ultimately overthrown in 1991 by the Ethiopian People's Revolutionary Democratic Front (EPRDF). Current president is Girma Woldegiorgis. In late 1990s, a war with Eritrea due to border problems broke out. In December 2000, a peace treaty was signed but final demarcation of the boundary is now suspended.

According to UNHCR figures, the number of refugees originating from the country is 63,105. There is an estimated 150,000 to 265,000 IDPs due to the war with Eritrea (1998-2000) and ethnic conflict in Gambela (most of them are in Tigray and Gambela Provinces).

ERITREA: Ethnic composition is: Tigrinya 50 percent, Tigre and Kunama 40 percent, Afar 4 percent, Saho (Red Sea coast dwellers) 3 percent, other 3 percent

Religions in the country are Muslim, Coptic Christian, Roman Catholic and Protestant.

Ethiopia's control over Eritrea (as a province) ended with the defeat of government forces by rebellion forces (1991) and a subsequent referendum approving independence (1993). Isaias Afwerki is the president. A border war with Ethiopia broke out in 1998 and ended under UN patronage in 2000. Demarcation of borders not finalized due to Ethiopian objections. The war damaged Eritrea's economy.

There are approximately 50,000 IDPs due to the war with Ethiopia (1998-2000); and an estimated 131,000 refugees.

CONGO: Ethnic composition: Kongo 48 percent, Sangha 20 percent, M'Bochi 12 percent, Teke 17 percent, Europeans and other 3 percent

Religious composition: Christian 50 percent, animist 48 percent, Muslim 2 percent

The Marxist regime ended in 1992 with democratic elections. Previous Marxist President Denis Sassou-Nguesso came to office after a brief civil war leading to ethnic and political conflict. A peace agreement with Southern rebel groups was finalized in March 2003, but peace is fragile.

There are 28,152 refugees originating from the country, posing a great humanitarian crisis.

The number of IDPs are estimated to be between 100,000 and 147,000, displaced primarily by multiple civil wars since 1992. A majority of them are of Lari origin.

BURUNDI: Ethnic composition in the country: Hutu (Bantu) 85 percent, Tutsi (Hamitic) 14 percent, Twa (Pygmy) 1 percent, Europeans 3,000, South Asians 2,000.

Religious composition: Christian 67 percent (Roman Catholic 62 percent, Protestant 5 percent), indigenous beliefs 23 percent, Muslim 10 percent.

In 1993, elected President Ndadaye was assassinated, which triggered ethnic conflict between Hutu and Tutsi factions. Nearly 300,000 people were killed; hundreds of thousands of were internally displaced or became refugees. With the help of international negotiation, an agreement between the Tutsi government and the Hutu rebels in 2003 led to the transition process. 2005 witnessed improvement in political stability and a peace settlement in Burundi. Although the country is now at peace, sporadic conflicts between Burundi's armed forces the remaining rebel groups continue.

There are an estimated 117,000 IDPs in the country (half of them clustered in the northern and central provinces – Gitega, Muyinga, Ngozi, Kayanza and Kirundo) mainly due to the psychology of "flee or be killed," violence used by the armed forces, and political or economical aims. There are 485,764 refugees.

SIERRA LEONE: Ethnic composition in the country is: 20 native African tribes: 90 percent (Temne 30 percent, Mende 30 percent, other 30 percent), Creole (Krio) 10 percent (descendants of freed Jamaican slaves who were settled in the Freetown area in the late-18th century), refugees from Liberia's recent civil war, small numbers of Europeans, Lebanese, Pakistanis, and Indians

Religious composition is: Muslim 60 percent, indigenous beliefs 30 percent, Christian 10 percent.

A decade of civil war that ended in 2002 resulted in the killing of tens of thousands of people and displacement of at least 2 million people. The government is gradually establishing stability with the assistance of the civilian UN office in the country. The president since 1996 is Ahmad Tejan Kabbah.

According to UNHCR 2005 figures there are 41,801 refugees originating from the country.

LIBERIA: Ethnic composition of Liberia is as follows: indigenous African tribes 95 percent (including Kpelle, Bassa, Gio, Kru, Grebo, Mano, Krahn, Gola, Gbandi, Loma, Kissi, Vai, Dei, Bella, Mandingo, and Mende), Americo-Liberians 2.5 percent (descendants of immigrants from the US who had been slaves), Congo People 2.5 percent (descendants of immigrants from the Caribbean who had been slaves). People adhering to indigenous beliefs are 40 percent, Christians are 40 percent, and Muslims make up 20 percent of the population.

National Patriotic Front of Liberia (NPFL) initiated an insurrection against the government which led to a 14 year civil war and ended with a peace agreement signed in 2003. Ellen Johnson-Sirleaf became the president in 2005 elections, following the rule by a transitional government. A major peacekeeping mission initiated by the UN in 2003 was extended in 2005. There are 13,941 refugees in Sierra Leone and 12,408 in Cote d'Ivoire. There have been 464,000 IDPs, displaced primarily because of the insecurity arising from the civil war, whose number is 15,000 at the moment. Although the peace agreement initiated optimism (nearly 300,000 refugees received assistance packages for return), continuing civil unrest worsens the situation.

8

The New International Migration and Migrant Women in Turkey: The Case of Moldovan Domestic Workers

SELMİN KAŞKA

INTRODUCTION

International migration has always been a complex phenomenon. However, the migratory flows during the last few decades have become more complex, diversified, and heterogeneous. On the one hand, new sending and receiving countries have started to become important in the migration scene. On the other hand, new migrant groups have started to join the migratory flows.

This research report aims to deal with the new international migration trends by looking at one aspect of the new movement, namely women migrants who come to work as domestic workers in a foreign country. The new global division of labor has certain significant impacts on migrant labor. For the majority of women migrants, domestic work, which is, mainly irregular and undocumented, has become the main employment opportunity in labor market niches of receiving countries.

In this research report I will present the findings of a research project on "The New International Migration and Migrant Women in Turkey: The Case of Moldovan Domestic Workers". In recent years

Turkey has become a host country for Moldovan women migrants who search for a better living after the transition process in their home country; this process can have dramatic consequences. In parallel to the worldwide tendencies, in Turkey, most Moldovan women migrants can find employment opportunities only in domestic work. This research project aimed to understand the dynamics of Moldova as a new sending country, Turkey as a new receiving country, and migration and working experiences of a new migrant group: Moldovan women domestic workers in Istanbul.

LITERATURE REVIEW

In the so-called "age of migration", the dynamics of international migration, i.e. its volume, forms and composition, have changed dramatically compared to the trends in the past. Turkey presents an example of this tendency. Known as a sending country in international migration movements, Turkey has become a receiving and a transit country in the last few decades. This new experience has many aspects which are in need of definition, investigation, and analysis. This paper will focus on one particular aspect of Turkey's new experience in international migration: irregular women migrants from Moldova who work as domestic workers in Turkish households. In other words, it will investigate migration, gender, and domestic work in Turkey as a host country.

It has been argued that movements of people are "globalizing, accelerating, diversifying and feminizing" (Castles and Miller, 2003: 8-9). Therefore, it is a very important task to develop a theoretical framework through which the gender aspect of the new migration movements can be analyzed. However, as Kofman et al. argue, "while there has been a dramatic speeding up of contemporary processes of feminization of migration, our conceptualization of these developments has not moved as fast" (Kofman et al., 2000: 21). Although there is no doubt that "birds of passage" have always included women (Morokvasic, 1984), migration theories have long been gender-neutral, with an implicit assumption that women are passive followers of their male relatives.

Nevertheless, in the last few decades there have been important attempts to include the gender dimension in migration theories. In this context, strictly connected to the "feminization of migration" trends, in recent years global domestic work has become a growing concern for scholars who study international migration. While theoretical attempts have been made to analyze this issue, case studies from different parts of the world have attempted to understand this new phenomenon in different settings (Anderson, 2000; Chang, 2000; Ehrenrich and Hochschild, 2003; Hogdagneu-Sotelo, 2001; Parrenas, 2001).

The general theoretical framework of this research project has been based on new theoretical attempts: firstly on the feminization of migration and secondly on the globalisation of domestic work. The focus of this research is on the immigration and work practices of Moldovan domestic workers in Turkey. I will focus specifically on the social, economic, legal and cultural environment in which Moldovan women immigrants live in Turkey.

Although it is quite common to employ local domestic workers in upper and middle class houses in urban areas, there are only a few works focusing on this issue (Ozbay, 1990a, 1990b, 2002; Kalaycıoğlu and Rittesberger-Tılıc, 2001; Ozyegin 2001, Bora, 2005). In addition, and parallel to the studies and research on the new international migration flows, the impact of the feminization of migration and globalisation of domestic work are generally under-researched fields in migration studies in Turkey.

However, Turkey has indeed experienced the impacts of these new tendencies. Since the 1990s, Moldovan domestic workers have been employed in Turkish households. Turkey is receiving mainly women migrants from Moldova. They are employed in middle or upper class Turkish houses, in health centers, in the entertainment sector and in the sex-trade. In this context, it can be argued that Moldovan women migrants present an example of the globalisation of domestic work in the Turkish setting.

Feminization of Migration and Globalisation of Domestic Work

It is recorded that women migrants overwhelmingly take up work as maids or domestic workers. This definitely applies to the Turkish case since Moldovan, irregular women migrants are identified with domestic work in the large cities in Turkey. The aim of this research is to examine this tendency in the Turkish context. Therefore, the general framework of this research has been established in order to understand the complex relationship between irregular migration and the globalisation of domestic work in the Turkish context by looking at the case of Moldovan domestic workers.

Increasing Demand for Domestic Work: "Care Deficit?"

According to Moors, modernization theory predicted in the 1970s that paid domestic work would wither away (Moors, 2003). In most of Europe, domestic workers have been disappearing since the beginning of the 20th century, and particularly after World War II (Lutz, 2005). What we see however is the worldwide trend that paid domestic work has grown rapidly in the last 20 to 30 years. Moors argues that paid domestic work has never been a "prestige zone" in social sciences. It is only recently that the number of studies in this field has started to increase (Moors, 2003).

There is strong evidence that the demand for paid domestic work has started to increase all over the world. As Lutz states, "domestic workers can be found working for dual earners, middle class families and single people, for double or single parents, for young urban professionals as well as for the elderly and invalid" (Lutz, 2005: 2). There are many different reasons for this development. Firstly, particularly in Northern Europe, as a result of neo-liberal policies there is a tendency towards the shrinking of the welfare state. In the 1980s, many countries saw a reduction in public services provisions. Secondly, demographic factors play an important role with the trend of an aging population being crucial in this respect. Thirdly, the changing social and economic roles of women and, by extension, feminization of the workforce, have generated increasing demand for paid domestic labor. Another factor is particularly related to the Southern European countries. In these countries, because of the decline of the extended family, the domestic work which was provided previously through the unpaid labor of women members of the family, has become commercialized. Finally, researchers point out the case of Middle Eastern countries, where the rate of women participation in the labor force is quite low, but where having a servant has become an important status symbol for middle-class families (Momsen, 1999: 4).

It should be stated that domestic work includes a variety of different tasks such as cleaning, cooking and caring, called by Anderson (2000, 2001) the "three C's". In care work there is also a variety of specialties, such as care for the elderly, children, the disabled or the ill.

Increasing Supply of Domestic Labor: Feminization of Migration
Due to the above-mentioned factors, the issue of paid domestic work has become important. But who undertakes domestic work? The recent tendency clearly shows that women migrants overwhelmingly take up domestic work. As researchers state, it is not the local women but the migrant women who are being hired for domestic work. For example, in 1984 the percentage of foreign females from outside European Union countries was 6% and 52 % in 1987 (Ehrenreich and Hochschild, 2003: 7).

Hogdagneu-Sotelo (2003) analyzes the reasons for the flourishing of domestic work and concludes that it mainly depends on the global economic system that generates gross inequalities between regions. In the global north, the movement of women into the paid labor force outside the home has created a demand for cleaning and childcare services to replace their own labor in the home. Meanwhile, in the south of Turkey, increasing numbers of households have been displaced from their usual means of subsistence, forcing members to emigrate in search of a livelihood.

Domestic work in private houses, particularly live-in, is the most important employment opportunity for newly arrived women, both regular and irregular (Anderson, 2001). It is well documented that Filipinos are global workers and can be found on all continents. Other nationalities of migrant workers are more regional in terms of where they are employed: Sri Lankans mainly in the Middle Eastern countries, Mexicans and Caribbean in the US, and Southern and Eastern Europeans and North Africans in Europe (Momsen, 1999).

As Moors states, sending countries have a strong interest in maintaining relations with labor migrants as they are a major source of foreign currency. "Some embassies... organize festivals and contests to promote the image of migrant domestic workers, defining them as 'economic heroes' who not only sacrifice themselves for their families but also for the nation" (Moors, 2003: 388).

There is no doubt that the ongoing developments relating to domestic work are very important for the social sciences. It is understood that if we consider domestic work, the so-called public/private distinction is not meaningful at all. As research on domestic work shows, we should acknowledge that "Worldwide, millions of homes are workplaces, and millions of workplaces are homes" (Colen and Sanjek, 1990, quoted in Dickey and Adams, 2000: 5).

In this framework, the literature which has been reviewed for this research reflects the complexity of the research topic, namely domestic work, gender and migration, and irregular migration. The review of the literature reveals that there is a vast range of studies which tackle the different dimensions of this complexity, among which gender, class, race and ethnicity play important roles. Some of the existing literature presents theoretical attempts to analyze the issue, while some contains case studies from different parts of the world which try to understand this new phenomenon in different settings. The general feature of most of the literature reviewed is that there is an important attempt to make migrant women visible.

Most of the literature refers to the concept of "transnationalism" when presenting a theoretical outline for study. Here the discussion on "transnationalism from below", and on "transnational families", is an important contribution in order to understand global domestic workers. On the other hand, since the new pattern of migration is different from the past, Morokvasic's (2004) concept, "settled in mobility", is very useful, and an alternative to the emigration/immigration perspective of the classical migration studies.

All the above-mentioned developments which have caused the globalisation of domestic work have led scholars to discuss this new tendency from different aspects. One of the dimensions of this tendency is related to, as Zimmerman and others term it, "global work transfer". They refer to Hochschild's concept, "global care chain". Hochschild defines this concept as a "...series of personal links between people across the globe based on the paid or unpaid work of caring', where each careworker depends for care work on another" (quoted in Zimmerman, Litt and Bose, 2006: 13).

One of the new concepts which explain the novelty of the new migration flows within the context of globalisation of domestic work is Hochschild's "care drain". According to her,

> in addition to (the) brain drain there is now a parallel but more hidden and wrenching trend, as women who normally care for the young, the old, and the sick in their own poor countries move to care for the young, the old, and the sick in rich countries, whether as maids and nannies or as day-care and nursing –home aides. It's a care drain (Hochschild, 2003: 17).

This concept implies an important and global trend: the importation of care and love from poorer to wealthier countries (Hochschild, 2003: 17).

By looking at recent case studies, and referring particularly to the well-educated domestic workers from East European countries, Lutz argues that the brain drain becomes "brain waste", since "destination countries are not interested in their professional expertise but rather in their 'experiental'" (Lutz, 2005: 7).

The general conclusion from the literature review is that the existing literature looks mainly at the increasing numbers of female migrants who are being sought for their labor in *advanced economies*. The peculiarity of Turkey in this context stems from the fact that it is not an advanced economy but nevertheless is a host country for foreign domestics.

Hogdagneu-Sotelo argues that in order to understand immigrant care workers, it is necessary to look at supply, demand, and the social network reference system. I follow this argument when I establish the framework of this research. In other words, I will look at the dynamics of the sending country, Moldova, the dynamics of the receiving country, Turkey, and the interrelations of these two dynamics by giving special attention to the networks of Moldovan migrants.

RESEARCH DESIGN

Two objectives have been followed while conducting this research. First, to understand and analyze the dynamics of migration flows from Moldova to Turkey. This objective will not only provide a detailed insight into the Moldovan case, but will also contribute to our understanding of the impact of irregular migration flows on Turkey. Second, to understand the gender dimension of migration in the Turkish context. Here, we will learn much about the gender dimension of migration from the Moldovan women migrants' experience. After analyzing their experience, we can develop our knowledge of the gender-specific aspects of migration.

Research Objectives, Research Questions and Hypothesis

This research aims to investigate the social, economic and cultural environment, and the legal framework in which Moldovan domestic female workers live. It has been designed to investigate the following specific aspects:

On the part of Moldovan domestic female workers themselves: Their socio-economic backgrounds, family structures, working conditions in Turkey, remittances, ways of recruitment, problem-solving methods, cultural interrelations with Turkish society and Turkish people, their relations with their immediate employers, their perceptions of Turkish society, turnover, their way of maintaining relations with their family members, their networks within Turkey, their legal status, and the problems stemming from their irregular situation, the stereotypes of Moldovan women as foreigners, their vulnerability as illegal foreign workers.

On the part of host country: Different aspects of the social environment in which Moldovan domestic workers live, such as attitudes to and perception of employers, the media, the public etc. In terms of economic factors, the extent to which the informal economy in Turkey plays a role. In terms of the legal dimension, the existing legal framework, and, given the fact that there is no special institution in Turkey which regulates migration movements or is responsible for migratory issues, the perspective for the future developments both in legal and institutional levels.

Depending on the researcher's observations from previous research in the UGINAR[1] and the IOM (Erder and Kaska, 2003) research projects, the following hypotheses have been formulated and questioned in this research:

a) Moldovan women migrants come to Turkey for mainly economic reasons and do not intend to remain in Turkey. Therefore, it seems to be a temporary migration movement.

---

[1] The UGINAR project (International Migration, Labour Force and Population Movement) was carried out by the academic staff from the Department of Labour Economics and Industrial Relations, Marmara University. It was funded by Marmara University Research Fund. The main aim of the UGINAR project was to study the complex character of new migration and population movements and their effects from a legal, social, economic, and industrial relations point of view within a multi-disciplinary approach. This researcher's sub-topic in the UGINAR project was "The New Foreign Female Labour in Turkey". The main aim of this sub-research was to examine the gender aspects of migration movements directed to Turkey. It aimed to explore particularly the presence of cultural bias and discrimination against women migrants through a survey research. Although it remains as a local project and limited in its scope, it has made important contributions to the researcher.

b) There is a potential risk of deception and trafficking, but this cannot be generalized and should not be confused with the network-type relationships which may act in fact as informal protection or as a problem-solving method. On the other hand, however, migration itself can be taken as an emancipatory movement for women. To this extent, the effects of migration on gender roles and power relations in the family can be investigated.

c) Since Moldovan domestic workers accept to be live-in servants and their local counterparts do not, there seems to be no competition between them.

Methodology

This research has been designed from a sociological perspective and aims to investigate the social, cultural, legal and institutional dimensions of migratory movements of Moldovan women migrants.

The methodology of this research depends on available statistical data, the related legislative framework, a review of the media and fieldwork. For fieldwork, semi-structured and unstructured interviews have been conducted.

All these methodological steps have be taken in order to outline the main characteristics of this movement and then to discuss the case of Moldovan women migrants in Turkey.

More concretely, the following methodological techniques have been used:

– Review of existing literature. This has provided information on the broad issue of gender and migration and will help to develop an appropriate conceptual framework. It has also provided information on the recent migration flows to Turkey and migration flows from Moldova.

– Documentary review, compilation of statistical data and official documents: this has provided the available documents related to migration flows from Moldova.

– Media review: the image of Moldovan women migrants in

Turkish society has been investigated through content analysis of the mass media, particularly a systematic review of two Turkish daily newspaper (*Sabah* and *Hurriyet*)

– Secondary data from the Turkish Government, particularly from the Ministry of Labor and Social Security, and Ministry of the Interior.

– Interviews with Turkish government officials: Through these semi-structured interviews it has been possible to follow the perceptions of Turkish government agencies and their future perspectives on migration movements in general and female migrants in particular.

– Interview with the representative of Moldova in Turkey: Through an unstructured interview it has been possible to obtain the perceptions of Moldovan officials in Turkey of Turkey's migration system, and of their citizens' conditions, their problems and solutions to them in Turkey.

– Interviews with Moldovan domestic workers. This is one of the most important parts of the fieldwork. Through in-depth interviews with the migrant women themselves it has been possible to answer the research questions and hypotheses outlined above.

– Interviews with employers of Moldovan migrants in Istanbul. In-depth interviews were conducted with the employers of Moldovan domestic workers in order to provide detailed information on the other side of domestic work.

– Interviews with private employment agencies and travel agencies in Istanbul. Through these in-depth interviews it has been possible to analyze the effects of networks of Moldovan migrants.

In this context, a total of 38 interviews were conducted.[2] The number of interviews is less than in the research proposal. In other words, when the research was first designed, the intention was to interview twenty Moldovan domestic workers. However during the conduct of the fieldwork, the research team experienced considerable

---

2 See the interview list in Appendix 8.10.

difficulty in accessing Moldovan interviewees. The research team accessed the respondents through their own personal references and through contact persons. Ultimately, these contacts were useful for 15 interviews only.

When the fieldwork was designed, it was expected that there would be some difficulties in conducting research on Moldovan migrants because of their lack of legal status. However the difficulties we came across during the fieldwork were more serious than expected.

These difficulties in finding Moldovan interview participants have stemmed from two main factors. Firstly, it was not possible to reach them through organizations or associations since they are not organized; they are mostly invisible in the public sphere. We asked anyone we knew if they were aware of any Turkish employers who employed Moldovans. This channel seemed to work in the beginning. Through our personal relations, we obtained information about many employers who employ foreign domestic workers. This indeed shows how common it is for the middle and upper-middle class families to employ foreign domestic workers. By using these contacts we accessed foreign domestic workers. However, in some cases it was impossible to obtain Moldovan women's permissions for interviews. We explained the purpose and scope of the research; if we were rejected in our first contact, we did not persist, in order to be sensitive to their undocumented status in Turkey. There were also some potential interview participants who initially accepted to speak to us but later changed their minds and sent their apologies by explaining their reasoning.

When this research project was designed, it planned to use snowball sampling. However this did not work properly. Almost all the women with whom we spoke expressed the view that they might help us in accessing their citizens if they wished to, but eventually we were informed that they did not want to speak. In some cases, we could not carry out the interview since the Moldovan domestic workers were about to leave Turkey. This is of course related to the fact that they are temporary migrants and that the turnover rate is quite high.

Secondly, during the fieldwork we observed a new tendency. We came across numbers of domestic workers from other former Soviet Union countries, particularly from Uzbekistan, Turkmenistan, and Azerbaijan but also from Bulgaria and Georgia. In order to understand this phenomenon and in order to obtain some information on Moldovans through domestic workers with different nationalities, we conducted five interviews with women from Turkic republic states.[3]

In addition to the interviews, two members of the research team had a chance to observe the work experiences of five foreign women. We did not conduct interviews with them. However, because of the intimate relations which we established during the course of time, we were able to have conversations with them.

Our interview participants were very helpful during the interviews. It was possible to establish trustful relations; therefore, during the interviews we could find a chance to gain information about some other women whom we did not have the chance to meet. Our interviewees talked about their sisters, daughters, and other female relatives who had already had migration and work experiences in Turkey. We conducted one interview with a female Moldovan undergraduate student in Istanbul. This interview was also very helpful in understanding the experiences of migrant women in Turkey.

All the interviews were conducted in Turkish. Since the interviewees (mostly from Gagauzia) could speak Turkish, we did not use an interpreter. We did not ask to tape-record the interviews; the research team took notes during and after them.

---

3 It should be noted that Turkish people do not generally differentiate between foreign women coming from the Eastern European and/or Former Soviet Union countries in terms of their nationality. Those women are called simply "them" regardless of their country of origin. For this reason, there were some cases to who were referred to us as 'Moldovan' domestic workers, but who eventually turned out to be women from other republics in the former Soviet Union.

We conducted some interviews in respondents' homes, some in our own homes and some in public places such as a fast food restaurant, coffee shops and public parks. We also had a chance to accompany a Moldovan domestic worker during her visit to Laleli to send money and packets to Moldova.

Although this is not a representative sample, I think that in terms of demographic characteristics and work experiences, I could obtain information which reflects the heterogeneity of Moldovan domestic workers.

ANALYTICAL PART

Setting the Context: Moldovan Women Domestic Workers in Turkey

Turkey: The Host Country for Irregular Migrants from Moldova

It is known that Turkey, as a traditionally migrant-sending country, has become a migration-receiving country in recent years. Since this is a new phenomenon, we have only limited information on this complex issue both in terms of academic studies and statistics.

In recent years this has become an important field in migration studies. Some of the studies look at the specific aspects of the migration flows, such as transit migration, human trafficking, asylum-seekers and refugees, while some others try to develop a general picture of irregular migration.

The existing research on migration to Turkey reveals that there are different categories of migrants in Turkey. As İçduygu (2005: 5) states, "Besides the migration of ethnic-Turks, often taking the form of asylum, there are four main types of inflows: asylum-seekers and refugees; transit migration; illegal labor migration; and registered migration of non-nationals. The first three types of inflow often overlap." In terms of irregular migration there are three types of flows directed to Turkey: immigration from Eastern Europe, transit migration and asylum-seekers (İçduygu, 2005: 6). The topic of this research is related to the third type, namely irregular labor migration.

Observation and limited research on the impact of the new international migration movements in Turkey in general, and irregular labor migration in particular, reveal that the growing phenomenon of irregular migration stems from several factors. Among these, geographical proximity between sending countries and Turkey, the role of the informal sector in the Turkish employment structure, the intensive commercial contacts between the sending countries and Turkey, known as "shuttle trade" (Yükseker, 2003), and the flexible visa regime[4] and border controls can be mentioned.

Due to these factors, increasingly large numbers of migrants participate in migration flows. It seems that to enter Turkey with a tourist visa is the main form of irregular migration. The main reason which gives an "irregular" character to this migration flow is the fact that, after their arrival, migrants remain in the country to work even after the expiration of their visas.

According to the estimates in 2001, over 254,000 foreign nationals were recorded as migrants in Turkey according to the four types of migratory flows, namely asylum-seekers and refugees; transit migration flows; illegal labor migration; and registered migration of non-nationals (İçduygu, 2005: 5).

Women Migrants in Turkey

The available statistics on migration are far from being sufficient. In addition, they are not classified by sex. Therefore it is not possible to calculate the number of women migrants in Turkey. Since they work informally, there is no record of the number of foreign domestics. Therefore we do not have any estimate of the number of women migrants. However we can easily observe that they constitute an important dimension of the migration flows directed to Turkey.

---

4   See Appendix 8.11 for the visa regulation for former Soviet Union Countries.

Existing research shows that women migrants from the Eastern European and the Former Soviet Union countries directed to Turkey do represent a heterogeneous group. It includes domestic workers, shuttle traders, service sector workers, and women in the entertainment sector. Although Turkey receives migration from all these countries, in terms of female migration, Moldova, Ukraine, Russia, Azerbaijan and Georgia have become particularly important (Erder and Kaska, 2003).

However in terms of domestic work, the most important country has been Moldova since the mid-1990s. Moldovan women migrants are recruited in Turkish households in order to perform cleaning, cooking and, more importantly, caring for children, the elderly, the infirm, or the disabled.

Domestic Work and Employing Domestic Workers in Turkey

Theoretical or empirical studies on domestic work in Turkey are very limited. Although it is quite usual to employ domestic workers in upper or middle-class houses in urban areas, there are only a few studies which focus on this issue. Among the limited work in this field, Özbay has analyzed the development of domestic work in Turkey through *evlatlıks* (Özbay 1999, 1999b, 2000 and 2002), Kalaycıoğlu and Rittersberger-Tılıç, and Özyeğin have analyzed local women with rural origins who work as domestics in Ankara. Bora has conducted an anthropological research on domestic servants in Ankara (Kalaycıoğlu and Rittersberger-Tılıç 2001, Özyeğin 2001, Bora, 2005).

In the context of the welfare regime in Turkey, caring for children, ill people, and house cleaning are usually organized through family and informal networks.[5] In other words, the number of formal public or private domestic services agencies is small. In this context,

---

5   See table in Appendix 8.1: Child Care in Turkey While Working. This table shows percentage of employed mothers of children under six years of age by a person who cares for the child while the mother is at work, according to background characteristics, Turkey 2003.

Moldovan women can find jobs quite easily in Turkish households. As Keough states, as in many global cities worldwide, domestic work in Istanbul, particularly certain types of domestic work, is no longer undertaken by upwardly mobile women, the extended family or the state, but by transnational migrants (Keough, 2003). Therefore foreign domestic workers have fitted easily into this development. Initially, migrants from Moldova who have Gagauz ethnic origins were preferred by Turkish employers because they speak Turkish. But as demand increased, people from Moldova with different ethnic origins have also been employed.

Since the phenomenon of foreign domestic work is new, there are only a few studies on the issue. Among the published works, Weyland (1997) analyses Filipino domestic workers in the households of foreign corporate executives in Istanbul; Keough (2003) presents the preliminary findings of her research on Gagauz women in Turkey and Gagauzia; Kumbetoglu (2005) analyses immigrant domestic workers in Istanbul; and İçduygu (2004) examines the issue of foreign domestic workers in his analysis of illegal migration in Turkey.

Relevant Legal Framework

Previous research on international migration directed at Turkey reveals that the legal framework in Turkey does not have a coherent character. There are more than seventy laws dealing with foreigners in Turkey. Therefore immigration, working regulations, and policies are not systematic. Parallel to this, it is also widely accepted that Turkey does not have a systematic migration policy to regulate the new migration movement.

Nevertheless it can be argued that there have been some important attempts in order to provide a migration regime which meets the necessities of the recent migration flows. Most of the ongoing efforts are related to the harmonization of the migration legislation within the European Union. In this context, there have also been some attempts to regulate migrant labor in Turkey. All these efforts are certainly related to the fact that Turkey has become an attractive destination for migrants, including asylum seekers, transit migrants, as well as irregular and regular migrants.

My intention here is not to focus on the details of the existing legal framework.[6] It seems that the most relevant pieces of legislation for Moldovan domestic workers are the *Passport Law*, the *Law Concerning Residence and Travels of Foreigners in Turkey*, *Turkish Citizenship Law*, and finally the *Law on Work Permits for Foreigners*. It is known that the rules concerning the entrance to and departure from Turkish territory are determined by the *Passport Law* (No.5682, of 1950), and that a foreigner's stay in Turkey is governed by the *Law Concerning Residence and Travels of Foreigners in Turkey* (No. 5683, of 1950). As I stated before, Moldovan domestic workers do obey the rules of these two pieces of legislation during their visa period. In other words, their irregular migrant status starts after their visa has expired. Therefore their irregularity stems from their stay and work in Turkey. However, according to the current rules, foreigners staying in Turkey with an expired visa must pay a fine at the border. Therefore their irregular migrant status has been sanctioned by this fine. The fine is calculated according to the duration of overstay.

Another relevant piece of legislation is related to acquiring Turkish citizenship. It is well documented in previous research that in order to obtain Turkish citizenship, and therefore to settle in Turkey with legal status, marriages of inconvenience were used by some irregular migrant women before the *Turkish Citizenship Law* (Law No. 403 of 1964) was amended in 2003. The Amendment to the *Turkish Citizenship Law* (No.4866) was enacted in order to eliminate this method by imposing a three-year waiting period before a foreigner obtains Turkish nationality.

Now I wish to turn to the most recent legal regulation on migration in Turkey, namely the law governing the issue of work per-

---

6   For the existing legal regulation on migration, see, İçduygu, 2004.

mits for foreigners. *The Law Concerning Work Permits for Foreigners* (No. 4817) was drafted in parallel to the European Union *Acquis*. It was enacted in March 2003 and put into force in September 2003. Before the law was put into effect, a six-month waiting period was envisaged.

This law is important because it has introduced some novelties to the Turkish system. Firstly, it aims to centralize the regulation of work permits. According to the law, the Ministry of Labor is the authorized body in regulating work permits. Before this law was enacted, various ministries and government institutions could grant work permits.[7] In practice, it is the Directorate General of Labor in the Ministry of Labor which is responsible for the regulation of work permits. The second aim of the law was to prevent illegal employment of foreigners, through effective controls and high fines for both the employer and employee. Thirdly, it abolished *The Law on the Specific Employment Conditions of Turkish Citizens in Turkey* (No.2007, of 1932) a law which provided a long list of professions reserved exclusively for Turkish citizens, thus making it harder for foreigners to find employment and obtain a work permit (Kaiser-Pehlivanoglu, 2001). Finally, with this law, foreigners are now allowed to be employed in domestic services. Under the previous legal regulation it was not possible for foreigners to work in domestic work. This law made it relatively easier for foreigners to work in Turkey.

---

7   As stated above, one of the aims of the law was to centralize the granting of work permits. This was one of the main problems in the regulation of employment of foreign domestic workers in the past. Legal experts argue that one of the reasons for irregular migration becoming widespread in Turkey has been the disorganized nature of the Turkish legal framework on the issue. Because of this complex situation, it has not been possible to produce reliable information and statistics on migrant labour and therefore to investigate the irregular employment of foreigners properly. However, the law could not remove the inconveniences in the previous legal framework, since it could not create a single authorized body. In other words, there are still some pieces of legislation concerning the jobs and professions in which foreigners will not be entitled to work and also some institutions which can still grant work permits to foreigners (Güzel and Bayram, 2006).

According to the law, foreigners are obliged to obtain permission before they start to work dependently or independently in Turkey. However, "in cases where the country's benefits require or depend on the force majeure, the work permits may be given after starting work, provided that information is given to the relevant authority beforehand, on the condition that the working period will not exceed one month and that Ministerial approval has been obtained."

According to Article 5 of Law 2007, "work permits for a definite period of time are given to be valid for at maximum one year, taking into consideration the situation in the business market, developments in the labor life, sectorial and economic conjuncture changes regarding employment, according to the duration of the residence permit of the foreigner and the duration of the service contract or the work, to work in a certain workplace or enterprise and in a certain job."

After the legal working duration of one year, the work permit may be extended to three years, on the condition that work will be continued in the same workplace or enterprise and at the same job. At the end of the legal working duration of three years, duration of the work permit may be extended up to six years, on condition of working in the same profession and at the disposal of a desired employer.

According to Article 20 of the law, foreign employees and employers are inspected by the Ministry of Labor and Social Insurances Institution inspectors whether or not they fulfill their obligations required by Law 2007. After the enactment of the law, the *Application Regulations for the Law on Work Permits of Foreigners* was issued. Therefore, a range of detailed rules on implementation, such as procedures and the bases regarding giving, restricting and canceling every kind of working permit on foreigners who are exempted from working permits, and on how the notification obligations are to be fulfilled, were arranged according to the regulations.

Statistical Information on Migration from Moldova to Turkey

Arrivals:[8] It is not possible to estimate the number of Moldovan migrants in Turkey. Official statistics state the number of arrivals, but we should keep in mind that irregular migrants enter Turkey with a tourist visa. The number of arrivals of Moldovans fluctuated between 47,000 and 90,000 in the period of 1997-2005. The figure for 2005 was 89,800. These are total numbers however, which include real tourists as well.

Residence and Work Permits:[9] The number of Moldovans living in Turkey with residence permits in 2001 was 855 (from a total of 161,254), and with work permits the number was 268 (from a total of 22,416). In 2005, the number of Moldovan citizens who had residence permit was 3,065 out of 178,964. As I mentioned earlier, since the enactment of the *Law on Work Permits of Foreigners* (2003), work permits have been granted by the Ministry of Labor and Social Security. According to the data obtained from the Ministry, at the beginning of March 2006, the number of citizens of the Republic of Moldova who had a work permit was 106 out of a total of 9,607 in that year. There is no doubt that these very low figures reflect a large informal labor market.

TABLE 8.1

Moldovans in Turkey with Residence Permits, 1998-2005

	1998	2001	2002	2003	2004	2005
Miscellaneous	233	371	472	661	1,224	2,618
Working	396	268	258	221	213	216
Student	177	208	160	173	200	231
Total	806	855	890	1,055	1,637	3,065

Source: Directorate of the General Security of the Ministry of Interior.

---

8   See table in Appendix 8.2 for the numbers of foreigners arriving in Turkey from former USSR (1997-2005) and, table in Appendix 8.3 for the numbers of foreigners from former USSR departing Turkey, by nationality (1997-2005).

9   See table in Appendix 8.5 for migrant groups from former USSR in Turkey with residence permits (1997-2005).

The Ministry of Labor has also started to classify the data on a sectorial basis. According to this, the number of foreign domestic workers who have work permit can be shown. The table below shows these figures by the end of 2005.

TABLE 8.2
Foreign Domestic Workers with Work Permit in Turkey (2.12.2005)

Country	Number
Moldova	20
Turkmenistan	4
Philippines	6
Romania	5
France	3
Uzbekistan	3
Others	7
Total	48

Source: Ministry of Labor and Social Security.

The numbers in the table are of course negligible. However they reflect the general tendency of informality in the Turkish context. In fact, local women who work in the domestic sphere, also work undocumented.

Marriages: In the period 1995-2005, the number of Moldovans who obtained Turkish citizenship through marriage was 3,207 out of a total of 41,430 foreigners who obtained Turkish citizenship throughout the ten year period. As is known, marriage has been seen as the only way for migrant women to legalize their undocumented status. It is quite early to observe the long-term impact of the recent amendment to the *Turkish Citizenship Law*; however, the recent statistics on this issue[10] reveal that it has been effective in discouraging marriages.

Deportation: Since most of the Moldovan citizens enter Turkey legally, they are not deported for violation of the entry rules, but for

---

[10] See table in Appendix 8.6: Foreigners Acquired Turkish Citizenship through Marriage, 1995-2005.

other offences. As shown in **Table 8.3,** in the period 1996-2001, a total of 16,251 Moldovans were deported. In 2001 the causes for deportation of Moldovans were as follows: visa expiration (2,215), prostitution and sexually transmitted diseases (938), illegal work (138), illegal entry (9), others (551); totaling 3,851. In the period of 1996-2001, the deportation number of Moldovans for prostitution and STDs was 4,933 from a total of 29,582. Therefore, the majority of Moldovans were deported for the reason of visa expiration. As is known, the visa period for Moldovans is one month.

Moldova: The Country of Origin of Irregular Migrants[11]

After the collapse of the USSR, the former Soviet Republic of Moldova was recognized as an independent state in 1991. Moldova is the second-smallest republic among the Soviet successor states, after Armenia, and comprises some 33,700 square kilometers. It is the neighbor of Romania and Ukraine. The country consists of two broad regions: to the west, Bessarabia, the area between the Prut and Dinestr Rivers, to the east, Transnistria. The total population of the country was 4.32 million in 1989.[12] About 83% of the population lives in Besarabia and 17 % in Transnistria, which has functioned as an autonomous state since a separatist conflict in 1991 through 1992 (King, 2000: xxvii-xxvvii).

Different ethnic groups live in Moldova: Romanian/Moldavans (64.5 %), Ukrainians (13.8 %), Russians (13 %), Gagauz (3.5%), Bulgarians (2.5%), Jews (1.5%) and others (1.7%). The majority is Romanian speaking, but some prefer to call themselves and their language Moldovan.

---

[11] There is a difficulty to access information and knowledge on Moldova. Scholarly information on Moldova is poor. In addition, there are unfortunately only a few academic studies on Moldova in English. Most of our information on Moldova depends on the reports of international organization such as the UN, IOM, World Bank etc. Needless to say, these reports have specific concerns; therefore they are not comprehensive academic studies. Nevertheless, they provide only a general picture of Moldova.

[12] For the population of Moldova between 1941-1989, see table in Appendix 8.8.

TABLE 8.3

Causes for Deportation of Moldovans (1996-2001)

	1996	%	1997	%	1998	%	1999	%	2000	%	2001	%
Visa Expiration	146	20.20	307	14.80	410	18.90	477	13.10	905	23.70	2,215	57.50
Prostitution	187	25.80	602	29.10	849	39.10	708	19.50	975	25.60	729	18.90
Sexually Transmitted Diseases	52	7.20	31	1.50	58	2.70	265	7.30	268	7.00	209	5.40
Illegal Work	23	3.20	65	3.10	429	19.80	442	12.20	288	7.60	138	3.60
Illegal Entry and Departure	–	–	17	0.80	5	0.20	2	0.05	3	0.10	9	0.20
Other	315	43.60	1,046	50.60	419	19.30	1,734	47.80	1,372	36.00	551	14.30
Total	723	100.00	2,068	100.00	2,170	100.00	3,628	100.00	3,811	100.00	3,851	100.00

Source: General Directorate for Foreigners, Ministry of Interior.

During its transition, Moldova suffered a deep economic recession, political turmoil, and worsening individual and social welfare (CBS-AXA 2005: 6). The economy suffered from many of the problems common to many post-Soviet states. Agriculture suffered from periodic droughts, continuing problems with transportation, and the disruption of export markets to the other post-Soviet countries (King, 2000: xxvvii). At the beginning of 2000, the Gross Domestic Product was 40% of that of 1990. As King states, this decline is far more dramatic than in some other republics. Real wages have decreased by 71%, resulting in a low purchasing capacity. Moldova has the lowest average salary among the CIS (Commonwealth of Independent States) countries, which is $30 per month, while the minimum consumer's budget is $65. Eighty percent of the population lives below the poverty line. Unemployment constitutes officially 1-2% of all engaged workers. The real rate, however, is 20-25% (HWWA, 2004: 75). The economically active population has declined from 1,809,000 in 1998 to 1,617,000 in 2001. In 2002, the economically active population was estimated at 1,615,000. The employed population in the last few years is decreasing. In 1993, the active population was about 1,688,000, and in 2001 it was 1,499,000 (HWWA, 2004: 75).

The proportion of urban population was 42% in 1998 (UN, 2000). The economy depends largely on agricultural production and, according to the HWWA Report, around 60.8 % of people working live in rural areas.

Migration from Moldova[13]

Moldova is experiencing mass migration. Confronted with political instability, collapsing incomes, and rapidly rising unemployment, people began to migrate from Moldova on a large scale in the first half of the 1990s. Moldova therefore is a net exporter of labor. Obviously, the labor migration of the Moldovan population became

---

13 The Republic of Moldova does not have a developed migration record system; therefore we can only rely on estimates of different institutions.

possible with the collapse of the socialist regime and liberalization of
entry and exit policies by former Soviet states. Low living standards,
limited possibilities of employment and other problems have resulted
in a mass migration of Moldovan citizens to various countries of the
world. The overall situation of the economy favored this intense labor
outflow from Moldova. In other words, low incomes, high unemployment, increased mobility and, apart from these push effects, pull
factors such as demand for cheap labor, are very significant causes of
Moldovan labor migration (Sleptova, 2003).

Because hardly any opportunities are available for legal migration from Moldova, most of this emigration has been irregular.
According to unofficial estimates, between 600,000 and 1,000,000
people are working abroad. The number of persons legally employed
abroad was 8,201 in 2000. (Sleptova, 2003). **Table 8.4** reveals the
main countries to which regular migration flows from Moldova are
directed to and which are outside of the Eastern European and Central
Asian countries and Baltic regions, in the period of 1998-2000.

TABLE 8.4

Emigration to the Countries outside the Eastern European and
Central Asian Countries (EECA) and Baltic Regions by Country 1998-2000

Country	1998		1999		2000	
	Persons	%	Persons	%	Persons	%
Canada	32	0.9	100	2.4	71	1.8
Germany	1,406	37.8	1,258	30.7	1,396	35.9
Israel	784	21.1	1,338	32.6	1,110	28.6
USA	1,350	36.3	1,241	30.2	1,115	28.7
Others	145	3.9	168	4.1	193	5.0
Total	3,717	100	4,105	100	3,885	100

Source: IOM 2002 –Migration Trends in EECA: Republic of Moldova, cited in HWWA, 79.

Today the biggest parts of Moldovan migrant workers are
employed in low-paid and low-skilled sectors. One of the main fields
is domestic service. Although there are some regularization efforts,

such as bilateral cooperation between Moldova and Italy, these efforts are small in scope since they have not significantly changed the undocumented status of Moldovans abroad (Sleptova, 2003).

TABLE 8.5
Destination Countries of Moldovan Migrants

	%
Greece	2.5
Italy	16.3
Portugal	4.5
Russia	61.9
Turkey	2.1
Ukraine	2.2
Other Countries	10.5
Total	100

Source: CBS-AXA, 2005.

The countries of destination for Moldovan immigrants are Russia as well as Central and East European countries. Turkey is among these countries, especially for the members of the Gagauz minority, which is a Christian community in the southern part of the country whose language is related to Turkish and enjoys substantial autonomy.

According to the report prepared by CBS-AXA Consultancy,[14] about 60% of the Moldovan migrants go to CIS countries, mainly Russia. "These destinations are cheaper in terms of monetary costs and cultural barriers are not as high as in the case of other countries. Italy absorbs more than 16% of the migrants. Far behind there is Portugal with 4.5, Greece with 2.5 and Ukraine and Turkey with about 2%" (CBS-AXA 2005, 6).

Current trends of migration from Moldova reveal that migration flows are rather circular in character. According to the HWWA

---

14 The CBS-AXA Consultancy report is based on research carried out in 2004. Data was collected using three distinct methodologies. These are an opinion poll with a sample of 1,000 households; qualitative data collection which depends on focus groups, in-depth interviews and mass media content-analysis; and a household survey involving 3,714 people.

Report, surveys show that Moldovan migrants maintain ties with their families at home and return home at least once or even several times over a period of a year. The destination countries targeted are normally countries with a segmentation of labor, which plays an ever-increasing role in driving migration. In many developed countries, people are unwilling to perform work that is low-paid, low in prestige, seasonal, or physically demanding (HWWA, 2004: 78).

Today most Moldovan migrant workers are employed in hard, low-paid and low-skilled sectors. Almost 70% state that their employment has nothing to do with their profession. The main fields of employment are construction, agricultural work, transportation, mining, household services, and the sex industry. Seasonal trends are notable, and the migration volume rises by 30-40% during the period of planting and harvesting in agriculture (HWWA, 2004: 78).

Feminization of Migration from Moldova

According to the CBS-AXA Report, fewer women than men migrate to Russia and more migrate to EU countries. The construction and renovation sector attracts more than half of Moldovan migrants, mostly men and mostly in Russia.

TABLE 8.6
Gender Structure of Moldovan Migrants in Receiving Countries

| | Gender Structure across Countries | | |
	Men %	Women %	Total
Greece	29.6	70.4	100
Italy	36.5	63.5	100
Portugal	67.9	32.1	100
Russia	74.3	25.7	100
Turkey	32.2	67.8	100
Ukraine	63.2	36.8	100
Total	100	100	100

Source: CBS-AXA, 2005.

According to the HWWA Report, available data on emigration from Moldova shows that more than 20,000 women of childbearing age leave Moldova every year. For instance, up to 70% of women from villages of the Gagauzia region are believed to have left for Turkey, Italy, Spain, and Portugal. Women working abroad are mostly active in the caring services such as nursing, domestic work, and entertainment. Feminization of migration has affected Moldova to a very great extent, since women make up about 65% (650,000 from 1,000,000) of the total estimated number of migrants from Moldova. When looking at the causes of feminized migration in Moldova, it becomes evident that mainly poverty and lack of opportunities have led to the development of this trend. The roots should be sought for in the challenges of the transition period in Moldova, which impacted both men and women. The situation of women, however, is worse than that of men. The number of women living in poverty is disproportionate to the number of men. In Moldova 68% of the unemployed are women, despite having the same level of training as men, and when employed their salaries in the national economy constitute just 60-70% of that of men[15] (HWWA, 2004: 79-80).

The scarce employment opportunities make women go abroad to work illegally, without social protection or insurance, leaving their children with elderly parents, relatives or neighbors. Furthermore, profiles of women becoming victims of trafficking from Moldova clearly indicate that the number of women who are mothers is the highest one (IOM, 2005).

Fieldwork Findings

Moldovan Domestic Workers in Istanbul
Socio-economic Backgrounds of Moldovan Domestic Workers
As shown in the table below (**Table 8.6**), the Moldovan domes-

---

15 See table in Appendix 8.10 for a summary of gender profile in Moldova in the period of 1980-2000.

tic workers interviewed for this research project are between the ages of 24 and 61. Twelve of them are between the age of 31 and 47. Except for one woman who has Moldovan ethnic origins, fourteen of them are of Gagauz ethnicity and define themselves as Gagauz Turks. They are educated women: five of them have university degrees and the rest have graduated from high school. All the interviewees have already worked in Moldova and their occupations varied. Some of them have been school teachers, two of them were employed as economists in state institutions in Moldova, one of them held an administrative post at a school, and one of them was an agricultural engineer. Some interviewees worked in agricultural jobs. It is worth noting that in their former job histories in Moldova, rural employment was followed by urban employment. This can be explained by the fact that most of them had a rural background, and their locations were villages or small towns in Moldova. Only five of them had an urban background.

The most remarkable, but not surprising characteristics of Moldovan domestic workers are that they have a formal education and worked outside the home before coming to Turkey. Therefore they have experienced downward occupational mobility in Turkey.

Their family structure also provides some useful information. Among the fifteen interviewees, nine women are married, including one who married a Turk and has Turkish citizenship through marriage. Three of them are widows, two of them are divorced and one of them is unmarried. Except for the one unmarried woman, all the migrants have children.

During the interviews we collected information about their husbands' jobs. There were nine interviewees who were married at the time of the interviews. Their husbands' jobs varied, from drivers and agricultural workers to construction workers; in some cases the husbands were unemployed or had experienced long-term unemployment.

Fourteen interviewees have children: the youngest is six and the

TABLE 8.7

Socio-economic Backgrounds of Moldovan Domestic Workers

Year of Arrival of Turkey	Age	Ethnicity	Education	Marital status	Occupation in Moldova	Location in Moldova	Number of Children
2000	51	Gagauz	High School	Married	Kindergarten teacher	Rural	4
1999	38	Gagauz	High School	Widowed	Agriculture	Rural	2
1999	49	Gagauz	High School	Married	Agriculture+ Kindergarten teacher	Rural	2
2003	24	Gagauz	High School	Unmarried	Factory worker	Urban	–
2002	52	Gagauz	High School	Widowed	Agriculture + Kindergarten teacher	Rural	3
1996	38	Gagauz	High School	Divorced	Kindergarten teacher	Urban	3
2001	38	Gagauz	University	Married	Agriculture Engineer	Urban	2
2000	31	Moldovan	High School	Married	Agriculture	Rural	1
1999	45	Gagauz	High School	Married	Factory worker	Rural	2
1999	44	Gagauz	High School	Married	Saleswomen	Rural	3
2000	46	Gagauz	High School	Married	Agriculture	Rural	6
1999	61	Gagauz	University	Married	Administrator of a school	Urban	2
1998	54	Gagauz	University	Widowed	Economist	Urban	2
1998	47	Gagauz	University	Married	Economist	Urban	2
2001	25	Gagauz	University	Divorced	Teacher	Rural	1

oldest is thirty eight years old. Among the children who have completed their education, there are married daughters who do not work; except for one case, and all their sons are employed. Four interviewees' children, both daughters and sons, have employment experiences in Istanbul.

Migration Practices of Moldovan Women in Turkey

Needless to say, the reason for Moldovan women to migrate is economic. One of the interviewees said that, contrary to the situation in Moldova, she can earn money when she works in Turkey. One woman had to come to Turkey after her husband died. The most commonly repeated reason for coming to Turkey is that their salary in Moldova was extremely low; so low that they could not make a living or even afford bread there.

Some women talked about their situation before the transformation in their country. The socialist period is well remembered by some of the interviewees and nine women had been in or visited other former socialist countries. This was of course related to the Soviet policies promoting holidays in different places in the former Soviet Union or in other socialist countries. Therefore most of them had already an experience of travelling abroad.

It seems that the decision to migrate and the choice of the destination country were made at the same time. The reasons for choosing Turkey as a destination country are related to the factors such as language and the information they had before migration. One of the respondents explained this:

> I heard that women from Moldova came to Turkey. The younger was going to Italy while women in my age came to Turkey (Interview no. 5).

Although some respondents came to Turkey without having any information, most of them had relatives and friends already in Turkey who had worked as domestics. The first arrivals obtained information about Turkey from various sources, for example from shuttle traders and Turkish people who were in Moldova or in the former Soviet Union countries.

All of the respondents confirmed that there were too many Moldovan women in Turkey. One of them said that half of the female population of her village was in Turkey. Some estimated their numbers at 1,000, some as 4,000. One of them said that if someone were to go to a village in Moldova he or she would find hardly any women. Even in the wedding ceremonies in Moldova it is hard to see women. Some said that it was not possible to estimate the real number of Moldovan women who have left Moldova, but they admitted that it was too many. One said that all Gagauz women were in Turkey.

When we asked our respondents if men came to Turkey, some replied that they wished to but that there were no jobs for Moldovan men here. They said that men usually go to Russia in order to work in construction work. One woman's husband came to Turkey and worked in a shop for one year, but he could not continue and returned home. The reason for this is that younger men are preferred for employment in shops. Two of the respondents' sons were working in Turkey at the time of the interview. Some of the women were aware of the fact that when men come to Turkey, they usually come with their spouse and they are employed in upper class houses as couples. Some women said that they already had friends who worked as couples.

After they had decided to migrate to Turkey, they did not mention any serious difficulties in organizing their journeys. They informed us that there are some agencies in Moldova which organize the passage. Some mentioned that the agencies also dealt with getting the visa paperwork. Some of women had travelled by ship but also by bus or minibus. The recent tendency is to travel by plane. This has been confirmed by the interviews we conducted with the representatives of travel agencies in Istanbul. Most of the women mentioned the difficulties of travelling by bus because Bulgaria has recently started to ask for visas. The reason for some women's preference to travel by ship is related to travel expenses; they find the air ticket quite expensive. Some stated they preferred to travel by bus in order to reduce the cost of travel. In order to enter Turkey they have to have a sufficient amount of money with them.

In their first journey, most of the respondents were not alone. They had their accompanying relatives, friends, or women from their own villages. Some of the migrants had experienced difficulty in their travel to Turkey:

> We came by a minibus via Bulgaria. They hardly let us enter. They asked, "Why did you come to Turkey? Are you coming to Turkey to work?" We said that we had a valid visa and we were going to Turkey to see the country (Interview no. 14).

According to the information obtained through the interviews, it is family members, including the fathers, who take care of children. However it seems that because most of the women do not have very young children, caring for children is not a serious problem. Some women's children are in Istanbul, some are in Moscow or Siberia.

Therefore, for this particular group of women, the "care deficit" does not seems to be a significant problem. This does not deny the fact that the most important consideration for respondents is their children. Their most important reason for being abroad is related to the well-being of their children. During the interviews they expressed how much they missed them. Although the majority of women had grown-up children, one of the respondents said that when she came to Turkey her daughter was 10 years old. She told us with regret that she was not with her daughter when she was growing up. They usually stay and work in Turkey for five or six months. After this time they go to Moldova for a short visit and then return to Turkey.

Working Practices and Conditions

There are different ways of finding jobs. I should preface this by saying that all of these are informal. First, there is a "worker's bazaar" in Laleli, Istanbul. Moldovans who want to find a job and employers who want to find a domestic worker can meet in the bazaar on Sundays. After having a short conversation about the conditions of work and the wages, and if they reach an agreement, the employer takes the worker to his or her house. This channel is still effective, but it may seem that it is not as effective as it was in the initial period of migration.

Secondly, there are some people who have different jobs, but at the same time act as an informal employment service or as "middle-men". They give information to people and arrange a meeting between the two parties. A commission is received from both parties. Before I conducted this fieldwork, during the UGINAR project, I had a chance to observe a shopkeeper acting as a middleman between foreign women and Turkish employers.

The third way to find a job is to apply to private domestic employment agencies. These also take commission. Contacting the private domestic employment agencies is possible through newspaper advertisements, but is mainly done through personal reference.

Finally, the informal network among Moldovan women is an important way to find jobs. Through these networks, for example, they recommend their relatives or friends to potential employers.

During our research, we did not come across the second channel. However, we have evidence that a Moldovan woman who herself works as a domestic worker also performs as an intermediary, and gets commission for this service. Yet overall we observed that it was quite common for Moldovan women to perform the intermediary role without receiving any commission. This is related to trust relations, and the purpose here is to help members of their community.

The findings of the current research show that the main channel for getting a job is to use informal networks. Most of the women found their jobs through a reference by their friends or relatives.

The role of the private employment agencies is also important. Most of the women talked about the agencies. Some of them had trust relations with particular agencies and thought that if they needed to change their job, they would apply to the agency, but only if they could not find a job through their networks. The reason for this is that the agency takes a commission/fee for its service.

Some of the respondents stated that they never looked for a job through intermediaries; therefore they never paid the fee for getting their job. It is our impression that all these migrant women are aware of, and make use of, the services of private employment agencies; they applied to the agencies particularly for their first job. This especially applies to the migrant women who came to Turkey in the relatively early period of migration flows. The fee that private employment agencies charge the employee varies between $35 and $100.

Now I want to turn to Moldovan domestic workers' job patterns. Among our interviewees there are four domestic workers who work on a live-out basis, while the rest were live-ins. I will deal with their job patterns separately.

In the fieldwork when we looked at the job patterns of live-in domestic workers, we observed that the tasks that they performed in Turkish households varied. Some were taking care of school children or working as baby-sitters, some of them were working as nurses and were taking care of ill or elderly people. But usually they were performing more than one job, for example: cleaning, cooking, and/or caring. In other words they were carrying out the three C's.

Although this research is not representative, the work the domestic workers performed indeed fits my argument and general observation. To put it more concretely, and by following their current job patterns, we see that among eleven live-in domestic workers only one woman undertakes cleaning and cooking, but in the other 10 cases the main task of the domestic worker is care work. Eight Moldovan women care for the elderly and two for children.

In order to investigate my argument that live-in foreign domestic workers in Turkey are demanded mainly for care work, I also asked the interviewees their job stories after they had arrived in Turkey. Since their turnover rate is quite high, in some cases jobs in five different households in three years, I have enough evidence to argue that most of the jobs they perform are care taking, particularly for the elderly, invalid, and young. There are only a few examples of people working exclusively as cleaners.

Among the fifteen Moldovan domestic workers we interviewed, four of them were working on a live-out basis. One of them was married to a Turk and was living with her husband. Among the others, one of them rented a house on her own, and the other two were living with their relatives.

One of the respondents who was working on a live-out basis said that she preferred to work as live-out because she could earn more. Although, she pointed out that it was more difficult because she had to travel to the houses in different areas. Besides, she believes, a live-in job is more comfortable. She said she started to work on a daily basis after her then-employers, whom she worked for as a live-in, refused to pay a wage increase. Now she is quite happy with the money she earns but complains about the hardship of the job. She sometimes stays during the night at the employer's house if she is asked to take care of the baby. She finds her multiple employers through the connections which she established at her previous live-in job. She works in their house three days a week, and every Saturday she cleans the husband's office. For the rest of the weekdays, she works as a daily cleaner in two different houses.

The second woman who is employed as a live-out, works for a single employer three days a week. She has been working with the same employer for six years.

The third live-out domestic worker, who is 61 years old and has Turkish nationality, has multiple employers. During the weekdays she works as cleaner in her employers' houses and on Saturdays she cleans an office. But she said she chooses each job; she does not accept job offers if the household is crowded or if the house is big.

The case of the fourth live-out domestic worker illustrates the fact that some domestic workers actually perform live-in and live-out jobs simultaneously. In this case, she works as a live-out five days a week for multiple employers, but also as a live-in during the weekend, staying three nights at a particular house.

I have also one case which illustrates the point that the same domestic worker performs live-in and live-out jobs in the same day. This worker takes care of an old couple for whom she works as live-in domestic worker between 6 pm and 9 am every evening. But she also works as live-out to take care of a child in the same apartment building during the daytime. She also works as a daily cleaner on her day off if she can find the work.

It appears that that there is no fixed wage for live-in domestics. The lowest wage is $300 and the highest is $450. Live-out domestics who have more than one employer earn between 45 -55 YTL per day.

The wage is determined either by the employer or the employee. However it seems that the amount of the wage depends on many factors including the difficulty of the job (i.e. multi-storey housing), the availability of benefits, and the relationship between the employer and the employee.

They usually get pocket money for their day off. It is between 10-20 YTL. Some employers pay the fine for the overstay penalty on their visas. Some give pocket money for religious holidays. Some of them were given clothes and food. Depending on the agreement between the employer and the employee, they are allowed to make phone calls to Moldova ones or twice in a month.

All the women who work on a live-in basis have their own rooms in the house. One of them has a television in her room, while the other has her own bathroom.

The day off is generally Sunday for live-in domestics. But, again, depending on the agreement between the employer and the employee, some have their day off on Thursday. Some domestics have 24 hours or more leave, and some have it during the daytime, not the night.

When we talked about their daily routine of the working day, Moldovan domestic workers generally did not complain about the hardships of their current jobs, although they admitted that the housework never ends. They said that they were usually happy with their jobs. Since they are used to doing difficult jobs in Moldova, when they compared their current situation to their jobs in Moldova, they found the job here in Turkey to be easy.

However, some had experienced hardship in their working life in Turkey, about which they overtly complained. Those who worked in multi-storey houses/villas said that that kind of job was extremely demanding.

> I worked in a villa in Cesme for five months. I did cleaning and took care of a paralyzed old man. It was the hardest job that I have had. Although there were two other domestic workers, I was really fed up with that job. I suddenly quit with a very short notice. Thank God, they paid my wage (Interview No. 4).

> I worked in a three-storey villa in Bahcesehir. I worked as nanny but at the same time I did the housework. It was very tiring (Interview No.7).

One of them complained about the pets at one of her previous jobs. One respondent said that she left one of her jobs because the couple at the house was gambling every night until late and they did not allow her to go to bed.

It is obvious from the work stories of Turkey that the turnover rate is relatively high. One of the reasons for this is that they need to depart from Turkey at relatively regular intervals in order to escape increasing rates of fines for overstay. Therefore when they leave their jobs to go to Moldova, they may not have a chance to continue to work in the same house.

The other reason for the relatively high turnover rate is related to the particular job they perform. For those who care for the ill or old persons, the job automatically terminates when their employers die. Similarly if they work as baby-sitters or child-carers, there is obviously a set period for the work. In some of these cases the domestics are offered a job by the relatives of a previous employer, but nevertheless this means a change in the workplace.

Bad or ill treatment by the employer is one of the reasons for quitting a job. The women sometimes prefer to terminate work in a particular house because their demand for a wage increase is not met by the employer.

For these reasons they may change their workplace relatively often. In our interviews we observed that the shortest period of employment in a particular house is fifteen days and the longest is four years for live-in workers.

I should state that all of the domestic workers spoke about how and why they quit a job. In all cases, they said they quit a job voluntarily. But I have some evidence of cases in which an employee was fired by the employer.

There is no doubt that relationships between the employer and employee is at the core of paid domestic work. At this point, I would particularly like to refer to domestic workers who undertake care work. As Lutz puts it, there is a distinction between performance-oriented (cooking, washing, cleaning, ironing etc) and care-oriented tasks. Care work requires emotional engagement and therefore care workers deliver an emotional surplus to their employers (Lutz, 2005). During the conduct of the fieldwork, we came across many cases in which domestics acted as intimate companions to their employers, who were old women and who lived alone. We also observed many different disciplinary practices implemented by the employers.

One of the interviewees was very happy with her recent job and explained her past experience:

> In my first job in Turkey I took care of an old man. My friends had found the job. I accepted because I did not want to be jobless. However his daughter behaved very poorly to me. She always shouted at me, she was calling me "fool". She claimed that the cookies I served were not fresh. When the old man asked her why she shouted at me she asked her father if he was in love with me. She sometimes had even beaten me. I was extremely insulted. I could not eat my meals. I lost 18 kg weight when I was working there.
>
> I worked there for months. I was forcing myself to continue to work two more months. And I was quite decisive about returning home after working there for a total of six months and not to come to Turkey ever again. In one of my days off, I told my friends that I had been enormously exploited. They found me another job.

> But I heard that nobody could work in that house more than a month. Actually what happened was that nobody could stand the daughter and the old man was placed in a nursing house (Interview. No.5).

In another case the worker had problems with her female employer:

> She was divorced. I was looking after her child, and also doing the housework. She came home with a different man every day. She also had very serious financial problems. She could not pay my salary. Then I complained about this. The neighbours did not like her at all. They did like me. They encouraged me to inform the police about her case. I went to the police station. I told them that I was an irregular migrant, but this woman was bad (meaning a sex worker). She blamed me for stealing her jewellery. The policemen listened to me and told me if I was a Turkish citizen, I would even get compensation. She actually had a record of being a prostitute. When I was working at her home, I also worked outside. Because she could not pay my wage, she found me daily cleaning jobs (Interview. No.14).

One of our respondents complained that her employers never acknowledged what she did. They just criticized.

The majority did not have serious problems and conflicts with their employers. Some of them did have close relations with the employer, especially with old women who they cared for. Some of them developed a kinship-like relationship and they called them "mother". They watched television together, and had their meals together.

In one case the domestic worker, in her last experience, did not have close contacts with the household members. She said she had her meals alone; she did not watch television with them. She preferred not to be close or over-familiar.

Above all, the expressions below may better explain the complex dynamics of domestic work:

> They pay us. We came here to work. It was too difficult during the first months. It is difficult if you complain (Interview No. 9).

> They pay us. We have to work. It is not our own house (Interview no.10).

> You are an apprentice. No matter how good they are to you, you should be aware of your status. (Interview)

The domestic workers who care for old people might often have two employers if the immediate employer has a daughter. We have much evidence that such a relationship between the employer and the employee is monitored and actually controlled by the daughter of the immediate employer.

One of the disciplinary practices of employers which can be applied only to the irregular domestic workers is to take the passport of their employee. The majority of our interviewees were quite clear about this. Only two women's passports were taken by the employer. The rest could keep their passports with them. They said that in their first years in Turkey employers took their passport. One of the women said that:

> In my first job, the employer's daughter wanted to take my passport. But I was recommended by my friends in the beginning that I should protect my passport and not to give it to the employers (Interview no.3).

> I keep my passport. The employers did not ask me. If any employer asked me to do so I would leave the job. I am not new anymore. I cannot stand it (Interview No.4).

Some women accepted the fact that employers are quite right to take the passports because they open their house to a foreigner.

Our interviewees save and send earnings to Moldova. Their earnings are used for various purposes, such as for medical care of their family members, to pay debts, expenses of a child's education, expenses for a child's marriage, to build their house, to support their parents, as an investment for their future, for the decoration of the house, to buy a house for their children, to support their unemployed husbands, and so on.

Moldovan migrants send their wages to their families. Recently, remittances sent by the irregular migrants have become an important issue in migration studies, but also for international organization such as the World Bank. The fact that Moldovan domestic workers, particularly live-ins, do not spend their earnings but send them home to their country, is also becoming a concern. For instance, according to a newspaper report, the amount of money transferred from Turkey to Moldova is around $ 35-40 million per annum.[16]

For the Moldovan domestic workers, the most popular way of money transfer is informal and located in Laleli. We observed that minibus drivers offered this service. They charge a 2% commission for this transaction. Although recently, transferring money through Western Union has become more popular. However, most of our interviewees told us that they sent the money through minibuses. They say they trusted them. They did not prefer to use the Western Union system because of the higher charge.

Just like money transfer, parcels are also sent by the minibuses. Moldovan domestic workers send various items to Moldova, including clothes, food, and sometimes diapers. The amount of the charge to send a parcel is determined according to the size and weight.

Networks within Turkey

It is observed that Moldovan women develop their own informal ties with other Moldovan women since they have relatives and friends in Istanbul. They meet each other, share their problems and spend time together. They also have close contacts with their family members through telephone conversations; they get regular information from them.

---

16 *Akşam*, "Moldovalı'nın Alamanyasıyız", 05.06.2000.

Among fifteen Moldovan domestics, thirteen have close female relatives including mothers, daughters, sisters and grandchildren, almost all of which are employed in domestic jobs. Parallel to the fact that it is mainly a female migration trend, only two of them have their sons here, and only one woman's husband came to Turkey, but he could not stay more than one year.

It would not be a surprise then to find some Gagauz women in Istanbul who have more than five relatives. We can observe a type of chain migration: information, particularly on work opportunities, is transferred within the family or kin group or the community members. This is one of the important elements in the migration dynamics of Moldovan women in Turkey. Including friends and acquaintances, we can easily observe that there is a female Moldovan community in Istanbul.

Their network relations are mostly mobilized for getting employment. Five of our respondents stated that they helped someone find a job. Actually more than five women recommended their friends or relatives to come and work in Turkey. But some said that they had never done so and would not do so, because they would not want to take the responsibility if there was a problem. It is our impression that almost all the women act in a way as intermediaries because before they go back to Moldova for a short period, they ask their friends or relatives cover their jobs for this certain time.

Mobility in Istanbul

It can be argued that, because of their irregular immigrant and work status, together with their gender status, physical mobility of Moldovan women is quite restricted in Istanbul. They represent a sample of the invisible migrant women. Ironically they are mobile at the international level, but immobile at the local level.

It has been observed that Moldovan women develop their own networks in Istanbul. Laleli, which has become a "transnational marketplace" (Yükseker, 2001 and 2003), plays an important role for various activities of Moldovan women and functions also as a central place in network relations.

Laleli, as Yukseker states, brings together female shuttle traders from the former Soviet Union countries and male Turkish shopkeepers, therefore buyers and sellers of different cultures and of opposite sexes (Yükseker, 2001, 1). For Moldovan domestic workers, Laleli is a central place for many reasons. Laleli is the only district that Moldovan women visit regularly in Istanbul. They go there for shopping, to send money or parcels to their families, to meet their relatives or friends. Most importantly, some of them find their jobs in Laleli. The Dadas parking area in Laleli actually functions as a gathering place for Moldovan women to find work, to see their friends and relatives. Remittances are transferred and parcels which contain gifts for their families are sent from this particular place.

Yukseker observed in Laleli that "Men and women build friendly and sometimes romantic relations that help facilitate transactions in an uncertain and informal economic environment" (Yukseker, 2001: 1-2). We also have similar observations from the Dadas car park. Moldovan women who want to send their parcels to Moldova bargain with the minibus drivers or their assistants about the cost. This bargaining may sometimes include short physical contacts like kissing, and in return for this, they pay less.

Moldovan live-in domestics generally have one day off in a week. Most of them have their day off on Sunday, but some have it on Thursday. In one case the domestic worker spends a longer time outside her employer's house, and spends this time with her children who are in Istanbul. On the other hand, in two cases domestic workers go out in the daytime. In one of these cases the worker is not allowed to spend the night outside, although she would like to.

The main activity of those who go out on their day off is to meet their relatives, friends and acquaintances. Most of them go to church. According to the information they gave, they sometimes go shopping and visit popular places in Istanbul.

Live-in Moldovan domestic workers generally have a day off once a week. How they spend their day off is important in order to understand their activities out of work and their geographical mobility in the city. For this reason we asked questions about leisure time activities. Most of them have never gone to the cinema or done other entertainment activities in Istanbul. Some of them said that they would not go to these places because they were afraid of being caught by the police. The youngest respondents told us that they go to the cinema if they find an opportunity. Some of them said that their employers took them to the cinema, theatre, or circus, or to dinner at a restaurant. One of the respondents told us that:

> I went to the cinema once. My employer took me. I fell asleep because I was too tired. I thought that it was free. But when I realized that it was not, I told my employer "the second time instead of taking me to the cinema, give the money to me" (Interview 14).

Some of those who have their day off on Sunday go to church in Istanbul. Some of them do not because of the police raids. But it seems that they do not go to church every Sunday. One of them for instance went to the church just once, while some of them go occasionally.

In order to understand their mobility in Istanbul, we also asked questions about where they went and where they most liked in Istanbul. Unsurprisingly Laleli is a very well-known place in Istanbul. But the workers' mobility is quite limited in the city. They mostly know the neighbourhood around their workplace. Although some have real fears about going out, one said that she would not get lost in Istanbul. She knew everywhere.

We also asked about other cities. Some of them had been to other cities in Turkey but these were mostly summer places such as Cesme, Yalova, Kartalkaya, Uludag and Bayramoglu, and they went to these places during the summer holiday and with their employers. There is only one case in which the domestic worker went to Bursa for one week's holiday with her friends. The woman, who is a Turkish citizen through marriage, went to her husband's hometown in one of the cities in the Black Sea region. Two women went to Ankara for their passports.

Problems Stemming from Being Irregular Migrant

Although some Moldovan domestic workers said that they never came across the police, the majority that we interviewed had had some bad experiences. They all said they feared the police. Even if they themselves had not had such an experience, they knew of their fellow-citizens' experiences. The most commonly expressed problem is related to bribery. They said that the police threatened them and forced the workers' to give bribes. One of the women said that she had to give $70 to two policemen; her friend had to give £200. Another interviewee had to give 10 YTL: she said they took away even the pennies by emptying her bags. Some of the women said they were afraid of going out on the weekdays. One of the respondents said that if she needed to buy something from the local market she asked the doorman, and that she preferred not to go out. One of the women for example goes out only once to make phone calls to her country and for only 5-10 minutes. Most of them said that they did not go to church because of the police raids.

On the other hand it seems that some local people act like policemen and take money from migrant women. For instance one of the women said that:

> Someone approached my aunt and her friends and introduced himself as a policeman and wanting money. My aunt and the other women gave the money to him without asking [to see] his identity card (Interview No.4).

All the interviewees were aware of their legal status as irregular migrants. Therefore, they somehow accepted the rule about the fines for expired visa. However they complained about the duration of the visa granted to Moldovan citizens.

One of the respondents said, "Actually I do not understand the fact that Bulgarian citizens can obtain a visa for three months, but we have only for one month. It is unbelievable. We also are Turks, Gagauz Turks" (Interview No. 14).

Keough, who conducted research on Gagauz women in Turkey and Moldova, points out the same policy and argues that, "As Christian Turks, they are not eligible for the privileged status of Muslims from the former Soviet Union who are able to gain citizenship in Turkey easily through their position as *soydas* or kin" (Keough, 2003).

One of our respondents, who was aware that Georgians can have a visa for three months and Ukrainians for two, implied that this policy is not fair:

> The fine is too high; in order to pay the fine and the air ticket we have to spend our one and a half [year] salary. They [the Turkish government] earn the most money from Moldovans because of the fine (Interview no.15).

All our respondents had some information about the work permit, and all were extremely enthusiastic about having it. But they all agree that it is very difficult, almost impossible to obtain one. Furthermore, their information about work permit is rather vague. One explained:

> They do not give us work permits. If they did I would apply for it. Actually they should consider about this. It would be good for everyone. People trust us; they see us as their daughters. I would pay for the work permit if it is affordable for me. If it is not I will work in the same status (Interview No. 4).

Another respondent stated that:

> I wish I could have one. Whenever I see the police I feel like I will have a heart attack. I have considered applying for one. I even have

considered an arranged marriage. I will pay money for the marriage, and then I can get Turkish citizenship (Interview No.14)

There is only one woman whose previous employer mentioned the work permit to her, but since she worked only for four months the employer did not apply for one. One of the women was aware of the fact that if she had a work permit she would have social security and annual leave. One of the respondents said that she knew some whose employers got the work permit for them.

Moldovans enter Turkey with a one-month tourist visa. Therefore until the end of this duration, they have tourist status, although they may start to work immediately after they enter Turkey. In other words, they do not have immigrant status during their visa period, although they actually are immigrants in this period.

Being Migrant Women: Gender Status

In her study on Germans in Turkey, Kaiser states that "most German residents in Turkey feel that they only face legal discrimination but no social discrimination on the part of the Turkish society. In fact many have underlined the phenomenon of positive discrimination that is to say, they perceive themselves to be held in high esteem solely on the basis of being a German citizen".

It is clear that women from the Former Soviet Union do not enjoy similar "positive discrimination". On the contrary, they are stigmatized as "Natashas", which refers to sex workers (Erder and Kaska, 2003). The stereotype against women from former Soviet Union also applies to the Moldovans. In fact, as I mentioned elsewhere in this report, in Turkish society the countries of origin of these women are not differentiated properly; they are simply perceived as Russians.

Our interviewees have also experienced vulnerability because of their gender. Regardless of their age they have received "offers" from Turkish men. This kind of practice makes them more cautious about their dress codes and behaviour.

One of our respondents who worked as a baby sitter stated that she was perceived as a sexual threat by the mistress of the house in her previous work and had to leave the job.

Problem-Solving Methods

Those women interviewed generally said that they did not have serious illnesses. However, most of the respondents had had some health problems. For example, one of them had had bronchitis and immediately after the diagnosis, she went to Moldova. She said it was her preference. "Who would take care of me here in Istanbul?" she said. In this case, the employer paid the air ticket to Moldova.

It seems that most of their employers helped them when they fell ill. For instance, some of them had quite serious health problems and in each case it was the employers who took them to the hospital and paid for the medical treatment expenses.

Some of them said that they preferred to go the dentist in Moldova, either because it is extremely expensive in Istanbul or the dentist's treatment was not proper medical treatment.

One of them had a dramatic experience with the health services in Istanbul. Her son came to visit her for Christmas, and because of the artificial alcoholic drink he had, he became seriously ill and was taken to the hospital by her. Unfortunately he died in the hospital. The woman is still trying to overcome the psychological effects of this dramatic loss, and complains about the bad and improper treatment in the public hospitals in Turkey. She compares the health services in Turkey and Moldova, and claims that there is no discriminatory treatment in Moldova.

Except for these cases, they said they sometimes suffered from colds or headaches, but not from serious problems.

The Republic of Moldova does not have a consular department in Istanbul. Due to this, Moldovan domestic workers in Istanbul apparently do not have strong relations with their embassy. Except for three women, they have not applied to the embassy for any reason.

The women who had already applied are those who had lost passports or who needed a document for a marriage certificate. Almost of all of the interviewees stated that if they needed to, they would apply to the embassy. But they did not foresee any reason to apply to the embassy other than concerning lost passports.

Cultural Interrelations with Turkish Society and Turkish People

All our respondents are aware that a considerable number of Moldovan women marry Turkish men. Some of them have relatives in Turkey who have married Turkish men.

One of our respondents is married to a Turk and already has Turkish citizenship. She has also converted to Islam. She is living with her husband. Although she is quite unhappy about the conservative and dominative behaviour of her husband, she nevertheless enjoys her legal and social status.

Some of our respondents who are widows have received marriage offers. But they said they did not want to accept because they did not have enough courage to do so. One of them said quite confidently that she did not want to; she preferred to pay the fine.

One woman who is divorced and has a Turkish boyfriend expressed her view: "Turkish men look for a 'clean' woman to marry", implying the fact that they look for a virgin.

The only unmarried woman among our respondents expressed her own experience and fears:

> I had a Turkish boyfriend. We went to the cinema twice. Later I went to Moldova. When I got back he sent me messages by his mobile phone. But I did not want to continue to see him. He asked me to go to the USA with him. I considered the consequences. If we would have a child what would happen? He is Muslim. He is a nice guy. But I do not have courage (Interview No.4).

On the other hand, one of the respondents who is married said that she had thought about a paper marriage.

Some of them feel themselves to be outsiders, some do not. Some said that they had gotten used to living in Turkey. They said they watched television, and read books in Turkish. Some said that "if you are in a foreign country you absolutely would feel as an outsider." Nevertheless it seems that this not a large problem for them. Some mentioned the similarity in terms of cultural events, such as wedding ceremonies.

We asked the respondents that if they knew ahead of time the situations they were experienced in Turkey, would they ever have come. Almost half of the women said that they would have done so. One asked "what would we do if there was no country like Turkey?" They said they would have come because life was too difficult in Moldova, they would come to earn money. One of the respondents said that she would have come but with her husband. This is a significant answer considering the fact that while she was working in Turkey, her husband left her and married another woman. Some emphasized that since there is no language barrier, they felt themselves closer to Turkey compared to Italy. Two interviewees were not sure about this. One of them said that she sometimes regretted her decision, but that there was no other alternative. She said, "We are not very much keen on coming here, it is difficult to come." And finally one said that if her life in Moldova had been of good quality she would not have come to Turkey at all: she came just for the money.

Future Expectations

Most of them said that they planned to continue working in Turkey for as long as they are healthy enough to work. There are two exceptions. One of them said that she might go back in a few months. The other thought that she stayed long enough; however since she was very happy with her employer who is an old woman, she might continue to work as long as her employer was alive.

It seems that for those who do not have a scheduled date to return, the duration of their stay depends on the circumstances. One of the interviewees said that it was likely that she would return to Moldova when there was welfare in the country. Some planned to go back when their children had completed their education.

Some of the interviewees prefer to stay in Turkey and do not have a plan to return at all. Some of the women hope to get retirement rights and benefits when they go back. They are women who have worked in Moldova for quite a long time before migrating, for instance 30 years. They plan to take care of their grandchildren, but they said they were not interested in paid work. One plans to work in Moldova either in a sanatorium or in agriculture. One plans to own a shop. One of our respondents plans to work either in a factory or on a farm. One said there was nothing to do in Moldova, and asked "What can you do in Moldova? There is scarcity there."

Most of them said decisively that they would like to live in their home country. One asked sincerely, "Why do we live such a life here?" Another, "Actually, what are we doing here?" And another, "Don't I want to stay in my home country in the last years of my life?"

The youngest interviewee expressed the view that:

> I think everybody should live in their home country. I am happy here, but not fully. Maybe I am wrong but I believe everybody should live in their own place. I wish I was born here and lived here. But it is not possible at all... If I had a satisfactory salary, a house and a car, I would certainly stay at home. I do not want to be here very much (Interview no.4).

One of the respondents articulated the view that she wished to live in Kazakhstan where she was born and brought up. Some women stated that they might live in Turkey only if they could take their children to Turkey.

Their dreams are mostly about their children's welfare, happiness and education. Some wanted to buy a house for their sons. It is the same for a woman who is in her mid-twenties. One of them said she just dreamed to be at home. Some of them dreamt of owning a house. The youngest interviewee had a dream about spending a New Year's Eve in New York.

One of the respondents' answers to this question is about return migration of Moldovan women in Turkey:

> I wish all our women could go back to Moldova. Children in Moldova have become too inclined to commit a crime like burglary, because they live without their mothers (Interview No. 14).

Employers

It is interesting to note why employers prefer to employ foreigners instead of Turkish domestic servants in their private houses. Generally, as mentioned above, middle-class women have a helper or cleaner who comes to do housework during the day. They are generally migrant women from rural Anatolia. The most important reason for employing foreign women is that they are accepted and indeed prefer live-in work. There are also other reasons. It is widely accepted that many foreigners and/or Moldovan migrants are unusually well-educated, some even having university degrees. Or they are skilled workers, for example some having diplomas from a nursing school. Additionally, their work discipline is an important reason. The employers generally stated that foreigners/Moldovans perform their job far better than Turkish women. And there is no doubt that the low wage is an important factor.

In order to understand the employers' views, we have conducted seven interviews. As I mentioned above, if the immediate employer is an old woman and if she has a daughter, the latter also acts as employer. We observed three cases in which the employee actually had dual employers. In those cases we interviewed the daughter and also spoke to the immediate employer, thereby also obtaining information from these employers.

One of the employer respondents is male, the rest are women. The youngest employer is 25 years old, the oldest is in her late fifties.

All but one of the employers work. One employer is a member of the upper-middle class, the rest have middle class backgrounds. Except for one employer, all have a university degree. Three of the employers employed foreign domestic workers as baby sitters, the others for caring for the elderly.

Two of the employer interviewees do not hire a foreign domestic worker anymore. Both had recruited Moldovan domestic workers for babysitting and both of them found the employee through their friends. The reason why they did not continue to employ Moldovans is related mainly to the conflicts arising from different cultural codes. The first employer had employed a 25 year-old Moldovan domestic worker earlier this year. The mistress did not approve of the employee's "liberal" code of behaviour, although her husband appreciated this. But the husband also was not satisfied with the employee's performance as a baby-sitter. One of the other reasons is that the employer claims that the Moldovan woman lied, and sometimes got drunk. The second employer employed a Moldovan in 1998. She was not satisfied with her work. Since it was the employee's first job in Turkey, she had problems adapting to her job. Apart from this, cultural differences which were reflected in dress also played a role.

Among the employers we interviewed, three of them still employ Moldovan domestics. They said they were generally happy with the employees' performance and did not talk about any serious conflict. All of them have been employing the same employee for quite a long time. All of them found the employee through the personal reference system.

Two employers currently employ domestic workers from Uzbekistan and Turkmenistan. Both of them found their employees through private employment agencies. One of them decided to fire the employee because of her behaviour at home. I have been informed that the employer found another domestic worker through a private employment agency immediately after the interview. She has been employing domestic servants from various countries of origin, including Moldovans, for quite a long time for cleaning work, and complained about the turnover rate. The other employer has also been employing these workers since 2003 and during that time she had employed five different domestic workers, including Moldovans. She also complained about the high rate of turnover.

Some employers implied a distinction between homemaking and housework. For example they said that they preferred to cook the meal themselves: they did not leave it to the domestic workers.

Employers who employ Moldovan domestics do not refer to the religious factor as a negative or positive aspect of the employment relationship.

Private Employment Agencies: Regulating Irregularity?

In 2004, the *Law on Turkish Employment Organization* (ISKUR) introduced a novel institution into the Turkish employment system (Law No. 4904). Before this law came into force, employment matters were organized only by the related government institution and therefore private employment agencies could not operate. This law eliminated the state monopoly in employment placement services, and opened the way to the launching of private employment agencies which serve as intermediaries between jobseekers and employers, with the stated goal of matching the employers' needs with the jobseekers' skills and interests. In fact some private agencies had already been operating before the law without having a legal basis.

According to this legal regulation, employment agencies which fulfill the necessary conditions can obtain licenses from the Turkish Employment Organization, and their operation is monitored by the ISKUR. The total numbers of licensed agencies were 23 in 2004, and 102 in 2005. According to the information provided by the Turkish Employment Organization, currently there are 161 licensed private employment agencies that are operating in Turkey.[17]

---

17 http://www.iskur.gov.tr/mydocu/bilgiedinme/iskuizin.html.

However, the services provided by these agencies are mostly directed at Turkish citizens, even though there are some exceptions. It is clear from the statistical data provided by ISKUR that the number of people who have found their jobs through these agencies is quite small. It is not my intention here to discuss the effectiveness of these agencies. What is relevant to the topic of this research is the relatively important role played by unlicensed private employment agencies which serve as intermediaries between employers who need full-time domestic workers and foreign women particularly from former socialist countries.

I have interviewed the owners of three private employment agencies, one with a license from ISKUR and two without, and therefore undocumented. The licensed agency actually provides employment services to foreigners in Turkey, including citizens of former Soviet Union countries, but its main area is tourism. It provides workers to hotels, motels, and fitness centers. The owner of the agency stated that they rarely provided services for domestic jobs, but that they did so if people who applied for them [for their business] asked for the domestic workers. One should not be surprised by the fact that the employment placement services which foreign domestic workers may need actually are provided by undocumented employment agencies.

The two agencies currently do not provide services to Moldovans, but do so to women from Turkic Republics such as Uzbekistan, Turkmenistan, and Azerbaijan. The owners of both agencies had worked with Moldovan women in the past but they stated that since their experiences with Moldovans were not positive at all, they preferred not to offer intermediary services to Moldovan women.

Even though they did not work with Moldovans, the interviews gave insights into the operation and functioning of the employment agencies in this field.

It is not possible to estimate the number of private employment agencies operating in Istanbul. But it has been observed that the turnover rate of these is quite high. They usually start business with a small amount of financial capital but certainly sufficient social capital. The stated reason for running the business without having a license, even though it is possible under the current legal regulation to apply for one, is the relatively high amount of money they have to pay when they apply for one.

It seems that it is not possible to start the business without having networks, particularly in order to provide foreign women. The owners of the two agencies interviewed depended on their networks: one has a business partner from Azerbaijan. This owner said that she had difficulties before the partnership, because she could not provide services to the potential employers due to insufficient numbers of job-seekers in her portfolio. After she met her Azeri partner, she did not have such a problem. She has been running the business for five years. The other did not talk about partnership but she talked about her close connections with the sending countries. She has been running the agency for three years. She talked about middlemen from the country of origin who come to Turkey for trade but also bring women with them when they are coming to Turkey. It is the middlemen who provide the passports and air tickets to these women. Women borrow the necessary amount from the middlemen. In return for this they pay money back to him, and work for him for one to two months.

It is possible to see agency offices in many middle or upper-middle class neighborhoods in Istanbul, but they are mostly located in Kadikoy. They usually have offices with at least three rooms, as well as a lounge, kitchen, and bathroom facilities. This spatial feature is important to stress because the office is also used as accommodation for foreign women when they are waiting to get a job. In addition foreign domestics who work on a live-in basis may spend their days off in the agency

The most striking thing about those agencies is that they set some standards for both parties: employers and employees, and also undertake the function of problem solving. It seems that the most important factor in determining the general rules of the job is the agency. This applies particularly to the wage. It is my impression that even if the employer and the employee do not meet through the intermediary of an agency, the almost fixed level of wage is followed by the two parties. The owners of one agency, who I interviewed, stated that the wage is determined according the size of the house and the job required. Therefore the wage ranges from \$400 – \$800. The second one said that according to her principle, she determined the wage in terms of YTL, and the maximum is 600 YTL. She said there are already some standards in Turkey: she simply follows those standards, and therefore if a potential employer offers to pay 700-800 YTL for cleaning and child caring, she would not trust them and would not provide the service. Furthermore she said that she would not provide services to a father and daughter. She said the strongest principle for her was to have an honorable reputation and the safety of the workers.

In the recent years it has been possible to read many advertisements of the agencies in daily newspapers. It has also been possible to receive flyers in mailboxes distributed by the agencies in the apartment buildings. But currently the numbers of the ads seem to be decreasing. This may be related to the inspections by the Ministry of Labor. The owners of the two unlicensed agencies informed us that they used to give ads to newspapers but they did not need to do so any more. They confirmed that it is not through ads but through word of mouth that employers and employees access them.

Although the private employment agencies operate informally, to a certain extent they run each agency by following some standard rules. For instance they usually have a written contract form and they ask both the employer and employee to sign the contract, even though each party is well aware that it does not have any sanction at all. In the contract, issues such as the duration of the trial period, the amount of the fee, the rights and obligations of both employer and employee are determined. The owner of the agency keeps a copy of the contract.

Travel Agencies

Travel agencies operating between Moldova and Turkey are another important actor for migrant women, although their role seems less important compared to the private domestic agencies. However for the researcher they are one of the most important sources of information about Moldovan women in Turkey.

In order to gain general information about the travel agencies operating between Moldova and Turkey we applied to The Association of Turkish Travel Agencies (TURSAB). The list of the travel agencies provided by TURSAB includes only the agencies which are members of TURSAB. We conducted two interviews with travel agencies which are included in the list. We also interviewed employees of two other agencies not included in TURSAB's list. Therefore we gathered information from four travel agencies.

From these interviews it can be argued that the agency's role may have been more important in the past compared to recent years. The reason for this is that currently, travel between Turkey and Moldova is mainly by air. Therefore travel agencies mainly deal with selling air tickets: they do not generally have further contacts with the passenger.

Two of the travel agencies have been offering their services since 1994: one of them started the business three years ago and the fourth agency one year ago. One of them works only between Moldova and Turkey, the other three also work between Turkey and other the former Soviet Union countries.

Between Moldova and Turkey there are two airlines organizing air flights: Turkish Airlines and Air Moldova. Turkish Airlines have flights five days a week, and Air Moldova every day. Therefore there are a total of twelve flights per week. It becomes apparent that the flow between Turkey and Moldova is increasing if one compares the fact that in 1994 there were only a few flights, but now they operate seven days a week. The travel agencies from which we obtained information sell Turkish Airlines' air tickets. The agencies organize flights mainly between Chisinau and Istanbul.

The flight takes approximately an hour and fifteen minutes. The cost depends on the season and the promotions of the airlines, but it is approximately $200 for a return ticket.

There are normally four to five staff employed in these agencies. All of them have employees from the former socialist countries: some of these people have obtained Turkish citizenship through marriage.

Travel agency employees confirm that most of their passengers from Moldova are women. They said that, for most of their passengers, it is not their first trip to Turkey: most of them have already traveled to Turkey before, many times.

I would argue that the travel agencies which only deal with selling tickets normally do have limited information about their passengers. Surprisingly however, some of the staff has extensive information about Moldovan women in Istanbul. This may be related to the fact that all of their offices are located in the Aksaray district, which is a high concentration place for foreigners from the ex-socialist countries. Therefore, they have information about the migration and working patterns of Moldovan migrants. They talked about the situation in Moldova quite confidently. One of the officers has already been to Moldova.

Although they said that they were just involved in selling the tickets, one said that they sometimes help in finding a hotel in Istanbul and this is within the scope of their business. They also help their passengers with whom they have personal contacts to find hotels in Moldova. One of them also said that they helped a woman who was working as a sex worker and asked them to help find her a "normal" job. He said that they found one.

The other employee said that he had helped a woman who needed a residence permit but who was rejected by the related department of the police. He said he helped her, since he knew some officers in the police department: he personally went there and eventually the woman obtained the permit.

Nevertheless, I would also argue that the experience of transport by plane and bus has different consequences in terms of the contact with the passengers. Given the fact that transport between Moldova and Turkey almost entirely depends on air flight, it has not been possible for us to have an interview with a driver or an employee of a travel agency which organizes travel by road.

In recent years travel between Moldova and Turkey depends on the air flights because of the new rule on the visa requirement of Bulgaria. The officers said that after Bulgaria started to implement this policy it became very difficult to organize travel. It takes too long and is too tiring.

There are still minibuses operating between Moldova and Turkey, but their function is limited to carrying cargo and to money transfer. All the officers confirmed this during the interviews.

The officers informed us that only small numbers of passengers are refused entry into Turkey. When we asked about the number of Moldovan passengers who traveled to Turkey in a year, their estimates varied between 15,000 and 75,000. According to the travel agents, most of the passengers traveled to Turkey in order to work, mainly in the entertainment sector, implying sex work, although there are women passengers who come for domestic work. They come to Turkey to earn money. They are educated women. According to their estimate the percentage of Gagauz passengers varied between 40 % and 80 %.

CONCLUSION

The growing body of literature has pointed to interconnections between the globalisation of domestic services and the recent pattern of gender-specific international migration. One observes that women migrants overwhelmingly take up work as maids or domestic workers. This definitely applies to the Turkish case, since Moldovan irregular migrants are identified as women within domestic work sectors in the big cities in Turkey.

Due to the trends strictly connected to globalisation, Turkey has become a host country for irregular migrants from different countries, but most notably from the ex-socialist countries in the region. As the Moldovan case reveals, this migration movement has an apparent gender dimension. Although Moldovan women are almost invisible in the public sphere, they are employed in the middle and/or upper class houses.

The phenomenon I have discussed above is therefore a migration movement of women, which means that it is a gender-selective migration. The existence of Moldovan women in Turkish households is visible, and it has almost become normal to employ Moldovan domestic workers in private households. As is known, Moldovan female migrants began to immigrate to Turkey in the 1990s for economic reasons. They have entered Turkey legally with tourist visas but stay illegally when they overstay the expiration of their visa period.

Up to now their migration and working processes and conditions have not come under a specific regulation, although through the *Law Concerning Work Permits for Foreigners (No.4817)* enacted in 2003 some limited attempts were made. Even though it is quite early to evaluate the impact of this law, it can be foreseen that there will be only a few applications of it. It seems that parallel to the structural nature of informal employment in Turkey, this law will probably have a very limited effect on the working status of irregular women migrants.

Except for their legal entry and departure from Turkey, almost all the processes are organized informally. Finding a job, working conditions, and problem-solving methods are all informal. Up to now the working processes and conditions have not come under a specific regulation, although by the *Law Concerning Work Permits for Foreigners* enacted in 2003 some limited attempts were made. With this Law it is possible for a migrant to apply for a work permit. However, it is observed that there have been only a few applications received by the Ministry of Labor for domestic workers. There is a general acceptance in Turkey that there is a need for domestic workers. For this reason, while the Ministry of Labor tries to prevent the employment of undocumented migrant labor, it is relatively tolerant of the migrant domestic workers. Therefore, it can be said that there has been no specific attempt at the regularization of domestic work, as seen in some other countries. In addition, there is neither a specific official institution in Turkey dealing with migration issues nor any formal organization for domestic workers.

It seems that migrant domestic workers from different countries of origin, particularly from the Turkic Republics, are increasingly becoming sources of competition. Based on the information gathered for this research, I can say that Moldovan migrant women have gained experience and confidence, and have developed a certain level of negotiating power relating to their labor. In a sense, I can argue that the respondents we spoke with for this research are mostly "successful" migrants.

REFERENCES

Abadan-Unat, N., 2002, *Bitmeyen Göç*, Istanbul: Istanbul Bilgi Universitesi Yayınları.

Ackers, L., 1998, *Shifting Spaces. Women, Citizenship and Migration within the European Union*, Bristol: The Polity Press.

Adams, K. M. and S. Dickey (eds.), 2003, *Home and Hegemony. Domestic Service and Identity Politics in South and Southeast Asia*, Ann Arbor: The University of Michigan Press.

Agustin, L. M., 2003, "A Migrant World of Services", *Social Politics*, 10(3): 377-396.

Andall, J., 2000, *Gender, Migration and Domestic Service. The Politics of Black Women in Italy*, Aldershot: Ashgate.

Anderson, B., 2000, *Doing the Dirty Work? The Global Politics of Domestic Labor*, London: Zed Books.

—, 2001, "Different Roots in Common Ground: Transnationalism and Migrant DomesticWorkers in London", *Journal of Ethnic and Migration Studies*, 27(4): 673-683.

Anthias, F. and G. Lazaridis (eds.), 2000, *Gender and Migration in Southern Europe. Women on the Move*, Oxford: Berg.

Apap, J., S. Carrera and K. Kirişci, 2004, "Turkey in the European Area of Freedom, Security and Justice", Centre for European Policy Studies, EU-Turkey Working Papers No.3.

Baldwin-Edwards, M., 2005, "Migration in the Middle East and Mediterranean", a regional study prepared for the Global Commission on International Migration (GCIM).

Bora, A., 2005, *Kadınların Sınıfı. Ücretli Ev Emeği ve Kadın Öznelliğinin İnşası*, Istanbul: İletişim Yayınları.

Boyle, P. and K. Halfacree (eds.), 1999, *Migration and Gender in the Developed World*, London: Routledge.

Boyle, P., K. Halfacree and V. Robinson, 1998, *Exploring Contemporary Migration*, New York: Longman.

Bridger, S. (ed.), 1999, *Women and Political Change. Perspectives from East-Central Europe*, London: Macmillan Press.

Castles, S. and M. J. Miller, 2003, *The Age of Migration*, 3rd ed., New York: Palgrave Macmillan.

CBS-AXA Consultancy, 2005, "Migration and Remittances in Moldova", report prepared by CBS-AXA Consultancy for International Organization for Migration mission to Moldova, European Commission Food Security Programme Office, Moldova: Chang, G., 2000, *Disposable Domestics –Immigrant Women Workers in the Global Economy*, Cambridge, Massachusetts: South End Press.

Chant, S. (ed.), 1999, *Gender and Migration in Developing Countries*, London: Belhaven Press.

Chin, B. N., 1997, "Walls of Silence and Late Twentieth Century Representations of the Foreign Female Domestic Workers: The Case of Filipina and Indonesian Female Servants in Malaysia", *International Migration Review*, 31(2): 353- 385.

DeLaet, D. L. and G. A. Kelson (eds.), 1999, *Gender and Immigration*, London: Macmillan.

Devlet İstatistik Enstitüsü (DİE), 2004, *Türkiye İstatistik Yıllığı*, Ankara: DİE.

Ehrenreich, B. and A. R. Hochschild (eds.), 2003, *Global Woman – Nannies, Maids and Sex Workers in the New Economy*, London: Granta Books.

Erder, S. and S. Kaska, 2003, *Irregular Migration and Trafficking in Women: The Case of Turkey*, Geneva: International Organization for Migration.

Erder, S., 2003, "Global Flows of Huddles: The Case of Turkey" in E. Zeybekoglu and B.Johansson (eds.), *Migration and Labor in Europe -Views from Turkey and Sweden*, Istanbul: Marmara University Research Center for International Relations (MURCIR & Swedish National Institute for Working Life (NIWL).

Ghosh, B., 1998, *Huddled Masses and Uncertain Shores. Insights into Irregular Migration*, London: Kluwer Law International.

Hamburg Institute of International Economics (HWWA), 2004, "EU-Enlargement, Migration and Trafficking in Women: The Case of South Eastern Europe", Report No.247, Hamburg.

Hondagneu-Sotelo, P., 2001, *Domestica –Immigrant Workers Cleaning and Caring in the Shadows of Affluence*, Berkeley: University of California Press.

İçduygu, A., 2004, *Türkiye'de Kaçak Göç*, Istanbul: Istanbul Ticaret Odası Yayını.

International Organization for Migration (IOM) and Sida, 2003, Migration Management /Moldova, Assessment 2003.

Kalaycıoğlu, S. and H. Rittersberger-Tılıç, 2001, *Cömert "Abla"ların Sadık "Hanım"ları – Evlerimizdeki Gündelikçi Kadınlar*, Istanbul: Su Yayınları.

Kasli, Z. U., 2005, "Changing Positioning and Coping Strategies – Undocumented Care Workers in Turkey", dissertation submitted for the degree of Master of Arts, University of Leeds, School of Sociology and Social Policy.

Kelson, G. A. and D. L. Delaet (eds.), 1999, *Gender and Immigration*, London: Macmillan Press.

Keough, L., 2003, "Driven Women: 'Reconceptualizing the Traffic in Women in the Margins of Europe through the Cse of Gagauz Mobile Domestics in Istanbul'", *Anthropology of East Europe Review*, 21(2): 14-26.

King, C., 2000, *The Moldovans. Romania, Russia and the Politics of Culture*, Stanford: Hoover Institution Press Publication.

Kivisto, P., 2001, "Theorizing Transnational Immigration. A Critical Review of Current Efforts", *Ethnic and Racial Studies*, 24(4): 549-577.

Kofman, E. et al., 2000, *Gender and International Migration in Europe: Employment, Welfare and Politics*, London and New York: Routledge.

Koser, K. and H. Lutz (eds.), 1998, *The New Migration in Europe. Social Constructions and Social Realities*, London: Palgrave.

Kümbetoğlu, B., 2005, "Enformelleşme Süreçlerinde Genç Göçmen Kadınlar ve Dayanışma Ağları", *Folklor/Edebiyat*, 11(41): 5-25.

Lazaridis, G. and J. Poyago-Theoky, 1999, "Undocumented Migrants in Greece: Issues of Regularization", *International Migration*, 37(4): 715-738.

Lazaridis, G., 2005, "Les Infirmieres Exclusives and Migrant Quasi-nurses in Greece", paper presented in International Workshop on Irregular Migration, Informal Labor and Community in Europe, Istanbul, December 2005.

Levy, A., 2003, "Moldova, Analysis of Institutional and Legal Frameworks and Overview of Cooperation Patterns in the Field of Counter Trafficking in Eastern Europe and Central Asia", research report, IOM.

Lindauer, D. L., 1998, "Labor and Poverty in the Republic of Moldova", Development Discussion Papers No.635, Harvard University: Harvard Institute for International Development.

Lutz, H., 2004, "Life in the Twilight Zone: Migration, Transnationality and

Gender in the Private Household", *Journal of Contemporary European Studies*, 12(1): 47-55.

Momsen-Henshall, J. (ed.), 1999, *Gender, Migration and Domestic Service*, London: Routledge.

Moors, A., 2003, "Migrant Domestic Workers: Debating Transnationalism, Identity Politics, and Family Relations. A Review Essay", *Society for Comparative Study of Society and History*, 45(2): 386-394.

Morokvasic, M., 2004, "'Settled in Mobility': Engendering Post-Wall Migration in Europe", *Feminist Review*, 77: 7-25.

Okur, A., 2004, "Ev Hizmetlerinde (İşlerinde) Çalışanların Sigortalılığı", *Kamu-İş İş Hukuku ve İktisat Dergisi (Yargıç Resul Aslanköylü'ye Armağan)*, 7(3): 347-368.

Öncü, A. and P. Weyland (eds.), 1997, *Space, Culture and Power –New Identities in Globalizing Cities*, London: Zed Books.

Özbay, F., 1999a, *Türkiye'de Evlatlık Kurumu: Köle mi Evlat mı?*, Istanbul: Boğaziçi Üniversitesi Matbaası.

—, 1999b, "Turkish Female Child Labor in Domestic Work: Past and Present", project report prepared for ILO/IPEC, Istanbul: Bogazici University Printing Office.

—, 2000, "Gendered Space: A New Look at Turkish Modernisation" in L. Davidoff et al. (eds.), *Gender and History*, Oxford: Blackwell.

—, 2002, "Evlerde El Kızları: Cariyeler, Evlatlıklar, Gelinler" in L. Davidoff (ed.), *Feminist Tarih Yazımında Sınıf ve Cinsiyet*, Istanbul: İletişim Yayınları.

Özyeğin, G., 2001, *Untidy Gender-Domestic Service in Turkey*, Philadelphia: Temple University Press.

Panayiotopoulos, P., 2005, "The Globalisation of Care: Filipina Domestic Workers and Care for the Elderly in Cyprus", *Capital & Class*, 86: 99-133.

Parrenas, R. S., 2000, "Migrant Filipina Domestic Workers and the International Division of Reproductive Labor", *Gender and Society*, 14(4): 560-580.

—, 2001, *Servants of Globalisation –Women, Migration and Domestic Work*, Stanford: Stanford University Press.

Phizacklea, A. (ed.), 1983, *One Way Ticket*, London: Routledge and Kegan Paul.

Pratt, G., 1999, "From Registered Nurse to Registered Nanny: Discursive Geographies of Filipina Domestic Workers in Vancouver, B.C.", *Economic Geography*, 75(3): 215-236.

Sabban, R., 2002, "United Arab Emirates: Migrant Women in the United Arab Emirates –The Case of Female Domestic Workers", GENPROM Working Paper No.10 (Series on Women and Migration), Genava: Gender Promotion Programme, International Labor Office.

Salt, J., 2002, "Current Trends in International Migration in Europe", CDMG 26, Council of Europe.

Salt, J., J. Clarke and P. Wanner, 2004, "International Labor Migration", *Population Studies*, 44, Strasbourg: Council of Europe Publishing.

Sleptova, E., 2003, "Labor Migration in Europe: Special Focus on the Republic of Moldova", available at (http://www.ipp.md/publications/St~ Sleptova~ fin.doc).

T.C. Çalışma ve Sosyal Güvenlik Bakanlığı, 2004, Yabancıların Çalışma İzinleri Hakkında Kanunun Uygulama Yönetmeliği, available at (http://www.calisma.gov.tr/birimler/cgm/yabancilarin_cal_izni1_htm).

T.C. Çalışma ve Sosyal Güvenlik Bakanlığı, 2004, Yabancıların Çalışma İzinleri Hakkında Kanunun Uygulama Yönetmeliğinde Değişiklik Yapılmasına Dair Yönetmelik, available at (http://www.calisma.gov.tr/birimler/cgm/degisiklik yont.htm).

T.C. Çalışma ve Sosyal Güvenlik Bakanlığı, 2004, Yabancıların Çalışma İzinleri Hakkında Kanun İle İlgili Bilgiler, available at (http://www.calisma.gov.tr).

T.C. Çalışma ve Sosyal Güvenlik Bakanlığı, Türkiye İş Kurumu Genel Müdürlüğü, 2005, Özel İstihdam Büroları Hakkında Duyuru. Yabancıların Çalışma İzinleri Hakkında Kanun (Kanun No.4817).

T.C. İçişleri Bakanlığı, Emniyet Genel Müdürlüğü, 2005, Vize Umumi Hükümleri, available at (www.egm.gov.tr).

T.C. Kültür ve Turizm Bakanlığı, 2001, Çıkış Yapan Yabancı Ziyaretçiler-Vatandaş Giriş Araştırmaları 2001 (http://www.turizm.gov.tr).

UNDP, 1997, "Common Country Assessment for the Republic of Moldova", available at (http://www.undg.org/documents/1733-Moldova_CCA_-_Moldova_1997.pdf).

United Nations, 2000, "UN in Moldova. Common Country Assesment-Republic of Moldova", available at (http://www.un.md/key_pub_documents/pic/ CCA_Moldova_2000.doc).

Wilford, R. and R. L. Miller (eds.), 1998, *Women, Ethnicity and Nationalism -The Politics of Transition*, London: Routledge.

Yeoh, B. S. A., S. Huang and J. Gonzalez III, 1999, "Migrant Female Domestic Workers: Debating the Economic, Social and Political Impacts in Singapore", *International Migration Review*, 33(1): 114-136.

Yükseker, D. H., 2003, *Laleli-Moskova Mekigi: Kayıtdışı Ticaret ve Cinsiyet İlişkileri*, Istanbul: İletişim Yayınları.

Appendices

TABLE

Child Care in Turkey While Working (Percent distribution of employed mothers of a child under six years of age by person who cares for child while mother is at work, according to background characteristics, Turkey 2003)

Background characteristics	Respondent	Husband/partner	Older female child	Women's mother	Husband's mother	Older male child	Other relative	Servant, hired help	Institutional care	No work since birth	Other	Missing	Total
Residence													
Urban	34.0	2.7	7.4	13.4	16.5	0.5	5.4	7.6	8.9	2.9	0.4	0.3	100
Rural	40.2	2.3	13.5	4.8	26.2	1.6	7.5	0.5	0.3	2.2	0.8	0.2	100
Region													
West	30.1	2.3	6.4	15.6	20.8	1.0	5.6	6.2	7.4	4.2	0.2	0.2	100
South	47.2	2.8	7.5	9.4	17.6	1.3	5.3	3.4	2.4	1.9	0.3	0.9	100
Central	35.7	3.3	7.2	9.3	24.1	0.8	7.3	4.1	5.6	1.8	0.7	0.0	100
North	34.9	4.8	11.8	2.3	31.1	0.9	7.4	1.8	3.4	1.2	0.0	0.3	100
East	43.1	0.6	20.2	2.7	17.4	1.3	7.2	2.3	1.6	2.0	1.5	0.1	100
Education													
No educ./prim.	39.8	0.7	28.3	3.2	15.7	3.4	6.6	0.0	0.0	0.7	1.3	0.4	100
First level prm.	44.4	3.1	7.3	8.9	24.4	0.3	7.2	0.7	0.3	2.7	0.6	0.1	100
Second level prm	43.7	7.7	1.5	9.1	21.2	1.6	7.2	0.0	4.0	3.3	0.0	0.6	100
High school and higher	13.3	1.6	0.2	16.2	20.2	0.0	4.4	18.5	21.3	4.0	0.0	0.4	100
Occupation													
Agricultural	35.7	1.6	14.9	6.5	28.8	1.3	7.8	0.2	0.0	2.1	0.5	0.4	100
Non-agricultural	38.2	3.1	7.2	10.9	16.0	0.9	5.5	6.7	7.9	2.9	0.7	0.2	100
Continuity of employment													
All year	28.8	1.8	11.7	10.1	20.0	0.5	5.7	8.3	9.2	2.9	0.7	0.2	100
Seasonal	39.0	2.1	11.4	5.7	27.4	1.2	8.3	0.1	0.7	2.8	0.8	0.4	100
Occasional	58.3	5.4	4.3	12.9	11.0	2.3	4.7	0.3	0.0	0.8	0.0	0.0	100
Total	37.1	2.5	10.4	9.0	21.3	1.1	6.5	4.0	4.6	2.6			

Source: HIPS, 2003.

APPENDIX 8.2

TABLE

Foreigners Arriving in Turkey from Former USSR (000 entrance), 1997-2005

	1997		1998		1999		2000		2001		2002		2003		2004		2005	
	Number	%	Number	%	Number	%	Number	%	Number	%	Number	%	Number	%	Number	%	Number	%
Armenia	18,0	1.2	20,3	1.6	19,2	1.8	17,7	1.3	7,0	0.5	17,4	1.0	23,6	1.1	33,0	1.2	36,6	1.0
Azerbaijan	93,5	6.1	125,0	9.7	122,6	11.9	182,1	13.0	189,3	12.6	166,2	9.8	193,3	8.9	331,0	11.7	411,1	11.8
Belarus	2,0	0.1	7,7	0.6	7,7	0.8	10,0	0.7	15,4	1.0	22,2	1.3	31,6	1.5	63,5	2.3	77,0	2.2
Estonia	2,3	0.2	4,0	0.3	2,2	0.2	4,3	0.3	5,3	0.3	6,5	0.4	6,1	0.3	13,0	0.5	16,6	0.5
Georgia	194,8	12.7	201,8	15.7	181,3	17.6	180,5	12.9	162,7	10.8	161,7	9.5	172,9	8.0	234,5	8.3	367,1	10.5
Kazakhstan	47,0	3.1	52,4	4.1	30,5	3.0	40,7	2.9	41,5	2.8	53,0	3.1	65,8	3.0	83,3	3.0	106,2	3.0
Kyrgyzstan	8,3	0.5	7,0	0.5	5,5	0.5	8,2	0.6	7,9	0.5	10,3	0.6	14,2	0.6	24,7	0.9	31,0	0.9
Latvia	1,5	0.0	0,6	0.0	2,0	0.2	6,7	0.5	10,2	0.7	12,2	0.7	15,2	0.7	24,0	0.8	23,6	0.7
Lithuania	7,6	0.5	11,3	0.9	11,3	1.1	12,1	0.9	13,0	0.9	18,8	1.1	23,1	1.1	37,2	1.3	50,5	1.4
Moldova	50,6	3.3	61,8	4.8	77,3	7.5	65,1	4.7	46,9	3.1	47,4	2.8	58,9	2.7	71,1	2.5	89,8	2.6
Russian Fed.	980,0	64.1	636,3	49.4	423,2	41.0	680,8	48.9	753,0	50.0	957,4	56.2	1,285,8	59.6	1,593,7	56.4	1,855,9	53.1
Tajikistan	—	—	—	—	—	—	1,0	0.0	2,0	0.1	2,5	0.1	3,6	0.2	4,9	0.2	6,8	0.2
Turkmenistan	5,7	0.4	6,2	0.5	7,3	0.7	11,1	0.8	14,9	1.0	21,2	1.2	16,7	0.8	26,6	0.9	34,3	0.1
Ukraine	100,5	6.6	138,3	10.7	127,6	12.4	153,7	11.0	214,0	14.2	184,5	10.8	227,3	10.5	278,0	9.8	367,1	10.5
Uzbekistan	16,9	1.1	14,4	1.1	13,8	1.3	21,7	1.5	21,4	1.4	20,7	1.2	19,5	0.9	20,3	0.7	24,6	0.7
Subtotal (Former USSR)	1,528,7	100	1,287,1	100	1,031,5	100	1,395,7	100	1,504,5	100	1,702,0	100	2,157,6	100	2,825,8	100	3,498.2	100
Others	-		-		-		-		-		-		-		-		20.275,2	—
Total	9,326,7	—	8,643,5	—	6,880,6	—	9,748,3	—	10,912,8	—	12,906,3	—	13,461.4	—	16.854,4	—		
% of former USSR in total	16.4		14.9		9.0		14.3		13.8		13.2		16.0		16.8		17.3	

Source: Directorate of the General Security of the Ministry of Interior.

APPENDIX 8.3

TABLE
Foreigners from Former USSR Departing Turkey, by Nationality (1997-2005)

	1997		1998		1999		2000		2001		2002		2003		2004		2005	
	Number	%	Number	%	Number	%	Number	%	Number	%	Number	%	Number	%	Number	%	Number	%
Armenia	14,238	1.00	16,565	1.80	14,518	1.10	6,997	0.50	16,594	1.00	16,594	1.00	22,994	1.10	31,335	1.10	36,340	1.00
Azerbaijan	81,688	5.70	86,034	9.30	153,319	11.60	144,818	10.10	151,678	9.20	151,678	9.20	191,048	8.90	325,220	11.70	400,132	11.50
Belarus	1,674	0.10	6,135	0.70	10,930	0.80	13,755	1.00	18,179	1.10	18,179	1.10	29,803	1.40	60,671	2.20	78,341	2.30
Estonia	2,099	0.10	1,945	0.20	4,609	0.30	4,993	0.30	5,040	0.30	5,040	0.30	5,683	0.30	11,681	0.40	16,315	0.50
Georgia	181,535	12.70	158,836	17.20	166,480	12.60	159,557	11.20	162,136	9.90	162,136	9.90	165,308	7.70	229,343	8.30	356,995	10.30
Kazakhstan	40,929	2.90	30,171	3.30	39,175	3.00	40,753	2.80	50,329	3.10	50,329	3.10	64,331	3.00	79,971	2.90	105,648	3.00
Kyrgyzstan	6,720	0.50	5,080	0.60	6,939	0.50	8,084	0.60	9,792	0.60	9,792	0.60	13,042	0.60	22,384	0.80	27,469	0.80
Latvia	1,235	0.10	2,317	0.30	6,889	0.50	10,000	0.70	9,676	0.60	9,676	0.60	13,066	0.60	21,915	0.80	23,507	0.70
Lithuania	6,954	0.50	10,201	1.10	12,122	0.90	12,405	0.90	17,197	1.00	17,197	1.00	21,451	1.00	34,522	1.20	49,984	1.40
Moldova	38,772	2.70	63,285	6.90	53,735	4.10	49,205	3.40	44,422	2.70	44,422	2.70	54,908	2.50	68,555	2.50	85,523	2.50
Russian Fed.	951,138	66.50	406,088	44.00	674,434	51.00	737,855	51.60	936,457	57.00	936,457	57.00	1,322,855	61.30	1,567,209	56.40	1,869,414	53.80
Tajikistan	*		*		912	0.10	2,037	0.10	2551	0.20	2,551	0.20	3,622	0.20	4,794	0.20	6,570	0.20
Turkmenistan	5,005	0.40	6,725	0.70	10,645	0.80	14,262	1.00	19,172	1.20	19,172	1.20	16,918	0.80	24,941	0.90	29,700	0.90
Ukraine	84,424	5.70	115,930	12.60	146,360	11.10	204,635	14.30	178,007	10.80	178,007	10.80	214,344	9.90	275,078	9.90	367,579	10.60
Uzbekistan	16,015	1.10	12,872	1.40	20,535	1.60	20,764	1.50	20,697	1.30	20,697	1.30	18,023	0.80	19,029	0.70	23,627	0.70
Subtotal (Former USSR)	1,429,406	100.00	922,184	100.00	1,321,602	100.00	1,430,120	100.00	1,641,627	100.00	1,641,627	100.00	2,157,096	100.00	2,776,648	100.00	3,477,144	100.00
Others	7,455,737	83.90	5,561,889	85.80	8,071,753	85.90	9,100,480	86.40	10,964,637	87.00	10,964,637	87.00	11,023,807	83.60	13,727,139	83.20	16,195,472	82.30
Total	8,885,143	100.00	6,484,073	100.00	9,393,355	100.00	10,530,600	100.00	12,606,264	100.00	12,606,264	100.00	13,180,903	100.00	16,503,787	100.00	19,672,616	100.00
% of former USSR in total	16.10		14.20		14.10		13.60		13.00		13.00		16.40		16.80		17.70	

Source: Directorate of the General Security of the Ministry of Interior.
(*) Not available.

APPENDIX 8.4

TABLE
Foreigners from Former USSR Departing Turkey, Distribution by Sex (2001)

	Male	%	Female	%	M+F	0-14 years	Total
Armenia	2,072	45.8	2,450	54.2	4,522	46	4,568
Azerbaijan	71,936	50.4	70,891	49.6	142,827	7.473	150,300
Belarus	5,508	33.8	10,801	66.2	16,309	4.683	20,992
Estonia	1,874	56.5	1,440	43.5	3,314	251	3.565
Georgia	89,147	60.4	58,334	39.6	147,481	4.084	151,565
Kazakhstan	11,951	31.5	25,996	68.5	37,947	6.083	44.030
Kyrgyzstan	4,737	47.6	5,224	52.4	9,961	691	10.652
Latvia	6,093	58.1	4,395	41.9	10,488	3.071	13.559
Lithuania	3,809	31.4	8,320	68.6	12,129	2.526	14.655
Moldova	10,524	25.5	30,689	74.5	41,213	1.527	42.740
Russian Fed.	229,830	36.1	407,098	63.9	636,928	104.806	741.734
Tajikistan**							
Turkmenistan	2,545	33.1	5,146	66.9	7,691	290	7.981
Ukraine	49,043	33.4	97,701	66.6	146,744	11.970	158.714
Uzbekistan	9,205	43.4	11,995	56.6	21,200	1.134	22.334
Total	498,681	40.3	740,480	59.8	1,239,161	148.635	1.387.796

Source: Republic of Turkey, Ministry of Culture and Tourism.

(*) In order to calculate the rate of men and women leaving Turkey, the ones at the age of 0-14 are excluded so that the outcome is determined over the total number of men and women.

(**) According to the source data, the total number of Tadzhikistan citizens leaving Turkey is 407, all of whom are men. Therefore, the distribution of Tadzhikistan citizens leaving Turkey regarding their sex could not be found and this figure could not be added to the grand total.

APPENDIX 8.5

TABLE
Migrant Groups from Former USSR in Turkey with Residence Permits, 1997-2005

	1997		1998		1999		2000		2001		2002		2003		2004		2005	
	Number	%	Number	%	Number	%	Number	%	Number	%	Number	%	Number	%	Number	%	Number	%
Armenia	30	0.2	43	0.2	43	0.2	48	0.2	51	0.2	59	0.2	73	0.3	130	0.4	350	0.9
Azerbaijan	4,587	25.5	6,439	27.9	7,930	31.4	10,564	33.5	10,044	34.3	9,935	33.7	9,502	32.7	10,508	32.4	10,477	28.3
Belarus	63	0.4	192	0.8	232	0.9	254	0.8	209	0.7	208	0.7	265	0.9	260	0.8	369	1.0
Estonia	5	0.0	5	0.0	4	0.0	11	0.0	14	0.0	11	0.0	26	0.1	27	0.08	30	0.08
Georgia	594	3.3	692	3.0	723	2.9	685	2.2	761	2.6	788	2.7	958	3.3	1,279	3.9	1,641	4.4
Kazakhstan	1,695	9.4	2,447	10.5	2,579	10.2	3,676	11.7	3,503	12.0	3,649	12.4	3,427	11.8	3,755	11.6	3,896	10.5
Kyrgyzstan	1,120	6.2	1,357	5.9	1,557	6.2	2,128	6.8	1,587	5.4	2,095	7.1	2,223	7.7	2,495	7.7	3,025	8.2
Latvia	9	0.0	20	0.0	8	0.0	14	0.0	20	0.0	13	0.0	23	0.0	20	0.06	39	0.1
Lithuania	27	0.2	54	0.2	79	0.3	50	0.2	47	0.2	55	0.2	65	0.2	82	0.3	126	0.3
Moldova	472	2.6	806	3.5	895	3.5	889	2.8	855	2.9	890	3.0	1,055	3.6	1,637	5.0	3,065	8.3
Russian Fed.	4,846	27.0	5,744	24.9	5,459	21.6	6,871	21.8	6,235	21.3	6,454	21.9	6,134	21.1	6,326	19.5	6,444	17.4
Tajikistan	226	1.3	305	1.3	364	1.4	332	1.1	309	1.1	279	0.9	264	0.9	302	0.9	351	0.9
Turkmenistan	2,332	13.0	2,371	10.3	2,397	9.5	2,529	8.0	2,242	7.7	1,821	6.2	1,645	5.7	1,794	5.5	2,087	5.6
Ukraine	1,314	7.3	1,862	8.1	2,064	8.2	2,326	7.4	2,290	7.8	2,150	7.3	2,312	8.0	2,621	8.1	3,422	9.2
Uzbekistan	652	3.6	806	3.5	896	3.5	1,118	3.5	1,099	3.8	1,108	3.8	1,082	3.7	1,232	3.8	1,726	4.7
Subtotal (Former USSR)	17,972	100.0	23,113	100.0	25,230	100.0	31,495	100.0	29,266	100.0	29,515	100.0	29,054	100.0	32,468	100.0	37,048	100.0
Other																		
Total	135,914		151,489		162,229		168,047		161,254		157,667		152,203		157,562		178,964	
% of former USSR in Total	–	13.2	–	15.3	–	15.6	–	18.7	–	18.1	–	18.9	–	19.1	–	20.6	–	20.7

Source: Directorate of the General Security of the Ministry of Interior.

APPENDIX 8.6

TABLE
Foreigners Acquired Turkish Citizenship Through Marriage, 1995-2005

	1995	1996	1997	1998	1999	2000	2001	2002	2003	2004	2005	Total	% in sub totals	% in total
Former USSR														
Azerbaijan	65	126	519	628	524	1,019	995	1,237	919	22	78	6132	39.0	14.80
Georgia	35	16	142	149	109	235	293	507	463	10	18	1,977	12.60	4.80
Russian Fed.	52	76	381	292	265	495	632	842	691	56	91	3,873	24.60	9.30
Turkmenistan	9	5	23	38	49	78	106	128	89	5	19	549	3.50	1.30
Moldova	-	2	65	100	78	319	728	965	902	14	34	3,207	20.40	7.70
Subtotal (Former USSR)	161	225	1,130	1,207	1,025	2,146	2,754	3,679	3,064	107	240	15,738	100.0	37.9
Balkans														
Bosnia-Herzegovina	13	14	33	22	15	17	12	22	20	4	14	186	1.70	0.4
Macedonia	29	16	60	65	57	82	100	73	60	25	55	622	5.80	1.50
Romania	39	70	321	371	246	760	1,087	870	434	32	64	4,294	39.8	10.40
Yugoslavia/ Serbia Montenegro	48	17	66	56	35	45	53	67	33	9	16	445	4.10	1.10
Bulgaria	259	147	489	459	385	499	1,398	755	808	4	39	5,242	48.6	12.70
Subtotal (Balkans)	388	264	969	973	738	1,403	2650	1,787	1,355	74	188	10,789	100.0	26.0
Middle East														
Syria	34	17	85	81	73	135	138	201	173	58	100	1,095	54.8	2.60
Iraq	24	20	29	27	55	36	60	68	38	18	34	409	20.50	1.0
Iran	21	21	34	35	17	52	77	75	55	35	71	493	24.70	1.20
Subtotal (Middle East)	79	58	148	143	145	223	275	344	266	111	205	1,997	100.0	4.80
Germany	74	55	87	61	54	61	70	90	57	8	24	641		1.50
Others	446	331	861	928	736	1,551	1,881	2,516	2,170	228	617	12,265		29.60
Total	1,148	933	3,195	3,312	2,698	5,384	7,630	8,416	6,912	528	1274	41,430	100.0	100

Source: Bureau of Population and Citizenship, Ministry of Interior.

APPENDIX 8.7

TABLE
Irregular Migrants from Former USSR Apprehended by Country of Origin, 1999-2005

	1999	2000	2001	2002	2003	2004	2005
Armenia	98	474	452	505	494	835	858
Azerbaijan	620	2,262	2,426	2,349	1,608	1,591	1,410
Belarus	82	281	273	197	142	88	98
Estonia	5	19	23	6	4	11	18
Georgia	809	3,300	2,693	3,115	1,826	2,294	2,348
Kazakhstan	185	294	489	396	414	367	296
Kyrgyzstan	35	200	161	274	285	410	333
Latvia	3	68	3	16	12	27	17
Lithuania	28	68	52	6	33	35	68
Moldova	5,098	8,312	11,454	9,611	7,728	5,728	3,462
Russian Fed.	1,695	4,554	3,893	2,139	2,130	1,266	1,152
Tajikistan	10	53	22	41	45	60	54
Turkmenistan	44	142	124	203	187	514	636
Ukraine	1,715	4,527	3,451	2,874	1,947	1,341	1,355
Uzbekistan	142	587	535	533	584	714	652
Subtotal (Former USSR)	10,569	25,141	26,051	22,265	17,439	15,281	12,757
Other	36,960	69,373	66,314	60,560	38,780	45,947	44,671
Total	47,529	94,514	92,365	82,825	56,219	61,228	57,428

Source: Directorate of the General Security of the Ministry of Interior, BFBA.

APPENDIX 8.8

TABLE
Population of Moldova (1941-89)

	1941	%	1959	%	1970	%	1979	%	1989	%
Moldovans	1,620,800	68.8	1,886,566	65.4	2,303,916	64.6	2,525,687	63.9	2,794,749	64.5
Ukranians	261,200	11.1	420,820	14.6	506,560	14.2	560,679	14.2	600,366	13.8
Russians	158,100	6.7	292,930	10.2	414,444	11.6	505,730	12.8	562,069	13.0
Gagauz	115,700	4.9	95,856	3.3	124,902	3.5	138,000	3.5	153,458	3.5
Bulgarians	177,700	7.5	61,652	2.1	73,776	2.1	80,665	2.0	88,419	2.0
Jews	—	—	95,107	3.2	98,072	2.7	80,127	2.0	65,672	1.5
Roma (Gypsies)	—	—	7,265	0.2	9,235	0.2	10,666	0.3	11,571	0.3
Romanians	—	—	1,663	0.06	—	—	—	—	2,477	0.06
Other	23,200	1.0	22,618	0.8	37,968	1.1	48,202	1.2	56,579	1.3
Total	2,356,700	100.0	2,884,477	100.0	3,568,873	100.0	3,949,756	100.0	4,335,360	100.0

Source: King, 2000, p.97.

APPENDIX 8.9

TABLE
Summary Gender Profile of Moldova

	1980	1990	1995	2000
GNP per capita (US$)	–	630	470	390
Population				
Total (millions)	4.0	4.4	4.3	4.3
Female (% of total)	52.7	52.3	52.2	52.5
Life expectancy at birth (years)				
Male	62	65	62	64
Female	69	72	70	71
Adult illiteracy rate (% of people aged 15+)				
Male	1.9	0.9	0.6	0.5
Female	7.8	3.9	2.6	1.7
Labor Force Participation				
Total labor force (millions)	2	2	2	2
Labor force, female (% of total labor force)	50	49	49	49
Unemployment				
Total (% of total labor force)	–	0.7	1.0	8.5
Female (% of Female labor force)	–	–	–	7.2
Education Access and Attainment				
Primary completion rates (% of relevant age group)				
Male	–	68	96	80
Female	–	65	94	81
Youth Illiteracy Rate (% of people aged 15-24)				

Source: http://genderstats.worldbank.org/ (Acess date: 23.05.2005)

Appendix 8.10

Interview List

1) 15 interviews with Moldovan domestic workers
2) 2 interviews with Turkmen domestic workers
3) 2 interviews with Uzbek domestic workers
4) 1 interview with Azeri domestic worker
5) 7 interviews with employers
6) 1 interview with a university student from Moldova in Turkey
7) 4 interviews with the representative of travel agencies operating between Turkey and Moldova
8) 2 interviews with the representative of employment agencies
9) 1 interview with an official from the Ministry of Labor and Social Security
10) 1 interview with an official from the Ministry of Interior
11) 1 interview with an official from the Embassy of Republic of Moldova
12) 1 interview with a bank officer responsible for the Western Union

APPENDIX 8.11

Visa Regulation for the Former Soviet Union Countries[1]

Armenia: Ordinary and official passport holders are required to have a visa to enter Turkey. Ordinary passport holders can obtain one-month multiple entry visas at the Turkish border gates.

Azerbaijan: Ordinary passport holders are required to have a visa to enter Turkey. They can obtain one-month multiple entry visas at the Turkish border gates. Official passport holders are exempt from visa for their travels up to 90 days.

Belarus: Ordinary passport holders are required to have a visa to enter Turkey. They can obtain two-month multiple entry visas at the Turkish border gates. Official passport holders are exempt from visa for their travels up to 90 days.

Estonia: Only diplomatic passport holders are exempt from obtaining a visa for their travels up to 30 days. Ordinary passport holders can obtain one-month multiple entry visas at the Turkish border gates.

Georgia: Ordinary and official passport holders are exempt from a visa for their travels up to 90 days.

Kazakhstan: Ordinary and official passport holders are exempt from a visa for their travels up to 30 days.

Kyrgyzstan: Ordinary and official passport holders are exempt from a visa for their travels up to 30 days.

Latvia: Ordinary passport holders are required to have a visa to enter Turkey. They can obtain one-month multiple entry visas at the Turkish border gates. Only diplomatic passport holders are exempt from a visa for their travels up to 30 days.

Lithuania: Ordinary passport holders are required to have a visa to enter Turkey. They can obtain one-month multiple entry visas at the Turkish border gates. Official passport holders are exempt from a visa for their travels up to 90 days.

Moldova: Ordinary passport holders are required to have a visa to enter Turkey. They can obtain one-month multiple entry visas at the Turkish border gates. Official passport holders are exempt from visa for their travels up to 30 days.

Russian Federation: Ordinary passport holders are required to have a visa to enter Turkey. They can obtain two-month multiple entry visas at the Turkish border gates. Only diplomatic passport holders are exempt from visa for their travels up to 90 days.

Tajikistan: Ordinary passport holders are required to have a visa to enter Turkey. They can obtain one-month multiple entry visas at the Turkish border gates. Only diplomatic passport holders are exempt from visa for their travels up to 90 days.

Turkmenistan: Ordinary passport holders are required to have a visa to enter Turkey. They can obtain one-month multiple entry visas at the Turkish border gates. Only diplomatic passport holders are exempt from visa for their travels up to 30 days.

Ukraine: Ordinary passport holders are required to have a visa to enter Turkey. They can obtain two-month multiple entry visas at the Turkish border gates. Official passport holders are exempt from visa for their travels up to 90 days.

Uzbekistan: Ordinary passport holders are required to have a visa to enter Turkey. Only diplomatic passport holders are exempt from visa for their travels up to 90 days.

---

1 http://www.mfa.gov.tr/MFA/ConsularInformation/ForForeigners/VisaInformation/Vis... Access date: 22.05.2006.

Appendix 8.12

Visa Fees at Border Gates for the Former Soviet Union Countries (2006)[1]

Azerbaijan   : 2 months 10$ – 10 Euro
Belarus   : 2 months 20$ – 15 Euro
Armenia   : 1 month 15$ – 10 Euro
Estonia   : 1 month 15$ – 10 Euro
Latvia   : 1 month 15$ – 10 Euro
Lithuania   : 1 month 15$ – 10 Euro
Moldova   : 1 month 15$ – 10 Euro
Russian Federation : 2 monhts 20$ – 15 Euro
Tajikistan   : 1 month 15$ -10 Euro
Turkmenistan   : 1 month 15$ -10 Euro
Ukraine   : 2 months 15$ -10 Euro

---

1   http://www.mfa.gov.tr/MFA/ConsularInformation/ForForeigners/VisaInformation/Vis... Access date: 22.05.2006

CONCLUSION

Challenges Facing Turkey as a 'Migration Transition' Country and a Future Research Agenda

After decades of being known as a country of substantial emigration, Turkey today is facing challenges to its immigration policies. Turkey's traditional immigration policy was shaped very much by nation-building concerns, as well as efforts to sustain a homogenous national identity. In this respect, Marcus (1985) and Zolberg's (1983) contributions to the literature on immigration that shows the relationship between state-nation formation and the often forced movements of people, help to better understand Turkey's experience with immigration in the first half of the century. However, this pattern of migration began to change after the Second World War; a period when Turkey acquired a reputation as a country of emigration. Pull and push factors played an important role in the shaping of this change. In the post Second World War era, the reconstruction of Europe followed by the economic boom of the 1960s created strong pull factors for Turkish labour emigration. In this context Castles and Kosack's (1973) classic contribution helps to better understand Turkey's experience in a broader framework. The push factors were very much related to Turkey's own demographic, economic and political trans-

formation. Abadan-Unat *et al.* (1976) and Keyder's (1987) books provide the background against which the "push" factors behind Turkish
labour emigration evolved. Castles and Miller's *Age of Migration*
(1997), on the other hand, shows how Turkish labour emigration was
very much a part of a broader phenomenon that was pulling "guest
workers" to Western Europe from the southern Mediterranean and
the Balkans.

Today the situation is very different. Here too external and
internal developments shaped Turkey's experience with immigration
in the post Cold War era. Globalisation clearly is a major external
force behind Turkey fast becoming a "migration transition" country.
This broader phenomenon is captured by *Age of Migration* and
Workers Without Frontiers.[1] İçduygu and Keyman (2000) demonstrate the impact of globalisation in the specific case of Turkey.
However, they also highlight the importance of internal developments
within Turkey as a factor transforming Turkey into a "migration transition" country. Turkey's liberal market economy characterized by
informality is another internal factor that attracts migration to the
country. Yet, another internal factor has been government policies that
have made entry into Turkey much easier than was the case during the
Cold War. Lastly, Turkey's current ambition to become a member of
the EU and the accompanying political liberalization is altering the
state's traditional conception of national identity. There is growing
pressure to adopt policies that recognize Turkey's own ethnic and cultural diversity. Inevitably, this is having a bearing on how Turkish state
and society are looking at foreigners and migrants. In turn, government policy is under growing pressure to be reformed and adapted to
the realities of Turkey becoming a "migration transition" country.

The early signs of a change of policy are becoming increasingly
apparent and the EU is an important driving force. For example,
Turkey, as part and parcel of pre-accession requirements, has to har-

---

1   See Stalker (2000).

monize its legislation in areas identified in the EU 'Accession Partnership' document.[2] Specifically, the *Action Plan on Asylum and Migration* adopted by the government in March 2005 lays out the tasks and time table that Turkey intends to follow in preparing for the development of a fully fledged national status determination system, lifting the geographical limitation and adopting EU directives on asylum and migration in general.[3] However, the uncertainty over Turkey's membership prospects is discouraging officials from advising the government to make these changes too precipitously. Furthermore, there is a deep-seated concern that Turkey may become a 'buffer zone' or a kind of a 'dumping ground' for the EU's illegal migrants and rejected asylum seekers. Yet, the pressures for policy reform are unequivocal. For example, the government has completely overhauled its work permit laws and regulations. Today it has become relatively easier for foreign nationals to seek work and to be employed in Turkey. Furthermore, the government has succeeded in cooperation with non-governmental organizations to provide protection and social services for victims of trafficking. Less than a decade ago such a policy would have been unimaginable.

Turkish society, which has always been aware of its ethnic and cultural diversity, will be facing challenges too, since Turkey's status as a 'migration transition' country is exposing her to a new kind of diversity involving foreigners. Sports are an area that manifests itself most conspicuously. Currently, in Turkey there are a large number of foreigners who are active and visible in various branches of sport and

---

2   "Accession Partnership" documents lay down the tasks that Turkey has to implement to harmonize its laws and policies with that of the EU *acquis*. There is a whole section relating to issues under immigration. The most recent one is *Accession Partnership Strategy for Turkey*, Council Decision, 18 February 2008.

3   The Action Plan on "Asylum and Migration" was officially adopted by the Turkish government on 25 March 2005. It is available with a book entitled *Asylum and Migration Legislation* (MOI and UNHCR, Ankara, February 2006). The document can be accessed from www.unhcr.org.tr. The Border Management Action Plan was adopted 27 March 2006, *National Action Plan towards the Implementation of Turkey's Integrated Border Management Strategy* (MOI, Ankara, March 2006). This Action Plan too touches upon issues to do with immigration.

Turks have become accustomed to seeing names in Turkish national teams that are not classic Turkish names.[4] These developments reflect a Turkish society that is evolving beyond the traditional definition of Turkish national identity. In turn this may facilitate the task of the government in its immigration policies yet at the same time provoke xenophobia especially among nationalist circles.

The prospects of Turkey loosening its traditional immigration policies seem less likely. The new Settlement Law of November 2006 continues to limit formal immigration to Turkey to individuals and groups of 'Turkish descent and culture'. This approach is very closely related with the traditional conception of 'Turkishness' reminiscent of the 1930s. The identifying features of 'Turkishness' are not solely related to Turkish ethnicity but also the ability and willingness to adopt the Turkish language and to be members of Muslim Sunni ethnic groups often closely associated with past Ottoman rule. Technically, Albanians, Bosnians, Circassians, Pomaks, Tatars, and Turks –mostly from the Balkans– who are included in this definition will be able to immigrate to Turkey. Minorities claiming a link to Turkey who are not Sunni Muslims, that is, everyone from Armenians and Assyrians to Greeks and Jews, as well as unassimilated Kurds and Alevis, are likely to face difficulties in immigrating to Turkey. Such a policy will not be in harmony with the emerging EU common immigration policy, which increasingly emphasizes civic connections to the host territory and employment prospects rather than ethnic or national origin as grounds for immigration. How will the government treat demands from descendents of former non-Muslim Turkish citizens to immigrate and settle in Turkey? Similarly, what will be the position of Turkey in the face of foreign individuals who may wish to immigrate on the grounds of family connections even if they are not of 'Turkish descent and culture'? What will happen to those Kurds or descendents that may have left willingly or unwillingly in the past wanting to return and resettle in Turkey? If

---

4   Some well-known examples are Mehmet Aurelio, Elvan Abeylegesse, and Mert Nobre.

and when Turkey lifts the geographical limitation to the 1951 Geneva Convention will recognized refugees have the right to "integrate" into Turkey and be allowed to become citizens?

Questions such as these will increasingly crowd the public policy agenda of Turkey. How will Turkey as a state manage immigration against the background of domestic pull and push factors accompanying globalisation? Hollifield (2004) in his article "The Emerging Migration State" refers to two types of states in respect to regulating migration: a state that follows relatively open door policies and extracts advantages from immigration compared to a state that builds walls around itself and restricts immigration. Which of these states will Turkey resemble? This is a topic that will deserve greater attention. It is however likely that Turkey will be caught between pressures in both directions. As the letter and spirit of the new Settlement Law suggests Turkey will remain relatively closed to formal immigration. Yet, the empirical reality suggests that in one way or the other people from abroad will increasingly come to Turkey as migrants for short or long durations. Turkey will be subject to contradictory forces from the outside too. A case in point is the day to day management of the movement of people into Turkey.

Turkey is in the process of adopting the EU Schengen visa system, which requires member countries to apply a common visa policy to third country nationals. This will require replacing Turkey's current, relatively liberal visa system with a much stricter one. Although this will align Turkish practice with that of the EU, it will also make it more difficult for nationals of neighboring non-EU countries to enter Turkey. This may actually result in a net cultural, economic, and social loss for Turkey (Kirişci, 2005). It may also exacerbate illegal migration by forcing people to circumvent visa restrictions. So far, in spite of the requirements of the EU, the Turkish government has been reluctant to adopt the Schengen visa system fully and has been allowing the movement of people between Turkey and neighboring countries to continue and grow. Actually, in the course of the last year Turkey has lifted visa requirements for the nationals of Georgia, Morocco and Tunisia. These three countries are on the Schengen so called "black list". If the EU does get serious about Turkey's membership this pattern may change and Turkey may restrict movement of people into Turkey.

One final aspect of Turkey as a 'migration transition' country is its relationship with the current Turkish immigrant stock in EU countries and the relations between the EU and Turkey in this regard. The nature of emigration that is likely to take place from Turkey to Europe will most probably change the nature and composition of Turkish migrant stock in Europe. The question of Turkish immigration to the EU will remain a hotly debated issue in the light of the growing need for immigration to compensate Europe's shrinking population. Münz and Reiterer (2007) strikingly demonstrate how demographic trends in most EU member countries are creating a need for immigrants and labor from abroad. They point out that the EU will inevitably need to attract labor from countries in the neighbourhood of the EU including Turkey. Even if Behar (2006) questions whether Turkish and EU demographics are compatible it is likely that the debate on the prospects of Turkish immigration to the EU will continue. What might be the composition of future Turkish immigration to Europe take? How might immigration to the EU be managed? What might be the ways in which Turkish immigration and the question of the integration of existing stocks of migrants be linked? What kinds of new forms of trans-national contacts are developing between the EU member countries and Turkey? In what different ways could the relationship between Turkish membership to the EU and immigration be managed? Might there be more attractive alternative destination of Turkish labor emigration than the EU? These are questions that are likely to crowd the public policy and research agendas of the future.

This volume aspires to constitute a first modest step towards addressing some aspects of the challenges associated with Turkey becoming a 'migration transition' country. Given the history of the eighty-five year old Turkish republic characterized by emigration and immigration flows, the chapters in this volume refer to both "relatively old" and "relatively new" cases of migration involving Turkey. The volume tries to bridge the two experiences in an effort to better understand Turkey becoming a 'migration transition' country. The chapters present a variety of challenges for further study. They provide insight and raise questions that can hopefully enhance understanding of emigration and immigration in the case of Turkey, as well as broaden knowledge on international migration in general.

International migration involving Turkey has not only changed Turkish society, but has also influenced the societies in neighboring regions profoundly. The historical case of Karamanlis in Greece, elaborated by Özdemir in Chapter 2, shows the interplay of identity politics and the legacy of the past migratory flows over the present day individual identity formations. Certainly, additional migration studies with historical perspective are required to illustrate the impact of old migration movements in the formation of identity in contemporary societies and communities. It is within this context, that careful comparisons are also needed. There is no doubt that comparisons in migration research can help broaden our generalizations and make historical research more scientific. For instance, it would be interesting to repeat such a study for the Cretan Muslims who were part of the Exchange. Moreover, the comparative method is largely dependent on the construction of the research project itself: indeed, the study of Yağmurlu in this volume provides us with an example of a research design in which a comparison of Turkish migrant and non-migrant mothers' long-term socialization goals are constructed. Only through such a comparative analysis can we possibly show the multi-dimensional aspects of the causes and consequences of migration. In terms of furthering the cause of comparative study Kaşka's study of Moldovan women in Turkey could be repeated in Moldova. This could help to increase our understanding of how demand and supply dynamics operate across a sending and a receiving country.

Beside issues of comparativeness this volume also addresses questions to do with data sets available for researchers interested in studying migration. For critical theoretical and empirical reasons it is important for researchers to probe the quality of data used in their migration research and seek to understand the strengths and weaknesses of a data-set. For instance, when Coşkun and Türkyılmaz analyze the 2000 Census data to estimate the international migration flows to Turkey, it becomes clear that there are certain shortcomings of the data used in their analyses. This may limit the conclusions drawn from the study conducted by them. In order to go beyond the dichotomies of "big-N studies" versus "ethnographic studies" or "qualitative studies" versus "quantitative studies" in migration research, further research should deal with the question of how to improve the quality of data in migration research regardless of their type. Most ethnographic studies in this volume, such as Soysal's chapter on Turks in Berlin, Danış, Taraghi, and Pérouse's chapter on irregular migrants, Brewer and Yükseker's chapter on Africans in Istanbul, Kaşka's chapter on the case of Moldovan domestic workers, and to a certain extent, Akçapar's study on brain drain, draw on in-depth interviews and participant observations in migrant communities. These studies will be enriched if, in the future, they are complemented with projects employing broad survey type of research methodology. Another fruitful methodological approach in migration research is to explore the use of triangulation. This is often considered to indicate that more than one method can be used in a study with a view to double-check the results. Such approaches will not only deepen our understanding of the status of migratory flows and the position of migrants, but also allow us to examine the relationship between theoretical abstractions and empirical realities of migratory processes, structures, and actors.

Indeed, the field of international migration research in Turkey is a fertile ground for further studies both of a theoretical and an empirical nature. The chapters in this volume are based mostly on empirical studies. However, obviously theory-building or theorizing through empirically based research remains a very important dimension of research. It should be noted that theorizing and agenda setting in research on international migration around the world has been almost completely in the hands of scholars and researchers in the receiving countries of the "North" and "West". It is in an attempt to encourage primary research as well as theorizing to take place in a traditionally emigration country such as Turkey that the Migration Research Program at Koc University (MiReKoc) was established with the support of the Foundation for Population, Migration and Environment (PME) of Switzerland. Since its inception in 2004 MiReKoc has supported 31 research projects dealing with various aspects of Turkey's experience with migration.[5] Although research on international migration in Turkey, and in many other countries of the "South" and the "East" is characterized by a richness of descriptive empirical material, it is also marked by a relative absence of new theoretical contributions. In other words, there seems to be a hegemonic setting in which research areas and questions are defined and formulated in the "core countries", and then are presented and inserted into the agendas of the "peripheries". Moreover, research concerns of the latter are less heard or their views are not aired effectively, while the interests of the former remain often high on the international research agenda. This phenomenon is deemed worthy of discussion, particularly in the light of the recent expansion of migration research in various countries of the "South" and the "East", including Turkey. The chapters in this volume do not only prove that there are genuine attempts of original empirical studies that voice a creative and unique research agenda (for instances, chapters by Yağmurlu, Danış, Taraghi, and Pérouse, and Brewer and Yükseker) but also, that there exist clear efforts to make theoretical contributions to the field of migration studies (such as chapters by Özdemir and Soysal). Yet there is still much to be done to voice an empirically and theoretically strong new research agenda in Turkey. We hope that *MiReKoc* and this volume is able to make a modest contribution to research on international migration in general.

---

5   A full list of these research projects can be reached from www.mirekoc.com.

REFERENCES

Abadan-Unat, N., R. Keleş, R. Penninx, H. Van Renselaar, L. Van Velzen and L. Yenisey, 1976, *Migration and Development: A Study of the Effects of International Labor Migration on Boğazlıyan District*, Ankara: Ajans-Türk Press.

Behar, C., 2006, "Demographic Developments and 'Complementarities': Ageing, Labor and Migration", *Turkish Studies*, 7(1): 17-31.

Castles, S. and G. Kosack, 1973, *Immigrant Workers and Class Structure in Western Europe*, London: Oxford University Press.

Castles, S. and M. J. Miller, 1997, *The Age of Migration: International Population Movements in the Modern World*, 2nd ed., New York: The Guilford Press.

Council of the European Union, 2008, "Accession Partnership Strategy for Turkey", Council Decision, 18th February.

Hollifield, J., 2004, "The Emerging Migration State", *International Migration Review*, 38(3): 885-912.

İçduygu, A. and F. Keyman, 2000, "Globalisation, Security and Migration: The Turkish Case", *Global Governance*, 6(3): 383-398.

Keyder, Ç., 1987, *State and Class in Turkey: A Study in Capitalist Development*, London: Verso.

Kirişci, K., 2005, "A Friendlier Schengen Visa System as a Tool of 'Soft Power': The Experience of Turkey", *European Journal of Migration and Law*, 7(4): 343-367.

Marcus, M. R., 1985, *The unwanted: European refugees in the twentieth century*, Oxford: Oxford University Press.

MOI and UNHCR, 2006, "The Action Plan on 'Asylum and Migration'" in *Asylum and Migration Legislation*, Ankara.

MOI, 2006, "The Border Action Plan", *National Plan towards the Implementation of Turkey's Integrated Border Border Management Strategy*, Ankara.

Münz, R. and A. F. Reiterer, 2007, *Wie schnell wächst die Zahl der Menschen?*, Frankfurt: S. Fischer Verlag.

Stalker, P., 2000, *Age of Migration and Workers without Frontiers*, London: Macmillan.

Zolberg, A., 1983, "The Formation of New States as a Refugee-generating Process", *ANNALS, AAPSS*, 467: 24-38.

Index